THE OXFORD HANDBOOK OF

# PLATO

# THE OXFORD HANDBOOK OF

# PLATO

*Edited by*

GAIL FINE

OXFORD

UNIVERSITY PRESS

2008

# OXFORD
UNIVERSITY PRESS

Oxford University Press, Inc., publishes works that further
Oxford University's objective of excellence
in research, scholarship, and education.

Oxford   New York
Auckland   Cape Town   Dar es Salaam   Hong Kong   Karachi
Kuala Lumpur   Madrid   Melbourne   Mexico City   Nairobi
New Delhi   Shanghai   Taipei   Toronto

With offices in
Argentina   Austria   Brazil   Chile   Czech Republic   France   Greece
Guatemala   Hungary   Italy   Japan   Poland   Portugal   Singapore
South Korea   Switzerland   Thailand   Turkey   Ukraine   Vietnam

Published by Oxford University Press, Inc.
198 Madison Avenue, New York, New York 10016

www.oup.com

Oxford is a registered trademark of Oxford University Press

Library of Congress Cataloging-in-Publication Data
The Oxford handbook of Plato / edited by Gail Fine.
p. cm.
Includes bibliographical references.
ISBN 978-0-19-518290-3
1. Plato.   I. Fine, Gail.
B395.O94 2008
184—dc22        2007017459

2 4 6 8 9 7 5 3 1
Printed in the United States of America
on acid-free paper

# PREFACE

........................

This volume consists of twenty-one newly commissioned essays by leading scholars in the field of ancient philosophy, along with a synoptic introduction and general bibliography. In keeping with the aim of the series of Oxford Handbooks, each essay is substantial and challenging, yet fully accessible; each is also an authoritative, original, and up-to-date discussion of either a major Platonic dialogue or a central topic in Plato. Each essay also provides some guidance to the voluminous secondary literature. Everyone from advanced undergraduates with little or no background in Plato to scholars in the field of ancient philosophy should be able to read these essays with pleasure and profit.

On a conservative estimate, Plato wrote twenty-six dialogues, many of which are unrivaled for their beauty, richness, and range of topics covered. No handbook of manageable size could provide a detailed discussion of every topic and dialogue; so I have had to be selective, while also aiming to be reasonably comprehensive. Hence I have chosen just some topics and dialogues for detailed discussion. However, some dialogues that do not receive their own chapters are discussed in various of the topical chapters; and some topics that do not receive their own chapters are discussed in the chapters on particular dialogues. Several topics and dialogues are discussed in more than one chapter, thereby providing different points of view on Plato's multifaceted thought.

In editing this volume, I have incurred various debts I am pleased to acknowledge. Thanks are due to Paul Moser for inviting me to edit the volume, and to Peter Ohlin and Linda Donnelly for overseeing its production. The staff in the Philosophy Center in the University of Oxford was of great help with various tasks. I gratefully acknowledge the generous research and administrative leave I've had from Cornell University. Financial assistance from the Department of Philosophy at Cornell University and from Merton College, Oxford helped defray my costs. I am also grateful for the friendly, supportive, and stimulating environment provided by both Cornell and Oxford.

Thanks are due to Kristin Inglis for help with the bibliography; to Jacob Klein for compiling the indexes; and to Jamie Brooks and Sydney Penner for filling in page references for the indexes.

Thanks too to Barbara Kretzmann for introducing me to the portrait of Plato that serves as the jacket design for this volume. It is part of a frieze of some 200 portraits in the Upper Reading Room of the Bodleian library. It's situated between portraits of Pythagoras and Aristotle; the portrait of Socrates is on the opposite wall, facing them.

I am enormously grateful to the contributors for the excellence of their essays, for their cooperative spirit, and for their friendly encouragement along the way. I am especially indebted to Malcolm Schofield for helpful advice at various stages, and to Lesley Brown, with whom I have been enjoying philosophical conversations for well over twenty years, to my great benefit. My greatest debt, for help with matters both large and small, in this project as in all else, is to Terry Irwin.

John Ackrill died while this volume was in press. I was fortunate to be John's student when I was a visiting graduate student in Oxford in 1972-3, and fortunate to remain in contact with him from then on. I admired, and benefited from, his incisive and clear mind, and appreciated his kindness. Many of the contributors to this volume were students, friends, or colleagues (nonexclusive 'or') of John's; and, like everyone who works on Plato, we are all the beneficiaries of his many contributions to the study of Plato. This volume is dedicated to his memory.

# Contents

# CONTRIBUTORS

........................................................

JULIA ANNAS is Regents Professor of Philosophy at the University of Arizona. Her many books include *Aristotle's Metaphysics M and N* (Clarendon, 1976), *An Introduction to Plato's Republic* (Clarendon, 1981; 2nd ed., 1984), *The Morality of Happiness* (Clarendon, 1993), *Platonic Ethics Old and New* (1999), and *A Very Short Introduction to Plato* (Oxford University Press, 2003).

CHRISTOPHER BOBONICH is Associate Professor of Philosophy and, by courtesy, Classics at Stanford University. He is the author of *Plato's Utopia Recast: His Later Ethics and Politics* (Clarendon, 2002), and coeditor with Pierre Destrée of *Akrasia in Greek Philosophy: From Socrates to Plotinus* (2007).

CHARLES BRITTAIN is Professor of Classics at Cornell University. He is the author of *Philo of Larissa* (Clarendon, 2001) and *Cicero: On Academic Scepticism* (2006), and translator, with Tad Brennan, of *Simplicius: On Epictetus' Handbook* (2002).

LESLEY BROWN is Centenary Fellow and Tutor at Somerville College, Oxford. She has published several articles on Plato's *Sophist*, as well as papers on ancient philosophy of language and on moral and political philosophy in Plato and Aristotle.

PAOLO CRIVELLI is Tutorial Fellow in Ancient Philosophy at New College, Oxford, and Lecturer in Philosophy at St Hugh's College, Oxford. He is the author of *Aristotle on Truth* (2004) and of various articles on Plato, Aristotle, and the Stoics.

DANIEL DEVEREUX is Professor of Philosophy at the University of Virginia. He has published articles on Plato and Aristotle, especially on their ethics and metaphysics. He is currently writing a book on Socratic and Platonic ethics.

GAIL FINE is Professor of Philosophy at Cornell University and Senior Research Fellow at Merton College, Oxford. She is the author of *On Ideas* (Clarendon, 1993) and of *Plato on Knowledge and Forms: Selected Essays* (Clarendon, 2003), and the editor of *Plato 1: Metaphysics and Epistemology* and of *Plato 2: Ethics, Politics, Religion, and the Soul* (Oxford University Press, 1999), both in the Oxford Readings in Philosophy series.

VERITY HARTE is Professor of Philosophy and Classics at Yale University and Honorary Research Professor in Philosophy, King's College London. She is the author of *Plato on Parts and Wholes: The Metaphysics of Structure* (Clarendon, 2002) and of various articles on Greek philosophy.

T. H. IRWIN is Professor of Ancient Philosophy in the University of Oxford and a Fellow of Keble College. From 1975 to 2006 he taught at Cornell University. His many books include *Plato's Gorgias* (translation and notes) (Clarendon, 1979); *Aristotle's Nicomachean Ethics* (translation and notes) (1999); *Aristotle's First Principles* (Clarendon, 1988); *Classical Thought* (Oxford University Press, 1989); *Plato's Ethics* (Oxford University Press, 1995); and *The Development of Ethics*, vol. 1 (Oxford University Press, 2007).

THOMAS K. JOHANSEN is University Lecturer in Ancient Philosophy in the University of Oxford and a Fellow of Brasenose College. His publications include *Plato's Natural Philosophy: A Study of the Timaeus-Critias* (2004) and *Aristotle on the Sense-Organs* (1998).

RACHANA KAMTEKAR is an Associate Professor of Philosophy at the University of Arizona. She writes on Plato, Stoicism, and moral psychology and is working on a book titled *The Powers of Plato's Psychology*. She has edited *Critical Essays on Plato's Euthyphro, Apology and Crito* (2004), and with Sara Ahbel-Rappe, *The Blackwell Companion to Socrates* (2006).

RICHARD KRAUT is Charles and Emma Morrison Professor in the Humanities at Northwestern University. He is the author of *Socrates and the State* (1984), *Aristotle on the Human Good* (1989), *Aristotle Politics Books VII and VIII*, translation with commentary (Clarendon, 1997), *Aristotle: Political Philosophy* (Oxford University Press, 2002), and *What Is Good and Why: The Ethics of Well-Being* (2007). He also edited *The Cambridge Companion to Plato* (1992).

MI-KYOUNG LEE is Associate Professor of Philosophy at the University of Colorado at Boulder. She is the author of *Epistemology after Protagoras: Responses to Relativism in Plato, Aristotle, and Democritus* (Clarendon, 2005).

HENDRIK LORENZ is Associate Professor of Philosophy at Princeton University. He is the author of *The Brute Within: Appetitive Desire in Plato and Aristotle* (Clarendon, 2006) and of several articles on Plato and Aristotle.

GARETH B. MATTHEWS is Professor of Philosophy (Emeritus) at the University of Massachusetts at Amherst. He taught previously at the University of Virginia and the University of Minnesota. He is the author of *Thought's Ego: Augustine and Descartes* (1992), *Socratic Perplexity and the Nature of Philosophy* (Oxford University Press, 1999), and *Augustine* (2005).

MARY MARGARET MCCABE is Professor of Ancient Philosophy at King's College London. She is the author of *Plato's Individuals* (1994) and *Plato and His Predecessors: The Dramatisation of Reason* (2000) and general editor of the series *Cambridge Studies in the Dialogues of Plato*. She currently (2005–2008) holds a Leverhulme Trust Major Research Fellowship.

CONSTANCE C. MEINWALD is Associate Professor of Philosophy at the University of Illinois at Chicago. She is the author of *Plato's Parmenides* (Oxford University Press, 1991) and of various articles in ancient philosophy. She is preparing the Plato volume for the series The Routledge Philosophers.

SANDRA PETERSON is Professor of Philosophy at the University of Minnesota, Twin Cities. She is the author of several articles on ancient philosophy.

MALCOLM SCHOFIELD is Professor of Ancient Philosophy in the University of Cambridge, where he has taught in the Faculty of Classics since 1972. He co-authored (with G. S. Kirk and J. E. Raven) *The Presocratic Philosophers* (1983). His many collaborative ventures include *The Cambridge History of Greek and Roman Political Thought* (2000), coedited with Christopher Rowe. His latest book is *Plato: Political Philosophy* (Oxford University Press, 2006).

DOMINIC SCOTT is Professor of Philosophy at the University of Virginia and an Emeritus Fellow of Clare College Cambridge. Between 1989 and 2007 he taught in the Philosophy Faculty at Cambridge University. He is the author of *Recollection and Experience: Plato's Theory of Learning and Its Successors* (1995) and *Plato's Meno* (2006).

CHRISTOPHER SHIELDS is Professor of Classical Philosophy in the University of Oxford and a Fellow of Lady Margaret Hall. His books include *Order in Multiplicity* (Clarendon, 1999), *Classical Philosophy* (2003), and *Aristotle* (2007). He also edited the *Blackwell Guide to Ancient Philosophy* (2002) and is editing the *Oxford Handbook of Aristotle* (Oxford University Press).

C. C. W. TAYLOR is Emeritus Professor of Philosophy in the University of Oxford and an Emeritus Fellow of Corpus Christi College. His publications include *Plato, Protagoras*, translated with notes (Clarendon, 1976, 2nd ed. 1991); *The Greeks on Pleasure* (with J. C. B. Gosling) (Clarendon, 1982); *Socrates* (Oxford University Press, 1998); *The Atomists: Leucippus and Democritus: Fragments,* a text and translation with a commentary (1999), and *Aristotle, Nicomachean Ethics II–IV*, translated with commentary (Clarendon, 2006).

THE OXFORD HANDBOOK OF

# PLATO

# CHAPTER 1

# INTRODUCTION

## GAIL FINE

## 1.

This volume falls into four parts. Chapters 2–3 discuss preliminaries to the philosophical study of Plato. Chapters 4–14 are devoted to central themes in Plato's work. Chapters 15–20 discuss individual dialogues. Chapters 21–22 explore Plato's legacy.

In principle, a handbook on Plato could be organized in different ways. One might have chapters just on individual dialogues; alternatively, one might have chapters just on particular topics. Instead, this volume contains both sorts of chapters. This makes the volume richer and more varied than it would otherwise have been, providing different angles from which to view Plato's multitextured thought. Each dialogue is an integral whole and should be read as such, with proper attention to and appreciation for its overall structure and the interconnectedncss of its various themes and arguments. If one reads a dialogue focusing just on what is said on a given topic, one misses much that is worthwhile. Indeed, one runs the risk of misinterpreting what is said on that topic, for discussion of it occurs as part of a larger whole; and understanding the part requires understanding that larger whole.[1]

---

1. For one illustration of this general point, see the discussion below of the structure of the *Republic*. Of course, some dialogues are more tightly interwoven than others; nonetheless, the default assumption should be that dialogues are to be read as wholes, not merely piecemeal. This enables one to see important connections that might otherwise be missed. For example, the *Theaetetus* contains a celebrated passage, important in later Platonism, enjoining one to become as much like god as possible; Plato marks the passage as a digression, and he has often been taken at his word. However, it is importantly connected to one of the dialogue's main themes: its defense of the objective nature of goodness.

On the other hand,, Plato discusses the same or related topics in many dialogues. Some dialogues seem to have the same, or similar, views; by considering
them together, we can paint a fuller picture of Plato's thought. For example, the
*Phaedo*, *Symposium*, *Republic*, *Phaedrus*, and *Timaeus* all develop views about the
nature of forms which, when read together, provide deeper insight into what Plato
might have had in mind. But sometimes dialogues seem to express quite different
views. This might be evidence of Plato's development, though whether his views
develop and, if they do, how they do so, are matters of controversy. For example,
the *Parmenides* criticizes a theory of forms; some commentators think it is criticizing the views of earlier dialogues, views that do not reappear after the *Parmenides*. However, this view has been disputed.

But a volume that contained a chapter on every dialogue, as well as on every
facet of Plato's variegated thought, would be too long to be practicable. Hence I had
to be selective.

It was easy to decide to include a chapter on the *Republic*. For it is probably
Plato's most famous dialogue; it is also one of his two longest dialogues (the other
being the *Laws*). As Scott explains in chapter 15, the *Republic* has a complex
structure; and a proper appreciation of the dialogue requires a grasp of that
structure. For example, it develops an elaborate analogy between justice in the city
and in the soul. In discussing justice in the city, Plato develops his political theory;
in discussing justice in the soul, he develops his ethical theory. If one looks at the
ethical and political theories in isolation from one another, one will miss
the parallels and interconnections that Plato develops between them. Or again, in
the middle books of the *Republic* (5–7), Plato discusses various issues in epistemology and metaphysics, partly by means of the famous images of the Sun, Line,
and Cave. Though the discussion of metaphysics and epistemology is important in
its own right, if one considers it just on its own one will miss the vital contribution
it makes to Plato's ethical and political theories. For his metaphysical and epistemological views play an important role in his defense of the controversial claim
that only philosophers can be virtuous or, therefore, happy, and that only they are
fit to rule in the ideally just city, precisely because only they are truly virtuous; and
the ideally just city must, in Plato's view, be governed by the truly virtuous.

Because the *Republic* engages with so many issues, it is discussed not only in the
chapter devoted solely to it but also in many of the topical chapters: Taylor discusses its epistemology; Harte discusses its metaphysics; Lorenz discusses its division of the soul; Annas discusses its ethical theory; Bobonich discusses its political theory; and Kamtekar discusses its views on art and education. Reading all
these chapters together will enhance one's understanding of the dialogue as a
whole.

In addition to the chapter on the *Republic*, there are also individual chapters
on some of the later dialogues. These dialogues are especially rich and complex
philosophically; they also pursue particular topics systematically and in detail.
Hence they especially benefit from sustained discussion. The *Parmenides* first
discusses and criticizes a theory of forms; it then conducts an exercise designed to

help one resolve some of the problems broached in the first part of the dialogue. The *Timaeus* discusses the nature of the material world, including the principles that explain its coming into being. The *Theaetetus* considers three main answers to the question "What is knowledge?," ostensibly rejecting all of them. The *Sophist* explores the nature of being and not-being which, in turn, allows Plato to provide a satisfying account of the possibility of falsehood. The *Philebus* asks about the relative value of pleasure and knowledge in the best life for a human being.

Some of these dialogues are also discussed elsewhere in this volume, sometimes in some detail. For example, in addition to Brown's chapter on the *Sophist*, Crivelli discusses the *Sophist* in the broader context of his philosophy of language as a whole. In addition to Lee's chapter on the *Theaetetus*, Taylor discusses the *Theaetetus* in the broader context of Plato's epistemology in general.

Some dialogues that do not receive their own chapters are nonetheless discussed in some detail in some of the topical chapters. For example, Schofield, Devereux, Annas, Lorenz, and Kamtekar all discuss the *Gorgias*. Devereux and Annas discuss the ethical views of the *Euthydemus*. Devereux, Annas, Lorenz, and Kamtekar discuss the *Protagoras*. Much of Kraut's chapter on Platonic love is devoted to the *Symposium*. Crivelli discusses the *Cratylus* at some length. Matthews and Taylor discuss the epistemology of the *Meno*. Various aspects of the *Phaedo* are discussed by Taylor (epistemology), Harte (metaphysics), and Lorenz (the soul). Bobonich discusses the political theory of the *Statesman* and *Laws*; Kamtekar discusses the *Laws'* views on education.

I hope that the fact that some articles discuss some of the same dialogues or issues, sometimes from different points of view, or within different contexts, or by focusing on different parts, will afford the reader a deeper insight into Plato's thought than would be possible in a volume that included chapters only on topics or only on individual dialogues.

In the rest of this introduction, I provide an overview of the issues discussed in subsequent chapters, as well as of the chapters themselves.[2]

## 2.

In chapter 2, Malcolm Schofield locates Plato in his place and time. Plato did not write in a vacuum. He was influenced by earlier philosophers (the so-called Presocratics, or early Greek philosophers), Greek drama, historians and historical

---

2. However, given the limitations of space, I discuss some issues and chapters in more detail than others; nor do I follow the order of the chapters. The reader is warned that I sometimes defend views at odds with those defended in one or another chapter. In places I have adapted the introductions to my *Plato* (Oxford: Oxford University Press, 2000), in the Oxford Readings in Philosophy series. This is a one-volume version of *Plato 1: Metaphysics and Epistemology* (1999) and *Plato 2: Ethics, Politics, Religion, and the Soul* (1999).

events, the medical writers, and more. Schofield discusses some of the philosophical and nonphilosophical influences on Plato; he also discuses Plato's life.

In chapter 3, T. H. Irwin discusses various features of the Platonic corpus: how it survived from Plato's time, how the earliest (Academic and Alexandrian) editions of his work came into existence, how and when the dialogues came to be arranged in tetralogies, and the order of the dialogues. According to the "standard" view, the dialogues may be divided into early (or Socratic), middle, and late dialogues.[3] Though the standard view has been challenged, Irwin defends it. However, as he notes, the relative dates of some dialogues are more controversial than those of others.

Acceptance of the standard view of the chronology of Plato's works is neutral as between "developmentalism" and "unitarianism": to say that Plato probably wrote his dialogues in a given order says nothing about how, if at all, his thought develops. Moreover, he may have revised various dialogues over time; this complicates the effort to arrive at a chronology or to assess development.

However, on one standard view, Plato's early dialogues represent the thought of the historical Socrates (as well as Plato's own first thoughts), whereas middle and later dialogues develop his own more independent views.[4] This is so in two ways. First, later dialogues engage in systematic discussion of issues that the early dialogues do not discuss in detail, such as metaphysics and epistemology.[5] Second, they defend different views from those to be found in the early dialogues. For example, from the *Gorgias* and *Republic* on, Plato countenances nonrational desires, which are not countenanced in earlier dialogues.[6] Or again, the middle dialogues articulate views about forms that are at least not explicit in earlier dialogues. The later dialogues, in turn, are sometimes thought to suggest yet a different view of forms. However, this "standard" view is controversial.

In chapter 4, Mary Margaret McCabe discusses Plato's various ways of writing. She asks to what extent the pictures in the dialogues (what is said) are affected by their frames (the setting in which something is said). She argues that even if one is primarily concerned with philosophical argument, one can't afford to ignore the frames, for the frames turn out to be part of the pictures. Her argument is developed not just in the abstract but also by attention to literary and dramatic details that influence our understanding of particular arguments. She also suggests that, while the dialogues are not dogmatic in the sense of claiming to present the final truth, subject to no revision, neither are they merely exploratory in the sense of articulating views to which Plato is not at all committed; nor yet does he intend to convey a hidden message. However, though McCabe thinks this explains some aspects of Plato's ways of writing—such as the puzzling nature of the endings of some of the dialogues, and the tentative way in which Socrates sometimes declares

---

3. A list is provided in Irwin, chapter 3 of this volume.

4. Hence some commentators contrast Socrates' and Plato's views, meaning thereby the views expressed in the early dialogues, on the one hand, and the middle and later dialogues, on the other hand.

5. Which is not to say that the early dialogues do not discuss these issues at all: see Matthews, chapter 5.

6. This assumes that the *Gorgias* is written after the *Protagoras*. It is controversial to say that earlier dialogues do not countenance nonrational desires. For the view that they do so, see Devereux, chapter 6.

his commitments—she also argues that it does not fully account for the multi-farious forms of the dialogues, for which she provides yet further explanations.

# 3.

In chapter 5, Gareth B. Matthews discusses the epistemology and metaphysics of the early dialogues. As is well known, Socrates often disclaims knowledge. For example, at *Apology* 21d he says that "neither of us knows (*eidenai*) anything fine and good (*kalon kagathon*)." However, sometimes he claims to have knowledge, including, it seems, knowledge of what's fine and good. For example, at *Apology* 29b he says: "I know (*oida*), however, that it is wicked and shameful to do wrong, to disobey one's superior, be he man or god." Socrates' account of his cognitive condition therefore seems to be inconsistent.

A variety of solutions have been proposed: for example, that Socrates simply is inconsistent; that he is insincere in denying that he has knowledge; that he claims to know in one sense of the term but not in another; that he thinks he knows some things but not others, in a single sense of the term.[7] On the usual version of the last of these views, he takes himself to know some particular truths, including some moral truths, but thinks he lacks knowledge of what, for example, virtue is: he can't provide a satisfactory answer to his characteristic "What is F?" question, which, as Matthews explains, asks for an explanatory set of necessary and sufficient conditions for being F, an account of the nature of F-ness.

It has been argued, against this last view, that Socrates accepts the priority of definition, according to which one cannot know what counts as either an example or a nonessential property of virtue unless one knows what virtue is. If so, one cannot know particular moral truths without knowing what virtue is. Matthews nonetheless argues that Socrates claims both to have some moral knowledge and not to know what virtue is, in a single sense of the term. If he is right, and if Socrates is also committed to the priority of definition, Socrates would seem to be inconsistent. Matthews argues, however, that, at least in the early dialogues, Socrates is not committed to the priority of definition. The passages that seem to espouse it are best read aporetically: Socrates wonders how he can have the knowledge he takes himself to have, given that he doesn't know what virtue is.

In chapter 7, C. C. W. Taylor also discusses Socrates' disavowal of knowledge. His solution is to say that Socrates recognizes two kinds of knowledge, expert and non-expert;[8] Socrates disclaims expert knowledge but takes himself to have

---

7. For one classic discussion, see G. Vlastos, "Socrates' Disavowal of Knowledge," *Philosophical Quarterly* 35 (1985), 1–31, reprinted in Fine, *Plato 1*, ch. 2.

8. Recognizing different kinds of knowledge is quite different from recognizing different senses of "knowledge." Horses and cows are different kinds of animals, but they are animals in the same sense of the term "animal."

non-expert knowledge. One cannot have expert knowledge of F unless one knows what F is; since Socrates claims not to know what virtue is, he disclaims expert knowledge of virtue. When he claims to have some moral knowledge, he is only claiming to have non-expert knowledge, which does not require knowing what virtue is.

In addition to the problem of how best to understand Socrates' disavowal of knowledge, there is a related problem, which Vlastos dubbed "the problem of the elenchus."[9] The problem has been formulated in various ways. On what Matthews calls the stronger version, the problem is to explain how the elenchus—Socrates' characteristic way of cross-examining interlocutors—can be used to achieve knowledge of what F-ness is, when all it seems to do is uncover inconsistencies in an interlocutor's belief set.

# 4.

Socrates doesn't explicitly raise the problem of the elenchus in the early dialogues, let alone offer an explicit solution. In the *Meno*, however, he both raises and resolves it. He and Meno have been asking what virtue is; after repeatedly failing to find the answer, Meno turns to the offensive and asks Socrates both how one can inquire into something if one does not know what it is, and how one would know if one had found what one was looking for should one happen upon it. Socrates adds that there also seems to be a problem about the possibility of inquiry if one knows what one is inquiring into. For one inquires only in order to gain knowledge one lacks; if one already knows what one is looking for, the inquiry is already at an end.

Meno is sometimes thought to raise two problems: the problem of inquiry and the problem of discovery.[10] The first asks how one can begin an inquiry; the second asks how one can complete an inquiry. According to Taylor, Socrates thinks one can solve the first problem only if one has some knowledge: one at least needs to know what question one is asking (though one does not need to know the answer to it). Here, however, one might ask whether Socrates would say that understanding the sense of a question constitutes anything he would call "knowledge"; perhaps, in his view, linguistic understanding requires no more than true belief. If this is right, then perhaps he thinks one can begin an inquiry on the basis of true belief, in which case knowledge is not necessary.[11]

9. G. Vlastos, "The Socratic Elenchus," *Oxford Studies in Ancient Philosophy* 1 (1983), 27–58; reprinted in Fine, *Plato 1*, ch. 1.

10. For this view, see D. Scott, *Plato's Meno* (Cambridge: Cambridge University Press, 2006), part 2; and Scott, *Recollection and Experience* (Cambridge: Cambridge University Press, 1995), 24–52.

11. For the view that Socrates requires no more than true belief for inquiry, see my "Inquiry in the *Meno*," in R. Kraut (ed.), *Cambridge Companion to Plato* (Cambridge: Cambridge University Press, 1992), 220–26, reprinted, with minor modifications, in my *Plato on Forms and Knowledge: Selected Essays* (Oxford: Clarendon Press, 2003), ch. 2.

One might argue that even if one can begin an inquiry without knowledge, one can not complete an inquiry without it. If that is right, and if Plato also accepts the priority of definition, then in the special case where one is attempting to discover what virtue is, it might seem that one must already know what virtue is to inquire what it is. But if one already knows what virtue is, then, it seems, one cannot inquire what it is for, again, one inquires only into what one does not know.

Matthews and Taylor suggest that Plato's solution is to distinguish latent from manifest knowledge: we all have latent innate knowledge of what virtue is but lack manifest knowledge of what it is; inquiry consists in making this latent innate knowledge manifest. Indeed, the *Meno* is often thought to offer the first account of innate knowledge.

It is clear that Plato posits *prenatal* knowledge; however, this does not imply that he posits *innate* knowledge. On an alternative view, he thinks that, at birth, we entirely lost the knowledge we once had. Though we no longer have knowledge, we have true beliefs; and these beliefs, along with a disposition to favor truths over falsehoods, are sufficient for allowing us to acquire knowledge.[12]

Be that as it may, Plato undoubtedly distinguishes knowledge from true belief, arguing at 98a that knowledge is true belief tied down with reasoning about the explanation (*aitias logismos*). Hence one can know *that* p is so only if one knows *why* p is so; all knowledge requires an account of the reason why what one knows is true. This might seem to be a more demanding conception of knowledge than a justified-true-belief account; for it is one thing to know why p is so and another to have a justification for believing that p is so. However, one might argue that one is justified in believing that p is so, in the way necessary for knowing that it is so, only if one knows why it is so. On this view, Plato's account of knowledge is a version of a justified-true-belief account of knowledge.[13]

At *Meno* 97aff., Plato says that one can know the way to Larisa; hence he seems to allow empirical knowledge.[14] He seems to suggest that one can know the way to Larisa simply by going there. One might wonder how this fits with the claim, also made in this part of the dialogue, that one can know something only if one can explain why it is so. One answer is that repeatedly traveling the route is not in conflict with understanding why this is the way to Larisa; rather, it is the means by which we achieve an understanding of why this is the way to Larisa— that is, why it is best to go this way, rather than that.[15]

12. I discuss this briefly in "Inquiry in the *Meno*" and in "Enquiry and Discovery," *Oxford Studies in Ancient Philosophy* 32 (2007), 331–67; cf. R. Dancy, *Plato's Introduction of Forms* (Cambridge: Cambridge University Press, 2004).

13. I defend this view in "Knowledge and True Belief in the *Meno*," *Oxford Studies in Ancient Philosophy* (2004), 41–81; contrast Taylor, chapter 7.

14. This assumes that he mentions the way to Larisa as a literal example of something one might know. However, it is sometimes thought that he mentions it only as an analogy, to explain how knowledge differs from true belief.

15. See my "Knowledge and True Belief in the *Meno*"; contrast Taylor, chapter 7.

## 5.

..................................................................................................................................................

The *Meno* says that to have knowledge, one must grasp an *aitia* of why what one knows is true. In the *Phaedo*, Plato argues that forms are, or are constituents of, *aitiai* (causes or explanations); hence all knowledge requires knowledge of forms. Plato doesn't merely say this: he proposes criteria for adequate explanations and argues that only explanations involving reference to forms satisfy those criteria.

To say that all knowledge requires knowledge of forms is not to say that knowledge is restricted to forms. However, Plato is often thought to argue this in the *Republic*, both in a celebrated but difficult argument at the end of Book 5, and also in Books 6–7 where, among other things, he develops the images of the Sun, Line, and Cave. On one version of this view, he takes the objects of knowledge and belief to be disjoint: knowledge is correlated with forms, belief with sensibles; one can't know sensibles or have beliefs about forms. On this view, knowledge, so far from implying true belief (as it does in the *Meno*) excludes it. On an alternative view, though Plato thinks all knowledge requires knowledge of forms, he doesn't restrict knowledge to forms but, as in the *Meno*, leaves room for empirical knowledge (and for mere belief about forms).[16]

What is involved in knowing forms? On one view, one grasps isolated individual forms through particular acts of nonpropositional acquaintance. According to Taylor, however, Plato is an epistemological holist, in the sense that he thinks one cannot know a single entity or proposition all on its own; rather, knowing one entity or proposition involves knowing related entities or propositions. This does not imply, however, that Plato takes knowledge to be irreducibly propositional; and, according to Taylor, Plato doesn't clearly distinguish propositional knowledge (knowledge that something is so) from knowledge of things. On an alternative view, Plato thinks knowing a thing requires or, more strongly, consists in knowing truths about the thing: one cannot know a form, for example, without knowing what it is, which is propositional knowledge (to know what a thing is, is to know that it is such and so). More strongly, knowing a form just is knowing what it is, where this is propositional knowledge. On the stronger view, knowledge of forms is a species of propositional knowledge. Even on the weaker view, knowledge of forms is at least partly propositional and so does not consist wholly in acquaintance.

## 6.

..................................................................................................................................................

The *Theaetetus* is Plato's longest systematic discussion of knowledge. Taylor discusses it in the context of Plato's epistemology in general. In chapter 17, Mi-Kyoung Lee discusses the dialogue as a whole, focusing on two related issues:

16. The *Theaetetus* also admits empirical knowledge. There is dispute about whether it is admitted in the *Timaeus*: contrast Taylor, chapter 7, and Johansen, chapter 19.

whether the dialogue espouses the view that epistemology can be done without metaphysics, and what if anything it suggests about the nature and existence of forms. She argues that some of the accounts of knowledge considered in the dialogue are supported with metaphysical theories that are incompatible with the existence of forms; but since Plato rejects those accounts of knowledge, he is not committed to the metaphysics used to support them. Though this falls short of positing forms, she suggests that Plato hints at requirements for knowledge that positing forms would allow us to satisfy.

The first and longest part of the dialogue asks whether knowledge is perception. The view that it is is linked both to Protagoras' measure doctrine, according to which things are (to one) as they appear to one, and to a Heraclitean flux doctrine. The refutation of Protagoras' measure doctrine is sometimes thought to be the first refutation (or attempted refutation) of relativism, though whether Protagoras is a relativist and, if he is, in what sense he is are disputed issues.[17] It is also disputed whether Plato's refutation of a Heraclitean flux doctrine in 181–83 refutes any sort of Heracliteanism he himself accepts in earlier dialogues,[18] or whether he's just refuting a flux doctrine that is needed to support Theaetetus' suggestion that knowledge is perception (or perhaps Theaetetus' suggestion, either on its own or when coupled with Protagoras' measure doctrine, implies some sort of Heracliteanism).

In 184–86, Plato presents his final refutation of the claim that knowledge is perception. On one view, which Lee is sympathetic to, he argues that when perception is conceived as being below the propositional threshold, it cannot constitute knowledge; indeed, when perception is so conceived, it does not even get as far as belief.[19] This is compatible with allowing—although it does not imply—that perceiving that something is so (which, in contrast to "pure" perception, involves identifying what one sees as being something or other) can be a case of knowledge.

In the second part of the dialogue, Plato asks whether knowledge is true belief. He eventually argues that it is not, on the ground that the members of a jury might have a true belief about who committed a crime, but, not having been eyewitnesses, they do not know who committed it; hence true belief is not sufficient for knowledge.

Before directly rejecting the view that knowledge is true belief, he embarks on a long discussion of whether false belief is possible. He proposes five explanations (including the famous image, which Lee discusses, of the mind as a wax tablet (191a–197a)); but each of them seems to fail. It has been argued that Plato's failure to explain false belief stems from his unclarity about being and not being, or about the distinction between naming and stating; it is only in the *Sophist* that he attains clarity on these issues and so is able to explain the nature of false statement and belief. Lee suggests, however, that the failure is due instead to the dialectical

17. For the view that he is a relativist, see M. F. Burnyeat, "Protagoras and Self-Refutation," *Philosophical Review* 85 (1976), 44–69. For the view that he is not a relativist, see G. Fine, *Plato on Knowledge and Forms*, chs. 6–8. Cf. M. Lee, *Epistemology after Protagoras* (Oxford: Clarendon Press, 2005), esp. ch. 3.

18. I discuss Plato's Heracliteanism below.

19. For this interpretation, see also M. F. Burnyeat, "Plato on the Grammar of Perceiving," *Classical Quarterly* 26 (1976), 29–51. For different views, see J. Cooper, "Plato on Sense-Perception and Knowledge (*Theaetetus* 184–6)," *Phronesis* (1970), 123–46, reprinted in Fine, *Plato 1*, ch. 13; and Taylor, chapter 7 in this volume.

context. In particular, it is an indirect indictment of the definition of knowledge as true belief. For in order to have a false belief about something, one must succeed in thinking about it, in which case one must have a true belief about it. If knowledge is true belief, it follows that whenever one succeeds in thinking about something, one thereby knows it. But, according to Plato, one cannot both know and not know the same thing. Hence if thinking about something involves knowing it, one cannot also have a false belief about it.[20]

In the third and final part of the dialogue, Plato asks whether knowledge is true belief plus an account. He explores this issue partly in terms of the famous dream theory, according to which there are basic elements that can be perceived and named but have no account and so are unknowable. Lee suggests that Plato deliberately leaves open the question of precisely what these elements are in order to focus on certain abstract questions about ontology and language that a more determinate account of the elements might obscure.

On one view, Plato accepts the dream theory's claim that some things can be known without an account; if so, he presumably rejects the *Meno*'s claim that knowledge is true belief tied down with an *aitias logismos*, as well as the claim made in the *Phaedo* (76b) and *Republic* (531e, 534b) that knowledge requires a *logos*. On another view, he continues to believe that knowledge requires an account, believes elements are knowable, and so rejects the view that they lack accounts. In order to adjudicate between these and other options, we need to know what an account is. Plato considers three possibilities, but appears to reject all of them. On one view, however, he at least hints that elements can be seen to have accounts once we realize that accounts need not consist in listing a thing's elements but can also consist in describing something's place in the larger whole of which it is a part. This leads to the sort of interrelation model of knowledge that is explicit not only in such later dialogues as the *Statesman* but also, according to some commentators, in earlier dialogues.[21]

## 7.

We've seen that in the early dialogues, a satisfactory answer to the "What is F?" question provides a set of necessary and sufficient explanatory conditions. The correct answer to the question "What is justice?," for example, will specify the

20. For a different version of the view that the failure to explain false belief is due to the dialectical context, see my "False Belief in the *Theaetetus*," *Phronesis* (1979), 27–80, reprinted, with minor modifications, in Fine, *Plato on Knowledge and Forms*, ch. 9. Cf. M. F. Burnyeat, Introduction to the *Theaetetus of Plato* (Indianapolis: Hackett, 1990), 65–123.

21. See the last paragraph of section 5 above. For my own view of these issues, see my "Knowledge and *Logos* in the *Theaetetus*," *Philosophical Review* 88 (1979), 366–97, reprinted, with minor modifications, in Fine, *Plato on Knowledge and Forms*, ch. 10. For criticism and alternative views, see D. Bostock, *Plato's Theaetetus* (Oxford: Clarendon Press, 1988); Burnyeat, Introduction to the *Theaetetus*.

necessary and sufficient conditions for anything's being just; it will also explain what justice itself—the nature or essence of justice—is. In the early dialogues, Socrates sometimes calls justice, piety, and so on—the referents of correct answers to "What is F?" questions—forms.[22] The form of piety, for example, is that "by which (*hô(i)*) all pious things are pious (*Eu.* 6d10–11), something that "is the same in every [pious] action" (5d1).

Since a form is some one thing, the same in all cases, it is a universal, in the Aristotelian sense of being a one over many (*De Int.* 17a38–b1). It is sometimes thought, however, that, at least in the middle dialogues, forms are particulars rather than, or as well as being, universals. In chapter 8, Verity Harte suggests that it is difficult to decide about this, partly because Plato lacks technical terms for "particular" and "universal," and partly because the contrast between universal and particular is not one of his central concerns. So, for example, he often contrasts forms and sensibles. But this is not the contrast between all universals, on the one hand, and all particulars, on the other. For there are nonsensible particulars, such as god and individual souls. There are also sensible universals, such as redness and being 3 inches, which are universals in the sense that they are repeatable, or can be had or shared by many things: there are many red things and many 3-inch-long things. Plato's primary concern is not to distinguish universals from particulars but to argue for the existence of a certain sort of nonsensible entity, the forms. This is compatible with the view that forms are universals, and not also or instead particulars: to say that forms don't exhaust the realm of universals is not to say that they are not universals (without also or instead being particulars). Hence one wonders why Aristotle says, or comes close to saying, that forms are both universals and particulars (see, e.g., *Met.* 13. 9). In chapter 21, Christopher Shields discusses this issue.

Why does Plato posit forms in the first place? As Harte and Shields explain, they play various functional and explanatory roles. Aristotle, for example, says that Plato introduced forms as basic objects of knowledge and definition, because he thought that entities in the sensible world are in flux or change, which disqualifies them from being the basic items of knowledge and definition. Hence there must be stable objects that can so serve, and these are the forms (*Met.* 1.6, 13.4, 13.9).

There is dispute about what, if any, sort of flux or change Plato appeals to in arguing that there are forms. For example, there is the broad distinction between the compresence and the succession of opposites. Compresence obtains when something is both F and not F at the same time:[23] for example, Helen is both beautiful (insofar as she is more beautiful than other women) and ugly (insofar as she is less beautiful than Aphrodite); bright color is both beautiful (in this painting) and ugly (in that one). The former is compresence in a particular (Helen

22. Although *eidos* is usually rendered as "form" and *idea* as "idea," the latter is misleading insofar as "idea" nowadays suggests some sort of mind-dependence, whereas forms are objectively existing, mind-independent entities.

23. Compresence can also be described in temporal terms: Helen is beautiful at t1 (when compared with me), but ugly at t2 (when compared with Aphrodite).

is both beautiful and ugly); the latter is compresence in a property or type (bright color is both beautiful and ugly, insofar as some of its tokens are beautiful, others ugly). Succession obtains when something is F at t1, and then ceases to be F, and becomes not-F, at a later time t2. For example, Helen is first short and then becomes taller as she grows older. There are also more radical sorts of succession, as encapsulated in Heraclitus' (alleged) famous remark that one can't step into the same river twice (DK B91), the idea being that it changes so rapidly that it doesn't persist over time.

On one view, Plato takes the sensible world to undergo the most radical sort of succession of opposites, according to which each sensible is, at every moment, changing in every respect. However, it has also been argued that even in the middle dialogues, Plato rejects the view that sensibles change in this radical way. Moreover, though they undoubtedly undergo some sort of succession—if of a more orderly sort—it is not clear that's what motivates the introduction of forms. Rather, as Harte argues, it is the compresence of opposites, especially in properties or types, that does so. For Plato accepts the oneness condition: he thinks that beauty, for example, is some one thing, the same in all cases. Beauty cannot be identified with any single sensible property; since beauty must be a single, nondisjunctive property, it must be a nonsensible one, and this is the form of beauty.

Though compresence in sensibles is a sufficient reason for positing forms, it may not be necessary. Any case where perception is inadequate for answering the "What is F?" question requires a corresponding form; hence Plato acknowledges forms for a broader range of cases than is licensed by compresence. This is not to say that there is a form for every linguistic predicate; rather, there are forms at most for every genuine nonsensible property (or, perhaps, just for a subclass of such properties: the basic ones).

Forms are sometimes thought to be necessary for the possibility not only of knowledge and definition but also of language. On one view, Plato thinks that grasping the meaning of a general term requires grasping a form; it is also sometimes thought that forms are just the meanings of general terms. If not every meaningful predicate has a corresponding form, then forms are not the meanings of general terms. Nonetheless, they might be central to thought and language in a different way. In chapter 9, Paolo Crivelli asks whether there is a linguistic dimension to the theory of forms. He also considers Plato's views about language more broadly, focusing on the *Cratylus* and *Sophist*.

To say that forms are (basic) nonsensible properties is to say that they are different from sensibles. Are they also separate from them? That is, can they exist whether or not sensibles do? Aristotle thinks Plato is committed to separation, and he argues that this is responsible for various difficulties in the theory of forms.[24]

It is sometimes thought that if forms are separate, they exist in another place than sensibles. However, if for forms to be separate is just for them to be able to

---

24. In chapter 21, Shields assesses some of Aristotle's criticisms.

exist whether or not any sensibles have them, then separation does not require forms to exist in a special realm.

It has also been argued that, so far from existing elsewhere, forms can, and sometimes do, exist in sensibles: for a sensible to be F is for either the whole, or a part, of the form of F (if there is one) to be in it. The view that either the whole, or a part, of the form of F is in each of its participants is subjected to criticism in the *Parmenides*; Sandra Peterson discusses this in chapter 16. As she notes, the criticisms construe immanence in a crudely physicalistic way. Perhaps there are other ways of conceiving of immanence on which it is possible for either the whole, or a part, of a form to be in its participants. One possibility is that to say that forms are in things is just to say that they are properties of them.[25] However, this view would be rejected by those who deny that forms are properties or universals. It is also rejected by some of those who take forms to be properties. For example, it has been argued that forms are perfect properties, whereas the properties of sensibles are imperfect. It has also been argued that forms are properties, but what is in sensibles are tropes (that is, individual instances of properties). To assess this issue, we need to know, among other things, what the so-called immanent characters countenanced in the *Phaedo* are (the largeness in us, for example, which is in some way distinguished from the form of largeness): Are they tropes, or forms when they are in things, or something else again?

Plato's metaphysics is not exhausted by his views about forms or by his view that some sensible properties and particulars suffer compresence (and some sorts of succession) of opposites. In the *Timaeus*, he provides a detailed account of the principles of becoming: the principles, that is, that govern the coming to be of the sensible world. He also describes its nature once in existence. In doing so, he develops the sort of teleological explanations he sought, but failed to find, in the *Phaedo*. The *Republic* goes further than the *Phaedo*, in positing the form of the good as the basic explanatory principle. But it is primarily in the *Timaeus* that Plato provides the details of his teleological vision of the whole of reality. Insofar as Plato thinks the sensible world and its coming into being can be explained, he presumably does not think it completely eludes our grasp, as it would if it were in the most extreme sort of Heraclitean flux described above. Thomas Johansen explores these and other aspects of the *Timaeus* in chapter 19.

# 8.

In the first part of the *Parmenides*, Plato discusses various issues about forms: reasons for positing them, their range, and difficulties they are allegedly liable to. Peterson explores these issues, along with the puzzling second part of the dialogue.

---

25. Aristotle canvasses a number of ways in which one thing can be in another in *Physics* 4.3; *Cat.* 1a24-25; and *Met.* 5.23.

At the beginning of the *Parmenides*, Socrates says that forms are introduced to solve a puzzle raised by the fact that things are both one and many, like and unlike: Simmias, for example, is one man with many limbs; he is like some things and unlike others. We can understand how this can be so, once we realize that he participates in both the form of one and the form of many, and in the forms of likeness and unlikeness. As in the middle dialogues, we can explain how sensibles can suffer compresence only by positing forms.

Socrates is also tempted to posit forms of man, fire, and water, but sensible men, fire, and water do not in any obvious way suffer compresence: Socrates is not both a man and not a man. Perhaps, then, as suggested above, compresence is sufficient but not necessary for positing forms.

Socrates denies that there are forms of mud, dirt, and hair; one of his reasons is that they are just what we see them to be. Perhaps this supports the suggestion, mentioned above, that his more general concern is with the limits of perception. So far, then, the *Parmenides* seems to capture at least one central line of thought in the middle dialogues.

The middle dialogues also seem to suggest that forms are Self-Predicative: any form of F is itself F; the form of beauty, for example, is itself beautiful. Self-Predication can seem absurd: how, for example, could the form of large be large? For, one might think, something can be large only if it has a size; yet forms are incorporeal. Self-Predication would indeed be absurd if it required the form of F to be F in the very same way in which sensible particulars are F, such that something can be large, for example, only if it has a size. However, as Peterson explains, Self-Predication can be understood as a much more plausible thesis. Indeed, in her view, if we were to reject it, we would also have to give up many ordinary statements we routinely accept, such as the biblical statement that "Charity sufferth long" and encyclopedia statements such as "the tiger is a carnivore." There are, however various accounts of the semantics of Self-Predications on which they are true, including the one Plato seems to assume.

Strenuous efforts have been made to argue either that Plato was never committed to Self-Predication or that, even if he was committed to it in the middle dialogues, he abandoned it in the wake of the *Parmenides'* criticisms. But if Self-Predication is at least plausible, then it is less clear that we should attempt to extricate Plato from it. If, rightly or wrongly, he remains committed to Self-Predication, he needs a different escape route from some of the arguments leveled in the first part of the *Parmenides*.[26]

Perhaps the most famous of these arguments is the so-called Third Man Argument.[27] It alleges that the, or a, theory of forms is vulnerable to a vicious infinite

26. I say "some of the arguments," because it is not clear that all of them assume Self-Predication.
27. "So-called" because Aristotle describes an argument that he calls the Third Man, and it is generally thought to be the same argument, from the logical point of view, as the argument Plato describes. See Aristotle, *Peri Ideôn*; *SE* 22; and *Met.* 7.13. However, whereas Aristotle describes a regress of forms of *man*, Plato describes a regress of forms of *large*. The classic discussion of the Third Man Argument in recent times is G. Vlastos, "The Third Man Argument in the *Parmenides*," *Philosophical Review* 63 (1954), 319–49.

regress: if there is even one form of F, there are infinitely many of them. This violates Plato's Uniqueness assumption, according to which there is at most one form for any given predicate.[28] The regress goes roughly as follows. Each form is a one over many; that is, whenever many things are F, there is one form in virtue of which they are F.[29] Consider the set of sensible large things. According to the One over Many assumption, there is one form of large—call it the form1 of large—over them. Since forms are Self-Predicative, we may posit a new set of large things, one consisting of the members of the original set, along with the form of large. The One over Many assumption tells us that there is one form of large over this set. This can't be the form in the set (= the form1 of large). For, or so the Third Man Argument alleges, nothing is F in virtue of itself: this is the so-called Non-Identity assumption. Hence there must be another form of large—call it the form2 of large—which is the form of large in virtue of which the members of our new set of large things are large. By Self-Predication, the form2 of large is large. We can now posit yet another set of large things, one consisting of the members of the previous set, along with the form2 of large. By the One over Many, there must be a form of large over this set which, by Non-Identity, must be nonidentical with anything in the set—and so on ad infinitum, and in violation of Uniqueness.[30]

The Third Man Argument can be reconstructed so as to validly generate a regress.[31] Hence Plato can avoid the argument only if he is not committed to all its premises. If Self-Predication is plausible, it is not a likely candidate for rejection. Plato also accepts *a* one over many premise, as well as the view that forms are different from, and perhaps separate from, sensibles. But these latter two views are not enough to commit him to the One over Many assumption or to the Non-Identity assumption at work in the Third Man Argument. It is debated, however, whether he is committed to these assumptions for other reasons.

It is sometimes thought that in the difficult second part of the *Parmenides*, Plato provides clues about how to answer at least some of the puzzles in the first part of the dialogue. But it remains a source of controversy whether—and if so, how—Plato revises his views about forms either there or in subsequent dialogues. The *Theaetetus*, *Timaeus*, *Sophist*, and *Philebus* all either mention entities called forms, or describe entities that seem similar, in at least some ways, to forms as they are described in the middle dialogues. But there is room for debate about the

---

28. I put it this way because Plato doesn't think there is a unique form corresponding to every predicate. There is a form of justice but not of barbarian (*Pol.* 262a–e; cf. *Phdrs.* 265e1–2).

29. If there is a form in this case at all: see preceding note.

30. This way of reading the argument is challenged by, among others, M. L. Gill; see her "Problems for Forms" in H. Benson (ed.), *A Companion to Plato* (Oxford: Blackwell, 2006), ch. 13. She suggests that one difficulty for it is that it is unclear what motivates the inference from positing *mia idea* (one form or idea) of largeness, to the claim that *hen to mega* (the large is one) (193). The answer is that the inference is from the One over Many to Uniqueness: from the claim that a given group of F things has just one form over it, to the claim that there is just one form of F *simpliciter*.

31. For a particularly lucid account, see S. M. Cohen, "The Logic of the Third Man," *Philosophical Review* 80 (1971), 448–75, reprinted in Fine, *Plato 1*, ch. 10.

precise connection between these entities and the forms countenanced in the middle dialogues.

# 9.

The ostensible main topic of the *Sophist* is the definition of a sophist; seven definitions are proffered, but each seems to fail. In exploring the seventh definition, various issues about being and not being are broached. Among the many issues considered within that broad compass is the nature of predication and correct speaking. The Late-Learners deny that one can predicate one thing of another. It is often thought that Plato can solve their problem only if he distinguishes between the identity and predication senses, or uses, of "is" ("Cicero is identical to Tully"; "white is predicated of snow"). Commentators then divide into optimists, who think he succeeds in doing so, and pessimists, who think he fails to do so. In chapter 18, Lesley Brown denies their common assumption, arguing, with the pessimists, that Plato does not distinguish different senses or uses of "is," but resisting their conclusion that he thereby fails to solve the Late-Learners' problem. For contrary to what is usually thought, distinguishing different senses or uses of "is" is not necessary for solving their problem. It can be solved by distinguishing between identity and predication *statements*; and Plato does so, by considering the "communion of kinds." This allows us to see how, for instance, Change is both the same and not the same. For to say that Change is the same, is to predicate "the same" of it; and to say that change is not the same, is to say that it is not identical with the kind, Sameness. Likewise, Change is both different (from other things) and also not different, in that it is not (identical with) the kind, Different.[32]

Another, related issue taken up in the "middle part" (as opposed to the "outer part") of the dialogue is the possibility of false statement (and belief). Showing that kinds mix is part of the solution, but it is not the whole of it. In addition, Plato provides an account of what a statement (*logos*) is: it involves interweaving a name (*onoma*) and a verb (*rhêma*); in particular, one names something, and then says something about it. Hence Plato distinguishes naming from stating.[33] This, in turn, allows him to explain the nature of both true and false statements: a true statement says of things that are, that they are; a false statement says different things from the

---

32. In explaining this, I've used "is" in a way that might encourage the view that Plato does distinguish senses or uses of "is." However, as Lesley Brown explains in chapter 18 of this volume, in the Greek not all the crucial sentences contain any form of *einai* (to be); this is one reason she suggests that the crucial distinction is between identity and predication *statements*, whether or not they include some form of *einai*.

33. It is sometimes thought that he failed to do so in earlier dialogues—including the *Theaetetus*—and thereby ran into difficulties. On an alternative view, the distinction is observed when he is speaking in his own right—as opposed to engaging in dialectical discussion with an opponent, as in the puzzles of false belief in the *Theaetetus*—even if it is not, until the *Sophist*, laid out in the same clear and explicit way.

things that are. Both a true statement, such as "Theaetetus sits," and a false statement, such as "Theaetetus flies," name Theaetetus and also say something about him; hence both count as statements. But the true statement says, concerning Theaetetus, that things that are are, while the false one says different things from the things that are. The precise interpretation of this account of false statement is disputed. Both Brown and Crivelli canvass and criticize a number of options; in the end, they favor different accounts.

# 10.

The main topic of the *Philebus* is the good human life: Is it pleasure, intelligence, or some combination thereof? In ways that interestingly anticipate Aristotle's *Nicomachean Ethics*, Plato argues that the good (i.e., the best) human life—that is, the happy (*eudaimon*) life—doesn't consist just in pleasure or just in intelligence but in a combination of them; intelligence is the more important component, but some pleasures (the good but not the bad ones) are also part of happiness. In rejecting the view that happiness consists in pleasure, Plato rejects hedonism, as he also does in the earlier *Gorgias* and *Republic*. (By contrast, it is sometimes thought that he endorses it in the *Protagoras*, though it is also sometimes thought that he there merely ascribes it to "the many.")[34] In rejecting the view that happiness consists in intelligence alone, Plato rejects a purely contemplative view of happiness which, according to some but not others, he favors in the *Republic* and *Symposium*.

In chapter 20, Constance C. Meinwald discusses these issues about the *Philebus* but she places special emphasis on its treatment of method and metaphysics, an understanding of which is necessary if we are to understand how Plato arrives at his final view of the constituents of happiness. In doing so, he introduces the Promethean Method, which is based on the fact that there is both limit (*peras*) and the unlimited (*to apeiron*) in things. This method involves dividing subjects into subkinds and knowing how they combine with each other.

In addition to the Promethean Method, Plato also describes a Four-fold division of things into limit (*peras*), the unlimited (*to apeiron*), what is mixed from them, and the cause of the mixture. Pleasure is put in the category of the unlimited, and mind in the category of cause; this helps explain their place in the good human life.

The so-called method of division, adverted to in the Promethean Method, is also described in other dialogues. But the *Philebus* is unique in linking it to *peras* and *to apeiron*. There are disputes about how to understand these notions. Indeed, it is not even clear that they have the same sense or reference in the Promethean Method and in the Four-fold division, though Meinwald argues that they do. In her view, the *apeiron* is best understood as a blurred condition in which kinds run

---

34. In chapter 11, Annas discusses Plato's views on pleasure.

together with no significant demarcations. So, for example, below the level of specific vowels there is a continuum of sounds; below the lowest division into kinds of cats, there is indefinite variation in softness, fur, and so on, all at the level of types. On this view, *apeira* are not, as is sometimes thought, particulars (this cat and that one) but types considered independently of their division into determinate kinds, which is the realm of limit, or *peras*. Limit involves proportion, which, in turn, involves explaining forms or kinds in a mathematicized way. But the *Philebus* is not unique in emphasizing the fundamentally mathematical nature of things. In the *Republic* (522b2–531d4), Plato makes the study of mathematics at least a necessary preliminary for understanding forms, but he also seems to envisage an even closer connection. The importance of mathematics for understanding reality is also emphasized in the *Timaeus*.

What are the kinds (*eidê*) that Plato discusses in the *Philebus*? Meinwald suggests that they are given by genus-species trees. Here it is worth asking (as one might also do about the "greatest kinds" in the *Sophist*) how these kinds compare with the forms described in the middle dialogues.

# 11.

Above we looked at the epistemological and metaphysical importance of the "What is F?" question. An answer to this question is also of moral importance. For according to Socrates, knowledge is necessary for virtue: in particular, if one does not know what virtue is, one cannot be a virtuous person.[35] Hence failure to answer the "What is F?" question indicates not just an epistemological but also a moral failing.

Socrates is generally thought to hold that knowledge is also sufficient for virtue.[36] If knowledge is both necessary and sufficient for virtue, then, in some sense, virtue is knowledge. This is one of two so-called Socratic paradoxes. (The other is that no one does wrong willingly or voluntarily; I discuss this below.) The knowledge that virtue consists in isn't any old knowledge; it isn't, for example, knowledge of how to make shoes. Rather, it consists in knowledge of good and bad.[37]

The virtuous person can presumably be relied on to do the virtuous thing.[38] But then, if virtue is knowledge of good and bad, it seems that anyone who knows

---

35. In this section, in speaking of Socrates I mean the Socrates of the early dialogues. For the view that knowledge is necessary for virtue, see, for example, *Eu.* 15d4–8; *La.* 196e; *Ch.* 176a–b; and *Ly.* 212a1–7. It's sometimes but not always thought that beginning with the *Meno*, the view that knowledge is necessary for virtue is rejected in favor of the view that true belief (but not knowledge) is necessary for virtue.

36. See, for example, *La.* 192c2–d11, where Laches suggests that courage is wise endurance; but the reference to endurance then drops out, though the view that courage is wisdom is retained.

37. See, for example, *La.* 199d–e.

38. Or, at any rate, can be relied on to try to do the virtuous thing; she might be prevented from doing so by factors beyond her control.

what it is good—that is, best overall—to do will do it.[39] Hence anyone who does what is bad must not have known what it was best to do. Indeed, Socrates holds an even stronger view: that no one even ever acts against his belief about what it is best to do. Not only will anyone who knows that it is best to do x, do x; if one even believes that it is best to do x, one will do it. This is the second Socratic paradox: that no one does wrong willingly or voluntarily. There is, then, no such thing as *akrasia*: no such thing, that is, as knowing, or believing, that it is better to do x than y, but doing y instead.[40] Yet it is often assumed that there is such a phenomenon. Socrates owes us an explanation of his denial of its possibility. He offers one in the *Protagoras*, which Daniel Devereux discusses in chapter 6.[41] Before considering it, it will be helpful to lay some groundwork.

Let us say that a rational desire is good-dependent: it is a desire one has because one believes it is in one's best overall interest to pursue a given course of action.[42] What is best for one overall is be *eudaimon*, which is conventionally translated into English as "happy." This translation is liable to mislead, since to a modern ear it suggests feeling pleased or content, whereas *eudaimonia* is doing well (*eu prattein*). *Eudaimonia* is a property of a life, not something fleeting; the *eudaimon* life is the best life possible for a human being, whatever that turns out to be.

Socrates assumes that all rational desires ultimately aim at one's own happiness. It is often believed that he also thinks that *all* desires ultimately aim at one's own happiness. If this is correct, he thinks that all desires are rational.[43]

Because Socrates takes all (rational) desires to be for happiness, he—like virtually all Greek moral philosophers—is a eudaimonist.[44] Devereux discusses the eudaimonist framework of the early dialogues; in chapter 11, Julia Annas discusses it as it figures in Plato's dialogues more generally.

It is useful to distinguish between rational and psychological eudaimonism.[45] Rational eudaimonism claims that happiness provides the only ultimate justifying reason for doing something: it is the ultimate answer to the question, "Why is x worth pursuing?" Psychological eudaimonism claims that happiness is the only

39. This makes it sound as though Socrates thinks that a purely cognitive condition can be action guiding, contrary to a common view according to which desire is also necessary for action. However, in the *Protagoras* (358c–d; cf. *Eud.* 278e) Socrates says that it is "not in human nature" to choose what one thinks is bad rather than what is good. Hence his view is that knowledge is sufficient for virtue, and so for virtuous action, once given the basic human desire to secure what is good.

40. This is just one way of characterizing *akrasia*. I shall not here distinguish between knowledge-*akrasia* and belief-*akrasia*; but for discussion of how Socrates may take them to differ, see Devereux, chapter 6.

41. See also Lorenz's discussion in chapter 10. It's worth noting that, though Socrates argues against the possibility of this phenomenon in the *Protagoras*, he doesn't there use the term *akrasia*. He asks, instead, whether someone can be "overcome by pleasure" (352e6–353a1).

42. The term "good-dependent" (like the term "good-independent," used below in connection with the division of the soul in the *Republic*) is due to T. H. Irwin, *Plato's Moral Theory* (Oxford: Clarendon Press, 1977), 192.

43. But contrast Devereux, chapter 6.

44. The Cyrenaics may be an exception. (Actually, as we shall see below, it's sometimes thought that the *Republic* is not altogether eudaimonist.) Though ancient moral philosophers generally agree that *eudaimonia* is in some sense the ultimate end, they disagree about how to achieve it and about what it consists in.

45. For this terminology, see T. H. Irwin, *Plato's Ethics* (Oxford: Oxford University Press, 1995), sec. 36.

ultimate explanatory reason for doing something: it is the ultimate answer to the question, "Why did you do x?." The early dialogues assume both sorts of eudaimonism. They assume, that is, not only that it is rational for me to do something only to the extent that it contributes to my happiness but also that whatever I do, I do because I believe it will most contribute to my happiness.

It follows from psychological eudaimonism that no one ever acts against what he believes it is best for him to do.[46] This is sometimes called the prudential version of the second Socratic paradox.[47] There is also a moral version, according to which no one ever does moral wrong willingly. This version is secured if we add Socrates' beliefs that (a) acting unjustly or immorally is bad for the agent, and (b) we only want what is actually good for us. It follows from (a) and (b) that if we act unjustly or immorally, it cannot be something we want to do, and therefore it is done unwillingly (see *Gorgias* 509e).[48]

Though Socrates takes psychological eudaimonism to be a fundamental fact about us, he doesn't just leave it there. Rather, he argues that *akrasia* is impossible. Hence, his own alternative (that no one does wrong willingly) is either implied or at least rendered more plausible. The argument against *akrasia* assumes hedonism, the view that the good—that is, happiness—is the same as pleasure (353c–354e); it also assumes that we always choose what we take to be the maximum pleasure. If the good consists in pleasure, and if we always choose what we think will yield the good—which, according to the sort of hedonism at issue here, is the maximum amount of pleasure—then, in choosing y over x, we must believe that y will yield more pleasure than x. But in a case of *akrasia*, we choose what we take to be less good, though more pleasant. So, in this alleged case of *akrasia*, we must think x is better than y. But then, given that the good just is pleasure, it's as though we chose y over x, thinking y more pleasant than x, but also thinking x more pleasant than y. This seems to involve inconsistent beliefs: we think both that y is more pleasant than x and that x is more pleasant than y. We can avoid this unpalatable result if we assume that, if we choose y over x, it isn't because of *akrasia* but because of a mistaken belief about what would yield the most pleasure. The phenomenon that some describe as *akrasia*, therefore, really just involves false beliefs (e.g., 358c1–5): there is a purely cognitive failure, not weakness of the will.[49]

The argument against the possibility of *akrasia* is open to question. Nor is it clear that, even in the *Protagoras*, Socrates accepts hedonism.[50] If he does not do so,

---

46. We saw earlier that Socrates takes virtue to consist in knowledge of what is good and bad. We can now say, more exactly, that it consists in, or at any rate involves, knowledge of what is good and bad for oneself. Of course, if one knows what is good and bad for oneself, one also knows what is good and bad as such (at least, this is so if Socrates accepts the priority of definition, discussed above). But that does not mean that virtue consists, either wholly or partly, in such knowledge; it could be presupposed instead.

47. For the distinction between the prudential and moral versions of the second Socratic paradox, see G. Santas, *Socrates: Philosophy in Plato's Early Dialogues* (London: Routledge and Kegan Paul, 1979), 183–94.

48. As we shall see, the highly controversial assumption that it is in one's best overall interest to be just is defended in detail in the *Republic*.

49. For a different account of the argument, see Devereux, chapter 6.

50. For discussion, see C. C. W. Taylor, *Plato's Protagoras*, 2nd ed. (Oxford: Clarendon Press, 1991), 162–70.

then the argument against *akrasia* is more ad hominem than offered in his own voice.[51] Be that as it may, Socrates is aware that his view that virtue is knowledge is controversial, and he defends it.

We saw above that the moral version of the second Socratic paradox assumes that what is best for one is being morally virtuous. More strongly, Socrates thinks that virtue is sufficient for happiness. This, too, is a highly controversial claim, one Socrates defends in the *Euthydemus*, where he argues that x is either a part of, or necessary for, happiness if and only if virtue secures it.

The claim that virtue is sufficient for happiness has been understood in two different ways. On one view, it means that virtue, all by itself, is sufficient for happiness. On another, weaker, view, it means that virtue is sufficient for happiness only given a sufficient (modest) amount of certain other goods, such as health. Annas argues that both views sit side by side throughout the corpus, without ever being clearly distinguished from one another.[52]

Suppose that virtue is literally sufficient for happiness. We can then ask whether virtue is sufficient for happiness by being its sole component, or by being an infallible means to happiness. An analogy will illustrate the difference between these two views. Milk, flour, and eggs are parts of, ingredients in, a cake; going to the store to buy these ingredients is an instrumental means of making the cake, but it is not part of the cake.

It is sometimes thought that the fact that Socrates takes virtue to be a craft (*technê*, also translated as "skill" or "art") supports the instrumental view: just as shoemaking is a craft with the distinct product of shoes, so virtue is a craft with the distinct product of happiness. But it has been argued that not all crafts have distinct products; music and dance have been thought to be counterexamples. If this is right, then the mere fact that Socrates takes virtue to be a craft does not imply that he takes it to be merely an instrumental means to happiness. We need to know what sort of craft he takes it to be: one that has, or lacks, an independent product. We might also ask how committed Socrates is to the craft analogy. Devereux suggests that he often accepts it as a working hypothesis but also has some doubts about it. Devereux also argues that happiness (unlike wisdom, that is, virtue, which consists in knowledge) is not a possession that can be used; rather, it consists in the use of assets guided by wisdom or knowledge. If this is right, then virtue is not the sole component of happiness, but neither is it a mere instrumental means to happiness. Devereux suggests that the relation between wisdom (knowledge), or virtue, on the one hand, and happiness, on the other, is closer than that between a craft like shoemaking and its product but is not quite the same as whole

---

51. It is sometimes thought that in the *Meno* (77–78), Socrates also argues against *akrasia* without assuming hedonism and in his own voice.

52. On the second, weaker, view, virtue is not literally sufficient for happiness; rather, it is just especially important to securing happiness. Hence it might be better to call the second view an alternative to the sufficiency thesis rather than a version of it. For the view that virtue is sufficient for happiness only given a sufficient (modest) amount of other goods such as health, see G. Vlastos, "Happiness and Virtue in Socrates' Moral Theory," in his *Socrates*, 200–32; and in Fine, *Plato 2*, ch. 4. For the view that virtue is literally sufficient for happiness, see Irwin, *Plato's Moral Theory*, esp. ch. 3, and *Plato's Ethics*, esp. chs. 3–4.

and part. Rather, it is similar to that between a *technê* like dancing, and its product, conceived as the exercise of the *technê*.

If virtue is the sole component of happiness, we have an account of what Socrates takes happiness to consist in. If, however, virtue is merely an instrumental means to happiness, we still lack such an account. If he endorses the hedonism described in the *Protagoras*, that would provide such an account; but, as we have seen, it is disputed whether he endorses it. Whether or not he endorses hedonism in the *Protagoras*, he firmly rejects it by the time of the *Gorgias* and subsequent dialogues. In these dialogues, though some pleasures—the good ones—are part of the happy life, happiness does not consist just in pleasure.[53]

# 12.

We have seen that the early dialogues assume rational eudaimonism: one has reason to do something only insofar as it contributes to one's happiness. One therefore has reason to be just only if that contributes to one's happiness. The early dialogues assume that being just contributes to one's happiness.[54] But the assumption is controversial. For justice seems to be other-regarding, in the sense that my justice seems to benefit you. As Thrasymachus says in Book 1, justice is "another's good" (343c): that is, my being just is good for you. But couldn't it harm me? What if any reason, then, does a rational eudaimonist have for being just? This is one of the main questions that Plato considers in the *Republic*. It is his version of the perennially fascinating, and absolutely fundamental, question: "Why be moral?"[55]

At the beginning of *Republic* 2, Glaucon challenges Socrates to show that justice is good not only for its consequences (it is agreed on all hands that it is good in this way) but also in itself, a view that, Glaucon says, is generally denied. To develop this point, he describes a thought-experiment: Gyges had a ring that made him invisible; this enabled him to commit injustice with impunity. Glaucon thinks that if we reflect on Gyges' situation, we will see that everyone would act as he did; we would all behave unjustly if we could get away with it. We practice justice

53. There is dispute about whether the version of hedonism described in the *Protagoras* is the same as the version(s) rejected in other dialogues. See, for example, J. C. B. Gosling and C. C. W. Taylor, *The Greeks on Pleasure* (Oxford: Clarendon Press, 1982); and Annas, chapter 11 of this volume.

54. In the *Crito*, for example, Socrates says that the good life is the same as the just life (48b). What about wisdom, courage, and temperance? Aren't they also part of the good life? Yes, but Socrates thinks that all the virtues are identical or, at least, that one can have one virtue if and only if one has them all. Hence if one is just, one is also courageous, and so on.

55. Plato's version of this question is sometimes thought to differ from another version of it. The question is sometimes taken to mean: Should one be moral for self-interested reasons, or for other reasons? Plato, by contrast, assumes that one has reason to be moral only if that promotes self-interest; his question is whether it does so. The difference between these two ways of understanding the question is part of what led H. Prichard to think that Plato's approach rests on a mistake; see his "Does Moral Philosophy Rest on a Mistake?," *Moral Obligation and Duty and Interest* (Oxford: Oxford University Press, 1968), ch. 1.

reluctantly, because we lack such a ring.[56] Acting justly involves, among other things, not harming others and, more positively, benefiting others.

To say that behaving justly involves not harming others and also benefiting them is not yet to say exactly what justice is. And Glaucon admits that most people might have an incorrect understanding of what it is; hence he asks Socrates to provide his own account. At the end of Book 4, Socrates offers a preliminary answer, according to which justice is a sort of psychic harmony. It has been argued that in so defining justice, Plato commits the fallacy of irrelevance:[57] Socrates was asked to explain why, for example, I have reason to benefit others; in reply, he explains why I have reason to promote my own psychic harmony. This definition of justice is sometimes thought to be too far removed from the ordinary understanding of it to provide an explanation of why one should be just, as the question was originally intended. Glaucon wanted to know why one should, for example, honor one's commitments and parents and not steal. Socrates explains why one has reason to want one's soul to be well ordered. What is the connection between the original question and Socrates' answer? In chapter 15, Dominic Scott canvasses a variety of ways of defending Plato against the charge of committing the fallacy of irrelevance. The basic strategy is to argue that one can achieve and maintain one's psychic harmony only if one benefits others, perhaps only if one benefits them for their own sakes; hence benefiting others turns out to be part of one's good. But there are many different versions of this general strategy.

Scott, for example, considers both psychological and metaphysical defenses. According to the psychological defense, conventionally unjust behavior is motivated by desires a person who has achieved platonic justice will lack; someone who has achieved platonic justice can be relied on to act, at least by and large, as a conventionally just person would. Hence, there is significant overlap between conventional and platonic justice; the fallacy of irrelevance is therefore avoided. According to the metaphysical defense, the platonically just person will both understand and love the form of the good; and this, in turn, will lead him to behave, at least by and large, as a conventionally just person would, if for different reasons (because of his love of the form of the good, rather than, for example, out of a fear of being caught). In Scott's view, Plato explicitly relies on the psychological defense. Though he may also intend the metaphysical defense, he does not explicitly offer it; commentators who appeal to it, in Scott's view, are engaged in "rational reconstruction."

Still, it is worth considering how this rational reconstruction would go. Here it is worthwhile to consider Plato's views on love, which Richard Kraut explores

---

56. But see 366c–d, where it is said that anyone who really knows what justice is will be just willingly. It is an overstatement to say that each of us would act unjustly whenever we could get away with it. Even on the ordinary view of justice that Glaucon describes, the social contract that arises when each of us agrees not to harm others in exchange for not being harmed ourselves is in our interests. Hence, even if I could be guaranteed to get away with doing an unjust act, I would not do it, if doing it would undermine the system that protects and benefits me. But most unjust actions would not have such serious consequences, or so we might think.

57. See, for example, G. Grote, *Plato and the Other Companions of Socrates*, vol. 4, new ed. (New York: Burt Franklin, 1973; reprint of the 1888 ed.), 99–106; and D. Sachs, "A Fallacy in Plato's Republic?," *Philosophical Review* 72 (1963), 141–58, reprinted in Vlastos, *Plato 2*, ch. 2.

(though not primarily in connection with Plato's reply to Glaucon) in chapter 12. If one loves something, one wants to be surrounded by it. Philosophers—who alone are platonically, hence truly, just—love goodness; hence they want to be surrounded by goodness. Hence they have reason to benefit others, by making them as good as their natures allow them to be. I return to this sort of consideration below.

Plato's views about love have been roundly criticized. For example, it has been argued that he thinks we do, or at any rate should, love others just for their admirable traits. And this might seem to have the unattractive consequence that we do not love others as the distinctive individuals they are; we love their admirable traits, not the people who have them.[58] Kraut argues that Plato's views on love should not be understood in this way; rather, Plato leaves room for loving individuals as the people they are.

To return to the *Republic*: Glaucon asks Socrates to show not only that justice is good in itself, but also that it is the greatest good (of the soul)—that is, that the just person is happier than anyone else could be. It is disputed whether, in reply, Socrates aims to show that virtue is the dominant component of happiness (its single most important constituent, though not one that, all by itself, is sufficient for happiness), or whether he aims to defend the more ambitious claim that virtue is sufficient for happiness. According to Annas, both the weaker and stronger claims can be found in the *Republic*, as well as throughout Plato's career. On an alternative view, the early dialogues defend the view that virtue is sufficient for happiness, whereas the main argument in the *Republic* (in Books 2–9) defends only the weaker view that justice is the dominant component of happiness.[59]

If justice is either the sole or dominant component of happiness, the *Republic* rejects the view that virtue is merely an instrumental means to happiness which, as we have seen, is a view the early dialogues are sometimes but not always thought to maintain. If the *Republic* argues that justice is the dominant component of, but not sufficient for, happiness, it rejects the view that virtue is sufficient for happiness which, as we have seen, is another view the early dialogues are sometimes but not always thought to maintain.

# 13.

Plato describes platonic justice in terms of his division of the soul into three "parts" or "kinds" (435e–441c): the rational (*to logistikon*), the spirited (*to thumoeides*), and the appetitive (*to epithumêtikon*). A person is just when each of these

---

58. For this view, see G. Vlastos, "The Individual as Object of Love in Plato," *Platonic Studies* (Princeton, N.J.: Princeton University Press (1973), 3–34, reprinted in Fine, *Plato 2*, ch. 5.

59. This alternative view is defended by Irwin, in both *Plato's Moral Theory*, ch. 7, and *Plato's Ethics*, esp. ch. 15.

parts fulfills its proper function, and when they are in the right sort of harmony with one another. In chapter 10, Hendrik Lorenz discusses Plato's division of the soul and compares it with his view of the soul in the *Protagoras*, *Gorgias*, and *Phaedo*.

On one view, the rational part is all reasoning, the appetitive all desire; if this is correct, there doesn't seem to be room for the third, spirited, part.[60] On another view, Plato's distinction is between three irreducibly different sorts of desires or motivating factors or, alternatively, between the subjects of those desires.[61] On this view, the rational part of the soul either consists of one's rational desires or is the subject for such desires; these are what, above, I called good-dependent desires. I have a rational desire to drink milk, for example, if I desire to do so because I think that's best for me, all things considered—because, say, I believe that it will promote my health, which I think is good for me.

Appetitive desires, by contrast, are good-independent: they do not consider what is best for me. I have an appetitive desire to drink milk, for example, if I just feel like drinking it. One can have an appetitive and a rational desire for at least some of the same things, if for different reasons. But these desires can also conflict: I might want to drink milk because I like its taste; but I might want not to drink it because I know it isn't healthy for me to do so (suppose I am lactose intolerant).

This way of conceiving of the parts of the soul—as types of desires, or as subjects for types of desires—leaves room for a third part, since the division between good-dependent and good-independent desires is not exhaustive. There are, however, different ways of conceiving of the spirited part. Lorenz suggests that it involves the desire to distinguish oneself and to be esteemed and respected by others, as well as an awareness of one's social position and of one's merits. This explains the spirited person's sensitivity to slights and insults; it also explains why Plato associates spirit with anger.

In acknowledging the existence of spirited and appetitive desires, Plato rejects the view, often associated with the early dialogues, according to which all desires are rational; he therefore rejects psychological eudaimonism.[62] In allowing that appetitive desires can not only conflict with but also overcome rational desires, he acknowledges the possibility of *akrasia*: again in contrast to the early dialogues.[63]

60. For this view, see T. Penner, "Thought and Desire in Plato," in Vlastos (ed.), *Plato 2*, 96–118.

61. Just as each part of the soul has its own sort of desire, so each part has its own distinctive kind of cognition, though there is dispute about what sort of cognition each part has. Lorenz argues that only the rational part is capable of means-end reasoning; contrast C. Bobonich, *Plato's Utopia Recast* (Oxford: Clarendon Press, 2002), 244.

62. *Rep.* 438a calls attention to this point. In the *Phaedo* and *Gorgias*, Plato also rejects the view that all desires are rational. In the *Phaedo*, nonrational desires seem to be ascribed to the body, whereas in the *Republic* they are ascribed to one part of the soul.

63. At least, he allows that one can believe that it is better for one to do x than y, yet do y instead. It is less clear whether he thinks that someone with full knowledge of what is best for one could ever act against that knowledge.

# 14.

Just as Plato divides the soul into three parts, so he divides the ideally just *polis*—city or state[64]—into three occupationally defined classes: the guardians or rulers; the auxiliaries or military class; and the workers or producers. And just as he argues that justice for an individual consists in the harmony of the three parts of the individual's soul, with each part fulfilling its proper function, so he argues that justice for a city consists in the proper harmony of its three parts (the three classes), with each part (class) fulfilling its function.

There is dispute over the precise interpretation of Plato's elaborate analogy between justice in a soul and in a city. According to the Whole-Part account, a city is just if and only if all or most of its members are just; but this view leads to considerable difficulties. For example, Plato thinks that even in the ideally just city, most people aren't just; only the guardians are. For they alone know what justice is; and one must have this knowledge to be just. (This is why, in Plato's view, philosophers should rule—a view he acknowledges as the greatest of the three waves of paradox that partly structure *Rep.* V (473d; cf. 484)).[65]

This suggests the Macro-Micro account, according to which there is a structural isomorphism between the justice of a person and a city. For a person to be just is for the parts of her soul to be in a particular sort of harmony, and for each part to fulfill its function; for a city to be just is for its occupationally defined classes to be in structurally the same harmony, and for each of its parts to fulfill its function. On this view, a city can be just even if not all or most of its citizens are just. All that is required is that each class fulfill its proper function, and that the classes stand in the appropriate harmonious relations to one another.[66]

# 15.

For each class to fulfill its function requires the members of that class to devote themselves to just one type of work; this is mandated by the principle of specialization laid down in Book 2. Those in the productive class will spend their time

---

64. *Polis* is variously translated as "city," "state," and "city-state."

65. For the view that, in the ideal city, only the philosophers are just, see J. Neu, "Plato's Analogy of State and Individual," *Philosophy* 24 (1971), 238–54. For the view that not only they are just, see R. Kraut, "Reason and Justice in Plato's *Republic*," in E. N. Lee, A. P. D. Mourelatos, and R. M. Rorty (eds.), *Exegesis and Argument* (Assen: Van Gorcum, 1973), 207–24.

66. For discussion of the Whole-Part interpretation, see B. A. O. Williams, "The Analogy of City and Soul in Plato's *Republic*," in E. N. Lee, A. P. D. Mourelatos, and R. M. Rorty (eds.), *Exegesis and Argument* (Assen: Van Gorcum, 1973), 196–206, reprinted in Fine, *Plato 2*, ch. 10. For a defense of the Macro-Micro account, see Neu, "Plato's Analogy of State and Individual"; and G. F. R. Ferrari, *City and Soul in Plato's Republic* (Sankt Augustin: Academia Verlag, 2003, and Chicago: University of Chicago Press, 2005). At 435e,

making shoes, producing food, and so on; the auxiliaries will devote themselves to defending the city from both external and internal enemies; and the guardians will contemplate forms and rule in the light of the knowledge that confers.

In restricting ruling to the guardians, Plato rules out democracy; the guardians are the only ones who have a say in how the city will be run. Hence most people are deprived of political autonomy. Their personal autonomy is also severely limited. For example, someone who is most suited to be in the working class cannot be an auxiliary, even if she wants to be. Both political and personal autonomy are often thought to be important goods; in depriving most members of the city of much of their personal and political autonomy, isn't Plato making them less happy than they could otherwise be? We might also ask, as Glaucon does at 519e, whether, in requiring philosophers, at least temporarily, to forgo contemplation of forms in order to rule, Plato is making them less happy than they could be; for contemplating forms is a greater good than ruling.[67]

In reply to the worry about the happiness of philosophers, Socrates says that he isn't aiming at the happiness of any one class but at the happiness of the whole (420b–421c; 519e–520a). According to Popper, Plato accepts the "organic theory," which involves both a metaphysical and a political component. The metaphysical component says that the state is an entity in its own right, distinct from its parts. The political component involves the view that individual citizens must sacrifice their interests for those of the city.

Scott argues, against Popper, that the city-soul analogy does not imply the metaphysical component. Rather, it implies only that the city and the soul are structurally similar. Though Scott also rejects Popper's version of the political component, he agrees that Plato thinks that the interests of individual citizens are subordinate to the greatest good of the state, which is its unity.[68] On an alternative view, in saying that he aims at the happiness of the whole, Plato means that he wants each citizen to be as happy as he can be. To say this is not to sacrifice individual happiness to the happiness of a distinct entity, the city; nor is it to give priority to the interests of the city over those of its citizens.[69]

How does Plato defend the view that he aims to make ordinary citizens as happy as possible, given that they have so little personal and political autonomy?

---

Plato says that characteristics of communities are derived from those of its members. This might seem to favor the Whole-Part account. However, the passage commits Plato only to the weaker view that *some* features of a community are *in some way* derived from features of its members. It doesn't commit him to the more specific view that a city is F if and only if all or most of its citizens are F.

67. At 419a, Adeimantus raises a further question about the guardians' happiness: Doesn't the fact that they live in relatively austere conditions make them less happy than they could be? Plato's answer is that thinking this involves overvaluing material possessions; the guardians have all they need for happiness, and they will know this.

68. See also L. Brown, "How Totalitarian Is Plato's *Republic?*," in E. Ostenfeld (ed.), *Essays on Plato's Republic* (Aarhus: Aarhus University Press, 1998), 13–27.

69. Nor is it to endorse utilitarianism. Plato's concern is to describe a city that allows each person to achieve the greatest amount of happiness they are capable of. In contrast to utilitarianism, he doesn't think it legitimate to sacrifice the happiness of a few in order to produce a greater overall aggregate amount of happiness.

And how does he defend the view that guardians are happy, when they are made to abandon the great good of contemplating forms for the lesser good of ruling?

On one view, Plato argues that the guardians must return to the cave to rule, despite the fact that it is not in their self-interest, because it is good to do so: not good for them, but impersonally good.[70] If this is right, then at this stage Plato abandons eudaimonism and does not show, as he undertook to do in Book 2, that it is always in one's interest to be just. On an alternative view, he retains eudaimonism and argues that it is in the guardians' best overall interest to rule.[71] To be sure, contemplating forms is a greater good than ruling. But it doesn't follow that the philosopher who has been trained in the ideal city would be better off, all things considered, if she continued to philosophize and thereby violated the just requirement that she rule, than if she spent some time ruling, thereby fulfilling a just requirement. Still, one wants to know why the philosopher is better off occasionally engaging in a less good activity than she would be if she more single-mindedly devoted herself to contemplating the forms.

One possibility is that ruling is instrumentally good for philosophers: if they don't rule, the city will be less stable than it would otherwise be, and that would harm them. By way of analogy, if philosophers don't eat, they will die and so could not contemplate the forms; hence even though eating is less good than contemplation, philosophers will spend some time eating, and for their own sakes.[72] Similarly, even if ruling is less good than contemplating, it may be in the philosophers' best interest to spend some time ruling.

One might also argue, more strongly, that ruling is not merely instrumentally good. For example, as we saw above, given their love of goodness, philosophers want, for their own sakes, to be surrounded by as much goodness as possible. In ruling, they make others as good as possible, which is in the intrinsic interests of those others. Hence in benefiting others for their own sakes, the guardians also benefit themselves; achieving the good of others is therefore part of their own happiness.

As to nonguardians, Plato thinks they will come as close to being happy as their natures allow only if they are ruled by the guardians, since only the guardians know what is truly good. In Plato's view, political and personal autonomy are less important to one's happiness than they are sometimes taken to be. Living in a stable, well-ordered city in which one devotes oneself to the task for which one is best suited contributes more to one's happiness than having more autonomy would. We may not agree with Plato's low estimation of the importance of autonomy or

---

70. Alteratively, one might argue that they must do so because, though it is not good for them, it is good for the city. For versions of the view that it is not in the philosopher's best overall interest to rule, see J. Cooper, "The Psychology of Justice in Plato," *American Philosophical Quarterly* 14 (1977), 151–57; J. Annas, *An Introduction to Plato's Republic* (Oxford: Clarendon Press, 1982); and N. P. White, "Plato's Concept of Good," in H. Benson (ed.), *A Companion to Plato* (Oxford: Blackwell, 2006), ch. 24.

71. For discussion, see R. Kraut, "Return to the Cave: *Republic* 519–21," in Fine, *Plato 2*, ch. 9, to which my discussion is indebted.

72. But this analogy is imperfect, since one can free ride on others' ruling, but not on others' eating.

with his defense of paternalism. Be that as it may, it is important to see that he limits personal and political autonomy neither in sacrifice to a superorganism nor for the interests of the state but to enable each individual to come as close to being happy as possible.

# 16.

For the ideally just city to come into existence, people's attitudes need to be radically transformed. For example, they need to learn what is truly of value: virtue, rather than material goods. They also need to learn to value true philosophers who, in turn, need to undergo the proper training so as to allow their natures to flourish. In chapter 14, Rachana Kamtekar considers the sort of education this transformation requires. She also considers Plato's views on art, which are intimately connected to his views on education since, for example, attending to certain sorts of art can inhibit proper development by arousing and encouraging inappropriate emotions.

Though Plato seems to think his ideally just city is possible,[73] it certainly isn't actual. We might then wonder what the best city we can hope for is, given people as they actually are. In chapter 13, Christopher Bobonich suggests that different dialogues defend different views. In the early dialogues, for example, Socrates thinks no one has the knowledge that is required for virtue; hence no one is qualified to rule in the way the guardians of the *Republic* are. Does he nonetheless think there should be absolute rulers, albeit less-qualified ones? Or does he think the city should be run in a different way? Presumably, he thinks the best city we can hope for, taking us more or less as we are, is one run according to his moral principles: for example, that it is better to suffer than to commit injustice; that if one commits injustice, it is better to be punished than to escape punishment; and so on. What would a city look like if it embodied these and other Socratic principles, but taking us more or less as we are? Such a city would need to impose some sanctions, which, in turn, might require a fair amount of coercion. What legitimates such coercion? Would all citizens benefit equally from living in a city founded on Socratic principles? How stable would such a city be? Does political activity, in such a city, compete with developing one's own virtue? Because the ethical views of the early dialogues are so underdeveloped, it is difficult to answer these questions in their case. But, Bobonich suggests, some questions receive fuller—and different—answers, beginning in the *Phaedo*. Bobonich traces Plato's answers to the various

73. See, for example, M. F. Burnyeat, "Utopia and Fantasy: The Practicability of Plato's Ideally Just City," in J. Hopkins and A. Savile (eds.), *Psychoanalysis, Mind and Art* (Oxford: Blackwell, 1992), 175–87, reprinted in Fine, *Plato 2*, ch. 13.

questions just mentioned, from the earliest through the latest dialogues. He also explores Plato's changing views of the nature of the ideally best city. He argues that the early, middle, and late dialogues espouse different ethical, epistemological, and metaphysical views, which, in turn, lead to differences in these dialogues' views about the best city, both for people as they are and for people who have undergone the necessary transformation to allow for a more radical change in society.

For example, according to Bobonich, the early dialogues deny the existence of nonrational desires, whereas later dialogues admit their existence. Hence, according to the early dialogues, one can persuade people to change their lives only by changing their beliefs. By contrast, admitting the existence of nonrational desires opens up the possibility that people can be trained to care about the right things not, or not only, by changing their beliefs but also by training their nonrational desires in such a way that they come to care about the right things, whether or not they can appreciate their true value.

According to Bobonich, Plato's views about the ideally just city, and about the best state for us more or less as we are, change again in the *Statesman*. For example, it seems to have more demanding qualifications for citizenship, and citizenship has greater ethical significance. In the *Republic*, the members of all three classes are citizens, though only the philosophers are just; in the *Statesman*, only just people can be citizens. However, this would allow nonphilosophers to be citizens if they are just, and Bobonich thinks that is Plato's view by the time of the *Statesman*. This could be so for one of two reasons: either Plato now thinks that nonphilosophers have knowledge, or he no longer requires knowledge for virtue.

The *Laws* has different views again. For example, it revises the *Republic*'s view of the nature of the ideally just city. It also allows, contrary to the *Republic*, that nonphilosophers can be educated so as to have a reasoned grasp of basic ethical and political truths. Hence nonphilosophers are now fit to rule; instead of philosopher rulers, Plato now posits an Assembly open to all citizens.

# 17.

Aristotle was Plato's student, or associate, in the Academy for nearly twenty years, and he is an important source of information about Plato, though there are disputes about his reliability.[74] In chapter 21, Shields explores some of Aristotle's criticisms of Plato, focusing on his claim that Platonic forms turn out to be both particulars and universals. Shields also explores a closely related, but possibly importantly different, claim: that "universals and particulars are practically the same natures" (*Met.* 1086b10–11). Shields argues that if Aristotle means to argue that forms are both universals and particulars, where these are taken to be exclusive

74. Irwin, chapter 3.

categories of being, his arguments fail; whereas, on some ways of understanding the claim that universals and particulars are practically the same natures, he has a more challenging criticism, one he himself needs to grapple with as well. In exploring these issues, Shields asks whether, as Aristotle sometimes seems to argue, the separation of forms would make them into particulars: a curious claim for Aristotle to make, given that he himself, in at least some phases of his career, admits universal substances (*ousiai*), as in the *Categories*, where the species and genera of individual substances count as secondary substances; yet species and genera are universals, not particulars.

Shields also explores Plato's account of participation in terms of mimeticism, asking whether, as Aristotle may believe, it commits Plato to the view that forms are particulars. Shields concludes that it does not do so. For these and other reasons, Shields argues, Aristotle has no easy route to the conclusion that forms are particulars. However, Shields argues, Aristotle also makes the good point that Plato seems to overtax forms, giving them too many roles to play, roles no single sort of entity could obviously play. Shields suggests, for example, that, according to Aristotle, Plato posits forms in order to explain both the knowability and the unity (both synchronic and diachronic) of sensible particulars. Insofar as they explain knowability, they must, in Aristotle's view, be universals; but insofar as they are principles of the synchronic and diachronic unity of particulars, it seems they must, according to Aristotle, be particulars. Shields suggests that this Aristotelian line of criticism is more promising, if not clearly devastating, than one that attempts to argue that forms are, impossibly, both universals and particulars.

More generally, Shields suggests that, though Aristotle does not succeed in delivering a knockout blow to Plato, he raises important criticisms that are well worth considering. In any case, we can understand both Plato's and Aristotle's views better by considering both Aristotle's objections and Plato's resources in the face of them.

Whether or not Plato was the first Platonist, he was by no means the last. In chapter 22, Charles Brittain describes the fascinating—though difficult and complex, and still relatively unexplored—history of how later Platonists appropriated, or claimed to appropriate, Plato's views. Though "Platonism" is often taken to involve a single, unified body of thought, Brittain shows how heterogeneous the tradition is. Nonetheless, he identifies three generally shared commitments: (1) to the authoritative status of Plato's work; (2) to the assumption that empirical experience is inadequate as a basis for understanding the world and that there are various primary immaterial principles, including forms, souls, and a transcendent god, that do explain it; and (3) to an increasing interest in a range of religious practices and concerns. As Brittain notes, the results of these commitments are likely to strike modern readers as remote from Plato's text, at least at first glance. However, as he also notes, even if we do not share the three commitments just mentioned, we can benefit greatly by reading the work of the philosophers who made them—not just because that work is intrinsically interesting but also because it sheds light on Plato, by providing a range of imaginative solutions to interpretative difficulties that are still with us. Just as exploring Aristotle's criticisms of Plato allows us to achieve further insight into Plato's and Aristotle's views, so comparing Plato's Platonism with later Platonism promises to shed light on both.[75]

# BIBLIOGRAPHY

Annas, J. *An Introduction to Plato's Republic* (Oxford: Clarendon Press, 1982).

Bobonich, C. *Plato's Utopia Recast* (Oxford: Clarendon Press, 2002).

Bostock, D. *Plato's Theaetetus* (Oxford: Clarendon Press, 1988).

Brown, L. "How Totalitarian Is Plato's *Republic?*," in E. Ostenfeld (ed.), *Essays on Plato's Republic* (Aarhus: Aarhus University Press, 1998), 13–27.

Burnyeat, M. F. *Introduction to the* Theaetetus *of Plato* (Indianapolis: Hackett, 1990).

Burnyeat, M. F. "Plato on the Grammar of Perceiving," *Classical Quarterly* 26 (1976), 29–51.

Burnyeat, M. F. "Protagoras and Self-Refutation," *Philosophical Review* 85 (1976), 172–95.

Burnyeat, M. F. "Utopia and Fantasy: The Practicability of Plato's Ideally Just City," in J. Hopkins and A. Savile (eds.), *Psychoanalysis, Mind and Art* (Oxford: Blackwell, 1992), 175–87; reprinted in Fine, *Plato 2*, ch. 13.

Cohen, S. M. "The Logic of the Third Man," *Philosophical Review* 80 (1971), 448–75; reprinted in Fine, *Plato 1*, ch. 10.

Cooper, J. "Plato on Sense-Perception and Knowledge (*Theaetetus* 184–6)," *Phronesis* (1970), 123–46; reprinted in Fine, *Plato 1*, ch. 13.

Cooper, J. "The Psychology of Justice in Plato," *American Philosophical Quarterly* 14 (1977), 151–57.

Dancy, R. *Plato's Introduction of Forms* (Cambridge: Cambridge University Press, 2004).

Ferrari, G. F. R. *City and Soul in Plato's Republic* (Sankt Augustin: Academia Verlag, 2003, and Chicago: University of Chicago Press, 2005).

Fine, G. "Enquiry and Discovery," *Oxford Studies in Ancient Philosophy* 32 (2007), 331–367.

Fine, G. "False Belief in the *Theaetetus*," *Phronesis* 24 (1979), 70–80; reprinted, with minor modifications, in Fine, *Plato on Knowledge and Forms*, ch. 9.

Fine, G. "Inquiry in the *Meno*," in R. Kraut (ed.), *Cambridge Companion to Plato* (Cambridge: Cambridge University Press, 1992), 200–26; reprinted with minor modifications in Fine, *Plato on Knowledge and Forms*, ch. 2.

Fine, G. "Knowledge and *Logos* in the *Theaetetus*," *Philosophical Review* 88 (1979), 366–97; reprinted, with minor modifications, in Fine, *Plato on Knowledge and Forms*, ch. 10.

Fine, G. "Knowledge and True Belief in the *Meno*," *Oxford Studies in Ancient Philosophy* (2004), 41–81.

Fine, G. (ed.) *Plato* (Oxford: Oxford University Press, 2000).

Fine, G. (ed.) *Plato 1: Metaphysics and Epistemology* (Oxford: Oxford University Press, 1999).

Fine, G. (ed.) *Plato 2: Ethics, Politics, Religion, and the Soul* (Oxford: Oxford University Press, 1999).

75. Thanks to Chris Bobonich, Lesley Brown, Dan Devereux, Terry Irwin, Chris Shields, and Christopher Taylor for helpful comments and/or discussion.

Fine, G. *Plato on Knowledge and Forms: Selected Essays* (Oxford: Clarendon Press, 2003).

Gill, M. L. "Problems for Forms," in H. Benson (ed.), *A Companion to Plato* (Oxford: Blackwell, 2006), ch. 13.

Gosling, J. C. B., and Taylor, C. C. W. *The Greeks on Pleasure* (Oxford: Clarendon Press, 1982).

Grote, G. *Plato and the Other Companions of Socrates*, vol. 4, new ed. (New York: Burt Franklin, 1973; reprint of the 1888 ed.).

Irwin, T. H. *Plato's Ethics* (Oxford: Oxford University Press, 1995).

Irwin, T. H. *Plato's Moral Theory* (Oxford: Clarendon Press, 1977).

Kraut, R. "Reason and Justice in Plato's *Republic*," in E. N. Lee, A. P. D. Mourelatos, and R. M. Rorty (eds.), *Exegesis and Argument* (Assen: Van Gorcum, 1973), 207–24.

Kraut, R. "Return to the Cave: *Republic* 519–21," in G. Fine (ed.), *Plato 2*, ch. 9.

Lee, M. *Epistemology after Protagoras* (Oxford: Clarendon Press, 2005).

Neu, J. "Plato's Analogy of State and Individual," *Philosophy* 24 (1971), 238–54.

Penner, T. "Thought and Desire in Plato," in Vlastos (ed.), *Plato 2*, ch. 6.

Prichard, H. "Does Moral Philosophy Rest on a Mistake?," *Moral Obligation and Duty and Interest* (Oxford: Oxford University Press, 1968), ch. 1.

Sachs, D. "A Fallacy in Plato's Republic?" *Philosophical Review* 72 (1963), 141–58; reprinted in Vlastos (ed.), *Plato 2*, ch. 2.

Santas, G. *Socrates: Philosophy in Plato's Early Dialogues* (London: Routledge and Kegan Paul, 1979).

Scott, D. *Plato's Meno* (Cambridge: Cambridge University Press, 2006).

Scott, D. *Recollection and Experience* (Cambridge: Cambridge University Press, 1995).

Taylor, C. C. W. *Plato's Protagoras*, 2nd ed. (Oxford: Clarendon Press, 1991), 162–70.

Vlastos, G. "Happiness and Virtue in Socrates' Moral Theory," in Vlastos, *Socrates*, 200–32; and in Fine, *Plato 2*, ch. 4.

Vlastos, G. "The Individual as Object of Love in Plato," *Platonic Studies* (Princeton: Princeton University Press (1973), 3–34; reprinted in Fine, *Plato 2*, ch. 5.

Vlastos, G. "Socrates' Disavowal of Knowledge," *Philosophical Quarterly* 35 (1985), 1–31; reprinted in Fine, *Plato 1*, ch. 2.

Vlastos, G. *Socrates, Ironist and Moral Philosopher* (Ithaca, N.Y.: Cornell University Press, 1991).

Vlastos, G. "The Socratic Elenchus," *Oxford Studies in Ancient Philosophy* 1 (1983), 27–58; reprinted in Fine, *Plato 1*, ch. 1.

Vlastos, G. "The Third Man Argument in the *Parmenides*," *Philosophical Review* 63 (1954), 319–49.

White, N. P. "Plato's Concept of Good," in H. Benson (ed.), *A Companion to Plato* (Oxford: Blackwell, 2006), ch. 24.

Williams, B. A. O. "The Analogy of City and Soul in Plato's *Republic*," in E. N. Lee, A. P. D. Mourelatos, and R. M. Rorty (eds.), *Exegesis and Argument* (Assen: Van Gorcum, 1973), 196–206; reprinted in Fine, *Plato 2*, ch. 10.

# CHAPTER 2

# PLATO IN HIS TIME AND PLACE

## MALCOLM SCHOFIELD

In this chapter, I attempt to situate Plato's philosophizing and literary production in its historical context. The evidence external to the dialogues that such an enterprise can rely on is either scrappy or suspect, or both. So what I offer here is a series of snapshots. They follow a chronological sequence, from Plato's relationship with Socrates and the Athens that executed him; through his momentous first visit to Italy and Sicily and its impact on his thinking about politics and philosophy; to the founding of the Academy, Plato's rivalry with Isocrates, and the birth of the theory of Forms; and ending with the worlds of the late dialogues.

## 1. SOCRATES AND THE FIFTH-CENTURY ENLIGHTENMENT

As a young man—perhaps as a teenager—Plato became a member of Socrates' intimate circle, something he is careful to indicate himself in both *Apology* (34A) and *Phaedo* (59b). After Socrates' death, a number of those who had belonged to the group started writing fictional dialogues (just how soon we don't know) designed to illustrate his character and personality, along with the distinctive themes and methods of Socratic conversation: Phaedo, Euclides, Aeschines, for example, and probably Antisthenes, already an intellectual heavyweight and prolific author, represented by Xenophon as quite inseparable from Socrates (*Mem.* 3.11.17). Plato was to compose many more "Socratic discourses" (*Sôkratikoi logoi*, as Aristotle calls them: *Poet.* 2, 1147b11) than anyone, over a much longer time span—about forty years, if we date *Ion* to the late 390s and *Philebus* to the late 350s. Socrates was with Plato a continuing and dominating obsession. Nearly the entire output of the most powerful and fertile thinker in the entire tradition of Western philosophy is conceived as an homage to Socrates and in re-creation of *his* philosophizing.[1]

At the very end of the *Phaedo* and its famous death scene, Plato has Phaedo say: "That was the way our friend met his end, Echecrates—a man, as we would say, who of all in his time that we had experience of was the best, and certainly wisest and most just" (*Phd.* 118a). Those attributes as Plato saw it were the keynotes of Socrates' life as they were of his philosophical conversation. The harmony between the two was evidently what made him irresistibly charismatic for those he captivated. In Plato's case, it was precisely those Socratic preoccupations—justice, the good, knowledge—that formed his notion of the philosophical life. Doing philosophy meant trying to understand how to live the life of a just person: getting rid of illusions about what we know or what we think we want, and coming to see what living well really consists in. That is the manifesto Socrates enunciates in his speech to the jurors in the *Apology* (*Ap.* 28a–33c). That is the theme Plato makes him elaborate and defend on a massive scale in the *Republic*, longest and most complex of all his *Sôkratikoi logoi*.

Fundamental in what he took from Socrates is the idea that philosophy is an *inquiry*, and inquiry best pursued in conversation with someone else. The conversation can be of different sorts and can accommodate flights of fancy, as well as close questioning of an interlocutor about the entailments of any views he may have advanced. Yet even when Plato's Socrates has ideas of his own to propound, they are expressly put forward for others to consider—for acceptance, qualification, or rejection—not as teaching imparted to those in need of instruction by someone secure in the knowledge of truth.[2] No doubt the young Plato was so much in thrall to Socrates that it never seriously occurred to him to think that philosophy ought to be more didactic or authoritarian, or a system of doctrines rather than an activity. In various of the early dialogues, his awareness of an alternative model of what education should be is nonetheless made crystal clear. Over and again, Socrates is represented as clashing with those who take education to be a matter of absorbing a *mathêma*, or body of knowledge, from someone who commands the relevant *technê*, or expertise—as though acquisition of moral understanding could be like learning medicine from a doctor or going to a sculptor to pick up his craft.[3]

1. A full discussion on *Sôkratikoi logoi* and their authors is in C. H. Kahn, *Plato and the Socratic Dialogue* (Cambridge, 1996), ch. 1. Brief information on the Socratic authors listed here (and on the many other thinkers mentioned in this chapter) is in D. Zeyl (ed.), *Encyclopedia of Classical Philosophy* (Westport, Conn., 1997). Also useful for the chapter in general are G. C. Field, *Plato and His Contemporaries* (London, 1930), and D. Nails, *The People of Plato* (Indianapolis, 2002).

2. A classic example is Socrates' introduction of his opinion about the Good in the *Republic* (*Rep.* 6.506b–507a).

3. This issue is a major preoccupation in, for example, *Laches*, *Protagoras*, and *Meno*. Socrates' classic disavowal of any claim to be a teacher is in *Ap.* 33a–c (he practices examination of those who think they know when they don't).

It is not that the Platonic Socrates rejects the conception of knowledge as *technê*. That conception is omnipresent in the dialogues, from the earliest (like *Ion* and *Hippias Minor*) to late works in which Socrates scarcely figures (notably, *Sophist* and *Statesman*). Indeed, he introduces it into discussion in contexts where a modern reader would be surprised to find it figuring at all. Take, for example, the idea expressed early in Book 1 of the *Republic* that justice is giving each individual his due, explicated as what is appropriate for him (*Rep.* 1.331e–332d). Socrates compares the *technê* which is called medicine: What does *it* give that is due and appropriate, and to what or whom does it give it? Having obtained an answer to that question and an analogous one about cookery, he frames a parallel question about justice: What would a *technê* have to deliver, and to what or whom, if it were to deserve the name "justice"? Socrates doesn't here necessarily assume himself that justice *is* a form of expertise comparable with medicine or cookery. His question is hypothetical in form. But it could not have been articulated as it is, except in an intellectual world where there was (i) a strong inclination to suppose that the value in any valuable activity must derive from its being practiced knowledgeably, and (ii) an assumption that such knowledge must constitute a *technê*, or form of expertise.

Just such a world came into existence in ancient Greece in the last decades of the fifth century—in other words, precisely during the period in which Plato sets the conversations that take place in his Socratic dialogues. The second half of the century saw an explosion of prose writing on all manner of technical topics, from horsemanship to perspective in painting for the dramatic stage. To this period belong the first medical surviving treatises in the Hippocratic corpus[4] and the first attempt we know of to articulate elements of geometry, by Hippocrates of Chios.[5] In a famous passage of the *Prometheus Bound* ascribed to Aeschylus, the Titan catalogues the skills and crafts he has taught mankind, from astronomy, numerical calculation, and writing to housing, animal husbandry, navigation and medicine, divination and sacrifice, and the knowledge and use of metals. "In one short word you may know all at once," he concludes (*PV* 506). "All *tekhnai* men owe to Prometheus." This text—perhaps from the 440s—is not the only piece of writing in this period to celebrate the range of *tekhnai* commanded by humans. It reflects growing confidence in human ability to make discoveries and master nature.[6]

4. On the Hippocratic corpus, see G. E. R. Lloyd (ed.), *Hippocratic Writings* (Harmondsworth, 1978), with useful bibliography. For general discussion, see G. E. R. Lloyd, *Magic, Reason and Experience* (Cambridge, 1979), ch. 1, and J. Jouanna, *Hippocrates* (Baltimore, 1999).

5. On Hippocrates of Chios, see Lloyd, *Magic, Reason and Experience*, 102–15, with more general discussion and bibliographical orientation in Lloyd, *Demystifying Mentalities* (Cambridge, 1990), ch. 3

6. A good survey of these fifth-century developments is in M. J. O'Brien, *The Socratic Paradoxes and the Greek Mind* (Chapel Hill, N.C., 1967), ch. 2. See also Lloyd, *Magic, Reason and Experience*, ch. 3. The *Prometheus* passage, together with a similar passage from Sophocles' *Antigone* (332–71), is presented in translation by W. K. C. Guthrie, *A History of Greek Philosophy*, Vol. 3 (Cambridge, 1969), 79–80. The authenticity and date of *Prometheus* are disputed: see M. Griffith, *The Authenticity of Prometheus Bound* (Cambridge, 1977).

The Hippocratic author of *On Ancient Medicine*, for example, explains in his opening chapters that medicine has made the discoveries he claims for it by following a principle and a procedure; in fact, in essence, this is just the same procedure that has been followed for generations, as people have gradually learned better what sort of food and drink prepared in what ways suit what sorts of constitution—not usually recognized as a *technê*, to be sure, but a *technê* nonetheless.[7] By the time Plato was writing, such self-consciousness about what it is for a *technê* to be a *technê* had evidently become commonplace. At the beginning of the *Gorgias* he parodies the mannerisms of writers of guides to this or that *technê* by having Polus (author of such a work—on rhetoric: 462b) declaim (448c): "Chaerephon, many forms of expertise among people have been discovered by experience from experiences. Experience is what makes our life proceed on the basis of expertise, inexperience on that of chance."

The period of intellectual revolution I have been describing is often referred to as the age of the Sophists.[8] The polymath Hippias, treated by Plato as one of the leading figures among the Sophists, certainly epitomized something of its spirit in his own person. Astronomy seems to have been his favorite subject, but he was prepared to teach virtually anything, from mathematics, grammar, and music to what we might call antiquarian subjects—although he has some claim to be considered the first historian of philosophy (*Hi. Ma.* 285b–e; cf. *Prot.* 318d–e). The word "sophist" originally signified (in George Grote's magisterial formulation) "a wise man—a clever man—one who stood prominently before the public as distinguished for intellect or talent of some kind."[9] Thus Herodotus in the fifth century BC calls the lawgiver Solon, the religious thinker Pythagoras, and the Homeric seer Melampus all sophists (*Histories* 1.29, 2.49, 4.95). "Sophist" never quite lost this general connotation, but in the pages of Plato, Xenophon, and Isocrates, it has come to have a more specific meaning: an expert who would teach you his subject for a fee.[10] Thinkers like Protagoras of Abdera, Prodicus of Keos, and Hippias (from Elis in the Peloponnese), who traveled the Greek world to do just that, were evidently salient presences in Athens around the time of the beginning of the Peloponnesian War (431 BC).

One of Plato's most elaborate dramatic masterpieces—the *Protagoras*—imagines them all assembled together in Athens shortly before the outbreak of the war. He pits Socrates in debate with Protagoras, initially on the subject of Prota-

---

7. There is a major edition of this treatise: M. J. Schiefsky, *Hippocrates* On Ancient Medicine (Leiden, 2005). Its defense of medicine as a *technê* has been much discussed. The topic is treated in two recent studies (which refer to previous bibliography): J. Barton, "Hippocratic explanations," and F. Dunn, "*On Ancient Medicine* and its intellectual context," both in P. J. van der Eijk (ed.), *Hippocrates in Context* (Leiden, 2005), 29–47 and 49–67.

8. The best guide to the Sophists is Guthrie, *History of Greek Philosophy*, Vol. 3, Part I. Another view is in G. B. Kerferd, *The Sophistic Movement* (Cambridge, 1981).

9. G. Grote, *History of Greece* (London, 1850), 8.479.

10. For example, Xen. *Mem.* 1.6.13; Guthrie, *History of Greek Philosophy*, Vol. 3, 35–40; and D. L. Blank, "Socratics versus Sophists on payment for teaching," *California Studies in Classical Antiquity* 1 (1985), 1–49.

goras's educational manifesto: the Sophist undertook to teach good decision-making, whether in running a household or in the public sphere, where those he taught were to be equipped with an exceptional capacity for the conduct and discussion of the affairs of the city (*Prot.* 318e–319a). How such a grandiose promise was to be honored is not clear.[11] Much of the Sophists' teaching seems to have been conveyed in sustained set-piece performances. Plato's Protagoras gives an impressive demonstration speech in the dialogue, and Prodicus (whose passion for precise distinctions between near synonyms is frequently satirized by Plato: e.g., *Prot.* 337a–c, 339d–342a, 358d–e; *Charm.* 163a–d; *Crat.* 384a–c) was celebrated for his lecture on the choice of Heracles, portrayed as a paradigmatic figure at a crossroads in life who wins the struggle of virtue over vice (Xen. *Mem.* 2.1.21–34).

Most people, says Plato's Socrates, think that some young men get corrupted by Sophists, and that there are some unprofessional Sophists who do the corrupting (*Rep.* 6.492a). His own line is that the whims of the Athenian people—in the assembly or in the courts, on huge public juries—do much more damage. And while Plato would probably not disagree that some Sophists harmed some individuals, the tone of the *Protagoras* is mostly one of urbane amusement at the antics of the Sophists and their followers, coupled with respect for Protagoras himself. Elsewhere, he has Socrates argue that it is just not credible that someone like Protagoras could have fooled the whole of Greece and got away with making his students more depraved than they were when he took them on, for more than forty years (*Meno* 91E). In short, the suggestion is that the Sophists' reputation for good or ill is much inflated. To be sure, Plato does himself engage with some of the ideas they generated (for example, Protagoras's famous slogan: "Man is the measure of all things," in the *Theaetetus*).[12] But in the early and middle dialogues, the one important line of thought with a Sophistic pedigree that he confronts (in different versions in the *Gorgias* and Book 2 of the *Republic*) is the antinomian claim that justice is a matter of convention (*nomos*) and will be ignored by anyone strong or adroit enough to pursue self-interest as nature (*phusis*) would dictate—although it is not clear that any Sophist actually advocated such behavior.[13] Otherwise, it cannot be said that the Sophists or their teaching loom that large in the dialogues, certainly by comparison with the massive presence of Socrates himself. As W. K. C. Guthrie says, Plato "was a post-war figure writing in an Athens of different intellectual temper. When he put on to his stage the giants of the Sophistic era, he was recalling them from the dead."[14]

---

11. See the quizzical reflections of A. Ford, "Sophists without rhetoric: the arts of speech in fifth-century Athens," in Y. L. Too (ed.), *Education in Greek and Roman Antiquity* (Leiden, 2001), 85–109.

12. See Taylor, chapter 17 in this volume.

13. On Sophistic pedigree, see the surviving fragments of Antiphon's *On Truth*, as presented in, for example, Guthrie, *History of Greek Philosophy*, Vol. 3, 107–13, or D. J. Furley, *Cosmic Problems* (Cambridge, 1989), ch. 6.

14. W. K. C. Guthrie, *A History of Greek Philosophy*, Vol. 4 (Cambridge, 1975), 6.

# 2. Philosophy, Politics, and Athens

Socrates' trial and condemnation by an Athenian court in 399 BC, on charges of impiety and immoral influence over young people, was devastating for Plato. It was not just a personal trauma. In his mind, it constituted a confrontation that crystallized the inevitability of conflict between philosophy and politics and their incommensurable assumptions. That issue, with its Socratic resonances, was to become one of central significance in Plato's treatment of the philosopher. It is highlighted at critical junctures in some of the most important dialogues in the corpus. Some particular passages serve to illustrate the point.

Nowhere are the rival claims of politics and philosophy more trenchantly advanced than in the *Gorgias*. The dialogue begins with Socrates' critique of rhetoric, but once Callicles enters the discussion he reciprocates with a politician's critique of philosophy. In his famous Nietzschean monologue he warns Socrates that philosophy makes a person helpless to defend himself in the public forum: if Socrates were brought before a court and faced with an unprincipled prosecutor, he would end up dead if the death penalty was what the prosecutor wanted (*Gorg.* 485E–486B).[15] This thinly veiled prediction of Socrates' actual fate is then reprised by Socrates himself near the end of the dialogue, where he imagines himself as a doctor prosecuted by a pastry chef before a jury of children—on a charge of ruining their health by his medicines and surgical interventions. The doctor could find nothing to say in such a court in his self-defense (521E–522C). Of course, Socrates *did* speak at his trial. Plato's point is that there was nothing he could have said then that could have begun to persuade the infantile citizenry of a self-indulgent democracy.

In the *Meno*, Plato actually makes Socrates' chief accuser—Anytus—a participant for a while in the dialogue. Conversation turns to the question whether, if you want someone to acquire virtue, you should send him to a Sophist for training and instruction. Anytus is outraged at the thought: Sophists corrupt the young—any decent father could do a better job. But when Socrates points out that the great and the good—statesmen like Themistocles, Aristides, Pericles—signally failed to turn out sons of the same caliber, Anytus advises Socrates to watch his tongue and his back, too. In Athens, as elsewhere, it's easier to do harm than good, he adds for good measure (*Meno* 94e). On that note, he leaves. The whole passage is coded commentary on what Plato saw as the incoherent malice motivating the charge of corruption brought against Socrates at his trial.

There is further general reflection on the plight of the philosopher in the city, again evoking the trial, in a famous passage in the Cave analogy in Book 7 of the *Republic*. Socrates imagines a philosopher escaping from the cave, acquiring a true

---

15. The Nietzschean affinities of Callicles' speech are explored in an appendix to the great modern edition of the dialogue: E. R. Dodds (ed.), *Plato: Gorgias* (Oxford, 1959).

understanding of reality—and then returning into the darkness once more. Such a person would find it hard to reacclimatize. People would think he had damaged his eyesight. And if he tried to free others, they would seize him and kill him if they could. He would make a fool of himself if before reacclimatization he was forced to compete over shadows or images of justice, in the law courts or anywhere else, with those who have never seen justice itself (*Rep.* 7.516e–517e). The theme is replayed once more, and in very similar accents, in the digression about the philosopher in the *Theaetetus*, a passage containing many echoes of the Cave. Philosophers, says Socrates again, will only make fools of themselves if they speak in the law courts (*Tht.* 172c). He goes on to develop—at length and in detail—a contrast between the truly important and the trivial, then to argue the mutual incomprehension with which the philosopher (preoccupied with the one) and the rest of humanity (mired in the other) view each other. The final words of the dialogue make the implicit reference to Socrates' own history all but explicit (210d): "Now I must go to the King's Porch to meet the indictment that Meletus has brought against me."

These Athenian texts—obsessively replaying the demise of an Athenian philosopher at the hands of the Athenian democracy—illustrate what Plato took to be the fundamental problem for all politics. But Athens and its democracy exerted over him a compelling fascination. He himself was born into the Athenian aristocracy. And his dialogues communicate an unforgettable sense of the high spirits, variety, and intellectual freedom of Athenian aristocratic life—in the gymnasium, at the symposium, at Sophistic performances, or just in private conversation—as Plato partly remembered and partly imagined them during the years in which his philosophical dramas are represented as being played out-that is, the last third of the fifth century BC. It may seem paradoxical that such a vigorous aristocratic culture flourished—as, of course, did Plato's own writing and thinking—under a democracy.

But, in truth, the Athenian political settlement was always a complex negotiation between mass and elite.[16] In his funeral speech of 429 BC, Pericles, the aristocrat who was the dominant figure in Athenian democratic politics in the 440s and 430s, remarked (in the words Thucydides attributes to him) that in Athens' meritocratic form of democracy "we have provided for the mind many relaxations from exertions," and again "we cultivate beauty with economy and philosophy without enervation" (*History* 2.38, 40). Loathe and despise democracy though he did, it is hard to suppose that Plato was altogether unaware that the vitality and range of his own writing owed much to Athenian intellectual life as he experienced it under the democracy during his formative years. Plato's vivid portrait of democracy and the democratic lifestyle in Book 8 of the *Republic* itself (*Rep.* 8.557a–564a) exhibits the color, energy, and variety that it is officially deprecating, and a kind of intimacy, too, all in marked contrast with the external and chilling account of oligarchy that has just preceded.

---

16. J. Ober, *Mass and Elite in Democratic Athens* (Princeton, 1989). Plato's own stepfather and guardian, Pyrilampes, was a friend of Pericles, active in the democracy's public life, and called his own son Demos.

One thing Plato certainly communicates is a sense of the precariousness of the world he describes. The dramatic date of the drinking party the inebriated Alcibiades bursts in on in the *Symposium* is deliberately set a few months before the public outcry provoked in 415 BC by events—the mutilation of the herms and the profanation of the mysteries—in which he was implicated (along with many others, including, among those present, Phaedrus, for example, and probably Eryximachus, too), and which were to be the catalyst for his political downfall.[17] The *Charmides*, set early in the Peloponnesian War, ends with some menacing words from Charmides (Plato's uncle) to Socrates. This is doubtless designed to remind us that Charmides, incidentally someone else implicated in the outrages of 415, would be involved with the oligarchic junta of the Thirty Tyrants that seized power briefly in 404 (and took pains to silence Socrates), and which was led by Critias, portrayed as Charmides' mentor in the dialogue.

The two generals who figure as main participants in the discussion of the *Laches*—Laches and C̶h̶a̶r̶m̶i̶d̶e̶s̶ *Nicias*—were both dead within a few years of its dramatic date. Nicias's acceptance in the dialogue of divination as a form of knowledge, and Socrates' question about its relation to generalship (*Laches* 195e–196a, 198e–199a), are clearly meant to prefigure the disastrous decision that triggered the final debacle of the Sicilian expedition in 413 BC: Nicias took an eclipse of the moon as a portent requiring delay in departure (Thuc. *Hist.* 7.50). The *Republic*, too, is set at some point in the war's duration. The first two of those mentioned as accosting Socrates as he is leaving the Piraeus at the beginning of the dialogue are Polemarchus and Niceratus. Both were to be executed by the Thirty, who also confiscated the immensely profitable arms factory Polemarchus's father Cephalus—Socrates' first main interlocutor in Book 1—had built up.[18]

So one could go on. Plato certainly did not think democracy (with the intellectual world it sustained at Athens) was the only system of government liable to collapse under the pressure of its own contradictory dynamic: witness the saga of regime change sketched brilliantly in Book 8 of the *Republic*. But the fragility of the world of the dialogues and of the political system at Athens that supported it is surely an insistent subtext. In the ideal communities delineated in *Republic* and *Laws*, life—including intellectual life—is to be strictly controlled at every point. There will simply be no potential for development of the exuberant proliferation of viewpoints of every kind, and of the social structures enabling debate between them, which makes the dialogues such attractive reading. Presumably, Plato concluded that that was the price that would have to be paid for a secure political order—in key respects, more

17. Brief accounts are in S. Price, *Religions of the Ancient Greeks* (Cambridge, 1999), 82–85, and P. J. Rhodes, *A History of the Classical Greek World 478–323 BC* (Oxford, 2006), 157–60. A full treatment is in W. D. Furley, *Andokides and the Herms: A Study of Crisis in Fifth-Century Athenian Religion* (London, 1996).

18. On these and similar resonances of the Peloponnesian War in Plato, see M. Gifford, "Dramatic dialectic in *Republic* Book 1," *Oxford Studies in Ancient Philosophy* 20 (2001), 35–106. Narratives and analyses of the war are in S. Hornblower, *The Greek World 479–323 BC*, 3rd ed. (London, 2003), chs. 12 and 13, and Rhodes, *History of the Classical Greek World*, chs. 8–15. A fuller account is in D. Kagan, *The Peloponnesian War: Athens and Sparta in Savage Conflict, 431–404 BC* (London, 2003).

reminiscent of unintellectual Sparta than of Athens—that would promote virtue and happiness. It was a conclusion perhaps already implicit in the enthusiasm for the Spartan social and political system fashionable among some Athenian aristocrats in his formative years and shared by Socrates and his mother's cousin Critias.


## 3. Light from the West

"When I first came to Syracuse, being then about forty years of age . . . " So writes the author of the Seventh Letter (*Ep.* 7.324a); and whether he really is Plato or not, the letter's evidence that Plato made a first visit to Sicily around his fortieth year is more or less universally regarded as reliable. Coupled with the usual dating of Plato's birth to 427 BC (D.L. 3.2), it yields a rough date of 387 for the visit, which on any reckoning must belong somewhere in the early to middle 380s. The letter's narrative focuses on the friendship he formed with the young Dion, brother-in-law of the tyrant of Syracuse, Dionysius I, by way of introduction to Plato's entanglements in Sicilian court politics twenty years later. He doesn't indicate his motivation in making the voyage west, but the most obvious reason is the one that has been transmitted and often repeated in ancient tradition: Plato was wanting to make contact with the Pythagorean philosophers in South Italy (probably his primary destination), and especially with Archytas in Tarentum.[19]

What was the outcome of that meeting of minds? Here is one way of telling the story[20]—which construes the encounter as a decisive moment with extraordinary impact on the future direction of Plato's thought. To put it in a nutshell, Plato converted to Pythagoreanism: to belief in the immortality of the soul; to a fascination with eschatology and myths of a last judgment; to a conviction that mathematics held the key to understanding the nature of reality; to the idea that politics might, after all, be reshaped by philosophy and philosophers; to the resolve to create in Athens his own community of friends dedicated to the pursuit of philosophy. From the conversion will have flowed much of the energy and vision that fueled the writing of dialogues such as *Gorgias, Meno, Phaedo,* and *Republic.* Its most practical consequence was to be the founding of the Academy.

If this book were about a famous philosopher of the modern period, there would probably be well-documented evidence of known date and in quantity supporting the interpretation—which might still, of course, be controversial. For ancient Greek thinkers, biographical facts are in short supply and hard facts almost

19. The following all give fairly similar variants of this account: Phld. *Acad. Ind.* X.5–11; Cic. *Rep.* 1.16; *Fin.* 5.87; V. Max. 8.7 ext. 3; and Olymp. *in Alc.* 2.86–93. Other variants include Apul. *Pl.* 1.3; D.L. 3.6 (which mentions not Archytas, but Philolaus and Eurytus); and Hier. *Contra Rufinum* 3.40. These and yet further texts on the subject are collected (and translated) in C. A. Huffman, *Archytas of Tarentum: Pythagorean, Philosopher and Mathematician King* (Cambridge, 2005), 272–74.

20. For example, Guthrie, *History of Greek Philosophy,* Vol. 4, 35–38 (with 9 n.1, 24 n.2, 284). But the effect of Archytas's personal influence is given greater stress, for example, by Dodds, *Plato,* 26–27, and G. Vlastos, *Socrates: Ironist and Moral Philosopher* (Cambridge, 1991), 128–30.

nonexistent. Diogenes Laertius tells us it was after returning from his travels abroad that the Academy gymnasium and its environs became the seat of his activities (D.L. 3.7). Otherwise everything is more or less insecure inference. We have no absolute or even relative dates for the four dialogues listed above. Issues relating to the chronology of the dialogues are discussed elsewhere in this volume: suffice to say here that all modern scholarship that is prepared to attempt a dating puts this quartet in that order, and (with some hesitation or disagreement over *Gorgias*) makes their production subsequent to Plato's return from Italy and Sicily. Quite how far Plato's preoccupation with mathematics or philosopher rulers or even eschatology has a major Pythagorean dimension could perhaps be disputed, as could the idea of a Pythagorean pedigree for the foundation of the Academy.[21] And we do not *know* that Plato met Archytas or other Pythagoreans on his visit, or, consequently, that discussions with them had any effect on his thought at all.

So the hypothesis about Plato's development sketched above is undeniably speculative. Nonetheless, it is reasonable speculation designed to give an economical explanation of something that certainly calls for explanation. It is a striking fact (here we *can* speak of fact) that the four dialogues under consideration share a preoccupation with mathematics and the ultimate origin and fate of the soul that is entirely absent from dialogues like *Ion*, *Hippias Minor*, *Euthyphro*, *Laches*, and *Protagoras* (for example), which are paradigmatically Socratic in method and content. What accounts for the difference? A simple answer suggests itself: the newly registered impact on Plato of powerful ideas encountered in an exotic non-Athenian religious and intellectual environment.

From as early as the eighth century BC, the Greeks had been establishing settlements on the coasts of South Italy and Sicily, which more or less rapidly achieved political control over the hinterland and its indigenous inhabitants, with more gradual cultural penetration. By the fifth century, cities such as Acragas and Syracuse, in Sicily, and Croton and Tarentum, in South Italy, had become among the richest and most powerful in the Greek world; "sybaritic" derives from the notoriously luxurious Sybaris, a city in South Italy already destroyed in 510 BC. In many respects, the cities of these western Greeks passed through phases of development comparable with those familiar from mainland Greece. In religion, they were more distinctive. The surviving evidence indicates a preoccupation with cults concerned with marriage, death, and the afterlife, often associated with Demeter and Persephone. There are burials indicating that the deceased were initiates into mysteries designed to achieve purification and a safe passage to a better life in the hereafter, with "other famous initiates and bacchants," as one gold plate of the late fifth century discovered at Hipponion puts it.[22]

---

21. For example, a Pythagorean model for the Academy is dismissed by M. Ostwald and J. P. Lynch, "The growth of schools and the advance of knowledge," in D. M. Lewis, J. Boardman, S. Hornblower, and M. Ostwald (eds.), *The Cambridge Ancient History*, Vol. 6, 2nd ed. (Cambridge, 1994), 604.

22. For the text of the Hipponion gold plate (and some discussion), see G. S. Kirk, J. E. Raven, and M. Schofield, *The Presocratic Philosophers*, 2nd ed. (Cambridge, 1983), 29–30. On western Greek religion, see G. Zuntz, *Persephone* (Oxford, 1971).

This was the world in which Pythagoras arrived, with Croton his destination, as a refugee from Samos in the eastern Aegean, perhaps somewhere in the decade 535–25 BC. He quickly became a charismatic figure whose life, work, and teaching are now the stuff of impenetrable legend. There is no doubt, however, that the main focus of his teaching was the soul and its place in the cosmic scheme of things—and the practices needed to ensure that, after death and judgment, its journey through an inevitable cycle of reincarnation will bring it eventually to the isles of the blessed. Not only in Croton, but elsewhere in South Italy, too, there formed groups of initiates into the austere Pythagorean way of life, instructed in its doctrines and practices, which encompassed everything from diet (where abstinence from beans was the most famous prohibition) to sacrificial and funerary rites.[23]

At Croton (and probably in other cities), the Pythagoreans acquired considerable political influence around the late sixth and early fifth centuries, although that dominance had long since ended by the time of Plato's visit; according to the fourth-century music theorist Aristoxenus (who came from Tarentum), Pythagoreanism petered out in South Italy (I think he means as a political force), with Archytas the one exception he mentions (Iamb. *VP* 249–51). Archytas seems to have achieved a prominence in democratic Tarentum, at the height of its considerable power, comparable with Pericles' at Athens, and like Pericles as general—probably seven years in succession, but probably also some time after Plato's visit (D.L. 8.79).

The name of Pythagoras is nowadays associated preeminently with a famous geometrical theorem about right-angled triangles. But there is no credible ancient evidence connecting him with the idea or practice of mathematics or with the identification or solution of mathematical problems. The pioneers here, as in so many other fields of inquiry, were the eastern Greeks in Asia Minor and the neighboring islands (the name of Hippocrates of Chios has already been mentioned).[24] What Pythagoras does seem to have pressed is the idea that number and proportion—particularly, in the fundamental harmonic ratios of 2:1 (the octave), 3:2 (the fifth), and 4:3 (the fourth)—were in some symbolic way the key to understanding the universe.

Mysterious generality started to give way to the new style of mathematical inquiry of the later fifth century in the work of the Pythagorean Philolaus (probably of Croton), who developed a complete mathematical analysis of the diatonic octave, apparently in the context of the theory of cosmic harmony.[25] Archytas,

23. For Pythagoras and the Pythagoreans, see Kirk et al., *Presocratic Philosophers*, ch. 7. The fundamental modern treatment is W. Burkert, *Lore and Science in Ancient Pythagoreanism* (Cambridge, Mass., 1972); a briefer treatment is in C. H. Kahn, *Pythagoras and the Pythagoreans: A Brief History* (Indianapolis, 2001).

24. On early Greek mathematics, see W. A. Heidel, "The Pythagoreans and Greek mathematics," *American Journal of Philology* 61 (1940), 1–33; Burkert, *Lore and Science in Ancient Pythagoreanism*, ch. 6; W. R. Knorr, "On the early history of axiomatics: the interaction of mathematics and philosophy in Greek antiquity," in J. Hintikka, D. Gruender, and A. Agazzi (eds.), *Theory Change, Ancient Axiomatics and Galileo's Methodology* (Dordrecht, 1981), 145–86.

25. On Philolaus, see Kirk et al., *Presocratic Philosophers*, ch. 11. Philolaus is discussed more fully in Burkert, *Lore and Science in Ancient Pythagoreanism*, ch. 3, and the major edition of C. A. Huffman, *Philolaus of Croton: Pythagorean and Presocratic* (Cambridge, 1993).

however, is the first Pythagorean known to us who was able to stand comparison with other leading mathematicians of his day. His musical theory was devoted to analysis of scale systems in terms of different means and proportions (arithmetical, geometrical, harmonic) and to physical explanation of pitch expressible in terms of ratios. He was famous for his solution of the problem of finding two mean proportionals to double the cube. Archytas presented the study of music programmatically as the sister science of arithmetic, geometry, and astronomy, as Plato seems to be acknowledging when he refers to this as the Pythagorean view in appropriating it in Book 7 of the *Republic* (*Rep.* 7.530d). And he claimed that "calculation" was the way to promote justice and political harmony.[26]

So when in a climactic passage of the *Gorgias* (*Gorg.* 507e–508a), utterly unlike anything in Plato before, Socrates reports "the wise" as saying that "heaven and earth and gods and men are bound together by community, friendship, orderliness, self-control and justice," which is "why they call the whole thing a world-order (*kosmos*)," and when he invokes at this point the power of "geometrical equality," his words are best explained as an echo of the conversations Plato had recently enjoyed with Archytas and other Pythagoreans. When the dialogue concludes with an eschatological myth about the contrasting fates of souls who have lived lives of justice or injustice, this new destination for a Platonic dialogue is again best explained as a reflection of the Pythagoreanism its author had assimilated on his western travels—however much or little of the detailed content of the story may owe to Pythagorean models. Most readers sense in *Gorgias* not just a shift in philosophical direction but an insistent and radicalized urgency of tone that was quite novel and perhaps unparalleled in Plato's work. That cannot all be put down to the passion of a new convert to Pythagoreanism, but conversion on his travels might well have been the catalyst.

# 4. Critique of Rhetoric and Rivalry with Isocrates

What the *Gorgias* is most urgent about is the choice between philosophy and politics (or politics as it is currently conceived and practiced): how radical it is, how much is at stake in making it. That is just the kind of focus we might have expected if the dialogue is the most immediate product of Plato's visit to Italy and Sicily, at any rate, given his reactions to the hedonistic lifestyle and the conception of happiness he found prevailing there (according to the Seventh Letter). *Gorgias* is the first of the dialogues to be preoccupied with tyranny and the tyrant (as the supreme lawless hedonist). Readers have often thought that the passage on the

---

26. Archytas is the subject of a major edition (with introductory essays) by Huffman, *Archytas of Tarentum*.

difficulty inherent in friendship with a tyrant (509c–511a) encapsulates Plato's reflections on Dion's relationship with Dionysius I.[27] But there is a sense in which the entire dialogue grapples with the problem of tyranny. It is as though Plato is now viewing Athens—which is foregrounded in the discussion with Callicles, in particular—through lenses sharpened in Sicily. He looks for tyranny at home, and he finds it in the ambitions of political rhetoric—which, as he portrays it, seeks not the good of city or citizens but the manipulation and control of the populace by flattery, as diagnosed by earlier writers such as Aristophanes and Thucydides. The Seventh Letter presents a Plato already primed for comparative political analysis at the time of his stay in Italy and Sicily. *Gorgias* shows us comparison in operation, as, for example, quite explicitly in the long section on the resemblances between the orator and the tyrant in the conversation with Polus (466a–471d).

The *Gorgias* attacks the credentials both of those who exercise political power by the practice of rhetoric and of those who teach it (whether by performance, like Gorgias, or through handbooks, like Polus). By starting with Gorgias and Polus (the teachers) and finishing with Callicles (the practitioner),[28] Plato makes a point: teaching, even by someone as apparently benign as Gorgias, and practice, with all its corrupting potential, form a dangerous continuum. For while Plato treats the Sophists mostly just as intellectual poseurs, he sees rhetoric as a real force for harm. The message is illustrated in some of the later pages of the dialogue, with what is effectively a counterhistory of Athenian imperialism. Here the greatest of the orators on its political stage—Themistocles, Cimon, Pericles—are accused of making Athens bloated and rotten and of deserving the blame for its eventual downfall (*Gorg.* 515b–519a). Plato's anger at the grossness of the deception and self-deception needed to sustain Athenian democratic rhetoric seems to have been fierce in the years after his return from Sicily. In the *Menexenus*, likely to have been written in about 385 BC, he puts in Socrates' mouth a pastiche funeral oration, said to have been learned from Pericles' mistress Aspasia (*Menex.* 235e–236c).[29] By virtue of blatant omissions and distortions, this blandly satirical composition paints a picture of Athens' entire history since the Persian Wars at the beginning of the fifth century right down to the ignominious King's Peace of 386 (some years after Socrates' death, of course) as one of noble and mostly successful endeavor. Rhetoric, we are to understand, is both agent and expression of Athenian political bankruptcy.

There was one specific reason why Plato might well have thought it timely to put the case against rhetoric with all the force he could muster: the Athenian speechwriter Isocrates' decision around 390 BC to start taking pupils, marked by

27. For example, Guthrie, *History of Greek Philosophy*, Vol. 4, 284 n.4.
28. On Gorgias, Polus, and Callicles as historical figures, see Dodds, *Plato*, 6–15; see also Guthrie, *History of Greek Philosophy*, Vol. 3, 101–7, 192–200, 269–74; Kerferd, *Sophistic Movement*, ch. 8; and R. B. B. Wardy, *The Birth of Rhetoric* (London, 1996), chs. 1–3.
29. For the *Menexenus*, see Guthrie, *History of Greek Philosophy*, Vol. 4, 312–23; see also the study of C. H. Kahn, "Plato's funeral oration: the motive of the *Menexenus*," *Classical Philology* 58 (1963), 220–34.

publication of his tract *Against the Sophists*.[30] The *Gorgias* is probably not a critique of Isocrates or *Against the Sophists* in particular,[31] although at least one significant passage (*Gorg.* 463A, on the psychological equipment of the orator) seems to turn Isocrates' specific claims for rhetoric (*Against the Sophists* 17) to its discredit. The dialogue is planned on an altogether grander design, as an assault on rhetoric itself. That is why it is named after Gorgias, the first famous exponent of rhetoric conceived as a *technê*, and why it makes this fifth-century figure the initial target. Plato turns his guns much more narrowly and explicitly on Isocrates in the *Euthydemus*, whose date of composition is disputed, but—echoing or pre-echoing the *Republic*'s distinction between the geometer and astronomer and the dialectician as it does— would probably have been written later than *Gorgias* and *Menexenus*.

The main body of the *Euthydemus* is devoted to a Socratic exposé of the logic-chopping of a later generation of Sophists, here represented by the brothers Euthydemus and Dionysodorus. But the frame dialogue is a conversation between Socrates and his old friend Crito, who is represented as having been present for the encounter but out of earshot (*Euthd.* 271a). In the final chapter at the end of the dialogue (304b–307c), Crito relates a conversation he had when leaving with an unnamed person, identified as a clever speechwriter who never appears in court himself, with a high sense of his own wisdom. This description fits Isocrates exactly,[32] and he is portrayed as confusing logic-chopping with philosophy—a fair charge against *Against the Sophists*. Socrates makes a damning assessment. Someone like that occupies the borderland between philosopher and politician—neither one thing nor the other, and inferior to both. However such people have a huge reputation for wisdom, except among real philosophers—whom it is therefore in their interest (especially when their own pretensions are exposed) to represent as no more significant than the likes of Euthydemus.

The likeliest reason why Plato decided he needed to rebut the insinuation (the *Euthydemus* makes the difference between Socratic philosophizing and logic-chopping crystal clear) is that Isocrates' school was by this time highly successful in training budding politicians in oratory, as, indeed, we know it became.[33] The dialogue doesn't advertise the contrasting merits of the Academy—in fact, it

30. The writings of Isocrates (436–338 BC) survive and are most conveniently consulted in the three-volume Loeb edition: G. Norlin (ed.), *Isocrates*, Vols. 1 and 2 (London, 1928 and 1929), and L. van Hook (ed.), *Isocrates*, Vol. 3 (London, 1945). More recent translations with good bibliography are D. Mirhady and Y. L. Too, (trans.), *Isocrates I* (Austin, Tex., 2000), and T. L. Papillon (trans.), *Isocrates II* (Austin, Tex., 2005). Good brief studies are Ostwald and Lynch, "Growth of schools and advance of knowledge," 595–602, and G. Kennedy, *The Art of Persuasion in Greece* (Princeton, 1963), 174–203. Interactions between Isocrates and other Athenian thinkers, above all Plato, in the first half of the fourth century BC are the subject of a valuable if often speculative monograph by C. Eucken, *Isokrates: Seine Positionen in der Auseinandersetzung mit den zeitgenössischen Philosophen* (Berlin, 1983).

31. But it is sometimes so taken, as in, for example, Ostwald and Lynch, "Growth of schools and advance of knowledge," 605.

32. For example, W. H. Thompson, *The Phaedrus of Plato* (London, 1868), app. 2.

33. Isocrates is not a gripping writer, and his identification of philosophy with training for political rhetoric (e.g., in *Antidosis* 270–96) is unlikely to appeal to most readers of this volume. But it seems clear that as a teacher he was highly effective: see the interesting study of R. Johnson, "Isocrates' methods of

concludes with an injunction to give serious consideration to philosophy itself and not bother with its practitioners, good or bad. But readers might be expected to draw their own conclusions, alerted, perhaps, by the reference to geometers and astronomers: geometry and astronomy are what Isocrates, at any rate, later represented as the distinctive ingredients in the educational program of the Academy (*Antidosis* 261–68).

Hard facts about the Academy are unsurprisingly in short supply.[34] We should not conceive of it as a school in any formal sense, with its own property and institutional structures. However, Plato did acquire a house and garden in the vicinity of the gymnasium, where communal meals were probably taken. Did Plato take pupils? If so, not (like Isocrates) for money. Ancient sources sometimes speak of "companions" (e.g., Plu. *adv. Col.* 1126C). Perhaps we should think of a more or less loosely defined society of friends (recalling the Pythagorean slogan, "friends share what they have"), with younger adherents learning from the conversation of their seniors. Doubtless, discussion would often be conducted in Socratic question and answer mode: in his early *Topics*, Aristotle—a member of the Academy for twenty years—formulated rules for its conduct. But mathematicians were among those attracted to the Academy, with Eudoxus of Cnidos notable among them.[35] While we should not assume that the mathematical curriculum of Book 7 of the *Republic* was in any way replicated in its modus operandi, anecdotes of Plato setting mathematical problems for Eudoxus and others (e.g., What uniform motions will account for the apparently disorderly motions of the planets?)[36] and the interest in it reflected in the dialogues (e.g., *Meno* 82b–87c and *Rep.* 7.529c–531c) suggest that mathematical questions will, indeed, have figured in the discussions a good deal.

The rivalry between Isocrates and Plato persisted. Isocrates seems to have responded to the *Euthydemus* by granting a distinction between those who (like the Socratic Antisthenes) deny the possibility of falsehood and contradiction,[37] and

teaching," *American Journal of Philology* 80 (1959), 25–36. A stimulating general study is that of Y. L. Too, *The Rhetoric of Identity in Isocrates: Text, Power, Pedagogy* (Cambridge, 1995).

34. Many accounts of the Academy as an institution in standard works on Plato are rather speculative: not exempt from the charge is Guthrie, *History of Greek Philosophy*, Vol. 4, 19–24. For a corrective, see, for example, H. Cherniss, *The Riddle of the Early Academy* (Berkeley, 1945), ch. 3. A lively and balanced brief treatment is that of J. Dillon, *The Heirs of Plato* (Oxford, 2003), 1–16.

35. Eudoxus was notable for his development of the general theory of proportion expounded in Book 5 of Euclid's *Elements* and for the elaborate theory of concentric spheres he devised to account for the apparently irregular motions of the planets. See further W. K. C. Guthrie, *A History of Greek Philosophy*, Vol. 5 (Cambridge, 1978), 447–57.

36. For the evidence, see A. Riginos, *Platonica: The Anecdotes Concerning the Life and Writings of Plato* (Leiden, 1976), 141–45. On the importance of problems in the development of Greek mathematics, see W. R. Knorr, *The Ancient Tradition of Geometric Problems* (Boston, 1986).

37. Antisthenes' intellectual activity spanned the fifth and fourth centuries; his literary output was huge (D.L. 6.15–19), although nearly all of it is lost. While ethics was the main preoccupation, he also engaged in Homeric interpretation and theorizing about language. He seems to have fallen under the influence of both Gorgias and the Sophists, before becoming a devoted Socratic. For him, virtue was sufficient for happiness—all that was needed was the strength of a Socrates (D.L. 6.11). See further, M. Schofield, "Antisthenes," in E. Craig (ed.), *Routledge Encyclopedia of Philosophy* (London, 1998), 1.314–17.

those who (like Plato's Socrates in the *Protagoras*) claim that all the virtues are a single form of knowledge (see the beginning of his *Helen*, which is of uncertain date). But this is a distinction without a difference: both groups are eristic paradox-mongers. It is much better, he says, to venture reasonable opinions on useful subjects than to have exact knowledge of useless ones. Plato, for his part, returned to a reconsideration of rhetoric in the *Phaedrus*. His Socrates projects a rhetoric reformed by philosophy. That would, indeed, be a *technê*, unlike the rhetoric of current theory and practice: "the art of speech by one who has gone chasing after opinions, instead of knowing the truth, will be a comical sort of art, in fact no art at all" (*Phdr.* 262c). The dialogue ends with some flattering words from Socrates about the natural powers of the young Isocrates and the promise of philosophy in him if he should become dissatisfied with his current activity (278e–279b)—a backhanded compliment, if ever there was one. But the *Phaedrus* paradoxically begins to exhibit in its prose style more of the deliberate avoidance of hiatus that had been Isocrates' constant trademark—and was clearly beginning to catch on more generally, with Plato himself a total convert in the late dialogues. Isocrates, in fact, had the last word, in his late and autobiographical *Antidosis* (353 BC). Here he makes the patronizing concession that the sort of "philosophy" practiced by those who occupy themselves with the exactness of geometry and astronomy is just training for the mind, a *preparation* for philosophy—more advanced than what boys do in school but similar in most respects (*Antidosis* 266).

## 5. PARMENIDES, HERACLITEANISM, AND THE THEORY OF FORMS

In chapter 6 of the first book of the *Metaphysics* (which surveys earlier thinkers' views on the first principles of things), Aristotle presents Plato as close to the Pythagoreans in making numbers occupy a key place in metaphysical foundations. He is looking at Platonic ontology through the lens of the late *Philebus* and Plato's oral discussions of the one and the indefinite dyad; more generally, Aristotle's perspective is informed by the Pythagorizing approach to metaphysics that prevailed in the Academy during his membership of it. But unlike Speusippus or Xenocrates, he was intent on stressing that there were important differences between Plato and the Pythagoreans. Above all, as he saw it, the Pythagoreans assimilate numbers and the contents of the sensible world, whereas Plato holds that numbers have an existence separate from sensible things.[38] The first main section

38. There are brief accounts of the work of Speusippus and Xenocrates in Guthrie, *History of Greek Philosophy*, Vol. 5, 457–83; more extended treatments are in Dillon, *Heirs of Plato*. Speusippus, Plato's nephew and successor, seemed to have been the more interesting thinker of the two, particularly notable for his hypothesis of different but analogous pairs of principles explaining successive levels of reality (e.g., numbers, magnitudes, soul)—on which see R. M. Dancy, *Two Studies in the Early Academy* (Albany, N.Y.,

of the chapter is accordingly devoted to a narrative explaining how Plato came to "separate" the Forms (how Forms relate to numbers is deferred until later).

Here is Aristotle's narrative (*Metaph.* A6, 987a32–b10):

> In his youth he [Plato] had become familiar first of all with Cratylus and with Heraclitean views to the effect that all perceptible things are always in flux, and there is no knowledge that relates to them. This is a position he later subscribed to in these terms. Socrates, on the other hand, engaged in discussion of ethics, and had nothing to say about the general system of nature. But he was intent on finding out what was universal in this field, and was the first to fix his thinking on definitions. Plato followed him in this, and subscribed to the position that definition relates to something else, and not to the perceptibles— on the kind of grounds indicated: he thought it impossible for there to be a common definition of any of the perceptibles, since they were always changing. Plato, then, called these kinds of realities "ideas," and claimed that the perceptibles were something in addition to them, and were all spoken of in terms of them—what he said was that by virtue of participation, the many shared their names with the forms.

The gist of Aristotle's account is clear. Plato accepts Socrates' view that knowledge as articulated in definitions must relate to something universal; takes over the Heraclitean view that there can be no such knowledge of perceptibles, because they are always changing—they have no definite or at any rate definable nature; and so posits Forms separate from perceptibles as the realities to which definitions do apply. But while the general thrust of the passage is not in doubt, it prompts questions:

1. What exactly is Aristotle claiming about Plato's relationship with Cratylus?
2. Whatever the claim, is it likely to be true?
3. Was subscription to Heracliteanism really a key component in Plato's motivation for positing Forms?

I shall deal summarily with points 1 and 2 and at greater length with point 3.[39]

1. Aristotle is certainly saying that when Plato was young he got to know Cratylus, and through him the Heraclitean theory of flux. Nevertheless, it is not claimed in so many words that Cratylus was his "teacher." Is it being stated or suggested that he got acquainted with Cratylus before joining Socrates' circle? The answer turns on what is meant by "first of all": first in temporal sequence, or the

---

1991), 63–119, 146–78. Xenocrates developed the *Symposium*'s idea of *daimones*, spiritual beings mediating between gods and humans (*Symp.* 202E–203A). Collections of the evidence are L. Tarán, *Speusippus of Athens* (Leiden, 1981), and M. Isnardi Parente, *Frammenti: Senocrate, Ermippo* (Naples, 1982).

39. On Cratylus, see D. N. Sedley, *Plato's* Cratylus (Cambridge, 2003), 16–23. A preoccupation with the flux of the perceptible world is not self-evidently what was fundamental in the philosophy of Heraclitus: for example, Kirk et al., *Presocratic Philosophers*, ch. 6; C. H. Kahn, *The Art and Thought of Heraclitus* (Cambridge, 1979). But Aristotle correctly interprets the way Heracliteanism was construed by Plato. See further, ch. 17 of this volume.

first point in Aristotle's exposition? I don't think we can be sure, although the second option better fits my sense of the flow of the passage. In any case, the issue will not be of much moment for our purposes.

2. It has been suspected that Aristotle doesn't really have biographical information at his disposal but is simply extrapolating from the end of Plato's *Cratylus*.[40] There Cratylus at least ends up a Heraclitean, and Socrates argues against a thoroughgoing Heracliteanism that if there were knowledge, it would have to relate to entities like "the beautiful itself," which is always such as it is and cannot therefore be in flux (*Crat.* 439b–440e). This passage is surely what Aristotle uses to *interpret* the way Plato came to use the Heracliteanism he learned about from Cratylus.[41] But Aristotle knows things about Cratylus—an obscure figure—not to be found in Plato (e.g., his famous criticism of Heraclitus: you can't step into the same river even once [*Metaph.* Γ5, 1010a7–15]); he doesn't actually need the biographical claim for his main purpose—to explain Plato's motivation for positing Forms; and the way he highlights it at the beginning of the passage suggests someone who thinks he has real news to impart. The verdict must be that Aristotle was told it by someone he had reason to think reliable—conceivably, Plato himself.

3. The reason for mentioning Plato's early familiarity with Cratylus and Heracliteanism is evidently its significance in the light of what later transpired. Plato had got to know the Heraclitean theory of flux and to understand its consequences for knowledge when young. But it was only later, when reflecting on Socrates' search for definitions (the focus of the early dialogues), and when puzzling about the nature of knowledge on his own account in consequence, that he came to put the Heracliteanism he had imbibed from Cratylus to philosophical work—in concluding that Forms, not perceptibles, must be the object of knowledge and definition. The key question is whether this is a believable account of the origin of the theory.

Nobody doubts that Plato posited Forms as a consequence of reflection on Socrates' definitional "What is X?" questions. One of his preferred locutions for referring to a Form is to have Socrates speak of "the very thing that X is." That formula is not itself a definition. Instead, it specifies what it is that would be captured by an adequate definition of X if we could find it. In other words, there has to be "the very thing that X is" if there is to be the kind of definitional knowledge of what all Xs have in common that Socrates was looking for. That, then, prompts the further question: What *kind* of thing is the very thing that X is?

Well-known texts in the so-called middle dialogues address themselves to this issue (notably, *Symp.* 211a–b; *Phd.* 65d–66a, 74a–c, 78c–79e). In doing so, they avail themselves of the radical thought—at the core of the argument of the great

40. For example, G. S. Kirk, "The problem of Cratylus," *American Journal of Philology* 72 (1951), 225–53, and Kahn, *Plato and the Socratic Dialogue*, 80–83.

41. Although if he did, he read somewhat more into Plato's text (even supplemented by, e.g., *Phd.* 78C–E) than it literally contains: see T. H. Irwin, "The theory of Forms," in G. Fine (ed.), *Plato 1: Metaphysics and Epistemology* (Oxford, 1999), 149–52—a study that explores different ways in which Heraclitean flux is understood by Plato.

metaphysical poem of the Presocratic Parmenides of Elea ("much of Plato's philosophy," especially his later philosophy, "is unimaginable without the towering figure of Parmenides")[42]—that if reality is to be the object of knowledge, then insofar as it is knowable, it must be what it is without qualification: it cannot *not* be in any respect at all (*Rep.* 5.476e–477a). Aristotle does not mention Parmenides in his account of the rationale underlying the theory of Forms (he confines himself to figures with whom Plato had significant early encounters). But Plato's encounter with Parmenides' *thought* was clearly decisive in this context. Parmenides' central argument is that only what is is an intelligible object of thought—use of the expression "is not" attempts something impossible: specifying not a something but nothing (Fr.2; cf. Fr.3, Fr.6.1–2). He then develops the consequences. Reality cannot come into being or pass away, or change or move, or exhibit any variation or imperfection, since to represent it as subject to any of these processes or conditions would require explicit or implicit use of "is not" (Fr. 8.1–49). The perceptible world as represented in ordinary human beliefs about reality fails to satisfy these constraints. "Mortal opinions," as Parmenides calls them, are desperately confused because they roll up "is" and "is not" together—they fail to make the critical decision between the two (Fr. 6 and 7; cf. Fr. 8.15–18).[43]

In Book 5 of the *Republic*, Plato follows Parmenides in his characterization of opinion as the mental condition of ordinary people who take what their senses tell them for knowledge (*Rep.* 5.474b–480a). Nonetheless, it sounds from his formulations as though he construes the state of the perceptible world primarily in terms of Heraclitean flux rather than any corresponding Parmenidean category—so that Aristotle may well have been right in construing reflection on Heracliteanism as a key metaphysical ingredient in the motivation for positing Forms. Thus in the account of the beautiful in the *Symposium*, Diotima begins (211a): "First, it always is and neither comes to be nor passes away, neither waxes nor wanes"; and there are generic formulations in terms of change or coming to be and passing away in the *Phaedo* (*Phd.* 78c–e) and the *Republic* (*Rep.* 6.485b). The reality with which philosophers are concerned in asking "What is X?" is specified in these texts by means of a contrast—implicit or explicit—with the Heraclitean flux of the perceptible world.

None of these texts makes the *argument* that there cannot be knowledge of what is in flux, so knowledge has to be concerned with entities—the Forms—quite separate from the coming to be and passing away of perceptible things. For anything like that, we have to wait until the end of the *Cratylus*. On the supposition

---

42. Guthrie, *History of Greek Philosophy*, Vol. 4, 35.

43. For presentation and discussion of the fragments of Parmenides' poem, see Kirk et al., *Presocratic Philosophers*, ch. 8. A good brief account is in Sedley, "Parmenides," 7.229–35. A seminal modern interpretation is G. E. L. Owen, "Eleatic questions," *Classical Quarterly* 10 (1960), 84–102. The major edition is A. H. Coxon, *The Fragments of Parmenides* (Assen, 1986). Philosophical studies that illuminate Parmenides' influence on Plato are I. Crystal, "Parmenidean allusion in *Republic* V," *Ancient Philosophy* 16 (1996), 351–63; P. K. Curd, *The Legacy of Parmenides: Eleatic Monism and Later Presocratic Thought* (Princeton, 1998), ch. 6.2; and J. A. Palmer, *Plato's Reception of Parmenides* (Oxford, 1999) (see ch. 4 on the Parmenidean dimension of *Rep.* 5.474B–480A).

that (as many scholars think probable) *Cratylus* postdates the three dialogues just mentioned, we might hypothesize that Plato here acknowledges the debt the metaphysics of those dialogues owes to the Heraclitean view of the perceptible world that he had first got to know in Cratylus's company all those years ago. Perhaps, indeed, it was only belatedly—after writing *Symposium*, *Phaedo*, and *Republic*—that he came to appreciate the importance of his conversations with Cratylus in shaping his approach to questions of metaphysics and epistemology when he turned eventually to tackle them. In general, Cratylus emerges from the *Cratylus* as one of the least impressive thinkers put on stage in the dialogues. It is at least a pleasant thought that Plato used its last couple of pages to flag up what he nonetheless now realized he learned from him.

# 6. THE ACADEMY AND THE LATE DIALOGUES

The literary and philosophical temper of Plato's late dialogues, as every reader notices, is much changed from the writings that precede them. Their hiatus-free prose can be extraordinarily crabbed and involved; they are comparatively lacking in dramatic life and color; anonymous and anonymized figures—the Eleatic Visitor (in *Sophist* and *Statesman*), the Athenian Visitor (in the *Laws*)—conduct most of the relatively wooden conversation (Socrates has a lead role only in *Philebus*), while Timaeus (in *Timaeus*) and Critias (in *Critias*) resort to uninterrupted monologue. There is less sense of contextualization of philosophical dialogue within a real world. Dialogues like the *Sophist*, *Statesman*, and *Philebus* (and, earlier, the *Parmenides*) read like texts for the Academy and, indeed, reflect discussion within the Academy.

In the case of the *Sophist* and *Statesman*, the argument for that hypothesis derives almost wholly from their combination of pedagogical and didactic concern to instill understanding of correct dialectical method with forbiddingly abstract or technical content. The *Parmenides* exhibits the same combination, but its preoccupation with the critique and proper interpretation of the theory of Forms locates it within a well-documented debate in the Academy about Forms, to which Eudoxus, Speusippus, Xenocrates, and Aristotle all contributed (neither Aristotle nor Speusippus accepted Plato's theory in any version).[44] Whether Plato wrote the

---

44. For accounts of the metaphysical issues and positions that preoccupied the early Academy, see W. D. Ross, *Plato's Theory of Ideas* (Oxford, 1951), chs. 9–17; Burkert, *Lore and Science in Ancient Pythagoreanism*, ch. 1; and J. Annas, *Aristotle's Metaphysics, Books M and N* (Oxford, 1976). For treatments of the contributions of Speusippus and Xenocrates, see also the literature referred to in n. 38 above; for Eudoxus, consult Guthrie, *History of Greek Philosophy*, Vol. 5, 452–53, and M. Schofield, "Eudoxus in the *Parmenides*," *Museum Helveticum* 30 (1973), 1–19; for Aristotle, see G. Fine, *On Ideas: Aristotle's Criticism of Plato's Theory of Forms* (Oxford, 1993).

*Parmenides* to initiate debate, or whether he was responding to an incipient or ongoing controversy already launched (as one might conjecture from the dialogue's consideration of the possibility—associated by Aristotle with Eudoxus—that Forms are immanent in particulars: *Metaph.* A9, 991a12–20), we do not know. But he must have intended it primarily for a readership within the Academy. The star example of such a dialogue, however, is the *Philebus*.

*Philebus* is a heady and often esoteric mixture of ethics, methodology, and metaphysics. The methodology and the ontology—couched as they are in terms of number, ratio, limit, the unlimited—reflect the Pythagorizing turn in Academic metaphysical speculation that is attested particularly in Books M and N of Aristotle's *Metaphysics*. This is especially true for Speusippus, but there is also Pythagorizing in Plato's own "unwritten doctrines," with which the ontology of the *Philebus* has an apparent affinity.[45] In making pleasure and arguments for and against hedonism the focus of the dialogue's ethical enquiry, Plato was not merely participating in an Academic debate but acting as adjudicator (in fact, the dialogue represents itself as awarding prizes—in rank order—to the most convincing candidates for what determines the goodness of a good life). We know—again primarily from Aristotle—that Eudoxus argued for hedonism and Speusippus against it. What Aristotle tells us about Eudoxus's hedonism (in Book 10 of the *Nicomachean Ethics*) makes it very probable that it is his account of pleasure as the good that Plato is reproducing for discussion in the *Philebus* (*Phlb.* 20c–21a). Later in the dialogue, various other thinkers who provide ammunition for anti-hedonist conclusions are referred to under designations such as the "difficult" people (44b–e) or the "subtle" people (53c). It is tempting to try to strip them of their anonymity (could "difficulty" be what Speusippus was known for?).[46] But whether identifications can be secured or not, there is no mistaking that Plato here introduces contemporary voices—presumably Academic—into the argument.

How much did Plato's own thinking as evidenced in the late dialogues owe to the other leading philosophers who worked with him in the Academy? Everything we have seen of Plato in this chapter suggests that he was someone whose philosophizing was invariably nourished by engagement with his immediate intellectual and political environment. His originality lies in the versatility and fertility of his response to it. So—to return for a moment to the *Philebus*—the very idea of writing once again about hedonism (already discussed in *Protagoras*, *Gorgias*, and

45. The music theorist Aristoxenus reports a famously unintelligible lecture by Plato on the Good (*Harmonics* 2.30.16–31.3), which is often connected with Aristotle's reference to "unwritten doctrines" of Plato (*Phys.* 4.2, 209b11–16). It is generally supposed that these must have included an idea he makes central to Platonic metaphysics in *Metaph.* A6 and debates at length in *Metaph.* M and N: that numbers (identified with Forms) are to be analyzed in terms of a formal principle (the one) and a material principle (the large and the small). The Tübingen school of Platonic interpretation sees this as the true centrepiece of Plato's entire philosophy, only hinted at in the dialogues; at the other extreme is the thoroughgoing skepticism of Cherniss, *Riddle of the Early Academy*, chs. 1 and 2. For a balanced and informative review of the evidence and the controversy (with ample bibliography), see Guthrie, *History of Greek Philosophy*, Vol. 5, ch. 8.

46. See M. Schofield, "Who were οἱ δυσχερεῖς in Plato, *Philebus* 44Aff?" *Museum Helveticum* 28 (1971), 2–20, 181.

Book 9 of the *Republic*), but within a framework shaped by Pythagorizing meta-physics, would surely never have occurred to him without the stimulus of arguments about these issues in the Academy. The great cosmological project of the *Timaeus* must owe much "to the research of and discussion with other members of the Academy in the 350s, especially mathematicians and astronomers."[47] It is possible to suspect the impact of much more specific ideas generated there, too. The *Statesman* makes central to its concept of statesmanship something that might well take the reader of the *Republic* by surprise: the idea that the knowledge required by someone involved in practical activity must be a capacity for measured judgment of what is appropriate and timely—in short, of what is "removed to the middle from the extremes" (*Statesman* 284b–e). Is this an entirely spontaneous innovation by the elderly Plato? Or is it his appropriation of a theory of virtue as occupying a mean determined by practical knowledge that had already been worked out by the young Aristotle?[48]

# 7. THE *LAWS* IN ITS TIME AND PLACE

The *Laws* was evidently designed for a wider public—although it has sometimes been suggested that, nonetheless, its existence bears an intimate relationship with the purposes for which the Academy existed. G. R. Morrow, one of the leading twentieth-century authorities on the dialogue, is one of many distinguished scholars convinced that the Academy was a school for statesmen, which prepared its members for the role "by the study of Greek law and politics," inter alia.[49] T. J. Saunders, another major authority on the *Laws*, believes we can infer from it the sorts of policies and procedures that Academic political "advisers" would have been taught to recommend to those who consulted them.[50] But while some who had associated with Plato in the Academy did become involved in the politics mostly of their home cities, as might be expected of aristocrats, the case is flimsy for seeing them as emissaries from the Academy primed for their task in the way Morrow and Saunders imagine, or for thinking the Academy had its own political agenda.[51] No doubt, its members talked politics during their stay in the Academy. To judge from the evidence of other late dialogues, however, *philosophical* dis-

---

47. Ostwald and Lynch, "Growth of schools and advance of knowledge," 609.

48. For example, M. Schofield, "The disappearance of the philosopher king," *Proceedings of the Boston Area Colloquium in Ancient Philosophy* 13 (1997), 224–26.

49. G. R. Morrow, *Plato's Cretan City: A Historical Interpretation of the* Laws (Princeton, 1960), 5.

50. T. J. Saunders, " 'The RAND Corporation in antiquity?' Plato's Academy and Greek politics," in J. H. Betts, J. T. Hooker, and J. R. Green (eds.), *Studies in Honour of T. B. L. Webster* (Bristol, 1986), 1.200–10.

51. For example, P. A. Brunt, "Plato's Academy and politics," *Studies in Greek History and Thought* (Oxford, 1993), ch. 10; M. Schofield, "Plato and practical politics," in C. J. Rowe and M. Schofield (eds.), *The Cambridge History of Greek and Roman Political Thought* (Cambridge, 2000), ch. 13.

cussion would have been devoted mostly to questions of metaphysics and ethics
and to the dialectical methods appropriate for tackling them.

What seems hard to doubt is that the *Laws* was written with practical intent, as
a guide to the principles that should inform the communal life of a well-ordered
Greek city and as a blueprint for their detailed implementation on a monumental
scale. "No work of Plato's," said Morrow, "is more intimately connected with its
time and with the world in which it was written than the *Laws*."[52] This huge
dialogue is dense with reference explicit and (more often) implicit to the political
and sociocultural institutions and practices of the Greek city-state, and, above all,
of Athens itself. In fact, Plato's extensive and intricate legal code is a reworking of
contemporary Athenian law, embodying a radical new utilitarian penology based
on the Socratic view that, since nobody does wrong willingly, criminality is a
disease (*Gorg.* 466d–480d). In consequence a much more inquisitorial form of
procedure before the courts was in his view required, reducing the scope for the
rhetoric the *Gorgias* thought so pernicious.

One particularly fascinating dimension of the code is its elaborate and un-
Athenian differentiation of penalties for offenses, according to whether the per-
petrator is a citizen, a slave, a temporary visitor, or a long-term resident alien (a
metic). As in Athens (but not Sparta), Plato allows for a class of metics: persons like
Cephalus in the *Republic*, needed for occupations regarded in the *Laws* as harmful
to the soul—notably commerce. But unlike at Athens, their residence is to be
subject to a time limit (twenty years). The way their alien status is marked can be
illustrated from the highly baroque structure of laws covering assault (*Laws*
9.879b–882c). Mostly, the metics are to be subject to more severe penalties than
citizens. Some prominence is given to the rule that if a foreigner whose assault on a
citizen can be proven—after an examination that pays proper respect to the god
who protects foreigners—to have been designed to insult and humiliate, he or she
is to be subjected to as many strokes of the lash as the blows he or she inflicted in
order to put a stop to "foreign uppitiness" (*thrasuxenia:* a word, as Saunders points
out,[53] that occurs nowhere else and was evidently coined for this occasion). There
is no rule covering citizen behavior of this sort (in Athens, imprisonment and loss
of citizen rights was probably the penalty).

Morrow went so far as to describe the society Plato was intent on defining
through his legislative template as "an idealized Athens."[54] Certainly, there is an
explicit preoccupation with Athens (as with Sparta and Persia) in Book 3, where a
historical approach is taken to the task of working out what the ideal social and
political system would be like. It begins with the flood and the emergence of the
first simple postdeluvian communities, and ends with a discussion of Athens and

---

52. Morrow, *Plato's Cretan City*, xxix.
53. T. J. Saunders, *Plato's Penal Code* (Oxford, 1991), 275 n.45.
54. Morrow, *Plato's Cretan City*, 592. But he did not underestimate the importance of the Spartan and
Cretan model for the ideal city of the *Laws*—it is, after all, to be a closed and tightly controlled society.
Uniquely, the dialogue is set not in Athens but in Crete, where the Solonian figure of the Athenian Visitor
can find sympathetic, if challenged, recipients for the blueprint he proposes.

Persia as societies that, in the past, combined the three prime desiderata of wisdom, freedom, and friendship by balancing in their system of government a monarchic with a democratic principle. Since the time of Cyrus the Great (in Persia) and, less explicitly, Solon (in Athens), the balance has become fatally disturbed. Persia has degenerated into tyranny, Athens into what Plato calls "theatocracy": the self-indulgence of a society under the control of the illusion that anybody's judgment is as good as anybody else's.

Thirty years on Plato here plays new variations on the old analysis of the malaise of Athenian democracy familiar from the *Gorgias*. But the contrast between Solonian Athens and the decline since the days of Marathon has a contemporary flavor. Around the time the *Laws* was being composed, Isocrates was vainly appealing for the reintroduction of what he called "the democracy bequeathed by our ancestors" in his *Areopagiticus*, written (probably in 355 BC) as a wake-up call to Athens in the aftermath of its second brief attempt to sustain an empire.[55] In the time of Solon and Cleisthenes, Athens enjoyed a balanced, well-ordered constitutional settlement, which did not as now educate the citizens "to regard licentiousness as democracy, lawlessness as freedom, outspokenness as equality, and the license to do these things as happiness" (*Areop.* 20). The *Laws* has a different agenda, but it breathes the same air.

An autobiographical dimension to the *Laws* has often been perceived.[56] In the 360s, Plato had made two further visits to Sicily, to the court of the young Dionysius II: one probably in 366, very soon after his accession to power after his father's death; the other in 361. Both were undertaken to oblige Dion, who had hopes of influencing the new tyrant and, initially (according to the Seventh Letter), of Plato's turning him into a philosopher ruler (*Ep.* 7.327b–328d). Both were wretched failures, with Dionysius turning out to be a dilettante in philosophy and interested only in using Plato in regional political machinations (again according to the Letter).[57] The *Laws* notoriously gives no room to the aspiration for rule by philosophers articulated in the *Republic*, and the dialogue insists that absolute power will almost inevitably bring about the moral corruption of anyone who wields it. Although the *Republic* itself has plenty to say about the corruptions of power, and the corruptibility especially of those naturally endowed for philosophy (*Rep.* 6.491a–495b), and although the *Laws* is designed to work out an *approximation* to what the *Republic* always conceived as a scarcely feasible ideal, readers have diagnosed personal disillusionment on Plato's part. It is certainly hard to think that his recent Sicilian experience did not somehow color his thoughts about tyrants in the *Laws*. At any rate, it is interesting that when in Book 4 he comes to sketch the preconditions that might favor the creation of a well-ordered polity, he

55. The political history of the period is a tangled tale: for example, Hornblower, *Greek World*, chs. 16 and 17. A helpful brief account of the "second Athenian confederacy" is available in S. Hornblower and A. Spawforth (eds.), *The Oxford Classical Dictionary*, 3rd ed. (Oxford, 1996), 1376–77.

56. A classic statement of this interpretation is G. Vlastos, "Socratic knowledge and Platonic 'pessimism,'" *Platonic Studies* (Princeton, 1973), ch. 9.

57. For a historical narrative, see Rhodes, *History of the Classical Greek World*, ch. 21.

specifies a location well inland, far from any port (Syracuse had a great harbor), and a young tyrant prepared to work with a lawgiver—thanks to his "orderly" character (that sounds ironic to the point of sarcasm).[58]

# BIBLIOGRAPHY

Annas, J. *Aristotle's* Metaphysics, *Books M and N* (Oxford, 1976).

Barton, J. "Hippocratic explanations," in P. J. van der Eijk (ed.), *Hippocrates in Context* (Leiden, 2005), 29–47.

Blank, D. L. "Socratics versus Sophists on payment for teaching," *California Studies in Classical Antiquity* 1 (1985), 1–49.

Brunt, P. A. "Plato's Academy and politics," *Studies in Greek History and Thought* (Oxford, 1993), ch. 10.

Burkert, W. *Lore and Science in Ancient Pythagoreanism* (Cambridge, Mass., 1972).

Cherniss, H. *The Riddle of the Early Academy* (Berkeley, 1945).

Coxon, A. H. *The Fragments of Parmenides* (Assen, 1986).

Crystal, I. "Parmenidean allusion in *Republic* V," *Ancient Philosophy* 16 (1996), 351–63.

Curd, P. K. *The Legacy of Parmenides: Eleatic Monism and Later Presocratic Thought* (Princeton, 1998).

Dancy, R. M. *Two Studies in the Early Academy* (Albany, N.Y., 1991).

Dillon, J. *The Heirs of Plato* (Oxford, 2003).

Dodds, E. R. (ed.) *Plato: Gorgias* (Oxford, 1959).

Dunn, F. "*On Ancient Medicine* and its intellectual context," in P. J. van der Eijk (ed.), *Hippocrates in Context* (Leiden, 2005), 49–67.

Eucken, C. *Isokrates: Seine Positionen in der Auseinandersetzung mit den zeitgenössischen Philosophen* (Berlin, 1983).

Field, G. C. *Plato and His Contemporaries* (London, 1930).

Fine, G. *On Ideas: Aristotle's Criticism of Plato's Theory of Forms* (Oxford, 1993).

Ford, A. "Sophists without rhetoric: the arts of speech in fifth-century Athens," in Y. L. Too (ed.), *Education in Greek and Roman Antiquity* (Leiden, 2001), 85–109.

Furley, D. J. *Cosmic Problems* (Cambridge, 1989).

Furley, W. D. *Andokides and the Herms: A Study of Crisis in Fifth-Century Athenian Religion* (London, 1996).

Gifford, M. "Dramatic dialectic in *Republic* Book 1," *Oxford Studies in Ancient Philosophy* 20 (2001), 35–106.

Griffith, M. *The Authenticity of Prometheus Bound* (Cambridge, 1977).

Grote, G. *History of Greece* (London, 1850).

Guthrie, W. K. C. *A History of Greek Philosophy*, Vols. 3, 4, 5 (Cambridge, 1969, 1975, 1978).

Heidel, W. A. "The Pythagoreans and Greek mathematics," *American Journal of Philology* 61 (1940), 1–33.

Hornblower, S. *The Greek World 479–323 BC*, 3rd ed. (London, 2003).

Hornblower, S., and Spawforth, A. (eds.), *The Oxford Classical Dictionary*, 3rd ed. (Oxford, 1996).

---

58. As is argued by Schofield, "Disappearance of the philosopher king," 230–41.

Huffman, C. A. *Archytas of Tarentum: Pythagorean, Philosopher and Mathematician King* (Cambridge, 2005).

Huffman, C. A. *Philolaus of Croton: Pythagorean and Presocratic* (Cambridge, 1993).

Irwin, T. H. "The theory of Forms," in G. Fine (ed.), *Plato 1: Metaphysics and Epistemology* (Oxford, 1999), 143–70.

Isnardi Parente, M. *Frammenti: Senocrate, Ermippo* (Naples, 1982).

Johnson, R. "Isocrates' methods of teaching," *American Journal of Philology* 80 (1959), 25–36.

Jouanna, J. *Hippocrates* (Baltimore, 1999).

Kagan, D. *The Peloponnesian War: Athens and Sparta in Savage Conflict, 431–404 BC* (London, 2003).

Kahn, C. H. *The Art and Thought of Heraclitus* (Cambridge, 1979).

Kahn, C. H. *Plato and the Socratic Dialogue* (Cambridge, 1996).

Kahn, C. H. "Plato's funeral oration: the motive of the *Menexenus*," *Classical Philology* 58 (1963), 220–34.

Kahn, C. H. *Pythagoras and the Pythagoreans: A Brief History* (Indianapolis, 2001).

Kennedy, G. *The Art of Persuasion in Greece* (Princeton, 1963).

Kerferd, G. B. *The Sophistic Movement* (Cambridge, 1981).

Kirk, G. S. "The problem of Cratylus," *American Journal of Philology* 72 (1951), 225–53.

Kirk, G. S., Raven, J. E., and Schofield, M. *The Presocratic Philosophers*, 2nd ed. (Cambridge, 1983).

Knorr, W. R. *The Ancient Tradition of Geometric Problems* (Boston, 1986).

Knorr, W. R. "On the early history of axiomatics: the interaction of mathematics and philosophy in Greek antiquity," in J. Hintikka, D. Gruender, and A. Agazzi (eds.), *Theory Change, Ancient Axiomatics and Galileo's Methodology* (Dordrecht, 1981), 145–86.

Lloyd, G. E. R. *Demystifying Mentalities* (Cambridge, 1990).

Lloyd, G. E. R. (ed.) *Hippocratic Writings* (Harmondsworth, 1978).

Lloyd, G. E. R. *Magic, Reason and Experience* (Cambridge, 1979).

Mirhady, D., and Too, Y. L. (trans.) *Isocrates I* (Austin, Tex., 2000).

Morrow, G. R. *Plato's Cretan City: A Historical Interpretation of the* Laws (Princeton, 1960).

Nails, D. *The People of Plato* (Indianapolis, 2002).

Norlin, G. (ed.) *Isocrates*, Vols. 1-2 (London, 1928, 1929).

Ober, J. *Mass and Elite in Democratic Athens* (Princeton, 1989).

O'Brien, M. J. *The Socratic Paradoxes and the Greek Mind* (Chapel Hill, N.C., 1967).

Ostwald, M., and Lynch, J. P. "The growth of schools and the advance of knowledge," in D. M. Lewis, J. Boardman, S. Hornblower, and M. Ostwald (eds.), *The Cambridge Ancient History*, Vol. 6, 2nd ed. (Cambridge, 1994), ch. 12a.

Owen, G. E. L. "Eleatic questions," *Classical Quarterly* 10 (1960), 84–102.

Palmer, J. A. *Plato's Reception of Parmenides* (Oxford, 1999).

Papillon, T. L. (trans.) *Isocrates II* (Austin, Tex., 2005).

Price, S. *Religions of the Ancient Greeks* (Cambridge, 1999).

Rhodes, P. J. *A History of the Classical Greek World 478–323 BC* (Oxford, 2006).

Riginos, A. *Platonica: The Anecdotes Concerning the Life and Writings of Plato* (Leiden, 1976).

Ross, W. D. *Plato's Theory of Ideas* (Oxford, 1951).

Saunders, T. J. *Plato's Penal Code* (Oxford, 1991).

Saunders, T. J. " 'The RAND Corporation in antiquity?' Plato's Academy and Greek politics," in J. H. Betts, J. T. Hooker, and J. R. Green (eds.), *Studies in Honour of T. B. L. Webster* (Bristol, 1986), 1.200–10.

Schiefsky, M. J. *Hippocrates* On Ancient Medicine (Leiden, 2005).

Schofield, M. "Antisthenes," in E. Craig (ed.), *Routledge Encyclopedia of Philosophy* (London, 1998), 1.314–17.

Schofield, M. "The disappearance of the philosopher king," *Proceedings of the Boston Area Colloquium in Ancient Philosophy* 13 (1997), 213–41.

Schofield, M. "Eudoxus in the *Parmenides*," *Museum Helveticum* 30 (1973), 1–19.

Schofield, M. "Plato and practical politics," in C. J. Rowe and M. Schofield (eds), *The Cambridge History of Greek and Roman Political Thought* (Cambridge, 2000), ch. 13.

Schofield, M. "Who were οἱ δυσχερεῖς in Plato, *Philebus* 44Aff?" *Museum Helveticum* 28 (1971), 2–20, 181.

Sedley, D. N. "Parmenides," in E. Craig (ed.), *Routledge Encyclopedia of Philosophy* (London, 1998), 7.229–35.

Sedley, D. N. *Plato's* Cratylus (Cambridge, 2003).

Tarán, L. *Speusippus of Athens* (Leiden, 1981).

Thompson, W. H. *The Phaedrus of Plato* (London, 1868).

Too, Y. L. *The Rhetoric of Identity in Isocrates: Text, Power, Pedagogy* (Cambridge, 1995).

van Hook, L. (ed.) *Isocrates*, Vol. 3 (London, 1945).

Vlastos, G. *Socrates: Ironist and Moral Philosopher* (Cambridge, 1991).

Vlastos, G. "Socratic knowledge and Platonic 'pessimism,' " *Platonic Studies* (Princeton, 1973), ch. 9.

Wardy, R. B. B. *The Birth of Rhetoric* (London, 1996).

Zeyl, D. (ed.) *Encyclopedia of Classical Philosophy* (Westport, Conn., 1997).

Zuntz, G. *Persephone* (Oxford, 1971).

CHAPTER 3
.....................................................................................................................................

# THE PLATONIC CORPUS

.....................................................................................................................................

## T. H. IRWIN

## 1. CONTENTS OF THE CORPUS
.....................................................................................................................................

This chapter is intended to answer some questions that may arise for new readers
of Plato, especially for those who are unfamiliar with Ancient Greek texts. They
may wonder how the Platonic Corpus has survived from Plato's time, why it
consists mostly of dialogues, when the different works were written, why they are
mostly about a character called Socrates, and why they are usually taken to express
Plato's views, even though Plato is never a character in them. Some answers—even
brief or conjectural answers or suggestions toward answers—to these questions
may help us to read more intelligently.

If we open a Greek text of Plato, such as the Oxford Classical Texts (OCT)
edition,[1] we find Plato's text divided into five volumes. These five volumes contain
thirty-six works,[2] nearly all dialogues, in nine "tetralogies" (groups of four works),
plus a collection of "Definitions" (probably spurious) and six works listed under
"spurious."[3] Each dialogue is supplied with marginal numbers and letters

---

1. *Platonis Opera*, ed. J. Burnet, 5 vols. (Oxford: Oxford University Press, 1900–1907). This edition is in
the process of being replaced by a new OCT. So far, vol. 1 (*Platonis Opera*, ed. E. A. Duke, W. F. Hicken, W.
S. M. Nicoll, D. B. Robinson, and J. C. G. Strachan, 1995) and the *Republic* (*Platonis Respublica*, ed. S. Slings,
2003) have appeared.

2. The two longest dialogues, the *Republic* and the *Laws*, are also divided into books. The divisions
into books are probably not derived from Plato. See n.62 below.

3. The six works listed as spurious are *De Iusto*, *De Virtute*, *Demodocus*, *Sisyphus*, *Eryxias*, and *Axiochus*. On the tetralogies, see sec. 3.

(beginning the *Euthyphro*, e.g., at 2a); these numbers and letters refer to "Stephanus pages."[4]

Not all the works in the Corpus are dialogues. The *Apology* purports to be Socrates' defense at his trial. The *Menexenus* is a funeral speech. Thirteen letters are included that purport to be by Plato. Most modern students reject almost all the letters as spurious. The most important letter about which serious dispute remains is Letter VII. If this letter is genuine, it is important, for two reasons: (a) It offers some autobiographical detail about Plato. (b) It puts forward philosophical claims that have no parallel in the dialogues. Probably, however, Letter VII is spurious and is not a reliable source for Plato's life or for his philosophy.

In addition to the six recognized spurious works, other works are "dubious," regarded as spurious by most or many modern students. Some of these dubious works are philosophically significant, including the *Hippias Major*, *Clitopho*, *Theages*, and *Alcibiades*. Of these, the first two are probably genuine, and the last two are probably spurious. No one has argued that any of the six acknowledged spurious works is authentic.

The Platonic Corpus is unusual among the works of Greek authors by being, as far as we know, complete. No reference in any ancient author attests the existence of any work by Plato that does not appear in our Platonic Corpus.[5]

The Corpus is found in the manuscripts of Plato, produced in the ninth century AD and later. In the 1,300 years between the lifetime of Plato and the production of our manuscripts, a canon of Plato's works was formed, someone tried to distinguish genuine from spurious works, and the works were arranged in a fixed tetralogical order. To see when and how this all happened, we need to consider the history of the Platonic Corpus from its creation to the production of our manuscripts. Many stages in this history are obscure, and the evidence is often fragmentary.

# 2. The Publication
## of the Dialogues

We normally think of "publication" as the dissemination of a finished written text by a publisher to bookshops and libraries. In Plato's time, there were no publishers, and it is not clear that the dissemination of a written text was the primary means of

---

4. The edition printed and published by Stephanus (the Latin name of Henri Estienne) in 1578 was the first edition of Plato to divide its pages into sections marked by letters. Modern editions of Plato still use these references.

5. According to Diogenes Laertius iii 5–6, Plato took up painting and writing poetry, especially tragic drama, before he met Socrates, but he burned his tragedies after he had heard Socrates. This "biographical" information may simply be invented on the basis of the dialogues. The authenticity of the short poems

making one's work known. Plato's first audience for his written compositions may have been a group of people who came for a private reading. We might compare a modern author delivering a talk or lecture before the publication of a written version. The next stage of dissemination would be to deliver the work to a bookshop; in Socrates' time, Athenian bookshops sold philosophical works even by non-Athenian writers (*Ap.* 26d–e).[6]

Sale by a bookshop did not replace oral dissemination. The *Parmenides* begins after Zeno the Eleatic has finished reading a treatise of his that he has brought to Athens for the first time (*Parm.* 127c–e). Similarly, Socrates mentions that he heard someone reading from a book of Anaxagoras (*Phd.* 97c). Bookshops were also centers for public reading where interested people might come to hear recent books read and to decide whether they wanted to read them often enough to buy a copy.[7] Before they could buy a copy, the original delivered by the author had to be copied by hand.

The Athenian philosophers we know of were associated with different public areas in Athens where they carried on philosophical discussion. Plato is associated with the public gymnasium (also a public meeting place) in the area called Academeia, after the precinct of the hero Hecademus. He bought land in this area and established a house and garden for himself. Here he began the association or fraternity that came to be called the Academy.[8] We might reasonably wonder whether the oral delivery of the dialogues (whether before or after they were available to booksellers) was connected with discussions in the Academy.[9]

Wherever these oral performances took place—in the Academy, in other invited gatherings, or in bookshops—Plato's dialogues were circulated widely enough in Athens to be the subject of parody and allusion in comedy.[10] One comic fragment alludes to discussions carried on the Academy, but it offers no help on their subject matter, apart from the suggestion that definitions were discussed.[11] If we could confidently accept the suggestion that Aristotle's *Topics* was designed for

---

attributed to him (see, e.g., DL iii 29–33) is questionable. W. Ludwig, "Plato's love epigrams," *Greek, Roman, and Byzantine Studies* 4 (1963), 59–82, argues that they are all spurious, except for the epigram on Dion. (They are collected at the end of Plato, *Collected Dialogues*, ed. J. M. Cooper and D. S. Hutchinson [Indianapolis: Hackett, 1997].)

6. On books in fifth- and fourth-century Greece, see *Oxford Classical Dictionary*, 3rd ed., ed. S. Hornblower and A. Spawforth (Oxford: Oxford University Press, 1996), 250–51; L. D. Reynolds and N. G. Wilson, *Scribes and Scholars*, 3rd ed. (Oxford: Oxford University Press, 1991), 1–5 (an admirably clear and instructive book); and B. M. Metzger, *The Text of the New Testament*, 3rd ed. (Oxford: Oxford University Press, 1991), ch. 1.

7. See, e.g., DL vii 2–3.

8. DL iii 7, 20, 41. On the character of the Academy, see J. M. Dillon, *The Heirs of Plato* (Oxford: Oxford University Press, 2003), ch. 1.

9. Favorinus (ca. AD 85–155) reports that when Plato read his work "On the soul," everyone got up and left before he was finished, except for Aristotle (DL iii 37). "On the soul" is sometimes used as a title for the *Phaedo*. Plato is reported to have given a public lecture on the good (not a reading of a dialogue); for reports, see Aristotle, *Complete Works*, ed. J. Barnes, 2 vols. (Princeton, N.J.: Princeton University Press, 1984), vol. 2, 2397–99.

10. DL iii 26 mentions an allusion to the *Phaedo* by the comic poet Theopompus.

11. See the fragment of Epicrates translated and discussed by Dillon, *Heirs of Plato*, 7–8.

the conduct of discussions within the Academy,[12] we would know some of what happened in the Academy, but we would not know whether the dialogues played any part in it.

After he had sold copies of the dialogues to booksellers, Plato seems to have continued working on them. He is said to have rewritten the first sentence of the *Republic* many times and to have been in the habit of revising dialogues he had already finished.[13] We do not know whether the revised versions were also sent to bookshops or whether they were used in later oral performances.

To ensure circulation of his works outside Athens, Plato would need someone to travel abroad with them, as Zeno the Eleatic did on behalf of his own works (according to the *Parmenides*). Hermodorus, a Syracusan member of the Academy, introduced Plato's works to Sicily, with Plato's permission.[14] It is not clear how widely the dialogues were circulated,[15] but some stories suggest that at least some of them were read or heard outside Athens.[16]

# 3. THE CIRCULATION OF THE CORPUS IN ANTIQUITY

After Plato's death, his nephew Speusippus became the head of the Academy. Plato's will does not say anything about his books and papers (DL iii 41–43), but we may reasonably assume that they passed into the custody of the Academy.[17] We have already mentioned the stories about his revisions of dialogues. Moreover, he

12. See G. Ryle, "Dialectic in the Academy," in *New Essays on Plato and Aristotle*, ed. J. R. Bambrough (London: Routledge, 1965), 39–68.

13. See Dionysius of Halicarnassus, *De Comp. Verborum* 25: "Plato kept on combing and curling and in every way braiding his dialogues even when he had turned eighty; for all lovers of literature (*philologoi*) are familiar with the stories told about this man's industry—including the story about the writing-tablet that is said to have been found after his death, the one that had many different versions of the beginning of the *Republic* that reads "I went down yesterday . . . "" DL iii 37 has the story about the *Republic*. One might wonder whether Dionysius' general claim rests on anything more definite than the story in DL about the *Republic*, combined with *Phdr.* 278de; see A. S. Riginos, *Platonica* (Leiden: Brill, 1976), 186. Both Dionysius' hairdressing metaphors and his one example suggest cosmetic changes rather than radical revisions of dialogues.

14. On Hermodorus, see *Academicrorum Philosophorum Index Herculanensis*, ed. S. Mekler (Berlin: Weidmann, 1902), 34. Cicero mentions Hermodorus, *ad Att.* xiii 21.4 (= Shackleton Bailey 327), remarking that (unlike Cicero's publisher) Hermodorus did not act without Plato's permission. See D. R. Shackleton Bailey ad loc. in Cicero, *Letters to Atticus*, vol. 5 (Cambridge: Cambridge University Press, 1966), 327.

15. DL vii 31 suggests a restricted circulation outside Athens.

16. Themistius 23, 295b (Teubner) mentions Axiothea of Arcadia (who, after reading the *Republic*, put on men's clothes and went to Athens to listen to Plato) and a Corinthian farmer (who, after reading the *Gorgias*, abandoned his farm and became a disciple of Plato).

17. A clear and lively account of this question appears in G. Grote, *Plato and the Other Companions of Socrates*, 4 vols. (London: Murray, 1888), vol. 1, ch. 6 ("The Platonic Canon"). A full account of the history of the Corpus is given by H. Alline, *Histoire du texte de Platon* (Paris: Champion, 1915). Much of the relevant evidence is collected by H. Dörrie, *Der Platonismus in der Antike*, vols. 1–2 (Stuttgart: Frommann-Holzboog, 1987–1990).

is said not to have finished his final corrections in the *Laws*.[18] If these stories are true, someone had access to his drafts, notes, and unpublished papers. The incomplete *Critias* was probably never published in Plato's lifetime, and the *Clitopho* also seems to be an incomplete work. Since these works are in our present Platonic Corpus, the Corpus must at some time have included published and unpublished works of Plato. Members of the Academy, therefore, seem to have decided on the publication of the *Laws*, perhaps after some editing, and of the unfinished *Critias*.

When Plato's works had recently been published, anyone who wanted to read them through had to pay a fee to the owners.[19] This restrictive policy suggests that the owners not only wanted to make money from the texts but also wanted to preserve their integrity by limiting the opportunities for copying, instead of simply selling the works to a bookshop for unrestricted copying. Since there was no law of copyright, and no legal means to prevent the production of inferior copies, deliberate restriction of circulation would be the only means, however imperfect, that the author or owner of a text could use to limit the deterioration of copies through circulation and recopying. According to one story, Aristotle's works suffered from inexpert copying; Plato's successors may have been doing their best to prevent similar damage to the Platonic Corpus.[20]

We may speculate that some acquaintance with Plato's work was fairly widespread in the century after his death in 347 BC, at least among those who attended private or public readings. But the serious readers of Plato may have been considerably fewer. Plato is said to have given Aristotle the nickname of "The Reader" (*anagnôstês*), perhaps because he was an unusually assiduous student of written texts, including the texts of Plato; his works contain many criticisms of points in the dialogues, and some complaints about their obscurities, but they contain no evidence of his having asked Plato to explain what he meant.[21] Perhaps Aristotle encouraged the practice of careful reading of philosophical texts. His surviving works show that he knew Plato's dialogues well.

18. See *Prolegomena in Platonis Philosophiam*, ed. L. G. Westerink (Paris: Les Belles Lettres, 1990), 24.12–15: "They say that the *Laws* were written last, because he left them uncorrected (*adiorthôtous*) and disordered (or "confused"; *sunkechumenous*), because he lacked the time to arrange them because of his death. And if they now appear appropriately arranged, that is because they were arranged not by Plato himself, but by a certain Philip of Opous, a successor in the Platonic school." In disputing the authenticity of the *Epinomis*, Proclus asks, "How could Plato have been unable to correct the *Laws* because he did not live long enough, and after that been able to write the *Epinomis*?" (25.6–8). According to DL iii 37, Philip of Opous "copied his [Plato's] *Laws*, which were written in wax." Wax tablets allowed easy erasure and revision. On these stories about the *Laws*, see G. R. Morrow, *Plato's Cretan City* (Princeton, N.J.: Princeton University Press, 1960), 515–18.

19. DL iii 66 attributes this information to Antigonus of Carystus (fl. c.240). Since it comes from Antigonus' life of Zeno, it may refer to the situation in Zeno's lifetime (335–263).

20. According to Strabo xiii 1.54, a damaged copy of Aristotle came into the hands of Apellicon, who filled the gaps he found in the text but did not know enough to fill the gaps correctly. This dramatic story about the fate of the (allegedly) sole copy of the Aristotelian Corpus is not to be taken too seriously, but it may indicate what could happen to texts in the process of circulation and recopying.

21. The story that Plato called Aristotle "the reader" comes from the *Vita Marciana* sec. 6. See I. Düring, *Aristotle in the Ancient Biographical Tradition* (Gothenburg: Almquist and Wiksel, 1957), 98. Düring comments on it at 108, 368. See also J. Annas, "Aristotle on inefficient causes," *Philosophical Quarterly* 32 (1982), 326.

Our knowledge of other people's use of the Platonic Corpus is limited by the fact that very few continuous philosophical works, apart from Aristotle's, survive from the period between the death of Plato and the lifetime of Cicero. But we have some evidence to show that Plato's works remained in general circulation. Zeno the Stoic was a student of Polemon, the head of the Academy.[22] Both Zeno and Chrysippus discuss and criticize Platonic dialogues.[23] While Arcesilaus (316–241 BC) was head of the Academy, the school turned in a skeptical direction, as a result of their interpretation of the dialogues and of the Socratic outlook.[24] The Epicurean school also seems to have been familiar with Plato.[25] When we come to Poseidonius (ca. 135–51 BC) and Cicero (106–43 BC), we have fuller evidence of knowledge of Plato's dialogues. Poseidonius discussed Plato's views on the division of the soul and examined passages in the *Phaedrus* and *Timaeus* in some detail. Cicero translated the *Timaeus* into Latin and partly imitated the *Republic* and *Laws* in two of his own works.[26] From Cicero onward we have evidence of familiarity with the dialogues in philosophical circles, both Platonic and Stoic.[27]

In what form did these readers read the Platonic Corpus? Once we have established the existence of an Academic edition, the next important question concerns the place of the Corpus in the library of Alexandria, the first major public library ever, collected during the reigns of the first two Ptolemies (305–246). The Alexandrian library was organized by Demetrius of Phaleron, a pupil of Theophrastus; its model was the library of Aristotle's school. It was well stocked with philosophical works and so probably included Plato's works from the start. Demetrius probably used the Academic edition in order to make the Alexandrian copy.[28]

# 4. Early Arrangements
# of the Corpus

Did either of the early editions (Academic and Alexandrian) divide the Corpus into tetralogies?[29] Plato may sometimes have composed in tetralogies. Internal references suggested to some ancient readers that the *Republic*, *Timaeus*, *Critias*, and

---

22. DL vii 2. On Polemon, see Dillon, *Heirs of Plato*, ch. 4.

23. Zeno's *Republic*; see DL vii 32. Chrysippus on Plato; see Plutarch, *Stoic. Rep.* 15–16.

24. DL iv 32 suggests that Arcesilaus' acquisition of the Platonic Corpus was a significant event, as though he had not always had easy access to it. Compare the story about Zeno above.

25. One of the spurious works in the Platonic Corpus, the *Axiochus*, presents a curious combination of Socratic and Epicurean views about death.

26. See Kidd's commentary on F 31, 85, 290–91 (in L. Edelstein and I. G. Kidd, eds., *Posidonius*, 4 vols. (Cambridge: Cambridge University Press 1972–1999); Dillon, *Heirs of Plato*, 216–31; A. E. Taylor, *A Commentary on Plato's Timaeus* (Oxford: Oxford University Press, 1928), 32–33.

27. A helpful short account of the treatment of Plato in Hellenistic philosophy is given by J. Barnes, "The Hellenistic Platos," *Apeiron* 24 (1991), 118–23.

28. Plato's works were in this library in the lifetime of Aristophanes of Byzantium (?ca. 257–180? BC; see sec. 4).

29. The titles of the works correspond to the titles in the catalogue of Plato's works that appears in DL iii 57–61. Each dialogue in the catalogue has an alternative title and a generic classification. Hence

*Hermocrates* were intended to form a group.[30] Of these four, the *Hermocrates* was apparently never written, and the *Critias* was left unfinished. Similarly, the *Theaetetus, Sophist, Politicus,* and *Philosopher* may have been intended to form a group;[31] the *Philosopher* was never written. These two planned tetralogies do not show that all the dialogues were intended to belong to tetralogies.

The evidence—or apparent evidence—of Plato's interest in tetralogies may have encouraged later readers and editors to arrange all the dialogues tetralogically and to believe that Plato had arranged them in this way. Thrasyllus (d. AD 36)[32] is said to have claimed that Plato himself had arranged his works in tetralogies, to correspond to the arrangement of tragedies performed at Athenian festivals (DL iii 56).[33]

The terminus post quem for the tetralogies seems to be the lifetime of Aristophanes of Byzantium, who proposed an arrangement in trilogies (DL iii 61–62).[34] It is difficult to see why he would have tried it if he was reading a Platonic Corpus already ordered in tetralogies. His order, unlike the tetralogical order, does not even cover the whole Corpus; but if he had tried to replace an existing tetralogical order, we might expect him to have ordered the whole Corpus. Since Aristophanes probably used the Alexandrian edition of the Corpus, it is unlikely that readers of this edition took the dialogues to be arranged in some canonical order. Since the Academic edition was probably the basis of the Alexandrian edition, it probably did not indicate any canonical order either.

Thrasyllus listed not only the nine tetralogies but also the acknowledged spurious works (DL iii 62). If modern critics are right, and some or all of the dubious works in the tetralogies are spurious, the compilers of the tetralogical list took some spurious works for genuine Platonic works. If the Alexandrian edition

---

the *Phaedo*, for example, is listed as *"Phaedo,* or *On the Soul;* ethical" (DL iii 58). Anon. *Prol.* 21.11–14 comments that it is not always easy to see how the dialogue deals with the subject matter mentioned by the second title.

30. See *Tim.* 17b–19a (summary of part of the *Republic*), 27ab, and *Crit.* 108ab (expecting a discourse by Hermocrates). It is by no means clear, however, that the reference to the *Republic* implies that Plato intended this dialogue to be the first member of a tetralogy. He may simply have intended to write a trilogy beginning with the *Timaeus.* See F. M. Cornford's reasonable doubts in *Plato's Cosmology* (London: Routledge, 1937), 4–5. Still the belief that Plato had intended a tetralogy beginning with the *Republic* may have encouraged the effort to divide all the dialogues into tetralogies.

31. See *Sph.* 253e, and *Pol.* 257a, 258a. As Cornford remarks, *Plato's Theory of Knowledge* (London: Routledge, 1934), 168, Socrates implies that he and Young Socrates will be the main speakers in the *Philosopher.*

32. On Thrasyllus' dates, see H. Tarrant, *Thrasyllan Platonism* (Ithaca, N.Y.: Cornell University Press, 1993), 215 (T1).

33. "But Thrasyllus says that he published his dialogues corresponding to the tragic tetralogy. For, they contended with four plays . . . , one of which was a satiric drama, and the whole four plays were called a tetralogy." Apparently, then, Thrasyllus did not represent himself as introducing the tetralogical arrangement. Albinus, *Eisagoge* 4, attributes a tetralogical arrangement to Dercyllidas (of uncertain date) and to Thrasyllus. For further discussion, see J. Mansfeld, *Prolegomena* (Leiden: Brill, 1994), ch. 2; Tarrant, *Thrasyllan Platonism*, esp. chs. 1–4.

34. The terminus ante quem for the tetralogies is the mid-first-century BC, since Varro (116–27 BC) refers to the *Phaedo* as "Plato in the fourth" (Varro, *LL* vii 37, published before Cicero's death in 43 BC). Cf. F. Solmsen ,"The Academic and Alexandrian edition of Plato's works," *Illinois Classical Studies* 6 (1981), 102–11.

of the Corpus included these spurious works, and it was closely related to the Academic edition, the latter probably also included spurious works. Some of them may belong to the fourth century and hence may have been written during or shortly after Plato's lifetime. Others were written later, including the Epicurean-influenced *Axiochus*.[35] The spurious works may have been exercises or essays on Platonic themes by members of the Academy.[36] If they were kept beside Plato's genuine works in the library of the Academy, their non-Platonic origin may have been forgotten. This suggestion becomes more plausible if we recall that Plato left fragments and abandoned introductions among his papers; spurious works might have intruded into this part of the Academy's collection. Alternatively, at least some of the supposedly spurious works may in fact be Plato's less successful efforts, retained in the Academy.

We should not suppose that the text of the Academic and Alexandrian editions was the only text of Plato in general circulation or the only one that underlies our manuscripts of Plato. The earliest papyrus fragments of Plato display considerable textual variation from the text of our manuscripts.[37] Moreover, Diogenes Laertius mentions that editions of Plato included editorial marks that recognized the possibility of spurious intrusions and textual corruptions (DL iii 65–66). This practice probably arose in Alexandria, where scholarly editing began.

In late antiquity, Plato was widely studied in the later Platonic schools (which modern writers refer to as "Middle Platonism" and "Neoplatonism"),[38] which also produced commentaries on the dialogues. Since demand for the texts led to frequent copying, it must have led to further transcriptional errors. Moreover, as we already see in Diogenes' report, readers "corrected" the text according to their views on what Plato must have said or ought to have said; no doubt, their views were sometimes mistaken (as the views of modern "correctors" often are). But this persistent interest in Plato also ensured the preservation of the text, and some of the efforts of scholarly editors may have removed errors and so may have tended to counteract the progressive corruption resulting from repeated copying.

---

35. Questions about the influence of Stoicism are more difficult to decide, partly because Stoic ethics is quite close to Socratic and Platonic ethics on many points, as we can see in the *Eryxias*.

36. The *Alcibiades*, for example, may have been composed for the purpose that it served for later Platonists (see Anon. *Prol.* 26.23–26), to introduce the main themes of Plato's philosophy, with a special emphasis on psychophysical dualism. The *De Virtute* is a short essay on the theme of the *Protagoras* and *Meno*, "Can virtue be taught?" Many passages recall these two dialogues.

37. The history of the Platonic Corpus in the Hellenistic period is discussed by G. Jachmann, "Der Platontext" in *Textgeschichtliche Studien*, ed. C. Gnilka, *Beiträge zur Klassischen Philologie* 143 (1982), ch. 2. His extreme skepticism about whether there was an Academic and Alexandrian "standard text" at all is endorsed by Barnes, "Hellenistic Platos." For a less skeptical view, see ch. 14, "The manuscript tradition of Plato's *Phaedo*," in Taran, *Collected Papers*, (Leiden: Brill, 2001), reprinted from *Gnomon* 48 (1976), 760–68.

38. On later Platonism, see Brittain, chapter 22 in this volume.

# 5. THE MANUSCRIPTS

Modern editions of a Greek text do not reproduce the text of any one manuscript; editors and textual critics try to establish the most probable Greek text by comparison of the different manuscripts. At the foot of each page in the OCT of Plato we find textual variants whose sources are indicated by letters referring to manuscripts or by the names of modern (sixteenth-century and later) critics who have proposed emendations not found in any manuscript. In some editions, we also find a list of "testimonia": lists of places in ancient authors where a given passage of Plato is quoted or closely paraphrased.[39] Why is all this apparatus necessary?[40]

The oldest sources for the text of Plato are papyri written in the second and third centuries AD. Unfortunately, these contain only fragments of text. Our main sources for the text are fifty-one Byzantine manuscripts, copied from the ninth century AD onward in the Greek-speaking areas ruled from Constantinople.[41] Our oldest surviving manuscript (normally referred to as B) was copied by John the Calligrapher, who finished his work (containing the first six tetralogies) in 895, on the orders of Arethas, a deacon in Patras who later became archbishop of Caesarea.[42]

Knowledge of Plato spread from the Byzantine Empire to Italy and the rest of Western Europe during the fourteenth and fifteenth centuries. The first manuscript of Plato to reach Italy may have been the (probably) eleventh-century manuscript W, which arrived in the fourteenth century.[43] A Latin translation of Plato by Marsilius Ficinus was published in 1484 and became a best-seller. The first printed edition of Plato in Greek did not appear until 1513.[44]

Modern printed editions from the sixteenth century onward choose their text from different manuscripts, testimonia, and conjectural emendations (by the current editor or by earlier editors). Our account of the transmission of the Corpus in antiquity shows why the manuscripts have different texts and why one needs to exercise some judgment in choosing among variant readings. Since our earliest manuscripts come from about 1,250 years after the lifetime of Plato, we cannot

---

39. See, e.g., the back of the new OCT i and of the new OCT of the *Republic*.

40. I have derived most of the information on texts and textual criticism from E. R. Dodds, ed. *Plato's Gorgias* (Oxford: Oxford University Press, 1959), 34–58; R. S. Bluck, ed., *Plato's Meno* (Cambridge: Cambridge University Press 1961), 129–47; G. J. Boter, *The Textual Tradition of Plato's Republic* (*Mnemosyne* Supp. 107 (1989)); Reynolds and Wilson, *Scribes and Scholars*.

41. For a list of the Plato manuscripts, see R. S. Brumbaugh and R. Wells, *The Plato Manuscripts* (New Haven, Conn.: Yale University Press, 1968). Boter, *Textual Tradition*, xx, suggests that still more Plato manuscripts may survive in uncatalogued libraries. According to G. Pasquali, *Storia della Tradizione e Critica del Testo*, 2nd ed. (Florence: Le Monnier, 1952), 247, Plato is the classical author with the richest textual tradition after Homer.

42. On Arethas, see Reynolds and Wilson, *Scribes and Scholars*, 64–65. Their Plate III shows part of Arethas' manuscript of Plato (now in the Bodleian Library, Oxford).

43. See Dodds, *Gorgias*, 39.

44. *Omnia Platonis opera*, published and printed by Aldus Manutius, Venice, 1513. On Ficinus, see Reynolds and Wilson, *Scribes and Scholars*, 155.

reasonably suppose that they contain all and only the very words that Plato wrote. Copyists make mistakes; later copyists multiply mistakes because of ignorance or inattention or illegible handwriting. Such mistakes were easy with Greek manuscripts. Copies of Plato were originally written in capital letters ("uncials"), without punctuation and without spaces between words. Small ("minuscule") letters were introduced, probably in the eighth century,[45] and eventually punctuation was also introduced.[46] In the face of apparent errors, some copyists tried to correct the real or imagined mistakes of their predecessors, and sometimes their attempted corrections introduced new errors.

The surviving manuscripts of Plato display variations that show the effects of these processes of textual corruption. Editors, both ancient and modern, have tried to undo some of these effects. If a particular sentence in manuscript $Z^*$ is so grossly ungrammatical as to be unintelligible, but the corresponding sentence in $Y^*$ is slightly different in ways that make it grammatical and intelligible, we may usually assume that $Y^*$ has preserved what Plato wrote.[47] But once we go beyond these relatively easy corrections, we may need to know more about the manuscripts. If $Z^*$ and $Y^*$ both offer a reading that makes sense, or if neither makes sense but we want to know which might be a better guide to what Plato wrote, we reasonably want to know something about the credentials of each manuscript. The study of Greek and Latin texts advanced significantly in the nineteenth century, when critics developed the systematic comparative study of manuscripts and their affiliations. Recent editions differ from the early printed editions because their textual proposals rest on a wider acquaintance with Plato, with Greek, and with the relations among manuscripts.

Our first thought might be that we simply need to find the earliest manuscript. Perhaps we should rely on $Y^*$ rather than $Z^*$ if and only if $Y^*$ is earlier, since, in that case, $Y^*$ will have been less affected by the process of corruption that inevitably follows repeated copying. We have enough information about the absolute dates of some manuscripts to form reasonable estimates of their relative dates. In some cases, the scribe helpfully adds a date at the end of his manuscript (as John the Calligrapher did with B, mentioned above). Sometimes we can find relevant information in library catalogues. On this basis, we can distinguish different Greek hands and can sometimes use this information to estimate the date and provenance of different manuscripts. This information about dates influences editors in their decisions about which manuscripts they should follow. A glance at an edition of Plato (e.g., OCT i p. 2) will show that editors regularly report the readings of only a few of the surviving manuscripts, listing the other manuscripts as "more recent" (*recentiores*) and citing only occasional readings from them. Since they separate the

---

45. On the difficulty of reading ancient books, see Reynolds and Wilson, *Scribes and Scholars*, 4. They discuss the transition from uncial to minuscule at 59f.

46. Slings in his edition of the *Clitopho* (Cambridge: Cambridge University Press, 1999), 342, maintains that ancient (i.e., pre-Byzantine) prose texts had punctuation.

47. I use asterisks to indicate imaginary manuscripts introduced for the sake of examples. Letters without asterisks are used to name actual manuscripts, following the names in the OCT.

earlier from the later manuscripts, should they not follow the earliest manuscript, since it is our earliest witness to the text of Plato? Some editors of modern editions have done just that and have based their text on the readings of the earliest manuscript, regarding the readings in later manuscripts as errors or (when they are probably correct) as conjectural emendations.

More recent editors, however, have rejected this rigid rule of following the earliest manuscript, arguing that it may not come closest to what Plato wrote.[48] Imagine this situation: (1) We have two surviving manuscripts, Y* and Z*. (2) Y* is earlier than Z*. (3) Z* was copied from an ancestor manuscript W*, and Y* from an ancestor X*. (4) W* is earlier than X*. Hence (5) the later manuscript Z* preserves an earlier form of the text (from W*) than the earlier manuscript Y* (derived from X*) preserves. And so the textual critic should try to find the readings of W* and X* and should not simply follow Y* or Z*.[49]

Some examples may suggest how we might have reason to believe that the lost manuscripts W* and X* underlie the surviving Y* and Z*. Manuscripts become corrupt because of human inability to copy long passages without making errors. But this tendency to error is also helpful to editors, since an error common to one group of manuscripts and absent from another group may show us that the first group descend from one earlier manuscript. One group of manuscripts, for instance, may contain the same lacuna (a shorter or longer passage omitted from a copy), because the scribe copying an earlier manuscript skipped a line (e.g.) in copying and transmitted his error to the manuscripts copied from his copy. If, then, the surviving manuscript Y* contains lacunae that are absent from Z*, this may suggest that Y* was copied from W* (which had the lacunae), whereas Z* was copied from X* (which lacked the lacunae). In that case, we should be more interested in the relative dates—if we can estimate them—of W* and X* than in those of Y* and Z*.

Some shared errors may indicate the relative dates of manuscripts. The change from uncials to minuscules is especially useful for this purpose. Errors that arise from misreading letters are different for uncials and for minuscules.[50] Hence if Z* seems to contain more errors arising from uncials than Y* contains, this is a reason for supposing that Z* and Y* were copied from different manuscripts, W* and X*, and that W* is earlier than X*. Hence the text preserved by Z* may be earlier than the text preserved by Y*.

Fortunately, this actually happens with the manuscripts of Plato. Some of them, notably the Vienna manuscript F and its affiliates, contain variants that seem to result from uncial errors.[51] Though these are not the earliest manuscripts, they

---

48. See, e.g., Boter, *Textual Tradition*, 7–10.

49. Boter, *Textual Tradition*, gives a detailed account of the manuscripts of the *Republic*, and of their relations; Slings, *Clitopho*, 340–43, states the conclusions briefly.

50. Since, for example, C and G in the Latin alphabet look more similar than c and g, we are more likely to confuse C and G than to confuse c and g.

51. The importance of F was pointed out by J. Burnet, "A neglected MS. of Plato," *Classical Review* 16 (1902), 98–101. See also Dodds, *Gorgias*, 41–47, and Boter, *Textual Tradition*, 12, 99–100.

may preserve an earlier text, and they may help us to correct the text offered by earlier manuscripts. This is only one small example of the sort of evidence that may reasonably persuade an editor to attend to the readings of one or another manuscript. Progress in the study of the Plato manuscripts has resulted from more accurate views of the relations between manuscripts, showing, for instance, that a manuscript previously thought to be simply an inferior copy is, in fact, an independent source.[52]

The text of Plato is generally sound. If we compare the critical apparatus on a random page of a modern edition of Plato and of most other Greek authors, we will see that the text of Plato contains many fewer variants that significantly affect the sense. The text of our manuscripts is generally confirmed by the abundant testimonia in other ancient writers.[53] A comparison of the old and the new OCT supports this claim about the general soundness of the text.[54] The critical apparatus in the new edition differs significantly from the old, partly because of further research (such as that just described) on the manuscripts and their relations. But the text printed in the two editions generally agrees, and the changes in the new edition are not radical. Moreover, some of the more significant changes do not result from further research on the manuscripts. In some cases, they result from closer consideration of the testimonia;[55] in other cases, they are conjectural (and sometimes questionable) alterations by the editors with no support in the manuscript tradition.[56]

This generally good condition of the text is no accident. The continuous interest in Plato in antiquity helped to preserve the text and to maintain its general integrity. It is instructive to notice the much inferior condition of the text of Aristotle, which suffered from the declining interest in him in the early Hellenistic period.[57]

52. The treatment of the manuscript tradition of Plato by various editors is discussed by Pasquali, *Storia della Tradizione*, 247–69. Boter, *Textual Tradition*, 22, on the *Republic*, argues that the relative value of different manuscripts is still not completely understood.

53. The quantity and distribution of the ancient testimonia for the *Republic* may be gathered from the seventy-page index in Boter, *Textual Tradition*, 291–365. At 366–76, Boter gives a list of the authors cited. In considering variations between the testimonia and the manuscripts of Plato, we need to bear in mind: (1) The testimonia are derived from manuscripts that may be less sound than the Plato manuscripts. (2) Ancient writers often quoted from memory. (3) Sometimes they emended the text of Plato on doctrinal grounds; see J. M. Dillon, "Tampering with the *Timaeus*," *American Journal of Philology* 110 (1989), 50–72. Hence the testimonia are not always to be preferred to the Plato manuscripts.

54. For some discussion of the new OCT i, see C. J. Rowe, "Plato re-edited," *Classical Review* 47 (1997), 272–74, and D. B. Robinson, "Textual notes on Plato's *Sophist*," *Classical Quarterly* 49 (1999), 139–60.

55. See, e.g., Slings, *Notes*, 126, cites Plotinus in defense of a convincing emendation of 518d10.

56. See, e.g., Slings's arbitrary deletion of *kaiper noêtôn ontôn meta archês* in *Rep.* 511d, defended in *Notes*, 114–19. At *Cra.* 385b3–d1, the editors of the new OCT unwisely follow M. Schofield ("A displacement in the text of the Cratylus," *Classical Quarterly* 22 (1972), 246–53) in bracketing the passage. They go even further than Schofield in believing it has no place in the dialogue as it now stands (note on 387c5). See also D. Sedley, *Plato's Cratylus* (Cambridge: Cambridge University Press, 2005), 10–13.

57. See n.20 above.

# 6. The Composition
## of the Dialogues

Having noticed these questions about the contents of the Corpus, we may ask about the order of the genuine dialogues. Though the tetralogical order appears in modern editions of the Greek text and in the most recent English translation of the collected works, it is worthless as a guide to the order in which the dialogues were written, or to the order in which they should be read. To fix the order of composition, we might try to establish the absolute date of each dialogue, or, if we cannot do this, the relative date.

If we ask about "the date" of a written work, we normally have in mind the date at which the author finished writing it, or the date at which it was published, or the date of a revised edition. But it may be difficult to apply these questions directly to Plato. We do not know the form in which the dialogues were "published." Their dramatic form has encouraged the conjecture that they may have originally been intended for public dramatic performance. Even nondramatic works were often presented orally before large or small audiences. Perhaps the written version of a dialogue was published some time after the first oral performance, or perhaps a second oral performance led to a further revision.[58] We do not know how many dialogues Plato intended to publish in the form in which we have them. He left the *Laws* unfinished at his death; we do not know whether he was also engaged in revising other dialogues that he had previously published or had performed. These possibilities remind us of our ignorance about the initial circulation or publication of the dialogues.

We are not completely ignorant, however. For we have some possible evidence of revisions or double versions of parts of different dialogues:

1. If the *Clitopho* is genuine, as it probably is, one might regard it as an alternative introduction to the *Republic* that was discarded in favor of Book i in the present version.[59]
2. If the *Minos* is genuine, one might regard it as an alternative introduction to the *Laws*.[60]
3. The author of an ancient commentary on the *Theaetetus* tells us that a spurious alternative prologue was in circulation.[61] Some have supposed that he is right to say it was an alternative prologue but wrong to say it was spurious.

---

58. Cf. the complicated history of Aristophanes' *Clouds*, discussed by K. J. Dover, *Aristophanes' Clouds* (Oxford: Oxford University Press, 1968), lxxx–xcviii.

59. The *Clitopho* is fully discussed by Slings in his edition. He takes a different view of its relation to the *Republic*.

60. On the *Minos*, see Morrow, *Plato's Cretan City*, 515.

61. See Anon. in *Tht*. 3.28–37; *Corpus dei Papiri Filosofici Greci e Latini*, vol. 3 (Florence: Olschki, 1995), 268–69, 486.

4. Even if we agree that Plato wrote alternative introductions to different dialogues, it by no means follows that he wrote different versions of the dialogues that they introduce. But some critics have claimed to find internal inconsistencies in Plato's longest works, the *Republic* and the *Laws*, from which they argue that our present versions of the dialogues do not carry out Plato's original plan. One might support such an argument by mentioning the evidence of separate publication of Books i–iv of the *Republic* (as we now divide it) and the story about the unfinished condition of the *Laws*.[62]

5. One manuscript of the *Cratylus* includes two apparent versions of one passage. If both versions are genuine, they may belong to two different editions of the dialogue.[63]

These pieces of possible evidence might be taken to suggest that Plato produced second editions of some of the dialogues. But we need not accept this suggestion. Plato may have taken a long time to compose the *Republic* and the *Laws*, and he may have changed his mind in the course of composing them; perhaps he even published parts of them before the whole works were completed. None of this implies that he went back over an earlier draft and composed a second edition.[64] Even if he was aware of inconsistencies or changes of direction in a published work, he may have lacked the time or enthusiasm to revise them substantially.[65] If we recall the unfinished tetralogies, we may well suppose that Plato's interest in new projects often diverted him from the completion of old projects (perhaps fortunately for us).

It is probably a hopeless task, then, to look for different layers of composition, or later revisions, or alternative versions, in a single dialogue. We have to see what we can find out about the dates of the dialogues, given our ignorance about how they were composed and circulated. We do not know when Plato began to write philosophical dialogues,[66] or when the latest dialogue was written.[67] The latest dateable event mentioned in the dialogues is the fighting around Corinth in 369, in which Theaetetus was fatally wounded (*Tht.* 142ab).[68]

---

62. See Aulus Gellius, *NA* xiv 3.3; Alline, *Histoire du texte*, 14–15. Ancient divisions into "books" seem to be determined by considerations about the most convenient (or profitable?) size for a roll of papyrus; that is why they are often made in inappropriate places.

63. See the new OCT at 437d10; Sedley, *Cratylus*, 7–10.

64. The *Cratylus* might be taken to offer the best evidence of a revised version, especially if one also believes that 385b3 ff does not belong to the dialogue in its present form; see n.56 above. But we do not know whether the intrusive passage is part of an earlier version or a section that Plato wrote and then deleted in the course of composing a single version.

65. The reference to "combing and curling" (n.13 above) suggests stylistic polishing and tinkering; it does not imply major revision of the content and argument.

66. Some critics assume, for no good reason, that Plato did not write any dialogues during the lifetime of Socrates. W. K. C. Guthrie, *History of Greek Philosophy* (Cambridge: Cambridge University Press, 1975), vol. 4, 54–56, surveys the unconvincing arguments that have been offered on each side.

67. Though Proclus tells us that the *Laws* was unfinished at Plato's death (see n.18 above), it need not have been the last dialogue to be written. Plato may have put it aside to work on other things.

68. The *Symposium* probably refers to events in the mid-380s. See Dover's edition (Cambridge: Cambridge University Press, 1980), 10. We might look for further historical references if we were unwise enough to rely on the Seventh Letter. Contrast Schofield, chapter 2 in this volume.

Since we have so little help in fixing the absolute dates of the dialogues, we have to see what we can find, or conjecture, about the relative dates. Ancient critics do not seem to have known much about the order of the dialogues.[69] But it is hazardous to ignore these questions. We would not make much sense of Kant, or Russell, or Wittgenstein, if we tried to explain all his works as the expression of a single philosophical outlook or as a series of independent essays, ignoring their relative dates. It is worth our while to see whether we can fix the order of Plato's works.

## 7. THE ORDER OF THE DIALOGUES

It may be helpful to sketch some of the arguments for the different (and to some extent separable) elements of an ordering of the dialogues that has received fairly widespread support over the past 150 years or so. This ordering has become popular enough to be described (usually pejoratively, by those who reject it) as "the standard view."[70]

The main sources of evidence for the relative dating of the dialogues are these:

1. *Style and language.* If we suppose that the *Laws* is the latest of the dialogues, we can order the others by the degree of linguistic and stylistic resemblance to the *Laws*.[71] Linguistic and stylistic tests pick out a fairly clear group of late dialogues and less-sharply defined groups of early and middle dialogues.

2. *Character.* Some dialogues are short, vividly characterized, and ostensibly negative in their conclusions. Some are more didactic than dramatic and seem to concentrate on the exposition of a doctrine rather than the cross-examination of interlocutors. We can see this contrast if we compare the *Charmides* and *Laches* with the *Sophist*, *Timaeus*, and *Laws*. The first type of

69. Though ancient critics consider the question of relative date, they offer nothing more helpful than the suggestion that the *Phaedrus* must have been the first dialogue, since the subject matter is suitable for a young man, and the *Laws* must have been the last, since it was left unfinished at Plato's death (Anon. *Prol.* 24.7–19; cf. DL iii 38). Most of the discussion in Anon., *Prol.* concerns the appropriate order for reading the dialogues (26.21–44). Anon. omits most of the "early" (or "Socratic") dialogues and treats the *Parmenides* as the culmination of Platonic doctrine (26.13–44). He follows Iamblichus, who picks out twelve dialogues, divided into two groups, "natural" and "theological." He picks out two "complete" (or "perfect," *teleioi*) dialogues, the *Timaeus* in the natural group and the *Parmenides* in the theological group. He remarks that some instructors also think it appropriate to discuss the *Republic* and the *Laws* (26.45–7). The *Alcibiades* often comes first because it introduces the central Platonic theme of the division between body and soul. On the order of reading dialogues, see A. J. Festugière, *Etudes de philosophie grecque* (Paris: Vrin, 1971), 533–50.

70. Annas and Rowe express skepticism about the "standard view" in J. Annas and C. J. Rowe, eds., *New Perspectives on Plato* (Cambridge, Mass.: Harvard University Press, 2002), ix.

71. The evidence and arguments are summarized by L. Brandwood, "Stylometry and chronology," in *The Cambridge Companion to Plato*, ed. R. Kraut (Cambridge: Cambridge University Press, 1992), and by C. H. Kahn, "On Platonic chronology," in Annas and Rowe, *New Perspectives*, ch. 4.

dialogue is earlier, by linguistic and stylistic tests, than the second type. But it is more difficult to apply this contrast to other dialogues. The *Phaedo*, *Republic*, *Phaedrus*, and *Philebus* include some dramatic and some didactic sections. Apparently, Plato switched between dramatic and didactic styles as it suited him within a single dialogue.

3. *Philosophical content.* On some central philosophical issues, different dialogues seem to reach or to suggest opposed conclusions. For example: (1) Some dialogues speak of 'forms' or 'ideas' as non-sensible, stable realities to be grasped by intellect rather than sense, and contrast them with the changeable things grasped by sense. Other dialogues speak of forms without this sharp contrast. (2) In some dialogues Socrates argues for the identification of virtue with knowledge and against the possibility of weakness of will. Other dialogues recognize different and potentially conflicting desires in the soul, apparently allowing the non-rational desires to overcome rational desires.

4. *Aristotle.* Aristotle claims that Socrates differs from Plato on some central points in metaphysics and ethics: (1) Socrates did not separate the forms from sensible things, but Plato did separate them. (2) Socrates treated virtue as knowledge, but Plato did not. Aristotle marks the division between the historical Socrates and the Socrates of Plato's dialogues in two ways: (a) He calls the historical Socrates simply 'Socrates', but calls the Platonic character 'the Socrates'. (b) He often uses the imperfect tense when he uses 'Socrates' ('Socrates used to say...'), but the present tense ('the Socrates says...') for the views of the character in a dialogue. [72]

5. *Convergence.* Broadly speaking, these different tests tend to divide the dialogues in the same way. With some exceptions, dialogues that appear to be early on linguistic tests also tend to be dramatic rather than didactic and tend to hold the doctrines that Aristotle ascribes to Socrates, whereas the apparently later dialogues tend to be didactic rather than dramatic and tend to hold the views that Aristotle describes as Platonic.

These arguments suggest that Plato began by agreeing with Socrates, and then gradually developed his distinctive, and in some respects non-Socratic, philosophical outlook. His outlook becomes non-Socratic insofar as he extends his philosophical range beyond Socrates' primary concern with ethics and rejects some central Socratic claims even within ethics.

If, then, we want to study the dialogues in a reasonably probable chronological order, we might follow this plan:

1. We might want to begin with the *Apology*, since it defends Socrates' life and work; we can test Socrates' claims about himself in the light of our reading of the shorter dialogues on ethical topics (*Laches*, *Charmides*, *Lysis*, *Euthyphro*, *Hippias Minor*, *Ion*, and *Crito*).

---

72. In (a) I take a disputed position on the legitimacy of "Fitzgerald's canon." For some further details and references, see T. H. Irwin, *Plato's Ethics* (Oxford: Oxford University Press, 1995), sec. 5.

2. The *Protagoras*, *Gorgias*, and *Euthydemus* are more elaborate works on similar themes; they also record confrontations between Socrates and (roughly speaking) professional intellectuals concerned with philosophical topics. These interlocutors are sophists, orators, and eristics, rather than the philosophical nonspecialists who appear in group 1.

3. The *Meno* reflects on some of the themes in these previous dialogues and introduces epistemological and metaphysical claims that are explored further in the *Cratylus, Hippias Major, Phaedo, and Symposium*.

4. The *Republic* (introduced by Book i and perhaps also by the *Clitopho*) is Plato's most elaborate effort to construct a broad philosophical theory that embraces the themes of most of the previous dialogues. The *Phaedrus* explores questions about rhetoric (raised in the *Gorgias*), love (raised in the *Symposium*), and moral psychology (raised in the *Republic*).

5. Some version of the metaphysics and epistemology of the previous dialogues (groups 3–4), and especially their Theory of Forms, are examined in the *Parmenides*. Interpreters disagree about whether this version is Plato's actual theory or a mistaken version that might easily be mistaken for his actual theory until its difficulties are pointed out. Plato's more systematic reflections on epistemology and metaphysics begin in the *Theaetetus*.

6. These reflections are continued in the *Sophist* and *Politicus*. In the *Timaeus*, these reflections are set in a broader cosmology and natural philosophy.

7. The *Philebus*, *Politicus*, and *Laws* are major works in moral and political philosophy that seem to reflect on some of the doctrines introduced in the previous dialogues.

Different parts of this arrangement rest on the different arguments mentioned above. Linguistic and stylistic evidence isolates groups 6 and 7 (not necessarily in that order) as the latest dialogues, and places groups 4 and 5 (not necessarily in that order) before them. It places groups 1–3 before the others without fixing any definite order of groups or within groups. Doctrinal considerations (mentioned in points (3) and (4) above) justify us in placing group 3 after groups 1 and 2.

Many students of Plato agree that something like this is a reasonable account of the order of the dialogues. In speaking of "early" or (because of Aristotle's testimony) "Socratic" dialogues, they normally have in mind groups 1 and 2. Groups 3 and 4 are usually called "middle" dialogues, and groups 5–7 are "late" dialogues.

It is helpful to distinguish questions about the "standard view" of the order of the dialogues from questions about a "developmental" account of Plato's philosophy. Students of Plato who deny that Plato's outlook can be shown to change radically in the course of his writing the dialogues reject a developmental account and sometimes tend to reject the standard view on chronology, as well. Conversely, those who accept the standard view often use it to argue that Plato's outlook developed and changed on major points. But the standard view of chronology and the developmental view of Plato's philosophy are not so closely connected.

Questions about chronology are connected to questions about philosophical development in two ways: (1) We cannot maintain a developmental view without some chronological hypothesis. The standard view offers the most plausible chronology, and so we are well advised to start from it, if we seek to trace Plato's development. (2) We have mentioned some apparent doctrinal variations (on non-sensible forms and on moral psychology) as evidence for chronology. These are variations that Aristotle takes to distinguish Socrates from Plato. To the extent that these apparent doctrinal variations seem to coincide with other chronological evidence, we may claim that the standard view of chronology supports belief in some degree of doctrinal development.

These connections, however, do not show that the standard view of chronology stands or falls with a developmental account of Plato's philosophy. For acceptance of the standard view does not imply that Plato's philosophical outlook changed radically. Different views have been held about how much he actually changed his mind from earlier to later dialogues. One might, for instance, decide that "Socratic" and "Platonic" moral theory are less-developed and more-developed versions of a single position rather than two different positions. Similarly, one might decide that the claims about nonsensible forms in the middle dialogues are never revised, because they do not need revision, in light of the criticism in the *Parmenides*.

Some particular dialogues have also been subjects of dispute among those who accept this division of the dialogues:

(a) Some place the *Euthydemus* and *Cratylus* in groups 5 or 6, contrary to stylistic evidence.

(b) Some place one or both of the *Protagoras* and *Gorgias* after the *Meno*. It is difficult to find clear stylistic or doctrinal grounds for fixing the order of these three dialogues.

(c) Most people take the *Parmenides* to presuppose the exposition of the Theory of Forms in groups 3 and 4. We will take a different view of its significance if we place it before some or all of these dialogues. Stylistic evidence places it later than the *Phaedo* and *Symposium*, so that it seems to be later than the formulation of the theory. But it is less obvious that it must follow the *Republic*.

(d) Since the *Timaeus* maintains central elements in the Theory of Forms, Plato does not seem to have thought that the criticisms in the *Parmenides* were fatal to his theory. Those who have supposed that the criticisms are fatal, and that Plato must have thought so, too, have placed the *Timaeus* earlier than the *Parmenides* and hence earlier than groups 5–7. This place for the *Timaeus* is inconsistent with the clearest stylistic evidence we have about the order of the dialogues.[73]

73. G. E. L. Owen, "The place of the *Timaeus* in Plato's dialogues," *Logic, Science and Dialectic* (London: Duckworth, 1986), ch. 4 (reprinted from *Classical Quarterly* 3 (1953), 79–95) defends an early date for the *Timaeus*. The reply by H. F. Cherniss, "The relation of the *Timaeus* to Plato's later dialogues," in *Studies in Plato's Metaphysics*, ed. R. E. Allen (London: Routledge, 1965), ch. 17 (reprinted from *American Journal of Philology* 78 (1957), 225–66) is generally (though not in every detail) convincing.

Acceptance of the "standard view," therefore, makes some difference to our understanding of the dialogues. If we accept it, we cannot, for instance, take the *Philebus* and the *Protagoras* to express, respectively, Plato's earlier and later views on pleasure; nor can we take the political theory of the *Politicus* to precede that of the *Republic*; nor again (as we have just seen) can we take Plato to have abandoned the Theory of Forms in his late dialogues. The order described in the "standard view" is a reasonable starting point for the reading and interpretation of Plato.

# 8. Questions about the Order of the Dialogues

The standard view has also aroused some doubts and objections. We need to consider some of these, to see how far the interpreter of Plato can rely on it. Some of the main grounds for doubt are these:

1. Features that we take to be evidence of chronology may simply mark Plato's stylistic choices. Perhaps he sometimes chose to write dramatic dialogues and sometimes to write didactic dialogues, and the different stylistic features may be results of such a choice.

2. Apparent doctrinal divergences are relevant to chronology only if we know (i) which doctrine came first; (ii) Plato was aware of the divergence; (iii) Plato intended to affirm a particular position, rather than simply to explore it. This third assumption depends on the controversial claim, which we must discuss later, that Plato's intention in the dialogues is (at least often) dogmatic rather than purely exploratory. But even if we accept the assumption, we need not take apparent conflicts at face value. Plato may, for instance, have set out a one-sided statement of the case for treating virtue as knowledge, so that he could answer it in another dialogue; or he may have outlined his own position in one dialogue, and then explored the opposite position in a later dialogue.

3. Aristotle may be wrong. Perhaps he noticed some differences between the dialogues and mistakenly inferred that they were to be explained by Plato's different attitudes to Socrates.

These doubts are worth considering insofar as they invite us to keep in mind the possibility that Plato's intentions may have been more complex than the intention simply to convey what he believed at the time of writing. If his intentions include the intention to write in his "early" or "late" style, or to present his "early" views for expository or argumentative purposes, we may be misled if we take "early" or "late" features as signs of a genuine chronological order. Perhaps, then, we ought not to concern ourselves about the order of the dialogues. Some critics who take this view treat the dialogues as different partial expositions of a philosophical system.[74] Others treat them as a series of explorations that Plato never intended to express a coherent doctrine.[75]

Warnings against naïve conclusions from allegedly "early" or "late" features are salutary. Many students of Plato have emphasized the complexity of Plato's intentions as an author, and the hazards of treating the dialogues as though they were philosophical texts of the sort we are used to. Questions about his literary intentions are relevant to many aspects of the interpretation of the dialogues, including the apparent evidence of chronology.

Still, the case against the chronological interpretation is not completely convincing. We may begin with stylistic and linguistic evidence. Some of the signs of the "late" style seem to be the result of conscious choice. For instance, in the *Phaedrus* and (allegedly) later dialogues, Plato sharply reduced the incidence of hiatus.[76] This was probably a conscious decision, given the sharp difference between the dialogues that allow it and those that avoid it. Hence one might argue that Plato could turn it on and off at will. Other stylistic features are less likely to be consciously adopted; but one might argue that they are unconscious results of the conscious adoption of a particular style.

It is doubtful, however, whether conscious decisions could underlie the common stylistic features of the later dialogues. The *Philebus*, for instance, has some of the characteristics of earlier dialogues, and so we might expect Plato to have decided to write it in the style of the *Gorgias* or *Republic* i, but it belongs stylistically with the late dialogues. Similarly, the *Phaedrus* differs linguistically and stylistically from the *Symposium*, in ways that connect it with the *Theaetetus* and the *Republic*.[77] Again, the *Philebus*, the *Timaeus*, the *Sophist*, and the *Laws* differ in their subject matter, dialogue form, and (in certain respects) style, but they share the features that mark out the late group. Apparently, then, the features of Plato's late style are constant across dialogues that are otherwise quite different. Their constancy makes it unlikely that they are a result of conscious decisions to adopt a style.

It is more difficult to decide whether apparent doctrinal conflicts can be explained away as the result of conscious decisions by Plato to present only one side of an issue on which he favors the other side. We need to decide, for instance, whether the "one-sided" discussion of incontinence in the *Protagoras* is likely to be the work of an author who tacitly recognizes the other side of the question but presents it only in *Republic* iv.[78] If we find (as I believe we do) that the "one-sided"

---

74. See P. Shorey, *What Plato Said* (Chicago: University of Chicago Press, 1933), 64–73.

75. This is Grote's view of the dialogues.

76. A word ending with a vowel followed by a word beginning with the same vowel creates a hiatus, as in "Carla Adams." Spoken English in England sometimes inserts "r" between the vowels to avoid such a hiatus.

77. See Brandwood, "Stylometry and Chronology," 113–15.

78. I have discussed this question further in "The parts of the soul and the cardinal virtues," in *Platon: Politeia*, ed. O. Höffe (Berlin: Akademie Verlag, 1997), ch. 6.

presentation does not even seem to take seriously the position that Plato defends in another work, we have good reason to believe that it is not intentionally one-sided. It is quite difficult to see why we should treat the arguments to show that virtue is knowledge as intentionally one-sided.

Aristotle's testimony is especially difficult to explain away. Admittedly, he is not always a reliable historian, and we should consider the possibility that his claims about Socrates are a result of inference from the dialogues rather than of any independent and reliable information.[79] But it is difficult to explain away all of Aristotle's claims. Why should reflection on the dialogues suggest to him that some of them are about the views of the historical Socrates? He recognizes that the character called "Socrates" in some of the dialogues puts forward the views that Aristotle attributes to Plato rather than Socrates. Aristotle cannot, then, have naively inferred that the character Socrates always puts forward the views of the historical Socrates. He must have supposed that he had some reason for distinguishing the position of the character Socrates in some dialogues from his position in other dialogues, and for treating only one of these positions as the position of the historical Socrates.

What could his reason be? He might have done what modern readers do, and noticed the apparent doctrinal conflicts between different dialogues. But why does he not resolve these simply by supposing that they reflect Plato's philosophical development without any reference to the historical Socrates? We might speculate that he thinks the dialogues with the fullest biographical remarks about Socrates are intended to present the historical Socrates. But this speculation does not fit the *Phaedo*. No other dialogue has as much to say about Socrates' life and philosophical development, but Aristotle takes it to present a Platonic, not a Socratic, theory of forms. It is not clear, then, how internal features of the dialogues could have persuaded Aristotle that some, and only some, are about the historical Socrates.

It is more plausible, then, to suppose that Aristotle ascribes some of the views of the Platonic Socrates to the historical Socrates because he believes he has some external evidence (i.e., evidence external to the dialogues) about the views of the historical Socrates. He probably had access to external evidence, and had a good reason to look for it and to use it. He joined Plato's Academy in 367, just over thirty years after the death of Socrates in 399. He knew people who had known the historical Socrates, and he could find out what they thought about Socrates. Since Plato was not the only one who wrote Socratic dialogues or expressed views about Socrates, Aristotle had good reason to try to find out what Socrates had actually thought. His claims about the Socratic elements in the dialogues match divisions that we would be inclined to mark on other grounds.

For these reasons, we may reasonably conclude that the cumulative arguments for the standard view of the order of the dialogues remain plausible. We can rely on them to show that the *Theaetetus*, for instance, is later than the *Protagoras*, and that

---

79. C. H. Kahn, *Plato and the Socratic Dialogue* (Cambridge: Cambridge University Press, 1996), 79–87, discounts Aristotle's testimony.

the *Timaeus* is later than the *Phaedo*. We cannot rely on them to settle every question that arises about the order of the dialogues. They do not settle, for instance, the relation of the *Gorgias* to the *Meno*. But we have good grounds for taking some version of the standard view as our starting point for discussion of the dialogues.[80]

# 9. The Dialogues and Plato's Philosophy

Since Plato wrote dialogues, he does not address his reader directly, as the author of a philosophical treatise would. We assume that Aristotle's *Metaphysics* and Aquinas' *Summa* present us with the views of their authors, except when the authors say (as they often do) that they are presenting the views of others. But we do not assume that because Oedipus is the leading character in two of Sophocles' plays, he presents Sophocles' views. We can learn something from Sophocles' plays about Sophocles' views; we may, for instance, find that he emphasizes some questions rather than others, and that he presents some points of view more fully or more sympathetically than others, and that he differs from other tragedians on these points (so that he is not simply following conventions of the genre). What should we believe about Plato's relation to his dialogues and to the character of Socrates?

It is reasonable to allow some weight to the views of Plato's contemporaries and immediate successors. Aristotle ascribes the views of the Platonic Socrates to Plato without suggesting that his doctrinal interpretation of the dialogues is un-usual or that it needs to be defended. Since he often cites these views in order to criticize Plato, he is probably confident that they are Plato's views. If most of his contemporaries had not assumed that the Platonic Socrates represented Plato's views, Aristotle's criticism would have seemed quite misguided. If we were to criticize Shakespeare for holding the views of Hamlet or Othello, or if we supposed Shakespeare held inconsistent views because Hamlet and Othello do not agree, we would be misunderstanding Shakespeare. But we have no reason to believe that anyone accused Aristotle of a similar misunderstanding of Plato.

The testimony of antiquity, however, is not unanimous. The Skeptical Academy rejected the doctrinal interpretation of Plato's dialogues and understood the dialogues as critical exercises, examining the arguments for and against each side in order to leave the reader in a puzzled condition (*aporia*). The point of these exercises is to induce suspension of judgment about dogmatic claims. According to the Skeptical Academy, the dialogues were primarily "peirastic" ("testing") rather

---

80. My discussion of the relative dates of the dialogues has ignored their dramatic dates, because they are entirely useless for fixing the absolute or relative dates of composition. D. Nails, *The People of Plato* (Indianapolis: Hackett, 2002), app. I, gives a useful chronological table of the dramatic dates of dialogues in their historical contexts.

than dogmatic. This description seems to fit the earlier dialogues (those usually called "Socratic" by modern students) but also seems to fit the *Parmenides* and *Theaetetus*. The people who gave generic titles to the dialogues called some of them "peirastic," thereby recognizing some plausible elements in the Skeptical interpretation of Plato.

As far as we know, however, the Skeptical interpretation was an innovation that tried to enlist Plato in a Skeptical project. We have no evidence that it goes back to Plato's contemporaries. The later Academy rejected it and returned to a doctrinal interpretation of the dialogues.[81] We may therefore claim the support of most ancient readers for a doctrinal interpretation, even though readers differed among themselves about what doctrines should be ascribed to Plato.

But the view of Aristotle and of other ancient readers is not decisive. They may have been wrong to treat the views of the Platonic Socrates as Plato's views. We would have good reason to disagree with Aristotle if we found that the views of the Platonic Socrates are so unstable, fragmentary, or inconsistent that they are better understood as starting points for inquiry than as firm conclusions. If, however, we find that a reasonably coherent philosophical outlook and a reasonably intelligible line of philosophical development can be ascribed to the Platonic Socrates, we have some grounds for claiming to have found Plato's views.

For this reason, the interpreter of Plato cannot do without philosophical reflection on the content of the dialogues. We might have preferred to establish a firm framework for philosophical interpretation by appeal to "extraphilosophical" evidence: the use of the dialogue form, chronology, characterization, dramatic dates, and so on. All of this evidence is useful, and indeed indispensable, for the understanding of the dialogues. But we cannot rely on it independently of philosophical interpretation. To understand the significance of the dialogue form, or the character of Socrates, or the use of characters and dramatic dates, we have to make our minds up about the doctrines, if any, that Plato reaches in different dialogues.[82]

# WORKS CITED

*Academicrorum Philosophorum Index Herculanensis*, ed. S. Mekler. Berlin: Weidmann, 1902.

Alline, H. *Histoire du texte de Platon*. Paris: Champion, 1915.

Annas, J. "Aristotle on inefficient causes," *Philosophical Quarterly* 32 (1982), 311–26.

81. A doctrinal interpretation of Plato apparently left its mark even on the ancient manuscripts of Plato. DL iii 66 mentions that an asterisk in the margin of manuscripts was used to indicate harmony (*sumphônia tôn dogmatôn*) in Plato. See Alline, *Histoire du texte*, 93. Alline (187–88) found fifteen asterisks in the surviving manuscript T, mainly in the myth in the *Phaedrus*. Solmsen, "Academic and Alexandrian edition," 107, doubts whether they really serve the purpose mentioned by DL.

82. I have benefited from helpful comments by the editor and by Charles Brittain on an earlier draft.

Annas, J., and Rowe, C. J., eds. *New Perspectives on Plato*. Cambridge, Mass.: Harvard University Press, 2002.

Anonymous. *Prolegomena in Platonis Philosophiam*, ed. L. G. Westerink. Paris: Les Belles Lettres, 1990.

*Aristotle, Complete Works*, ed. J. Barnes. 2 vols. Princeton, N.J.: Princeton University Press, 1984.

Barnes, J. "The Hellenistic Platos," *Apeiron* 24 (1991), 115–28.

Bluck, R. S., ed. *Plato's* Meno. Cambridge: Cambridge University Press, 1961.

Boter, G. J. *The Textual Tradition of Plato's Republic*. Mnemosyne Supp. 107 (1989).

Brandwood, L. "Stylometry and chronology," in *The Cambridge Companion to Plato*, ed. R. Kraut. Cambridge: Cambridge University Press, 1992.

Brumbaugh, R. S., and Wells, R. *The Plato Manuscripts*. New Haven, Conn.: Yale University Press, 1968.

Burnet, J. "A neglected MS. of Plato," *Classical Review* 16 (1902), 98–101.

Cherniss, H. F. "The relation of the *Timaeus* to Plato's later dialogues," in *Studies in Plato's Metaphysics*, ed. R. E. Allen. London: Routledge, 1965, ch. 17; reprinted from *American Journal of Philology* 78 (1957), 225–66.

Cicero. *Letters to Atticus*, ed. D. R. Shackleton Bailey. Cambridge: Cambridge University Press, 1966.

Cornford, F. M. *Plato's Cosmology*. London: Routledge, 1937.

Cornford, F. M. *Plato's Theory of Knowledge*. London: Routledge, 1934.

*Corpus dei Papiri Filosofici Greci e Latini*, vol. 3. Florence: Olschki, 1995.

Dillon, J. M. *The Heirs of Plato*. Oxford: Oxford University Press, 2003.

Dillon, J. M. "Tampering with the Timaeus," *American Journal of Philology* 110 (1989), 50–72.

Dodds, E. R., ed. *Plato's Gorgias*. Oxford: Oxford University Press, 1959.

Dörrie, H. *Der Platonismus in der Antike*, vols. 1–2. Stuttgart: Frommann-Holzboog, 1987–1990.

Dover, K. J., ed. *Aristophanes' Clouds*. Oxford: Oxford University Press, 1968.

Dover, K. J., ed. *Plato: Symposium*. Cambridge: Cambridge University Press, 1980.

Düring, I. *Aristotle in the Ancient Biographical Tradition*. Gothenburg: Almquist and Wiksel, 1957.

Festugière, A. J. *Etudes de philosophie grecque*. Paris: Vrin, 1971.

Grote, G. *Plato and the Other Companions of Socrates*, 4 vols. London: Murray, 1888.

Guthrie, W. K. C. *History of Greek Philosophy*, vol. 4. Cambridge: Cambridge University Press, 1975.

Irwin, T. H. "The parts of the soul and the cardinal virtues," in *Platon: Politeia*, ed. O. Höffe, ch. 6. Berlin: Akademie Verlag, 1997.

Irwin, T. H. *Plato's Ethics*. Oxford: Oxford University Press, 1995.

Jachmann, G. "Der Platontext," in *Textgeschichtliche Studien*, ed. C. Gnilka. *Beiträge zur klassischen Philologie* 143, 1982.

Kahn, C. H. "On Platonic chronology," in J. Annas and C. J. Rowe, eds. *New Perspectives on Plato*, ch. 4. Cambridge, Mass.: Harvard University Press, 2002.

Kahn, C. H. *Plato and the Socratic Dialogue*. Cambridge: Cambridge University Press, 1996.

Ludwig, W. "Plato's love epigrams," *Greek, Roman, and Byzantine Studies* 4 (1963), 59–82.

Mansfeld, J. *Prolegomena*. Leiden: Brill, 1994.

Metzger, B. M. *The Text of the New Testament*, 3rd ed. Oxford: Oxford University Press, 1991.

Morrow, G. R. *Plato's Cretan City*. Princeton, N.J.: Princeton University Press, 1960.

Nails, D. *The People of Plato*. Indianapolis: Hackett, 2002.

*Omnia Platonis Opera*. Venice: Aldus Manutius, 1513.

Owen, G. E. L. "The place of the *Timaeus* in Plato's dialogues," *Logic, Science and Dialectic*, ch. 4. London: Duckworth, 1986; reprinted from *Classical Quarterly* 3 (1953), 79–95.

*Oxford Classical Dictionary*, 3rd ed., ed. S. Hornblower and A. Spawforth. Oxford: Oxford University Press, 1996.

Pasquali, G. *Storia della Tradizione e Critica del Testo*, 2nd ed. Florence: Le Monnier, 1952.

Plato. *Collected Dialogues*, ed. J. M. Cooper and D. S. Hutchinson. Indianapolis: Hackett, 1997.

*Platonis Opera*, ed. J. Burnet. 5 vols. Oxford: Oxford University Press, 1900–1907.

*Platonis Opera*, vol. 1, ed. E. A. Duke, W. F. Hicken, W. S. M. Nicoll, D. B. Robinson, and J. C. G. Strachan. Oxford: Oxford University Press, 1995.

*Platonis Opera quæ extant omnia*, ed. H. Stephanus. Geneva, 1578.

*Platonis Respublica*, ed. S. Slings. Oxford: Oxford University Press, 2003.

*Poseidonius*, ed. L. Edelstein and I. G. Kidd, 4 vols. Cambridge: Cambridge University Press, 1972–1999.

Reynolds, L. D., and Wilson, N. G. *Scribes and Scholars*. 3rd ed. Oxford: Oxford University Press, 1991.

Riginos, A. S. *Platonica*. Leiden: Brill, 1976.

Robinson, D. B. "Textual notes on Plato's Sophist," *Classical Quarterly* 49 (1999), 139–60.

Rowe, C. J. "Plato re-edited," *Classical Review* 47 (1997), 272–74.

Ryle, G. "Dialectic in the Academy," in *New Essays on Plato and Aristotle*, ed. J. R. Bambrough, 39–68. London: Routledge, 1965.

Schofield, M. "A displacement in the text of the *Cratylus*," *Classical Quarterly* 22 (1972), 246–53.

Sedley, D. N. *Plato's Cratylus*. Cambridge: Cambridge University Press, 2005.

Shorey, P. *What Plato Said*. Chicago: University of Chicago Press, 1933.

Slings, S. R. *Critical Notes on Plato's Politeia*. Leiden: Brill, 2005

Slings, S. R., ed. *Plato's Clitopho*. Cambridge: Cambridge University Press, 1999.

Solmsen, F. "The Academic and Alexandrian edition of Plato's works," *Illinois Classical Studies* 6 (1981), 102–11.

Taran, L. "The manuscript tradition of Plato's Phaedo," ch. 14, in L. Taran, *Collected Papers*. Leiden: Brill, 2001; reprinted from *Gnomon* 48 (1976), 760–68.

Tarrant, H. *Thrasyllan Platonism*. Ithaca, N.Y.: Cornell University Press, 1993.

Taylor, A. E. *A Commentary on Plato's* Timaeus. Oxford: Oxford University Press, 1928.

# CHAPTER 4

# PLATO'S WAYS OF WRITING

## MARY MARGARET McCABE

## 1. THE DIALOGUE FORM: A PROSPECTUS

Plato's writing scintillates. And most—if not all[1]—of what comes down to us from Plato's hand is in the dialogue form, somehow or other. But should we speak of "the" Platonic dialogue form? After all, the dialogues come in all sorts of different forms: some are dramatic, others merely formalized discussion (compare the *Phaedo* and the *Statesman*); some are in direct speech, others narrated (compare the *Gorgias* and the *Symposium*); some seem to have a beginning, a middle, and an end, whereas others begin, or end, in the middle of things (compare the *Euthydemus* and the *Philebus*); some have Socrates in the central role, and others are dominated by less engaging, but more authoritative figures (compare the *Theaetetus* and the *Sophist*).[2] We may miss the complexity of Plato's ways of writing if we reduce his dialogues to a single and canonical shape. Such reduction might be hopelessly banal (because vastly general), or else simply false.[3]

1. This depends on whether we take the *Letters* to be genuine; compare K. Sayre, *Plato's Literary Garden: How to Read a Platonic Dialogue* (Notre Dame, 1995). I include *Apology* by virtue of the passage of dialogue within it, see sec. 7.
2. For all the figures who take the leading role, strong claims to authority are made: Parmenides at *Parmenides* 127–29, the Eleatic Stranger at *Sophist* 216, Timaeus at *Timaeus* 20, the Athenian Stranger in his authoritative leading of the discussion from the beginning of *Laws* I. The position of Socrates is more complicated, see sec. 3.
3. See A. Long, "Character and Dialectic: The Philosophical Origins of the Platonic Dialogue," Ph. D. dissertation (University of Cambridge, 2004); Long, "The Form of Plato's *Republic*," in R. Osborne, ed., *Debating the Athenian Cultural Revolution* (Cambridge, 2007).

Still, we rightly call them dialogues. Plato's characters *talk* to each other: about where they are going (e.g., *Euthyphro* 2–4), who they met yesterday (e.g., *Euthydemus* 271), where they are planning to have dinner (e.g., *Symposium* 174); and about virtue (e.g., *Meno*), about knowledge (e.g., *Theaetetus*), about truth and falsehood (e.g., *Sophist*), about what there really is (e.g., *Parmenides*). Some of what they say seems utterly trivial, but some seems universal and of abiding importance. So, for example, in the *Protagoras*, the short conversation between Socrates and his friend at 309c–310a has the air of gossip, while the discussion about the virtues between Socrates and Protagoras at 332a–333b appeals to general principles and seeks an abstract conclusion. Does the dramatic detail of the dialogues have any bearing on their philosophical purposes?

I shall say that it does—that, indeed, we cannot properly make sense of what Plato does if we ignore the effect on the arguments of dramatic context, allusion, characterisation—indeed, of all the aspects of the style and drama of a dialogue. This effect is felt both particularly (where the dramatic detail alters radically how we understand individual arguments) and generally (where various strategies render the reader carefully reflective on what is said). I shall conclude that the philosophical content of a dialogue is to be found, at least, in the dialogue as a whole. How Plato writes, therefore, is indissoluble from what he is trying to say.

## 2. A DIFFERENT VIEW: PICTURES AND FRAMES

But this conclusion does not command universal assent. For many suppose that the philosophical picture of a dialogue lies just in its arguments, while the fictional apparatus—the "who said what to whom"—is only the frame in which they are presented.[4] So, for example, the *Euthyphro* is constituted by sections of argument, clearly demarcated, about what is the holy (5d–11b, 11e–15e), exhibited in a frame discussion about Socrates' meeting with Euthyphro as they are both hurrying to court, and Euthyphro's retreat at the end (2a–5d; 15e–16a). These argumentative sections of the dialogues can, often, be formalized. For example, *Parmenides* 152a–e purports to show that the one both is and becomes both older and younger than itself, and it can be formalized as a linear sequence without the answers that young Aristotle gives to Parmenides' questions.[5] If those answers make little difference, is

4. The "frame/picture" contrast is an old one; compare, for example, D. Gallop, *Plato: Phaedo* [*Phaedo*] (Oxford, 1975), 74. Gail Fine rightly reminds me that the relation between frame and picture is a variable one. I retain the terminology in what follows, to mark the difference between what is said and the setting in which it is said, while noting that my conclusion—that philosophical significance is to be found in each dialogue as a whole—supposes that the frames are, indeed, a part of the picture.

5. F. M. Cornford, *Plato and Parmenides* (London, 1939), misses them out. This is not, surely, the Aristotle who wrote the *Metaphysics*—but who is to say that Plato did not choose this name for his character with deliberation?

the rest of the descriptive material of a dialogue irrelevant to its arguments save as their frame?

One answer would be that some parts of a dialogue give us the emotive cast, the tone, of what will follow.[6] Thus the *Republic* opens with an optimistic discussion of how Socrates and Glaucon fell in with Polemarchus, Adeimantus, and friends and how their long conversation about justice ensued. The *Symposium* describes—in delightful detail—Socrates' wayward progress to Agathon's dinner party and what happened next. In darker contrast, several dialogues turn on Socrates' trial and execution: the *Phaedo* describes Socrates' death, surrounded by friends, whose grief Socrates finds inappropriate. This theme is picked up in other dialogues, too: Meno (*Meno* 80b) warns Socrates of the dangers of practising his puzzling method of examination; in the *Hippias Major*, Socrates' alter ego tells him that he will never make a really fine speech in court until he knows what fine really is (304c–e); and the *Theaetetus*, presented as a memorial to Socrates' young lookalike, Theaetetus, ends with Socrates going off to court (to his meeting, we suppose, with Euthyphro in the King's Porch; *Theaetetus* 210d). All this affects us, makes us care about what we read. However, it makes no substantial difference to the real philosophical business in hand—or so this account of the dialogue form would go.[7] Perhaps, then, discussions about issues of abstract generality (virtue, knowledge, truth) count as the philosophical content of the dialogues; and details, such as where Socrates was sitting in the gymnasium when his friends arrived, do not. Instead, those details may serve to seduce and attract us into reading, to please and sometimes anger us—so that we set foot on the harsh road to understanding the arguments beyond; but they are not—so this account would say—otherwise part of the dialogue's philosophical destination.

Is the frame so easily separated from its picture, or the emotional tone of Plato's writing from its content?[8] We might think Parmenides' comparison of himself to an aged racehorse unimportant (*Parmenides* 136e–137a) and yet be quite sure that there is some significance to the arguments of the theme that Socrates is a young man (127c, 130e, 135d).[9] Or we might suppose that Socrates' impending death makes no difference to the *Phaedo*'s arguments about the immortality of the soul, even if it adds urgency, but still wonder whether the calmness of Socrates' death by hemlock is an anomaly that tells us something important about the nature

---

6. Compare here the dramatic opening of the *Theaetetus* and the ancient story that there existed another, "more frigid" introduction that was not used by Plato: *Anonymous Commentary on the Theaetetus*, 3.28–37.

7. Emotion, one might say, does not affect truth-value; compare Jonathan Barnes's view of the poverty of Plato's arguments, *The Cambridge Companion to Aristotle* (Cambridge, 1995), xvi.

8. In recent years, many have argued that it is not: see, for example, M. C. Stokes, *Plato's Socratic Conversations* [*Conversations*] (London, 1980), and R. Blondell, *The Play of Character in Plato's Dialogues* [*Play*] (Cambridge, 2002). A subtheme of this line of interpretation is the question of Plato's attitude to tragedy: see M. C. Nussbaum, *The Fragility of Goodness: Luck and Ethics in Greek Tragedy and Philosophy* (Cambridge, 1986), and S. Halliwell, *The Aesthetics of Mimesis: Ancient Texts and Modern Problems* [*Mimesis*] (Princeton, 2002); compare D. Roochnik, *The Tragedy of Reason* [*Tragedy*] (New York, 1990).

9. This is a commonplace in accounts of how the arguments against forms are to be construed: for example, R. E. Allen, *Plato's Parmenides, Translation and Analysis* (Oxford, 1983), 100.

of a philosopher.[10] How are we to decide which bits of the dialogue to include in a philosophical interpretation, and which we may safely leave out? I suggest that if we treat the settings as dispensable frames for the arguments, we miss both the ways in which the frames are involved in particular arguments and how the frames determine the reader's reflective stance.

## 3. THE INTERLOCUTORS

In the dialogues, people talk to each other. Some are richly characterized and act accordingly. Euthyphro, for example, comes to the discussion on his way to court, to prosecute his father for the murder of a slave (4a–d); in this extraordinary act[11] he has complete confidence, by virtue of the expertise he claims in matters moral and religious (4e–5a). This comes across as an arrogance so deep-seated that even when Socrates shows it to be unfounded, Euthyphro cannot forsake it but quits the scene in haste (15c–e). Charmides is introduced as a young man as noble of spirit as he is handsome (*Charmides* 154d), and his discussion with Socrates reveals that his character is appropriately modest for a discussion of the virtue of self-control or temperance, *sôphrosunê*. Ctesippus is said to be headstrong (*Euthydemus* 273a); accordingly, he is the first to succumb to the attractions of sophistic argument (298b ff.).

And there is Socrates: regularly the protagonist, but variously portrayed. Sometimes he is Socrates the expert in erotics (e.g., *Lysis* 204b–c, *Symposium* 177e)—at times apparently inflamed by beautiful young men (*Charmides* 155c–e, *Symposium* 216), at times coldly self-controlled (*Symposium* 217b ff.). Sometimes he is a solitary (late for dinner because he is thinking alone, *Symposium* 174–75; compare *Euthydemus* 272e); but sometimes he insists on the company of friends as the best way to proceed in philosophy (e.g., *Charmides* 166d; *Gorgias* 486e ff.; *Cratylus* 391a). He is regularly described as brave (e.g., *Laches* 181), and he certainly seems to have the courage to discuss anything with anyone; but at times he is apparently terrified by the arguments against him (*Euthydemus* 293a). Sometimes he is modest (e.g., *Euthydemus* 272c–d), sometimes arrogant (*Gorgias* 482)—and sometimes the modesty seems to be a ploy, designed to flummox those to whom he presents himself (compare *Euthyphro* 5a–c with 15d–16a).[12] He is the self-deprecating inquirer after knowledge who proposed to the Athenians that as a

10. C. Gill, "The Death of Socrates," *Classical Quarterly* 23 (1983): 25–28, and E. Bloch, "Hemlock Poisoning and the Death of Socrates: Did Plato Tell the Truth?" in T. Brickhouse and N. Smith, eds., *The Trial and Execution of Socrates* (Oxford, 2001).

11. The historical context is vital here to understanding just how extraordinary this would be in ancient Athens; see Schofield, chapter 3 in this volume.

12. Socrates' apparent irony, however, does not merely entitle us to negate whatever he says (note Alcibiades' remarks at *Symposium* 216): see, for example, G. Vlastos, *Socrates, Ironist and Moral Philosopher* [*Socrates*] (Cambridge, 1991); A. Nehamas, *The Art of Living: Socratic Reflections from Plato to Foucault* [*Art*] (Berkeley, 1998); and M. M. McCabe, "Irony in the Soul: Should Plato's Socrates Be Sincere?" in M. Trapp, ed., *Socrates* (London, 2007).

punishment he should be given a state pension (*Apology* 36). And his tone often seems insincere when he sets up some opponent for a fall—however much he may demand sincerity from others.[13] In this, he seems less of the cooperative friend than a competitor, and often readers of a dialogue are incensed by his pride in his own "human wisdom" and his apparent contempt for the terminal ignorance of everyone he meets (*Apology* 21–23).

This figure of Socrates is often unattractive and always difficult to interpret;[14] it might properly deter us from seeking a single and uniform account of the dialogues, as much as from looking for a single Socrates persisting through the dialogues.[15] For its Socrates may be particular to each dialogue and may both remind us of the other Socrateses and discourage us from supposing that any portrait aims for verisimilitude. Still, Socrates is usually a vivid figure. Some dialogues, by contrast, present their main figures in an exiguous way. The Eleatic Stranger, for example, is introduced as "godlike" (*Sophist* 216); that may be why he has little individual character.[16] His interlocutors, Young Socrates and a subdued Theaetetus, are as thinly characterized. The contrast between these dialogues and those rich dramas of character has tempted commentators to posit a difference in their dates: to suggest that "the" dialogue form was a literary device that lost its appeal later in Plato's life, to be replaced by an inadequate gesture in the direction of style. But maybe we should pause: How are we to understand the relation between the richly portrayed Theaetetus of his eponymous dialogue and his thin counterpart in the *Sophist*? Or, within a single dialogue, the benign figure of "father" Parmenides in his eponymous dialogue, compared with his meager portrayal in the second half of the same dialogue? Is the line of demarcation between character and argument to be drawn so easily? And is it so to be drawn for Plato?

# 4. IDENTIFICATION AND TRANSPARENCY

For those cases where philosophical discussion is directly and richly portrayed—the *Meno*, for example, or the *Phaedo* or the *Philebus*—we might think we should *imagine ourselves as one of the* characters in question: should sympathize with their

---

13. For example, at *Euthyphro* 9d; *Protagoras* 331c–d; *Republic* 346a. See M. M. McCabe, *Plato and His Predecessors: The Dramatisation of Reason* [*Predecessors*] (Cambridge, 2000), ch. 2.

14. Nehamas, *Art*.

15. The debate on the date of composition of the dialogues and the development of Plato's thought has been much at issue in the past fifty years or so; see, for example, G. E. L. Owen, "The Place of the *Timaeus* in Plato's Dialogues," *Logic, Science and Dialectic* (London, 1986). Vlastos, *Socrates*, had the effect of focusing recent attention on the question of Plato's attitude to the "historical" Socrates. On some of this see, for example, R. Kraut, "Introduction to the Study of Plato," in R. Kraut, ed., *The Cambridge Companion to Plato* (Cambridge, 1992), 1–50; C. H. Kahn, *Plato and the Socratic Dialogue: The Philosophical Use of a Literary Form* [*Dialogue*] (Cambridge, 1996); J. M. Cooper, *Plato: Complete Works* [*Plato*] (Indianapolis, 1997), xii–xviii; J. Annas and C. Rowe, eds., *New Perspectives on Plato, Modern and Ancient* (Cambridge, Mass., 2002); and the sane observations of D. N. Sedley, *The Midwife of Platonism: Text and Subtext in Plato's Theaetetus* (Oxford, 2004).

16. His austerity is anticipated, perhaps, in the digression of the *Theaetetus* 172–78: he is a philosopher.

positions, should take up the point of view they espouse. So we might share Cebes' worries about whether the soul is immortal, while sympathizing with his earnest desire that it be so, indeed (*Phaedo* 88a ff.). The arguments that follow, then, would engage with that position and show us where it should be modified and resolved. Or we might imagine ourselves as Meno, or Laches—and feel for them as their less than rigorous collections of beliefs are subjected to Socratic argument, feel with them the sense of puzzlement (of *aporia*), of frustration and irritation, or just sheer embarrassment (*Meno* 80a ff.; *Laches* 194a ff; and compare Protarchus' more robust response, *Philebus* 20).[17] We may feel some sympathy, even, for rebarbative characters such as Protagoras or Critias (*Protagoras* 333–34; *Charmides* 166). And we can empathize with the characters thus just because they are portrayed in vivid ways, such that we can clothe ourselves, as we read, with their character and attitudes. But we then find the attitudes and views that we thus adopt subjected to dialectical scrutiny, and this serves a direct philosophical purpose. So—we could say—the point of having these characters represented to us is that the representation is somehow transparent,[18] available for us to identify with the characters on the dialogue's stage and to suffer their philosophical fate.

Well, who has not sympathized with the squirming embarrassment sometimes felt by Socrates' interlocutors (e.g., Hippocrates, *Protagoras* 312a; Nicias, *Laches* 200)? Who has not felt Callicles' irritation (*Gorgias* 489 ff.) or Thrasymachus' annoyance (*Republic* 336–37, 343) that Socrates is merely manipulating the arguments against them, missing the heart of the problem of justice for the individual? Our emotional sympathy is engaged, indeed, by the brilliance of Plato's writing: as Socrates supposes to occur when we hear recitations of Homer:

> When even the best of us hear Homer or some other tragedian imitating one of the heroes sorrowing and making a long lamenting speech or singing and beating his breast, you know that we enjoy it, give ourselves up to following it, sympathize with the hero, take his sufferings seriously, and praise as a good poet the one who affects us most in this way (*Republic* 605c–d).[19]

And then the dialogue's effect might be somehow therapeutic:[20] the examination of these views we have adopted is beneficial to us (at least it purges us of error). By the end of the dialogue, we may be brought to identify, instead, with Socrates, peculiar figure though he may be. So in our imaginative engagement with the dialogue, our views are transformed. Is that what we should say about these rich dialogues? And if it is, what should we say about those dialogues that seem obstinately poor?

---

17. The same seems to happen to Socrates himself: for example, *Protagoras* 339, *Euthydemus* 293.

18. A. Nehamas, "Plato and the Mass Media," *The Virtues of Authenticity* [*Authenticity*] (Princeton, 2000); Halliwell, *Mimesis*, 91.

19. Translations throughout are from Cooper, *Plato*.

20. D. N. Sedley on the Anonymous Commentator on the *Theaetetus* in "The *Theaetetus*: Three Interpretations" ["Interpretations"], in C. Gill and M. M. McCabe, *Form and Argument in late Plato* (Oxford, 1996).

## 5. THE TROUBLE WITH IMITATION

Imaginative identification may prove problematic, however, even where it might seem plausible (identifying with the Eleatic Stranger, or with Young Socrates of the *Statesman* is a harder task). In the *Republic*, Socrates is disapproving of dramatic performance (605e ff.), since it takes over our emotions under reason's inadequate guard.[21] Socrates denies that this kind of sympathy is intellectually healthy—especially sympathy with those who are not exemplary characters (as many of Socrates' interlocutors are not)—for in imitating poor or uncontrolled characters, we shall ourselves practise their inadequacy, and so much the worse for us.

But even the imitation of good characters will be problematic as a means of learning wisdom. For wisdom—or so, at least, Socrates seems to say on several occasions—is not something that is transmitted by our passive absorption of what we learn (for example, *Protagoras* 313–34; *Symposium*, 175; compare *Euthydemus* 285, *Republic* 345b). Instead, the search for wisdom is a hard road, whose traveling we cannot delegate to anyone else (see *Apology* 23a–b; *Euthydemus* 281). So neither imaginative identification with Socrates' interlocutors nor even with Socrates himself seems to be the right way of going about philosophical inquiry. If we read, in the dialogues, representations of philosophy being done, that tells us nothing about how we should do philosophy with the dialogues. How far, then, does either the criticism of poetry and drama that Socrates puts forward in the *Republic*, or the repudiation of a passive model of learning, target Plato's own writing, too?

## 6. DOCTRINES AND IMPASSES

To answer this question, we may ask another. In the recent explosion of discussions about Plato's literary skills, the question "Who speaks for Plato?"[22] has been posed, asking what we may suppose to be the views of Plato, transmitted through his representations of others in dialogue. *Is* the point that we should end up switching our allegiance away from the interlocutor toward either Socrates or the Eleatic Stranger? Are we to think, then, that Socrates (or the Eleatic Stranger, or Timaeus, or the Athenian Stranger), by occupying the protagonist's role, is the mouthpiece of the author?[23] What Socrates says, on this account, would be what Plato himself believes.[24]

---

21. On this complex issue, see, notably, M. F. Burnyeat, *Culture and Society in Plato's Republic: The Tanner Lectures on Human Values* (Harvard, 1999); Nehamas, *Authenticity*; Halliwell, *Mimesis*.

22. G. A. Press, ed., *Who Speaks for Plato? Studies in Platonic Anonymity* (Lanham, 2000), and D. Clay, *Platonic Questions: Dialogues with the Silent Philosopher* [*Questions*] (University Park, Penn., 2002).

23. Of course, we should not say so for a drama—is King Lear Shakespeare?

24. But see, for example, J. Beversluis, *Cross-Examining Socrates: A Defense of the Interlocutors in Plato's Early Dialogues* (Cambridge, 2000), and C. Gill, "Speaking up for Plato's Interlocutors," *Oxford Studies in Ancient Philosophy* 20 (2001): 297–321.

And in that case, the importance of everything else in the dialogue may diminish, turning, at worst, into the "merely" literary curlicues to make the doctrines put forward by the master palatable.[25]

But this explanation cannot be universal. After all, in many dialogues Socrates ends up without a doctrine—or, at least, without a doctrine that has withstood serious critical attack[26]—but only a state of impasse, *aporia*. In some dialogues, further, it is not clear just what has happened to some thesis employed along the way (a good example is the theory of perception from *Theaetetus* 156[27]). And in some dialogues, it appears that progress genuinely is made, but it is circumscribed by caution (for example, the account of false statement in *Sophist*, see 261; the account of the mixed life in the *Philebus*, see 67b; the "likely story" of the *Timaeus*).

Instead, the dialogue form may be meant to offer us something that is not Platonic doctrine. Some have seen there a thoroughgoing, nondogmatist, skepticism: any view, even the view of a Socrates, is liable to be overturned, and so the best thing to do is to suspend judgment.[28] Some have found the dialogues to be in some other, vaguer way, "open-ended"—noncommittal, indeterminate about what we should say about these big questions: committed, merely, to the project of going on looking.[29] But neither of these broad views takes seriously enough the determinate differences that do occur within the arguments: between a view that is denied—for example, that justice is the interest of the stronger; *Republic* 343a—and one that is not—for example, that justice is where each does his own; *Republic* 433.

Perhaps, instead, the different attitudes to different arguments imbue the positive conclusions with a kind of (variable) provisional status, so the frequently puzzling nature of the endings, the tentative way in which Socrates declares his commitments en route would be meant to disavow authority for them.[30] "This," the protagonist may sometimes be understood to be saying, "is a likely story; but still open to critical attack." Socrates' arguments (and even the procedures of the Eleatic Stranger) are presented to make clear this disavowal of authority, to advance the conclusions as tentative, but as conclusions nonetheless.[31] To identify, by

25. Some ready-made contrast between the "literary" and the "philosophical" begs the very question I am asking.

26. This happens not only in the dialogues conventionally labeled "Socratic" (such as *Laches, Charmides, Lysis,* and *Protagoras*) but also in *Theaetetus* and *Parmenides*.

27. See M. F. Burnyeat, "Plato on the Grammar of Perceiving," *Classical Quarterly* 26 (1976): 29–51; Burnyeat's magisterial *The Theaetetus of Plato*, trans. M. J. Levett (Indianapolis, 1990); and J. M. Cooper, "Plato on Sense-Perception and Knowledge (*Theaetetus* 184–6)," *Phronesis* 15 (1970): 123–65.

28. See Sedley on the *Theaetetus* as interpreted by Academic skepticism, in "Interpretations."

29. See, for example, Roochnik, *Tragedy*, and Clay, *Questions*; compare H. Gadamer, *Dialogue and Dialectic: Eight Hermeneutical Studies of Plato*, trans. P. C. Smith (New Haven, 1980), with the comments by C. Gill in. "Critical Response to the Hermeneutical Approach from an Analytic Perspective" in G. Reale and S. Scolnicov, eds., *New Images of Plato: The Idea of the Good* [*Good*] (Sankt Augustin, 2002).

30. Stokes, *Conversations*; M. Frede "The Literary Form of the *Sophist*," in C. Gill and M. M. McCabe, eds., *Form and Argument in Late Plato* (Oxford, 1996).

31. The change of protagonist might be designed to produce this tentativeness in itself; that would account, perhaps, for the apparently dogmatic conclusions of the *Timaeus*.

the dialogue's end, with Socrates is to agree with him, with reservation, and to take this view of the nature of philosophical progress seriously.

This would not make the dialogues weapons of skepticism or leave them "open-ended." It explains the differences between what the characters say in different dialogues, while at the same time allowing the reader an active role in the process of reading: the reservation. So it does, I suggest, tell some of the story. It grants to Plato genuine commitment to—and responsibility for[32]—the views about, for example, politics and psychology presented by Socrates in the *Republic*, while allowing them to be subject to revision. And it tells us something about the appropriate general response to the explicit arguments when we read. But it still does not account for the multifarious forms of the dialogues, nor for how we should respond to that multifariousness when we read.

# 7. PHILOSOPHICAL FICTION

It would be an obvious mistake to take the *Symposium*, or the *Gorgias*, or even the *Parmenides*, to describe some historical event, just as it happened. For each dialogue is a work of fiction, somehow artfully composed in such a way that we notice the artistry itself.[33] Consider, for example, the pastoral tone of the *Phaedrus*—a work set ostentatiously outside Athens (whither Socrates allegedly only ventured twice[34]); or the high tragedy of the *Phaedo* (apparently recorded by Plato, even though he was away sick; 59b); or the logically low comedy of the *Euthydemus* (Socrates' encounter with a pair of sophists with poor historical credentials[35]). Even those works that make vigorous claims to historicity at the same time bear the marks of fiction. The *Apology* claims to be Socrates' speech in his own defense, but it includes an improbable philosophical discussion with his accusers (24d–28a).[36] The *Parmenides* describes a visit to Athens paid by the two great Eleatics, Parmenides and Zeno, and their discussion with the young Socrates: *bien trouvé*, but are we meant to think it actually happened?[37] The dramatic dates and places of the dialogues, therefore, may be trickier than at first appear.[38] And what of those

32. See M. F. Burnyeat, "Sphinx without a Secret?" ["Sphinx"], *New York Review of Books* (May 30, 1985).

33. See, for example, A. Nightingale, *Genres in Dialogue: Plato and the Construct of Philosophy* (Cambridge, 1995); R. Rutherford, *The Art of Plato* (London, 1995); and Blondell, *Play*.

34. On campaign at Potidaea and Delium, see *Symposium* 219e ff and *Crito* 52b. We should be attentive, therefore, to how the *Phaedrus* makes play with his being out of place, 230d; see G. R. F Ferrari's classic *Listening to the Cicadas: A Study of Plato's Phaedrus* [*Cicadas*] (Cambridge, 1987).

35. See D. Nails, *The People of Plato* (Indianapolis, 2002), 152. At *Euthydemus* 271–72, it is suggested that the brothers are "new-fangled."

36. On the genre of Socratic *logoi*, see Kahn, *Dialogue*.

37. The dialogue takes care with the relative ages of the interlocutors (127a–b), echoing the elaborate timing of the transmission of the story itself, but there is no independent evidence that the meeting actually took place.

38. R. Hunter, *Plato: Symposium* (Oxford, 2004), 3 n.1.

dialogues that somehow lack location in particular time and place? For example, the *Sophist* and the *Statesman*—led by the anonymous Eleatic Stranger[39]—appear to be dramatically tied to the *Theaetetus*; but they are oddly bereft of particular detail. I suggest that there are explanations—both general and particular—for a dialogue's elaborate fictionality and that those explanations are philosophical ones.[40]

So the dialogues are not merely verbatim reports of actual events; but artful presentations of conversation. We may distinguish, therefore, between:

- The philosophy that is represented in the fictional encounters of the dialogues: Do the discussions between Socrates (often) and various interlocutors constitute a dialogue's philosophical content?
- The representing of those encounters: Or is Plato doing more—from a philosophical point of view—than merely recording these discussions when he writes?

If there is some kind of contrast thus to be drawn between what is represented and its representation, what happens when we read that representation? Is it that we take it in, envisage it, so that the representation is somehow directly transmitted to the reader? Or is there a more complex relation between what Plato writes and what happens when we read? If the dialogues are fiction, and we are brought to notice it, then the business of reading may be a more active process than merely absorbing whatever it is that the representation is meant to "say." So there is a third point of contrast:

- Reading these representations: When we read, are we passive to what is represented there, or actively and critically engaged?

That Plato saw these three things—the represented, the representation, and the business of reading—to be distinct may be attested by the *Phaedrus'* story, in which Thamus, king of Egypt, castigates Theuth for rejoicing at his discovery of writing. For:

Writing shares a strange feature with painting. The offsprings of painting stand there as if they are alive, but if anyone asks them anything they remain most solemnly silent. The same is true of written words. You'd think they were speaking as if they had some understanding, but if you question anything that has just been said, because you want to learn more, it continues to signify just that very same thing forever. When it has once been written down, every discourse rolls about everywhere, reaching indiscriminately those with understanding no less than those who have no business with it and it doesn't know to whom it should speak and to whom it should not. And when it is

---

39. *Xenos* may mean "stranger" or "visitor"; in antiquity, visitors were often strangers.

40. It is impossible, of course, to demonstrate this for every word in every dialogue, and it is a fortiori impossible to do so in a short essay such as this. My hope, merely, is to shift the burden of proof onto those who suppose that some bits of the Platonic dialogues are easily dispensible by the philosophical reader.

faulted and attacked unfairly, it always needs its father's support; alone, it can neither defend itself nor come to its own support. 275d–e.

The story is told by Socrates, who wrote no philosophy (this is the direct representation). His telling of the story, however, is represented in such a way that we notice as we read that the story somehow undermines its own mode of representation (it is told in writing). This is not, then, mere reportage. Instead, the writing of a tale told against writing shatters the confidence of his readers that what they read here can be taken on trust.[41] But now this gets worrying. If writing is somehow unreliable, why—if we are searching for wisdom—should we read the dialogues?

Some would say that the dialogues are somehow inherently contradictory, testimony to the deep down slipperiness of the way we write—or even talk.[42] Others would say that they are somehow second best to the oral tradition of philosophy within the Academy.[43] Maybe their surface meaning is even the disguise for a coded message underneath.[44] Each of these suggestions, however, may underplay the overt self-consciousness of the paradox about writing. For in challenging its own mode of presentation, it asks how the search for wisdom should proceed, and this question, itself a philosophical one, is provoked by, and so reflective on, the written dialogue itself. In what follows, I suggest that the dialogues have this philosophical quality through and through—not only the represented dialogues, but also Plato's representing of them—and that this should determine our reading of them. Even the most unlikely aspects of their composition[45] may be best understood from the default position that Plato writes nothing in vain.

# 8. QUESTION AND ANSWER

In almost all the dialogues, people talk about big abstract questions: the nature of reality, truth, virtue, knowledge. These conversations come in all sorts of shapes and sizes, but they are often conducted by question and answer, by one person asking questions of another.[46]

Why does Plato use conversation like this? Is it the compulsion of culture, the regular practice of classical antiquity for theoretical discussion? Compare, for

---

41. Compare *Protagoras* 329a–b, and *Epistulae VII* 341 ff.

42. J. Derrida, "Plato's Pharmacy," in *Dissemination*, trans. Barbara Johnson (Chicago, 1981), and Ferrari, *Cicadas*.

43. For example, H. J. Krämer, *Plato and the Foundations of Metaphysics*, trans. J. R. Caton (Albany, N.Y., 1990), and T. A. Szlezak, *Reading Plato* (London, 1999); see also Reale and Scolnicov, *Good*.

44. For example, L. Strauss, *The City and the Man* (Chicago, 1964), but see Burnyeat, "Sphinx."

45. Aristotle's answers in the *Parmenides* are still a challenge, though . . .

46. The three-sided conversation of *Laches* 194 ff. is an exception.

example, the debates in Thucydides,[47] or the formalized conversations of drama,[48] or the *dissoi logoi* of the sophistic tradition.[49] Or is it—more strongly—a philosophical claim: that theoretical discussion can only be carried out within a particular culture?[50] (Tough luck for us, reading Plato from a distance.) This might condemn in advance any attempt by us to abstract arguments from the dialogues or to find some kind of disengaged philosophical viewpoint therein. Can there be a view from outside the culture upon what happens within, whether an Archimedean point from which to make judgment about the arguments represented there, or a way for us here and now to read the dialogues?[51]

Well, it seems that the business of question and answer is an explicit method of proceeding in philosophical inquiry. Socrates sometimes suggests that question and answer is either the right way to proceed or the only way *he* is able to proceed:[52] consider the extraordinary moment in the *Protagoras* (334c–d) where he complains that he cannot remember long speeches—even though he is the narrator of the whole dialogue. Other protagonists have the same commitment to question and answer: for example, the Eleatic Stranger at *Statesman* 285 and Parmenides at *Parmenides* 137. And many interlocutors explicitly accept this way of going about the business in hand (for example, Gorgias at *Gorgias* 457 ff. ; Protarchus at *Philebus* 19; and Euthydemus and Dionysodorus at *Euthydemus* 275–76[53]), even if others refuse, either in practice, or directly (for example, Protagoras, at *Protagoras* 335c, 348b–c; compare *Hippias Major* 291a). As a consequence of this self-consciousness, proceeding by question and answer is itself subject to scrutiny: What recommends it?

First, the process is sequential: one answer provokes another question, and so on (compare *Symposium* 204d). So the salience of answer to question, and of question to the preceding answer, brings order to the discussion.[54] This shows up in the limiting cases, where what the interlocutor says precludes his answering any further question: for example, the monists of *Sophist* 244c are unable to sustain a conversation at all, and this is taken to be so successful a rebuttal that it amounts to murder.

47. For example, the Mytilenean debate, 3.37 ff., and the Melian debate, 5.87 ff.

48. For example, the debate between the right and the wrong arguments at Aristophanes' *Clouds*, 900 ff., or between Antigone and Creon at Sophocles, *Antigone* 435 ff.

49. Diels/Kranz 90.

50. See R. Rorty, *Philosophy and the Mirror of Nature* (Princeton, 1979).

51. Compare B. A. O. Williams, *Ethics and the Limits of Philosophy* (London, 1985), with Williams, *Shame and Necessity* (Berkeley, 1993).

52. On the "Socratic method," see, among many others, Vlastos, *Socrates*; T. Brickhouse and N. Smith, *Socrates on Trial* (Princeton, 1989); Brickhouse and Smith, *The Philosophy of Socrates* (Boulder, 2000); H. H. Benson, *Essays on the Philosophy of Socrates* (New York, 1992); and Benson, *Socratic Wisdom: The Model of Knowledge in Plato's Early Dialogues* (New York, 2000).

53. Here the process is subverted and made even more self-conscious: the brothers claim, 275e, that whatever their interlocutor says he will be refuted.

54. For example, the connectives at *Charmides* 159c–160b, and the explicit conclusions at 160b3 and 7; or the way in which the method of collection and division is allied to questioning to produce order at *Statesman* 281.

Second, this order is connected to a constraint on both answer and question: the views put forward by any discussant should be internally consistent (*Charmides* 164c–d; *Gorgias* 491b–c; *Euthydemus* 287a–b; *Euthyphro* 15c). This seems, indeed, to be a constraint on what is said or believed that is somehow fundamental to the interlocutors themselves (*Gorgias* 482b–c). Inconsistency, that is to say, is somehow a fault or a danger, so much so that its discovery provokes all sorts of emotional anguish, evidenced by physiological effects: blushing (*Republic* 350d), gaping (*Charmides* 169c); and psychological disturbance, including irritation (*Gorgias* 489) and confusion (*Meno* 80).

Third, as a consequence both of the ordered nature of question and answer and of its demand for consistency, the process is also reflective. If a later answer is inconsistent with an earlier one, or out of order, this causes trouble, which is then explicitly discussed (for example, *Phaedo* 92c; *Charmides* 164d; *Laches* 193e). Contrariwise, some sophists notoriously reject this condition on conversation (Euthydemus and Dionysodorus at *Euthydemus* 283–88, Protagoras at *Theaetetus* 151–71), but Socrates supposes that rejection to be self-defeating (*Euthydemus* 288a; *Theaetetus* 178–79). As these conversations are presented, then, they are presented under reflective scrutiny, not only for the content of what is said but also for its integrity and good order.

But, fourth, there is not merely a demand for consistency at all costs—mere consistency might just give us a coherent collection of someone's beliefs, with no claims on the truth, or it could be secured at the price of refusing to engage in philosophical conversation at all. On the contrary, the burden of the questioning is repeatedly to elicit the reasons that some earlier claim might be true: the dominant question is a demand for some kind of explanation (for example, *Euthyphro* 10–11; compare *Phaedo* 96 ff.). Explanation is fundamental, indeed, to the structure of question and answer, or at least as it is practiced in these Platonic conversations.

# 9. CONVERSATION AND DIALECTIC

Conversations, then, could be analyzed formally in terms of sequence, order, consistency, and explanatory structure. Just as the discussions between Parmenides and Aristotle could be restated as linear arguments, the same might be done for more complex passages: for example, the last argument for the immortality of the soul at *Phaedo* 102–7[55] or the argument to deny the possibility of weakness of will at *Protagoras* 353–58.[56] In that case, could we edit out a great deal of the individual

---

55. This argument is demarcated by the interruption of the frame at 102a–b and terminated with Simmias' qualified agreement at 107a. Compare the formal analysis of Gallop, *Phaedo*.

56. This argument is demarcated by the imagined participation of "the many," expressly begun at 353a and terminated at 358a. Compare the formal analysis of G. Santas, *Socrates: Philosophy in Plato's Early Dialogues* (London, 1979), ch. 7.

dialogues, forsaking the conversational details altogether? This would be a mistake. For it misses, not only the variety of the dialogue form but also the way in which the argumentative material extends—I say indefinitely—beyond the passages that seem to be the best candidates for formalization. And it misses the way in which this breadth brings the conditions for argument themselves into philosophical view.

To repeat the point with which I began, these dialogues are not uniform. And they are not committed to conversations of a particular sort, or even to conversation at all. Conversation predominates when Socrates is engaged on the inquisition of some unfortunate acquaintance—encountered going about his business, and falling into the trap of explaining what he is doing to the indefatigable Socrates (Euthyphro or Ion, for examples). In such cases, one party seems to have—to begin with, at least—some definitive and determinate point of view, which comes under scrutiny in the questions and answers that follow.[57] Here, then, the person who answers is being examined. Sometimes, both interlocutors seem to have a view: for example, in the *Gorgias*, Callicles maintains that natural justice is the exercise of power without the control of reason, while Socrates denies it (482 ff.); in the *Philebus*, Socrates starts out as the advocate of the life of pure reason, Protarchus the advocate of some kind of hedonism (12–22). On other occasions, it is the questioner who seems to occupy the philosophical position, but still his interlocutors perform a pivotal role. For example, the two objections made by Simmias and Cebes at *Phaedo* 84d ff. dictate the course of the rest of the dialogue; Glaucon's challenge at *Republic* 357a ff. informs the nine books that follow. In other dialogues, where the role of the answerer seems exiguous (e.g., *Sophist* or *Statesman*),[58] the significance of question and answer is brought into sharp relief at the moments when the interlocutor does actually say something that matters (for example, *Statesman* 299e, *Euthydemus* 290).[59]

Sometimes, instead, there is a striking contrast between lengthy exegesis and conversation. The most notable example may be the paratactic structure of the *Symposium*, which presents a series of separate speeches about love[60] but whose final speech contains a dialogue between Socrates and Diotima, the role of protagonist sharply reversed.[61] On other occasions, one question and answer session is oddly embedded in another; this occurs when the interlocutors imagine some third party responding to questions (e.g., *Apology* 26b ff; *Republic* 476–80; *Protagoras*

---

57. Sometimes, as in the cases of Euthyphro or Ion, this is a claim to knowledge—the same goes for the sophists Socrates talks to: Gorgias, Protagoras, Hippias, Euthydemus, and Dionysodorus. Sometimes the view to be examined has to be teased out of him: as in Charmides, at *Charmides* 158, or Lysis and Menexenus at *Lysis* 207.

58. Aristotle is introduced as someone "who will give the least trouble" (*Parmenides* 137b); likewise, Theaetetus at *Sophist* 217c–d.

59. At *Sophist* 252d, Theaetetus is positively prolix; this has the effect of emphasizing his claim there about contradiction; and compare 256b (although the text there is suspect).

60. The arrangement is emphasized by Aristophanes' famous attack of the hiccups that displaces the planned order of the speeches.

61. The *Euthydemus* has a similar paratactic construction.

351 ff.; *Theaetetus* 170). Differently again, in the *Timaeus*, the long speech of Timaeus is preceded by a prologue between Socrates and the others present.[62] Yet again, some dialogues make play with other forms of discourse: the *Phaedrus* offers the reading of some speeches—of which at least one is ostentatiously spurious; the *Gorgias, Phaedo,* and *Republic* close with elaborate myths.[63]

These differences—both within and between dialogues—matter. For the display of different modes of argument goes along with a discussion of how arguments should work, and this discussion is provoked even by those cases where conversation either ostentatiously fails or just runs out (e.g., *Euthydemus* 303; *Protagoras* 334–35; *Gorgias* 523a; *Phaedo* 90–91). In these cases, there is a critical relation between what is said (about the serious significance of conversation for philosophical discussion) and how it is said (in conversation, or failing conversation), and this relation is itself the focus of philosophical attention. As Socrates suggests at *Republic* 534d8–535a1, conversation is the way that philosophy should proceed:

"So you would legislate, would you, that they should most of all receive that education through which they would be able to ask and answer questions in the most knowledgeable way?"

"Yes, I would so legislate—and you with me, too. "

"So do you suppose," I said, "that dialectic lies at the top for us, like a coping-stone on our studies, and that there is no other subject that should rightly be put higher than it, but that it provides now the end to our inquiries into education?"

It should proceed that way, it seems, both by dialogue between persons and by dialogue within a person—for that is what thinking is: a "silent dialogue within the soul":

Socrates: A talk which the soul has with itself about the objects under its consideration. Of course, I am only telling you my idea in all ignorance; but this is the kind of picture I have of it. It seems to me that the soul when it thinks is simply carrying on a discussion in which it asks itself questions and answers them itself, affirms and denies. And when it arrives at something definite, either by a gradual process or a sudden leap, when it affirms one thing consistently and without divided counsel, we call this its judgment. (*Theaetetus* 189e–190a)[64]

The paradigm of philosophical activity, then, is dialectical discussion;[65] this is portrayed and reflected on by the dialogues. Philosophical discussion thus takes

62. See M. F. Burnyeat, "First Words" ["Words"], *Proceedings of the Cambridge Philological Society* 43 (1998): 1–20. The *Menexenus* has the same form.

63. On Platonic myths, see, for example, J. Annas, "Plato's Myths of Judgement," *Phronesis* 27 (1982): 119–43, and K. Morgan, *Myth and Philosophy: From the Presocratics to Plato.* (Cambridge, 2000).

64. *Theaetetus* 189–90; *Philebus* 38c ff.; and *Sophist* 263e. On *Republic* 523–25, see M. M. McCabe "Dialectic Is as Dialectic Does," in *The Virtuous Life in Greek Ethics*, ed. B. Reis (Cambridge, 2006).

65. The technical expression *dialektikē* is derived from *dialegesthai*, "to converse"; see especially *Republic* 454a; 511b–c; 532–33. Aristotle follows in the same tradition: *Metaphysics* B1.

place at both levels of discourse within the dialogues—it takes place, therefore, across frame and picture, so it involves both what is represented and its representation. What is more, the contrast between different modes of discourse becomes evident when we read, just because the dialogues are composed in ways that make us notice their composition—such as, for example, their fictionality. The conditions for philosophical discourse, as a consequence, are themselves subject to the reader's active and reflective scrutiny.

# 10. THE PSYCHOLOGY OF DIALECTIC

Should we still say that this allows us to select those parts of the dialogues that constitute argument, of the general, abstract sort, and to dispense with the rest? Plato's conversations, in their variety, cannot be reduced to an impersonal form, however. For built in to these models of conversation are (at least) four psychological conditions.

The first is the way in which views are *held* by the interlocutors. Sometimes someone offers a thesis that they hold dear (for example, Critias at *Charmides* 164d). This leads the characters to difficulties in the sequel: when their claim is attacked, they themselves mind about it.[66] At other times, responsibility for the views in question is delegated to someone not present (for example, at *Republic* 476e ff.), but these absent characters are themselves characterized as committed to the view (*Republic* 476d). How far is this feature of the dialogues ineluctably ad hominem? How far does it fail a demand that philosophical discussion should be somehow general? And what does it have to do with us at a distance, as we read?

The second psychological condition invites the same objection. Sometimes an interlocutor is reduced by Socrates to puzzlement, to *aporia*. Meno, for example, complains that Socrates has reduced him to numbness by showing that the views he thought he held consistently cannot be sustained together (*Meno* 80a ff.). This puzzlement, Socrates protests, has its own dynamic: for puzzlement is part of what compels one to continue to search for the answers to the questions with which one began. It seems, then, a part of the psychology of the drama we see: a feature attributed to one (or both) of the interlocutors and particular to them. Formal arguments don't feel puzzled.

Third, more happens in the dialogues than simply the reduction of someone to *aporia*. For the interlocutor is sometimes able to rethink his position, to alter his allegiance, to change his mind. This reflects a feature of some conversations: that they represent two different points of view, in tension with each other, and that it is possible, engaged on such a conversation, to take up different positions, to shift perspective (e.g., Protarchus at *Philebus* 23a). This, indeed, seems to be what the

66. Of course, since these are fictional characters, the sense of "themselves" minding about it is odd.

"silent dialogue" claims: that we are able, when we think, to occupy different viewpoints (or to have different parts of our souls do so), to conduct an internal conversation in which one side asserts and the other denies the same thing—without risking contradiction or psychological damage. This suggests, further, that we are able to entertain a view, instead of committing ourselves to it.[67] Likewise, engaged on a conversation, we may find ourselves stepping outside the position we originally occupied and understanding a different point of view.

Fourth, this "stepping outside" may occur at a remove. For not only do the characters of a dialogue engage on a conversation and reflect on their own and their interlocutor's positions from outside. They are also able to notice, inspect, think about the whole process of a conversation. Consider occasions where the interlocutors imagine a conversation with someone else—imaginary or otherwise absent: for example, the conversation with the "other Socrates" at *Hippias Major* 286c ff.[68] Here the frame interlocutors imagine the two different points of view and their resolution, from the outside. Their position need not be committed to either point of view; instead, it is broadly reflective on both. This is a psychological phenomenon, not merely a logical one: call it detachment.[69]

# 11. DETACHMENT

Detachment, this reflection at a remove, is neither limited to the characters within the dialogues nor just exemplified therein. For it is also something we do when we read: we look at the conversations represented in the dialogue, and at the reflections on them provided by the dialogue, from outside. This, I suggest, is the role of the elaborate play between history and fiction in which some dialogues engage: in puzzling about whether this or that story is true, we bring into focus the relation between ourselves (reading here and now) and whatever did or did not happen then. The dialogues' tension between historicity and fiction thus renders our role as readers self-conscious. Then we are not passive spectators, not mere recipients of some knowledge conveyed by one character or another. On the contrary, we are actively engaged in reflection, both on the represented dialogue and on the way the dialogue is written for us to read.

Consider some generic differences in the way conversation is presented from dialogue to dialogue. Some are directly presented: the *Laches*, for example, offers us a play-like conversation between Lysimachus, Laches, Nicias, and Socrates (compare, for example, *Meno*, *Euthyphro*, *Cratylus*, and *Philebus*). Indeed, this formula

---

67. Compare the occupation of a position for the sake of argument, as by Glaucon at *Republic* 358, and by Simmias and Cebes at *Phaedo* 77e.

68. Compare *Republic* 476–80, or the framing of the *Parmenides* in an outer narrative.

69. On detachment, in the context of two independent discussions, see McCabe, *Predecessors*, e.g. 125; Halliwell, *Mimesis*, 79 ff.

may encourage us to identify with one or another character, as well as to change our identification to Socrates, as the dialogue proceeds. Three dialogues reinforce this thought, for they are narrated by Socrates, told from his perspective: *Charmides*, *Lysis*, and *Republic*. Here we might imagine that Socrates is speaking to an imaginary audience—or even that he speaks directly to us as we read. Should we think, then, that his privileged voice is the only one we should hear or obey; or should we notice the contrivance itself?

The *Sophist* and the *Statesman*, too, proffer the philosophical discussion directly in dialogue, but now the privileged voice is that of the Eleatic Stranger. These two dialogues are explicitly tied to the *Theaetetus*, which has an elaborate opening of a quite different sort. For the story is told—years later—within a direct dialogue between Euclides and Terpsion. Euclides has a written record (with good credentials: it was checked by Socrates, 143a) of the encounter between Socrates, Theodorus, and Theaetetus, and he proposes to read it out, but as if in direct speech, missing all the "and he said . . ." bits. This frame dialogue should frame not only the discussion that follows but also the two sequels, even though Euclides makes no promise to tell us about the meeting with the Eleatic Stranger. This could be mere carelessness, of course: the connection between the three dialogues is trivial, a surface matter and of no significance to how we understand the dialogue. But the opening of the *Theaetetus* calls our attention to how the dialogue is presented, especially to the difference between direct and indirect reportage. At the very least, this makes us notice the contrivances of the fiction, as well as the differences of style, and reflect on our distance from the story we are told.

In the *Phaedo*, too, the story is told by two people (Echecrates and Phaedo) and provoked by a death and its circumstances. But later in the dialogue the frame interrupts the narration, twice. First, at 88c, the two objections of Simmias and Cebes against the arguments for the immortality of the soul, have been voiced, and Phaedo and Echecrates discuss the devastating effect of those objections, *both* on Socrates' friends as they sat in prison *and* on Echecrates and Phaedo as they consider it from their later viewpoint. Second, at 102a, when Socrates has just pronounced some of the most vexed and impenetrable arguments of the dialogue, Echecrates interrupts again, saying that "he made these things wonderfully clear to anyone of even small intelligence."[70] Both interruptions reflect on the state of mind of the people *hearing* the arguments: both the audience within the narrated story and those who hear it later. But they also serve to remind the reader of her own position. For while the first interruption may underline our sympathy for the characters of the dialogue, the second emphasizes our alienation from them. In so doing, the pair of interruptions provokes us to think more directly about our own perspective on what we are being told.

The same device of the interruption of the frame dialogue is found at the central point of the *Euthydemus*. Socrates, narrating the previous day's events to

---

70. The existence of a vast literature on the interpretation of the method of hypothesis bears witness to the impenetrability of Socrates' words: this interruption, then, should surprise us.

Crito, says that Cleinias has made a certain objection to Socrates' argument and (disingenuously, perhaps) that the objection is a good one. Crito interrupts with a vigorous disagreement (*Euthydemus* 290), incredulous that it could have been Cleinias who made the objection. As a consequence, the framed argument continues in the frame, between Socrates and Crito, and discussing not only who could have said what but also what constraints on argument and agreement there should be (291b, 292e). The shift to the frame both adds this methodological reflection and brings to our attention the framing procedure itself. We are shaken from merely identifying with the characters (since we are no longer sure who said what) into something far more detached and reflective—and the reflection is focused not only on the original subject but also on the nature of argument itself.[71]

In cases such as these, the reader may have two different views of what she reads. The rich portrayal of character and situation—Socrates, his friends, his opponents, at dinner, in prison, at the gymnasium—encourages her to identify with one or another of the characters (sometimes alternating, as they speak) and to feel their theoretical commitments, either as if they were her own or at least with sympathetic understanding. In this way, we come to understand different arguments and philosophical positions, to consider, at first hand, the arguments put forward in the dialogue. By contrast, when we are shocked, by devices in the frame, into looking *at* what is going on, we do so from this position of detachment, contemplating both points of view from the outside. We both consider the sorts of conditions that will come to bear on either point of view, including the conditions for argument as such, and think about the subject in question from a position of detached reflection. So, I suggest, the active role of the reader is crucial to understanding why the dialogue is multiform.

## 12. ETHICAL RATIONALISM

Still, does this reflectiveness account for the dialogue form in its particularity, or of the local purposes of Plato's varied use of dialogue? Suppose that there are some central philosophical issues addressed in each dialogue—the nature of virtue, the possibility of knowledge, the structure of reality. Allow, further, that in some dialogues Plato focuses attention on just how we may address those issues—by thinking, for example, about either the possibility of discovery (*Meno* 80 ff), or the nature of truth and the possibility of falsehood (*Theaetetus* and *Sophist*), or the constraints on contradiction (*Euthydemus*), or the nature and significance of philosophy itself (for example, *Phaedo*, *Republic*, *Theaetetus* 172–77, and in the *Sophist/Statesman/[Philosopher]* trilogy). How are these aspects of the dialogues connected? We might think that the dialogue form gives us access to the general,

---

71. Compare the elaborate frame of the *Parmenides*, which vanishes by the end of the dialogue and leaves us with an extreme, and unresolved, contradiction.

methodological questions but that this is quite separate from the issues of virtue and reality, which are tackled by Plato's characters. How are we to make the connection between detached reflection, and what we should reflect *about?*

I have suggested that the questions about how to do philosophy, the general methodological questions raised in the frame dialogues, are not to be construed as generating merely formal constraints on argument, for, I argued, these formal constraints include psychological conditions. The methodology, therefore, already has considerable content. But there is more.

Return to those dialogues where we see Socrates investigating the views of his interlocutor—the dialogues where Socrates seems to advance little that is positive of his own—apart, of course, from the vital discussions we find in each case of how to go about answering the questions. In the *Crito*, for example, the discussion between Socrates and Crito about the nature of moral justification affects the action they are considering: Should Socrates escape from prison? Or Euthyphro's false claims to expertise underpin, and undermine, what he does: If he has no expertise, how can he justify prosecuting his father? As the frame dialogue articulates the long sections of argument by asking just what the conditions for knowledge are (at 6d, 8a, 9c, 11b, 14c, 15c), it addresses what both Socrates and Euthyphro should do. Here claims to knowledge are connected to what should be done; if they fail, this should have an immediate effect on what is done. But the claims about knowledge themselves are subject to the constraints about explanation and consistency governing the formality of dialectic. The formal conditions for argument and for explanation, therefore, are not separable from the ethical questions that are the content of the arguments.

This is not merely an issue for those who lay direct claim to knowledge about moral matters. After all, in many passages, Socrates suggests that all knowledge is integrated (for example, *Euthydemus* 281; *Republic* 508d ff.). This, at least, asks how we should understand the relations between knowledge of one sort (of shoemaking, for example) and of another (of the good, for example), or the relation between knowledge and the virtue of wisdom. And it is a question that seeks an ethical answer, as well as an epistemological one. But the relation between moral matters and formality goes deeper.

Consider the attack by the sophists of the *Euthydemus* on the possibility of contradiction (285d–288a). They take the view (if a view it could be called) that—since everything they say is true—no one can contradict anyone else, or even themselves. If this is correct, consistency does not matter and they themselves cannot be refuted. The consequence of this, of course, is that the rules for argument break down altogether, including the rules for the argument that would rebut it. How, in the face of this, are we to reclaim the possibility of argument? Socrates offers metaphysical suggestions—suggestions about the persistence and integrity of the person[72] to

---

72. At *Protagoras* 311b, Socrates asks of Hippocrates: "Who would you become [if you learn from the sophist]?" At *Euthydemus* 291a, Crito is incredulous that Ctesippus could have said what Socrates reports: "What sort of Ctesippus [said that]?" The opening word of the *Phaedo* is "yourself"; see Burnyeat, "Words."

whom the rules of argument apply—to support his claim that the sophists are wrong. But those metaphysical suggestions are compelling because they are based on ethical considerations: without persistence and integrity, there would be nothing that it is for us to live a life. Since a life—the best life—is what we seek, we are bound to suppose that we persist and then to agree that consistency matters. The constraints—if this is right—on argument come from a complex network of theory: from assumptions about knowledge, about reality and identity, and about value, which provide the content of the individual discussions of individual dialogues. I call this "ethical rationalism," and it runs through the dialogues, in frame and picture alike. As a consequence, Plato commits himself—in his ways of writing—to a substantial philosophical position: that there is no line of demarcation between the constraints of logic and those of ethics, of psychology or metaphysics, or epistemology. The dialogues, in different ways, with different interests, with varying assumptions and starting points, suppose that the relation between what is said, how it is said, and who said it is intimate.

## 13. Representation and Reading the Dialogues

We can still draw a line between where the characters represented stand and where Plato stands as he represents them: the line between the frame and the picture is not a contrast between what does and what does not matter to philosophy but between the orders of reflection on what is said. Equally, therefore, we can draw a line between what Plato writes and what stance we may occupy in reading. For as we read, we identify with different positions, and then—also as we read—we are shocked out of that identification into a position of detachment, of reflection *on* the positions with which identification is possible. What happens to us then is exactly parallel to—but not identical with—what happens to any interlocutor: we take a position, then look at it from without. This detachment allows us to see just how complex a matter it is to occupy a philosophical position at all and how to do so—if ethical rationalism is true—involves all our various commitments.

This, we may now see, gives us an account of why the dialogues represent people in conversation with one another, and in quite different ways. There may be no single story to be told of how, for example, personal identity, or psychological unity, is maintained for all the dialogues. The questions each dialogue asks range over a wide range of abstract questions, and they do so by virtue of setting direct conversations in a dramatic context, in all the many ways in which that is done.

This means, in the first instance, that we should read the dialogues one by one, alert to the internal nuances of context and reference, and read them whole. This is not, I have been arguing, merely a matter of tone or of emotional engagement but, rather, a matter of the constraints on argument and, connectedly, on what arguments can reasonably maintain. Consider how the first part of the *Parmenides* (127–136)—where, notoriously, the venerable figure of Parmenides puts apparently lethal objections to Socrates' theory of forms—portrays Socrates as a young man. Frequently, this is construed as a coded message, that we should not take Parmenides' arguments to be decisive. But we should avoid reading such coding piecemeal: What, in the same context, are we to say of the figure of Parmenides, apparently a committed monist (and so opposed to Socrates' theory), who announces that without the theory of forms we lose the power of dialectic—the power that he himself wields throughout the dialogue (when he loses it in the *Sophist*, he dies)? The setting of this dialogue makes our response to the arguments indeterminate because both sides are loaded. The framing of the dialogue, striking as it is, makes this indeterminacy itself the focus of critical attention and reflects, in turn, on the standing of the arguments against the forms.

Or the *Theaetetus* finds itself unable to say just how someone could come to believe falsely, at least in the absence of perception (200b–c). The puzzle about falsehood, in this dialogue, is partly a problem in the philosophy of mind—a problem of explaining just how we could *come to be* wrong about things. But it follows the denial of Protagoras' claim that everything is true—a denial that rests on a dialectical refutation of Protagoras' view. That refutation, in turn, relies on the suggestion that if dialectic is possible, then we can be wrong about things and can disagree. If the interlocutors engage in conversation, then disagreement is possible; if we disagree, then the disagreement is realized as we read.

The *Philebus* opens (and closes) in the middle of a discussion of the best life, which should be perfect and self-sufficient (20d–21a). Discussion should have the same characteristics, and be determinate, complete, and sufficient (19e–20a), but discussion with Philebus can never be so since his extreme hedonism admits of no limitation at all. The way the discussion with Philebus fails[73] is designed to show that the preferred life, the life rationally chosen, must be itself susceptible to rationality and that extreme hedonism is intolerable. It does so once we reflect on the conditions for this dialogue: it does so when we read, reflectively and detached.

## 14. INTERTEXTUALITY

But there is something else again: for the dialogues invite us not only to be self-conscious readers of any one dialogue but also to attend to others, in an equally self-conscious way. The interconnections between *Theaetetus*, *Sophist*, *Statesman*, and the missing *Philosopher*, for example, are peculiar. The *Theaetetus* is a story told years later about the discussion between Socrates, Theodorus, and Theaetetus

73. See McCabe, *Predecessors*, ch. 4.

(along with some of Theaetetus' friends). The *Sophist* continues the same conversation (now in direct speech; the recall of the *Theaetetus* has vanished) the following day, with a new character, the Eleatic Stranger. Then the *Statesman* continues the conversation (at some unspecified time) but fails to complete the discussion: the dialogue of the *Philosopher* does not exist.[74] There is, therefore, a formal continuity between the three extant dialogues, so that we are asked to notice that they are related. But the relation is very much more complicated than just that the *Sophist* and the *Statesman* provide us with more of the same. Instead, the *Sophist* reflects vividly back on places where the *Theaetetus* failed (e.g., at 236e) and also, perhaps, on places where the *Theaetetus* asks questions the *Sophist* does not answer (there is nothing in the *Sophist* that explains how we could *come to* make a mistake about an unrealized state of affairs, even if it tells us what it is to *have made* the mistake: false beliefs are false statements in our heads[75]). And the *Statesman* wonders, in its turn, just how—or whether—the reflections on dialectic to be found in the *Sophist* are to be integrated into life lived in the state.[76]

We might say the same of the relation between the *Republic* and the *Timaeus*,[77] dialogues that at first seem to be describing the same event—a two-day conversation Socrates had after the festival of a goddess (*Republic* 327a, *Timaeus* 21a). But then it becomes clear that the *Republic*'s goddess is the Thracian Bendis, while the *Timaeus*' is Athena, the patron of Athens.[78] Is this mere carelessness? Well, once this forces the reader to think harder about the relation between the *Republic* and the *Timaeus*, she should notice, too, that what seems like a summary of the *Republic* at the opening of the *Timaeus* in fact leaves out all the central metaphysical and epistemological material of books V–VII. The "compare and contrast" that this invites is critical: What is the importance of the central books to the theory advanced by Socrates in the *Republic*? How is that altered by the account of cosmic teleology offered by Timaeus? How are the two accounts of the way things really are consistent? The setting of the *Timaeus* prevents us from restricting our reading of it to the *Timaeus* alone, and it brings the *Timaeus*' relation to the *Republic* into philosophical view.

We may say the same of the extraordinarily large intertextuality of other dialogues. Sometimes the trick is turned by the same sort of language (e.g., the motif of sticks and stones at *Phaedo* 74b ff, *Parmenides* 129d); sometimes by the allusion to some particular person (e.g., Euthydemus, whose theory of total assimilation is described at *Cratylus* 386d); and sometimes in ways that are rather more specific (e.g., the reference to an argument for recollection at *Phaedo* 72e[79]).

---

74. Of course, Plato might have died before he wrote it, but the complex interconnections between *Theaetetus*, *Sophist*, and *Statesman* suggest that its omission was deliberate.

75. See sec. 9 on the silent dialogue.

76. Notice the unclarity of the myth about just what constitutes the best life, or even about what constitutes a life at all: 269–74.

77. The *Republic* does not specify Socrates' audience; this is not inconsistent with the *Timaeus*' representation that Socrates was, on the occasion to which he alludes at *Timaeus* 17a, talking to Timaeus, Critias, and Hermogenes.

78. See *Republic* 354a10 and *Timaeus* 26e.

79. This cross-reference invites the reader to remember, in a context where what it is to remember is at issue.

Sometimes one passage seems to offer a critique of another (e.g., *Euthydemus* 293b-296d on *Meno* 81 on recollection), sometimes the point, or the direction, of an allusion remains obscure.[80] The one characteristic of these passages is that they are allusive, inexact, puzzling. They run true to what I have described as the detaching effect of the dialogues—for they urge not only a similarity between the two passages in question but also a difference. In so doing, they militate against the thought that what we have here are somehow references to a single body of fixed doctrine, underpinning all the dialogues. They equally, and for the same reasons, militate against the thought that we are being offered here coded references to some esoteric thinking, private to the initiated. For, on the contrary, the critical reflection to which we are invited by these cross-references is symmetrical with the reflection invited in us by other passages and with the reflection portrayed in the characters at the many levels of the narration. Nothing here requires us to suppose, that is to say, that we have here merely a vehicle for Platonic doctrine or, contrariwise, to suppose that the dialogues repudiate positive views altogether. Instead, views are indeed put forward in the dialogues, and for some of those views, the author must take responsibility. But in writing the way he does, he engages his readers, too, in active scrutiny of what is said: a large part of the philosophical work, therefore, is done by us, the readers of what Plato writes.[81]

# BIBLIOGRAPHY

Allen, R. E. *Plato's Parmenides, Translation and Analysis* (Oxford, 1983).

Annas, J. "Plato's Myths of Judgement," *Phronesis* 27 (1982): 119–43.

Annas, J., and Rowe, C., eds. *New Perspectives on Plato, Modern and Ancient* (Cambridge, Mass., 2002).

Barnes, J. *The Cambridge Companion to Aristotle* (Cambridge, 1995).

Benson, H. H. *Essays on the Philosophy of Socrates* (New York, 1992).

———. *Socratic Wisdom: The Model of Knowledge in Plato's Early Dialogues* (New York, 2000).

Beversluis, J. *Cross-Examining Socrates: A Defense of the Interlocutors in Plato's Early Dialogues* (Cambridge, 2000).

Bloch, E. "Hemlock Poisoning and the Death of Socrates: Did Plato Tell the Truth?" in T. Brickhouse and N. Smith, eds., *The Trial and Execution of Socrates* (Oxford, 2001).

Blondell, R. *The Play of Character in Plato's Dialogues* (Cambridge, 2002).

Brickhouse, T., and Smith, N. *The Philosophy of Socrates* (Boulder, 2000).

———. *Socrates on Trial* (Princeton, 1989).

---

80. What is the relation between the sudden mention of dialecticians at *Euthydemus* 290c and the account of the philosopher-kings of the central books of the *Republic*?

81. I have, as always, benefited from discussion with many people about these topics: my particular thanks to Peter Adamson, Hugh Benson, Sarah Broadie, Gail Fine, Christopher Gill, Verity Harte, Dominic Scott, Nick Smith, Raphael Woolf, and especially to Owen Gower, Jonas Green, Alex Long, and Imogen Smith. My thanks, also, to the Leverhulme Trust for the Major Research Fellowship during the tenure of which I wrote this essay.

Burnyeat, M. F. *Culture and Society in Plato's* Republic. The Tanner Lectures on Human Values (Harvard, 1999).

———. "First Words," *Proceedings of the Cambridge Philological Society* 43 (1998): 1–20.

———. "Plato on the Grammar of Perceiving," *Classical Quarterly* 26 (1976): 29–51.

———. "Sphinx without a Secret?" *New York Review of Books*, May 30, 1985.

———. *The* Theaetetus *of Plato*, trans. M. J. Levett (Indianapolis, 1990).

Clay, D. *Platonic Questions: Dialogues with the Silent Philosopher* (University Park, Penn., 2000).

Cooper, J. M. *Plato: Complete Works* (Indianapolis, 1997).

———. "Plato on Sense-Perception and Knowledge (*Theaetetus* 184–6)," *Phronesis* 15 (1970): 123–65.

Cornford, F. M. *Plato and Parmenides* (London, 1939).

Derrida, J. "Plato's Pharmacy," in *Dissemination*, trans. Barbara Johnson (Chicago, 1981).

Ferrari, G. R. F. *Listening to the Cicadas: A Study of Plato's* Phaedrus (Cambridge, 1987).

Frede, M. "The Literary Form of the *Sophist*," in C. Gill and M. M. McCabe, eds., *Form and Argument in Late Plato* (Oxford, 1996).

Gadamer, H. *Dialogue and Dialectic: Eight Hermeneutical Studies of Plato*, trans P. C. Smith (New Haven, 1980).

Gallop, D. *Plato:* Phaedo (Oxford, 1975).

Gill, C. "The Death of Socrates," *Classical Quarterly* 23 (1973): 25–28.

———. "Speaking up for Plato's Interlocutors," *Oxford Studies in Ancient Philosophy* 20 (2001): 297–321.

———. "Critical Response to the Hermeneutical Approach from an Analytic Perspective" in G. Reale and S. Scolnicov, eds., *New Images of Plato: The Idea of the Good* (Sankt Augustin, 2002).

Gill, C., and McCabe, M. M., eds. *Form and Argument in Late Plato* [*Form*] (Oxford, 1996).

Halliwell, S. *The Aesthetics of Mimesis: Ancient Texts and Modern Problems* (Princeton, 2002).

Hunter, R. *Plato: Symposium* (Oxford, 2004).

Kahn, C. H. *Plato and the Socratic Dialogue: The Philosophical Use of a Literary Form* (Cambridge, 1996).

Krämer, H. J. *Plato and the Foundations of Metaphysics*, trans. J. R. Caton (Albany, N.Y., 1990).

Kraut, R. "Introduction to the Study of Plato," in R. Kraut, ed., *The Cambridge Companion to Plato*, 1–50 (Cambridge, 1992).

Long, A. G. "Character and Dialectic: The Philosophical Origins of the Platonic Dialogue," Ph.D. dissertation, University of Cambridge (2004).

———. "The Form of Plato's Republic," in R. Osborne, ed., *Debating the Athenian Cultural Revolution* (Cambridge, 2007).

McCabe, M. M. "Dialectic Is as Dialectic Does," in B. Reis, ed., *The Virtuous Life in Greek Ethics* (Cambridge, 2006).

———. "Irony in the Soul: Should Plato's Socrates Be Sincere?" in M. Trapp, ed., *Socrates*, (London, 2007).

———. *Plato and His Predecessors: The Dramatisation of Reason* (Cambridge, 2000).

Morgan, K. *Myth and Philosophy: From the Presocratics to Plato* (Cambridge, 2000).

Nails, D. *Agora, Academy and the Conduct of Philosophy* (Dordrecht, 1995).

———. *The People of Plato* (Indianapolis, 2002).

Nehamas, A. *The Art of Living: Socratic Reflections from Plato to Foucault.* (Berkeley, 1998).

———. *The Virtues of Authenticity* (Princeton, 2000).

Nightingale, A. *Genres in Dialogue: Plato and the Construct of Philosophy* (Cambridge, 1995).

Nussbaum, M. C. *The Fragility of Goodness: Luck and Ethics in Greek Tragedy and Philosophy* (Cambridge, 1986).

Owen, G. E. L. *Logic, Science and Dialectic* (London, 1986).

Press, G. A., ed. *'Who speaks for Plato?': Studies in Platonic Anonymity* (Lanham, 2000).

Reale, G., and Scolnicov, S., eds. *New Images of Plato: The Idea of the Good* (Sankt Augustin, 2002).

Roochnik, D. *The Tragedy of Reason* (New York, 1990).

Rorty, R. *Philosophy and the Mirror of Nature* (Princeton, 1979).

Rutherford, R. *The Art of Plato* (London, 1995).

Santas, G. *Socrates: Philosophy in Plato's Early Dialogues* (London, 1979).

Sayre, K. *Plato's Literary Garden: How to Read a Platonic Dialogue* (Notre Dame, 1995).

Sedley, D. N. *The Midwife of Platonism: Text and Subtext in Plato's* Theaetetus (Oxford, 2004).

———. "The *Theaetetus*: Three Interpretations," in C. Gill and M. M. McCabe, *Form and Argument in Late Plato* (Oxford, 1996).

Strauss, L. *The City and the Man* (Chicago, 1964).

Stokes, M. C. *Plato's Socratic Conversations* (London, 1980).

Szlezak, T. A. *Reading Plato* (London, 1999).

Vlastos, G. *Socrates, Ironist and Moral Philosopher* (Cambridge, 1991).

Williams, B. A. O. *Ethics and the Limits of Philosophy* (London, 1985).

———. *Shame and Necessity* (Berkeley, 1993).

CHAPTER 5

....................................................................................

# THE EPISTEMOLOGY
# AND METAPHYSICS
# OF SOCRATES

....................................................................................

## GARETH B. MATTHEWS

THE portrayal of Socrates in the early dialogues of Plato is the most vivid picture we have of any ancient philosopher. Prominent in that depiction is the story Socrates tells us in the *Apology* about his reaction to being told that, according to the oracle at Delphi, no one was wiser than he (21a). Socrates responded to this news, he says, by trying to find someone of whom he could say, "This man is wiser than I, but you said I was [wiser]" (21d).[1] At least part of his test for determining whether a given candidate was wiser than he was to determine if the candidate knew something "noble and good" (*kalon kagathon*). Socrates himself claimed to know nothing of that sort (21d).

Another part of his test was to see whether candidates thought they knew things that, in fact, they did not know. At *Apology* 22cd, Socrates says of the craftspeople that they knew many noble things [or fine or beautiful things, *polla kalla*], and so were, in that respect, wiser than he. But in the end, he concluded that they were not really wiser because they mistakenly thought themselves to be wise in other things. "This error of theirs," he explains, "overshadowed the wisdom they had" (22de). His own wisdom, he had already said, lay in his not thinking he knew what he did not know (21d). Apparently, no one excelled him in that!

On the face of it, the project of determining whether someone knows something noble and good is, at least in part, an epistemological project. So is the project of determining whether one thinks one knows something one does not really

---

1. All translations of Plato are taken from Cooper, *Plato: Complete Works*.

know. Both projects presuppose an understanding of what is to count as knowledge.

Some commentators claim that Socrates, as he is portrayed in the early dialogues of Plato, has no epistemology at all, or at least no epistemological *theory*. Thus Gregory Vlastos, the dean of Socrates scholars in the twentieth century, writes: "In fidelity to our texts no *epistemological theory* at all can be ascribed to Socrates."[2] Vlastos is equally dismissive of the suggestion that Socrates has a metaphysics. Socrates, he writes, "is as innocent of epistemology as of metaphysics." It is part of my purpose in this chapter to show how it can be appropriate to speak of the epistemology and the metaphysics of Socrates, but another part is to make clear why someone might also have doubts or reservations about whether Socrates even has an epistemology or a metaphysics at all.

An even more fundamental issue dogs the project of this chapter: namely, the problem of how we can know anything about the philosophy of the historical Socrates. We can call this "the problem of the historical Socrates." As I have already said, Plato has certainly given us an extremely vivid picture of Socrates in his early dialogues.[3] But one may well ask how we can know that the picture Plato has given us is historically accurate.

The answer is surely that we cannot know. As Charles Kahn so vividly puts the point, "The Socrates of the dialogues is an ambiguous figure, at once Plato's historical master and his literary puppet."[4] Still, the picture of Socrates in the early dialogues is a memorably coherent portrait of a philosopher whose views deserve careful interpretation, analysis, and criticism. It is the epistemology and metaphysics, if any, of the figure that emerges from that portrait that I discuss here. I leave aside the issue of whether we have good reason to think that that figure is, in fact, the historical Socrates.

In discussing the epistemology of Socrates, I focus especially on these three topics: Socratic Ignorance, the Priority of Definitional Knowledge, and the Problem of the Elenchus.

# SOCRATIC IGNORANCE

Socrates makes his claim of ignorance, or, more accurately and pedantically, his disclaimer of knowledge, in various forms. Here, from the *Apology*, is the example[5] of that disclaimer already mentioned above:

2. Vlastos, *Socrates: Ironist and Moral Philosopher*, 15.

3. I follow Vlastos in counting these as the early dialogues of Plato: *Apology, Charmides, Crito, Euthyphro, Gorgias, Hippias Minor, Ion, Laches, Protagoras, Republic* I (Vlastos, *Socrates: Ironist and Moral Philosopher*, 46–47).

4. Charles H. Khan, "Did Plato Write Socratic Dialogues?," in Benson, *Essays on the Philosophy of Socrates*, 35–52.

5. Other relevant passages include these: *Apology* 29b, *Charmides* 165bc, *Laches* 200e, *Gorgias* 509a, and *Hippias Minor* 372be.

T1. I am wiser than this man; it is likely that neither of us knows anything worthwhile [or: noble and good, *kalon kagathon*], but he thinks he knows something when he does not, whereas when I do not know, neither do I think I know. (21d)

We can distinguish at least two claims of ignorance in this passage:

C1. I do not know anything worthwhile (or: noble and good, *kalon kagathon*).
C2. I do not know, nor do I think I know, things that others think they know.

For another statement of Socratic ignorance, we can look to this passage from the dialogue, *Charmides*, where Socrates is speaking:

T2. "But Critias," I replied, "you are talking to me as though I professed to know the answers to my own questions and as though I could agree with you if I really wished. This is not the case—rather, because of my own ignorance, I am continually investigating in your company whatever is put forward. However, if I think it over, I am willing to say whether I agree or not. Just wait while I consider." (165bc)

In T2, Socrates seems to be making the following claim:

C3. I do not profess to know the answers to my own questions.

If we put these three claims, C1, C2, and C3, together, we get the picture that Socrates claims ignorance of (i) things noble and good, (ii) which others think they know, and (iii) which are the subject of his investigations when he questions his fellow Athenians. Although it is not immediately clear how extensive this knowledge disclaimer is, it seems to fall short of being a claim not to know anything at all. Indeed, a few pages later in the *Apology* Socrates says this about his practice of questioning his fellow Athenians:

T3. I know well enough [*oida schedon*] that this very conduct makes me unpopular. (24a)

And five pages later, he makes this morally significant claim:

T4. I do know [*oida*], however, that it is wicked and shameful to do wrong, to disobey one's superior, be he god or man. (29b)

Finally, the confident and well-targeted way in which he questions his interlocutors at least suggests that Socrates must know quite a bit about what he is inquiring into, even though he does not know what he most wants to know.

## COMPLETE IGNORANCE?

There is, however, at least one passage in a Platonic dialogue in which, astoundingly, Socrates claims total ignorance of what he is clearly most interested in—namely, virtue. What I have in mind is this passage from near the beginning of the dialogue, *Meno:*

> T5. Socrates: "I myself, Meno, am as poor as my fellow citizens in this matter, and I blame myself for my complete ignorance [literally, not knowing at all, *to parapan*] about virtue. If I do not know what something is, how could I know what qualities it possesses? Or do you think that someone who does not know at all [*to parapan*] who Meno is could know whether he is good-looking or rich or well-born, or the opposite of these? Do you think that it is possible?" (71b)

Socrates adds that he has never met anyone who did know what virtue is (71c).

What T5 commits Socrates to *seems* to be nothing less than this:

> C4. Neither I nor, as it seems to me, anyone I have met, knows at all what virtue is.

The fact that Socrates here claims not to know *at all* what virtue is, and repeats the "at all" [*to parapan*], should not be taken lightly. This is, in fact, the only dialogue in which Socrates claims not to know *at all* what F-ness is. It is natural to conclude that Socrates is here disclaiming knowledge that, for example, bravery is a virtue or that any token person or action is virtuous. Can this claim of complete ignorance of what virtue is be taken seriously?

Before we draw any rash conclusions from T5, we should note that the *Meno* seems to be a transitional dialogue. The first part of the dialogue is fairly typical of the early dialogues. But we soon come to the Paradox of Inquiry, which threatens the very rationality of Socratic inquiry:

> T6. How will you look for [virtue], Socrates, when you do not know at all [*to parapan*] what it is? How will you aim to search for something you do not know at all? If you should meet with it, how will you know that this is the thing that you did not know? (*Meno* 80d)

A few lines later, Socrates introduces, apparently in response to the Paradox of Inquiry, a grand epistemological and metaphysical hypothesis:

> T7. As the soul is immortal, has been born often and has seen all things here and in the underworld, there is nothing which it has not learned; so it is in no way surprising that it can recollect things it knew before, both about virtue and other things. As the whole of nature is akin, and the soul has learned everything, nothing prevents a man, after recalling one thing only—a process men call learning—discovering everything else for himself, if he is brave and

does not tire of the search, for searching and learning are, as a whole, recollection. (*Meno* 81cd)

T7 seems to entail the denial of T5. The idea it expresses is that, instead of Socrates being completely ignorant of virtue, "there is nothing which the soul has not learned."[6] In the context, the implication of this claim seems to be that "the soul," and so, presumably, the soul of Socrates, as well as the souls of his interlocutors, have already learned, among other things, what virtue is. The knowledge that "the soul" has may, at any given time, be only latent, until it is made manifest through recollection.[7] However, since "the whole of nature is akin," it seems that one who can manage to recollect a single bit of relevant knowledge may be able to regain manifest knowledge of what he latently knows about other things—provided "he is brave and does not tire of the search."

If we now read T5 in light of T7, we see that we should probably understand Socrates' claim in T5 to be in "complete ignorance" about what virtue is to be only this: he does not know at all *manifestly* what virtue is, even though he knows *latently* everything there is to know.

Let's return now to claims C1, C2, and C3. Putting them together, and adding a reference to the distinction we get in the *Meno* between manifest and latent knowledge, we get something like this as the claim of Socratic ignorance:

C5. Socrates claims that (i) he does not know (manifestly) anything noble and good, where (ii) knowing something noble and good would bring with it the ability to answer satisfactorily Socrates' "What is F-ness?" questions and (iii) his interlocutors (at least initially) think they know how to do that.

# EXAMPLES

In the early dialogues, Socrates is unwilling to accept an example of a thing that is F, or even a list of examples of F-things, as a satisfactory answer to his "What is F-ness?" question.[8] Thus, when he asks Euthyphro what piety is, Socrates refuses to accept the answer, "Doing what I am doing now." Here is part of the exchange:

6. Exactly how this passage is to be understood is subject to debate. Indeed, the question of how to understand the doctrine of recollection is far from settled. Vlastos, "*Anamnesis* in the *Meno*," is an important early article on the subject. Fine, "Inquiry in the *Meno*," is an important later contribution, which includes references to other interpretations. And Scott, *Plato's Meno*, see especially pp. 96–97, is the most recent contribution.

7. "Recollection" may be taken "thinly" or "thickly." On a very thin reading, "what Plato means by "recollection" in the *Meno* is *any enlargement of our knowledge which results from the perception of logical relationships*" (Vlastos, *Studies in Greek Philosophy*, vol. 2, 155–56). I suspect we should go for a reading at least somewhat thicker than that.

8. There is scholarly debate about whether the examples in question are types of action or action tokens. See Nehamas, "Confusing Universals and Particulars," and Benson, "Misunderstanding the 'What Is F-ness?' Question."

T8. Socrates:     For now, try to tell me more clearly what I was asking just now, for, my friend, you did not teach me adequately when I asked you what the pious was, but you told me that what you are doing now, prosecuting your father for murder, is pious.

Euthyphro:     And I told the truth, Socrates.

Socrates:     Perhaps. You agree, however, that there are many other pious actions.

Euthyphro:     There are.

Socrates:     Bear in mind then that I did not bid you tell me one or two of the many pious actions but that form itself [*auto to eidos*] that makes all pious actions pious, for you agreed that all impious actions are impious and all pious actions pious through one form, or don't you remember?

Euthyphro:     I do.

Socrates:     Tell me then what this form itself is, so that I may look upon it, and using it as a model, say that any action of yours or another's that is of that kind is pious, and if it is not that it is not. (*Euthyphro* 6ce)

So what would Socrates require before he would recognize that he had been "taught adequately"? That is, what would Euthyphro have to do to tell Socrates "what the form of piety itself is," so that Socrates could use the response as a "model" or pattern [*paradeigma*] to determine which actions are pious? From the evidence of the early dialogues, it seems that what Socrates requires as an adequate answer to his "What is F-ness?" question is some privileged set of *necessary and sufficient conditions* for something to count as an F. The set of necessary and sufficient conditions cannot just be features that *happen to belong* to all and only people or things that are F; they must reveal that *by which* x is F—that is, what *makes* x F. To put the point another way, they must reveal the *nature (ousia)* of what it is to be F (*Euthyphro* 11a). Let's call a set of necessary and sufficient conditions that reveals the nature of what it is to be F an "*explanatory* set of necessary and sufficient conditions." My suggestion, then, is that the things "noble and good" mentioned in T1 that Socrates is most interested in knowing, and that he thinks neither he nor his interlocutors know, are an explanatory set of necessary and sufficient conditions for an action or a person to count as being brave, pious, temperate, wise, just, and, more generally, virtuous.

In the commentary literature, knowing an explanatory set of necessary and sufficient conditions for something to be F is called definitional knowledge of F-ness. I use that terminology, however, with the warning that the definitional knowledge under discussion is not the meaning of a lexical item, say, a word in Greek. It is, rather, an account of what it is that makes something or someone brave, or temperate, or virtuous, or whatever. Put another way, definitional knowledge of virtue, or one of the individual virtues, is having an account of a moral kind that reveals its nature.

Socrates' recognition of his own lack of definitional knowledge seems to be at least one thing that motivates the "What is F-ness?" questions he asks his interlocutors. He seems to want to learn whether his interlocutors know what F-ness is, when he himself does not know. Moreover, he seems to want to learn for himself what F-ness is through questioning his interlocutors.

We are now in position to state what I shall call the "moderate interpretation" of the claim of Socratic ignorance:

> *Socratic Ignorance* (Moderate Interpretation): Socrates claims that (i) he does not know (at least not manifestly) anything noble and good, where knowing something noble and good would be (ii) having definitional knowledge of virtue, or one of the virtues, such as piety or bravery, and (iii) his interlocutors (at least initially) think they have satisfactory knowledge of virtue itself, or whichever one of the virtues Socrates asks them about.

# Senses of "Know"

The claim of Socratic Ignorance, even on this moderate interpretation, expresses a significant disclamer. Some commentators have thought the Socratic disclaimer to be far less radical than this. Prominent among the efforts to understand the Socratic disclaimer in a less radical way than this is the interpretation offered by Vlastos. Vlastos writes:

> In Plato's earliest dialogues, when Socrates says he has no knowledge, does he or does he not mean what he says? The standard view has been that he does not. What can be said for this interpretation is well said in Gully, 1968: Socrates's profession of ignorance is "an expedient to encourage his interlocutor to seek out the truth, to make him think that he is joining with Socrates in a voyage of discovery" (p. 69). More recently the opposite interpretation has a clear-headed advocate. Terence Irwin in his *Plato's Moral Theory*[9] holds that when Socrates disclaims knowledge he should be taken at his word: he has renounced knowledge and is content to claim no more than true belief.[10]

After considering these two alternatives—(i) Socrates is being insincere as a way of drawing his interlocutor into discussion, and (ii) Socrates really means that he knows nothing—Vlastos proposes a way to go between the horns of the di-

---

9. The reference is to Irwin, *Plato's Moral Theory*, 140. In Irwin, *Plato's Ethics*, we find this: "If [Socrates] says he has knowledge, but in a context in which he has made it plain that he claims only human wisdom, his apparent claim to knowledge may simply amount to a claim that he recognizes that his convictions do not really count as knowledge" (28).

10. Vlastos, *Socratic Studies*, 39.

lemma. He distinguishes two senses of "know" or, better, two senses of the Greek verbs we translate as "know." In what we can call the "strong sense" of the verbs for "know," which Vlastos marks with a subscript as "know$_c$," we know all and only what we are infallibly certain of. In the weak sense, by contrast, which Vlastos marks with a subscript as "know$_e$," we can know whatever has survived elenctic examination.

Vlastos then explains how we are to understand the apparent clash between Socratic claims of knowledge and Socratic disavowals of knowledge this way:

> When he says he know something he is referring to knowledge$_E$; when he says he is not aware of knowing anything—absolutely anything, "great or small" . . . —he refers to knowledge$_C$ ; when he says he has no knowledge of a particular topic he may mean *either* that in this case, as in all others, he has no knowledge$_C$ and does not look for any *or* that what he lacks on that topic is knowledge$_E$, which, with good luck, he might still reach by further searching.[11]

So now we have this interpretation of the claim of Socratic ignorance:

> *Socratic Ignorance* (two-senses interpretation): Socrates knows$_C$ (i.e., is infallibly certain of) very little, even though Socrates knows$_E$ (i.e., has found to survive elenctic examination) quite a bit.

The proposal is ingenious. But it faces several difficulties. First, and most obviously, Socrates never says anything in the early dialogues about using one or more of his verbs for "to know" in different senses. Nor does he say anything of this form: "In one sense I know this, but in another sense I do not."

There is a second difficulty. It turns on the specific senses that Vlastos assigns to the relevant Greek verbs for "know." Here is the problem. In T1, Socrates says of himself and his interlocutor, "It is likely that neither of us knows [*eidenai*] anything worthwhile [*kalon kagathon*]." How are we to use Vlastos's disambiguation proposal to clarify the meaning of Socrates' verb here for "to know," *eidenai*? We have these two options:

1. It is likely that neither of us knows$_C$ anything worthwhile.
2. It is likely that neither of us knows$_E$ anything worthwhile.

According to Vlastos's proposal, Socrates will certainly think (1) is true, on the grounds that there are so few things that anyone could be infallibly certain of. But that conclusion seems irrelevant to the practice of interrogating his interlocutors. After all, the elenchus is not aimed at determining whether there is something that he is infallibly certain of, such as the fact that he exists. It is, rather, aimed at determining whether the interlocutor has any beliefs that will survive elenctic examination: that is, whether the interlocutor knows$_E$ anything. So let's turn to (2).

The trouble with (2) is that, according to Vlastos, (2) will be false, or at least Socrates will consider it false. For according to Vlastos, the set of moral beliefs

11. Ibid., 58

Socrates holds at any given time[12] has survived elenctic examination. Those beliefs are then, presumably, things that Socrates knows$_E$. So, on this reading, Socrates will consider his own statement false. What all this means, I think, is that the Vlastosian proposal fails to make room for a plausible reading of T₁.[13]

# LIMITED KNOWLEDGE

Hugh Benson accepts the Socratic claims of ignorance as the implication of a very strong and restrictive conception of what it is to know something. Indeed, as Benson remarks at the end of his book on the Socratic conception, knowledge is "very difficult to obtain. Indeed, we should be surprised to discover that anyone has it."[14]

Benson must, of course, explain away the passages in which Socrates claims to have knowledge, such as T3 and T4. Here is T3 in its broader context:

> T3*. To fear death, gentlemen, is no other than to think oneself wise when one is not, to think one knows what one does not know. No one knows whether death may not be the greatest of all blessings for a man, and men fear it as if they knew that it is the greatest of evils. And surely it is the most blame-worthy ignorance to believe that one knows what one does not know. It is perhaps on this point and in this respect, gentlemen, that I differ from the majority of men, and if I were to claim that I am wiser than anyone in anything, it would be in this, that, as I have no adequate knowledge of things in the underworld, so I do not think I have. *I do know* (*oida*), however, that it is wicked and shameful to do wrong, to disobey one's superior, be he god or man. (*Apology* 29b1–7; emphasis mine)

This passage includes a qualified claim of ignorance ("I have no adequate knowledge of things in the underworld"), as well as a clear claim to knowledge of an important moral truth. Socrates does not explain here why he thinks his knowledge of the "underworld" is inadequate. It is plausible to assume that he thinks it is inadequate because, as yet, he has had no experience of the underworld.

12. After Socrates has engaged in a number of elenctic examinations, anyway.

13. There might, of course, be other two-sense interpretations that would avoid this difficulty. A related interpretative move is to distinguish, not senses of Socrates' words for "know," but rather kinds of knowledge. Woodruff, "Plato's Early Epistemology," distinguishes expert and nonexpert knowledge, where expert knowledge must include definitional knowledge. Other interpreters (e.g., Taylor, *Socrates*, 50ff.) follow Woodruff. Brickhouse and Smith, *Plato's Socrates*, distinguish "knowing how something is" from a lesser sort of knowledge (38–45). These latter lines of interpretation are more congenial to the view of Socratic Ignorance I present here. On the importance of keeping views about senses distinct from views about kinds, see Matthews, "Senses and Kinds."

14. Benson, "Misunderstanding the "What Is F-ness" Question," 221.

By contrast, he claims to know "that it is wicked and shameful to do wrong, to disobey one's superior, be he god or man."

On the moderate interpretation of Socratic Ignorance I advanced above, Socrates can consistently claim to know that it is wicked and shameful to disobey one's superior and also claim not to know anything worthwhile [*kalon kathagon*], if, for example, he realizes that he lacks definitional knowledge of what it is to be wicked or shameful. Indeed, on the moderate interpretation of Socratic Ignorance, Socrates can consistently (a) claim to know certain moral facts, but (b) deny that he has definitional knowledge of the elements of those moral facts (e.g., what it is to be shameful, wicked, etc.), and (c) express puzzlement over how it is he can know such moral facts without having the appropriate definitional knowledge. This is, in fact, the situation of many analytic philosophers today. They will claim to know that 7 is a number but at the same time admit that they have no definitional knowledge of what it is to be a number. Furthermore, they may also be puzzled over how they can know that 7 is a number without having the appropriate definitional knowledge. They may be puzzled because they find plausible a principle that Socrates seems to accept.

# The Priority of Definitional Knowledge

According to a principle many commentators[15] have thought Socrates is committed to, one could not know that 7 is a number without having definitional knowledge of number. Peter Geach once called this principle "the Socratic fallacy" and claimed it to be a morally pernicious fallacy.[16] Hugh Benson, In a more recent formulation, calls it the "Priority of Definitional Knowledge" and states it as the conjunction of (P) and (D):

> (P) If A fails to know what F-ness is, then A fails to know, for any x, that x is F.
> (D) If A fails to know what F-ness is, then A fails to know, for any G, that F-ness is G.[17]

According to (P), if Socrates and his interlocutor fail to know—that is, to have definitional knowledge—of what, say, beauty is, they will fail to know of any given instance of beauty, say, Helen of Troy, or the Parthenon, that Helen is beautiful or the Parthenon is beautiful. According to (D), if Socrates or one of his interlocutors

---

15. But certainly not all. Among the dissenters are Nehemas, "Socratic Intellectualism"; Beversluis, "Does Socrates Commit the Socratic Fallacy?"; and Brickhouse and Smith, *Plato's Socrates*, especially pp. 45–55.

16. Geach, "Plato's *Euthyphro*."

17. Benson, *Socratic Wisdom*, 113.

fails to have definitional knowledge of bravery, they will not even know that bravery is a virtue.

(P) and (D), both individually and jointly, threaten to undermine the reasonableness of thinking one might ever come to *know* what F-ness is through a Socratic elenchus. To see that this is so, consider, for example, the way the elenchus proceeds in the dialogue, *Laches*. When Laches proposes that courage is standing fast in the face of an advancing enemy, Socrates asks whether one couldn't be brave in retreat. (191a) Laches, like anyone who reads this dialogue, recognizes immediately that a soldier might be brave in retreat and that such a soldier would be a counterexample to the suggested analysis of courage. But, according to (P), one could not know that this example is a genuine counterexample unless one already knew what courage is—that is, had definitional knowledge of bravery. But, if one had that, there would be no point in conducting the elenchus.

Again, when Charmides suggests that temperance might just be a certain quietness, Socrates gains his agreement that temperance is one of the noble, or admirable, things [*tôn kalôn*] (*Charmides* 159bc). Socrates then points out that quietness is sometimes noble, sometimes not, and concludes that temperance cannot be just a certain quietness (160bc). But if they do not actually know that temperance is a noble thing, they will not know that it is not a certain quietness.

Perhaps, however, it is not the aim of the Socratic elenchus to provide knowledge of what F-ness is. Perhaps the aim is only to determine what F-ness is. Or perhaps it is not even that. Before we can make a reasonable judgment concerning the aim of the Socratic elenchus, we need to consider what the form of an elenchus is and then what it would be reasonable to take the aim of inquiry in that form to be.

# THE ELENCHUS

Vlastos describes the steps that make up the "standard" Socratic elenchus this way:

1. The interlocutor asserts a thesis [*p*], which Socrates considers false and targets for refutation.
2. Socrates secures agreement to further premises, say *q* and *r* (each of which may stand for a conjunct of propositions). The argument is ad hoc: Socrates argues from *q* and *r*, but not to them.
3. Socrates then argues, and the interlocutor agrees, that *q* and *r* entail *not-p*.
4. Thereupon Socrates claims that *not-p* has been proved true, *p* false.[18]

A quarter of a century before Vlastos wrote "The Socratic Elenchus," he had maintained that "Socrates never meant to go beyond (3) in his elenctic

---

18. Vlastos, "Socratic Elenchus," 39.

arguments—that their object was simply to reveal to his interlocutors muddles and inconsistencies within themselves."[19] In "The Socratic Elenchus," however, Vlastos argues that Socrates makes two powerful assumptions that enable him to assert, with justification, that *not-p*—that, for example, what his interlocutor had said piety (or bravery, or whatever) is—is simply false. The powerful assumptions Vlastos attributes to Socrates are these:

> A. Anyone who ever has a false moral belief will always have at the same time true beliefs entailing the negation of that false belief.[20]
>
> B. The set of moral beliefs held by Socrates at any given time is consistent.[21]

These two assumptions, Vlastos maintains, entail this:

> C. The set of moral beliefs held by Socrates at any given time is true.[22]

Almost all commentators have declined to follow Vlastos in attributing these particular assumptions to Socrates.[23] Nevertheless, the problem Vlastos uncovered, and tried to solve, has dominated Socratic scholarship for the past two decades.

## THE PROBLEM OF THE ELENCHUS

Vlastos states the problem this way: "... how is it that Socrates claims to have proved a thesis false when, in point of logic, all he has proved in any given argument is that the thesis is inconsistent with the conjunction of agreed-upon premisses [*sic*]?"[24]

I call this the "Weaker Version" of the problem and state it this way:

> *The Problem of the Elenchus* (Weaker Version): How can the elenchus establish anything more than inconsistency between a thesis about what F-ness is and certain premises that have been agreed to by the interlocutor?

In his article, Vlastos makes heavy use of the dialogue *Gorgias* for clues to the methodology of the elenchus. One of the passages he quotes is this one:

> T9. For I think that we should all be contentiously eager to come to *know* [*to eidenai*] what is true and what is false about the things we assert; for it is a common good for all that this should be made evident. (505e)

19. Ibid., 45.
20. Ibid., 52.
21. Ibid., 55.
22. Ibid.
23. For example, Kraut, "Comments on Gregory Vlastos"; Brickhouse and Smith, "Vlastos on the Elenchus"; and Polansky, "Professor Vlastos's Analysis of Socratic Elenchus."
24. Vlastos, "Socratic Elenchus," 49.

This passage suggests that it is *knowledge* of what is true and what is false that the elenchus aims to establish. It presents us with a stronger version of the Problem of the Elenchus:

> *The Problem of the Elenchus* (Stronger Version): How can the elenchus be used to achieve knowledge of what F-ness is?

# RESPONDING TO THE PROBLEM
# OF THE ELENCHUS

Vlastos does not mark off the stronger version of the Problem of the Elenchus from the weaker version. As we have already noted, his general response to the Problem of the Elenchus is to say that Socrates relies on assumptions A, B, and C. If, indeed, Socrates does rely on these assumptions, then he does have available a response to the weaker version of the Problem of the Elenchus. That is, given these assumptions, Socrates can claim to have established truths about the virtues through his use of the elenchus. Moreover, given Vlastos's two-sense construal of Socratic Ignorance, Socrates can be said to *know* whatever has survived elenctic examination. And so Vlastos also has a response to the stronger version of the Problem of the Elenchus.

Suppose, however, we find it implausible to attribute assumptions A, B, and C to Socrates. What response would be available to us to resolve the Problem of the Elenchus?

Terence Irwin suggests that Socrates makes other assumptions, what he calls the "Guiding Principles of Socratic Inquiry."[25] According to Irwin, "If [Socrates] has good reasons for believing these principles, then he has good reason to accept the conclusions of elenctic inquiry."[26]

Among the five principles Irwin supposes that Socrates' interlocutors agree to is one that begins this way:

> [The interlocutor] agrees that a virtuous action must always be "fine" (*kalon*), "good" (*agathon*), and "beneficial" (*ophelimon*). If an action is shameful or harmful, the interlocutor agrees that it cannot be virtuous, and that a state of an agent producing such an action cannot be a virtue.[27]

Irwin adds:

> These are guiding principles of the elenchos, not simply Socrates' own beliefs. For he assumes—and his assumption is proved right in the dialogues we have

---

25. Irwin, *Plato's Ethics*, 48–49.
26. Ibid., 48.
27. Ibid.

examined—that the interlocutor will accept these principles and be influenced by them in answering Socrates' questions.[28]

It is Irwin's view that Socrates does not attempt to argue for these guiding principles of the elenchus until we get to the *Gorgias*. In that dialogue, Irwin tells us, Socrates claims to demonstrate truths, even though he still does not "know how things are." Irwin unpacks that paradox this way: "By showing how anyone disagreeing with him becomes ridiculous, [Socrates] has shown enough to prove his own position, but not enough to justify him in claiming to know how things are."[29] In this way, Irwin offers a response to the weaker version of the Problem of the Elenchus while rejecting the stronger version on the grounds that Socrates does not suppose he has acquired any knowledge through the elenchus.[30]

## REJECTING THE PROBLEM OF THE ELENCHUS ALTOGETHER

Some commentators reject both the stronger version and the weaker version of the Problem of the Elenchus. The clearest way to do that is to argue that Socrates never claims to establish any positive conclusions through his use of the elenchus. Hugh Benson is one commentator who takes this position. Benson reconstructs eight elenchi from early dialogues, each of which shows only that the premises of that elenchus are inconsistent. After discussing whether the *Gorgias* alters the picture significantly, Benson comes to this conclusion:

> I have shown, then, that "the problem of the elenchus" need not arise in Plato's early dialogues. A careful examination of the elenchoi employed in the *Euthyphro*, *Laches*, and *Charmides*, three paradigmatic elenctic dialogues, requires only that Socrates understands each of these elenchoi as establishing the inconsistency of the interlocutor's beliefs. The passages of the *Gorgias* that have been claimed to suggest otherwise do not in fact require an alternative interpretation of Socrates' understanding.[31]

28. Ibid., 49.

29. Ibid., 122.

30. Perhaps, however, this is not Irwin's own view about whether one can acquire knowledge through an elenchus. In his earlier work, *Plato's Moral Theory*, he writes: "Socrates should not believe, then, that the elenchus can never in principle meet his demand for definition and knowledge. Naturally the definitions it finds will rely on the agreement between Socrates and the interlocutor; one interlocutor might be wrong to agree, but answers can be confirmed by other people's agreement. This all looks a feasible programme for Socrates; when he and his interlocutors, after repeated tests, are satisfied with an account, he can claim knowledge derived from the elenchus" (68–69).

31. Benson, *Socratic Wisdom*, 92.

There are lots of good things to be said in favor of Benson's interpretation. But there is also something odd about it. As Socrates tells his story in the *Apology*, he set out to discover whether others are wiser than he is (21be). What would be a reasonable way of doing that? Trapping someone in a contradiction to show that the interlocutor actually has inconsistent beliefs might be a reasonable way to show that the interlocutor is not wise at all, and so is not wiser than Socrates, assuming, of course, that Socrates cannot be trapped in such contradictions. But setting out to determine whether people are wise by simply determining whether they have consistent beliefs seems to be a hopeless way to determine whether they are wiser than Socrates. It is quite conceivable that a very simple-minded person with very few beliefs might actually have consistent beliefs. But finding, after a thorough examination, no inconsistency in a simpleton's belief set would hardly tend to show that the simpleton is wise, let alone wiser than Socrates.

Socrates, moreover, often presents himself as deeply interested in finding out for himself, through the examination of an interlocutor, what courage is, or holiness, or virtue, or friendship, or whatever the item up for discussion might be. In fact, Benson agrees that Socrates himself wants to find out the nature of courage and virtue and holiness and friendship and all the other things he discusses with his interlocutors.[32] But he thinks Socrates wants to find out what these important things are by finding someone who knows what they are who can teach him.

This suggestion is also rather troubling. Testing putative experts on, say, bravery, for the consistency of their beliefs about bravery seems a very unpromising way of determining whether they know what bravery is. For all we know, there are many distinct belief sets about bravery that are internally consistent, yet incompatible with each other and therefore not all correct. Thus trying to find out for oneself what bravery is by seeking to identify a teacher who has merely consistent beliefs about bravery is hardly a promising strategy. In the absence of solid textual evidence, we should be reluctant to attribute it to Socrates.

## TESTING BELIEFS FOR CONSISTENCY

Is it plausible to suppose, as Benson does, that testing the interlocutor's beliefs for consistency is the sole, or even the chief, aim of the Socratic elenchus? Only rarely does Socrates himself suggest that he may be testing his interlocutor's beliefs for their consistency. In one such instance, Nicias had proposed that "courage is knowledge of the grounds of fear and hope" (*Laches* 196cd). Socrates mentions, as a possible counterexample to Nicias's proposal, a ferocious beast, the fabled

---

32. "I do not deny that these passages indicated that Socrates aims to uncover truths and acquire knowledge and to encourage his interlocutors to do the same as well. (How could one?)" (Benson, "Problems with Socratic Method," 107).

"Crommyon sow" (196). Nicias responds by rejecting the counterexample. He says, simply, "By no means . . . do I call courageous wild beasts or anything else that, for lack of understanding, does not fear what should be feared" (197a). In this case, one could certainly say that Socrates is testing his interlocutor for the consistency of his beliefs. Moreover, Nicias passes the test!

Yet it is quite unusual in the early dialogues for an interlocutor to reject a counterexample that Socrates has suggested. Moreover, Socrates typically claims outright that he is asking what F-ness is in the hope of finding out for himself what it is. Thus when Euthyphro, near the beginning of the dialogue named after him, claims to "know accurately" (*akribôs eideiên*) what piety is (5a), Socrates offers to become Euthyphro's pupil. The clear implication, whether ironical or not, is that he might come to know what Euthyphro knows. This thought is repeated later in the dialogue, for example, at 14bc.

Similarly, the *Laches* unfolds as an unsuccessful search for what bravery is, not as a determination that the beliefs of Nicias and Laches are inconsistent. Thus when Socrates and Nicias consider whether bravery might be analyzed as knowledge of what it is be feared and hoped for (196d), Socrates points out that such a conclusion would be in conflict with a rather obvious assumption they had made earlier namely, that courage is only a part of virtue:

T10.

| | |
|---|---|
| Socrates: | Then the thing you are now talking about, Nicias, would not be a part of virtue but rather virtue entire. |
| Nicias: | So it seems. |
| Socrates: | And we have certainly stated that courage is one of the parts of virtue. |
| Nicias: | Yes, we have. |
| Socrates: | Then what we are saying now does not appear to hold good. |
| Nicias: | Apparently not. |
| Socrates: | Then we have not discovered, Nicias, what courage is. (*Laches* 199e) |

One might have expected at this point a confirmation that the most an elenchus can establish is inconsistency of belief. The relevantly inconsistent beliefs would be these:

B1. Courage is only a part of virtue.
B2. Courage is the whole of virtue.

But Socrates does not say, "So, Nicias, you will have to give up at least one of your beliefs." Instead, he says, "Then we have not discovered [*êurêkamen*] what courage is." That is, they have not come to *know* what courage is.

# REJECTING THE PRIORITY
# OF DEFINITIONAL KNOWLEDGE

If we suppose Socrates is firmly committed to the Priority of Definitional Knowledge, and we are unhappy about making the Socratic elenchus presuppose either the assumptions Vlastos makes or those Irwin proposes, we may see no alternative to limiting the aim of the elenchus to establishing inconsistency in the interlocutor's beliefs, as Benson does. But do we have to suppose that Socrates is committed to the Priority of Definitional Knowledge?

Near the end of the *Hippias Major*, there is a long passage that seems to commit Socrates to the Priority principle. Here is part of it. (Socrates is speaking.)

> T11. I hear every insult from that man (among others around here) who has always been refuting me . . . ."Look," he'll say, "How will you know whose speech—or any other action—is finely presented or not, when you are ignorant of the fine? And when you're in a state like that, do you think it's better for you to live than die?" (304c1–e1)

The project in this dialogue is to investigate what *to kalon* is: that is, what the beautiful, or the fine, or the noble, is. Socrates and Hippias have not been able to come up with a successful analysis. Socrates says in T8 that he expects to be ridiculed by a neighbor when he talks about a fine speech, since he cannot give a satisfactory analysis of what it is for something to be fine. But before we immediately conclude that Socrates is committed to (P) and (D), we should see how the speech that begins with T11 ends:

> T12. That's what I get, as I said. Insults and blame from you, insults from him. But I suppose it is necessary to bear all that. It wouldn't be strange if it were good for me. I actually think, Hippias, that associating with both of you has done me good. The proverb says, "What's fine is hard"—I think I know *that*. (304e3–9)

On a natural, and I think correct, reading of T12, Socrates here says that he thinks he *knows* that what is fine is hard (more literally, that "noble things are difficult"—*chalepa ta kala*). But if he did know about fine (or noble) things that they are difficult, he would know something, indeed, something very important, about the fine, or the noble (*to kalon*) without, as the dialogue amply demonstrates, having definitional knowledge of the noble or the fine. So, just after he seems to have accepted the Priority of Definitional Knowledge, he seems to flout it. What is going on?

# AN APORETIC READING

It is important, I think, to recognize that a standard way in which Socrates expresses (P) and (D) is by asking a question. "How can I know that x is F," he asks, "if I don't know what F-ness is?" "How can I know that F-ness is G," he asks, "if I don't know what F-ness is?" [33]

It is, indeed, natural to suppose that, if I really do know that the bird on the tree in front of my window is a robin, I must know the identifying features of robins and be able to "tick them off" as I look at the bird in the tree to be sure that it has all these identifying features. Suppose, however, that someone asks me something more basic, say, whether a robin is a bird, or whether 7 is a number. Surely I know that a robin is a bird and that 7 is a number. Yet it is overwhelmingly unlikely that I can specify an explanatory set of necessary and sufficient conditions for the truth of "x is a number" or even for "y is a bird." But how can I know those basic things without being able to "tick off" the right necessary and sufficient conditions? It is puzzling.

If we read the passages in which Socrates is taken to commit himself to (P) or (D) as expressions of puzzlement or perplexity over how he can know that a speech is fine when he can't informatively define "fineness"—or, in general, how he can know that x is F without having definitional knowledge of F-ness—then we can understand such passages, as I think we should, as motivating the elenchus without immediately undermining its chance of success in yielding knowledge. I suggest we read those passages this way: that is, give them an "aporetic reading."

Giving an aporetic reading to the passages in which Socrates asks how we can know that x is F or F-ness is G without having definitional knowledge of F-ness makes this part of the epistemology of Socrates relevant to recent discussions of natural kinds and natural-kind terms. Both Saul Kripke[34] and Hilary Putnam[35] have argued that we do not, in general, recognize instances of gold or elm trees by applying the necessary and sufficient conditions for something to be gold or an elm tree. Their conclusion has seemed radical to many readers because of the plausibility of the very picture of instance recognition we find in T8.

If we do give the passages that suggest (P) and (D) an aporetic reading, we should not be surprised to find Socrates himself making claims that violate (P) or (D), or both. In addition to T9, we might consider another passage from the *Apology*. The one I have in mind comes after the jury at the trial has just ruled that Socrates is guilty as charged. To understand this passage, we must understand a certain feature of the Athenian system of justice. According to that system, if the defendant in court is found guilty, the party who brought charges proposes a penalty and the party found guilty proposes an alternative penalty. The jury then

---

33. In addition to T11 and T12, see, for example, *Charmides* 176ab and *Laches* 190bc.
34. Kripke, *Naming and Necessity*.
35. Putnam, "Meaning of "Meaning," 215–71.

has to accept one of the two proposals; it cannot come up with some completely different penalty. Meletus, Socrates' accuser, proposes death, and Socrates needs to propose an alternative. Should he propose some sort of prison term? The jury might accept that rather than the death penalty. This is part of what Socrates says:

> T13. Since I am convinced that I wrong no one, I am not likely to wrong myself, to say that I deserve some evil and to make some such assessment against myself. What should I fear? That I should suffer the penalty Meletus has assessed against me, of which I say I do not know whether it is good or bad? Am I then to choose in preference to this something that I know very well [*eu oida*] to be an evil and assess the penalty of that? Imprisonment? Why should I live in prison, always subjected to the ruling magistrates the Eleven? (*Apology* 37b2–c2)

At the end of his trial Socrates gives reasons for explaining his uncertainty about whether death is good or evil. But he thinks he knows very well, as he says here in T13, that imprisonment would be an evil. Does he think he has definitional knowledge of evil? We have no early dialogue in which he tries to get an interlocutor to say what evil is. But one can be quite confident that he would not think he could say, in the rigorous way he demands, what it is for something to count as being evil. On my aporetic reading of the Principle of Definitional Knowledge, he might well have asked, "How can I know that imprisonment would be an evil, if I cannot say what it is for something to be an evil?" But he would not have been forced, on pain of inconsistency, to take back what he had just said about knowing that imprisonment would be an evil on the ground that he did not have Definitional Knowledge of evil.

# THE *MENO* RESPONSE TO THE PROBLEM OF THE ELENCHUS

I stated earlier that the *Meno* is a transitional dialogue and so should not be assumed to be a reliable guide to the views of the figure of Socrates we have focused our attention on here. One innovation in this dialogue is an analysis of knowledge as true belief that has been "tied down" by giving "an account of the reason why" (*aitias logismô*) (98a). This analysis of knowledge seems to be at least an ancestor of the familiar modern suggestion that knowledge is justified true belief.[36] It is clearly

---

36. For a full and careful discussion of this passage and its relation to recent analyses of knowledge, see Fine, "Knowledge and True Belief in the *Meno*."

an epistemological theory. It could be argued to be implicit in the early dialogues we have focused on, but it is not explicitly stated in any of them. They offer no explicit analysis of knowledge.

On one plausible interpretation of the *Meno*, it also offers, among other things, Plato's own reflections on the Socratic elenchus and on what assumptions are needed to justify thinking that it can produce positive conclusions, and perhaps even knowledge. If one reads the *Meno* this way, then the fact that Socrates begins the dialogue by insisting in T5, not just that he doesn't know what virtue is, which would be a standard profession of Socratic Ignorance, but that he doesn't know *at all* (*to parapan*) what virtue is, is significant. Meno then sets up the Paradox of Inquiry in T6 so that it is not knowing *at all* what virtue is that would make inquiry impossible. As commentators have been quick to point out, we are usually in the position of knowing something, but not enough, about the subject of our inquiry. But then the Paradox of Inquiry does not apply to us, at least if it is stated in the strong form in which Meno first presents it. The application to the Socratic elenchus, in particular, is this: We can't reasonably expect the elenchus to carry us from having no knowledge at all about what virtue is to having definitional knowledge of what it is.

According to the Doctrine of Recollection as presented in T7, however, each of us does have some knowledge of what virtue is, though our knowledge may be purely latent. A reasonable task for the elenchus is then to help us make our latent knowledge manifest. Socrates' interrogation of the slaveboy is meant to show us that this can happen through asking questions rather by making assertions. Socrates gives this explanation of how it can happen:

> T14. So the man who does not know has within himself true opinions about the things that he does not know? [Meno agrees.] These opinions have now just been stirred up like a dream, but if he were repeatedly asked these same questions in various ways, you know that in the end his knowledge about these things [*epistêsetai peri toutôn*] would be as accurate as anyone's. (85cd)

If we apply this suggestion to the Socratic elenchus, the idea is not that the elenchus itself establishes positive conclusions through some logically coercive chain of reasoning, let alone produces knowledge in interlocutors by having them internalize such reasoning. Rather, the idea is that repeated elenctic questioning about F-ness, asking "these same questions in various ways," may eventually lead an interlocutor not simply to "recollect" true beliefs about F-ness but, finally, to gain knowledge of what F-ness is.

On this interpretation of the *Meno*, then, we are meant to conclude that the Problem of the Elenchus, both in its weaker and in its stronger forms, can be resolved positively. However, it will not be resolved by seeing how a bit of stand-alone elenctic reasoning establishes what F-ness is. Rather, it will be resolved by seeing that repeated elenctic questioning can eventually lead an interlocutor to recollect true beliefs about F-ness and finally gain manifest knowledge of what F-ness is.

# METAPHYSICS

Plato's grandest metaphysical theory is his Theory of Forms. Does Socrates also have a theory of forms? Gail Fine, in her monumental study of Aristotle's *On Ideas*, maintains that he does. She writes:

> As I interpret Socrates—an interpretation that basically agrees with, but goes beyond Aristotle's—he introduces forms for epistemological and metaphysical, but not for semantic reasons. Further, Socratic forms are universals in the sense that they are explanatory properties. The fact that they are self-predicative paradigms does not jeopardize their status as explanatory properties; on the contrary, they are self-predicative paradigms because they are explanatory properties.[37]

When Fine refers to Aristotle's interpretation, she seems to have in mind especially remarks Aristotle makes in his *Metaphysics* M3, which she translates this way:

> T15. Now Socrates was concerned with the moral virtues, and he was the first to seek universal definitions in connection with them. . . . It was reasonable for Socrates to try to find what a thing is, because he was seeking to argue deductively, and the starting-point of deductions is what a thing is. . . . For there are two things one might fairly ascribe to Socrates—inductive arguments and universal definitions, both of which are concerned with the starting-point of knowledge. But Socrates did not make universals or definitions (*horismous*) separate (*chōrista*), but they (the Platonists) separated them, and they called these sorts of beings "ideas." (1178b12–32)[38]

Fine points out that in the *Laches*, Socrates maintains that "speed is some one thing, the same in running, playing the lyre, speaking, learning, and so on."[39] Similarly, as Socrates says in the *Euthyphro*, piety is one thing in all its instances. As pointed out above, Socrates seeks definitional knowledge of piety—what is called a "real definition" of piety, rather than just a nominal definition.[40]

According to Fine, "Socrates offers an epistemological argument for the existence of forms: the possibility of knowledge requires explanation, and this, in turn, requires the existence of forms—real properties and kinds."[41] What Fine seems to have in mind here is this passage from the *Euthyphro*, which we have already discussed:

> T3. Tell me then what this form itself is, so that I may look upon it, and using it as a model [or template or pattern, *paradeigma*], say that any action of

37. Fine, *On Ideas*, 53–54.
38. Ibid., 48.
39. Ibid.
40. Cf. Penner, "The Unity of Virtue," and Irwin, *Plato's Ethics*, 25–27.
41. Fine, *On Ideas*, 50.

yours or another's that is of that kind is pious, and if it is not that it is not. (6e3–6)

In this way, the metaphysics of Socrates seems to be driven by his epistemology.

I have said that, before the *Meno*, Socrates does not offer an analysis of knowledge. Although he has an epistemology, we might be reluctant to credit him with an epistemological theory. Is the situation similar with regard to his metaphysics? In particular, does Socrates really have a theory of forms?

According to Aristotle in T12, Socrates, unlike Plato, did not consider his universal forms to be separate. Reginald Allen has challenged Aristotle's assertion. With special reference to what Socrates has to say about the form of piety in the *Euthyphro*, Allen mounts this argument:

> Ontologically, the priority of Forms is implied by the fact that they are essences and causes by which things are what they are; their existence is a condition for the existence of their instances. That priority implies existential independence. If Euthyphro's action in prosecuting his father is holy [that is, pious], its existence as holy depends upon the existence of the Form of holiness, by which it is holy; it would be merely queer to think that the Form of holiness depends for its existence on Euthyphro's action in prosecuting his father being holy.[42]

Allen's reasoning may be persuasive to many of us who have read the middle dialogues of Plato. But it does seem to go beyond anything made entirely explicit in the *Euthyphro* or in any of the other early dialogues. Perhaps we could say there is a theory of forms "immanent" in the philosophy of Socrates.

# SOUL-BODY DUALISM

In the *Apology* Socrates characterizes his mission this way:

> T16. For I go around doing nothing but persuading both young and old among you not to care for your body or your wealth in preference to or as strongly as for the best possible state of your soul. (30ab).

But did Socrates think of the soul as an entity distinct and separable from the body? According to a speech he gives near the end of the *Gorgias*, he did. He says to Callicles:

> T17. Death, I think, is actually nothing but the separation of two things from each other, the soul and the body. (524b)

Socrates goes on in the *Gorgias* to describe the separated soul this way:

---

42. Allen, Plato's "Euthyphro," 136.

T18. All that's in the soul is evident after it has been stripped naked of the body, both things that are natural to it and things that have happened to it, things that the person came to have in his soul as a result of his pursuit of each objective. (524d)

In the *Apology*, however, Socrates insists,

T19. To fear death . . . is no other than to think oneself wise when one is not, to think one knows what one does not know. (29a)

And in his final speech at his trial he offers these two alternatives:

T20. Either the dead are nothing and have no perception of anything, or it is, as we are told, a change and a relocating for the soul from here to another place. If it is a complete lack of perception, like a dreamless sleep, then death could be a great advantage. . . . If death is like this I say it is an advantage. If, on the other hand, death is a change from here to another place, and what we are told is true and all who have died are there, what greater blessing could there be, gentlemen of the jury? (40ce)

Thus, in the *Apology*, Socrates remains explicitly agnostic about whether the soul survives death. Still, whether Socrates believed in an afterlife, as he is given to say in the *Gorgias*, or remained agnostic on this issue, he does seem to have conceived the soul as a thing distinct from the body—something that might conceivably survive bodily death.

On the other hand, Socrates never gives any arguments for soul-body dualism. In the middle dialogue *Phaedo*, Socrates offers quite explicit arguments for not only the forms but also the soul and its immortality. But the Socrates of the *Phaedo* is not our concern here. Vlastos summarizes the situation this way:

The queries, "Is the soul material or immaterial, mortal or immortal? Will it be annihilated when the body rots?" are never on his elenctic agenda. The first question he never addresses at all. He does allude to the second at the close of the *Apology* but only to suggest that it is rationally undecidable: both options—total annihilation or survival in Hades—are left open. In the *Crito* he reveals his faith in the soul's survival. In the *Gorgias* he declares it. Nowhere does he try to prove it in the earlier dialogues.[43]

So what can we say about the metaphysics of Socrates in Plato's early dialogues? Socrates seems to have believed in forms, which Aristotle called "universals" and which we might today call "properties." He thought of these forms as distinct from, if not separate from, the concrete particulars that have them. He was at least inclined to think that we cannot know that something has one of these forms unless we can specify the nature of that form. He believed that one's soul is something distinct from one's body. It is something that may survive one's body.

---

43. Vlastos, *Socrates: Ironist and Moral Philosopher*, 55.

# BIBLIOGRAPHY

Allen, R. E. *Plato's "Euthyphro" and the Earlier Theory of Forms* (London, 1970).

Benson, Hugh H. "Misunderstanding the "What Is F-ness?" Question," *Archiv für Geschichte der Philosophie* 72 (1990), 125–42.

———. *Socratic Wisdom: The Model of Knowledge in Plato's Early Dialogues* (New York, 2000).

———. "Problems with Socratic Method," in Gary Alan Scott, ed., *Does Socrates Have a Method?* (University Park, Penn., 2002.

———. ed., *Essays on the Philosophy of Socrates* (New York, 1992).

Beversluis, John. "Does Socrates Commit the Socratic Fallacy?," *American Philosophical Quarterly* 24 (1987), 211–23; reprinted in Benson, *Essays on the Philosophy of Socrates*, 107–22.

Brickhouse, Thomas C., and Nicholas D. Smith. *Plato's Socrates* (New York, 1994).

———. "Vlastos on the Elenchus," *Oxford Studies in Ancient Philosophy* 2 (1984), 185–95.

Cooper, John M., ed. *Plato: Complete Works* (Indianapolis, 1997).

Fine, Gail. "Inquiry in the *Meno*," in Richard Kraut, ed., *The Cambridge Companion to Plato*(Cambridge, 1992), 200–26.

———. *On Ideas: Aristotle's Criticism of Plato's Theory of Forms* (Oxford, 1993).

———. "Knowledge and True Belief in the *Meno*," *Oxford Studies in Ancient Philosophy* 27 (2004), 41–81.

———. *Plato on Knowledge and Forms* (Oxford, 2003).

Geach, P. T. "Plato's *Euthyphro:* An Analysis and Commentary," *Monist* 50 (1966), 369–82.

Gulley, Norman. *The Philosophy of Socrates* (London, 1968).

Irwin, Terence. *Plato's Ethics* (Oxford, 1995).

———. *Plato's Moral Theory* (Oxford, 1977).

———. "Socratic Puzzles," *Oxford Studies in Ancient Philosophy* 10 (1990), 24–66.

Kahn, Charles H. "Did Plato Write Socratic Dialogues?" in H. H. Benson, ed., *Essays on the Philosophy of Socrates* (New York, 1992), 35–52.

Kraut, Richard. "Comments on Gregory Vlastos, 'The Socratic Elenchus,' " *Oxford Studies in Ancient Philosophy* 1 (1983), 59–70.

Kripke, Saul. *Naming and Necessity* (Cambridge: Harvard University Press, 1980).

Lesher, James H. "Socrates' Disavowal of Knowledge," *Journal of the History of Philosophy* 25 (1987), 275–88.

Matthews, Gareth B. "Senses and Kinds," *Journal of Philosophy* 69 (1972), 44–57.

———. *Socratic Perplexity and the Nature of Philosophy* (Oxford, 1999).

Matthews, Gareth B., and Thomas A. Blackson. "Causes in the *Phaedo*," *Synthese* 79 (1989), 581–91.

McPherran, Mark L. *The Religion of Socrates* (University Park, Penn., 1996).

Nehamas, Alexander. "Confusing Universals and Particulars in Plato's Early Dialogues," *Review of Metaphysics* 29 (1975), 287–306.

———. "Socratic Intellectualism," *Boston Area Colloquium in Ancient Philosophy* 2 (1986), 275–316.

Penner, Terry. "The Unity of Virtue," *Philosophical Review* 82 (1973), 35–68; reprinted in Benson, *Essays on the Philosophy of Socrates*, 162–84.

Polansky, Ronald M. "Professor Vlastos's Analysis of Socratic Elenchus," *Oxford Studies in Ancient Philosophy* 3 (1985), 247–59.

Prior, William J. "Socrates Metaphysician," *Oxford Studies in Ancient Philosophy* 27 (2004), 1–14.

Putnam, Hilary. "The Meaning of "Meaning," in *Mind, Language and Reality*, Philosophical Papers, vol. 2 (Cambridge, 1975, 215–71).

Reeve, C. D. C. *Socrates in the Apology* (Indianapolis, 1989).

Scott, Dominic. *Plato's* Meno (Cambridge, 2006).

Taylor, C. C. W. *Socrates: A Very Short Introduction* (Oxford, 1998).

Vlastos, Gregory [1965]. "*Anamnesis* in the *Meno*," *Dialogue* 4 (1965), 143–67; reprinted in Gregory Vlastos, *Studies in Greek Philosophy*, vol. 2 (Princeton, 1995), 147–55.

———. "Is the 'Socratic Fallacy' Socratic?," *Ancient Philosophy* 10 (1990), 1–16.

———. "The Socratic Elenchus," *Oxford Studies in Ancient Philosophy* 1 (1983), 27–58.

———. *Socrates: Ironist and Moral Philosopher* (Ithaca, 1991).

———. *Socratic Studies*, ed., Myles Burnyeat (Cambridge, 1994).

———. *Studies in Greek Philosophy*, 2 vols. (Princeton, 1993, 1995).

Woodruff, Paul. "Plato's Early Epistemology," in S. Everson, ed., *Epistemology* (Cambridge, 1990), 60–84; reprinted in Benson, *Essays on the Philosophy of Socrates*, 86–106.

CHAPTER 6

# SOCRATIC ETHICS AND MORAL PSYCHOLOGY

## DANIEL DEVEREUX

## 1. SOCRATES AND PLATO

Our knowledge of Socrates' ethics and moral psychology is based chiefly on Plato's dialogues. Socrates did not write any philosophical works; but since he is the main speaker in most of Plato's dialogues, we have plenty of information to work with. In a sense, Plato gives us *too much* information: it is generally agreed that, in some dialogues, the dramatic figure "Socrates" represents the views and style of discussion of the historical Socrates; in others, "Socrates" speaks for Plato, setting out and arguing for views that are not always in agreement with those of the historical Socrates. If Plato is our main source of knowledge about Socrates, how can we tell when Plato's "Socrates" speaks for Socrates and when he speaks for Plato? As we shall see, Plato's student, Aristotle, provides the key to an answer.

Among Plato's thirty-five dialogues,[1] there is a group of eleven or twelve that share certain features setting them apart from the rest. In these dialogues, which are considerably shorter than the others, Socrates always has the role of questioner. The questions he discusses are mostly about specific virtues and how they are related to each other: for example, piety is discussed in the *Euthyphro*, courage in the *Laches*, temperance in the *Charmides*, and justice and temperance in the

1. A few of these dialogues are not accepted as genuine by most scholars. For a comprehensive discussion of the nature and composition of Plato's works, see Irwin, chapter 3 in this volume.

*Gorgias.* Socrates and his interlocutors never reach satisfactory answers to the questions discussed, and because the dialogues end in puzzlement, or (in Greek) "aporia," they are often called "aporetic." Nevertheless, there are clear indications that Socrates favors an "intellectualist" view of the virtues, according to which they consist in a kind of knowledge. The other, longer, dialogues are generally more didactic: Socrates (or, in some cases, a different main speaker) lays out and argues for ambitious theories, and the range of subjects discussed is greatly expanded, encompassing the full range of topics that define the main areas of philosophy as we know it today. And in these dialogues, Socrates argues for a more balanced view of the virtues, a view according to which such virtues as courage, temperance, and justice involve both intellectual *and* emotional elements.

Aristotle, in several brief passages, draws contrasts between the views and interests of Socrates and Plato, contrasts that correspond closely to the differences just noted between the two groups of dialogues. For instance, he says that Socrates "asked questions and did not answer" because he claimed not to have knowledge, and that he differed from Plato in focusing his inquiries exclusively on the virtues (*Sophistical Refutations* 183b7–8; *Metaphysics* 987a29–b7; cf. *Apology* 38a1–7). He also reports that Socrates viewed the virtues as purely intellectual qualities—as different forms of knowledge—whereas Plato took account of the emotional and appetitive aspects of the psyche in his treatment of such virtues as courage, temperance, and justice (*Magna Moralia* 1182a15–30). These contrasts between Socrates and Plato match the differences between the shorter, aporetic dialogues, such as the *Protagoras, Laches,* and *Charmides,* and the longer didactic works like the *Republic, Phaedo,* and *Symposium.* Although Aristotle was not yet born at the time of Socrates' death, he spent some twenty years in Plato's school, the Academy, and he undoubtedly came in contact with many people besides Plato who had firsthand knowledge of Socrates. If we accept Aristotle's reports as trustworthy, they provide strong evidence that the shorter, aporetic dialogues present the views of the historical Socrates, while the longer dialogues put forward the different conception of the virtues developed by Plato—in conscious disagreement with the intellectualist view of his mentor.

Most scholars today are in agreement that the shorter dialogues portray the characteristic views and arguments of the historical Socrates; for this reason, these dialogues are also called "Socratic." In fact, a number of scholars believe that these dialogues contain a Socratic "theory" of the virtues: a *unified, systematic* account of their nature and value. According to this view, one of Plato's intentions in writing these dialogues was to set out this systematic account of the virtues and to defend it with arguments used by Socrates. The claim is not that Plato gives us verbatim reports of Socratic discussions: the discussions may well be fictional, but the views and arguments they contain derive from Socrates. As we shall see, there are problems with this view: later in this essay, I suggest that while these dialogues are "Socratic" in the sense that they focus on the views and style of discussion of the historical Socrates, they were not intended to give us a unified Socratic theory of the virtues—for the good reason that Socrates in all likelihood *did not have* a unified theory of the virtues.

# 2. SOCRATES AND THE SOPHISTS

A prominent theme in the Socratic dialogues is Socrates' opposition to the "sophists," a varied lot with different interests and claims to fame, who shared certain characteristics that justified their common designation.[2] They all claimed to be experts (*sophistai*) in political affairs, public speaking, and debating, and they offered to teach these skills, *for a fee*, to young men who were anxious to achieve success in the political arena. They advertised themselves as "teachers of virtue," or excellence, and they regarded virtue as an art or skill—a *technê* in Greek (*Gorgias* 519c3–d1; *Protagoras* 319a3–b1, 320b4–5; *Hippias Major* 282b1–e8, 283c3–5). The claim that virtue is an art or skill clearly served their purpose, for if it's a skill, it ought to be teachable in the way that arts and skills generally are.

Many Athenians were suspicious of the sophists. They regarded them as subverters of traditional morals, and they were skeptical of the claim that virtue could be acquired through the sort of teaching offered by the sophists (*Protagoras* 357e4–8; cf. *Meno* 90e10–91c5 and *Gorgias* 519c2–520e11). In view of Socrates' opposition to the sophists, it is ironic that he was considered to be one of the clan by many of his contemporaries. He makes this clear in his *Apology* when he says that Athenian public opinion is biased against him because of slanderous reports that he engages in the same activities as the sophists (18a7–20c3). Actually, it is not so surprising that Socrates was lumped together with the sophists by the general public. His interests were more or less defined by the sophists' claims and activities. For example, he questioned whether virtue could be taught and inquired into the nature of virtue. His discussions typically involved refuting his interlocutor, and refutation was part of the sophists' stock in trade. Although Socrates denied having any special expertise or "wisdom," he reports that his success in refuting his interlocutors gave others the impression that he had superior knowledge of the matters under discussion (*Apology* 22e7–23a5). Moreover, some of his claims (his "Socratic paradoxes") were strikingly at variance with common opinion, and this may have led many to think that he, like the sophists, was undermining traditional moral beliefs. Socrates also seems to have accepted the sophists' view that virtue is an art or skill. It is true that Socrates never claimed to *teach* virtue, as the sophists did, and he never asked for payment from those who associated with him. Nevertheless, to a casual observer, he might well have seemed a fellow traveler, if not a bona fide member of the group (cf. *Sophist* 226b1–231b8).

Socrates' opposition to the sophists was focused mainly on their claim to teach virtue. Although he seems to have accepted their view that virtue is an art or skill (a *technê*), he argues in both the *Protagoras* and *Meno* that virtue is not teachable. He realizes that his position is puzzling: if virtue is an art or skill, then it ought to be

---

2. For background on the sophists, see R. Barney, "The Sophistic Movement," in M. L. Gill and P. Pellegrin (eds.), *A Companion to Ancient Philosophy* (Malden, Mass., 2006), 77–97; see also Schofield, chapter 2, and Johansen, chapter 20, in this volume.

teachable; and if it is not teachable, this would seem to cast doubt on the claim that it is an art or skill (*Meno* 94b4–8; *Protagoras* 319c7–d7, 361a3–b7). Socrates finds himself in the following quandary at the end of the *Protagoras*:[3]

1. If *X* is an art or skill, then it is teachable.
2. Virtue is a kind of knowledge—that is, an art or skill.
3. Virtue is not teachable.

It is possible that Socrates was genuinely perplexed and thought he had good reasons for maintaining each of these three propositions. It is also possible that he had doubts about one or more of them. Let us take a brief look at a couple of his arguments to see if there is a way out of the quandary.

One of Socrates' main arguments against the teachability of virtue (in both the *Protagoras* and *Meno*) is that those who possess virtue are unable to pass it on to others, in the way that skilled craftsmen can pass on their expertise to apprentices (*Meno* 90b3–e8). He cites the examples of Pericles and Themistocles, famous Athenian statesmen, who had every reason to pass on their political skill and excellence to their sons but were apparently unable to do so (*Protagoras* 319d7–320b5; *Meno* 93a5–94e2). If these great leaders were unable to teach their virtue to others, surely it's because virtue is not teachable.[4]

The main target of Socrates' argument is the sophists' claim to teach virtue. The "virtue" he has in view is the ability to achieve success in politics—that is, to become a powerful and influential leader like Pericles or Themistocles—and this ability is just what the sophists promised to teach their students (*Protagoras* 318e4–319a7; *Meno* 91a1–b5). However, there are good reasons to doubt that Socrates considered this ability to constitute genuine virtue. In another dialogue, the *Gorgias*, he contends that Pericles and Themistocles did not exercise good political leadership—they maintained their power by pandering to the people and did nothing to improve them (515c4–517a6). He also suggests in several places that someone who possessed genuine virtue would be able to explain its nature, and he claims that he has never met anyone who was able to do this (*Meno* 71b1–c4; cf. *Charmides* 158d8–159a4 and *Apology* 29e3–30a3). This is a pretty clear indication that he did not regard the prominent political leaders of his day as examples of genuine virtue. Socrates apparently regards genuine virtue as an extremely rare commodity—something he has never encountered in his many years of searching.

Socrates' argument for the unteachability of virtue is ad hominem in the sense that it relies on a conception of virtue accepted by his opponents, the sophists, but not by him. He says to them in effect: "Let us suppose for the sake of argument that virtue is the sort of thing you say it is, that is, the abilities that enabled leaders like

---

3. See, for example, R. Kraut, *Socrates and the State* (Princeton, N.J., 1984), 285–86.

4. In the *Meno*, Socrates argues more generally that, since there are no teachers of virtue and no learners, it would seem that virtue is not teachable (89d3–96c10). He first points out that those who are regarded as most virtuous, leaders like Pericles and Themistocles, were unable to pass on their excellence to others; he then considers those who claim to be teachers of virtue, the sophists, and notes that their claim is highly disputed, which is not the case in other recognized arts and skills. (Of course, if to be a teacher of virtue one must first possess it, and if "virtue is an extremely rare commodity" (see below), then virtue might be teachable even if there are not, at present, any teachers of it.)

Pericles to gain power and influence in their communities and to secure the admiration of their fellow citizens. I contend that this 'virtue' is not teachable, for those who possess it are unable to pass it on to others." If the argument is ad hominem in this way, we may conclude that Socrates did not see it as a real threat to the view that genuine virtue is an art or skill and therefore teachable. We have found an escape route from the quandary at the end of the *Protagoras*.

1. If $X$ is an art or skill, then it is teachable.
2. (Genuine) virtue is an art or skill.
3. (Sophistical) virtue is not teachable.

If the virtue that the sophists claim to teach is not teachable, it cannot be an art or skill (*Protagoras* 319b3–d7, esp. c1–8; cf. *Meno* 94b4–6). But Socrates believes there is a genuine art of politics, an art quite different from what the sophists profess to teach.[5]

We have seen that Socrates' arguments against the teachability of virtue are not intended to undermine the view that (genuine) virtue is an art or skill. There are some indications in other Socratic dialogues that Socrates may have had doubts about this view, however. For instance, in the *Hippias Minor*, he argues that an art is a "capacity for opposites": that is, the knowledge involved in an art or skill can be used for evil as well as good purposes—medical skill can be used to spread disease as well as to cure it. Perhaps someone who uses her medical skill to harm others should not be called a doctor, but she can be just as skillful as the doctor who cures; it's precisely the skill that enables her to harm others in the way that she does. Now if a virtue like justice were a skill and a capacity for opposites, it could be used for evil purposes as well as good: a just person could use her justice to harm an innocent person (365d6–369a2, 375d7–376b6). But this seems perverse: someone who possessed the virtue of justice could not manifest that justice by harming an innocent person. If a skill *is* a capacity for opposites, it seems that justice cannot be a skill.

Another way of expressing this contrast between virtue and skill is that certain aims or motives are essential to virtue but not to skill. In order to determine whether someone has a skill, we can simply observe them at work: if they perform in a skillful manner and produce the desired results, it is safe to conclude that they possess the skill. But if someone consistently acts justly when called on to do so, it doesn't follow that they possess the virtue of justice: they might act justly out of fear of being punished, or for appearance, or in order to further their career; acting justly for these reasons falls short of what is expected of a just person.[6]

Socrates also argues in the *Hippias Minor* that in the case of an art or skill, one who errs voluntarily is better or more skillful than one who does so *involuntarily* (372c8–376b6). For instance, a mathematician might deliberately make a mistake in a proof in order to see if his students are paying close attention; such a deliberate mistake would not count against his knowledge or skill. But if someone made the same mistake without realizing it ("involuntarily"), it would indicate a gap in his

5. For example, *Gorgias* 464b2-c3, 521d6–8; *Meno* 99e4–100b. Socrates' claim about the sophists is parallel to his claim about the rhetoricians in the *Gorgias*: while there may be a genuine art of rhetoric (504d5-e4, 517a4–6), this art is quite different from the pseudo-art that Gorgias and other contemporary rhetoricians profess to teach.

6. Aristotle makes a similar distinction between virtue and skill; see *Nicomachean Ethics* II 4, 1105a26–b5.

knowledge. If justice were an art or skill, then someone who erred voluntarily—that is, performed an unjust act voluntarily—would be better or more just than one who did something unjust involuntarily. But here, in contrast with arts and skills, voluntarily performing an unjust act *would* seem to count against being a just person.[7]

Socrates admits to being perplexed by these arguments: he is drawn to the view that virtue is an art or skill; at the same time, he sees that it leads to a consequence that he regards as clearly unacceptable (376b8–c6; cf. 372d3–e1). Some have suggested that Socrates points to a way out of the dilemma when he says, in the concluding lines of his argument, "Then the one who goes wrong voluntarily and does base and unjust things, Hippias—*if there is such a person*—would be none other than the good man" (376b4–6). The suggestion is that since Socrates argues elsewhere (as we shall see) that *no one* voluntarily acts unjustly, he would regard the unacceptable consequence of the argument as an impossibility. And yet Socrates seems genuinely perplexed at the end of his argument, and, on reflection, it seems that he has good reason to be. For if voluntary unjust action is impossible, this would be a consequence of our psychological makeup, not of the nature of justice itself: for if justice were an art or skill, there would be nothing in its nature that would rule out someone displaying justice by voluntarily committing some terrible injustice. But this seems clearly unacceptable: deliberately and willingly committing injustice is simply incompatible with our understanding of what it is to be a just person.

To sum up, Socrates is inclined to agree with the sophists' view that virtue should be understood as an art or skill; indeed, he relies on it as a working hypothesis in many of his arguments. But he also has doubts about the sophists' view because of certain striking disanalogies between the virtues and arts or skills. If virtue is not an art or skill, it is no longer clear that it is teachable, at least in the way that arts and skills are: Socrates' doubts about virtue being an art or skill would carry over to its teachability. However, he has no doubts about whether the "virtue" which the sophists claim to teach is teachable; he believes that this pseudo-virtue—the ability to achieve status and power in the political arena—is not teachable since those who have it are unable to pass it on to others.

# 3. SOCRATES' DENIAL OF *ACRASIA*

If virtue is an art or skill that involves knowing what is truly good and evil, the virtuous person should be able to "size up" a situation and determine what sort of action is called for (*Laches* 199d4–e1). But will this knowledge guarantee performance? Isn't it possible to know what one ought to do in a given situation, but fail to do it because of a strong desire to do something else instead? Don't we sometimes act against our better judgment because of weakness of will? Socrates believes

---

7. Aristotle cites this contrast as a reason for denying that virtue is an art or skill; see *Nicomachean Ethics* VI 5, 1140b21–25. Another contrast noted by Aristotle is that to have a virtue is to have achieved a standard of excellence in whatever the virtue is concerned with, but this is not the case with an art or skill—one can possess a skill without having achieved a standard of excellence; see *Nicomachean Ethics* VI 5, 1140b21–25; cf. VI 7, 1141a9–12. This contrast is perhaps alluded to in the *Protagoras* at 327c1–d4.

that a virtuous person will consistently act in a virtuous manner. If so, he must hold that knowledge of the good guarantees performance: if you know what is good, you will always do it. Socrates' conception of virtue thus seems to rule out weakness of will (*acrasia* in Greek). But how can he deny what seems to be a common, everyday occurrence?

Socrates takes up this question in the *Protagoras* and tries to show that the common understanding of *acrasia* is mistaken.[8] The sorts of cases he considers are familiar ones—for example, we are tempted to do something that promises immediate gratification, but we realize that this pleasure is not worth the undesirable consequences that would inevitably follow. Socrates recognizes that most people would say that we sometimes "give in" to such temptations even though we know we shouldn't (352b3–c2), but he suggests that this is a misdescription of what actually happens; in these situations, we only *appear* to be acting against our knowledge: we are actually acting in ignorance.

Socrates' celebrated argument against *acrasia* has been picked apart and analyzed in great detail by scholars over the past half century. I will not be able to go through the argument in detail;[9] instead, I focus on Socrates' overall strategy and attempt to clarify how he understands apparent cases of *acrasia*. His argument has three parts: he first sets out three claims that make up the "Common View"; he then points out that this Common View leads to an absurd consequence; and finally he argues for an alternative description of apparent cases of *acrasia* that avoids the problem with the Common View. As we will see, he does not give a *proof* of his claim that *acrasia* does not occur; rather, he tries to show that the usual way of understanding apparent cases of *acrasia* is problematic and that there is another, less problematic, way that is compatible with his view that knowledge of the good guarantees performance.

At the beginning of the argument, Socrates contrasts his own view of the "power" of knowledge with the Common View.

> Come now, Protagoras, and reveal how you think about this: How do you stand in regard to knowledge? Do you take the same view of it as most people? Most people do not regard it as something strong and controlling and ruling—they don't think of it in this way at all. They think that often knowledge is present in a man, but that something else rather than this knowledge is in control: sometimes anger, sometimes lust, sometimes pleasure or pain, often fear—they think of knowledge as no more than a slave, dragged around by everything else. Is this also your view of knowledge, or do you take it to

---

8. "*Acrasia*," like our expression "weakness of will," covers more than just acting contrary to *knowledge*: for example, we might believe, mistakenly, that a certain kind of good-tasting drink is bad for one's health and occasionally give in to a temptation to have some; this would be an instance of *acrasia*, as well as of weakness of will.

9. For some recent detailed discussions, see G. Santas, *Socrates, Philosophy in Plato's Early Dialogues* (London, 1979), 195–217; C. C. W. Taylor, *Plato's Protagoras*, 2nd ed. [*Protagoras*] (Oxford, 1991), 170–200; T. Penner, "Knowledge vs. True Belief in the Socratic Psychology of Action," *Apeiron* 29 (1996), 199–230, and Penner, "Socrates on the Strength of Knowledge: *Protagoras* 351b–357e" ["Strength"], *Archiv für Geschichte der Philosophie* 79 (1997), 117–49; and R. Singpurwalla, "Reasoning with the Irrational: Moral Psychology in the *Protagoras*" ["Reasoning"], *Ancient Philosophy* 26 (2006), 243–58.

be something noble—the sort of thing that rules a man; and if someone *knows* what's good and what's bad, he would not be overpowered by anything so as to act contrary to what knowledge commands—wisdom is powerful enough to come to his aid. (352a8–c7)

According to the Common View, people sometimes find themselves in the grip of psychological conflict: their knowledge tells them to do one thing, but they are led by passion or desire to do something different. Socrates focuses on the case of doing something you know to be bad because you are "overcome by [a desire for] pleasure"; he argues that when most people call an action or experience "good" or "bad," they consider only the pleasure or pain that it brings: an action or experience is "good" if it brings pleasure or takes away pain and "bad" if it brings pain or takes away pleasure (353c4–354e2).[10] Thus the Common View has three elements:

1. People sometimes do things they know to be bad.
2. They do these bad things *because* they are "overcome by pleasure."
3. What is good = what is pleasant; what is bad = what is painful.

Socrates believes that there is something incoherent or absurd in the combination of these three claims. For according to (3), we should be able to substitute "good" for "pleasure," and vice versa; but if we substitute "good" for "pleasure" in (1) and (2) we get:

4. People sometimes do things they know to be bad because they are overcome by good. (355a5–d3)

But how could good be the cause of bad? Socrates thinks this is "laughable" or absurd. The Common View's explanation of the alleged cases of acting contrary to knowledge, combined with its equation of the good with pleasure, leads to an absurd consequence. This does not mean that defenders of the Common View must give up their belief that people sometimes act contrary to their knowledge; they can look for another possible explanation, or they can give up the equation of good with pleasure. But Socrates has shown that the Common View as it stands is problematic, and he thinks he has another way of describing these cases that is not problematic.

At the very beginning of his argument, Socrates explains what he hopes to show. According to the Common View, there is a certain *experience* that people describe as acting against our knowledge because of "being overcome by pleasure"—an apparent case of *acrasia*. Let us call this experience an "apparently *acratic* experience." Where the Common View goes wrong is not in claiming that there is such an experience; Socrates accepts the existence of the experience, but not the Common View's description of it.

10. Does Socrates agree with the hedonism that he attributes to the Common View? For an affirmative answer, see Taylor, *Protagoras*, 162–70, and T. H. Irwin, *Plato's Ethics* (New York, 1995), 82; for dissent, see D. J. Zeyl, "Socrates and Hedonism," *Phronesis* 25 (1980), 250–69.

> Come, then, [Protagoras,] and let us together attempt to persuade these
> people and explain to them what this experience is which they call "being
> overcome by pleasure," which is the cause of their not doing what they know
> to be best. For perhaps if we told them that they are not speaking correctly and
> that what they say is false, they would ask us: "But Protagoras and Socrates, if
> this experience is not being overcome by pleasure, what can it possibly be—
> what do you say it is? Tell us." (352e5–353a6)

After he has pointed out the absurd consequence of the Common View, Socrates
proceeds to build a case for a revised description of the experience; at the end of the
argument, he formulates his revised description as follows.

> At that point you asked us: "But Protagoras and Socrates, if this experience is
> not being overcome by pleasure, what can it possibly be—what do you say it
> is? Tell us." If we had then said straightaway that it is *ignorance*, you might
> have laughed in our faces; but if you laugh at us now you will be laughing at
> yourselves. For you agreed with us that those who err in their choice of
> pleasures and pains do so through lack of knowledge.... And you must know
> that the erring act done without knowledge is done through ignorance. So this
> is what "being overcome by pleasure" is—ignorance in the highest degree.
> (357c6–e2)

What exactly does Socrates mean by saying that "ignorance" is a more accurate
description of the experience? He is clearly denying that in an apparently *acratic*
experience, the agent *knows* that the action chosen is a bad one: he says that the
person who chooses wrongly does so under the influence of a false opinion or belief
(358c1–5). He is suggesting, then, that the agent believes that the act chosen is good
rather than bad: that is, the agent chooses the present pleasure in the belief that it is
the best option available.

Advocates of the Common View might wonder how this is a more accurate
description of the experience that they have in mind. Recall that a crucial aspect of
an apparently *acratic* experience is psychological conflict: the agent's knowledge
dictates doing X, but he chooses to do Y, instead, because he is overcome by a
strong desire for immediate gratification. According to Socrates' revised description, the agent's desire to do Y is in accord with his (false) belief that Y is the right
thing to do in the situation—there is no longer any conflict. Instead of a more
accurate description of an apparently *acratic* experience, Socrates seems to have
given a description of a different sort of experience. Is he simply denying the
existence of psychological conflict in apparent cases of *acrasia*?

If we look at Socrates' argument leading up to his revised description, it becomes clear that his description does not eliminate psychological conflict. Central
to the argument is an analogy between our judgments regarding pleasure and pain
and our perceptual judgments about things that we see and hear. Socrates points
out that when we are looking at objects close at hand or far away, we may make
mistakes in judging their size; similarly, when pleasures or pains are near at hand or

in the future, we may misjudge them and think that they are greater or smaller than they really are (356c4–357b3). He suggests that just as there is an art of measuring the size of objects, which saves us from being taken in by misleading appearances, so there is an art of measuring pleasures and pains that provides a similar protection.

Socrates' analogy implies that pleasures and pains present misleading appearances when they are near at hand or off in the future; when they are in the middle range, we are less prone to misjudge them. Suppose we are considering the possibility of going to a movie with friends, and we decide, correctly, that it would be foolish to go since we have an important exam the next morning. But when the possible pleasure is there for the taking—say, our friends stop by on their way to the movie—we might waver and then decide that it would be all right to join them; the proximity of the pleasure leads us to overestimate its value in relation to its cost (or underestimate its cost in relation to its value). The next day, after a disastrous performance on the exam, we regret our ill-considered decision. Socrates seems to have just such experiences in view in the following passage:

> The power of appearance makes us wander back and forth, frequently
> changing our minds about the same things and regretting our actions and
> choices of things large and small; the art of measurement, on the other
> hand, would render the appearance ineffective, and by showing us the truth
> would bring peace to the soul abiding in that truth, and would save our lives.
> (356d4–e2)

Socrates suggests that the agent in apparent cases of *acrasia* changes his mind; he makes the wrong choice under the influence of a false belief (358c3–5), but he later "has regrets": in retrospect, he sees that he made the wrong choice. The false belief or "ignorance" is only a temporary, passing, condition (this is also implied by equating the ignorance with an *experience*—something that happens to one; see 357c6–d3). It's not that the agent has a standing belief that going for immediate gratification is the right thing to do: in cooler moments of reflection, before and after the choice, the agent's judgment is clear-headed; but at the moment of choice when the pleasure is near at hand (356a5–7; cf. 353c9–d4), the "power of appearance" clouds his judgment and leads him to believe that taking the present pleasure is the right choice.[11]

The distinction between knowledge and belief—in particular, between knowledge and *true* belief—is an important element in Socrates' account of apparent cases of *acrasia*. The person with knowledge can be counted on to make the

---

11. What does Socrates mean by "the power of appearance"? Does he hold that the distorted appearance is a "purely intellectual" mistake that gives rise to a desire for the immediate gratification? Or is it the other way around—that the desire aroused by the anticipated pleasure causes the distorted appearance? Or is the desire equivalent to a belief about the value of the present pleasure based on the distorted appearance? For the first view, see Penner, "Strength," 117–49; for the second, D. T. Devereux, "Socrates' Kantian Conception of Virtue," *Journal of the History of Philosophy* 33 (1995), 381–408, and T. Brickhouse and N. Smith, "The Socratic Paradoxes," in H. H. Benson (ed.), *A Companion to Plato* (Malden, Mass., 2006), 263–77; for the third, Singpurwalla, "Reasoning," 249–54.

right judgments about pleasures and pains and to act accordingly. At the opposite extreme is the vicious, self-indulgent person whose judgment has been permanently corrupted, and who has standing false beliefs about the relative values of various pleasures and pains. Such a person will not typically waver back and forth but will consistently act in accordance with his standing beliefs. In the middle is the person who wavers: the person who has true beliefs but not knowledge and whose judgment can be turned around by the "power of appearance." This is the person who has the apparently *acratic* experience: he seems to know that $X$ is the right choice but chooses $Y$, instead, because of a strong desire for immediate gratification. According to Socrates' account, knowledge is not vulnerable to the power of appearance, but belief is; in apparent cases of *acrasia* the agent's true belief about the relative values of the pleasures and pains (or goods and evils) in a course of action is overcome by the misleading appearance of the present pleasure—that is, the agent "changes his mind" at the time of choosing and (mis)judges that $Y$ is the right choice. Afterward, he sees his mistake and "regrets" his choice.

This way of understanding Socrates' account of apparent cases of *acrasia* preserves the element of psychological conflict: the agent's desire for immediate gratification contends with and "overcomes" his belief that he should resist.[12] As we have seen, the account involves a contrast between the stability of knowledge, which can withstand the "power of appearance," and the instability of true belief, which can be temporarily suppressed and replaced by a false belief that supports the desire for immediate gratification. Socrates' description of apparent cases of *acrasia* is similar to what is sometimes called "rationalization": fabricating a justification for some action that goes against our better judgment—if, under the influence of passion or desire, we manage to persuade ourselves that it is a good thing to do, we will have (temporarily) acquired a false belief supporting the action.

Does Socrates provide a convincing account of what happens in apparent cases of *acrasia*? In view of the familiar phenomenon of rationalization, we might agree that sometimes what seems like "acting against knowledge" is more accurately described as acting under the influence of a temporary false belief that rationalizes our action. But we might also question whether it is only true opinion that gets pushed aside or suppressed in rationalization: Why can't the same thing happen to knowledge? Furthermore, some might argue that our experience testifies to the fact that we sometimes succumb to temptation without any rationalization—we "know full well" that we are making a bad choice and that we will come to regret it. Socrates might reply that *knowledge* must have a stronger hold on us: if we had genuine knowledge of the good, it would exert such a powerful influence on us that we would never act against it.[13] And it is worth noting that philosophers continue to find the

---

12. The conflict ceases at the moment of choice, if not before; when the agent chooses the *acratic* action, his judgment accords with his desire. In the *Republic*, Plato apparently concedes that conflict can occur even at the moment of choice; see the story of Leontius in Book IV, 439d6–440a4.

13. Cf. Aristotle, *Nicomachean Ethics* VII 2, 1145b23–24: "Socrates thought it would be astonishing (*deinon*) if knowledge, being present in a man, could be overpowered by something else"; see also *Magna Moralia* II 6, 1200b34–37.

phenomenon of *acrasia* puzzling, and many are sympathetic toward Socrates' view. But it also seems clear that he gives no argument for his claim that knowledge, or "the art of measurement," cannot be overcome by passion or desire; as I mentioned earlier, Socrates does not give a *proof* of his claim that *acrasia* does not occur.

Socrates' thesis that knowledge of the good guarantees performance of right action is closely related to another paradoxical claim, which he argues for in the *Protagoras*: the doctrine of the "Unity of the Virtues." If each of the virtues requires knowledge of good and evil, and if this knowledge guarantees that one will always perform the virtuous action in the appropriate situation, then one couldn't have one virtue without having all the rest (see *Laches* 199d4–e1). Some scholars believe that what Socrates means by the Unity of the Virtues is that, while each virtue has its own distinct essence, they are all *inseparably* linked to each other through the knowledge of good and evil. Others argue that he makes a stronger claim: that the virtues are *identical* with this knowledge and that there is just one essence and one definition for all the virtues.[14] I will not pursue this dispute, but it is worth noting that whether unity is understood as identity or inseparability, the basis for the doctrine is the claim that knowledge of the good guarantees performance of right action.

# 4. Desire and the Good

As we have seen, Socrates does not deny that there is an experience of psychological conflict in apparent cases of *acrasia*. On one side is a desire for immediate gratification; on the other is the correct belief that the gratification is not worth the undesirable consequences that will inevitably follow. As the conflict plays out, Socrates suggests that the agent "rationalizes" the choice of the present pleasure by temporarily suppressing the judgment that it is a bad choice. In giving this account, Socrates seems to accept the Common View's assumption that we can desire things we recognize to be bad (bad for us, or bad in some other way). However, in both the *Gorgias* and the *Meno*, he claims that we only desire what is good—no one desires what is bad.[15] In the *Gorgias*, Socrates makes this claim in attempting to

---

14. Socrates seems to argue for *identity* in the *Protagoras*, but in the *Laches* he appears to claim that the virtues are distinct parts of a whole. For a defense of the identity interpretation for both dialogues, see T. Penner, "The Unity of Virtue," *Philosophical Review* 82 (1973), 35–68, reprinted in G. Fine (ed.), *Plato 2* (New York, 1999), 78–104; for the inseparability interpretation, see G. Vlastos, "The Unity of the Virtues in the *Protagoras*," *Review of Metaphysics* 25 (1972), 415–58, reprinted with additional notes in Vlastos, *Platonic Studies*, 2nd ed. (Princeton, 1981), 221–69, 418–23; for a "fence-straddling" interpretation, see M. Ferejohn, "The Unity of Virtue and the Objects of Socratic Inquiry," *Journal of the History of Philosophy* 20 (1982), 1–21; and for the view that the two dialogues present conflicting views, see D. Devereux, "The Unity of the Virtues," in *A Companion to Plato*, ed. H. H. Benson (Malden, Mass., 2006), 325–40.

15. In both contexts, it is clear that Socrates' claim is that we only desire what is good *for us*. This would seem to commit him to Psychological Egoism—that is, to the view that all of our actions are motivated by self-interest. However, as we shall see, Socrates' claim is not about what *motivates us to act*; thus it is not clear that he is committed to Psychological Egoism. It is also worth noting that many of his statements about his own motives do not seem to fit comfortably with such a doctrine (e.g., *Apology* 31a9–c3, *Euthyphro* 3d5–9).

show that tyrants do not have great power because they do not do what they want to do. It will be useful to survey the main steps of his argument.

1. Having great power is doing whatever one wants to do.
2. We only want what is good for us, not what is bad or indifferent.
3. Doing unjust acts is bad for us.
4. Tyrants do many unjust acts, thinking they are best for them.
5. Thus, by (3) and (4), tyrants do what is bad for themselves.
6. Thus, by (2) and (5), tyrants do not do what they want to do.
7. Thus, by (1) and (6), tyrants do not have great power.[16]

The most questionable parts of the argument are steps (2) and (3): What exactly is meant by the claim that "we only want what is good for us," and what is its basis; and why does Socrates think doing unjust acts is always bad for us? We return to the latter question toward the end of our discussion.

It seems that (2) would not leave room for the psychological conflict we noticed in Socrates' discussion of *acrasia* in the *Protagoras*: if we recognize that a tempting present pleasure would be bad for us, then, according to (2), it cannot be something that we want or desire. In fact, what Socrates means by (2) is that, *whether or not we recognize it*, if something is bad for us, we cannot be said to want it. This is clearly implied by his claim that when the tyrant, for example, does away with a potential rival, he does what seems best to him but not what he wants (since it is bad for him). Socrates' claim in (2) is not that we only want what we take to be good, but that we only want what is *in fact* good for us.

The assertion that all of our desires are directed toward what is actually good clearly conflicts with Socrates' view in the *Protagoras* that we sometimes have desires for things that are bad for us; moreover, the claim seems clearly false—it seems obvious that we *do* have desires for things that are bad for us. Socrates claims, in effect, that if we don't know what is good for us, then we also don't know what we want. Suppose that we believe that *X* would be a good thing for us to do, but, actually, it would be bad; according to Socrates, we might believe that we want to do *X*, but, in fact, we don't, since it would be bad for us. We sometimes say things that seem to fit with Socrates' claim: for example, we might say to someone who is very thirsty, "You don't want that sugary stuff you're about to drink. What you want is something that will satisfy your thirst: this glass of cool water is what you really want." Similarly, Socrates might say that the tyrant wants what will make him happy; being unjust will make him miserable in the long run, whereas being just will make him happy; therefore, he (really) wants to be just—he only *thinks* that he wants to act unjustly.

Although we sometimes speak this way, it still seems extremely implausible to say that the tyrant doesn't want to do *X* even though he thinks it's best and freely

16. Steps (1)–(4) are argued for at 467c5–481b5. The inferences in steps (5), (6), and (7) are not explicitly drawn by Socrates, perhaps because Callicles breaks in at 481b5. But it's clear that these steps follow from the preceding and that Socrates' intention from the outset is to argue for (7); see 466e13–467a10, 509e2–7.

chooses to do it. Sometimes we think that $X$ would be the best thing to do in a situation, but we don't really want to do it. But this doesn't seem to be true of the tyrant when he decides to get rid of a hated rival: he has no hesitation, no misgivings. Socrates' claim about desire, as noted, also seems to clash with the *Protagoras'* view that we can desire things that are bad for us because of the lure of immediate gratification. What is even more puzzling is that the claim conflicts with some of Socrates' statements later in the *Gorgias*. One of the important themes in his discussion with Callicles is the value of self-discipline and the need to resist certain desires. He mentions at one point, for example, that doctors often tell their sick patients they must refrain from satisfying their desires for the things they are used to eating and drinking (505a6–10). In another place he says that we should only satisfy those desires that make us better, not those that make us worse (503c6– d3, 505b1–12; cf. 517b2–c2). In these passages, he takes it for granted that not all of our desires are directed toward what is actually good for us. There appears to be a clear inconsistency between Socrates' earlier claim that we only desire what is good for us and his later insistence on the need to curb and restrain certain desires.

For a reader of the Greek text, there is an interesting difference between the earlier and later passages, which may help resolve the apparent inconsistency. Throughout the earlier discussion in which Socrates claims that we only want what is good for us, he uses a verb that is usually translated as "wish" or "want"; in his later discussion of desires that need to be curbed, he uses a different verb that is usually translated as "desire."[17] Although these verbs are often used interchangeably (and are so used in parts of the *Gorgias* that are not concerned with claims about desire), they do have somewhat different meanings. In another Socratic dialogue, the *Charmides*, Socrates differentiates between the two by pointing out that the object of *wanting* is the good, while the object of *desiring* is what is pleasant—which may or may not be good (167e1–5). The notion that *desire* (*epithumia*) is directed toward things that are pleasant but may or may not be good seems to fit the examples of "desires" in the discussion with Callicles: Socrates refers to bodily appetites like hunger and thirst—*appetitive* desires whose satisfaction is pleasant (496c6–e9). Given this difference between the two verbs, it is probably no coincidence that in the *Gorgias* "wanting" (*boulesthai*) is used in the argument for the claim that all desires are for the good, and "desiring" (*epithumein*) is used in the discussion of appetitive desires that are aimed at pleasure and need to be restrained: in these contexts, it seems likely that Socrates is using the verbs in their special senses. If so, the apparent inconsistency is resolved: if his statements are about two distinct types of desire, "wanting" and "appetitive desire," there is no inconsistency. If, alternatively, the claims are about a single notion of desire, then we are faced with an obvious inconsistency.

---

17. The two verbs are *boulesthai* (= "to want" or "to wish") and *epithumein* (= "to desire"); in the later discussion, Socrates more often uses the noun, *epithumia* (= "desire") instead of the verb. (In the later discussion, Socrates does use *boulesthai* once in referring to appetites, in speaking of the healthy person's appetites that do not need to be curbed (505a6–10); these are appetitive desires that are, at the same time, desires for what is good.)

Let us suppose, charitably, that Socrates is not guilty of an obvious inconsistency. We might then sum up his view as follows. There are two types of desire, one of which ("wanting") is always directed toward what is actually good, while the other ("appetitive desire") is always directed toward what is pleasant. Some appetitive desires need to be resisted, since satisfying them would be bad for us. Thus we can only *want* what is good for us, but we can *desire* what is bad. The tyrant doesn't *want* to do something unjust since it would be bad for him, but he may *desire* to do it if he believes it will bring him pleasure (or fend off future pain). This way of understanding Socrates' claims eliminates the apparent inconsistency in the *Gorgias*, and leaves room for the sort of psychological conflict presupposed in the *Protagoras*—a conflict between our appetitive desire for immediate gratification and our judgment that it isn't worth the cost. But we are still left with a puzzle: What is Socrates' reason for distinguishing between the two types of desire in the way that he does? The distinction seems somewhat artificial, and the claim that there is a type of desire that is directed only at what is actually good is particularly problematic.[18] Does Socrates make this claim simply in order to support his paradoxical thesis that tyrants do not have great power?

Later in the discussion with Callicles, it becomes clear that the problematic claim about wanting the good is also related to Socrates' well-known paradox that "all unjust action is involuntary."

> Why don't you at least answer me this, Callicles—Do you or don't you think Polus and I were correct in being compelled to agree in our previous discussion that no one acts unjustly wanting to do so, but all unjust action is done involuntarily? (509e2–7)

Actually, Socrates and Polus did not agree that "no one acts unjustly wanting to do so" or that "all unjust action is done involuntarily." However, these claims do seem to follow from two of their earlier agreements: (i) if a tyrant does *X*, which is actually bad for him, he cannot be said to *want* to do *X*; and (ii) a tyrant's unjust actions are bad for him in that they bring about a corrupt, unhealthy condition of the soul. From these it follows that tyrants (or anyone else, for that matter) cannot *want* to do the unjust actions that they do; and if they don't want to do them, they do them involuntarily. Since it is the "not wanting" that makes the actions involuntary, Socrates must establish that no one wants to act unjustly in order to support his claim that all unjust action is done involuntarily.[19]

Socrates' controversial thesis about wanting the good serves two important purposes: it allows him to argue that tyrants do not have great power, and it provides a basis for his paradox that all unjust or immoral action is done involuntarily. But it

---

18. Aristotle also connects "wanting" (*boulesthai*) with the good but in a more plausible way: he argues that for each individual, the object of wanting is what *appears* good rather than what is actually good, but also that what appears good to the good person is actually good; see *Nicomachean Ethics* III 4, 1113a15–31.

19. For a different view of how the controversial claim about wanting relates to the paradox, see K. McTighe, "Socrates on Desire for the Good and the Involuntariness of Wrongdoing," *Phronesis* 29 (1984), 193–236, reprinted in H. Benson (ed.), *Essays on the Philosophy of Socrates* (New York, 1992), 263–97.

seems likely that the thesis is also attractive to Socrates in its own right, as expressing an important truth about our relationship to the good.[20] The thesis implies that we have an innate, natural attraction to what is actually good. When we mistakenly choose something that only appears to be good, we are still pursuing what is actually good (*Meno* 77d7–e4; cf. *Republic* 505d5–9). Socrates would perhaps say that when we attain the object of our misguided desire, we are not satisfied—we have a sense that this is not what we really wanted (cf. *Gorgias* 493d5–494a3).

Plato speaks of our innate orientation toward the good in the following passage in Book VI of the *Republic*.

> Every soul pursues the good and does whatever it does for its sake, having an intuition of its existence but unable to form an adequate grasp of what it is or to acquire the sort of stable beliefs about it that it has about other things, thus missing out on whatever benefit other things may provide. (505d11–e4)

Since this passage comes from the *Republic*, a later "Platonic" dialogue, we cannot assume that it expresses a view that Socrates would agree with. However, it does seem to accord with Socrates' thesis that what everyone *wants* is the good, and it captures the idea that even when our choices are misguided, we are still pursuing what is actually good. But we should also remember that Socrates recognizes another type of desire, *appetitive* desire, which can be directed toward what is pleasant but bad. It is this type of desire that overcomes our better judgment in apparent cases of *acrasia*.

# 5. WISDOM, VIRTUE, AND HAPPINESS

Socrates maintains, as we've seen, that those who know what is truly good will be virtuous and will always act rightly. He also holds that everyone wants the good. But what exactly *is* the good? In a well-known passage in the *Apology*, he chastises his fellow Athenians for caring too much for such things as wealth and status and too little for the things that really matter: wisdom, truth, and the perfection of the soul (29d7–30b4; cf. 36c3–d1). This suggests that he regards virtue and wisdom as the highest goods. But Socrates also boasts that he confers "the greatest benefit" on his fellow citizens by making them truly happy (36c3–d10; cf. 38a1–7, 41b7–c4). So happiness, too, is a paramount good.

How does Socrates understand the relationship between wisdom and virtue, on the one hand, and happiness, on the other? In several places, he claims that they are inextricably linked: one cannot be happy without virtue, and if one has virtue one cannot fail to be happy (*Gorgias* 470e4–11, 507b8–c5, 508a8–b3; *Crito* 48b4–6). Is virtue a good because it contributes to happiness, or does it have some value in

20. For development of this suggestion, see R. Kamtekar, "Socrates on the Attribution of Conative Attitudes," *Archiv für Geschichte der Philosophie* 88 (2006), 127–62.

itself, apart from its contribution to happiness (as some modern moral philoso-phers have argued)? There is general agreement that Socrates subscribes to a form of "eudaimonism"—that is, the view that happiness (*eudaimonia* in Greek) is "the good," or the highest good, and that every other good, including virtue, derives its goodness from its contribution to happiness. Scholars disagree, however, about the way in which virtue contributes to happiness, some holding that it "produces" happiness as a separate product, others that it contributes by being a part of happiness.[21]

According to the first view, the value of virtue would be purely "instrumental," and this seems to fit well with the idea that virtue is an art or skill, similar to carpentry, medicine, or shipbuilding; for these arts have a product separate from the art itself, and the art derives its value from the product. But there are passages, as we shall see, that are hard to square with a purely instrumental understanding of the value of virtue; in these passages, Socrates seems to regard virtue as having value in its own right, not simply as something that produces happiness as a distinct product. Socrates' views on these questions are obviously fundamental to his ethics, so we must try to clarify how he understands the nature of happiness and its relationship to virtue and the good.

Socrates takes up the question of the nature of happiness in the *Euthydemus*. He points out to his young interlocutor, Cleinias, that there is no need to ask whether everyone wants to "do well" and be happy—the answer is obvious; what is not clear is how one goes about "doing well" and being happy. Socrates begins by citing commonly held views, and then proceeds to "correct" them in certain ways (just as he does in the discussion of *acrasia* in the *Protagoras*). People generally believe that to be happy is to possess an abundance of goods such as wealth, health, power, and status, along with the virtues of justice, temperance, courage, and wisdom (278e3–c2). But is possession of these goods a guarantee of happiness? It seems that one also needs a certain amount of luck or good fortune; for even if someone had all of these goods, she might be deprived of happiness by tragic misfortunes. But Socrates manages to persuade Cleinias that there is no need to add good fortune to the list of goods, since wisdom, like any art or skill, guarantees success in one's activities—it ensures "doing well"—so if one is wise, one will have no need of good fortune (279c4–280b3).[22]

21. For Socrates' commitment to eudaimonism, see C. D. C. Reeve, *Socrates in the Apology* (Indianapolis, 1989), 126–30; G. Vlastos, *Socrates, Ironist and Moral Philosopher* [*Socrates*] (Ithaca, N.Y., 1991), 200–32; Irwin, *Plato's Ethics*, 52–53; T. Brickhouse and N. Smith, *The Philosophy of Socrates* [*Socrates*] (Boulder, Colo., 2000), 127–29. For the view that virtue produces happiness as a separate product, see T. H. Irwin, *Plato's Moral Theory* (Oxford, 1977), 92–93; for a defense of virtue as a part of happiness, see Vlastos, *Socrates*, 209–32.

22. But suppose an expert ship captain is blown off course and shipwrecked by an unforeseen storm: Has he "done well"? "Doing well" for Socrates consists in the skillful exercise of one's craft, or of wisdom; we may "do well" even if we fail to achieve the goal of our skillful actions. Socrates' discussion of the relationship between doing well and good fortune has interesting connections with Stoic views; on the relationship between the *Euthydemus* and Stoic ethics, see J. Annas, "Virtue as the Use of Other Goods," in T. Irwin and M. C. Nussbaum (eds.), *Virtue, Love and Form: Essays in Memory of Gregory Vlastos* (Edmonton, 1993), 53–66.

But Socrates is still not satisfied. He points out that even if we have all of these goods, we will not be happy unless we benefit from them, and this means that we must *use* them (280b5–d7). Moreover, we must use them rightly—that is, wisely— for if goods are used *unwisely*, they will result in more harm than good. Happiness and "doing well" will therefore consist in the wise use of such goods as wealth, health, power, and so on. Wisdom turns out to be the key to happiness (280d7– 281b4).[23] In fact, Socrates goes on to argue that, strictly speaking, wisdom is the only thing that is good. For if a good is something we are *always* better off having, wisdom seems to be the only thing that qualifies as a good. Someone who lacks wisdom would not be better off with wealth or power, or any of the other things on the list of "goods," for if these things are used unwisely (as they can be), they turn out to be harmful rather than beneficial. To underline the fact that the other "goods" apart from wisdom are not genuine goods, let us call them "assets." Happiness, then, will consist in the wise use of assets: one must have some assets to "use wisely,"[24] but the most important factor is wisdom.

In the course of his discussion with Cleinias, Socrates revises or corrects the common view of happiness as "the possession of many goods" in two ways. First, he drastically prunes the list of goods: only wisdom qualifies as a genuine good, since it is the only thing we are *always* better off having. Second, he points out that happiness does not lie in the *possession* of wisdom and other commonly recognized "goods" but in the wise *use* of these "goods" in activity. We should also note that Socrates treats wisdom and virtue as equivalent (282d8–283b3; cf. 278d1–3). Wisdom/virtue is distinct from happiness in that it is a "possession" that can be used in activity, whereas happiness is not a possession that can be used—it is the *use itself* of wisdom/virtue (and other assets) in activity.

In the second stage of the argument, Socrates and Cleinias attempt to clarify the nature of wisdom/virtue (288d5–292e5). It was earlier agreed that wisdom is the only genuine good and that it is beneficial insofar as it guarantees the correct use of "assets." Socrates now points out that among the various arts or skills there is generally a separation of production and use: some arts are concerned with pro- duction but not use (it is not part of flute-making to know how to play the flute), while others are concerned with use but not production (the art of flute-playing is not concerned with how flutes are made) (289b7–d7). Given the preceding argu-

---

23. There is a puzzle about Socrates' claim that possession of goods is not sufficient for happiness. If we possessed wisdom and a sufficient supply of assets, it seems clear that we would use those assets wisely— after all, it would be *foolish* not to. Hence, contrary to Socrates' claim, it seems that the possession of wisdom and these assets would be a guarantee of doing well and living happily. Perhaps Socrates wants to emphasize that, while doing well is guaranteed by the possession of goods, it *consists in* the activity of using them. The claim that happiness consists in activity is standard in Socratic dialogues: see, for example, *Charmides* 171e7– 172a5, 173c7–d5; *Crito* 48b2–8; *Gorgias* 507b8–c5; *Republic* I, 353d11–354a2.

24. See, for example, 280c3–d7: the craftsman cannot do well unless he has tools and materials to work with. The necessity of having assets in addition to wisdom/virtue seems to conflict with the claim noted above that wisdom/virtue is sufficient for happiness. Perhaps in making the claim for the sufficiency of virtue, Socrates presupposes that the virtuous person has at least some assets, for example, health (*Crito* 47e4–6; *Gorgias* 505a2–4, 512a2–5; cf. Brickhouse and Smith, *Socrates*, 139–49).

ment, one would expect wisdom to be classified as one of the arts concerned with use. But Socrates surprisingly claims that wisdom is concerned with both production and use: it has its own characteristic product and knows how to use that product (289b4–6). He and Cleinias then set off on a search for an art that combines production and use. After considering and eliminating various possible candidates, they decide that the "political" or "royal" art is most likely to be the one they're looking for (289b4–291c2).[25]

But their attempt to identify the product of this art leads to an impasse. Socrates points out that if the political art is beneficial, its product must be something good; but the earlier argument showed that the only genuine good is wisdom. So if the political art produces a genuine good, it must reproduce itself: the function of the political expert would be to "produce" others who are wise and good in the same way that he is (292b1–d6). But if these "products" of the political art are good in the same way, then they will be good insofar as they make others good, and these will be good insofar as they make others good, . . . and so on. If the question is "How is wisdom beneficial?" the answer, "It is beneficial insofar as it produces itself," is of no help at all; as Socrates puts it, the search for the valuable product of the political art has landed them in a "labyrinth" with no way out (291b7, 292d8–e5). The rest of the dialogue provides no hints as to how this impasse or aporia might be avoided.

It might seem as if Socrates has overlooked an obvious solution. At the beginning of the second stage, he says that wisdom is the art that "provides and produces happiness" (291b4–7). And in the first stage of the argument, it was agreed that wisdom guarantees correct use of assets, thereby ensuring that we will "do well" and be happy. Isn't it clear that happiness is the good product provided by wisdom or the political art? Perhaps this is the solution that Plato had in mind, but there are a couple of reasons for skepticism. First, let us recall that the product they are looking for is something that the political art knows how to *use*. If happiness is the product, then the political art must know how to use happiness. But is happiness something that can be used? If happiness consists in the wise use of assets, can we make sense of this *wise use of assets* itself being something that can be used?

A second reason for doubting that happiness provides the solution to Socrates' aporia has to do with the distinction between the exercise of an art or skill and the goal at which it aims. In a typical art or skill like carpentry, its "exercise" will be the various activities involved in the production of, say, a table. Socrates says that "doing well" for the carpenter is a matter of *using* appropriate tools and materials in a skillful manner (280c3–d1, 281a2–6). The product aimed at is not the activity of

25. The assimilation of wisdom to the political art follows naturally from Socratic premises: (i) if wisdom is an art, and if it is characteristic of an art that its possessor can transmit it to others, then someone who is wise will be able to make others wise; (ii) if the wise are virtuous, then someone who is wise will be able to make others virtuous; (iii) the function of the political art is to make others virtuous; (iv) hence someone who is wise will have the ability to carry out the function of the political art: that is, they will possess the political art.

production but the result—for example, a table. Even in the case of an art like flute playing that is concerned with the use of something produced by another art, there is a distinction between the use and the result aimed at—between the flutist's playing of the flute and the melody produced. So if wisdom is an art, there should be a product or result, which it aims at in its use of assets. The very expression "wise *use* of assets" implies a goal or product: when we use something, it is always with a view to some end or goal. Since happiness is identified with the *use* of assets, it cannot be the product of the political art. If wisdom is equated with the political art, and happiness consists in the exercise of that art, there must be something else that is its product or goal.[26]

If we turn to the *Gorgias*, keeping in mind the aporia of the *Euthydemus*, we find clear suggestions pointing to a solution. In the *Gorgias*, Socrates claims that the goal of any genuine art is a certain virtue or excellence in the thing to which the art is applied (503d6–504e4, 506c5–e4). Medicine and "gymnastic" (physical training) are concerned with the body, and their aim is to bring about and maintain the excellence or "virtue" of the body—health and strength. Socrates divides the political art into two parts corresponding to gymnastic and medicine: the art of legislation and the art concerned with the administration of justice (464b2–c5, 520b2–3). The political art tends to the soul: its aim is to bring about and maintain the soul's excellence or virtue. In his discussion with Callicles, Socrates introduces a very general and simplified concept of virtue: the virtue or excellence of a thing has to do with how its parts are related to each other; a thing will be an excellent specimen of its kind—it will possess virtue—if its parts are ordered in the appropriate way for a thing of its kind (506c5–e4, 503d5–504d3). Thus the virtue of the body, health, consists in the various parts of the body being appropriately ordered (504b7–c9).

The virtue of the soul is analogous to physical health: it consists in the parts of the soul being ordered in the appropriate way. But what are the "parts" of the soul? Socrates does not take up this question directly, but he indicates what he has in mind in a couple of brief remarks: in one passage he mentions "that [part] of the soul in which appetitive desires are found" (493a1–b3), and in another he refers to a part that should exercise rule over these desires—presumably the rational, thinking part of the soul (491d7–e1). The virtue of the soul, then, and in particular justice and temperance (504d1–e4), will be the condition in which the appetitive and the rational parts of the soul are properly ordered: that is, the condition in which the rational part rules the appetitive. Just as the goal of medicine and gymnastic is to bring about and maintain the virtue of the body, health, so the goal of the political art is to bring about and maintain the virtue of the soul: that is, the proper order of its parts. (Let us call this "psychic order.")

---

26. According to this scheme, the wise person does not aim at happiness in exercising his or her wisdom, but happiness is nonetheless something "produced" by wisdom (291b4–7, 292b6–c1); we might call it a "by-product" of wisdom.

In the *Gorgias*, in contrast with the *Euthydemus*, Socrates does not treat virtue as equivalent to wisdom or the political art. Virtue as psychic order is the *product* of the political art, as health is the product of the art of medicine. The analogy between virtue and health clearly implies that virtue is distinct from the political art—it is not identical with a form of knowledge but consists in a relationship between the rational and the appetitive parts of the soul. The analogy suggests that, just as one doesn't need to acquire the art of medicine to be healthy, so one doesn't need to acquire the political art to possess virtue; the good political leader will work to bring about virtue (especially justice and temperance) in the souls of his fellow citizens, but this will not necessitate teaching them the political art (504d1–e4, 515a1–d1, 517b2–c2).[27]

The treatment of the political art in the *Gorgias* provides what is missing in the *Euthydemus*: a product distinct from the art itself, and also distinct from happiness. But is the product of the political art, virtue, a good in its own right? Recall that the aporia of the *Euthydemus* demands that the product be a genuine good. Does the *Gorgias* recognize a distinct kind of good embodied in virtue understood as psychic order? Socrates seems to give an affirmative answer in the following passage.

> Socrates: Listen, then, as I take up the discussion from the beginning. Is the pleasant the same as the good?—It is not, as Callicles and I have agreed.— Should the pleasant be done for the sake of the good, or the good for the sake of the pleasant?—The pleasant for the sake of the good.—And *pleasant* is that by which, when present, we experience pleasure, and *good* is that through which, when it is present in us, we are good?—That's right.—But surely we are good, both we and everything else that's good, when some virtue has come to be present in us?—Yes, this seems to me necessary, Callicles.—But the way in which the virtue of each thing comes to be present in it, whether it's the virtue of an artifact, a body, a soul, or of any living thing—the best way it comes to be present is not at random but through the order, correctness, and art that has been bestowed on each of them. Isn't this right?—I for one would say so.—So it is through ordering that the virtue of each thing is ordered and organized?—I would agree.—Each thing, then, is rendered good by the presence in it of a certain organization, an organization that is appropriate for that thing?—I think so. (506c5–e4)

Socrates here treats virtue as a *source* of goodness: it is the presence of the appropriate virtue in a thing that makes that thing good (cf. *Charmides* 161a8–9, *Gorgias* 497d8–e3, *Meno* 87d8-e1). As a source or principle of goodness, virtue itself must be good, and it would seem to be a good in its own right.

---

27. See T. H. Irwin, *Plato, Gorgias* (Oxford, 1979), 214. At 507a5–c5, Socrates enumerates the virtues that make one a good person: temperance, justice, piety, and courage; the striking absence of wisdom may be explained by the fact that Socrates here has in view the virtue that a good political leader works to instill in the populace at large (504d5–e4, 515b8–c3, 517b2–c2). Being just and acting justly may require a knowledge of which actions are just and which unjust (509d7–e2), but this would be only a part of the knowledge that a good political leader uses to instill virtue in his fellow citizens.

We have seen that the *Gorgias* provides a possible solution to the aporia of the *Euthydemus* by identifying a distinct product of the political art, a product that is a genuine good in its own right.[28] We might say that the *Gorgias* "corrects" the *Euthydemus* by introducing a conception of virtue that is distinct from wisdom or the political art—virtue understood as psychic order. Wisdom is a virtue, but there is another kind of virtue, psychic order, which is exemplified most clearly in justice and temperance (504d1–e4, 506e1–507a2).

We began this section by noting that Socrates in the *Apology* considers both happiness and wisdom/virtue as the most important or highest goods, but he doesn't indicate how these are related to each other. Our examination of the *Euthydemus* and *Gorgias* has provided some clarification. Let us sum up our results.

1. Happiness or "doing well" is not a possession that can be used;[29] it consists in *use*—the use of assets guided by wisdom.

2. Wisdom *is* a possession that can be used, but it differs from other things that can be used in that it can only be used well or rightly, whereas they can also be used badly or wrongly.

3. Wisdom, understood as the political art, not only guides the use of assets (including the products of other arts: *Euthydemus* 291c4–9, *Gorgias* 517c7–518a7) but also has the function of producing virtue in human souls.

4. The virtue produced by the political art consists in the proper order of the parts of the soul—the rational part ruling the appetitive part—and it is distinct from the political art in the way that health is distinct from the art of medicine.

5. Virtue as psychic order is not like an asset that may or may not be beneficial; it is like wisdom—it is always beneficial, it always contributes to our happiness.

6. Virtue as psychic order is also a good-making characteristic: it "makes" those who possess it good specimens of their kind—that is, good human beings. As a "good-maker," it must be good in its own right.

Happiness is also a good in its own right, of course, but not a "good-maker" in the way that virtue is; happiness is a good insofar as it is a kind of activity and life that fulfills the desires of a person whose soul has psychic order (*Gorgias* 492c4–494a5, 504e6–505b1; cf. *Symposium* 204e1–205a3). We noticed earlier that Socrates speaks of happiness as something "produced" by wisdom or virtue. Does this mean that happiness is related *instrumentally* to its "producers"? This depends on how one understands the relationship between a state or condition of the soul (wisdom or virtue) and its exercise or expression in activity (happiness). The relationship seems closer than that between a typical art and its product but not quite the same

---

28. What about the demand that the political art know how to *use* its product? The product of the political art is virtuous citizens. We may surmise that a wise statesman will know how to "use" these products in the sense that he knows how to direct their activities for the overall good of the civic community.

29. Cf. Aristotle, *Nicomachean Ethics* IX 9, 1169b28–30.

as that between whole and part; perhaps the relationship is similar to that between an art like dancing and its "product": the product simply is the exercise of the art.[30]

# 6. SOCRATES AND PLATO REVISITED

Some of the claims made in the preceding section are controversial. For example, the claim that Socrates views virtue, understood as psychic order, as having value in its own right apart from its contribution to happiness, would be disputed by those who believe that Socrates subscribes to a strong form of eudaimonism, the view that happiness is "the good," or the highest good, and that every other good, including virtue, derives its goodness from its contribution to happiness. These scholars might argue that, although there are passages in the *Gorgias* that link the goodness of virtue to the notion of "proper order," the value of this proper order, for Socrates, is tied to its contribution to happiness. And it must be admitted that there are passages in other dialogues that seem to support the eudaimonist interpretation (cf. *Meno* 88c1–d3).[31]

Another controversial aspect of our interpretation is the claim that Socrates distinguishes between wisdom and virtue—that is, virtue understood as psychic order—and the further suggestion that these are separable in the sense that one can have virtue as psychic order without possessing wisdom or the political art. The latter view would imply a rejection of the Unity of the Virtues, a doctrine that is generally believed to be a standard fixture of the Socratic dialogues.

While it seems clear that a conception of virtue as psychic order is introduced in the final section of the *Gorgias*, some have argued that this is a Platonic innovation and should not be attributed to Socrates.[32] This is linked to the view that the *Gorgias* is a "transitional" dialogue—that is, a dialogue that shares many features with the other Socratic dialogues but also includes some Platonic elements that are not in harmony with Socrates' views.[33] In fact, the *Gorgias* contains both the "Platonic"

---

30. Cf. Aristotle, *Eudemian Ethics* II 1, 1219a11–18.

31. According to a number of recent scholars, Socrates regards happiness as the single ultimate end of action—that every deliberate action is done for the sake of happiness (see n. 21, above). But even if this were true, it would not rule out the possibility that virtue as psychic order has value in its own right, apart from its contribution to happiness: virtue may be choiceworthy for its own sake, as well as for the sake of happiness, while happiness is choiceworthy only for its own sake. It is questionable, however, whether Socrates *does* hold that happiness is the single ultimate end of all choices and actions. At *Gorgias* 499e7–500a3, he characterizes "the good" as "that for the sake of which everything that we do should be done"; then at 506c5–e4, he picks up this line of thought (see c5), and argues that "the good" is virtue understood as proper order. Nowhere does he characterize happiness as "that *for the sake of which* everything is done (or should be done)"; instead, he says that virtue (or wisdom) is necessary for one who "wants to be happy" or "is going to be happy" (507c8–d6 and *Euthydemus* 280d4–6; cf. *Republic* 358a1–3, 427d1–7, 498b8–c4). See above, n. 26.

32. For example, W. H. Thompson, *The Gorgias of Plato* (New York, 1973), viii–x.

33. For example, A. Gomez-Lobo, *The Foundations of Socratic Ethics* (Indianapolis, 1994), 109–11; J. M. Cooper, "Socrates and Plato in Plato's *Gorgias*," *Reason and Emotion: Essays on Ancient Moral Psychology and Ethical Theory* (Princeton, N.J., 1999), 29–75; and Irwin, *Plato, Gorgias*, 7–8.

conception of justice as psychic order (504c5–d3, 507e6–508a4; cf. 525a3–6), and the "Socratic" view that it is an art or skill (460a5–c6)—and we are given no hints as to how we are supposed to fit these views together. But this is nothing new. We noticed, for instance, that Socrates assumes in many arguments that virtue is an art or skill, but in the *Hippias Minor* he raises difficulties for this view. He also seems to argue for inconsistent views about how the virtues form a unity.

If the conception of virtue as psychic order appeared only in the *Gorgias* and not in any of the other Socratic dialogues, it would be plausible to regard it as a Platonic innovation. But the analogy between virtue and health (and vice and sickness) that underlies the conception of virtue as psychic order appears in other Socratic dialogues. In the *Crito*, for instance, Socrates suggests that just as "healthful" things promote the good condition of the body while "diseaseful" things tend to cause its destruction, so just actions promote the good condition of the soul (virtue) while unjust actions corrupt and destroy it (47c8–48a4).[34] And when he claims in the *Apology* that his accusers are doing more harm to themselves than to him by their unjust actions, and that through their unjust actions they acquire vice and wickedness, he seems to have the same view in mind (30c7–d6, 39a6–b6; cf. *Gorgias* 479b3–c4, 480a6–b2). The health analogy and the associated conception of virtue as psychic order are not "Platonic" innovations: they already appear, at least in rudimentary form, in the Socratic dialogues. Perhaps the *development* of the health analogy in the *Gorgias* is "Platonic," but if so, Plato probably thought of himself as developing a Socratic idea.

The intellectualist conception of the virtues as forms, or a single form, of knowledge is clearly dominant in the Socratic dialogues. But there is another conception, virtue as psychic order, which appears in several of these dialogues and is developed in some detail in the *Gorgias*. These different ways of understanding virtue do not fit together to form a unified conception. The presence of the two incompatible conceptions of virtue in the Socratic dialogues is just one of several inconsistencies and ambivalences we have noticed. The lesson to be drawn is that Plato is not setting out a systematic, unified, "Socratic" theory of the virtues in these dialogues; rather, he is exploring and developing the provocative claims and ideas of his mentor—claims and ideas that are not always consistent with each other. An implication of this way of understanding Plato's project in the Socratic dialogues is that the break between "Socratic" and "Platonic" may not be as sharp as modern scholars tend to believe; for example, Plato may have viewed his elaborate account of the virtues in terms of psychic order in the *Republic* as a departure from Socrates' intellectualism and, at the same time, as a development of another aspect of his mentor's conception of virtue.[35]

---

34. For "healthful" (*hygieinon*) and "diseaseful" (*nosôdes*) as the things that *produce* health or disease, see also *Gorgias* 504c5–9 and *Republic* 444c8–d10. The notion that a virtue like justice can be acquired by performing just actions goes hand in hand with the analogy between virtue and health and does not fit comfortably with the intellectualist conception of virtue as a kind of knowledge (cf. *Euthydemus* 283a1–4; *Gorgias* 507c9–d1, 527c6–e5; *Republic* 444c1–d1, 518d9–519a1).

35. My thanks to Tom Brickhouse, Gail Fine, and Rebecca Stangl for helpful comments on an earlier version of this chapter.

# BIBLIOGRAPHY

Annas, J. *Platonic Ethics, Old and New* (Ithaca, N.Y.: Cornell University Press, 1999).

———. "Virtue as the Use of Other Goods," in T. Irwin and M. C. Nussbaum (eds.), *Virtue, Love and Form: Essays in Memory of Gregory Vlastos* (Edmonton: Academic Printing and Publishing, 1993), 53–66.

Barney, R. "The Sophistic Movement," in M. L. Gill and P. Pellegrin (eds.), *A Companion to Ancient Philosophy* (Malden, Mass.: Blackwell, 2006), 77–97.

Benson, H. (ed.) *Essays on the Philosophy of Socrates* (New York: Oxford University Press, 1992).

Brickhouse, T., and Smith, N. *The Philosophy of Socrates* (Boulder, Colo.: Westview, 2000).

———. "The Socratic Paradoxes," in H. H. Benson (ed.), *A Companion to Plato* (Malden, Mass.: Blackwell, 2006), 263–77.

Carone, G. R. "Calculating Machines or Leaky Jars? The Moral Psychology of Plato's *Gorgias*," *Oxford Studies in Ancient Philosophy* 25 (2004), 55–96.

Cooper, J. M. "Socrates and Plato in Plato's *Gorgias*," *Reason and Emotion* (Princeton, N.J.: Princeton University Press, 1999), 29–75.

Devereux, D. T. "Socrates' Kantian Conception of Virtue," *Journal of the History of Philosophy* 33 (1995), 381–408.

———. "The Unity of the Virtues," in H. H. Benson (ed.), *A Companion to Plato* (Malden, Mass.: Blackwell, 2006), 325–40.

Ferejohn, M. "Socratic Thought-Experiments and the Unity of Virtue Paradox," *Phronesis* 29 (1984), 105–22.

———. "The Unity of Virtue and the Objects of Socratic Inquiry," *Journal of the History of Philosophy* 20 (1982), 1–21.

Gomez-Lobo, A. *The Foundations of Socratic Ethics* (Indianapolis: Hackett, 1994).

Guthrie, W. K. C. *Socrates* (Cambridge: Cambridge University Press, 1971).

Irwin, T. H. *Plato, Gorgias* (Oxford: Clarendon Press, 1979).

———. *Plato's Ethics* (New York: Oxford University Press, 1995).

———. *Plato's Moral Theory* (Oxford: Clarendon Press, 1977).

Kahn, C. *Plato and the Socratic Dialogue* (Cambridge: Cambridge University Press, 1996).

Kamtekar, R. "Socrates on the Attribution of Conative Attitudes," *Archiv für Geschichte der Philosophie* 88 (2006), 127–62.

Kraut, R. *Socrates and the State* (Princeton, N.J.: Princeton University Press, 1984).

McTighe, K. "Socrates on Desire for the Good and the Involuntariness of Wrong-doing," *Phronesis*, 29 (1984), 193–236; reprinted in H. Benson (ed.), *Essays on the Philosophy of Socrates* (New York: Oxford University Press, 1992), 263–97.

Penner, T. "Knowledge vs. True Belief in the Socratic Psychology of Action," *Apeiron* 29 (1996), 199–230.

———. "Power and Desire in Socrates: The Argument of *Gorgias* 466a-468e that Orators and Tyrants Have No Power in the City," *Apeiron* 24 (1991), 147–202.

———. "Socrates on the Strength of Knowledge: *Protagoras* 351b–357e," *Archiv für Geschichte der Philosophie*, 79 (1997), 117–49.

———. "The Unity of Virtue," *Philosophical Review* 82 (1973), 35–68; reprinted in G. Fine (ed.), *Plato 2* (New York: Oxford University Press, 1999), 78–104.

Reeve, C. D. C. *Socrates in the Apology* (Indianapolis: Hackett, 1989).

Rudebusch, G. *Socrates, Pleasure, and Value* (New York: Oxford University Press, 1999).

Santas, G. *Socrates, Philosophy in Plato's Early Dialogues* (London: Routledge and Kegan Paul, 1979).

Singpurwalla, R. "Reasoning with the Irrational: Moral Psychology in the *Protagoras*,"
    *Ancient Philosophy* 26 (2006), 243–58.
Taylor, C. C. W. *Plato's Protagoras*, 2nd ed. (Oxford: Oxford University Press, 1991).
Thompson, W. H. *The Gorgias of Plato* (New York: Arno Press, 1973).
Vlastos, G. *Socrates, Ironist and Moral Philosopher* (Ithaca, N.Y.: Cornell University Press,
    1991).
———. "The Unity of the Virtues in the *Protagoras*," *Review of Metaphysics* 25 (1972), 415–
    58; reprinted with additional notes in Vlastos, *Platonic Studies*, 2nd ed. (Princeton,
    N.J.: Princeton University Press, 1981), 221–69, 418–23.
Zeyl, D. J. "Socrates and Hedonism," *Phronesis* 25 (1980), 250–69.

# CHAPTER 7

......................................................................................

# PLATO'S
# EPISTEMOLOGY

......................................................................................

## C. C. W. TAYLOR

A convenient starting point for consideration of Plato's treatment of knowledge is Socrates' notorious disavowal of knowledge; we can hope to arrive at a conception of how knowledge is seen in the Socratic dialogues if we can see what it is that Socrates claimed not to have. In antiquity, Socrates was widely supposed to have claimed that he knew nothing or, in some versions, that he knew only this one thing, that he knew nothing.[1] But in Plato's dialogues, Socrates never makes either claim. The nearest he comes to the former is at *Apol.* 21d, where he describes himself as having shown that someone who claimed to have wisdom (which, in context, amounts to wisdom in organizing his life as a whole) did not, in fact, have the wisdom which he claimed. Socrates remarks that while it is likely that neither he nor the person whom he has just exposed knows anything fine and good, he (i.e., Socrates) is wiser in that he is aware of his ignorance (*ha mē oida oude oiomai eidenai*), while the other is not. Assuming that "is likely" is an intentional understatement, this is naturally taken as asserting that Socrates knows nothing fine and good. But in this same work Socrates twice claims to know that it would be wrong for him to abandon his divine mission to improve the souls of his fellow citizens by philosophical criticism (29b, 37b); that implies that he knows that carrying out his mission is fine and good, which I take it he would count as a case of knowing something fine and good. So either Plato depicts Socrates as inconsistent within a single work, or the assertion that he knows nothing fine and good is to be interpreted as to be consistent with the knowledge claim just mentioned.

---

1. Cicero, *Academica* I, 16 and 45, II, 74.

The context readily suggests such an interpretation. Socrates is explaining how he was prompted to his mission by the pronouncement of the Delphic oracle that no one was wiser than he. He was puzzled by this because he was conscious of not being wise about anything, great or small (21b)—that is to say, of not being an expert in any subject matter—and he tried to show that the oracle could not have meant what it seemed prima facie to mean by seeking genuine experts, whether experts in the conduct of life as a whole, as the sophists claimed to be (20a–c), or experts in particular areas, such as builders. The result was that neither kind of expert proved wiser than Socrates: the former because they had no expertise at all, the latter because they mistakenly believed that the technical expertise which they did possess extended to the conduct of life as a whole. I suggest, then, that the assertion at 21d that neither Socrates nor the supposed expert knew anything fine and good is to be interpreted as "neither knows anything fine and good in that way," that is in the way that the supposed expert had claimed: the possession of expertise in how to live. Lacking such expertise, Socrates may still be able to know some particular moral truths, such as that mentioned above, though how he knows them is as yet unexplained.

So far, the texts warrant a distinction between the highest level of epistemic achievement, wisdom or expertise, which Socrates claims not to possess, and a lower level, exemplified by knowledge of particular moral truths, which he does claim.[2] It has been suggested[3] that this amounts to the distinction between knowledge and true belief. That distinction is certainly important in Plato's epistemological thought (see below), but it is not the distinction drawn in the *Apology*. In that work, Socrates is made to claim particular moral knowledge without qualification, or any other indication in the text that the verbs rendered "know" are not the most appropriate terms to use. The contrast between that knowledge and the wisdom which Socrates disavows is never explicitly spelled out, but it is evidently connected with the fact that the possessor of wisdom is thereby qualified to impart that wisdom to others, and regularly does so, whereas Socrates insists that he does not have any wisdom to impart: that is to say, that he does not teach anyone anything (19d–20c). What the expert is typically qualified to teach is a systematic body of knowledge, both theoretical and practical, the relative importance of the two aspects depending on the nature of the expertise.

---

2. For a similar, though different, view, see G. Vlastos, "Socrates' Disavowal of Knowledge," *Socratic Studies*, ed. M. Burnyeat (Cambridge, 1994), 39–66, reprinted in G. Fine, ed., *Plato 1: Metaphysics and Epistemology* [*Plato 1*] (Oxford, 1999), 64–92. He claims that what Socrates disavows is certainty, and that what he claims is a form of knowledge falling short of certainty, derived from successful application of elenctic argument. My claim is that what Socrates disavows is systematic knowledge, and that what he claims is unsystematic—that is to say, piecemeal knowledge. I see nothing in the texts to suggest that wisdom requires certainty or that Socrates gives any general account of what grounds his particular claims to knowledge, beyond the claim that he has arguments for them. I discuss the matter more fully in *Socrates* (Oxford, 1998), 42–48.

3. By T. Irwin, *Plato's Moral Theory: The Early and Middle Dialogues* (Oxford, 1977), 40–41, and Irwin, *Plato's Ethics* (Oxford, 1995), 28–29.

It is that kind of expertise which Socrates disavows; he is not expert in any specific subject or in the kind of general expertise in running one's life which the sophists claimed to have. But he does not argue that expertise is impossible. He recognizes experts in specific areas, and, as far as general expertise goes, he does not argue that there can be no such expertise, merely that those who claim to possess it, including sophists and statesmen, fail to meet the ordinary standards for possessing expertise, notably the ability to impart it to others. In various dialogues, we see Socrates in conversation with self-styled experts in different areas (e.g., Euthyphro claims to be an expert on religious matters (4e–5a), and Meno on virtue in general (81b)), and as the conversation progresses, we find their claims to knowledge of the subject evaporating. A notable feature of these discussions is that they reveal that Plato is using a specific conception of expert knowledge. Central to any expertise is the knowledge of what that expertise is concerned with, and that knowledge consists in the ability to specify those things. The requirements for such a specification are exacting; it must apply to all and only the things in question, it must reveal the feature or features in virtue of which things count as of that kind, and that feature (or those features) must be the same in all cases. For example, the expert in holiness must be able to specify a feature or set of features such that (a) all and only holy things possess that feature and (b) it is in virtue of possessing it that those things count as holy (6d–e).

The ability to give that kind of specification is primary in a number of ways. In the *Euthyphro*, it serves as a template for the solution of disputed cases; anything which satisfies the specification of holiness is holy, and anything which does not satisfy it is not holy (6e). The specification is thus explicitly said to be sufficient for resolving disputes, and one may plausibly suppose that it is assumed to be necessary also. In the *Meno*, having the specification of what virtue is is necessary for knowing further things about virtue, specifically how it is to be acquired (71b). In at least one dialogue, the *Hippias Major*, Socrates maintains that it is impossible to know whether anything is an instance of a property (the example is that of beauty) unless one is able to specify what that property is (304d–e), and that seems also to be the implication of the conclusion of the *Lysis* (223b), where Socrates says that he and his young friends appear ridiculous in thinking that they are friends, though they have proved unable to say what a friend is. It is clearly implied that in that situation they do not *know* that they are friends and, perhaps, even suggested that they are not entitled to believe that they are.[4]

The evidence surveyed so far has not suggested any general account of knowledge or any concern with how knowledge is acquired or how it relates to other mental states such as belief or activities such as perception or thought. What has emerged is the view that a certain kind of knowledge is primary. This is, roughly,

4. For a defense of the thesis that Socrates maintains a strong form of the principle of the priority of definition—"If A fails to know what F-ness is, then A fails to know anything about F-ness"—see H. H. Benson, "The Priority of Definition and the Socratic Elenchus," *Oxford Studies in Ancient Philosophy* 8 (1990), 19–65, revised version in Benson, *Socratic Wisdom* (New York, 2000), ch. 6. This article contains copious references to other literature on the topic.

knowledge of what things are, where things are conceived as universals of one sort or another, chiefly properties (holiness, temperance) or states (virtue), but also kinds, not sharply differentiated from properties and states. (I take it that the question "What is a friend?" may be expressed without change of meaning as "What kind of thing is a friend?" or as "What is it to be a friend?"—that is to say, what is the property of being a friend?) Knowledge of "things" consists in the ability to specify them as set out in the preceding paragraph. Apart from the formal characteristics set out there, specifications take various forms, some approaching to conceptual definitions, as in "speed is the ability which achieves many things in a short time" (*Laches* 192a–b), others to scientific accounts, such as "Color is an efflux of shapes adapted to (the sense of) sight and (hence) perceptible" (*Meno* 76d). Plato never makes any explicit theoretical discrimination between these types of specification, and it is a moot point how far he was aware of the distinction.[5]

This kind of knowledge is primary in that it is presupposed by any other kinds of knowledge in the respective area (e.g., knowledge that friendship is good presupposes knowledge of what friendship is). As is clear from the citations so far, this paradigm is found in a number of dialogues generally regarded as written early in Plato's career, as well as in the *Meno*. There we find it brought into connection with a number of questions about knowledge not raised in any of the others cited, including a puzzle about how it is possible to acquire knowledge, and the question of how knowledge relates to true belief. These questions require closer examination.

# MENO

The dialogue opens abruptly with the question how virtue or excellence (*aretē*) is to be acquired: that is to say, How is one to become an outstanding individual and thereby achieve overall success in life? Socrates immediately turns the question to that of what virtue or excellence is, in accordance with the primacy thesis elucidated above, and various attempts at specification are explored and rejected. When Socrates says (80d) that though he and Meno do not know what excellence is, they should continue to try to find out, Meno asks how it is possible to try to find out anything which you do not already know. He poses two specific problems:

5. Of the extensive literature on Socratic definition, the following may be particularly mentioned (see bibliography for full citations):

T. Penner, "The Unity of Virtue"

G. Vlastos, "What Did Socrates Understand by His 'What Is *F*?' Question?"

C. C. W. Taylor, "Socratic Ethics"

H. H. Benson, "The Priority of Definition and the Socratic Elenchus"

D. Charles, "Definitions in the Meno"

1. Of the many things which you do not know, which one will you set up as the object of your inquiry?
2. Even if you were to happen upon what you were looking for, how will you know that that is what you did not know? (80d6–8).

The first problem makes the point that, in order to undertake any inquiry, one must know what inquiry one is undertaking, and therefore understand the terms in which that inquiry is identified. To undertake an inquiry is to ask a question, and one must know what question it is that one is asking. (Knowing what question one is asking is of course distinct from knowing the answer to that question.)

The second problem asks how you will know whether you have found what you were looking for, with the implication that you will never know. If you did not know the answer to the question in advance of inquiry, how will you recognize any answer as the one you were looking for? In general, the answer to the second problem is that the understanding of what question one is asking provides a specification of what counts as a correct answer to it, and that one recognizes an answer as correct when one recognizes that it satisfies that specification. Thus understanding the question "What is the cube root of 27?" involves knowing that one has correctly answered it when one has found a number $n$ such that $((n \times n) \times n) = 27$, and understanding the question "Who is the murderer of Smith?" involves knowing that one has correctly answered it when one has identified an individual of whom it is true that that individual murdered Smith. (The question of how one knows that one *has* found the right number, or the right individual, is not a question about how doing so is in principle possible, but about how one knows that one has employed the right method of inquiry and employed it correctly.)

The general answer to the second problem—that the phrasing of the question provides a specification of the correct answer—poses a particular problem in the special case where the question is itself a request for a specification. Prior understanding of what a cube root is specifies the correct answer to the question "What is the cube root of X?" but if one's question is "What is X?" (e.g., "What is virtue?"), it is problematic what prior understanding might be supposed to specify the correct answer. It is tempting to think that that prior understanding could be nothing other than understanding of what virtue is: that is to say, in the special case of the kind of knowledge which Plato regards as primary (see above), Meno's second problem is unanswerable. In fact it is not. The prior understanding in question is the pre-theoretical understanding of the concept which is presupposed by the ability to pose and to understand the request for a specification, and the specification itself consists either in sharpening that pre-theoretical understanding via a conceptual definition or in providing a substantive account satisfying the requirements indicated in that pre-theoretical understanding. (There is a residual problem—namely, which type of specification is (a) sought and (b) appropriate for the particular case.)[6]

In response, Socrates represents Meno as arguing that it is impossible to try to find out anything; he poses the dilemma that either one already knows what one is

---

6. For example, Charles, "Types of Definition," 118–19.

trying to find out, in which case one cannot try to find it out, or one does not already know it, in which case one does not know what one is trying to find out (and hence cannot look for it) (80e). This "captious argument," as Socrates describes it, does not do justice to the genuine problems which Meno has raised or to the insights about the presuppositions of inquiry which those problems reveal. The dilemma which Socrates ascribes to Meno is solved simply by the distinction between knowing what question you are asking and knowing the answer to that question. Contrary to his description, however, Socrates does not treat Meno's problem as a facile sophism but as a deep problem whose solution involves an ambitious theory not only of the acquisition of knowledge but also of the nature of the soul. The essence of the solution is that it is possible to find out what you (by ordinary standards) do not know, provided that in a deeper sense you do already know it. What we think of as discovery is in fact the recovery of knowledge which the soul has previously possessed but which it has forgotten. The detailed exposition in which that broad outline is spelled out raises a number of difficult questions about precisely what cognitive resources it is that the soul has previously possessed, how it has come to possess them, and how its mode of possession relates to the distinction between knowledge and belief.

Socrates begins by simply stating the theory on the authority of priests, priestesses, and poets; the human soul is immortal and undergoes many incarnations, in the course of which it has "seen everything here and in Hades" and has thereby learned everything. Hence it is not surprising that it should be able to recall what it previously knew about virtue and other things (81c). This suggests a simple model of the revival of experiential knowledge; knowledge is originally acquired by experience, whether of things in the world, experienced, presumably, via the senses, or of things in Hades. What those things might be, and what kind of experience apprehends them, we are not told. We are told, however, how this theory allows for the process of arriving at knowledge via some sequence of mental acts; since the whole of nature is akin, and one has learned everything, recalling one thing allows one to find out everything else, provided one perseveres in one's search (81d). This sounds like a description of the acquisition of knowledge by inference from things known by experience, but a key feature of inferential knowledge is that previous experience of what one knows by inference is no part of the explanation of one's knowledge. One is not reminded of what one knows by inference.[7]

Socrates' explanatory account of this kind of knowledge, in contrast, includes the repetition of the claim that the soul has learned everything (d1), and he concludes (d4–5) with the assertion that seeking and learning is just recollection (or, in other words, being reminded (*anamnēsis*)). That is not, then, inferential knowl-

---

7. One might have inferential knowledge of something one had already experienced, provided that the previous experience is not causally productive of one's inferential knowledge. For example, if one saw a dog running over a snow-covered lawn, but then forgot having done so, one might infer from the tracks that a dog had run over the lawn. But if one remembered seeing the dog run over the lawn, one's knowledge that a dog ran over the lawn is not inferential, even if one did, in addition, infer from the tracks that a dog ran over the lawn.

edge. Rather, what is envisaged is something more like sequential revival of experiences via association of ideas. Suppose that I have been previously acquainted
with every member of a given family. Since they all share a family resemblance,
recalling what Robert Smith looks like serves to *remind* me of what his brother
Richard looks like, and that, in turn, of what their cousin Winifred looks like, and
so on. There is no inference here, merely serial reminding.

Challenged to show that this theory is true, Socrates conducts the famous
experiment with the slave, which he claims to be an instance of the process he has
just described. This, however, appears to be an instance of the acquisition of
knowledge by inference. The slave certainly works out the answer to the problem of
doubling the square by inference, specifically inference from the premises that the
diagonal of a given square bisects it; that the square on the diagonal contains four
triangles, each equal to half the area of the given square; and that $4 \times \frac{1}{2} = 2$. Insofar
as his reaching the correct solution is to be explained by recollection, it is quite
unnecessary to suppose that the slave is recollecting the solution of that particular
problem, a solution which, ex hypothesi, he had arrived at in some previous
existence. It suffices to suppose that he recollects the crucial properties of the
square and the diagonal, from which he now (for the first time) infers the solution.
But it is unclear whether that is how Plato sees the matter. It is possible that he does
not distinguish the acquisition of knowledge by inference from what I have termed
serial reminding and therefore intends what, in fact, is a description of the latter to
apply to both indifferently.

This raises the important question of what it is that one recollects. On the
model of serial reminding, one recollects literally everything that one finds out by
any kind of investigation, and everything that one recollects one has previously
experienced. Even if we restrict the application of the theory to a priori investigation (a restriction for which there is no explicit textual warrant), it is still a vastly
uneconomical theory and one which depends on a quite obscure conception of
experience. It is uneconomical in supposing that every particular arithmetical or
geometrical truth which anyone discovers has previously been known by that
person, and obscure in attributing that knowledge to experience. To stick to the
example of doubling the square, what would it be for the slave to have "seen" that
the area of the square on the diagonal of a given square is double the area of the
original square? Ex hypothesi, that would be to recognize that particular truth
without inference; but that leaves us quite in the dark how the slave knows that
truth (he "just knows," it seems) and darker still how the process of thought which
he undertakes together with Socrates revives that particular item of immediate
knowledge. These difficulties are at least alleviated if we suppose that what is
recollected is some restricted set of items (elements, principles, or basic entities),
knowledge of which provides the basis for inferential knowledge of further truths.
The idea that there might be such a thing as immediate apprehension of
the properties of, say, the square or the even seems not an obviously hopeless
suggestion. It remains problematic how closely that notion of immediate apprehension can be modeled on perception.

This question connects with the topic of the distinction between knowledge and true belief. When the slave has reached the correct answer to the problem, Socrates says that he has true beliefs about it (which are his own, not imposed on him by someone else) but that he does not yet know the answer. His true beliefs have been stirred up as if in a dream, and if he is subjected to repeated and varied questioning, he will eventually attain exact knowledge (85b–c). Yet, immediately, Socrates describes him as having recovered his *knowledge* (my italics) from within himself, without anyone's having taught it to him (d3–4) and proceeds to argue that the knowledge which he now has[8] he must always have had, since he could not have acquired it during his present life (d9–13). That is clearly incompatible with the suggestion that all that he now has is true belief and that he is yet to acquire knowledge, which he will do as a result of subsequent questioning. True belief, it appears, presupposes the permanent possession of knowledge (86a–b), and the transition from true belief to knowledge is in fact the transition from a state of partial recovery of the knowledge which we have always possessed to its full recovery.

The connection with the perceptual model of knowledge arises from Socrates' argument (86a6–9) that since the slave's true beliefs are always in his soul, both in its incarnate and in its discarnate state, his soul is always in a state of "having learned" (*ton aei chronon memathēkuia estai hē psuchē autou.*) If the soul is always in a state of having learned (i.e., *having acquired* knowledge), there was no time at which it *did acquire* that knowledge; "always having learned" is thus equivalent to "never having *learned*, but always knowing." And since the knowledge we have was never acquired, but was always possessed, it follows that it was not acquired by experience.

The distinction between knowledge and true belief reappears at the end of the dialogue, when Socrates points out that true belief is as good a guide to action as knowledge (97a–b). The crucial difference is one of stability; true beliefs are as useful as knowledge as long as one retains them, but they are liable to be lost, "until one ties them down by reasoning about the cause" (*aitia*).[9] That (i.e., tying down true beliefs by reasoning concerning the cause) is recollection, and when true beliefs are thus tied

---

8. It may be, as G. Fine suggests (*Plato on Knowledge and Forms* [*Knowledge*], [Oxford, 2003], 5 and 69), that "now" at d9 refers not to the actual time of Socrates' utterance but to the envisaged future time at which the slave has achieved complete knowledge. But even if that is so, the argument still requires that the slave has never acquired knowledge but has always possessed it.

9. Following on from G. Vlastos's influential discussion of the meaning of *aitia* in Plato and Aristotle, G. Fine suggests that *aitia* should be rendered "explanation" rather than "cause." Fine explains that she reserves the term "cause" for an event that is sufficient for bringing about change and points out, correctly, that Plato's *aitiai*—for example, the *aitia* of the correct solution of the geometrical problem in the *Meno*—are not restricted to events. See Vlastos, "Reasons and Causes in the *Phaedo*," *Philosophical Review* 78 (1969), 291–325, reprinted in Vlastos, ed., *Plato I: Metaphysics and Epistemology* (Garden City, N.Y., 1971), 132–66, and in Vlastos, *Platonic Studies*, 2nd ed. (Princeton, 1981), 58–75; Fine, "Knowledge and True Belief in the *Meno*" ["Knowledge and True Belief"], *Oxford Studies in Ancient Philosophy* 27 (2004), 56.

In common with some other writers on Plato and Aristotle, I use "cause" more widely, to apply to whatever answers the question "Why?" and hence as virtually interchangeable with "reason" and "explanation." For this usage, see, for example, D. Bostock, *Plato's* Phaedo [Phaedo] (Oxford, 1986), 135; for a defense of the translation of *aitia* as "cause," see D. Furley, "What Kind of Cause Is Aristotle's Formal Cause?" in M. Frede and G. Striker, eds., *Rationality in Greek Thought* [*Rationality*] (Oxford, 1996), 60–62. Given that usage of "cause," the issue of whether *aitia* should be rendered "cause" or "explanation" is stylistic rather than substantial.

down, they become stable items of knowledge (98a). This brief passage contains a cluster of problems. The first is how we are to understand "reasoning about the cause"; the cause of what? Reasoning about the cause of one's having a belief does not seem appropriate to turn true belief into knowledge. On the other hand, reasoning about the cause of the belief's being true makes good sense of the point about stability, as well as giving a good account of the example of the slave. Someone who understands why a given belief is true—for example, because it follows from the basic principles of the discipline to which it belongs—is not liable to be persuaded by apparent counterarguments. And we can see why frequent and varied questioning would be needed to give the slave the systematic grasp of geometry which would enable him to see not just *that* this is the correct solution of this problem but *why* it is.

It is problematic, however, whether reasoning about the cause is required for every case of knowledge or only for some. In this passage, someone who has traveled the road to Larisa is said to know it, which presumably implies that his or her true beliefs about the road amount to knowledge about it. But acquaintance with the road is surely insufficient to give one understanding of why one's beliefs about it are true; one may know that the road passes a certain hill on the north side because one has been there but still not understand why the road passes the hill to the north rather than to the south. Again, the acquisition of this kind of knowledge seems to have nothing to do with reasoning; experience of the actual road (together with memory of what one has experienced) is sufficient for knowledge of it. It seems plausible, then, that perceptual knowledge is not supposed to be explained by recollection, which is what we should expect, especially in light of the assertion that knowledge which is recollected was not acquired at any time but was always possessed. No one can believe that knowledge of the road to Larisa, or knowledge that Socrates is now standing in front of me, has been in my soul as long as my soul has been in existence.

Recollection, then, provides an explanation of a special kind of knowledge, which contrasts with perceptual knowledge.[10] It is characteristic of that kind of knowledge to be grounded in an understanding of what makes the beliefs constitutive of that knowledge true, an understanding which is reached via reasoned inquiry.[11] The objects of that understanding are most plausibly to be thought of as whatever function as principles or elements of reasoning. At this point, we should

10. Alternatively, only the kind of knowledge which is explained by recollection is knowledge, strictly speaking. On that supposition, perceptual knowledge counts as knowledge in a reduced sense, perhaps on the strength of some resemblance to knowledge properly so called (e.g., that it gives one's true beliefs the same degree of stability as "reasoning about the cause" does). On either view, knowledge grounded in recollection is primary in the evaluative sense.

11. Some commentators (e.g., Fine, *Knowledge*, 5–6, 50, and Fine, "Knowledge and True Belief," 61–67) interpret the requirement that knowledge involves tying down true beliefs by reasoning concerning the cause as amounting to the definition of knowledge as justified true belief (a view shared by E. L. Gettier in his epoch-making article "Is Justified True Belief Knowledge?" *Analysis* 23 (1963), 121–23). But the requirement that one should have a grasp of what makes one's beliefs true is a stronger requirement than that one's true belief should be justified. At the conclusion of his discussion with Socrates, the slave is justified in his true belief that the square is doubled by constructing the square on the diagonal, since he has constructed (or at least followed) a sound argument leading to that conclusion, but Socrates insists that he does not yet

recall Socrates' methodological principle that knowledge of what things are is primary in the investigation of the properties of those things. In the *Meno*, Plato seems to be moving toward a systematization of that principle in an ambitious combination of epistemology and metaphysics.

On this theory, the transformation of true belief into knowledge via intellectual inquiry is, in fact, the recovery of knowledge which the soul has always possessed. Souls are created with a grasp of the basic principles of reality, including an understanding of what are the primary things, and the task of systematic intellectual inquiry is to reactivate that knowledge, which includes both formulating those principles, including definitions of the basic things, and drawing consequences from them. This program is admittedly hinted at, rather than made explicit, in the *Meno* itself. It is displayed more explicitly in other dialogues, especially the *Phaedo* and the *Republic*.[12]

# PHAEDO

The thesis that the objects of recollection are basic principles, including basic entities, which was suggested for the *Meno* by considerations of economy and fit with the text, is explicitly confirmed by the text of the *Phaedo* (72e–77a). Forms (see ch. 8), which are not explicitly mentioned in the *Meno*, are central to the epistemology and metaphysics of the *Phaedo*, and they fill two gaps in the schematic theory sketched in the *Meno*, first as objects of recollection and second as the causes, reasoning about which transforms true belief into knowledge. Recollection of Forms is presupposed by the ability to give philosophical accounts of properties such as equality; we are prompted to give such accounts by experience of instances of them, and that experience prompts us to think of the properties as something over and above the instances themselves.[13] The instances, then, remind us of

---

know the conclusion. (In fact, some of Gettier's counterexamples show how one can be justified in having a true belief yet lack knowledge, since one does not grasp why one's belief is true. Someone who has excellent evidence that Jones owns a Ford may believe on the strength of that evidence that either Jones owns a Ford or Brown is in Barcelona, and that might be true despite the fact that Jones no longer owns a Ford, because Brown is, as it happens, in Barcelona.)

Fine responds by tightening the requirements for justification to include the grasp of what makes one's belief true as a necessary condition for justification. As she points out ("Knowledge and True Belief," 64, 78), the question whether the *Meno* provides an account of knowledge as justified true belief then turns on the question (still disputed in contemporary discussions) of how demanding the standard for justification is.

12. The most recent comprehensive discussion of the *Meno* is D. Scott, *Plato's* Meno (Cambridge, 2006), which contains a full bibliography.

13. I accept the interpretation of recollection in the *Phaedo* proposed by D. Scott, *Recollection and Experience* (Cambridge, 1995), part 1 (condensed version reprinted in Fine, *Plato 1*, 93–124), according to which recollection explains the ability to give theoretical accounts of Forms. The more traditional view that what recollection explains is ordinary concept formation is maintained by, among others, J. L. Ackrill,

something distinct from them, as a picture may remind us of its subject, and what we are reminded of in each case is the appropriate Form. That confirms the more economical interpretation proposed for the *Meno*. The explanation of the slave's solving the puzzle is his ultimate recollection not of that very solution but of the square and the diagonal to which he was prompted by Socrates' rough representation of them and from which he was able to work out the solution itself.

For a case where what is sought is itself the account of some Form, the doctrine that all nature is akin allows us to see how such an account may be worked out. Since Forms are systematically connected with one another, recollection of the properties of one may lead by inference to recollection of the properties of another. That Forms are the causes of things is central to the *Phaedo*'s account of explanation, where the first stage in the explanation of anything's being F is that it shares in the Form of F. Admittedly, that is only the first stage, which Socrates describes as a "safe and ignorant" answer (105c1); a more subtle answer explains the thing's being F via the presence of an entity or the instantiation of a property such that anything in which that entity is present, or anything instantiating the property, necessarily is F—for example, whatever contains fire is necessarily hot (105c2–6). The explanatory entities and properties are of various types, and while some may themselves be conceived as Forms, not all can be; fire and snow are perceptible stuffs which come to be and cease to be, not changeless and eternal Forms.[14] It is then obscure how the theory in which they play a central role is supposed to be radically superior to the empirically based theories of the physicists of the sixth and fifth centuries.

I have two suggestions on this point. First, Socrates' principal objection to his predecessors is their neglect of teleological explanation, and though the theory sketched in the *Phaedo* is not explicitly teleological, it is unlikely that Plato had simply abandoned that ideal. Second, the *Timaeus*, which is Plato's fullest sketch of a theory of the physical world,[15] (a) depicts the world as teleologically designed,

---

"*Anamnesis* in the *Phaedo*: Remarks on 73C–75C," in E. N. Lee, A. P. D. Mourelatos, and R. M. Rorty, eds., *Exegesis and Argument: Studies in Greek Philosophy Presented to Gregory Vlastos* (Assen, 1973), 177–95, reprinted in Ackrill, *Essays on Plato and Aristotle* (Oxford, 1997), 13–32, and Bostock, Phaedo, 66–69. Scott gives a lucid account of the controversy.

14. For fuller discussion, see C. C. W. Taylor, "Forms as Causes in the *Phaedo*," *Mind* 78 (1969), 45–59; Bostock, Phaedo, ch. 7; and Fine, *Knowledge*, ch. 14, "Forms as Causes: Plato and Aristotle."

15. At *Timaeus* 27d–28a and 51d–52a, Plato asserts that there can be no knowledge, but only belief, about the physical world since knowledge requires stable objects, whereas the physical world is in a state of systematic instability. Hence the account which he proceeds to give of it is only a "likely story" (*eikota muthon*, 29d2). But that should not be taken as an expression of epistemic despair about the physical world. I take it that the teleologically grounded mathematical physics is intended to be, given the pervasive instability of matter, the closest approximation to knowledge of which that subject matter is capable. Mathematical and evaluative Forms are universal principles of intelligibility, which, instantiated in various subject matters, make that subject matter knowable or the nearest approach thereto. In "The Philosophical Economy of Plato's Psychology: Rationality and Common Concepts in the *Timaeus*," in Frede and Striker, *Rationality*, 29–58, D. Frede gives a persuasive account of how those universal principles permeate the flux of sensible phenomena in the *Timaeus*, allowing the achievement, if not of knowledge of phenomena at least of true and reliable beliefs about them (37b4–8).

In different contexts, Plato expresses mutually inconsistent views about whether there is any knowledge of the sensible world. It is certainly recognized in the *Meno* (see above, though note the reservation

specifically as the best material approximation to the Form of the Living Being, and (b) gives a basic explanatory role to the geometrical properties of the fundamental particles of matter. Physical stuffs and their properties thus fit into an overarching theory which is both teleological and mathematical. Ultimately, matter behaves the way it does because it instantiates mathematical structure, and mathematical structure is as it is because that is the best way for it to be. Mathematical and evaluative Forms are thus the ultimate *aitiai*, and it is by reasoning about them that we achieve the systematic understanding of reality which constitutes knowledge.

# REPUBLIC

That systematic understanding is further elucidated in the two principal treatments of knowledge in the *Republic*, in book V and in books VI–VII. In the former passage, Socrates, in defending his claim that the ideal state can come into existence only if it is ruled by philosophers (473c–e), argues that only the person with knowledge of the Forms is entitled to be called a *philosophos* (lover of wisdom). The first argument for this conclusion (475e–476d) presupposes the existence of the Forms, but the second (476d–480a), which is designed to convince someone who does not antecedently accept the existence of Forms, argues from the generally accepted premise that knowledge is a grasp of what is to the conclusion that only the person who knows the Forms grasps what is. The main rival, the person who lacks knowledge of the Forms, but is restricted to acquaintance with sensible instances of them, is thereby confined to what is intermediate between being and not-being, and hence to a grade of cognition lower than knowledge—namely, belief.

Both the premise and the argument itself are highly problematic.

The premise is that knowledge is a grasp of what is. Someone who knows (*gignōskei*) knows something (rather than nothing), and what he knows is (476e7–477a1). The range of uses of the Greek verb "to be" admits three interpretations of "what he knows is":

1. What he knows is true.
2. What he knows is something (e.g., is beautiful).
3. What he knows exists.[16]

---

expressed in n. 10) and in the *Theaetetus* (see below). In the *Republic*, it is assumed that the philosopher-rulers know particular truths about good and bad (520c). The *Phaedo* seems more optimistic about the possibility of knowledge of the sensible world than the *Timaeus*; Socrates is dissatisfied with the theories of his predecessors, not because they were attempting something impossible in principle but because they failed to give the right kind of explanation of physical events, and he appears to envisage that the theory of Forms will ultimately make good that deficiency. And even in the *Timaeus*, though knowledge is apparently impossible, true and reliable belief is attainable (see above).

16. So G. Fine, "Knowledge and Belief in *Republic* V," *Achiv für Geschichte der Philosophie* 60 (1978), 121–39, reprinted as Fine, *Knowledge*, ch. 3. (The passage cited occurs at 69 in the latter volume.) My discussion of *Rep.* V owes a great deal to hers, though she distinguishes senses (1) and (2) more sharply than I do.

All three are appropriate marks of knowledge: if someone knows that p, it must be true that p, and if someone knows something (e.g., knows Socrates), then what he knows must be something (e.g., be a man) and must exist. This elucidation indicates that the three interpretations apply most readily to different types of knowledge: (1) is a characteristic of propositional knowledge, where what is known is a proposition, capable of truth and falsehood, and linguistically represented by a sentence, such as "Plato knows that Socrates is wise." Interpretations (2) and (3), on the other hand, apply primarily to what is traditionally called "knowledge by acquaintance," or familiarity with some object. But (a) neither here nor elsewhere does Plato show a firm grasp of that distinction, and (b) in this discussion, he is chiefly concerned with cases such as that of "knowing beauty" (i.e., knowing what beauty is), where the distinction becomes blurred. Someone who knows beauty may be conceived as being familiar with something which is such-and-such and which exists, and as being ipso facto aware of the true proposition that beauty is such-and-such. We should not expect this discussion to focus on truth as a mark of knowledge, then, if such a focus is assumed to presuppose a sharp distinction of truth from the other marks.

Plato's thought is not well represented by interpretation (3), "what is known must exist." He goes on immediately (477a2–7) to describe things as being more or less, and some things as "such as to be and not to be" and hence intermediate between "being unqualifiedly" and "not being in any way." The notion of degrees of existence is not only unintelligible in itself; nothing suggests that Plato accepted it. "Degrees of being" in 479a–d fit readily with interpretation (2), being such-and-such, and also with (1), being true, but not at all with (3), existence. It is best, then, to assume that Plato's argument is to be interpreted in terms of (1) and (2), to the exclusion of (3), while bearing in mind that (1) and (2) are unlikely to be sharply distinguished from one another.

On this undifferentiated interpretation, the argument proceeds fairly smoothly. At 477a–b, Plato correlates degrees of being with degrees of knowability; what totally or unqualifiedly is is totally or unqualifiedly knowable, what is not in any way is totally unknowable. Anything which both is and is not is in between the totally knowable and the totally unknowable and is the object of a mental state in between complete knowledge and total ignorance or error, if there is such a state.

This argument may be understood either in terms of truth (Elucidation A) or in terms of being something (Elucidation B). For the reasons given above, I incline to think that Plato does not distinguish between the two elucidations.

Elucidation A:
Any proposition which is totally or unqualifiedly true (e.g., "$2 + 2 = 4$") is capable of being known without qualification; any which is totally or unqualifiedly false (e.g., "$2 + 2 = 5$") expresses nothing but ignorance or error. But any proposition which is sometimes (in some contexts) true and sometimes false, (such as "Englishmen are phlegmatic,") is neither an expression of unqualified knowledge (since it is not true without qualification that

Englishmen are phlegmatic, it cannot be known without qualification) nor of total ignorance or error.

Elucidation B:
Something which is totally or unqualifiedly such-and-such (e.g., "Cruelty is bad") is capable of being known as such without qualification; something which is not such-and-such at all can be said to be such only in error (e.g., "Cruelty is good"). But suppose we have something which is such-and-such qualifiedly; e.g. "Swimming is good for you." Someone who accepts that without qualification does not have knowledge but is not totally wrong, either.

Plato's strategy is to try to show that the *philotheamōn* (the person who is acquainted only with sensible instances of Forms) cannot escape from that situation. The only general beliefs available to him are characterized as much by falsehood as by truth. That claim is not distinguished by Plato from the claim that the objects of the *philotheamōn*'s general beliefs are characterized by not being F (e.g., beautiful) as much as by being F.

Plato has already assumed that distinct capacities are directed onto (*epi*) distinct objects; belief is a distinct capacity from knowledge (477b5), so belief is directed onto one thing and knowledge onto another (b7–8). This assumption is spelled out at 477b11–478a4. At 477c6–d5, Plato's Principle of Differentiation of Capacities is stated: capacities are differentiated by two factors, their object and their effect (i.e., what possession of the capacity enables its possessor to do). Capacity A and capacity B are one and the same capacity if they have the same object and the same effect, and they are distinct capacities if they have different objects and different effects. It is apparently assumed that objects and effects cannot vary independently of one another: it is impossible that the same object should be subject to distinct effects or the same effect applied to distinct objects. Plato, then, must assume that there is a necessary connection between objects and effects. That result would be achieved if the object were itself specified in terms of the effect, as what is susceptible of the effect—for example, the capacity to see has as its object the visible, and the capacity to touch has its object the tangible. But that would merely yield the trivial result that the concept of the knowable is distinct from the concept of the believable, which is compatible with its being the case that the application of the two concepts is identical. Plato is not aiming at the trivial connection between knowledge and the knowable but at the connection, necessary but nontrivial, between knowledge and the character of what is known—namely, that knowledge is of what is true and/or real, whereas belief lacks those necessary connections with truth and reality.

He is correct to distinguish the two concepts in that way but wrong to try to derive that distinction from his general Principle of Differentiation of Capacities. That general principle is either trivial or false. Heating is a distinct effect from cooling, but there is no nontrivial sense in which the object of the one effect, the heatable, is distinct from the object of the other, the coolable.

By 478d, belief has been established as a capacity intermediate between knowledge and error or ignorance. Objects intermediate between being and nonbeing will be objects appropriate to that intermediate capacity (478d5–9).

Arguments familiar from, for example, *Rep.* I, 331c and *Hippias Major* 289a–c show that the instances of Forms, which are all that the *philotheamōn* is familiar with, are so characterized. These instances include both kinds (e.g., paying back what you borrowed) and particulars (e.g., a beautiful woman). Beliefs about these things, such as "Justice is paying your debts" and "Helen is beautiful" will be neither unqualifiedly false nor unqualifiedly true but sometimes true and sometimes false; in Plato's words, "the many beliefs (*nomima*) held by the many about beauty and the rest roll about, as it were, between not being and being without qualification" (479d3–5). So those who are familiar with nothing beyond the instances of Forms, lacking any grasp of the Forms themselves, must recognize that they have nothing more than belief, and therefore accept the title "lovers of belief" (*philodoxoi*) instead of that of *philosophoi* which they had attempted to usurp (479e–480a).

But the *philotheamōn* can have unqualifiedly true particular beliefs—for example, "In these particular circumstances, paying back this particular debt was just." As such beliefs will simply be true, they will be *epi tōi onti* (literally, "onto what is"; i.e., they will latch onto what is so). So why will they not amount to knowledge?

To defend Plato against that objection, we must return to the *Meno*'s distinction of knowledge from true belief, by the criterion that, in order to count as knowledge, true beliefs have to be grounded in "reasoning about the cause"—that is to say, in a grasp of the grounds of their truth. In order to have knowledge, the *philotheamōn* must understand what makes his beliefs true, e.g., why this particular repayment was unqualifiedly just. And in order to do that, he must have a systematic grasp of the standards which govern the characterization of types and particular instances: he must be familiar with the Forms, as well as the instances. Knowledge, even of particular cases, must be grounded in understanding of why things are as they are, and that understanding requires knowledge of Forms. Hence the *philotheamōn*, who has no knowledge of the Forms, lacks the understanding which is necessary for knowledge.

This suggestion does not claim to represent Plato's actual argument but to reply to an objection on the part of the *philotheamōn*. It has the advantage of assimilating *Rep.* V to the *Meno* and thereby removing an apparent difficulty: that whereas in the *Meno* (and *Tht.* 201b) knowledge and belief can have the same objects, in *Rep.* V they have, by the Principle of the Differentiation of Capacities, different objects. In fact, the two positions are compatible; the thesis in the *Meno* and *Theaetetus* concerns particular items of knowledge, while that of *Rep.* V concerns the objects of the capacities as such. Plato does not claim in *Rep.* V that there can be no knowledge which is not knowledge of Forms (which would deprive philosopher-rulers of knowledge of events in the sensible world). He does (implicitly) claim that there can be no knowledge of anything which is not grounded in knowledge of Forms.[17]

---

17. However, this does imply that perceptual knowledge such as knowledge of the road to Larisa either is not knowledge (or, at least, not knowledge strictly speaking) or is somehow grounded in knowledge of the Forms. Does Plato perhaps think that you cannot know the road unless you know what a road is, and that knowing the latter is (or involves) knowing the Form of the Road?

Teleology and mathematics are central to the discussion in books VI–VII, whose context is the description of the advanced education of the philosopher-rulers. The "greatest subject" of their education is the Form of the Good, since their grasp of what is beneficial in the political sphere depends on their understanding of goodness as such (505a). Since Socrates does not know what goodness (506c) is, he cannot give a scientific account of it, but he states his beliefs in the form of the famous images of the Sun (506e–509d), the Divided Line (509d–511e), and the Cave (514a–517a). The central point of the first of these is that just as the sun is both the ultimate generative force and the primary source of illumination in the visible world, so the Form of the Good is primary, both epistemologically and ontologically, in the intelligible world of the Forms (509a–b). That is to say, the other Forms exist, and are what they are, because it is best that they should be, and understanding what any Form is involves understanding why it is what it is—that is to say, understanding how that is the best way for it to be.

This immediately raises the difficulty that teleological explanation requires that what is actual is the best of a range of alternative possibilities, whereas the Forms exist, and are what they are, necessarily. I suggest that we can best approach Plato's meaning if we take it that his starting point is the ordinary conception of goodness as consisting in order and proportion, as illustrated in *Gorgias* 504a–b, where goodness in a range of things, from a house to the soul, consists in order and arrangement of parts, whereas badness consists in disorder. To be good, then, is to manifest rationally satisfactory order; so to say that the intelligible Forms are as they are because that is best is to say that they are what they are because that system is maximally intelligible.

It seems fairly clear that Plato believed that order and proportion were ultimately to be understood mathematically. Hence the curriculum which is to lead the philosophers to the systematic study of the Forms is mathematical, not merely because mathematics leads the mind from reliance on the senses to abstract thought (524b) but because the grasp of the basic principles common to the various mathematical sciences is useful in leading to the search for the beautiful and the good (531c–d). To understand goodness is to understand order, and fundamental to the understanding of order is the understanding of its mathematical basis; hence the understanding of goodness is to be sought via the basic principles of mathematics.[18] Some confirmation of this suggestion is provided by Aristotle's evidence of Plato's lecture on the Good, which was all to do with mathematics and which culminated (on the most likely interpretation of the text) in identifying the Good with Unity.[19]

18. For a fuller exposition and defense of this view, see M. Burnyeat, "Plato on Why Mathematics Is Good for the Soul," *Proceedings of the British Academy* 103 (2000), 1–81.
19. The evidence comes from the *Elements of Harmony* of Aristoxenus (a pupil of Aristotle), II.30–31:

This, as Aristotle was always saying, was the experience of most of those who heard Plato's lecture *On the Good*. Each of them attended on the assumption that he would hear about one of the recognised human goods—such as wealth. health, strength, and in general some marvellous

This suggestion is open to some obvious objections. According to the simile of the Sun, the Form of the Good is epistemologically primary; according to the image of the Divided Line, the principles of the mathematical sciences are themselves fully intelligible only when they are derived from the "unhypothetical principle of everything" (510c–511d), which, in context, must be the Form of the Good. Yet, on this suggestion, the Form of the Good is itself elucidated as a fundamental principle of mathematics, specifically the Form of Unity. The difficulty arising from the Divided Line is comparatively superficial; the principles of the individual mathematical sciences, when taken in isolation from one another, have the status of mere hypotheses. Only when they are derived from a single unhypothetical principle (i.e., when they are tied down by reasoning concerning their cause) are they themselves known, and are hence the grounds of the knowledge of what is derived from them.

The other difficulty is deeper. Ex hypothesi goodness was the basic explanatory concept, but if understanding what goodness is requires that one explain what it is in terms of other concepts, those concepts are now more basic than goodness. We have here an instance of the classic problem of the hierarchical structure of knowledge. If knowledge of X is founded on knowledge of Y, and that, in turn, on knowledge of Z, then either we have an infinite regress of knowledge or we have some foundations of knowledge, knowledge of which is grounded on nothing but themselves. Plato's insistence that we must be able to give an account of what we know seems to rule out self-evident foundations of knowledge; he asserts the necessity of a *logos* in many passages,[20] notably in *Rep.* 534b–c, where the philosopher's task is that of giving the *logos* of each of the Forms and his ultimate aim that of differentiating the Form of the Good (*tōi logōi*[21]) from the other Forms. In

---

happiness. When Plato's lectures turned out to be about mathematics—numbers, geometry, astronomy—and to crown all about the thesis that the good is one, it seemed to them, I fancy, something quite paradoxical, and so some people despised the whole thing, while others criticised it. (Translation from J. Barnes, *The Complete Works of Aristotle: The Revised Oxford Translation*, 2 vols. [Princeton, N.J., 1984], 2:2397.)

The crucial phrase, translated above "the good is one," is *agathon estin hen*, which would most naturally be rendered "there is one good" (presumably as opposed to many). The translation given above assumes the emendation *tagathon estin hen*, "the good is one" (presumably, again, as opposed to many different things). But it is hard to see why the thesis that there is a single supreme good should have seemed so paradoxical as to provoke the reactions mentioned; it is clear from the context that the disappointed audience was expecting to hear that one of the recognized goods was *the* (i.e., the supreme) good. What was so outrageous must have been not the claim that the good was one as opposed to many but the account of *what* it was, and that must have been such as to require the mathematical build-up described. I propose that we should adopt the reading *tagathon estin hen*, understanding that as "the Good is the One," the article before *hen* being omitted (as is standard in Greek) when an expression with the definite article is the complement of the verb *einai* (to be).

20. *Rep.* 510c, 531e, 533b–c; *Phaedo* 76b; *Symp.* 202a; *Tht.* 202c; *Tim.* 51e; *Laws* 966b, 967e.

21. The phrase *tōi logōi* may be translated either "by (its) definition" or "by reasoning." The translation does not affect the doctrine; Forms have to be distinguished from one another by reasoning (since reason alone grasps them), but what reasoning does is to reach accounts of them which differentiate one from another.

contrast, the account at the end of book VI of the priority of the Good—and the simile of the Sun, in particular—strongly suggest traditional foundationalism. Just as the sun makes everything else visible by its own light, and is itself visible by that same light, so the Good makes the other Forms intelligible and, we should expect from the analogy, is itself intelligible in and of itself.

Holistic (alternatively, coherentist) pictures of knowledge offer an escape from this dilemma.[22] To give an account of a concept is not to explain it in terms of anything more basic but to locate it in a coherent structure of concepts, and specifically to show the explanatory role which each concept plays within that structure. The suggestion that Plato identifies goodness with unity can be seen as instantiating that model. The basic explanatory role of goodness in a teleological scheme of explanation is adapted to unity, in that goodness is order, harmony, symmetry, and so on, those features are understood mathematically, the mathematical understanding of them is grounded in basic mathematical principles, and, given the holistic model, the account of those principles consists in showing their contribution to the system as a whole.

This discussion of *Rep.* VI–VII is doubly speculative, first in suggesting that Plato intends the nature of goodness to be understood mathematically, and then in raising the possibility that the type of account of it which he intends is a holistic one. Both suggestions are recommended by the extent to which they achieve plausibility; neither can claim direct textual confirmation. The problem which the second suggestion attempts to meet is also prominent in the *Theaetetus*, the only dialogue of Plato's to be devoted to the topic of knowledge. We shall therefore return to it in the context of that dialogue.

# THEAETETUS

The topic of the dialogue is the question "What is knowledge?" Three answers are proposed, and examined in turn:

1. Knowledge is perception (*aisthēsis*).
2. Knowledge is true belief.
3. Knowledge is true belief with an account (*logos*).

Each answer is rejected, and the dialogue ends aporetically. The discussion of the first suggestion, which is considerably longer than the other two combined, is largely devoted to a complex and sophisticated treatment of two theses, which Socrates argues to be logically connected with the proposed account of knowledge

---

22. As suggested by G. Fine, "Knowledge and Belief in *Republic* V–VII," in S. Everson, ed., *Companions to Ancient Thought 1: Epistemology* (Cambridge, 1990), 85–115, reprinted as ch. 4 of Fine, *Knowledge*, and in Fine, *Plato 1*, 215–46.

as perception—namely, Protagoras' thesis that things are as they appear to each individual, and a thesis derived from Heraclitus that everything is in a state of total flux. I shall not discuss the treatment of these theses (for which see ch. 17) but shall confine myself to the direct discussion of the proposed account of knowledge as perception. This is undertaken in a brief section (184b–186a) whose central point is a distinction between, on the one hand, properties apprehended by the individual bodily senses (colors by sight, acoustic properties by hearing, flavors by taste, etc.) and on the other formal properties (being, sameness and difference, likeness and unlikeness, number, etc.), which are not specific to any individual sense.[23]

Socrates says (185a6–7) that the soul discerns or apprehends (*episkopein*) the sensible properties "by means of the powers of the body," and the formal properties "itself by means of itself" (i.e., solely by its own power). The appplication of those concepts is not the work of any individual sense, or of the senses collectively, but of the integrating capacity of the mind, which unifies the data of the several senses into a single coherent diachronic picture (186a10–b1), and which also applies evaluations, such as beautiful and ugly, good and bad (a8). Perception, identified as the apprehension of the sensible properties, is thus distinguished from judgment, which is the work of the mind, and since being is one of the properties which belong to judgment, it is judgment, not perception, which grasps truth, since truth belongs to being (186b–c).[24] And since knowledge implies truth (c9–10), the conclusion is reached that "Knowledge is not in our experiences, but in our reasoning about them; for it is here (i.e., in reasoning) that it is possible, it seems, to attain being and truth, but it is impossible there (i.e., in experiences)" (d2–5).

At first, this seems very straightforward: knowledge is propositional, knowledge that p. And propositions are the objects of judgment: judgment is always judgment that p. Perception, by contrast, lacks propositional content. Hence, knowledge cannot be perception. If that is the argument, it is a bad one, since the premise that perception lacks propositional content is just false. Some perception at least has propositional content: for example, I can see *that* the table has already been laid. Even if we restrict ourselves to perception of the proper objects of the senses, one sees *that* the color sample is green. Moreover, Socrates himself says just that, when he points out that, asked to examine (*skepsasthai*) whether something is salty or not, one does so by taste (185b7–c2). A great deal of perception, then, is perception that something is the case, and it is plausible that that was part of what Theaetetus had in mind in his original suggestion (151e1–3) that "someone who knows something perceives what he knows, and as it now seems to me, knowledge

23. On this section, see, in addition to the works cited below, M. Burnyeat, "Plato on the Grammar of Perceiving," *Classical Quarterly*, n.s. 26 (1976), 29–51, and J. M. Cooper, "Plato on Sense Perception and Knowledge: *Theaetetus* 184 to 186," *Phronesis* 15 (1970), 123–46, reprinted in Fine, *Plato 1*, 355–76, and in Cooper, *Knowledge, Nature and the Good: Essays on Ancient Philosophy* (Princeton, 2004), 43–64.

24. The crucial sentence is 186c7, "Is it possible for what cannot even attain to being to attain to truth?" to which Theaetetus answers, "It is impossible." The connection between being and truth is presumably made via the idiomatic use of *to on* and *ta onta* in the sense of "what is true"; the ordinary Greek for "speak the truth" is *to on* (or *ta onta*) *legein*.

is nothing other than perception." And certainly, when Socrates immediately equates Theaetetus' suggestion with Protagoras' doctrine that things are as they seem to each individual, that seeming has propositional content; the wind's seeming (feeling) cold to me is its seeming (feeling) to me that the wind is cold. So if Socrates' final argument is the straightforward one set out above, it assumes a conception of perception which is not the one intended by the original proposal. In that argument, propositional content is assigned exclusively to judgment, leaving perception to be construed as contentless, i.e. as the reception of raw data whose interpretation is the work of a distinct faculty. But no one could conceivably maintain that knowledge is perception thus conceived.

That may, however, be the argument. Socrates' claim would then be that, *strictly speaking*, perception is nothing more than the contentless reception of stimuli[25] and talk of perceiving *that* p is an illegitimate conflation of perception itself with judgment consequent on perception. The proponents of the thesis that knowledge is perception would then have misdescribed their own position. There are, however, some indications in the text that Socrates' argument may be different. First, in the statement of his conclusion quoted above (186d2–5), he says not that knowledge is in judgment about our experiences (which would presumably be *doxa*) but that it is in reasoning (*sullogismos*) about them. That suggests that knowledge is to be found not in the class of conceptualized judgments about perception but in some more restricted class of judgments arrived at by reasoning.[26] That is supported by what immediately precedes (186b–c). The soul perceives by touch the hardness of what is hard and the softness of what is soft, but certain other properties it attempts itself to judge by examination and comparison; these properties are "their being and what they are (or that they are)[27] and their opposition to one another and again the being of their opposition."

By contrast with perception, which is innate in humans and animals, "reasonings (or "calculations," *analogismata*) about them with reference to their being and their utility" are arrived at through a long and arduous process of education. It is hard to see that it takes such a process to arrive at the judgment, concerning something hard, that it is hard, but easier to see that it might take such a process to be able to understand what hardness is, that hardness is not just different from but opposite to softness, and again what oppositeness is. For these tasks, one needs not just experience of hardness and softness but a theory of the nature of those properties and of the properties of those properties (such as oppositeness). The references to evaluation may make the point that evaluation, like understanding

25. Which is presumably all that animals and infants experience (186b11–c1).

26. The reminiscence of the *Meno*'s "by reasoning concerning the cause" (*aitias logismōi*) is highly suggestive.

27. The Greek is *hoti estin*, which may be translated either as "what they (both) are" or "that they (both) are," "both" referring to the experienced instances of hardness and softness. For the reasons given in what immediately follows, I think that "what they are" is more likely. For the opposite view, see D. Bostock, *Plato's Theaetetus* [Theaetetus] (Oxford, 1988), 139–40. Given that translation "being" (*ousian*) is best understood in the same way: as equivalent to "nature," the *kai* connecting the two expressions being epexegetic, "their nature, i.e. what they are."

what things are, requires not just experience but theory; one cannot determine whether something is good or bad, or beautiful or ugly, just by experiencing it but needs to understand the appropriate standards of evaluation.[28]

It is, then, at least possible that the conclusion of the first main section of the dialogue is that knowledge is not perception, not because knowledge is always propositional, whereas perception lacks propositional content, but because knowledge is primarily knowledge of what things are, whereas perception is never sufficient to reveal what things are.[29] That suggestion is not without its difficulties,[30] but it is worth keeping in mind when we turn to the remaining sections.

The second proposed definition is that knowledge is true belief. Since perception cannot be knowledge, the latter must be found in the activity of the soul "by itself" (see the distinction above), which is said to be belief or judgment (187a), and since there can be false belief, knowledge cannot be belief as such but must be true belief (187b). This proposal is threatened by the claim that false belief is impossible (in which case, knowledge would collapse into belief), and the bulk of this section (to 201a) is devoted to discussion of how false belief is possible (for details, see ch. 17). The substantive suggestion is dealt with only briefly, being refuted (201a–c) by the distinction between an eyewitness's knowledge of some event, say an assault, and the true beliefs that a member of the jury has about that event. The latter cannot have knowledge of what "only the person who saw" can know (b7–8). Socrates describes the jury as having only a short time to decide the matter and as being persuaded, but not "taught" or "instructed" by the litigants (201a–b), which conveys the suggestion that they are unfairly manipulated rather than being presented with evidence sufficient to reach a proper verdict, but the insistence that only the eyewitness can know what occurred clearly implies that testimony, however compelling, and however fairly presented, can never produce that knowledge. We have returned to the distinction between the person who knows the road to Larisa from experience and the person who has true secondhand beliefs about it. Knowledge by experience is admitted without qualification as knowledge, and there is no suggestion that the eyewitness is better placed epistemically than the jury member because the former has some "reasoning about the cause" of the event which the latter lacks.[31]

It is clear that the eyewitness's knowledge is knowledge *that* such and such occurred. But it is less clear how sharply Plato distinguishes that from knowledge *of* the event. Just as the person who knows the road knows various things about it— for example, that it passes to the north of such and such a hill—whereas the person who merely "has the road in mind" merely believes those things, so the person who

28. Experience is necessary, but not sufficient, for correct evaluation; to the untutored ear, a piece by Stockhausen may sound ugly, but it takes understanding of the genre and its conventions to determine whether it is really beautiful or ugly.

29. This suggestion was originally made by J. McDowell, *Plato, Theaetetus* (Oxford, 1973), 188–93.

30. See, for example, Bostock, Theaetetus, 140–42.

31. On the jury passage, see M. Burnyeat and J. Barnes, "Socrates and the Jury," *Proceedings of the Aristotelian Society, Supplementary Volume* 54 (1980), 173–91 (Burnyeat) and 193–206 (Barnes).

knows the event knows various things about it, whereas the person who relies on testimony merely believes those things. The suggestion that knowledge *that* and knowledge *of* things are not seen by Plato as two distinct kinds of knowledge is supported by the fact that the dialogue passes immediately to the final suggestion, that knowledge is true belief with an account (*logos*), which is primarily a discussion of knowledge of things, in the sense of knowledge of what things are. The basic idea is that knowing what something is is having a true belief about that thing together with an account of it. The kinds of account discussed are the enumeration of the elements of a thing, illustrated by the example of the analysis of a syllable into its component letters; the statement of one's true belief; and a description of the thing sufficient to distinguish it from everything else.

The first suggestion is rejected on the strength of the regress difficulty discussed earlier; if knowledge requires an enumeration of the elements of the things known, then the elements themselves must be unknown. But it is impossible that unknown elements can be the basis of knowledge of what they compose. On the contrary, the elements must be better known than the things composed of them (206b), but that is impossible on this compositional model. Stating one's true belief is immediately rejected on the ground that since everyone with a true belief is able to state it, this proposal merely restates the previously rejected suggestion that knowledge is true belief (206d–e). Finally, the suggestion that knowledge of something is true belief of or about that thing together with a distinguishing mark of that thing is rejected on two grounds. First, true belief about anything requires that one already possesses a distinguishing mark of it (otherwise one's belief would not be about it specifically); hence, once again, knowledge adds nothing to true belief. Second, if one responds to the first objection by requiring knowledge of the distinguishing mark, the proposed account of knowledge is circular (208c–210a). The dialogue thus ends inconclusively.[32]

This outcome raises the question whether the aporia reflects genuine uncertainty on Plato's part, or whether his intention is to suggest some positive answer to the original question. Specifically, is the reader to infer that, given some other sense of "account," knowledge will indeed prove to be true belief with an account? An obvious suggestion is that we should revive the *Meno*'s proposal, defining knowledge as true belief with reasoning concerning the cause. But that proposal fits derivative, rather than basic, knowledge. One has the kind of knowledge defined in the *Meno*'s terms when one has some true belief together with understanding of what makes that belief true. But that understanding is itself a sort of knowledge, and application of the *Meno*'s formula to it raises the dilemma which we have already encountered: either it, too, has to be accompanied by understanding of something else which makes it true, which leads to a regress, or there are some beliefs which are true in virtue of nothing other than their own truth—in other words are self-evident. If there is a distinction between basic and derivative

---

32. On the final section of the dialogue, see G. Fine, "Knowledge and *Logos* in the *Theaetetus*," *Philosophical Review* 88 (1979), 336–97, reprinted as Fine, *Knowledge*, ch. 10, and Bostock, Theaetetus, ch. 6.

knowledge, and if we assume that Plato is looking for an account of the former, then that would need to be an account of self-evidence; but "true belief with reasoning concerning the cause" cannot be an account of self-evidence. An alternative is the suggestion which we have already encountered: that the understanding of what makes any belief true is provided by the whole conceptual structure into which that belief fits. The regress is halted by the abandonment of the distinction between basic and derivative knowledge; "reasoning concerning the cause" would then have to be construed as "elucidation of the conceptual scheme to which the belief belongs."

This certainly has some affinities with some things said about knowledge in the *Phaedrus*, *Sophist*, *Statesman*, and *Philebus*, all plausibly regarded as later than the *Theaetetus*. Of these, the *Phaedrus* and *Philebus* describe,[33] and the *Sophist* and *Statesman* exemplify,[34] a method of specifying what things are by a process of constructing definitions *per genus et differentiam*. A genus is collected together from many different things, and then successively divided into species and subspecies until indivisible species are reached. But while that method provides systematic knowledge of the various species and of their connections with their higher genera and therefore with each other, it does not avoid the problem of basic knowledge. For knowledge of being an X as being an F which is G presupposes that we know what being an F and being G is. It will not do to say that being an F is being a member of that genus which is constituted by the species, F which is G, F which is H, and so on. For that assumes that we know which species constitute a unity, and it seems that, for that, we have to have some way of identifying the genus independently of the species. We cannot identify the genus as the genus which is collected from the different things we started from, for that requires that we know what different things to collect. If we begin by collecting indivisible species, then how can we know which species to collect? And if we begin from individuals, then how shall we know which individuals to collect?

A system of classification cannot by itself be adequate to provide knowledge of reality but has to be supplemented by means of fixing the application of the classificatory terms, whether by observation, or by taking as primitive some pretheoretical categories, or in some other way. The *Sophist* gives some intriguing hints in this direction in the suggestion that one of the principal tasks of philosophy is working out the conceptual interrelations of what it calls the "Greatest Kinds"—that is to say, some of the most general and abstract concepts: namely, Being, Sameness, Difference, Change, and Stability (251c–261b). It may have been Plato's view that a full specification of these interrelations will amount to an account of what each of these kinds is and thus to identifications of these highest genera, which will then be divisible via the method of division. But that is speculation; there is nothing in the text to connect the discussion of the Greatest Kinds with the method of collection and division.

---

33. *Phaedr.* 265d–266c; *Phil.* 16b–18d.
34. *Soph.* 219a–232a, 264b–268d; *Statesm.* 258b–268d, 279a–311c.

# CONCLUSION

The overall picture of Plato's views on knowledge is not particularly tidy. While some themes remain constant from his earliest dialogues throughout, there are a number of important points on which he does not appear to have reached a fixed position. The following are constant themes.

I. Knowledge is systematic. Over specific areas, such as mathematics and morality, and even conceivably for reality as a whole, items of knowledge are systematically interconnected, and it is the task of inquiry in those areas to reveal those connections.

II. For any department of knowledge (and, conceivably, for reality as a whole), the primary knowledge is knowledge of what things are. Given the metaphysical theory of Forms as the basic things that there are, Forms are the primary objects of inquiry. Changes in (or uncertainties about) that theory are reflected in corresponding changes in Plato's views (or uncertainties) about knowledge.

III. Knowledge of what things are is achieved a priori, by critical reflection. Empirical investigation has at best a secondary role in the achievement of knowledge (see below).

Those themes may be summed up as the doctrine that the aim of inquiry is to achieve systematic understanding of the intelligible principles of reality. While that remained Plato's constant ideal for philosophy, his conception of how, and how completely, it might be achieved seems to have fluctuated, in various ways.

a. The Theory of Recollection expresses the view that the soul has been in permanent possession of a total grasp of the principles of reality and that the task of critical inquiry is to recover that grasp. But that theory is found only in the *Meno*, *Phaedo*, and *Phaedrus*, and even in those dialogues it appears in different versions.

b. The *Republic* presents the ambitious ideal of a single all-embracing system, on the model of a mathematical axiomatic system, founded on a single fundamental principle, the nature of goodness. It is plausible that goodness was itself conceived mathematically. No other dialogue gives that universal role to any single principle.

c. There is no single view of the status—or, indeed, the existence—of empirical knowledge. In the *Timaeus*, Plato denies that knowledge of the sensible world is possible but allows that there can be reliable belief about it. Knowledge of the sensible world is recognized in numerous dialogues, but there is no uniform view how it is achieved. In *Rep.* V, knowledge of the sensible world appears to be admitted, provided that it is grounded in knowledge of Forms, and the same view is indicated by the thesis in the *Meno* that knowledge requires reasoning concerning the cause of one's true beliefs. But in the *Meno* and *Theaetetus*, we find instances of knowledge acquired by direct perception, where it is not clear how, or whether, knowledge of Forms is presupposed. Equally, it is not clear how, or whether, such items of knowledge are systematically connected to others. It may be that such knowledge is thought of as knowledge of a secondary kind or as not, strictly speaking, knowledge, but no distinction of that kind is explicitly drawn.

d. Plato asserts repeatedly that in order to know what something is one must be able to give an account or definition of that thing. He is clearly aware of the difficulty that that requirement leads to an infinite regress of accounts, but his response to that difficulty is disputed. On some views, he modified the requirement to the extent of recognizing some things, perhaps including the Form of the Good, which were self-intelligible. On others, he extended the notion of an account to include the system in which such alleged primitives have their place, so that knowledge of the primitive elements and knowledge of what is derived from them is mutually self-supporting. There are traces of such views in some of the later dialogues, but they are not explicitly related to the regress problem.

e. Some of the later dialogues exhibit definitions in genus-species hierarchies. The method raises a number of questions, including how these hierarchies are supposed to apply to the sensible world, and how the method is supposed to account for knowledge of the *summa genera* and the *infimae species*. It is possible that the former kind of knowledge is somehow grounded in the kind of investigation of the interrelation of basic formal concepts conducted in the *Sophist*, but there is no explicit connection in the texts between these two kinds of investigation.

# BIBLIOGRAPHY

Ackrill, J. L. "*Anamnesis* in the *Phaedo*: Remarks on 73C–75C," in E. N. Lee, A. P. D. Mourelatos, and R. M. Rorty, eds., *Exegesis and Argument: Studies in Greek Philosophy Presented to Gregory Vlastos* (Assen, 1973), 177–95; reprinted in Ackrill, *Essays on Plato and Aristotle* (Oxford, 1997), 13–32.

Barnes, J. *The Complete Works of Aristotle: The Revised Oxford Translation*, 2 vols. (Princeton, 1984).

Benson, H. H. "The Priority of Definition and the Socratic Elenchus," *Oxford Studies in Ancient Philosophy* 8 (1990), 19–65; revised version in Benson, *Socratic Wisdom* (New York and Oxford, 2000), ch. 6.

Bostock, D. *Plato's* Phaedo (Oxford, 1986).

———. *Plato's* Theaetetus (Oxford, 1988).

Burnyeat, M. "Plato on the Grammar of Perceiving," *Classical Quarterly*, n.s. 26 (1976), 29–51.

———. "Plato on Why Mathematics Is Good for the Soul," *Proceedings of the British Academy* 103 (2000), 1–81.

Burnyeat, M., and Barnes, J. "Socrates and the Jury," *Proceedings of the Aristotelian Society, Supplementary Volume* 54 (1980), 173–91 (Burnyeat) and 193–206 (Barnes).

Charles, D. "Definitions in the Meno," in V. Karasmanis, ed., *Socrates 2400 Years since His Death* (Athens, 2004), 357–66; revised version, entitled "Types of Definition in the *Meno*," in L. Judson and V. Karasmanis, eds., *Remembering Socrates: Philosophical Essays* (Oxford, 2006), 110–28.

Cooper, J. M. "Plato on Sense Perception and Knowledge: *Theaetetus* 184 to 186," *Phronesis* 15 (1970), 123–46; reprinted in G. Fine, ed., *Plato 1: Metaphysics and Epistemology* (Oxford, 1999), 355–76, and in Cooper, *Knowledge, Nature, and the Good: Essays on Ancient Philosophy* (Princeton, 2004), 43–64.

Fine, G. "Knowledge and Belief in *Republic V*," *Archiv für Geschichte der Philosophie* 60 (1978), 121–39; reprinted in Fine, *Plato on Knowledge and Forms* (Oxford, 2003), ch. 3.

———. "Knowledge and Belief in *Republic V–VII*," in S. Everson, ed., *Companions to Ancient Thought 1: Epistemology* (Cambridge, 1990), 85–115; reprinted in Fine, *Plato on Knowledge and Forms* (Oxford, 2003), ch. 4, and in Fine, ed., *Plato 1: Metaphysics and Epistemology* (Oxford, 1999), 215–46.

———. "Knowledge and *Logos* in the *Theaetetus*," *Philosophical Review* 88 (1979), 336–97; reprinted in Fine, *Plato on Knowledge and Forms* (Oxford, 2003), ch. 10.

———. "Knowledge and True Belief in the *Meno*," *Oxford Studies in Ancient Philosophy* 27 (2004), 41–81.

———. *Plato on Knowledge and Forms* (Oxford, 2003).

———. ed. *Plato 1: Metaphysics and Epistemology* (Oxford, 1999).

Frede, D. "The Philosophical Economy of Plato's Psychology: Rationality and Common Concepts in the *Timaeus*," in M. Frede and G. Striker, eds., *Rationality in Greek Thought* (Oxford, 1996), 29–58.

Furley, D. "What Kind of Cause Is Aristotle's Formal Cause?" in M. Frede and G. Striker, eds., *Rationality in Greek Thought* (Oxford, 1996), 59–79.

Gettier, E. L. "Is Justified True Belief Knowledge?" *Analysis* 23 (1963), 121–23.

Irwin, T. *Plato's Ethics* (Oxford, 1995).

———. *Plato's Moral Theory: The Early and Middle Dialogues* (Oxford, 1977).

McDowell, J. *Plato, Theaetetus* (Oxford, 1973).

Penner, T. "The Unity of Virtue," *Philosophical Review*, 82 (1973), 35–68; reprinted in H. H. Benson, ed., *Essays in the Philosophy of Socrates* (New York, 1992), 162–84, and in G. Fine, ed., *Plato 2: Ethics, Politics, Religion, and the Soul* (Oxford, 1999), 78–104.

Scott, D. *Plato's* Meno (Cambridge, 2006).

———. *Recollection and Experience* (Cambridge, 1995).

Taylor, C. C. W. "Forms as Causes in the *Phaedo*," *Mind* 78 (1969), 45–59.

———. *Socrates* (Oxford, 1998).

———. "Socratic Ethics," in B. S. Gower and M. C. Stokes, eds., *Socratic Questions* (London, 1992), 137–52.

Vlastos, G. "Reasons and Causes in the *Phaedo*," *Philosophical Review* 78 (1969), 291–325; reprinted in Vlastos, ed., *Plato I: Metaphysics and Epistemology* (Garden City, N.Y., 1971), 132–66, and in Vlastos, *Platonic Studies*, 2nd ed. (Princeton, N.J., 1981), 58–75.

———. "Socrates' Disavowal of Knowledge," in Vlastos, *Socratic Studies*, ed. M. Burnyeat (Cambridge, 1994), 39–66; reprinted in G. Fine, ed., *Plato 1: Metaphysics and Epistemology* (Oxford, 1999), 64–92.

———. "What Did Socrates Understand by His 'What Is F?' Question?" *Platonic Studies*, 2nd ed. (Princeton, N.J., 1981), 410–17.

CHAPTER 8

................................................................................

# PLATO'S
# METAPHYSICS

................................................................................

## VERITY HARTE

## I. IDENTIFYING OUR TOPIC

................................................................................

Any attempt to write about Plato's metaphysics must be, to some extent, a work of construction and runs the risk of artificial separation between topics that are, for Plato, naturally related. Plato's writings are not themselves shaped in reflection of modern subdivisions of philosophical areas and the form in which they are shaped—the often heavily and self-consciously crafted dialogue form—does not naturally invite separate identification and treatment of the writings' often tightly interwoven philosophical threads. With the possible exception of the *Parmenides*, no work of Plato presents itself as being as a whole on a topic that we could without distortion understand as metaphysics narrowly construed, although it is fair to say that some works are more obviously metaphysical in character than others. In what follows, therefore, readers should understand that there is an engagement with the works of Plato from a perspective that, in certain respects, may differ from his own.

"Metaphysics" is a heading under which a range of topics might be considered. In discussions of Plato's metaphysics, what takes center stage is, typically, a certain feature of Plato's ontology: his commitment, at least in certain works, to the existence of a special class of entities, once known in English as "Ideas," these days more commonly referred to as "Forms." The present essay is no exception in this regard. This narrowing of the subject has some justification. Forms are seen to play a central role in Platonic counterparts to many of the topics one might expect to find discussed in a modern course on metaphysics (topics, for example, such as the nature of reality, the metaphysics of properties, and causal responsibility), while not all the topics one might find in such a course (topics, for example, such as possible worlds or paradoxes of time travel) have obvious counterparts in the work of Plato. There are, however, recognizably metaphysical topics, Plato's treatments of which would undoubtedly be valid and interesting objects of study but which are not considered in any detail here. Examples include the metaphysics of composition, the nature of time and space, personal identity, and the existence and nature of god(s).[1] Omission of such topics is partly due to the limitations of space and partly due to the desirability of having a relatively unitary focus.

This narrowing of the topic of Platonic metaphysics to Plato's *ontology* itself has some advantage as regards locating Plato's metaphysical theorizing within his own immediate tradition. For, unlike metaphysics as such, *ontology*—understood as the rational investigation of what there is or of being—is a branch of study for which Plato could find obvious precursors in his philosophical predecessors, perhaps most notably, the Eleatic philosopher, Parmenides, in whose *Way of Truth* one finds an account of a subject identified only as "being" (in Greek: *to eon*), which, as has often been noted, attributes to being many of the characteristics that Plato would subsequently ascribe to Forms.[2] In Plato's works, Forms themselves are identified most generally as "the beings" (in Greek: *ta onta*, or at least in many places apparently equivalently: *ousiai*).[3]

Plato's place in this tradition provides the overall focus of this essay. Like Parmenides, and like Democritus, the atoms of whose atomic theory are also noticeably Parmenidean, at least on common understandings of these two Presocratic thinkers,[4] Plato is a philosopher for whom reality differs from the way in which it presents itself to us in perceptual experience and must be rationally discovered. Plato is a realist, at least in one common use of the term "realist"; he is committed to the existence of a world that is objective and mind-independent.[5] But he is a realist, we might say, of an essentially optimistic variety. Given the existence of a world that is genuinely objective and independent of human thinking, there are, we might think, no very good reasons to suppose that human thinking will have *any* means of access to the character of the world. Plato, like rationalist-minded philosophers before and after him, believes that our most prominent apparent sources of access to the world—our senses—are often radically mistaken about it. Nevertheless, he nowhere doubts that knowledge—through rational inquiry—is possible.[6] This metaphysical orientation underlies the

---

1. There has also, it's fair to say, been rather less discussion of these topics in the literature on Plato generally. However, on composition, see my discussion in Harte 2002; on time and space, see Algra 1995, Owen 1966a, Sorabji 1983 and 1988; on personal identity, see Bostock 1999, Gallop 1982, Gerson 2003, Gill 1996, McCabe 1994, ch. 9, and 2000; on the existence and nature of god(s), see Menn 1995, Morgan 1992.

2. For a sophisticated treatment of Plato's relations to Parmenides, see Palmer 1999.

3. See, for example, *Phaedo* 65d13, 66a3.

4. For an introduction to Parmenides and Democritus, see Long 1999, chs. 6 and 9.

5. This, if anything is, is a point on which there is now broad consensus, although this has not always been the case: see Natorp 2004.

6. Again, there is now broad consensus that Plato is not skeptical about the possibility of knowledge. In antiquity, however, there was a long-standing tradition of skeptical readings of Plato, on the history of which, see Brittain 2001.

central contrast in his metaphysical theorizing, a contrast between what is intelligible and what is perceptible. It is this contrast and no other, I argue, that shapes the contours of his ontology.

## II. Is There a *Theory* of Forms? And Does That Theory *Develop* over the Course of Plato's Writings?

Our focus is on Forms. But we must first consider what sort of evidence is available to us about Plato's views about Forms. In addition to talking about Forms, discussions of Plato's metaphysics commonly talk of Plato's Theory of Forms. But not everyone agrees that Plato has what should be described as a *theory* of Forms,[7] and many people who are content to talk in terms of a theory find that theory only in one or other subset of Platonic works. Discussion of Plato's Theory of Forms thus gets quickly caught up in controversies regarding the development of Plato's thought. Indeed, on one view, the Theory of Forms, its development and its subsequent rejection, is the central narrative in this development, whose transitions are marked, first, by the introduction and elaboration of a theorized account of Forms in central works of Plato's so-called middle period—works such as the *Symposium*, *Phaedo*, and *Republic*, in particular—and, second, by Plato's signaled rejection of this account of Forms in the *Parmenides*.[8] A few words on these matters are in order, then, although my remarks are made with the intention of setting such questions about development aside so far as is possible.

The answer to the question of whether or not there is a Theory of Forms will depend on one's criteria for theory. What does seem clear is that Forms are *theoretical* entities. By this, I do not mean simply that they are not given in perception, nor are they among the data of "commonsense," although, at least prima facie, they are not. Rather, Forms are theoretical entities in the sense that they do some theoretical work. I give four (what seem to be the) central examples. As I have already said, Forms have a role to play in Plato's theory of being or what there is:

1. Forms are (among the primary) beings.
2. Further, especially in the *Phaedo* (96–106), Forms are identified as having causal responsibility[9] for things other than Forms having some of the character they do; the Form of beauty, for example, has causal responsibility

---

7. For example, consider the doubts expressed in Annas 1981, ch. 9.

8. Contrast, for example, Ryle 1966 and Owen 1953 and 1966b with Kahn 2007; and see Peterson, chapter 16 in this volume.

9. I choose "causal responsibility" as the least misleading translation of the Greek terms under discussion in this passage of the *Phaedo*: the adjective *aitios* and the noun *aitia*. For discussion of the terminology, see Frede 1980, and for the notion in Plato, see Sedley 1998.

for the beauty of anything else that is beautiful. In this way, Forms are not only themselves beings, they are causally responsible for at least certain other aspects of the character of the world, as well.

Given these roles in Plato's theory of being, it comes as no surprise that Forms have central roles to play in Plato's theories about the ways in which we talk and think about the world also.

3. In the case of language, it seems from several works that Forms play a special role in relation to the language we use to describe the world; they are in some way privileged bearers of the terms that we use to describe those aspects of things for which they turn out to be causally responsible.[10]

4. In Plato's theory of knowledge, Forms turn out to be objects of knowledge and of a privileged sort.[11]

It is, of course, conceivable that Plato started out with some (independently motivated) commitment to this favored sort of entity—the Form—and then sought out contexts in which to put it to theoretical work. More likely, however, is that Forms are theoretical entities in the sense of being entities whose claim to existence is justified or defended in light of the theoretical work they do. One might defend this view by appeal to a passage of the *Parmenides* (130b1–e3) in which Socrates, invited to answer questions about the range of Forms to which he is committed and finding himself uncertain, suggests that the reason not to subscribe to a Form for such items as hair, mud, and dirt is that these are things that are "just as we see them to be" (130d3–4). Socrates appears to reason here in the following (reasonable) way: where there is no theoretical work for Forms to do, there is no reason to posit them.[12] In general, this understanding of the theoretical status of Forms gains support from the fact that, within the Platonic corpus, there are no clear examples of direct arguments for the existence of Forms.[13]

Given this understanding of Forms as theoretical entities, when it comes to possible lines of development, one might expect that any developments in the conception of Forms would be driven by developments in his views on questions associated with the various theoretical roles that Forms play, developments in his views about the nature of language or knowledge, for example. This makes the task of considering whether Plato's theorizing about Forms is something that develops over the course of his writings considerably more complicated. In what follows, questions about development are left outside the frame of this discussion, to the

10. See *Phaedo* 102b11, *Republic* X 596a7–9, *Parmenides* 130e5–131a2. Passages like these have sometimes led people to think that Platonic Forms are meanings; see Bostock 1986. See also Crivelli, chapter 9 in this volume.

11. See *Phaedo* 73b–76e and *Republic* 476a–480a. I take no stand here on the controversial question of whether, especially in this *Republic* passage, Forms are assumed to be the *only* objects of knowledge. Contrast Annas 1981, ch. 8, and Fine 1978 and 1990; see also Taylor, chapter 7 in this volume.

12. For this understanding of his reasoning and its significance, see McCabe 1994, 78–81.

13. Arguments for the existence of Forms can be found in Aristotle's *On Ideas*, together with his criticisms of them. See Fine 1993.

considerations elsewhere in this handbook of the larger topics within which Forms have theoretical work to do.

# III. The Language of Forms

This still leaves open the question of where we should look for evidence of Plato's views about Forms. As far as use of language goes, the central terms used to identify Forms in indisputably canonical accounts of Forms—in particular, the Greek terms *idea* and *eidos*[14]—turn up in a wide range of works across the corpus that cut across candidate boundaries between developmental stages in Plato's thought. In some places, these go along with comparatively rich characterizations of the nature and role of the objects picked out by these terms, in others not; in some places, these characterizations are obviously similar, in others less obviously so.

For example, in Socratic dialogues of definition, such as the *Euthyphro*, for example—works that on widely accepted chronologies of the order in which Plato's works were written were produced earlier rather than later—we find the language of Forms, including hallmarks of what, as we have already indicated, are Forms' central roles.[15] In *Euthyphro* 6d11, for example, Socrates indicates that he is looking for "that form (*eidos*) in virtue of which all the pious things are pious," using causal language comparable to that found in the explicit theory of Forms as causally responsible set out in *Phaedo* 96–106. But the Socratic dialogues provide no real detail as to the ontological character of Forms. Had an accident of survival left us in a position where these and only these works of Plato survived, it would, I think, be something of a challenge to reconstruct from them the Theory of Forms of scholarly conception or, indeed, of the sort that could warrant Aristotle's much publicized objections.

This lack of detail might be taken to indicate that these works constitute an early stage in the development of Plato's theory, where later works develop or extend the account of Forms so as to provide the metaphysical underpinnings for Socrates' search for definitions.[16] Alternatively, one might view it as a consequence of a presentational strategy that takes you through an ordered sequence in which the picture does not develop but is gradually filled out.[17] The evidence does not

---

14. On the terminology, see Motte et al. 2003.

15. The dialogues of definition I have in mind are *Euthyphro, Charmides, Laches, Lysis*, and *Hippias Major; Republic* I and *Theaetetus* share the general form but for different reasons do not naturally go with this group—*Republic* I because it opens the *Republic; Theaetetus* because it is generally viewed as a later return to the form and is much more elaborate. Not all the works that would typically be identified as early works are dialogues of definition; to name just two examples, the *Apology* and *Crito* are not works of this type.

16. On the idea of "Socratic" Forms in contrast to "Platonic" Forms and the possible relations between them, contrast Vlastos 1991, Irwin 1999, and Penner 1987.

17. Kahn 1996.

seem to me clearly to decide between these positions. Nor do we need to, for there are pragmatic reasons not to consider the evidence about Forms from these Socratic dialogues. Precisely because they do not offer a rich characterization of the ontological character of Forms, it is difficult to derive much of our view about the nature of Forms from them. Note, however, that this is in reality only a matter of degree. Even in the "canonical treatment" of Forms in the *Phaedo*, the *Republic* or *Symposium*, the characterizations of Forms are *richer*, but not *rich*; at the least, they leave open many unanswered questions, a fact the *Parmenides'* searching "reprise" might be thought to acknowledge.

More difficult is the question of what *other* dialogues to include; the *Timaeus*, *Sophist*, *Politicus*, and *Philebus*, for example, all have discussion involving the language of Forms. These are dialogues generally held to be among the later group of Plato's writings, postdating not only the discussions of Forms in the *Phaedo*, *Symposium*, and *Republic* but also those in the critical examination of the *Parmenides*.[18] Their discussion is in certain respects like and in certain respects unlike the discussions of Forms in these earlier works, so that it is unclear the extent to which it indicates a departure from their view of Forms. These later works do not play a central role in the discussion here, again for pragmatic reasons. Both they and the *Parmenides*, the nature and import of whose treatment of Forms would be critical to any attempt to tackle the question of where these later discussions fit within the context of Plato's treatment of Forms, are considered in detail elsewhere in this handbook.[19] So far as is possible, however, I attempt to remain neutral on the question of development related to the characterizations of Forms therein.

For better or worse, then, our (main, if not exclusive) focus is the somewhat, but by no means fully rich characterizations of the ontological character of Forms in the canonical discussions of the *Phaedo*, *Symposium*, and *Republic* (to which we might add also the *Phaedrus*).

# IV. WHAT FORMS ARE THERE?

One striking feature of discussion of Forms in both *Phaedo* and *Republic*, especially, is that discussions of Forms are typically framed as though all participants in the conversation are already familiar with Forms and have some idea of what Forms there are. This is somewhat surprising if Forms are here being introduced and theorized for the *reader* for the first time, although it is possible that the

18. In the case of the *Timaeus*, this dating has been disputed, however, by Owen 1953, precisely on grounds related to questions concerning the developments in Plato's attitude to Forms. Contrast Cherniss 1957.

19. For the view that Plato abandons Forms in light of the *Parmenides'* criticisms, see, for example, Owen 1953 and 1966b. For an alternative, more "unitarian" approach to Plato's treatment of Forms, post-*Parmenides*, see now Kahn 2007.

mismatch between reader and participant is precisely designed to draw the reader's attention to the novel features of what is being said. Whatever its intended purpose may be, one effect of the strategy is resulting unclarity as to what the scope of the theory is intended to be.

Consider, for example, the following passage that occurs early in the *Phaedo* and is its first introduction of Forms:

> What about the following, Simmias? Do we say that there is such a thing as the Just itself, or not?—We do say so, by Zeus.—And the Beautiful, and the Good?—Of course.—And have you ever seen any things of this sort with your eyes?—Not at all, he said.—Or have you grasped them with any of your bodily senses? I'm speaking of them all, for example, of Largeness, of Health, of Strength, in sum of the being of all of the others that each happens to be.[20] (*Phaedo* 65d4–e5)

Here, we have a list of examples of Forms:[21] Just, Beautiful, Good, Largeness, Health, and Strength. This list, in itself, is a rather odd assortment of items, including values, a size property, and physical characteristics. It is completed by a generalization—"all the rest"—whose scope is utterly opaque.

Somewhat better is the generalizing move that follows Socrates' subsequent argument, in the *Phaedo*, to the effect that the soul can be shown to preexist its embodiment on the grounds that, when embodied, it has cognitive abilities requiring that, prior to embodiment, it had knowledge of Forms. The argument takes the Form of Equality as example, but it applies, Socrates says, to Forms in general, whose range is indicated as follows:

> For our present argument is no more about the Equal than about the Beautiful itself, the Good itself, the Just, the Pious, and, as I say, about all the things on which we put as a seal this mark "what is," and about which we ask and answer in our questions and answers. (*Phaedo* 75c10–d5)

Socrates here ties the scope of Forms to the scope of Socratic questions and answers. Socratic questions ask "What is F?" for some range of properties. The Form is identified as "What is [F]"—that is, as the referent of the answer to this Socratic inquiry. In this way, he fixes the scope of Forms. But this fixing is not very informative, since we are no clearer on the intended scope of such Socratic questions and answers than on the scope of Forms.

If the passages containing examples and generalizations of this sort are not helpful in fixing the scope of Forms, we might turn to the arguments in which we find them. As I have said, the Platonic corpus does not provide us with direct arguments for the existence of Forms, which we might use to establish their scope.

---

20. Translations of Plato here and elsewhere are taken from or take as a starting point those in Cooper 1997, although in some cases I have modified them more or less extensively.

21. The passage does not refer to the items mentioned as Forms, but it seems clear that this is what they are.

Forms do play roles in a number of arguments, however, and we might turn to these arguments to investigate what range of Forms they could be used, indirectly, to establish. The results of such investigation, however, turn out not to be straightforward.

Commonly, Forms are introduced as pairs of opposites. In both *Phaedo* 102b–105b and *Republic* 475e–476e, for example, we find as examples of Forms a series of pairs of opposites: in the *Phaedo*, Largeness and Smallness, Hot and Cold, Odd and Even; in the *Republic*, Beautiful and Ugly, Just and Unjust, Good and Bad.[22] And it is a central feature of Forms, in these passages, that a Form cannot be characterized by its own opposite, something that isn't the case for other, perceptible bearers of the same name as the Form (this point is central to the *Phaedo* passage cited above; see especially 102d–103c).[23] And it is sometimes suggested that a passage of *Republic* VII makes explicit a restriction of Forms to opposite properties.[24]

In *Republic* 523b ff., in preparation for the establishment of the educational curriculum for the philosopher-rulers, Socrates contrasts two sorts of sense perception: one sort does not summon the understanding to investigate, and one sort does exhort it to investigate. Socrates illustrates this contrast by the example of looking at three fingers: the smallest, ring, and middle fingers. Perception of a finger *as a finger* is an example of the sort of perception that does not summon the understanding to investigate, precisely because perception does not deliver up two opposing perceptions at the same time: "sight doesn't suggest to [the soul] that the finger is at the same time the opposite of a finger" (523d5–6). In the case of perception of the finger as having certain opposing properties, by contrast, as being, for example, large or small, thick or thin, hard or soft, Socrates says that perception precisely reports that the very same thing that the sense reports as large, thick, or hard, it says to be the opposite also (524a6–10 especially). And perception of opposing properties like these is the sort of perception that, for this reason, *does* summon the understanding to investigate.

> Sight, however, saw the large and small, not as separate, but as mixed up together. Isn't that so?—Yes.—And, for the sake of clarity on this, understanding was compelled to see in turn large and small, not mixed up, but distinguished, in the opposite way from that.—True.—And isn't it from these sort of cases that it first occurs to us to ask what the large is and what the small.—Absolutely.—And thus we called one intelligible, the other visible.—That's right. (*Republic* 524c3–d1).

The investigation that is initiated by perceptions that summon is an investigation of the sort that lead to the recognition and identification of Forms. Hence the contrast between those properties perception of which summons and those

---

22. Are these contraries or contradictories? The examples suggest that opposing Forms are contraries, not contradictories, but whether this distinction is observed throughout is unclear.

23. This feature of Forms is central to the contrast between Forms and their perceptible counterparts, which I consider in detail below.

24. Annas 1981, ch. 9.  pp 221–222

properties perception of which does not summon could be taken as an indication of a restriction upon the range of Forms to that of the summoning properties: that is, to Forms that are opposites.[25] However, if this passage is understood to imply such a restriction in the scope of Forms, it is inconsistent both with examples of Forms we find elsewhere and with another passage of the *Republic* that has also been taken to indicate the scope of Forms.

First, the examples: even without going outside the works on which we are focusing (and which are indisputably home to the canonical Theory of Forms), it is easy to find at least candidate examples of Forms that do not have opposites: in *Republic* X, Forms of Couch and Table (596b1–2); in the *Phaedo*, Forms of Fire and Snow (103c13). And if we were to consider works throughout the corpus, examples would come easier still. But these latter examples will be moot, because of questions about development, and the first group of examples can all be brought into doubt, if doubt is sought. *Republic* X is an unusual context, and it is just not clear what we should make of this talk of a Form of Couch and of Table, which plays a role in Socrates' development of an elaborate analogy between painting and poetry in the service of his notorious criticisms of mimetic art.[26] And there is some external evidence (for what this is worth) that Plato did not, in fact, believe in Forms of artifacts.[27] As to the *Phaedo*'s examples, the passage does not provide unequivocal evidence that Fire and Snow are themselves understood as Forms, as opposed to being entities that stand in some necessary relation to a Form, which Form conforms to the restriction of Forms to opposites.[28]

Turning from the examples to the other passage of the *Republic* that appears to speak to the question of the scope of Forms, we find, at least on the face of it, a different result from the book VII passage. In book X, immediately before the introduction of a Form of Couch and of Table, Socrates offers what appears to be a procedure for generating Forms, which is commonly translated along the following lines:

> Do you want us to begin our examination, then, by adopting our usual procedure? As you know, we customarily hypothesize a single form in connection with each of the many things to which we apply the same name. (*Republic* 596a5–7)

Read in this way, the passage proposes a range of Forms far wider than that implied by reading the scope off the distinction in *Republic* book VII. Indeed, the range

25. So Annas (ibid.).

26. Annas (ibid.) remarks on the unusual context; for the salience of couches and tables to this context, see Burnyeat 1999, 232–36.

27. For the evidence and discussion, see Fine 1993, ch. 6. This same external evidence would not restrict Forms to opposites, however, since it would include Forms of natural kinds.

28. *Phaedo* 104d1–7 is the best evidence that Three, and so, arguably, by analogy, Fire, Snow, and so on, are indeed Forms, but it is not indisputable. The *Timaeus* does provide unequivocal evidence as to the existence of a Form of Fire (see especially 51b7–d3), but the *Timaeus* is an unusual work in many respects and, as I have said, one whose dating has been controversial in light of views about the ways in which Plato's views about Forms develop.

*[handwritten margin note: to which we apply / word except / a custom of applying / a bit of natural language]*

would be wide to the point of potential absurdity: Do we really want a Form for *any* general term, no matter how unnatural, gerrymandered, or empty it might be? Again, however, the evidence is not decisive, again because of the unusual context and also because the passage need not be translated in this way. Smith proposed that the passage should be construed, rather, as making the claim that we commonly assume, "[as a rule of procedure,] that the Idea which corresponds to a group of particulars, each to each, is always one, in which case we call the group of particulars by the same name as the [Form]."[29] On this construal, the passage does not carry any implication about the scope of Forms.

My view is that it is a mistake to seek to use either of the *Republic* passages considered (book X or book VII) to settle the question of the scope of Forms, and not simply because they appear to answer the question in ways that are inconsistent with each other. For all practical purposes, the book X passage is unavailable for use to settle this question. Its construal is vexed, and its context is such that it is hard to know what more general use can be made of the points that are made therein. In the case of book VII, I think it mistaken to view the passage either as making or implying a point about the scope of Forms. Notice the care with which Socrates puts his claim, at 523d4–5: in the case of those properties, like being a finger, perception of which does not summon the understanding, "the soul *of the many* is not *compelled* to question what a finger might be" (emphasis mine). What could and should be questioned by the soul of the few (the author of the *Parts of Animals*, for example) is another matter.

It thus does not follow from what Socrates says in book VII that properties like being a finger are ones whose content does not merit rational inquiry of the sort that would discover and identify a Form. And it certainly does not follow—as Socrates does not claim, anyway—that the distinction he draws between properties that summon and those that do not corresponds to an ontological distinction between Forms and other non-Formal properties. What follows is just what Socrates emphasizes and the sort of point that the passage's educational context requires: properties that summon are those for which the fact that an understanding of them needs rational inquiry is conspicuous or obvious in a way that it is not in other cases; such properties are thus well chosen for use in the design of an educational curriculum that has as its object the turning of attention away from perception to reason.

Suppose, nevertheless, that we ask ourselves what this passage can tell us about the intended scope of Forms. Its moral, I suggest, is the contrast from which we began: between reason and perception. The scope of Forms is set by the limits to the unproblematic deliverances of perception, if unproblematic deliverances there be. But this passage has not told us what these limits might be, and the limits may themselves be things about which Plato has shifting conceptions, according as his views of the respective contributions of perception and reason develop and change. This general claim may not satisfy, inasmuch as it fails to deliver a determinate

---

29. Smith 1917; translation put together from pp. 70–71.

answer as to what Forms there are. However, it has the merit of being consistent with the verdict arising from the one passage in which Plato explicitly raises, without settling, the question of the scope of Forms for our consideration. This is the passage of the *Parmenides* mentioned above that gives indications of the sort of criteria that ought to be used to settle the question. Forms are not needed in those cases where things are "just as we see them to be." What cases these are may be for us to discover.

# V. How, in General, Are Forms Characterized?

When Forms are characterized, it is, as often as not, as part of a contrast between the characteristics attributed to Forms and the characteristics attributed to certain perceptible counterparts to Forms. These perceptible counterparts are generally called "particulars," but I argue below that this label is importantly misleading. Typically, Forms are identified as having features that their perceptible counterparts prominently lack (such as unity and stability, for example) or as lacking features that their perceptible counterparts prominently have (a susceptibility to qualification by conflicting pairs of opposite qualities most notably among them). Questions about the characteristics of Forms are thus bound up with questions about the differences between Forms and their perceptible counterparts.

Consider, for example, the contrast drawn in the following passage from the *Phaedo*:

> Let us then return to those same things with which we were dealing earlier. That being of whose being we give an account in our questions and answers, is it always in the same condition in the same respects or does it vary from one time to another? Does the Equal itself, the Beautiful itself, each thing itself—that which is—ever admit any change whatever? Or does each of these things that is, being of a uniform character taken by itself, remain the same in the same respects and never in any way admit any sort of change whatsoever?—Necessarily, said Cebes, it remains the same in the same respects, Socrates.—But what about the many beautifuls, such as people or horses or clothing or any other things of this sort, or about the equals, or about all those sharing a name with those things? Do they remain the same, or, in complete contrast to those others, do they, practically never in any way remain the same as themselves or each other?—The latter is the case, said Cebes, they never remain the same.—Then, is it the case that, whereas you could touch and see and perceive with the other senses these latter, there is no way to grasp those that always remain the same than by reasoning of the mind; rather, such things are invisible and not seen?—You're absolutely right. (78c10–79a5)

Socrates uses this contrast to establish that there are two sorts of being: one visible, the other invisible (79a6–7). And this is the overarching contrast between Forms and their counterparts: Forms are not perceptible, but intelligible; their counterparts are perceptible. These two sorts of beings are further characterized in terms of their respective stability or instability. Intelligible Forms are invariant; they do not change. Their perceptible counterparts, by contrast, are in no way invariant but subject to change. It is unclear quite how these two contrasts are meant to be related, but the shape of the passage suggests that the receptivity to change of their perceptible counterparts is intended to support the view that changeless Forms are intelligible as opposed to perceptible.

The passage raises a number of questions. First, how should we understand the terms of the contrast here and elsewhere—the contrast between the "many beautifuls" and the Form with which they share a name? This is a question I return to later. Second, how should we understand the comparative instability of the perceptible counterparts to Forms? Is the suggestion that Forms' perceptible counterparts "never in any way remain the same" meant to imply that they are, instead, subject to variation *in every respect*? Plato has sometimes been regarded as taking such an extreme view of the condition of perceptible things. However, if this extreme view were in question, it would be hard to see why Cebes would immediately agree with this picture without any question. Still, even if we do not suppose that Plato's view is extreme in this way, we must still ask ourselves what sort of change is at issue.[30] This is linked to the third question, which is how susceptibility to change of this sort (or these sorts) would support the view that (insusceptible) Forms are intelligible as opposed to being perceptible.

The change to which the perceptible counterparts to Forms, unlike Forms, are subject may include such unproblematic examples of change as coming into being or perishing, growth or diminution, and so on. But it seems likely, also, to include a phenomenon that we might not be immediately inclined to think of as an example of change. This is the phenomenon generally known as "the compresence of opposites." Certainly, when, in the *Symposium*, Diotima seeks to explain to Socrates the Form of Beauty's manner of "always being," she denies both that it is subject to ordinary sorts of changes and that it is subject to the compresence of opposites; this is in implied contrast to its perceptible counterparts.

> First, it always is and neither comes to be nor passes away, neither waxes nor wanes. Second, it is not beautiful this way and ugly that way, nor beautiful at one time and ugly at another, nor beautiful in relation to one thing and ugly in relation to another, nor is it beautiful here but ugly there, as it would be if it were beautiful for some people and ugly for others. (*Symposium* 210e6–211a5)

At its most general, the compresence of opposites is a situation in which it would be true to say of some subject both that it is F and that it is un-F (the

---

30. A now classic discussion of these questions is Irwin 1977. See also Irwin 1999.

opposite of F): that it is, for example, both beautiful and ugly. This is among the things here denied of the Form of Beauty. A simple example of the occurrence of the compresence of opposites in a perceptible counterpart to a Form might take the form of the following example from *Phaedo* 102b3–6: Simmias is both large and small (or, perhaps, both larger than and smaller than—it is the comparative terms that Socrates himself uses at b5): large in comparison with Socrates (larger than Socrates), small in comparison with Phaedo (smaller than Phaedo). This example may be misleadingly simple. Whether it illustrates the only or central form of example and the manner in which it might be expected to provide support for the intelligibility of Forms are matters I return to later.

The respective invulnerability and vulnerability to the compresence of opposites of Forms and their perceptible counterparts is one candidate, and, in my view, the best candidate explanation of what is meant by another broad contrast between them, which has prominence in the *Phaedo* especially. This is the view that the perceptible counterparts to Forms are in some way deficient in comparison with the perfection of Forms. Consider, for example, the following agreement between Socrates and Simmias, applied to the Form of Equal and its perceptible counterparts:

> Well, then, he said, do we experience something like this in the case of the equals among sticks and the other equals we mentioned just now? Do they seem to us to be equal in just the same way as what is Equal itself is? Is there some deficiency in their being such as the Equal, or is there not?—A considerable deficiency, he said. (*Phaedo* 74d4–8)

Equality here means geometrical (rather than, as it might be, political or social) equality, that property in virtue of which things are of the same measurement in some dimension of measurement. Socrates and Simmias agree that the perceptible counterparts of the Form of Equal have some deficiency in respect of this property when compared with the Form itself. This deficiency has been interpreted in one of two ways.[31] On the Approximation View, Socrates and Simmias agree that two sticks, for example, cannot be exactly equal in any dimension of measurement; they may *look* equal, but, with sufficiently accurate measuring equipment, we would find they are not. On the Compresence of Opposites View, by contrast, Socrates and Simmias agree that equal sticks are both equal and unequal (albeit in different respects); they may, for example, be equal in length but not in weight; equal to each other but not to some third stick of different dimensions.[32] Notice that Plato cannot simultaneously maintain both of these views, for they are inconsistent with each other. By Approximation, sensible equals are not in any respect exactly equal; they merely approximate equality. By Compresence, in contrast, sensible equals are, indeed, exactly equal, *in some respect*; they are also unequal in some (other) respect.

---

31. For the contrast, see Nehamas 1975.

32. For Approximation, see, for example, Ross 1951; for Compresence, see, for example, Nehamas 1975 and Irwin 1977, 1999.

I favor the Compresence of Opposites view of deficiency for the following reasons. First, it seems to me that it would at the least be hugely controversial to claim that, as a matter of fact, no two perceptible objects could have exactly the same measurements as each other in some dimension of measurement. The very existence of one case of the dimension in some perceptible object seems to prove the possibility of its occurring twice. The claim at issue, it should be noted, is much stronger than the possibly trivial claim that we are often fast and loose in our identification of things as being equal, and that many things we identify as such turn out to fall short of equality upon closer examination. It is, however, the stronger claim that is needed for the Approximation View. And it seems to me that we should avoid the attribution of controversial claims where none are needed. Second, the Approximation View seems unable to deal with those instances in which there are Forms for each of a pair of (binary) opposites. The Form of Equal is one example, if there is a Form of Unequal also.[33] The problem for the Approximation View is that whatever is only approximately equal seems to be something exactly unequal. The view cannot thus be simultaneously maintained for each of a pair of (binary) opposites.

These first two reasons have been illustrated with reference to the *Phaedo*'s own example, but both would appear to generalize across at least a wide range of candidate Forms. It also seems important that both reasons do apply so readily to the very Form that Socrates chooses as an example when making the point about the deficiency of sensibles in comparison with Forms; the greater plausibility of one or other view with respect to this very example should count in its favor. The final reason to favor the Compresence View is that it seems to cohere much better with those passages in which there seems undeniable interest in the compresence of opposites, both in the *Phaedo* and elsewhere (*Phaedo* 102b3–6, mentioned above; more controversially, but, I think, plausibly, in a vexed passage in the immediate context, 74b7–c3;[34] and, for example, *Republic* V, 478e7–479d5), especially since, as we have seen, Plato cannot consistently maintain *both* views of the status of Forms' perceptible counterparts.

Notice, however, that we now find ourselves confronted once more by the question of the scope of Forms—in particular, by the question of whether there are Forms only for pairs of opposites. If perfection is a defining characteristic of Forms in contrast to their perceptible counterparts, and if what perfection amounts to is an invulnerability to the compresence of opposites with which their perceptible counterparts are afflicted, then it looks as if there can be Forms only of opposites.[35]

---

33. Perhaps this might be doubted, if one thinks that Formal pairs of opposites are *contraries* (see n. 22 above). The reference to "inequality" at *Phaedo* 74c2, identified using the abstract noun *anisotês*, might be taken as evidence for a Form of Unequal.

34. For recent discussion of this vexed passage, see Sedley 2007.

35. This problem arises on the Compresence of Opposites View of the imperfection of Forms' perceptible counterparts, but it is not clear that we would be in a much better position if we, instead, adopted the Approximation View of their imperfection, for it seems at least less obvious what would be meant by the claim that perceptibles approximate nonoppositional features such as humanity, for example, than that they do so for oppositional features such as equality or beauty.

As it is, however, there seems no clear evidence for this restriction in the scope of Forms (which would have been easy enough to state). And there is some evidence against such a restriction in scope, in candidate examples of Forms that do not have opposites.

Faced with this question, there seem to be three different options for keeping the scope of Forms broader than the focus on compresence of opposites might be taken to suggest. First, one might decide that Plato thinks the phenomenon of compresence of opposites is found more broadly than we might think.[36] Second, one might deny that the contrast between perfect Forms and imperfect sensible counterparts is, in fact, a defining characteristic of Forms.[37] In this way, we need not take imperfection, so understood, to constrain our understanding of the scope of Forms. But we would still need to explain the prevalence of interest in the presence or absence of the compresence of opposites, whether or not it is part of a contrast between imperfect perceptibles and perfect Forms. Finally, then, in a manner similar to the point made above in connection with *Republic* book VII, one might suggest that the compresence of opposites is given attention as an especially conspicuous aspect of some broader phenomenon that has the potential to apply to a broader range Forms, under which broader phenomenon compresence may be subsumed.

How might this final strategy be cashed out? Without pretending to the sort of detailed examination one would really need of this question, two possibilities suggest themselves. One is to recall that Forms are contrasted to their perceptible counterparts as being invulnerable to ordinary sorts of change, as well as to the compresence of opposites (as in the *Symposium* passage quoted above). Suppose that Plato shares with Aristotle the view that negative predicates like "is not human" are true not only of presently existing things that are not human but also of things that previously existed as humans, but which no longer exist.[38] Then, it is as true to say, today, that Socrates is not human, as it would have been true to say of him that he was human, on the fateful day recorded in the *Phaedo*.[39] This is not a case of compresence of opposites. But it is a case of something of which compresence of opposites might be construed as a more vivid example.

A second, possibly related way in which to cash out the strategy would be to draw on one final broad contrast associated with the difference between Forms and their perceptible counterparts: the contrast between being and becoming, a key, but unclear statement of which is found in the *Timaeus*:

> In my judgement, then, we must first make the following distinction: what is that which is always, having no becoming, and what is that which becomes always, never being? The former is such as to be grasped by thought with

36. For indications of this sort of strategy, see Fine 1993, 100–101.
37. This strategy has recently been defended by Sedley 2006.
38. For this view in Aristotle, see *De Interpretatione* 3, 16b11–15 and *Categories* 10, 13b14–19.
39. I set aside the complications raised by questions about the possible humanity of Socrates' putatively immortal soul.

reason, being always in the same condition, whereas the other is such as to be grasped by judgement with unreasoning perception, becoming and ceasing to be, but never really being. (27d5–28a4)

While the relation between the *Timaeus* and the discussions of Forms on which we have been focusing has been left an open question, the contrast drawn here seems clearly in some way related to the contrast drawn at *Phaedo* 78–79, quoted above.[40] Consider, then, one persuasive interpretation of what Plato may mean by the contrast between that which becomes and that which is, put forward by Michael Frede.[41] Things that become are things that, relative to some specific times, contexts, or relations take on the character or marks of some formal feature, F, but not in virtue of having or being some nature that *is* F. Only Formal natures—that which is captured by a definition of "F"—*are*, as opposed to *become*, F. Occurrence of the compresence of opposites, in respect to some F, is one conspicuous, but not the only, indication that perceptibles fail to satisfy the requirements on things that *are* (what is) F, and hence merely *become* F, at some times and in some contexts or relations.

# VI. *Where Are Forms?*

The question "*Where* are Forms?" may seem an odd one, but it seems to me worth considering, insofar as it will sharpen our understanding of the questions there are about the relation between forms and their perceptible counterparts. Further, odd though the question may be, it is one that, even in popular thought about Plato, as found in a nonspecialist encylopedia, is commonly given an answer: Forms exist in some "Platonic heaven."[42] This answer may be intended metaphorically, since Forms are also (and with justification) commonly understood to be immaterial, nonspatially extended objects of a sort that are not naturally thought of as having spatial location. Nevertheless, the metaphor implies the existence of a location or quasilocation for Forms, which is distinct from that of the location of ordinary material objects. Since Forms are the objects of intellect and material objects are the objects of perception, the metaphor often extends to talk of two quasi-spatially distinct "realms": the sensible realm and the intelligible realm.

Such talk, of course, reflects the sort of contrast between two sorts of being—the perceptible and the intelligible—on which we have focused thus far. And the "location" of these two sorts of beings in two different "realms" undoubtedly reflects

---

40. Note that the dual contrast will be further complicated, as the *Timaeus* proceeds, by the introduction of the receptacle. See, for example, 50c7–d2, 51e6–52b5.

41. Frede 1988. See also response by Code 1988.

42. See, for example, the entry on Wikipedia, the Free Encyclopedia: http://en.wikipedia.org/w/index.php?title=Theory_of_Forms&oldid=73131620%Wikipedia.

some of Plato's own choices of image and language. In the *Republic*'s analogy of the cave, for example, the intellectual ascent involved in turning one's attention from the perceptible to the intelligible is depicted as a journey out of a cave to an environment outside. And the *Phaedrus* talks of the "place beyond heaven" (247c3) as the location of truth. But there are questions as to what is the best way in which to understand this sort of language and image.

One direction we should be careful to avoid being led is in the direction of talking as though Plato is somehow committed to two different *realities*. Assuming that reality is what there is—whatever that turns out to be—then it is hard to see that it makes any sense to talk of *two* realities; Plato's view, rather, should be understood as the view that the deliverances of perception do not exhaust (and may in some way distort) the contents of reality. There remain, however, two rather different ways to understand this view. On one, the view is that there is in reality what we ordinarily think that there is (the perceptibles), but that there is, *in addition*, an aspect of reality besides what is evident in perceptual experience and which is in various ways metaphysically explanatory of what is evident in experience. On another, the view is that the evidence derived from perceptual experience in certain respects *distorts* our understanding of what there is in reality, and that the reality discovered through rational inquiry corrects or replaces aspects of what our experience suggests to us there is. On the first view, perceptibles and intelligibles work in tandem, though in distinction from each other; on the second, perceptibles and intelligibles are more like rivals.

The second view is more in line with the rationalist tradition antecedent to Plato, from which I began. On this view, Plato (like Parmenides and Democritus before him) is best understood as proposing that it is only by using our intellect, as opposed to our senses, that we will come to understand what there really is in the (single) world around us, the world with which we are, indeed, in contact through perception, but about which perception to a greater or lesser extent misinforms us. And, we may note, in the case of Democritus, for example, there is no parallel temptation to talk of a distinct "atomic realm." Of course, the prevalence of this temptation with regard to Plato may be a reflection of (another) respect in which Plato differs from Democritus (one of many). But it may also be a hazard arising from an overly literal interpretation of spatial imagery that is, in fact, designed to accentuate the intelligibility—as opposed to the perceptibility—of Forms.

A second potential hazard of an overly literal reading of the talk of Forms as residing in some "Platonic heaven" is the assumption that, if Forms are separate, as Aristotle suggested, they are therefore not immanent, not *in* the things that have them. However, as Fine has argued, these matters are far from clear.[43] Even if Plato does assume that Forms are in some sense separate—not literally spatially, but in the sense of being capable of independent existence—it is not at all clear that he concludes from this that Forms are not also *in* certain things. In the *Phaedo*, presence (*parousia*, 100d5) is among the candidate relations that Socrates canvases

43. Fine 1984 and 1986. Contrast Devereux 1994.

for the relation between participant and Form, and he is prepared to license inferences of the following sort:

> When you then say that Simmias is larger than Socrates but smaller than Phaedo, do you not mean that there is *in* Simmias both Largeness and Smallness? (102b3–5)

It is disputed whether, in this passage, Socrates has in mind that the Forms, Largeness and Smallness, are themselves in Simmias, or whether there are, in addition to Forms, additional corresponding items, so-called Immanent Forms or Immanent Characters, and it is one of these Immanent Forms or Characters that is, for example, the Largeness in Simmias.[44] On a credible reading of the passage, however, Forms do turn out to be items that can be located.[45] But they are not located off in some remote "Platonic heaven"; they are located where everything else is, around here, sometimes in (at least some of) the things we see.[46]

# VII. What, Metaphysically Speaking, Are Forms? And What, for That Matter, Are "Particulars," the Perceptible Counterparts to Forms?

Are Forms universal in character, or are Forms particular? That is, are Forms repeatable items—not only located, but multiply located in many spaces and times in the things that have them in common—or are they unique and nonrepeatable in character? Both views of the metaphysical character of Forms have been defended.[47] On balance, there seems to me reason to favor the view that Forms are universal in character. This is, in part, because Forms appear to perform the central function that is typically adduced as the reason for introducing a universal, the performance of which has some claim to be constitutive of being a universal; Forms underlie genuine similarities in the character of things by being (in some

---

44. Contrast Fine 1986 and Vlastos 1969.

45. Does the idea of their being located call into question their immaterial character? No: no more than does the claim that the immaterial soul is to be found—at least some of the time—*in* a body.

46. "Sometimes": if Forms' capacity for independent existence includes (or amounts to) the capacity to exist even if no perceptibles participate in them, then Forms need not always be located *in* some perceptible object(s). But it does not follow from this that they are—as well or instead—in some alternative location, a Platonic heaven; it may be that in this case they exist without any specific location(s).

47. For the view that Forms are universals, see, for example, Fine 1993; for the view that Forms are particulars, see, for example, Geach 1956 (at least implicitly); yet another view is that Forms are best understood as something like chemical elements, for which, see Denyer 1983.

way) common to them. But it does not follow from this that the Theory of Forms is itself a *Theory* of Universals. After all, it is not clear that their performing this function, if they do, constitutes the central reason for their introduction as Forms, and performing this function is not the sole function of Forms.

If, in the Theory of Forms, Plato were giving us a Theory of Universals, then he would, in all likelihood, be the first to do so (and, indeed, he is cited as such by Armstrong,[48] for example). One of the consequences of being the *first* to offer a theory of the existence of a certain sort of metaphysical object is that the metaphysical terrain is not already carved up in such a way that distinctions of the sort that might emerge from such a theory are readily available to draw on. I argue that the distinction between universal and particular, understood as the distinction between items that are repeatable and those that are not, is not, in fact, central to the contours of Plato's ontology as he conceives them, if, that is, he would recognize the distinction at all. This fact may go some way toward explaining why these two, as it seems to us, fundamentally different metaphysical characters, universal and particular, have both seemed feasible in characterizations of Forms.

There are two main reasons to suppose that the distinction between universal and particular is not, in fact, central to Plato's ontology (at least, not in his construction of the Theory of Forms). These two reasons complement each other. The first is that Forms do not appear to be the only item in Plato's ontology that are universal in character, so it would seem that, if he does think of Forms as being universal in character, this cannot be what he takes to be especially distinctive of them. The second is that when Plato constructs the "other" to Forms, he does so in a way that encompasses both items that are particular and items that are universal. By the "other" to Forms, I mean, of course, not merely whatever is different from Forms but the items that are typically contrasted with Forms in arguments centrally involving features of Forms—that is, in the type of argument that one might take to indicate Plato's reasons for positing Forms (with the features proposed). Misleadingly, these "other" to Forms are often referred to as "particulars"; Plato's "particulars," however, are not all metaphysically particular, or so I argue.

I take the first reason first. In saying that Forms are not the only items in Plato's ontology that appear to be universal in character, I follow an interpretation according to which, in talk of the perceptible counterparts to Forms, Plato at least sometimes refers to perceptible universals. Consider, for example, the following central passage from *Republic* book V:

> (S) Now that these points have been established, I want to address a question to our friend who doesn't believe in the beautiful itself or any form of the beautiful itself that remains the same in all respects but who does believe in the many beautiful things—the lover of sights who won't allow anyone to say that the beautiful is one or the just or any of the others; and let me ask him this: of these many beautiful things, friend, is there one which will not also appear

---

48. D. M. Armstrong in his entry on "universals" in Kim and Sosa 1995, 502.

ugly? Or, of the many just, one which will not appear unjust? Or, of the many things that are holy, one that will not appear unholy? (G) No, he said, rather they must appear in some way both beautiful and ugly, and the same goes for the others you asked about. (S) What about the many doubles? Do they appear less halves than doubles? (G) No. (S) And the many large and small things, or light and heavy things, is any one of these any more whichever of these we say it is than the opposite? (G) No, each will always be both. (S) Then *is* each of the many any more whatever someone says it is than it *is not*? (478e7–479b10)

According to the interpretation I follow, the items referred to here as, for example, "the many beautifuls" are universal perceptible properties such as "being brightly colored" of the sort that might (erroneously, in Socrates' view) be offered as a candidate explanation of the beauty of some perceptible beautiful object (a lithograph by Miró, for example).[49] Such properties are universal, insofar as they are themselves repeatable items. Many Miró lithographs, for example, have in common being brightly colored. But they are clearly distinguished from Forms, which are *nonperceptible* universals.[50]

This brings us on to the second reason for supposing that the distinction between universal and particular is not central to Plato's ontology. For it is these very items—the perceptible universals of, for example, *Republic* book V—that turn out to be included in Plato's construction of the "other" to Forms. They are included in, but, in my view, do not exclusively constitute the other to Forms, which elsewhere seems to include things that are metaphysically particular in character. Consider, for example, a portion of the *Phaedo* passage quoted before:

> But what about the many beautifuls, such as people or horses or clothing or any other things of this sort, or about the equals, or about all those sharing a name with those things? Do they remain the same, or, in complete contrast to those others, do they, practically never in any way remain the same as themselves or each other? (*Phaedo* 78d10–e4)

Here again, we have mention of "the many beautifuls." On this occasion, however, the expression would appear to refer to metaphysically particular items—people, horses, clothing.[51] Part of the difficulty is that Plato does not have explicit terminology with which to mark the particular-universal distinction, a fact which itself is grist to my mill. Further, as we have seen, he is prepared to use the very same expression—"the many beautifuls," for example—for items on both sides of this metaphysical divide. Neither the lack of explicit terminology nor the indifferent use of terminology across the division shows that Plato could not draw the distinction. But it does support my case that the distinction, if he has it, is not

49. For this reading, see Gosling 1960 and compare Irwin 1977 and Fine 1993. For doubts, see Silverman 2002, ch. 4.

50. Or: nonsensible universals. So, for example, Fine 1993.

51. But, contrast here, Irwin 1977.

central to his own conception of the contours of his ontology, nor to where he puts the fault lines in his arguments about Forms.

Further, from the point of view of his theorizing, the heterogeneity apparent in Plato's construction of the "other" to Forms has certain advantages. I focus on two. The first takes us back to some questions left outstanding in section V above about the compresence of opposites. It is clear from the *Republic* V passage already quoted that perceptible universals can take a prominent role in arguments involving compresence of opposites. I now argue that, even when not directly referred to, it is the perceptible universals that do the lion's share of the philosophical work involved in appeals to compresence.

While sometimes more nuanced, claims about the occurrence of the phenomenon of compresence of opposites are sometimes put as the claim that all "perceptibles" (of the relevant sort) necessarily give rise to compresence of opposites. Our *Republic* V passage has this tone.[52] But what does this mean? Is it the claim (PC) that, for any particular perceptible having some relevant feature, F, necessarily, that particular perceptible also has the opposing feature un-F? Or is it the claim (UC) that, for any perceptible type, a token of which is F, for some relevant feature, necessarily that type has un-F tokens also?

Plato would certainly be well advised not to commit himself to (PC) as stated, which seems an implausibly strong claim. Could there not, for example, be an action that was *just* and that was not, in any respect, *unjust*?

We may make this point (and the force of (UC) more concrete) with an example exploiting the *Phaedo*'s chosen Formal exemplar, Equality. Consider the following (apparently reasonable) possibility that (PC) rules out. Imagine a world in which there are exactly two objects that, as a matter of fact, are equal in every dimension. *Ex hypothesi*, they are not unequal in any respect, contra (PC). However, just because these equalities of length, weight, and so on involve specific lengths, weights, and so on, then clearly there *could* be an object to which these objects were unequal, although, in fact, there is not.[53]

But what does it mean to say that there *could* be an object to which the equals of this world were unequal? One aspect of the possibility in question is a possible object that does not, but could, exist in the actual world we're considering. Call it *U* (for unequal). Another aspect relates to the objects that do exist in the actual world considered in view of the possibility of *U*. It is this aspect that matters as far as the actual equals are concerned, and this is their *possible inequality to U* (a possibility realized in all those worlds in which both they and *U* exist). Such *possible inequality to U* must have some basis in some (actual) feature of the equal objects in every (relevant) world, including the actual.[54] But what this feature amounts to is just the claim that there is some type that these equals instantiate,

52. The "sometimes" of *Phaedo* 74b8 may be an example of nuance.

53. The advisability of stepping down to a modal claim about (particular) compresence is noted in Kelsey 2000, 105 (where the thought is attributed to Sarah Broadie, n.26).

54. The domain of worlds must be fixed to those in which the equal objects (or their counterparts) exist and where all relevant dimensions bearing on their equality in the actual world are constant.

and that this type has equal and unequal tokens across the relevant worlds.[55] Once considered across worlds, then, it becomes easier to see that the *possibility* of compresence is grounded in (UC). But any actual occurrence is possible and thus open to the same explanation. Both actual and possible occurrences of compresence in perceptible particulars may thus be grounded in the occurrence of the phenomenon at the level of types.

A second advantage of the heterogeneity of Plato's "other" to Forms is the effect it has on our understanding of predicates, in particular as applied to their perceptible counterparts and to Forms. Given the existence and pertinence of certain perceptible universals, metaphysically particular beautiful objects—such as a lithograph by Miró—turn out often to be instances both of a perceptible universal (being brightly colored) and of a Form (the Beautiful). They are not instances of the Form in virtue of being instances of the perceptible universal (because the perceptible universal is vulnerable to compresence). And this leaves open how we should understand the relation between the particular's instantiation of the perceptible universal (its bright color) and its instantiation of the Form (beauty). This question approaches, albeit somewhat indirectly, one of the most controversial features of Plato's Theory of Forms: self-predication.

Self-predication is the view that a Form can in some sense be predicated of itself: that the Form of Beauty can have the predicate "beautiful" applied to it. Self-predication might occur in certain specific cases without being a matter of theory. For example, if every Form is one and if there is a Form, One, then this Form self-predicates. The interesting question, however, is whether Forms self-predicate systematically and as a matter of theory. And there are grounds for thinking they do. Consider, for example, the following passage from the *Phaedo*:

> Consider, then, he said, whether you share my opinion as to what follows, for I think that, if there is anything beautiful besides the Beautiful itself, it is beautiful for no other reason than that it shares in that Beautiful, and I say so with everything. Do you agree to this sort of cause? (*Phaedo* 100c2–7)

Since this passage assumes that the Beautiful itself *is* beautiful—and goes on to make a claim about what must be true about anything *besides* the Form that counts as beautiful—we have here a pretty clear statement of self-predication in what looks to be a sample case: the Form, the Beautiful itself, is beautiful. Further, it is sometimes thought that the theory of causal responsibility that Socrates is here in the process of developing and illustrating requires that a cause resemble its effect in the relevant causal respect.[56] This would provide a theoretical motivation for

55. The argument proceeds on the assumption that (at least in some cases) compresent opposite properties are attributed on the basis of one and the same feature of the object(s) in question. The case of Simmias, who, while remaining the same in height, can be viewed as large in relation to Socrates and small in relation to Simmias is of this type.

56. See Sedley 1998; for discussion of the causal principle itself, see Makin 1990.

systematic self-predication. Notoriously, self-predication plays some central role in the so-called Third Man Argument at *Parmenides* 132a1–b2.[57]

If there are good grounds for supposing that Forms self-predicate, it is nevertheless hard to deny the apparent absurdity of some pictures of how this would work. (No doubt, this is one reason that, among *Parmenides* interpreters, self-predication is high on the list of targets for attitudes to Forms to be repudiated or revised.)[58] The apparent absurdity is brought out nicely by Fine: self-predication would have the consequence that "the form of White (if there is one) is coloured white; the form of dog (if there is one) can scratch its ears."[59] And, lest we think absurdity occurs only in cases where it is disputable whether there are Forms, consider two very clearly evidenced Forms, the Large and the Small. Is the Large some *massive* object? And *how small* would the Form of Small have to be?[60]

The absurdity arises on what Fine describes as "Narrow Self-Predication," the view that "the Form of F is F in roughly the same way in which F sensibles are F."[61] This is probably why attempts to rescue (or revise) self-predication have focused on identifying some different way in which the Form "is F." Without rejecting this strategy, I want to suggest that we should have in mind a question about the way in which perceptible Fs *are* F, Forms aside.

Think once again about my lithograph, a perceptible beautiful (metaphysically particular) object. It is an instance both of a perceptible universal (being brightly colored) and of a Form (the Beautiful). But it is not an instance of the Form in virtue of being an instance of the perceptible universal (because the perceptible universal is vulnerable to compresence). Being brightly colored cannot be the explanation of my lithograph's beauty, because these same bright colors have ugly instances (such as the sweater I bought, but never wear). Not only that: many cases of beauty will not be brightly colored—in the case of beautiful souls or beautiful theories, for example, the beautiful items in question will not be colored at all. But Plato is committed to the view that an explanation of beauty must be capable of covering all cases.[62] Bright coloration, then, is at most coextensive with some cases of beauty. But this would appear to leave it an open question how, if at all, the *beauty of my lithograph* relates to its being an instance of this perceptible universal? The (salient) perceptible features of my lithograph could be either (a) in no way constitutive of the beauty of my lithograph or at least (b) not constitutive of it in any way that invites the drawing of the absurd parallel when it comes to

57. This was originally brought out by Vlastos 1954 and has been the subject of much discussion; see, among many others, Meinwald 1992, Peterson 1973, Sedley 1998.

58. This is the strategy of Meinwald 1992, for example.

59. Fine 1992, 25. And see discussion of self-predication in Peterson, chapter 16 in this volume.

60. This sort of picture is only encouraged—to its discredit—by the Approximation View of imperfection, rejected in section V above.

61. Fine 1992, 25.

62. At least he often appears so committed, although it is not clear how well this would work in the case of the "more subtle" forms of explanation endorsed in *Phaedo* 105b ff., for while it may be the case that, for example, fever, when present in a body, always makes it sick, it is far less clear that whenever a body is sick, fever is present.

considering the way of being beautiful that applies to the Form. Self-predication might be defended from evident absurdity, that is, by supposing that the basis for the application of predicates to perceptible particulars is already somewhat different from what we might have been ordinarily inclined to think. Indeed, I take this to be one way to understand the claim that Socrates makes at *Phaedo* 100c (quoted above).

Finally, therefore, this raises a question about the perceptibility of the properties corresponding to Forms. In adjudicating between the two options regarding my lithograph presented above, we may be concerned about proving too much. It proves too much, one might think, if the beauty of my lithograph turns out to be nonperceptible, just like the Form. Or perhaps this is not too much. After all, if Forms *are* immanent, the beauty of my lithograph is brought about by the presence of the nonperceptible Form of Beauty within it. This issue has arisen, indirectly, more than once over the course of my discussion. Take, for example, some particular beautiful human being. This is a metaphysically particular object that I can directly perceive. In some sense, I can directly perceive it as human and as beautiful. But it seems to me far from clear whether, on Plato's view, I can directly perceive its humanity or its beauty. While it may seem unsatisfactory for me not to be able to answer this question, it does have the merit of being consistent with the emphasis of my overall theme: Plato as metaphysician for whom the fact that Forms are intelligible rather than perceptible is the primary point of focus, and who, in positing Forms, is concerned to argue that many aspects of the (single, local) world that appears to us in perception are not in reality how they appear.[63]

# REFERENCES

Algra, K. (1995) *Concepts of Space in Greek Thought* (Leiden: Brill).

Annas, Julia (1981) *An Introduction to Plato's Republic* (Oxford: Clarendon Press).

Bostock, D. (1986) *Plato's Phaedo* (Oxford: Clarendon Press).

Bostock, D. (1999) "The Soul and Immortality in Plato's *Phaedo*," in Fine 1999b, 404–24.

Brittain, Charles (2001) *Philo of Larissa* (Oxford: Oxford University Press).

Burnyeat, M. F. (1999) "Culture and Society in Plato's *Republic*," in *Tanner Lectures on Human Values*, vol. 20, ed. G. B. Peterson (Salt Lake City: University of Utah Press).

Cherniss, H. F. (1957) "The Relation of the *Timaeus* to Plato's Later Dialogues," *American Journal of Philology* 78, 225–66.

Code, A. (1988) "Reply to Michael Frede's 'Being and Becoming in Plato,'" *Oxford Studies in Ancient Philosophy*, supplementary volume, ed. Julia Annas and Robert H. Grimm, 53–60 (Oxford: Clarendon).

Cooper, J. M., ed. (1997) *Plato: Complete Works* (Indianapolis: Hackett).

Denyer, N. C. (1983) "Plato's Theory of Stuffs," *Philosophy* 58, 315–27.

63. For helpful discussion of the issues and/or comments on drafts of this essay, I am grateful to the editor, Gail Fine, and to Ursula Coope, Melissa Lane, M. M. McCabe, and Dominic Scott.

Devereux, D. T. (1994) "Separation and Immanence in Plato's Theory of Forms," *Oxford Studies in Ancient Philosophy* 12, 63–90.

Everson, S., ed. (1990) *Epistemology*. Companions to Ancient Thought No. 1 (Cambridge: Cambridge University Press).

Fine, Gail (1978) "Knowledge and Belief in *Republic* V," *Archiv für Geschichte der Philosophie* 60, 121–39.

Fine, Gail (1984) "Separation," *Oxford Studies in Ancient Philosophy* 2, 31–87.

Fine, Gail (1986) "Immanence," *Oxford Studies in Ancient Philosophy* 4, 71–97.

Fine, Gail (1990) "Knowledge and Belief in *Republic* V–VII," in Everson 1990, 85–115.

Fine, Gail (1992) "Aristotle's Criticisms of Plato," *Oxford Studies in Ancient Philosophy*, supplementary volume ed. James C. Klagge and Nicholas D. Smith (Oxford: Clarendon Press), 13–41.

Fine, Gail (1993) *On Ideas: Aristotle's Criticism of Plato's Theory of Forms* (Oxford: Clarendon Press).

Fine, Gail, ed. (1999a) *Plato 1: Metaphysics and Epistemology*. Oxford Readings in Philosophy (Oxford: Oxford University Press).

Fine, Gail, ed. (1999b) *Plato 2: Ethics, Politics, Religion and the Soul*. Oxford Readings in Philosophy (Oxford: Oxford University Press).

Frede, M. (1980) "The Original Notion of Cause," in Schofield et al. 1980, 217–49.

Frede, M. (1988) "Being and Becoming in Plato," *Oxford Studies in Ancient Philosophy*, supplementary volume, ed. Julia Annas and Robert H. Grimm (Oxford: Clarendon Press), 37–52.

Gallop, D. (1982) "Plato's "Cyclical" Argument Recycled," *Phronesis* 27, 207–22.

Geach, P. T. (1956) "The Third Man Again," *Philosophical Review* 65, 72–82.

Gerson, Lloyd P. (2003) *Knowing Persons* (Oxford: Oxford University Press).

Gill, Christopher (1996) *Personality in Greek Epic, Tragedy, and Philosophy* (Oxford: Clarendon Press).

Gosling, J. C. B. (1960) "*Republic* V: *Ta Polla Kala*, etc.," *Phronesis* 10, 151–61.

Harte, Verity (2002) *Plato on Parts and Wholes: The Metaphysics of Structure* (Oxford: Clarendon Press).

Irwin, T. H. (1977) "Plato's Heracleiteanism," *Philosophical Quarterly* 27, 1–13.

Irwin, T. H. (1999) "The Theory of Forms," in Fine 1999a, 143–70.

Kahn, C. H. (1996) *Plato and the Socratic Dialogue: The Philosophical Use of a Literary Form* (Cambridge: Cambridge University Press).

Kahn, C. H. (2007) "Why Is the *Sophist* a Sequel to the *Theaetetus?*" *Phronesis* 52, 33–57.

Kelsey, S. (2000) "Recollection in the *Phaedo*," *Proceedings of the Boston Area Colloquium in Ancient Philosophy* 16, ed. J. J. Cleary and G. M. Gurtler (Leiden: Brill), 91–121.

Kim, J., and Sosa, E., eds. (1995) *A Companion to Metaphysics* (Oxford: Basil Blackwell).

Kraut, R., ed. (1992) *The Cambridge Companion to Plato* (Cambridge: Cambridge University Press).

Long, A. A., ed. (1999) *The Cambridge Companion to Early Greek Philosophy* (Cambridge: Cambridge University Press).

Makin, S. (1990) "An Ancient Principle about Causation," *Proceedings of the Aristotelian Society* 91, 135–52.

McCabe, Mary Margaret (1994) *Plato's Individuals* (Princeton, N.J.: Princeton University Press).

McCabe, Mary Margaret (2000) *Plato and His Predecessors* (Cambridge: Cambridge University Press).

Meinwald, C. (1992) "Good-Bye to the Third Man," in Kraut 1992, 365–96.

Menn, Stephen (1995) *Plato on God as* Nous (Carbondale: Southern Illinois University Press).

Morgan, M. L. (1992) "Plato and Greek Religion," in Kraut 1992, 227–47.

Motte, A., Rutten, C., and Somville, P. (2003) *Philosophie de la Forme: Eidos, Idea, Morphé dans la philosophie Grecque des origines à Aristote* (Louvain-la-Neuve: Éditions Peeters).

Natorp, P. (2004) *Plato's Theory of Ideas: An Introduction to Idealism*, ed. Vasilis Politis (Sankt Augustin: Academia Verlag).

Nehamas, A. (1975) "Plato on the Imperfection of the Sensible World," *American Philosophical Quarterly* 12, 105–17.

Owen, G. E. L. (1953) "The Place of the *Timaeus* in Plato's Dialogues," *Classical Quarterly* NS 3, 79–95.

Owen, G. E. L. (1966a) "Plato and Parmenides on the Timeless Present," *Monist* 50, 317–40.

Owen, G. E. L. (1966b) "The Platonism of Aristotle," *Proceedings of the British Academy* 51, 125–50.

Palmer, J. A. (1999) *Plato's Reception of Parmenides* (Oxford: Clarendon Press).

Penner, T. (1987) *The Ascent from Nominalism* (Dordrecht: Reidel).

Peterson, S. (1973) "A Reasonable Self-Predication Premise for the Third Man Argument," *Philosophical Review* 82, 451–70.

Ross, D. (1951) *Plato's Theory of Ideas* (Oxford: Clarendon Press).

Ryle, G. (1966) *Plato's Progress* (Cambridge: Cambridge University Press).

Schofield, M., Burnyeat, M., and Barnes, J., eds. (1980) *Doubt and Dogmatism: Studies in Hellenistic Epistemology* (Oxford: Clarendon Press).

Scott, D., ed. (2007) *Maieusis: Studies on Greek Philosophy in Honour of M. F. Burnyeat* (Oxford: Clarendon Press).

Sedley, David (1998) "Platonic Causes," *Phronesis* 43, 114–32.

Sedley, David (2006) "Form-Particular Resemblance in Plato's *Phaedo*," *Proceedings of the Aristotelian Society* 106, 309–25.

Sedley, David (2007) "Equal Sticks and Stones,' in Scott 2007, 68–86.

Silverman, Alan (2002) *The Dialectic of Essence: A Study of Plato's Metaphysics* (Princeton, N.J.: Princeton University Press).

Smith, J. A. (1917) "General Relative Clauses in Greek," *Classical Review* 31, 69–71.

Sorabji, R. K. (1983) *Time, Creation and the Continuum* (London: Duckworth).

Sorabji, R. K. (1988) *Matter, Space and Motion* (London: Duckworth).

Vlastos, G. (1954) "The Third Man Argument in the *Parmenides*," *Philosophical Review* 63, 319–49.

Vlastos, G. (1969) "Reasons and Causes in the *Phaedo*," *Philosophical Review* 78, 291–325.

Vlastos, G. (1991) *Socrates, Ironist and Moral Philosopher* (Cambridge: Cambridge University Press).

# CHAPTER 9

# PLATO'S PHILOSOPHY OF LANGUAGE

## PAOLO CRIVELLI

IDEAS in and problems of philosophy of language surface frequently in Plato's dialogues. Some passages briefly formulate, or presuppose, views about names, signification, truth, or falsehood; others are extended discussions of important themes of philosophy of language.

It is impossible, within the limits of this essay, to follow all the leads. I focus on three topics. The first is the linguistic dimension of the theory of forms; the second is the discussion of names in the *Cratylus*, Plato's only dialogue almost completely dedicated to linguistic themes; the third is the examination of semantic and ontological issues in the *Sophist*, whose linguistic section (259d9–264b10) presents Plato's most mature reflections on statements, truth, and falsehood.[1]

---

1. I have benefited greatly from remarks by the editor and Francesco Ademollo. The responsibility for the remaining deficiencies is only mine.

# Linguistic Dimension
# of the Theory of Forms

## Are there forms corresponding to every predicative expression? The case for

Several considerations suggest that for every predicative expression there is a corresponding form:

1. In the *Phaedo*, in the context of his earliest extensive presentation of the theory of forms, Plato says that "each of the forms exists and the other things that partake of these derive their names from these themselves [*autōn toutōn tēn epōnumian ischein*]"[2] (102b1–2; cf. 78d10–78e2, 103b5–103c2; *Prm.* 130e5–131a2, 133c8–133d5; *Ti.* 52a4–7; Arist. *Metaph.* A6, 987b9–10).

2. In *Republic* X, Socrates announces that he will begin his inquiry by the "usual method," whereby he is accustomed "to assume that each form [*eidos hekaston*] corresponding to each set of many things [*hekasta ta polla*] is one, in which case we apply the same name to the many things [*sc.* as to the form]" (596a6–8).

3. In the *Meno*, Socrates adduces the fact that "you address these many things [*sc.* roundness and the other shapes] by a single name [*sc.* 'shape']" (74d5–6) as a reason for believing that there is a single item that "occupies" (74d8) all shapes and has "shape" as its name (74e11).

These texts induce some commentators to attribute to Plato the view that for every predicative expression there is a corresponding form.[3] For the sake of precision, let me pin down the terminology: a form *F corresponds to* a predicative expression *P* just if the range of *F* is identical with the extension of *P*; the *range* of a form *F* is the set whose elements are all and only the items that partake of *F*; and the *extension* of a predicative expression *P* is the set whose elements are all and only the items of which *P* is true.[4]

## Are there forms corresponding to every predicative expression? The case against

In the *Politicus* (262a3–263b12), Plato denies the existence of a form corresponding to "barbarian" (i.e., "non-Greek human being"). In the *Parmenides* (130b1–130e3), the young Socrates, after endorsing the existence of the forms *like, one, many, just,*

---

2. For *epōnumian ischein* + gen. meaning "to derive the name from," see *Criti.* 114a5–6.

3. D. Ross, *Plato's Theory of Ideas* [*Theory*] (Oxford, 1951), 79.

4. Other passages that appear to bear witness to a linguistic dimension of the theory of forms (*Prm.* 135b5–135c2; *Phdr.* 249b5–249c3, 266b3–5) are vague: they do not show that, according to Plato, for every predicative expression there is a corresponding form.

*beautiful, good,* "and everything of that sort," hesitates to admit the forms *man, fire,* and *water* and is disinclined to accept forms of undignified things like hair, mud, and dirt. Parmenides comments that philosophy has not yet gripped the young Socrates as it will later, when he will not despise the items last mentioned. To be sure, one must be cautious in using the *Parmenides* as evidence for reconstructing Plato's own earlier views. Nevertheless, it is not unreasonable to regard our *Parmenides* passage as alluding to a development in Plato's theory of forms. Since the position held by the young Socrates denies that for every predicative expression there is a corresponding form, it is tempting to infer that at some stage Plato did not think that for every predicative expression there is a corresponding form.[5]

These facts tell against attributing to Plato the view that for every predicative expression there is a corresponding form.

## Forms and predicative expressions

Let us then examine again the passages that appear to provide evidence for this interpretation. A bit of reflection shows that the passages under (1) and (2) commit Plato to the claim that if many perceptible particulars partake of the same form, then they bear its name, and, therefore, to the claim that if many perceptible particulars partake of the same form, then they bear the same name as one another. What these passages do not commit Plato to is the converse claim: that if many perceptible particulars bear the same name as one another, then they partake of the same form. Only this last claim would point toward (without, however, entailing) the thesis that for every predicative expression there is a corresponding form. Let me stress that the rendering of the passage from *Republic* X given above is not the only possible one, and it differs from those endorsed by translators and most commentators.[6] It has been defended on philological grounds, however.[7]

The passage under (3) provides stronger support for the interpretation in question: even if it mentions only one example (the name "shape" and the corresponding form), it is paving the way for an understood generalization. How far does this generalization go? Since a form in the *Meno* is a single cause (*sc.* item that can be mentioned in providing an explanation) of why all things partaking of it are in a certain way (cf. 72c7–8),[8] the generalization cannot go as far as to cover all predicative expressions. For, in the case of certain predicative expressions, there is no single cause of why all things they are true of are in the way the predicative expressions say they are. (Consider the predicative expression "triat," an abbreviation of "triangle or cat": there is no single cause of why every triat is a triat.)

So, the passages mentioned fail to prove that, according to Plato, for every predicative expression there is a corresponding form. In view of the considerations of the last subsection, one ought to avoid crediting Plato with such a view.

5. D. Bostock, *Plato's* Phaedo [Phaedo] (Oxford, 1986), 201–2.
6. Bostock, Phaedo, 198.
7. J. A. Smith, "General Relative Clauses in Greek," *Classical Review* 31 (1917), 70.
8. G. Fine, *On Ideas: Aristotle's Criticism of Plato's Theory of Forms* [Ideas] (Oxford, 1993), 48, 50.

## Forms corresponding to basic predicative expressions

Plato might nevertheless hold a less ambitious theory: that for every basic predicative expression there is a corresponding form, whereas nonbasic predicative expressions have no corresponding forms and are to be analyzed by appealing to forms that correspond to basic predicative expressions. For instance, the theory could acknowledge the existence of the forms *Greek*, *triangle*, and *cat*, which correspond to the basic predicative expressions "Greek," "triangle," and "cat," but deny the existence of forms corresponding to the nonbasic predicative expressions "barbarian" and "triat," which are to be analyzed by appealing to the forms *Greek*, *triangle*, and *cat*.

Such a theory invites the question of what makes a predicative expression basic. One possible answer is that whether a predicative expression is basic depends on whether its extension is a genuine group. Intuitively, "Greek," "triangle," and "cat" satisfy this condition, while "barbarian" and "triat" do not. Obviously, one would like to go beyond intuitions: that is, to know what makes a set of items into a genuine group.

There is evidence that Plato allows only forms whose ranges are genuine groups (*Phdr.* 265e1–3; *Plt.* 262a5–263b11). *If* Plato endorses the converse claim—that every genuine group is the range of a form—*then* he is committed to the view that for every basic predicative expression (i.e., every predicative expression whose extension is a genuine group) there is a corresponding form. The evidence does not warrant crediting Plato with the converse claim.


## Forms as missing standards

What remains beyond doubt is that there is a linguistic dimension to Plato's theory of forms: Plato does say that perceptible particulars derive their names from the forms they partake of. What does Plato precisely mean when he says this?

A deflationary explanation is possible. The view it attributes to Plato is simply that a form and the perceptible particulars that partake of it share the same name.[9]

One might feel that this explanation is too deflationary, however. Specifically, one might complain that this explanation does not make enough of Plato's point that perceptible particulars *derive* their names from the forms they partake of. An alternative, more substantive explanation rests on attributing to Plato two assumptions.[10] The first, intuitively plausible but never formulated in the dialogues, is that the mastery of a predicative expression is acquired by confronting an *unambiguous standard* for it—that is, something to which that predicative expression applies, whereas its negative counterpart does not. For instance, the

---

9. Fine, *Ideas*, 318, 326.

10. N. P. White, *Plato on Knowledge and Reality* (Indianapolis, 1976), 75–77; Bostock, Phaedo, 94–115, 194–96.

mastery of the predicative expression "red" is acquired by confronting an unambiguous standard for "red," something to which "red" applies, whereas its
negative counterpart "not red" does not. The second assumption, often made in
Plato's early and middle dialogues, is that for some predicative expressions, including those from the all-important spheres of ethics and aesthetics (e.g., "good,"
"just," and "beautiful"), there are no unambiguous standards among perceptible
particulars: for instance, to any perceptible particular to which "beautiful" applies,
"not beautiful" also applies, in some different respect or context (cf. *Hp. Ma.*
289a8–289b3; *Smp.* 210e2–211b5; *Rep.* V 478e7–479c5).[11]

How, then, is the mastery of these predicative expressions acquired? The
*Phaedo* can plausibly be taken to be committed to the view that in the case of these
predicative expressions, too, mastery is acquired by confronting unambiguous
standards, which, however, are not perceptible particulars but intelligible forms.
For instance, the form *beautiful* is something to which "beautiful" applies, whereas
its negative counterpart "not beautiful" does not (in any respect or context). Forms
can be contemplated by the soul when it is disembodied. They are forgotten at
birth, but they leave latent memory traces, which can be triggered when perceptible
particulars are encountered that partake of them. Such a triggering ignites a disposition to apply the predicative expression whose mastery had been acquired by
confronting the form whose latent memory trace has been triggered. In this sense,
perceptible particulars derive their names from the forms they partake of.

Let me pause for a few remarks.

1. Rather few forms are required by the view that forms function as missing
   standards—specifically, only forms corresponding to predicative expressions for which there are no unambiguous standards among perceptible
   particulars. Obviously, other considerations might postulate the existence
   of more forms.
2. The view that forms function as missing standards does not make forms
   into meanings. One should have no more inclination to regard the form
   *beautiful* as the meaning of "beautiful" than to regard the finger one
   was shown when learning to use "finger" as the meaning of "finger."
3. According to the view that forms function as missing standards, the soul
   learns to use certain predicative expressions in its disembodied existence.
   Did my disembodied soul learn to use "beautiful," "beau," or "schön"? The
   beginnings of an answer can perhaps be gleaned from the *Cratylus*, where
   Plato assumes that there are forms of names (cf. below). So, my soul
   became perhaps acquainted with the association of the form of the name
   "beautiful" with the form *beautiful*. Since not only "beautiful" but also
   "beau" and "schön" partake of the form of "beautiful," having grasped the

11. Some commentators (e.g., Fine, *Ideas*, 56; T. H. Irwin, "The Theory of Forms" ["Forms"], in G.
Fine (ed.), *Plato 1: Metaphysics and Epistemology* (Oxford, 1999), 156–65) take Plato's view to be that it is
perceptible *properties* (rather than *particulars*) that instantiate certain predicative expressions and their
negative counterparts.

form-to-form association enables me to apply "beautiful" (or the translation of it in whatever language I happen to be speaking) to beautiful things.

4. The evidence for crediting Plato with the view that forms function as missing standards is shaky (for instance, as I pointed out earlier, the assumption that the mastery of a predicative expression is acquired by confronting an unambiguous standard for it is never formulated in the dialogues). Some commentators therefore refrain from attributing this view to Plato.[12]

# NAMES IN THE *CRATYLUS*

## Theme and structure

The *Cratylus* examines the problem of the correctness of names: if a name is correctly given to something, what is the source of this correctness? Plato discusses two contrasting solutions, associated with two of the speakers, Hermogenes and Cratylus. The third speaker, Socrates, is called to adjudicate.

The *Cratylus* is an aporetic dialogue: Socrates discloses difficulties for the views defended by both of his interlocutors, but he reaches no positive conclusion. To be sure, this does not exclude the possibility that the dialogue might contain some of Plato's positive views on the correctness of names and other themes of philosophy of language. Nevertheless, one should be cautious in one's attempt to unearth such positive views.

## The problem addressed

There is something woolly about the problem of the correctness of names. One reason is that names constitute a loose category: they comprise not only proper nouns like "Cratylus" (383b2–3) but also common nouns like "man" (399c1), adjectives like "large" (433e8), participles like "flowing" (421c5), and infinitives like "to grow" (414a8) (words of primarily syntactic function are excluded).

There is a further, deeper source of woolliness. What is it for a name to be correctly given to something? Is it for a certain usage of a name to be established correctly (as when the stipulation is made that "hydrogen" will be the name of a certain element, or "splash" of events of a certain sort), or for a name whose usage has already been established to be employed correctly? In the second alternative, is

---

12. For example, Fine, *Ideas*, 59, 137–38; Irwin, "Forms," 155–65.

it for a name whose usage has already been established to be applied truly (as when someone applies "hydrogen" to hydrogen, or "splash" to splashes), or for a name whose usage has already been established to be employed correctly to convey the intended point, independently of whether this is true or false (as when someone happens to employ "hydrogen" to mean a certain element, or "splash" to mean events of a certain sort)? In the second alternative, is it the case that a name whose usage has already been established is employed correctly to convey the intended point just if it is being employed in conformity with its previously established usage? Or is it the case that a name whose usage has already been established is employed correctly to convey the intended point just if its previously established usage, in accordance with which it is being employed on this specific occasion, is appropriate to the intended point? On the first of these last two alternatives, the use of "public," in accordance with British English, to express a point concerning private schools of a certain sort, is correct; on the second alternative, it is (arguably) incorrect.

These alternatives are not explicitly mapped in the *Cratylus*. However, the problem of the correctness of names is sometimes connected with the first kind of correctness, sometimes with the last. In other words, sometimes it is the problem of what the source is of the fact that a certain usage of a given name is correctly established; sometimes it is the problem of what the source is of the fact that a certain name whose usage has already been established is, in its being employed in accordance with this previously established usage, adequate as an expression of the intended point. These two issues are close.[13]

## Conventionalism versus naturalism

Hermogenes favors a conventionalist solution: "the correctness of names is determined by . . . convention and agreement" (384d1–2), "any name you give a thing is its correct name" (384d2–3), and "if you change its name and give it another, the new one is as correct as the old" (384d3–5). Something like this conventionalism is the position likely to be endorsed by most people, nonphilosophers and philosophers alike, and Hermogenes seems to lack an elaborate linguistic theory to support it.[14]

Cratylus defends a naturalist solution: "there is a correctness of name for each thing, one it is endowed with by nature" (383a4–5), and "a thing's name isn't whatever people agree to call it, . . . but there is a natural correctness of names,

13. N. Denyer, *Language, Thought and Falsehood in Ancient Greek Philosophy* [*Falsehood*] (London, 1991), 69–71.

14. Here I follow D. Sedley, *Plato's Cratylus* [*Cratylus*] (Cambridge 2003), 51–54, against the widely held view that Hermogenes' conventionalism is a philosophically extreme position (e.g., B. Williams, "Cratylus' Theory of Names and Its Refutation" ["Theory"], in M. Schofield and M. Craven Nussbaum (eds.), *Language and Logos: Studies in Ancient Greek Philosophy Presented to G. E. L. Owen* (Cambridge, 1982), 90).

which is the same for everyone, Greek or foreigner" (383a5–383b2). Such a naturalism is counterintuitive. Cratylus seems to have a linguistic theory to back it, but he is unwilling to expound it.

## Socrates' criticism of conventionalism

Cratylus' naturalism and Hermogenes' conventionalism are presented in the dialogue's initial exchange (383a1–384e2). The next section (385a1–391a1) contains an extended criticism of Hermogenes' conventionalism.

After a preliminary skirmish (385a1–385e3), Socrates inquires about Hermogenes' view on Protagorean relativism (385e4–386d2), according to which things are for each subject in the way they appear to him or her. To paraphrase a famous example from the *Theaetetus* (152b2–9): whenever a wind feels cold to a person, it is cold for that person, and whenever it does not feel cold to a person, it is not cold for that person (different people can be involved, or the same person at different times). Hermogenes rejects Protagorean relativism (386a5–7). Socrates offers a brief argument for the rejection: were Protagorean relativism correct, there would be no difference between experts and laymen (because things would be for all subjects in whatever ways they appear to them). An annihilation of the difference between experts and laymen would also follow if Euthydemus were right when he claims that "everything always has every attribute simultaneously" (386d4), a position quickly dismissed.

Having done away with Protagorean relativism, Socrates and Hermogenes conclude that things are what they are "by nature" (386e4)—that is, neither relatively to subjects nor dependently on what appears to them. From this they infer (386e6–9) that actions also are what they are by nature (the grounds of this inference are unclear).[15] This result is taken to hold also for that aspect of actions which is the use of tools: it is by nature that given actions are performed by using certain tools. For instance, what instrument weaving is performed with is a matter that is neither relative to subjects nor dependent on what appears to them: it is a natural matter. And, however things may seem to you, by nature, weaving is not performed with a drill but with a shuttle.

This applies also to speech acts, since they, too, are actions. So, it is by nature that given speech acts are performed by using certain tools. Specifically, since "naming is a part of speaking" (387c6), it is by nature that given acts of naming are performed by using certain tools. But the tools of naming are names. So, it is by nature—neither relatively to subjects nor dependently on what appears to them—that given acts of naming are performed by using certain names.

---

15. For different interpretations, and the difficulties they face, see J. L. Ackrill, "Language and Reality in Plato's *Cratylus*" ["Language"], *Essays on Plato and Aristotle* (Oxford, 1994), 38; C. D. C. Reeve (trans.), *Plato: Cratylus* [Cratylus] (Indianapolis, 1999), xv–xvi; Sedley, Cratylus, 55–58.

So far, the argument has been rather abstract: it has concluded that naming is what it is by nature and that, by nature, given acts of naming are performed by using certain names. But what is it that naming by nature is? Socrates and Hermogenes agree that by using names "we instruct [*didaskomen*] one another and we separate [*diakrinomen*] objects according to how they are" (388b10–11), so that "a name is a tool for giving instruction and separating being" (388b13–388c1). The concept of instruction introduces, in one go, two fundamental features of language: communication and truth.[16] As for the concept of separating being, at first one might regard it as connected with reference: we use names to "separate being" in that we isolate certain specific beings from others as topics of discussion (as the name "snow" in the statement "snow is white" isolates snow from other beings as a topic of discussion). However, Plato later indicates that the art of instruction involving the use of names coincides with dialectic (390c2–12) and that certain names imitate not sounds, shapes, or colors but the essence of their nominata (423b9–424a1; cf. below). These later hints suggest that the separation of being is the taxonomic division of genera into subordinate species,[17] and perhaps also the analysis of kinds into their constituents (genera and differentiae) performed by definitions. The ideas of reference, taxonomic division, and analysis are probably operating jointly in Plato's description of names as separating being.[18]

Since speech acts of naming are what they are by nature—neither relatively to subjects nor dependently on what appears to them—it follows that people can be more or less successful at naming. Most successful will be those who possess the relevant art. As with other kinds of action, so with naming: craftsmen make the best use of the tools—in this case, names. Moreover, again in analogy with what happens with other kinds of action, in the case of naming, the tools (i.e., names) are also produced by another art, the art of the legislator (*nomothetēs*), who lays down the rules governing the use of names. The idea of a legislator who lays down rules for names is strange for us, but it was probably well known in Plato's time, thanks to the many (now almost completely lost) Sophistic discussions of the correctness of names: Plato could mention it without causing surprise in his readers.[19] Names are therefore at the crossroads of two arts: that of the user (who gives instruction and separates being) and that of the producer (the legislator).[20]

Socrates and Hermogenes make two points concerning the legislator's art. The first (389a5–390a10; cf. *Rep.* X 596a10–596b10; *Ti.* 28a6–28b2, 28c2–29b2) is that, like

16. N. Kretzmann, "Plato on the Correctness of Names" ["Correctness"], *American Philosophical Quarterly* 8 (1971), 128; Ackrill, "Language," 42.

17. Taxonomic division is mentioned at 424c5–424d4.

18. Sedley, *Cratylus*, 59–61.

19. *Chrm.* 175b3–4; Sedley, *Cratylus*, 66–74. Some commentators regard the legislator as a mythical personification of an accepted linguistic authority: see, for example, Kretzmann, "Correctness," 128–29, and M. Schofield, "The Dénouement of the *Cratylus*" ["Dénouement"], in M. Schofield and M. Craven Nussbaum (eds.), *Language and Logos: Studies in Ancient Greek Philosophy Presented to G. E. L. Owen* (Cambridge, 1982), 66.

20. *Euthd.* 289b7–289c4; *Rep.* X 601d1–3; T. Borsche, "Platon," in P. Schmitter (ed.), *Sprachtheorien der abenländischen Antike*, 2nd ed. (Tübingen, 1996), 143.

other tool-producing craftsmen, so also the legislator produces names by looking at forms and realizing them in certain materials—namely, syllables and letters. Forms of names are presupposed: both a generic form and specific forms (like the form of the name for dogs and that of the name for horses). It is also presupposed that syllables and letters play the role of materials. As blacksmiths can produce tools of the same kind by looking at the same form and embodying it in different kinds of iron, so legislators can produce names of the same kind by looking at the same form and embodying it in different syllables and letters. As not every kind of material is apt for the blacksmith to produce (say) a drill, so not all syllables and letters are apt to realize a certain name. Nevertheless, there is some flexibility in the choice of syllables and letters: this explains away the obvious fact (which at first blush tells against Cratylus' naturalism) that distinct linguistic communities have equally adequate names that sound differently.

The second point concerning the legislator's art (390b1–390d8; cf. *Rep.* X 601d1–601e3) also relies on an analogy with other tool-producing arts: the person in the best position to know whether the tool has been properly produced is the skilled user. In the case of names, the skilled user is the person who is able to ask and answer questions—that is, the dialectician (implicitly identified with the person who gives instruction and separates being). The dialectician will therefore supervise the legislator's production of names.

In the end, Hermogenes gives up his conventionalism, and Socrates concludes that Cratylus' naturalism is correct (390d9–391b3). This seems too sweeping a conclusion. For the result established by the argument is rather abstract: it only requires that certain general aspects of naming should be by nature, and it says nothing with regard to particular aspects of the process. As far as we have been told, convention could still play an essential and abundant part in these particular aspects. Perhaps Plato intends his readers to see that Hermogenes and Socrates are hasty in reaching their conclusion.

## Etymology and imitation

Having established that names have a natural correctness, Socrates and Hermogenes proceed to "inquire what correctness of names is" (391b4–5). First (391c10–421c2), they examine many *derivative* names: names that can be analyzed by etymological techniques whereby they are brought back to further names out of which they are composed. Then (421c3–427d3) they investigate the correctness of *primary* names: the basic names that are not composed out of further names. They begin this investigation by assuming (422c7–10) that the correctness of names is the same for all—for primary as for derivative names. By reflecting on what their examination of derivative names has shown, they agree that the correctness of derivative names consists in being "fit for revealing what each being is like" (422d2–3). They then infer (422d5–7; cf. 393d3–4) that the correctness of primary names also consists in the capacity to reveal what their nominata are like. However, in the case of primary names, this revelatory capacity cannot be based on being composed out of further names—for primary names are not thus composed. All names are composed out of syllables and letters: while derivative names are also composed out of further names, primary names are only composed out of syllables and letters. Accordingly, primary names are analyzed by applying mimetic techniques whereby the single letters in them are phonetic imitations of basic features of reality: for instance, the sound "r" is "a tool for all motion" (426c1–2) because the tongue "is most agitated and least at rest in pronouncing this letter" (426e4–5); since "the tongue glides in the highest degree in pronouncing 'l'" (427b2–3), this sound reveals gliding and smoothness. The whole primary name describes its nominatum as exhibiting the basic features of which its letters are phonetic imitations.

Not every imitation—indeed, not every vocal imitation—is a name; otherwise, "we would have to agree that those who imitate sheep, cocks, or other animals are naming the things they imitate" (423c4–6). Socrates (423d4–424a6) distinguishes the vocal imitations that are names from those that are not by assuming that the former imitate the being (*ousia*) of their nominata, whereas the latter imitate their models' sounds, shapes, or colors—their qualities, as we would call them. Socrates does not explain what the being of the things imitated by names is. The likeliest hypothesis is that the being of a thing is whatever can be truly and appropriately mentioned in answering the "What is it?" question asked about it (even if my car is white, it is not appropriate to say "It is white" to answer the question, "What is it?" asked about my car). Given that this is correct, the being of the things imitated by names is their essence, in a somewhat weak sense of "essence" ("weak" in that it ignores matters of identity over time). So, Socrates' attempt to distinguish the vocal imitations that count as names from those that do not comes to the requirement that names should imitate the essence of their nominata.

The natural correctness of a name, therefore, consists in its describing the essence of its nominatum. But the descriptive content of a name cannot be identified with its ordinary meaning, if by meaning we understand what competent speakers would mention in answering the question, "What does it mean?": for the essence described by the name can only be discovered by means of an art, not by simply examining the intuitions of competent speakers.

Many of the *Cratylus*'s analyses of names are awkward, and modern linguists would regard them as ridiculous. This induces many commentators to think that Plato is not serious when he produces these analyses.[21] However, throughout Antiquity, the analyses of the *Cratylus* were regarded as serious. Moreover, passages from other dialogues where Plato seems earnest present analyses that sound to us no less implausible than those of the *Cratylus*.[22]

21. For example, Schofield, "Dénouement," 63; Williams, "Theory," 92; Reeve, *Cratylus*, xxx–xxxiii.
22. Sedley, *Cratylus*, 25–50.

## Socrates' criticism of naturalism

In the last part of the dialogue (427d4–440e7), Cratylus is persuaded to join the discussion. He agrees with Socrates' account of the natural correctness of naming (428c1–8). In particular, he agrees that the correctness of a name consists in "displaying what the object is like" (428e2), that "names are therefore spoken for the sake of instruction" (428e5), and that there is an art of giving names—that of the legislator (428e7–429a1).

The natural correctness of naming introduced by Socrates might seem to amount to a descriptive theory of naming, according to which a name $n$ names whatever has the nature revealed by $n$. But, in fact, Socrates and Cratylus disagree on whether the natural correctness of naming has such an implication (429a2–433b7). Cratylus thinks that it does and is therefore committed to the claim that whatever is named by a name $n$ is named correctly by $n$. (Since the nature revealed fixes the nominata, the nominata must have the nature revealed.) Socrates, instead, is committed to denying that his account of the natural correctness of names implies a descriptive theory of naming: he is committed to denying that a name $n$ names whatever has the nature revealed by $n$. Socrates seems to believe that what $n$ names does not depend on the nature revealed by $n$. For this reason, there are better and worse names: they are better to the extent that they manage to reveal the nature of their nominata, worse to the extent that they fail to do this. And there are two ways in which a name can be poor at revealing the nature of its nominatum: either by revealing partially or somewhat unfaithfully the nature that its nominatum has or by revealing (in whatever way) a nature that its nominatum does not have. In this last case, the name is downright false.

Although some commentators criticize Plato's view that names can be false,[23] the view is actually reasonable. An analogy (admittedly, far from what we find in the *Cratylus*) can help illustrate the competing views of naming defended by Cratylus and Socrates. Cratylus' position is analogous to that of someone recognizing only the "attributive" use of definite descriptions: if a definite description denotes anything, what it denotes is the only thing satisfying the condition expressed by its descriptive component. Socrates' position is analogous to that of someone allowing the "referential" use of definite descriptions. This may be explained by means of an example. Suppose that you and I are at a party. We are looking at a man, Smith, who is holding a glass of yellowish liquid. Since we had earlier heard Smith uttering the sentence, "Could I have some beer?," we assent to the sentence, "That man over there is drinking beer" (uttered while pointing at Smith). Later, I make a statement to you by using the sentence, "The man who is drinking beer is German." My utterance successfully refers to Smith, and this successful reference is achieved by using the definite description "the man who is drinking beer." But, as a matter of fact, Smith is not drinking beer (he is drinking champagne, like everyone else; his earlier request to have some beer had been unsuccessful).[24] My use of the definite description "the man

23. For example, R. Robinson, "A Criticism of Plato's *Cratylus*," *Philosophical Review* 65 (1956), 328.
24. For the distinction between the "attributive" and the "referential" use of definite descriptions, see K. Donnellan, "Reference and Definite Descriptions," *Philosophical Review* 75 (1966), 285–89.

who is drinking beer" may be fairly described as a case of false naming and seems analogous to the sort of case Socrates has in mind.

Cratylus also agrees with another thesis of the theory set out earlier by Socrates and Hermogenes: that names reveal what their nominata are like by imitating them by means of their component letters (433b8–433c2). But he dissents from Socrates on one point: while Socrates holds that names can be more or less accurate in their imitation of their nominata, Cratylus states that every name imitates perfectly its nominatum and there is no place for a name to be an inaccurate imitation of its nominatum (433c3–10). In order to refute this position, Socrates first (433d1–434b9) rehearses together with Cratylus the main claims of the mimetic account of the natural correctness of names. He then (434b10–434e1) focuses on the name *sklērotēs* ("hardness"). He points out that the Eretrians pronounce it *sklērotēr*. To avoid admitting that the Attic version of the name is less accurate than the Eretrian, Cratylus claims that the sounds "r" and "s" imitate the same characteristic. By making this move, Cratylus implicitly commits himself to regarding *sklērotēs* as a correct name of hardness. But now, when Socrates points out that the sounds "l" and "r" give opposite indications ("l" imitates smoothness, "r" hardness),[25] Cratylus finds himself forced to concede that *sklērotēs* is not, after all, a perfectly accurate name of hardness: *skrērotēs* would have been more accurate. This concession already suffices to refute Cratylus' position that every name imitates perfectly its nominatum.

But Socrates seems to think that he has found a loophole in the naturalist position, and he pushes the argument further (434e1–435d1). He remarks that we do understand one another when we use *sklēron* ("hard"), but how does this come about? Cratylus replies that it is "because of habit" (434e4). This answer damages naturalism because it points toward acknowledging a role for habit, and perhaps also for convention, at the very heart of the naturalistic theory: that is, in the link of primary names to their nominata. Cratylus could retreat by claiming that *sklēron* is not a name of what is hard (just as, in his view, "Hermogenes" is not the name of Hermogenes; cf. 383b4–7). Such a line would clash with his earlier commitment to *sklērotēs* being a correct name of hardness, however, and if *sklēron* is, after all, a name of what is hard, it is difficult to see how this could be the case otherwise than through habit.

In the last section of the dialogue (435d1–440e2), Socrates subjects Cratylus' views to further criticism. Cratylus claims (435d1–436a8) that names are not merely "the best and only way" of giving instruction (*didaskalia*) but also the only means of making discoveries (*heuresis*) about things. This adds an epistemological dimension to Cratylus' naturalism. It is on this epistemological dimension that the last part of the dialogue focuses, with a battery of three objections (436a9–437d8, 437d8–438c3, and 438c4–440e2).

25. Earlier (426d3–426e6) "r" was said to imitate motion, whereas hardness was not mentioned (cf. Schofield, "Dénouement," 74).

# SEMANTICS AND ONTOLOGY
# IN THE *SOPHIST*

## Why a discussion of statement in the *Sophist?*

The *Sophist*'s stated purpose is to define the sophist (218b7–218c1). An Eleatic Stranger (ES) and Theaetetus pursue this project by applying the method of division, but they encounter difficulties connected with the concept of falsehood. For they attempt to define the sophist as someone who produces verbal imitations that seem to be like their models (i.e., faithful to them) but really are not like their models (i.e., are not faithful to them) (235b8–236d4). In other words, the ES and Theaetetus describe the sophist as someone who makes statements that seem to be true but really are not true; they are false statements that seem to be true. Since they seem to be true, the sophist's false statements induce those who hear them to believe them and therefore to form false beliefs. Thus, the sophist makes false statements and induces false beliefs.

This description of the sophist clashes with the falsehood paradox, which is summoned by way of objection (236d5–241b4). The falsehood paradox is a family of arguments whose conclusion is that there are neither false statements nor false beliefs. I say "a family of arguments" because there are many subtly different arguments with this same counterintuitive conclusion. Accordingly, I often speak of a "version of" the falsehood paradox. Versions of the falsehood paradox appear in other dialogues (*Euthd.* 284b1–284c6; *Cra.* 429c6–430a5; *Tht.* 167a6–8, 187c7–200c7, esp. 188c9–189b9; cf. *Rep.* V 478b5–478c2): only in the *Sophist* does Plato solve it, but his earlier presentations of it already suggest some awareness of how it is to be disarmed.[26]

As for statements, the main version of the falsehood paradox in the *Sophist* goes as follows: to make a false statement is to state what is not, which amounts to stating nothing, which, in turn, amounts to making no statement. So, making a false statement amounts to making no statement. Therefore, there are no false statements. Parallel steps lead to the result that holding a false belief amounts to holding no belief and thereby to the conclusion that there are no false beliefs.

The *Sophist*'s core section (236d5–264b10) is devoted to showing that there are false statements and false beliefs. Since the main version of the falsehood paradox deals with not being, a crucial move is the development of an account of not being. This is done by bringing in the concept of otherness (257b10–257c3): roughly, for $\sigma$ not to be $\pi$ is for $\sigma$ to be other than everything that is $\pi$ (where "$\sigma$" and "$\pi$" are schematic letters to be replaced by syntactically appropriate expressions).[27]

---

26. Cf. M. F. Burnyeat, "Plato on How Not to Speak of What Is Not: *Euthydemus* 283a–288a," in M. Canto-Sperber and P. Pellegrin (eds.), *Le style de la pensée: Recueil de textes en hommage à Jacques Brunschwig* (Paris, 2002), 40–66.

27. Plato's account of not being in terms of otherness is variously interpreted. The exegeses are recorded by F. J. Pelletier, *Parmenides, Plato, and the Semantics of Not-Being* (Chicago, 1990), 45–93, and

After the account of not being has been developed, the ES declares that he and Theaetetus must "agree what statement is" (260a7–8)—that is, define statement. Theaetetus wonders why this is needed (260b3–4). The ES explains (260b5–261c10) that since to state, or believe, a falsehood is to state, or believe, what is not, the sophist could still adopt a last defense based on denying that not being combines with statement and belief: only by defining statement and belief will it be possible to show that not being combines with them. At first glance, this last defense of the sophist seems a silly and desperate move. An account of not being in terms of otherness has been offered; we have been hearing all along that to state, or believe, a falsehood is to state, or believe, what is not; why on earth should we doubt that not being combines with statement and belief?

The subsequent discussion divides into three parts: a definition of statement (261d1–262e10), a proof that statements can be false (262e11–263d5), and a definition of belief on the basis of which it can be easily established that beliefs can be false (263d6–264b5).

## Words, names, and verbs

When it comes to defining statement, the ES and Theaetetus do not apply the method of division. Instead, they describe statements of the simplest kind. Does this suffice to yield a definition? The Socrates of Plato's early dialogues would probably have denied it.

The ES distinguishes (261e4–262a8) two kinds of words (*onomata*, 261d2), or vocal indicators (*tē(i) phōnē(i) dēlōmata*, 261e5): verbs (*rhēmata*), which signify actions (*praxeis*), and names (*onomata*), which signify objects (*pragmata*, 262e13), "those who perform the actions" (262b10).[28] When words of only one kind are combined, the resulting string signifies nothing: only if words of one kind are combined with words of the other is the resulting string endowed with signification (261d9–261e2). More specifically, when words of only one kind are combined, the resulting string does not constitute a statement (*logos*) (262a9–11): if only verbs are combined, the resulting string fails to be a statement (e.g., the string of verbs "walks runs sleeps" is not a statement) (262b2–8); if only names are combined, the resulting string again fails to be a statement (e.g., the string of names "lion stag horse" is not a statement) (262b9–262c2). Only if verbs are combined with names does the resulting string constitute a statement (262c4–6). For instance, "Man understands" is a statement (262c9–262d1), and it is obtained by combining the verb "understands" with the name "man."

---

P. Crivelli, "Il *Sofista* di Platone: non essere, negazione e falsità" ["Negazione"], *Atti e Memorie dell'Accademia Toscana di Scienze e Lettere "La Colombaria"* 55 (1990), 41–58 (at pp. 59–62 I defend an interpretation close to that in the main text above).

28. The expressions used to describe the relation of words to what they stand for are the nouns "indicator" (*dēlōma*, 261e5, 262a3) and "sign" (*sēmeion*, 262a6, 262d9) and the verb "to signify" (*sēmainein*, 262b6).

Let me pause for a few remarks.

1. *Onoma* is used in two ways, a narrow and a broad one. On its narrow usage, on which it is best rendered by "name," *onoma* denotes the vocal indicators that signify objects. On its broad usage, on which it might be translated by "word," it denotes all vocal indicators (including those that signify actions as well as those that signify objects).

2. The distinction between actions and objects is unclear. Is it an exhaustive ontological classification, so that every being is an action if and only if it is not an object?

3. The distinction between verbs and names also is unclear. Is it contrasting the grammatical categories of verbs and names, or the syntactic categories of predicate expressions and subject expressions? Both alternatives face difficulties. For, arguably, not every member of the grammatical category of verbs signifies an action (consider "is carried," to which in Greek corresponds a single word, *pheretai*). Analogously, it looks as if not every predicate expression signifies an action, unless the category of actions is larger than expected (consider "is tall").

4. Although verbs signify actions, the contribution made by a verb to a statement of which it is a component cannot be exhausted by its signifying an action; otherwise, the statement "Man understands" would be perfectly equivalent to the string of names "man, understanding."[29]

## Naming and stating

The ES and Theaetetus agree that one name and one verb make up a statement that is shortest (*smikrotatos, elachistos, brachutatos*) and primary (*prōtos*) (262c5–262d1, 263c1–4). This presupposes that there are statements of other kinds, in particular, longer and nonprimary statements that do not consist of merely one name and one verb. These other kinds of statement are not described. The use of "primary" suggests that statements of other kinds are composed out of primary ones (whose components are not statements, but names and verbs), much in the same way as, according to the *Cratylus* (422a1–422e1), derivative names are composed out of primary ones (whose components are not names, but syllables and, ultimately, letters). Statements can concern not only the present but also the past and the future (262d2–3).

The ES remarks that when a string composed only of names, or one composed only of verbs, is pronounced, "either way the utterance reveals no action nor inaction nor being of what is or of what is not" (262c2–4). The part of this remark about the failure to reveal the "being of what is or of what is not" is obscure. It probably involves the predicative elliptical use of "to be" (whereby "to be" is

---

29. Cf. Denyer, *Falsehood*, 164–67.

employed as a copula to be completed with a predicative expression, which, however, is suppressed and remains understood): the point made is probably that a string of words of the sort described fails to signify the being so-and-so of what either is so-and-so or is not so-and-so. This sounds like an anticipation of the account of truth and falsehood given later.

The ES says that a speaker[30] producing a primary statement, namely a statement composed of one name and one verb, "does not only name something [*onomazei*], but accomplishes something [*ti perainei*]" (262d3–4):[31] a speech act is brought to completion.[32] He adds that in producing a primary statement, a speaker "does not only name something [*onomazei*], but also states something [*legei*]" (262d5). This remark presupposes that naming and stating are different. No explanation of what they are is offered. The ES and Theaetetus then agree (262e4–8) that every statement must be "of," or "about," something. Their later observations (262e13–263a11, 263c1–12) on the primary statements introduced as examples, "Theaetetus is sitting" and "Theaetetus is flying," show that the item a primary statement is about is the object signified by its name. In the face of these data, let me indulge in some speculation.

1. What is it that a speaker producing a primary statement names? Does such a speaker name both the object signified by the primary statement's name and the action signified by its verb? Or only the object? The ES and Theaetetus do not address this problem, but the etymological link between *onomazein* ("to name") and *onoma* ("name") suggests that the last alternative is the right one: a speaker producing a primary statement names only the object signified by its name.[33]

2. Granted that this result is correct, a further point can be plausibly inferred: in a primary statement, the name is what mainly contributes to the speaker's performing the speech act of naming, whereas the verb is what mainly contributes to the speaker's performing the speech act of stating.[34]

3. Given that a speaker producing a primary statement names only the object signified by its name, and given that the item a primary statement is about

30. Taking *tis* at 262c9 as the grammatical subject of *ti perainei* at 262d4.

31. Cf. *Cra.* 425a2–3. For the phrase *ti perainein*, cf. *Grg.* 472b8; *Smp.* 217c1–2; *Rep.* IV 426a2; *Tht.* 180a6–7.

32. Cf. G. Nuchelmans, *Theories of the Proposition: Ancient and Medieval Conceptions of the Bearers of Truth and Falsity* (Amsterdam, 1973), 15–17. Other commentators (e.g., G. Rudebusch, "Does Plato Think False Speech Is Speech?," *Noûs* 24 (1990), 601–2) take the ES to be claiming that a speaker producing a primary statement *ti perainei* in the sense of *limiting* something: such a speaker limits both the object signified by the primary statement's name (by specifying what action it is performing) and the action signified by the primary statement's verb (by specifying which object is performing it).

33. It is less likely that *onomazein* should be connected to *onoma* in its broad usage (in which case, a speaker producing a primary statement would probably name both the object signified by the primary statement's name and the action signified by its verb): for the wide usage of *onoma* appears only at the beginning of the linguistic section (261d2, 261d4) and is then superseded by the narrow usage.

34. Cf. M. Frede, "Plato's *Sophist* on False Statements" ["Statements"], in R. Kraut (ed.), *The Cambridge Companion to Plato* (Cambridge, 1992), 413–14.

is the object signified by its name, it follows that a speaker producing a primary statement names only the item the primary statement is about. On the plausible assumption that a speaker producing a primary statement *refers* only to the item the primary statement is about, a further inference can be plausibly drawn: for a speaker who produces a primary statement to name an item is to refer to it.

4. One reason for insisting that every statement must be about something is probably the need to do away with an assumption made by one version of the falsehood paradox—that is, the assumption that a false statement is about nothing (because it is about what is not). Note that two different uses of "about" are around: that whereby "about" expresses the relation of a statement to its referent (in this use, "Theaetetus is flying" is about Theaetetus) and that whereby "about" expresses the relation of a statement to what is stated (in this use, "Theaetetus is flying" is about Theaetetus' flying).

5. Plato is probably committed to the claim that strings of words which one might be inclined to describe as singular predicative statements with empty subject expressions (e.g., "Pegasus is flying") are not genuine statements. Some modern philosophers of language (e.g., Frege) explicitly endorse this claim.

6. Verbs signify actions. Therefore, the action signified by a verb within a primary statement probably plays a role in the speech act of stating carried out mainly by means of that verb. What role? According to the ES, a speaker makes a primary statement "by putting an object together with an action [*suntheis pragma praxei*] by means of a name and a verb" (262e13–14). So, here is a plausible answer: when in producing a primary statement a speaker carries out a speech act of stating mainly by means of the primary statement's verb, what he or she does is to *put* the object which he or she has named—the object signified by the primary statement's name—*together* with the action signified by the primary statement's verb.

7. To put two items together is to set them into some relation or other. When a speaker makes a primary statement, and thereby puts an object together with an action, into what relation does he or she set them? It cannot be the relation of partaking: by saying "Theaetetus is flying," the ES does not create a flying Theaetetus (apart from being absurd, this would immediately entail the impossibility of false statement). The relation into which action and object are set by the speaker must be a different one: perhaps a relation like that of being-stated-by-this-speaker-about.

8. Let me go back to the question asked under (6): What role does an action play in a speech act of stating carried out mainly by means of a verb that signifies it? An answer perhaps different from the one just offered is based on some points made in the *Cratylus*, in connection with a version of the falsehood paradox (*Cra.* 429c6–430a5). Socrates and Cratylus agree (430a6–431c3) both that one can assign[35] names to objects and that such

---

35. The verbs used are *dianemein* (430a7–8, 430e1), *prospherein* (430a8), and *apodidonai* (431b4).

an assignment[36] can be carried out correctly, and therefore truly, as well as incorrectly, and therefore falsely. One is tempted to modify this *Cratylus* account to fit the situation of the *Sophist* by substituting actions for names. The result is that, when in producing a primary statement a speaker carries out a speech act of stating mainly by means of the primary statement's verb, what he or she does is to *assign* the action signified by the primary statement's verb to the object that he or she has named, that is, the object signified by the primary statement's name.

9. If the judge assigns the house to Smith, then the judge, on the basis of the authority he or she is endowed with within a certain legal system, brings it about that a certain relation (the relation of being-a-property-of) obtains between the house and Smith. Similarly, if a speaker assigns a certain action to a certain object, then the speaker, on the basis of the authority he or she is endowed with within a certain linguistic system, brings it about that a certain relation obtains between the action and the object. After all, putting together and assigning have much in common.

## True and false statements

The ES and Theaetetus agree that a statement must be "of a certain quality": either true or false (*Sph.* 262e9–10, 263a12–263b3; cf. *Phlb.* 37b10–37c2). Plato occasionally contrasts the qualities of a thing with what it is, namely its essence (cf. *Men.* 71a1–71b8, 86d8–86e1, 87b3; *Grg.* 448e6–7; *Tht.* 152d3–4, 152d6). Therefore, by saying that truth and falsehood are qualities of statements, the ES and Theaetetus are probably hinting that neither truth nor falsehood is essential to statements as such (some statements are true and not false, others false and not true).[37]

Two examples are brought in: the true statement "Theaetetus is sitting" and the false statement "Theaetetus is flying."[38] Here is the relevant passage:

| 262e | ES | Now let us fix our attention on ourselves. |
|------|------|--------------------------------------------|
|      | THT. | We will. |
|      | ES | I shall make a statement to you by putting an object together with an action by means of a name and a verb. You are to tell me what the statement belongs to. |
| 263A | THT. | I shall do my best. |
|      | ES | "Theaetetus is sitting"—not a lengthy statement, is it? |
|      | THT. | No, of a just length. |

---

36. The nouns used are *dianomē* (430d3, 431b1), *dosis* (430d6), and *epiphora* (430d6).

37. Cf. Frede, "Statements," 417.

38. The English phrases "is sitting" and "is flying" render the Greek words *kathētai* and *petetai* (the English words "sits" and "flies" convey the wrong sense).

ES  Now it is for you to say what it is about and what it belongs to.

THT.  Clearly it is about me and mine.

ES  What about this one?

THT.  Which one?

ES  "Theaetetus—with whom I am now speaking—is flying."

THT.  This one also can only be described as mine and about me.

ES  Besides we say that it is necessary for each of the statements to be of a certain quality.

263B  THT.  Yes.

ES  Of what quality then must one say each of these is?

THT.  One is, somehow, false, the other true.

ES  And the true one states of the things that are that they are about you.[39]

THT.  Certainly.

ES  Whereas the false one <states> things other than the things that are.

THT.  Yes.

ES  Therefore it states the things that are not as things that are.

THT.  I suppose so.

ES  But things that are other than things that are[40] about you. For we said[41] that about each thing there are many things that are and many that are not.

THT.  By all means.

Shortly before embarking on defining statement, the ES and Theaetetus had agreed that "statement has come to us thanks to the reciprocal interweaving of forms" (259e5–6). They were thereby probably committing themselves to the claim

---

39. Alternative translation: "And the true one states the things that are as they are about you." For a defense of the rendering in the main text above, see D. Keyt, "Plato on Falsity: *Sophist 263B*" ["Falsity"], in E. N. Lee, A. P. D. Mourelatos, and R. M. Rorty (eds.), *Exegesis and Argument: Studies in Greek Philosophy Presented to Gregory Vlastos* (Assen, 1973), 288–91, and Frede, "Statements," 418. "About you" is to be construed in common with "states," "things that are," and "are" (cf. D. Robinson, "Textual Notes on Plato's *Sophist*" ["Notes"], *Classical Quarterly*, n.s. 49 (1999), 159). "About you" must be mentally supplied in the next two remarks by the ES.

40. I adopt Cornarius's emendation *ontōn* (263b11), printed also by all recent editors. The main manuscripts read *ontōs* (cf. Robinson, "Notes," 159).

41. Cf. below, n.51.

that every statement involves the reciprocal interweaving of at least two forms. In the case of "Man understands," the reciprocally interwoven forms probably include the forms *man* and *understanding*; in the case of "Theaetetus is sitting," there are perhaps exactly two reciprocally interwoven forms—namely, the forms *being* (which functions as a connector; cf. 253c1–3, 256e6) and *sitting* (*being* is perhaps also involved in "Man understands").[42] Near the beginning of the passage translated above, the ES says that he will make a statement "by putting an object together with an action by means of a name and a verb" (262e13–14). In view of these facts, it can be plausibly inferred that if a speaker produces a primary statement by putting an object, signified by a name, together with an action, signified by a verb, the action in question is always a form (one of a special type, like the forms *understanding*, *sitting*, and *flying*), whereas the object in question can be anything (e.g., a form like the form *man*, signified by the name "man" within "Man understands," or a perceptible particular like the boy Theaetetus, signified by the name "Theaetetus" within "Theaetetus is sitting" and "Theaetetus is flying"). It can also be plausibly assumed that "to be about" (in some of its occurrences in the passage translated above) expresses the relation that in modern philosophical jargon is expressed by "to hold of."[43]

As for true statements, the above passage suggests the following account: a statement composed of a name $n$ and a verb $v$ is true just when[44] the action signified by $v$ is about the object signified by $n$. For example, "Theaetetus is sitting" is true just when *sitting*, the action signified by the verb "is sitting," is about Theaetetus, the object signified by the name "Theaetetus."

The account of false statement is controversial. At least four different exegeses have been suggested.[45]

1. According to the "Oxford interpretation," a statement composed of a name $n$ and a verb $v$ is false just when the action signified by $v$ is other than everything that is about the object signified by $n$. For instance, "Theaetetus is flying" is false just when *flying*, the action signified by the verb "is flying," is other than everything that is about Theaetetus, the object signified by the name "Theaetetus."[46]

---

42. Cf. J. M. E. Moravcsik, "Being and Meaning in the *Sophist*," *Acta Philosophica Fennica* 14 (1962), 60. The form *being* is not expressed by a separate word in the Greek sentences *anthrōpos manthanei* and *Theaitētos kathētai*, but Plato perhaps agrees with Aristotle that every finite form of any verb is equivalent to the phrase consisting of the corresponding finite form of *einai* and the participle of that verb (see Arist. *Int.* 12, 21b9–10; *Ph.* 1. 2, 185b28–30; *Metaph.* Δ7, 1017a27–30).

43. M. Frede, *Prädikation und Existenzaussage: Platons Gebrauch von "...ist..." und "...ist nicht..." im Sophistes* [*Prädikation*] (Göttingen, 1967), 52–55, 94–95; Frede, "Statements," 418; B. E. Hestir, "A 'Conception' of Truth in Plato's *Sophist*," *Journal of the History of Philosophy* 41 (2003), 8–10.

44. I use "just when" in the strictly temporal sense of "at all and only the times at which."

45. Classifications of the interpretations of Plato's account of false statement are also in Keyt, "Falsity," 293–95, and Crivelli, "Negazione," 81–91.

46. D. Peipers, *Ontologia Platonica: Ad Notionum Terminorumque Historiam Symbola* (Leipzig, 1883), 173–77; Ross, *Theory*, 116; Frede, *Prädikation*, 95; G. E. L. Owen, "Plato on Not-Being" ["Not-Being"], in G. Vlastos (ed.), *Plato: A Collection of Critical Essays*, vol. 1 (Garden City, N.J., 1971), 237–38; Frede, "Statements," 419.

2. According to the "incompatibility interpretation," a statement composed of a name $n$ and a verb $v$ is false just when the action signified by $v$ is incompatible with some form that is about the object signified by $n$ (two forms are incompatible just if their very nature makes it impossible for them to be about the same particular). For instance, "Theaetetus is flying" is false just when *flying* is incompatible with some form that is about Theaetetus.[47]

3. According to the "quasi-incompatibility interpretation," a statement composed of a name $n$ and a verb $v$ is false just when the action signified by $v$ is other than, but in the same incompatibility range as, some form that is about the object signified by $n$ (an incompatibility range is an exhaustive set of incompatible forms). For instance, "Theaetetus is flying" is false just when *flying* is other than, but in the same incompatibility range as, some form that is about Theaetetus.[48]

4. According to the "extensional interpretation," a statement composed of a name $n$ and a verb $v$ is false just when the object signified by $n$ is other than everything of which the action signified by $v$ holds. For instance, "Theaetetus is flying" is false just when Theaetetus is other than everything of which *flying* holds.[49]

The incompatibility interpretation may be ruled out because it implausibly presupposes that at some points in the *Sophist* the Greek word *heteron* expresses (not otherness, as it does elsewhere in the dialogue, but) incompatibility. The extensional interpretation cannot be easily reconciled with the wording of the above passage (although, as I have argued elsewhere, a reconciliation is not impossible).[50] It is difficult to decide between the two remaining contenders. The issues here are too many and too complicated to be addressed in this essay. I restrict myself to expressing my preference for the Oxford interpretation, a preference due to the fact that this interpretation fits well with the earlier account of not being in terms of otherness: given that for $\sigma$ not to be $\pi$ is for $\sigma$ to be other than everything that is $\pi$, it follows that for a certain action not to be about a certain object is for that action to be other than everything that is about that object.[51]

---

47. Cf. K. M. Sayre, *Plato's Late Ontology: A Riddle Resolved* (Princeton, 1983), 236–38 (cf. 229–34).

48. Cf. M. T. Ferejohn, "Plato and Aristotle on Negative Predication and Semantic Fragmentation," *Archiv für Geschichte der Philosophie* 71 (1989), 258–62, and Lesley Brown's contribution to this volume, chapter 18.

49. Cf. P. Crivelli, "Plato's *Sophist* and Semantic Fragmentation," *Archiv für Geschichte der Philosophie* 75 (1993), 73–74.

50. As in note 49 above.

51. At 263b11–12, the ES remarks: "We said that about each thing [*peri hekaston*] there are many things that are and many that are not." The cross-reference is to 256e6–7, where the ES and Theaetetus agreed that "about each of the forms [*peri hekaston . . . tōn eidōn*] what is is a lot whereas what is not is of indefinite multitude." The argument leading to this agreement (256d11–256e5) shows that the ground for claiming that "about each of the forms what is is a lot" (256e6) is that each form partakes of many forms, and that the ground for claiming that "about each of the forms . . . what is not is of indefinite multitude" (256e6–7) is that for each form $F$ there are indefinitely many forms such that for every $K$ from among them, $F$ is other than everything that *is K* by being identical with $K$ (cf. *kata panta . . . hē thaterou phusis heteron apergazomenē*

The idea that to state a falsehood is to state what is not resurfaces—but, thanks to the analysis of statement and the account of not being in terms of otherness, it is now innocuous. The venom is taken out in two steps. In the first, we realize that a false statement *states what is not* in that it *states* about an object *what is not* about it. This first step, whose main achievement is to replace the intractable notion of "complete" not being with the manageable one of "specific" not being (e.g., not being about Theaetetus), is based on the analysis of statement. At last we understand why there was a need to define statement in order to realize that not being combines with it: the sophist's last defense was not as silly as it appeared at first— what the sophist wanted was an explanation of whether and how the manageable notion of "specific" not being is relevant to false statement. In the second step, we capitalize on the manageability of the notion of "specific" not being: we realize that to state about Theaetetus what is not about him is to state about Theaetetus what is other than everything that is about him. This second step relies on the account of not being in terms of otherness.

## Paradoxes that arise from confusing naming with stating

As I noted earlier, a remark made by the ES presupposes that stating and naming are different. Moreover, the ES and Theaetetus stress that the two statements offered as examples, "Theaetetus is sitting" and "Theaetetus is flying," are about the same object: Theaetetus. These facts are probably due to one version of the falsehood paradox being based on confusing stating with naming. Were one to confuse stating with naming, one would be likely to identify the statement "Theaetetus is flying" with the complex name "the flying Theaetetus" and to conclude that "Theaetetus is flying" is not false but meaningless (because the absence of a flying Theaetetus allegedly makes the complex name "the flying Theaetetus" meaningless).[52] Hence the point of indicating that stating and naming are different. Moreover, were statements identical with complex names, then not only would "Theaetetus is flying" be identical with "the flying Theaetetus" but also "Thcactctus is sitting" with "the sitting Theaetetus." The two statements would

---

*tou ontos hekaston ouk on poiei* at 256d12–256e2, where *kata panta* is to be construed in common with *ontos* and *ouk on*; cf. Owen, "Not-Being," 233–34). The earlier passage (256e6–7) displays the converse of the *identity* use of "not to be": π is not about σ if and only if σ is not π in that σ is other than everything that *is* π by *being identical with* π. The account of false statement in which the later passage (263b11–12) is embedded requires the converse of the *predicative* use of "not to be": π is not about σ if and only if σ is not π in that σ is other than everything that *is* π by *partaking of* π. Plato expects the reader to carry out the minor modification of the earlier analysis of what it is for π not to be about σ (the one involving the converse of the *identity* use of "not to be") so as to obtain the analysis of what it is for π not to be about σ that is required by the account of false statement (the one involving the converse of the *predicative* use of "not to be"). Note that we get two (equivalent) analyses of what it is for π not to be about σ that fit the account of false statement: first, for π not to be about σ is for π to be other than everything that is about σ; second, for π not to be about σ is for σ to be other than everything that π is about.

52. According to some commentators (e.g., Owen, "Not-Being," 245), Plato himself earlier succumbed to such a version of the falsehood paradox.

then be about different items (the flying Theaetetus and the sitting Theaetetus) and would therefore not contradict one another. Hence the point of emphasizing that the two statements are about the same object.

## From false statement to false belief

The ES and Theaetetus define thought (*dianoia*) as "the inner conversation of the soul with itself that occurs without voice" (263e4–5) and belief (*doxa*) as the soul's inner silent (affirmative or negative) statement that concludes an inner silent conversation (263e10–264a3; cf. *Tht.* 189e6–190a6, 196a4–7; *Ti.* 37a2–37c5; *Phlb.* 38c5–38e8). Given that an account of false statement has been attained, an account of false belief comes as a bonus.

What is the language of the soul's inner silent conversation? Is it a divine language? A language of images? Or the language the speaker feels most comfortable with at the moment? No answer is forthcoming from Plato's works.[53] Another important unasked question is: Can thinkers always tell, by introspecting their consciousness, what the contents of their beliefs are?[54]

# CONCLUSION

Many of Plato's views in philosophy of language have had a remarkable impact on later thinkers. Aristotle picked up and developed some of these views, such as the idea that truth and falsehood are qualities of statements (*SE* 22, 178b27–28), the distinction between primary and nonprimary statements (*Int.* 5, 17a8–9, 17a20–24), and the analysis of primary statements into names and verbs (chs. 2–5 of *de Interpretatione*); others he criticized, such as the claim that linguistic expressions are tools (*Int.* 4, 17a1–2). The falsehood paradox never surfaced again as a serious threat: the *Sophist* laid it to rest. Alongside these elements of success in the area of philosophy of language, a conspicuous absence in a neighboring field should be mentioned: the study of argument and of its validity does not appear in Plato. Its development is perhaps the most notable of the many achievements of his most distinguished pupil.

---

53. P. Crivelli, "ΑΛΛΟΔΟΞΙΑ," *Archiv für Geschichte der Philosophie* 80 (1998), 21–23.

54. N. P. White, "Plato (427–347)," in M. Dascal, D. Gerhardus, K. Lorenz, and G. Meggle (eds.), *Sprachphilosophie—Philosophy of Language—La philosophie du langage*, vol. 1 (Berlin, 1992), 241.

# REFERENCES

Ackrill, J. L. "Language and Reality in Plato's *Cratylus*," *Essays on Plato and Aristotle* (Oxford, 1994), 33–52.

Borsche, T. "Platon," in P. Schmitter (ed.), *Sprachtheorien der abenländischen Antike*, 2nd ed. (Tübingen, 1996), 140–69.

Bostock, D. *Plato's Phaedo* (Oxford, 1986).

Burnyeat, M. F. "Plato on How Not to Speak of What Is Not: *Euthydemus* 283a–288a," in M. Canto-Sperber and P. Pellegrin (eds.), *Le style de la pensée: Recueil de textes en hommage à Jacques Brunschwig* (Paris, 2002), 40–66.

Crivelli, P. "ΑΛΛΟΔΟΞΙΑ," *Archiv für Geschichte der Philosophie* 80 (1998), 1–29.

———. "Il *Sofista* di Platone: non essere, negazione e falsità," *Atti e Memorie dell' Accademia Toscana di Scienze e Lettere "La Colombaria"* 55 (1990), 9–104.

———. "Plato's *Sophist* and Semantic Fragmentation," *Archiv für Geschichte der Philosophie* 75 (1993), 71–74.

Denyer, N. *Language, Thought and Falsehood in Ancient Greek Philosophy* (London, 1991).

Donnellan, K. "Reference and Definite Descriptions," *Philosophical Review* 75 (1966), 281–304.

Ferejohn, M. T. "Plato and Aristotle on Negative Predication and Semantic Fragmentation," *Archiv für Geschichte der Philosophie* 71 (1989), 257–82.

Fine, G. *On Ideas: Aristotle's Criticism of Plato's Theory of Forms* (Oxford, 1993).

Frede, M. "Plato's *Sophist* on False Statements," in R. Kraut (ed.), *The Cambridge Companion to Plato* (Cambridge, 1992), 397–424.

———. *Prädikation und Existenzaussage: Platons Gebrauch von "... ist ..." und "... ist nicht ..." im Sophistes* (Göttingen, 1967).

Hestir, B. E. "A 'Conception' of Truth in Plato's *Sophist*," *Journal of the History of Philosophy* 41 (2003), 1–24.

Irwin, T. H. "The Theory of Forms," in G. Fine (ed.), *Plato 1: Metaphysics and Epistemology* (Oxford, 1999), 143–70.

Keyt, D. "Plato on Falsity: *Sophist* 263B," in E. N. Lee, A. P. D. Mourelatos, and R. M. Rorty (eds.), *Exegesis and Argument: Studies in Greek Philosophy Presented to Gregory Vlastos* (Assen, 1973), 285–305.

Kretzmann, N. "Plato on the Correctness of Names," *American Philosophical Quarterly* 8 (1971), 126–38.

Moravcsik, J. M. E. "Being and Meaning in the *Sophist*," *Acta Philosophica Fennica* 14 (1962), 23–78.

Nuchelmans, G. *Theories of the Proposition: Ancient and Medieval Conceptions of the Bearers of Truth and Falsity* (Amsterdam, 1973).

Owen, G. E. L. "Plato on Not-Being," in G. Vlastos (ed.), *Plato: A Collection of Critical Essays*, vol. 1 (Garden City, N.J., 1971), 223–67.

Peipers, D. *Ontologia Platonica: Ad Notionum Terminorumque Historiam Symbola* (Leipzig, 1883).

Pelletier, F. J. *Parmenides, Plato, and the Semantics of Not-Being* (Chicago, 1990).

Reeve, C. D. C. (trans.) *Plato: Cratylus* (Indianapolis, 1999).

Robinson, D. "Textual Notes on Plato's *Sophist*," *Classical Quarterly*, n. s. 49 (1999), 139–59.

Robinson, R. "A Criticism of Plato's *Cratylus*," *Philosophical Review* 65 (1956), 324–41.

Ross, D. *Plato's Theory of Ideas* (Oxford, 1951).

Rudebusch, G. "Does Plato Think False Speech Is Speech?," *Noûs* 24 (1990), 599–609.

Sayre, K. M. *Plato's Late Ontology: A Riddle Resolved* (Princeton, 1983).

Schofield, M. "The Dénouement of the *Cratylus*," in M. Schofield and M. Craven Nussbaum (eds.), *Language and Logos: Studies in Ancient Greek Philosophy Presented to G. E. L. Owen* (Cambridge, 1982), 61–81.

Sedley, D. *Plato's* Cratylus (Cambridge, 2003).

Smith, J. A. "General Relative Clauses in Greek," *Classical Review* 31 (1917), 69–71.

White, N. P. "Plato (427–347)," in M. Dascal, D. Gerhardus, K. Lorenz, and G. Meggle (eds.), *Sprachphilosophie—Philosophy of Language—La philosophie du langage*, vol. 1 (Berlin, 1992), 234–44.

———. *Plato on Knowledge and Reality* (Indianapolis, 1976).

Williams, B. "Cratylus' Theory of Names and Its Refutation," in M. Schofield and M. Craven Nussbaum (eds.), *Language and Logos: Studies in Ancient Greek Philosophy Presented to G. E. L. Owen* (Cambridge, 1982), 83–93.

# CHAPTER 10

# PLATO ON THE SOUL

## HENDRIK LORENZ

PLATO'S central contribution to psychology is his theory of the tripartite soul. This is at once a theory about the nature of the embodied human soul and a theory of human motivation. Its implied theory of motivation was accepted with little or no modification by Aristotle. It remained influential into the later ancient period and beyond, not only among Platonists but also in the Aristotelian tradition. The theory is introduced and put to extensive use in the *Republic*. As a theory of motivation, it has noteworthy antecedents in the *Phaedo* and supersedes an incompatible theory that is in play in earlier dialogues such as the *Protagoras*, the *Meno*, and, arguably with notable signs of strain, the *Gorgias*. As a theory about the nature of the human soul, it significantly departs from ideas presented in the *Phaedo*, raising questions about the immortality of the soul of which Plato is keenly aware. The *Phaedrus* and the *Timaeus*, both of them written after the *Republic*, revisit the theory and bear witness to Plato's ongoing reflection about the nature of the soul.

In this chapter, I focus on the *Republic*, whose psychological theory is discussed in considerable detail in section 4. I begin by discussing the *Protagoras* (section 1), the *Gorgias* (section 2), and the *Phaedo* (section 3), insofar as speakers in those dialogues express views about human motivation or about the nature of the soul.

## 1. *PROTAGORAS*

In the course of an elaborately constructed discussion with Protagoras, Socrates presents an outline of a remarkable theory of human motivation. The central and most famous tenet of that theory is that "if someone were to know what is good and bad, then he would not be forced by anything to act otherwise than knowledge dictates"[1] (352c4–6). Let us call this the claim that Knowledge Reigns Supreme (KRS). Socrates takes that claim to be one that is not shared by the majority of people. The majority view, he thinks, is that people can, and frequently do, act contrary to knowledge of good and bad, being mastered by emotions such as anger, pleasure, pain, lust, or fear (352b3–8). KRS underlies Socrates' strikingly optimistic assessment that knowledge of good and bad, if only we had it, "would save our lives" (356d7–e2), at least ensuring that our lives would go as well as, given the circumstances, they possibly could.

KRS, in turn, rests on two key assumptions: first, that knowledge of good and bad would be consistently effective in affording its bearer an accurate view of how it would be best to act in the circumstances; second, that a given person's knowledge of how to act would be fully in control of his or her actions. Socrates says disappointingly little about the nature and structure of the knowledge of good and bad (cf. 357b5–6) or about how it might be attained. It is clear, however, that he thinks of it in quantitative terms: as an expertise of measurement concerning matters of value. He says that such expertise would give us "peace of mind firmly rooted in the truth" (356d7–e2) and would render powerless any mistaken appearances about good and bad that may arise in the varied circumstances of life. One thing this makes clear is that he thinks the person of practical knowledge may, on occasion, find herself with inaccurate, preliminary impressions about how to act in a given situation, in a way that he likens to perceptual illusions. Having a dull, run-of-the-mill doughnut right now might strike even a sage as a greater pleasure than having her favorite dessert tomorrow after dinner, much as the truck in the distance does look smaller than the car near at hand. However, Socrates thinks that, whereas those who lack practical knowledge tend to be fooled by illusions about matters of value, the person who is knowledgeable about such things is in no danger of acting on illusory appearances. "The art of measurement," he says, "would make the appearances lose their power by showing us the truth" (356d7–e1).

For the knowledge of good and bad to save our lives, or at least to ensure that they go as well as they can in the circumstances, this knowledge must not only afford a steady, accurate view of how to act; it must also be the case that the bearer of such knowledge acts entirely in accord with that steady, accurate view. Socrates clearly thinks that people can be fully relied on to act in accord with such practical knowledge as they may have. He goes further than that, holding that "no one who knows *or believes* there is something else better than what he is doing, something possible, will go on doing what he had been doing when he could be doing what is better" (358b6–c1; italics added). Thus he takes the view that no one will pursue a given course of action if at the time she knows, or merely believes, that the circumstances allow a better course of action.

1. Translations of Plato's works are as in J. M. Cooper (ed.), *Plato: Complete Works* (Indianapolis, 1997), with some modifications.

On some conceptions of *akrasia*, that amounts to a denial of *akrasia*. In fact, Socrates seems to go further even than that, holding that practical knowledge or belief governs not only what one ends up trying to do but even what one wants to do. "No one," he claims, "goes willingly towards the bad or what he believes to be bad," adding the noteworthy further claim that "it seems not to be in human nature, either, to want to go towards what one believes to be bad instead of to the good" (358c6–d2). On that view, believing that *φ*-ing is bad, and that a good, or better, course of action is available, ensures that one is not even going to want to *φ*, at any rate as long as one retains the relevant beliefs.

It is worth noting that one can accept KRS without accepting what is known as "Socratic intellectualism." For the sake of clarity, let that be the view that every desire to do something or other aims at the pursuit of a course of action that the person in question knows or believes is at least no worse than any other course of action she takes to be available. One could reject Socratic intellectualism and nonetheless uphold KRS. One might hold that people can, and frequently do, want to do things that they realize it would be better not to do, but that genuine knowledge of good and bad is a psychological condition in which, among other things, one's motivational and affective states have settled into unison with one's thoughts about good and bad. Something like this may be Plato's view in the *Republic*. However, the basis on which the Socrates of the *Protagoras* endorses KRS would seem to be a simpler one. As we have seen, he presents it as a fact of human nature that people will not even want to do something they believe to be bad when they believe a good, or better, course of action is available. Presumably, his basis for holding that is the thought that desires to act in some way or other always aim at the pursuit of what the person in question knows or believes to be the best course of action available, or at least a course of action no worse than any other option he or she takes to be available. It would seem, then, that the Socrates of the *Protagoras* endorses KRS because he subscribes to Socratic intellectualism.

As has been noted already, the *Protagoras'* theory of human motivation rules out *akrasia*, if *akrasia* is conceived of as a matter of acting contrary to one's currently held judgment about how it would be best, or anyhow better, to act. But that is by no means the only way one can conceive of *akrasia*. In the classical tradition, it is not before Aristotle that we get a conception of *akrasia* according to which *akratic* action is specifically a matter of action that runs counter to a practical judgment, currently held by the agent. In earlier writers such as Xenophon, the language of *akrasia* is tied to a rather loose notion of being mastered by emotions like pleasure, pain, anger, or fear, as well as by sources of pleasure such as food, drink, or sex (e.g., *Memorabilia* 1.5). It is not required by that notion that the person who is mastered or overcome in this way, in acting as he should not, all the while retains a judgment that he should not act as, in fact, he does. It may well be that he experiences a lapse in judgment, brought on by intense emotion or the prospect of indulgence. At the time of action, he may be deluded enough to believe that acting as he does is best. Or, at the time of action, he may have no belief at all about the rather complicated matter of how it would be best for him to act in the circumstances, busy as he is enjoying himself or being in the grip of fear that focuses all his attention on whatever it may be that terrifies him.

Against that background, Socrates in the *Protagoras* should not be interpreted as arguing against the possibility of *akrasia*, understood as being overcome by emotions or sources of pleasure. Rather, his main target is the view that people can know that something is less good than something else they might pursue, and they pursue it all the same. This, of course, is the view he is ascribing to "the many." His view is not, then, that there is no such thing as being overcome by emotions or by things that are pleasant or painful. Rather, his view is that being overcome in this way is always a matter of adopting, or finding oneself in the grip of, false practical beliefs and hence is always a manifestation of ignorance (cf. 357e2, 358c1–3). Thus knowledge of good and bad, if only we had and maintained it, would reliably protect us from acting as we should not. It would do this, moreover, by reliably affording us accurate views of how we should act in the circumstances in which we find ourselves. With those views steadily in place, we would never even want to act as we should not.

## 2. GORGIAS

The Socrates of the *Gorgias* seems to operate within a robustly intellectualist framework, at least for much of the dialogue. He assumes that anyone who knows what is just and unjust cannot possibly act unjustly or even want to act unjustly. He also seems to assume that every desire to do something or other aims at the good in the sense that every such desire rests on a judgment that it is (in the circumstances) better to do the thing in question than not to. Presumably, the latter assumption underlies the former: knowing what is just brings with it knowledge that acting unjustly is always worse than not to, and so no one who knows what is just can ever even want to act unjustly.

Gorgias tells Socrates that if a student of rhetoric lacks knowledge about matters of value, such as what is good, fine, and just (459c8–e1), "he will learn those things from me as well" (460a3–4). But, says Socrates, just as a person who has learned carpentry, music, or medicine is a carpenter, musician, or doctor, so a person who has learned what is just is a just person (460b7). Moreover, a just person wants to do just things, and, in fact, he will never want to act unjustly (460c1–3). Since a trained orator knows just things, then, he is incapable of using oratory unjustly or even of wanting to act unjustly in any way at all (461a4–7). Thus Gorgias is contradicting himself when he holds that orators must know what is just and also that some orators use their art unjustly. Socrates evidently sees no gap at all between having learned what is just and unjust, in the way one might learn such things by a teacher's instruction, and being wholeheartedly motivated to pursue justice and avoid injustice. This is best explained by the conjecture that, much like the Socrates of the *Protagoras*, the Socrates of the *Gorgias* assumes that since people already are wholeheartedly motivated to pursue the good, knowledge of what precisely effective pursuit of the good involves and requires is fully sufficient to ensure proper motivation.

That the Socrates of the *Gorgias* operates with some such picture of human nature is confirmed by what he says in his discussion with Polus. During that discussion, he claims that whenever we do something that we do not take to be good in itself, we are acting "for the sake of the good," by which he seems to mean that we do the thing in question because we suppose that doing it is better for us than not doing it. Thus he holds that "it's because we pursue the good that we walk whenever we walk; we suppose that it's better to walk" (468b1–2); and again: "we put a person to death, if we do, or banish him and confiscate his property because we suppose that doing these things is better for us than not doing them" (468b4–6). He also operates with a conception of desire that serves to explain and underwrite his remarkable claims about human behavior and motivation. Moreover, that conception of desire explains why people like tyrants "do just about nothing they want to do" (466d6–e2). According to that conception, all desires to do something or other aim at doing something that it is good for the person to do, presumably in that it is better for the person to do the thing in question than not to. Since every human desire aims at doing something that it is good for one to do, Socrates seems to think, one can only do what one wants to do by doing something that it is, in fact, good for one to do. In doing something that it would be better for one not to do, one is inevitably frustrating the very desire on which one is acting. People who rarely, if ever, do something that it is good for them to do, such as tyrants, will thus rarely, if ever, do what they want to do, even if they are in a position to do everything they see fit.

This is a reasonable view for Socrates to take, if he thinks that every desire to do something or other aims at the good in the strong sense that one thing that any such desire is so constituted as to aim at is the doing of something that it would be genuinely good for the person to do in the circumstances. On that view, forming a desire to do this or that necessarily involves envisaging doing this or that as being something that it is, or would be, good for one to do in the circumstances. Moreover, it is the relevant course of action envisaged in this particular way that constitutes the object of the desire in question. On that view, if it seems best to a tyrant, say, to kill a dissident, a full specification of the tyrant's object of desire will be something like "killing that dissident, as something that it is good for me to do in the circumstances." Of course, there is no way for the tyrant to perform an action that matches that specification. But that is as it should be. It is precisely why the tyrant quite definitely fails to do what he wants to do, even though he may well succeed in killing the dissident.

Interestingly enough, we have independent evidence that it is part of the Socratic conception of desire, at any rate as Plato thinks of it, that desire aims at the good in something like the strong sense just explicated. In arguing for the theory of the tripartite soul in book 4 of the *Republic*, Plato relies on what is known as the Principle of Relatives (*Republic* 4, 437d7–439b1). The principle says, in effect, that if A and B are a pair of relatives, A and B bear the same degree of complexity. For instance, knowledge without qualification and what can be learned without qualification are relatives, and so are medical knowledge and what can be learned about health and disease. Likewise, thirst and drink are relatives, and so are, say, small thirst and little drink. Thirst, then, is a kind of desire that by itself is simply for drink but not, says Socrates, "for much or little, good or bad drink, or, in a word, for drink qualified in some way or other" (*Republic* 439a4–7).

The Socrates of the *Republic* rejects an imaginary interlocutor's claim that thirst is desire for drink qualified as good, "on the grounds that everyone desires good things" (*Republic* 438a3–4; cf. *Meno* 77c1–2). When Glaucon remarks that "the person who says that has a point" (*Republic* 438a6), Socrates enunciates and explains the Principle of Relatives. He then refutes, as being a violation of that principle, the idea that thirst by itself is desire for drink qualified as good. On what is philosophically the most natural and attractive construal of the view that is being rejected, any desire to obtain this or that (say, food) necessarily involves envisaging the thing in question as being a good thing to obtain. On this view, it is the relevant thing envisaged in this particular way that constitutes the object of the desire in question. But that view of how desire aims at the good looks to be a notational variant of the view employed by the Socrates of the *Gorgias*, put in terms of desires to obtain this or that rather than in terms of desires to do this or that.

It may seem that the Socrates of the *Gorgias*, in his discussion with Callicles, abandons Socratic intellectualism by allowing that at least some desires do not aim at the good but, for instance, at pleasure. In his discussion with Callicles, Socrates speaks of the part of the soul to which the person's desires belong (493a3–4), and stresses the need to maintain control over one's pleasures and desires (491d4–E 1). He recommends self-control (491d10–e1) and warns of its lack (525a3–6). Moreover, Callicles advocates enlarging one's desires as much as possible and satisfying them with bravery and intelligence (491e6–492a3; cf. 491b2–4), apparently thinking that without that bravery one might find oneself with a suitably enlarged desire for some gratification, with access to the object of one's desire but without the determination or ruthlessness needed to achieve (what one would take to be) satisfaction.

However, nothing that Socrates says in the *Gorgias* entails the rejection of Socratic intellectualism. The jar that stands for the part of our soul that houses our desires or appetites is presented as part of a story that Socrates says he heard some clever person tell (493a5–c3). In turn, it seems to be an elaboration of something Socrates claims to have heard from some wise person (493a1–5). Socrates notes that "the story is on the whole a bit strange" (493c3–4). The story does not contain a determinate psychological theory, and in any case Socrates keeps plenty of distance from it both by reporting it as a story told by someone else and by noting its strangeness.

As we have seen already, Socratic intellectualism is compatible with accepting the possibility of lack of self-control, understood as weakness in relation to affects like lust or anger or in relation to pleasant things such as food, drink, or sex. The Socrates of the *Protagoras* does not deny the possibility of *akrasia*, understood in this way. Rather, he is rejecting the view of "the many" that people can be overcome by emotions or objects of desire all the while knowing, or correctly believing, that what they are doing is bad for them to do. Being overcome in this way, Socrates holds, is always a matter of finding oneself in the grip of a false practical belief, and hence is always a manifestation of ignorance.

In his discussion in the *Gorgias* with Callicles about the superior individuals who Callicles thinks should rule their cities, Socrates asks him whether they should rule themselves, as well as their fellow citizens (491d4–8). Callicles claims not to understand what Socrates means by self-rule, and Socrates clarifies: "Nothing very subtle. Just what the many mean: being temperate and in control of oneself, to rule over the pleasures and desires within oneself" (491d10–e1). But in the *Protagoras*, Socrates has offered "the many," and us, an analysis of what control over oneself really is: nothing other than wisdom, the knowledge of good and bad (*Protagoras* 358c1–3).[2] Wisdom ensures that not only in one's pursuit and enjoyment of pleasures but quite generally in all one's actions, one is invariably guided by one's own accurate, stable, and unified view of what is good and bad. The unwise person, by contrast, tends to find himself riddled with false beliefs about what is good and bad, arising from misleading appearances about pleasures and pains that he is unable to correct in anything like a reliable way. He is always vulnerable to having pleasures and desires forced on him by false appearances about good and bad that he fails to render powerless.

This intellectualist construal of self-control and its lack is on display in the *Protagoras*. If Socrates' remarks about self-rule in the *Gorgias* are interpreted along such intellectualist lines, as they certainly can be, what he says in his discussion with Callicles chimes in well with what he has said in the earlier discussions with Gorgias and Polus. On the alternative, nonintellectualist interpretation of those remarks, Socrates acknowledges, in his discussion with Callicles, the existence of human desires that do not aim at the good and that stand in need of being controlled or repressed. In that case, however, it becomes mysterious why it should be the case, as Socrates claims it is in his discussion with Gorgias, that it is impossible for anyone who has learned by instruction what is just and unjust even to want to perform an act he or she recognizes is unjust (461a4–7; cf. 460c3). If it is a fact of human nature that we find ourselves with desires that aim not at the good but at pleasure, what could possibly guarantee that Jones, who has learned what is just and unjust, cannot form a pleasure-directed desire, say, to eat the last piece of chocolate cake when he knows perfectly well that in the circumstances it would be

2. That the *Protagoras* articulates a "Socratic" conception of *akrasia* is duly noted in J. Cooper, *Reason and Emotion* (Princeton, 1999), 63 n.54.

unjust for him to do so? Worse still, Socrates falls into outright incoherence if he allows it to be a psychological possibility that Jones can, say, steal his neighbor's money while judging that doing so is worse, and worse for him, than not doing so, having been overcome by a pleasure-directed desire for greater wealth. This is because in his discussion with Polus, Socrates plainly holds that even when we do things that we do not take to be good in themselves, we still always act for the sake of the good, doing what we do "because we suppose that doing these things is better for us than not doing them" (468b1–8).

Better, then, to interpret Socrates' remarks about self-rule in the *Gorgias* along the intellectualist lines familiar from the *Protagoras*. That is not to say, however, that Callicles is likely to interpret Socrates' remarks about self-rule along those lines. Naturally enough, Callicles' idea of self-control is one of abstaining from pleasures and repressing desires because of lack of resources, a sense of shame or scruple, or conventional and misguided thoughts about matters of value. But that is Callicles' outlook, not Socrates'. To say that the Socrates of the *Gorgias* operates within a robustly intellectualist framework is not to deny that the dialogue has a notable undercurrent of psychological complexity. Callicles' interest in bodily pleasures and desires—in particular, his idea that one should enlarge one's desires by indulging them—raises awkward questions for Socratic intellectualism. Since desires like hunger and thirst plainly have both physiological and habitual aspects, it seems clear that one can find oneself with such desires, even intense, pressing ones, regardless of whether or not one thinks that it would be good for one to eat or drink in the circumstances. Socrates considers the bodily desires of sick people, noting that doctors often do not allow them to fill themselves with what they want (505a6–10). What to say about a sick patient who fully understands and appreciates that he should not now drink, intensely thirsty though he is?

Furthermore, both Callicles and Socrates show interest in people's sense of shame and, more broadly speaking, in their sensitivity to the values of their community.[3] Callicles envisages a psychologically interesting case of mental conflict, in which someone has an enlarged desire for gratification but cannot bring himself to act on it "because of softness of spirit," by which he presumably means some kind of scruple or sense of shame (491b2–4). How do such psychological factors relate to one's thoughts about good and bad? Is it a psychological possibility for Jones to think, firmly and without any wavering, that his eating the last piece of cake would be best and yet to be unable to get himself to take it because he is worried that he might be perceived as greedy? Those and other such questions seem close to the surface of the *Gorgias*. It is tempting to think that Plato, by foreshadowing the psychological complexities of the middle dialogues, means to prepare the reader for the developments that culminate in the *Republic*'s theory of the tripartite soul.

---

3. Socrates' appeals in the *Gorgias* to his interlocutors" sense of shame are discussed in J. Moss, "Shame, pleasure, and the divided soul," *Oxford Studies in Ancient Philosophy* 29 (2005), 137–70.

# 3. *Phaedo* and the *Immortality* of the *Soul*

The Socrates of the *Phaedo* accepts the possibility of psychological conflict without accepting that the soul, even the embodied soul, is a thing of parts. One of his arguments against the *harmonia* theory of the soul, put forward by Simmias (85e3–86d3), relies on the occurrence of conflicts between desires and also of conflicts between how one decides to act and how anger or fear incline one to act. Among other things, he points out that people who are thirsty may nonetheless be averse to drinking (94b8–10). According to his characterization of such a conflict, the soul opposes the affection in question and impels the person "towards the opposite, not drinking." It is presumably part of the picture that being thirsty involves experiencing an impulse toward drinking, which the soul may thwart by opposing it.

Socrates adds that the soul may oppose the body and its parts harshly and painfully, as in athletic exercise or medical treatment, or, more gently, when it converses with one's emotions by issuing threats or exhortations (94c9–d6). To illustrate that more gentle form of opposition, Socrates refers to a passage from Homer's *Odyssey* (20, 17–18), which also features in the argument for the tripartition of the soul in *Republic* 4. The Socrates of the *Republic* takes the passage to provide an example of a conflict between reason and the spirited part of the soul (*Republic* 441b5). Confronted with the disloyal behavior of Penelope's maids, Odysseus is furious and is sorely tempted to punish them there and then. However, he also realizes that it would be unwise to reveal himself at this time as the legitimate king of Ithaca. In an effort to control his anger, he addresses his heart, saying "Endure, my heart, you have endured worse than this" (94d7–e1). The more gentle form of opposition is characterized as a matter of the soul's conversing with desires, anger, or fear, "as one thing that talks to another" (94d5–6).

It is important to note that in the picture of conflict that Socrates presents, the conflicting parties are the soul on the one hand and the parts of the body on the other. Socrates construes the *harmonia* theory as claiming that the soul is a certain kind of arrangement or composite of bodily parts (92a7–b2, 92e5–93a9). He holds that no arrangement could oppose the parts that compose it (93a8–9, 94c3–7). Since the soul frequently opposes the various bodily parts (94c10–d2) and the affections that reside in them (94b7–c1), it follows, Socrates argues, that the soul could not be any kind of arrangement of the parts that compose the body. The argument presupposes that the bodily parts that compose our organisms are able to form impulses to eat or drink, as well as emotions such as anger or fear. This idea is nicely illustrated by the *Odyssey* passage that Socrates is quoting: there it is Odysseus' heart that is said to growl in anger and that Odysseus addresses with soothing words.

The Socrates of the *Phaedo*, then, takes the body, at any rate while it is ensouled, to be the subject of what we would call "mental states" of various kinds. In doing so, he may seem to foreshadow Aristotle's psychological theory, according to which it is the ensouled organism, not the soul, that is the subject of mental states (*De Anima* 1.4, 408b12–15). However, it should be noted that Socrates takes the soul, too, to be a subject of mental states and acts. After all, he takes the soul to oppose the bodily affections in various ways—for instance, by pulling one away from drinking when one is thirsty or by confronting one's anger or fear with threats and exhortations.

In arguing against the *harmonia* theory, the Socrates of the *Phaedo* is recognizing forms of psychological conflict that Socratic intellectualism cannot accommodate. In the *Odyssey* passage to which Socrates refers, Odysseus is determined not to pounce on the maids there and then, plainly because he is aware that the time has not yet come to disclose his presence in Ithaca to Penelope's suitors. Nevertheless, he still feels driven to kill the maids right away, furious as he is at their flagrantly disloyal and shameless behavior. That is why he has to oppose his anger, exhorting his heart to endure. To put things schematically, Odysseus finds himself with a desire to kill the maids at once, without in the least believing that doing so would be as good as, or better than, any other course of action that is available in the circumstances. He has a firm and unwavering grasp of the fact that killing the maids at once would be immeasurably worse than not doing so. Nonetheless, he feels a pressing urge to do so. To accept this as a genuine psychological possibility, as the Socrates of the *Phaedo* shows every sign of doing, is to abandon Socratic intellectualism. It seems out of the question that Plato is not aware of this.

It is unclear whether the Socrates of the *Phaedo* is prepared to accept that impulses of the body may prevail over contrary impulses of the soul. Might Odysseus' soul have failed to master his heart's anger? Might he have proceeded to slaughter the maids, all the while knowing or believing that it would have been better to keep quiet? We do not know, but Socrates does say that the soul leads all the bodily parts, "opposing nearly all of them throughout life and mastering them in all sorts of ways" (94c10–d2). Thus he might think that although the body can form various kinds of emotion and desire, it is always the soul that determines what is done, accommodating or thwarting the body's inclinations as it sees fit.

In that case, he might think that people can, and frequently do, want to act as they recognize they should not but that they never act on such urges, at any rate not without revising their views about how it would be best, or better, to act in the circumstances. As we shall see, this view would amount to a halfway house between Socratic intellectualism and the psychological theory of the *Republic*. One thing to note about a view along such lines is that it seems unstable. If people more or less frequently find themselves with irrational urges, what guarantees that they never act on them, contrary to their better judgment? What ensures the control of people's better, more thoughtful, desires over how they end up behaving? If Plato favored such an intermediate view while writing the *Phaedo*, it seems easy to see how that view gave way to the psychological theory of the *Republic*, according to which people are capable not only of irrational desire but also of acting contrary to their own better, more thoughtful, desires.

One striking difference between the *Phaedo* and the *Republic* is that while the latter famously introduces the claim that the embodied soul is a composite of three parts, the Socrates of the *Phaedo* seems committed to thinking that even the embodied soul is incomposite. In the context of the so-called affinity argument (78b–80b), Socrates gets his interlocutor Cebes to agree that

> it is naturally appropriate for what has been combined and what is a composite to undergo this, to be divided up in the way in which it has been combined. But if something turns out to be incomposite, for that alone, if for anything, it is appropriate not to undergo these things. (*Phaedo* 78c1–5)

Socrates is aware that the affinity argument is not sufficient to prove that the soul is indissoluble. But he is firmly committed to the immortality of the soul, of course. He goes along with Simmias and Cebes (77b–e) in thinking that for a given soul to be divided up, or dispersed, is to be destroyed (80d5–e1). Thus he must think that souls will, for whatever reason, not be divided up. If he thinks that souls are composites, he owes an explanation of why they will not be divided up, even though, being composites, they are naturally such as to be vulnerable to division. He shows no concern at all to offer such an explanation. This seems best explained by supposing that he takes each soul to be incomposite. In any case, there is no sign in the text that the Socrates of the *Phaedo* takes the soul to be a combination or composite of constituent parts.

At this point, it is important to recall that the *Phaedo* treats the body as a subject of impulses and emotions. Conflicts that the *Republic* conceives as taking place within the soul and hence as showing the existence in the soul of distinct and conflicting parts are treated in the *Phaedo* as conflicts in which the soul opposes suitable parts of the body, such as the heart. On this picture, such conflicts may leave the soul itself entirely undivided.

One might think that the *Phaedo* can preserve the unity of the soul only by sacrificing the unity of the psychological subject, ascribing some psychological states to the soul and others to a distinct subject, the body or some suitable part of it. One might also think that forming even the simplest desire is a task that could never be accomplished by a mere body or bodily part, but only by a soul (cf. *Philebus* 34d10–35d6). We do not know whether these considerations were among Plato's reasons for abandoning the *Phaedo*'s picture of motivational conflict; however, we do know that the Socrates of the *Republic* ascribes all psychological states to the soul and none to the body, conceiving of the soul, at least in its embodied state, as a composite of three parts.

When he turns to the soul's immortality in *Republic* 10, Socrates confronts the question how a thing of parts could turn out to be everlasting. "We must not think," he says, "that the soul in its truest nature is full of multicoloured variety and unlikeness or that it differs with itself. . . . It isn't easy for a composite of many parts to be everlasting if it isn't composed in the finest way, yet this is how the soul now appeared to us" (*Republic* 611a10–b7). What he goes on to say (at 611b–612a) is indeterminate between two significant alternatives. Once separated from the body, the soul might be a composite that is composed finely enough to be everlasting; or it might then be incomposite and wholly rational, because reason is the only part of it that is immortal. The *Timaeus* operates with the second of these alternatives, conceiving of reason alone as immortal and of appetite and spirit as together constituting the soul's mortal part (*Timaeus* 69c5–d4). The *Phaedrus*, by contrast, seems to explore the first alternative: it likens the disembodied human soul to a charioteer in charge of two horses—one good, the other bad—which plainly stand for spirit and appetite (*Phaedrus* 246a–250c). In the disembodied condition, there may be no room for conflict between the driver's directives and any desires the horses might have. In the case of human souls, as opposed to divine ones, the driver has a hard time maintaining control over his chariot (247b3–6, 248a1–6). But the driver's troubles may arise simply from the disparity of his horses and the heaviness of the bad horse (247b3–5) rather than from any irrational desires that the horses might have.

# 4. REPUBLIC

It is time to turn to *Republic* 4, in which Socrates attempts to establish by argument that the embodied human soul is composed of three parts. The argument is better than its reputation.[4] Its conclusion is momentous. It follows validly from premises that Socrates provides. And each of those premises would have seemed to an intelligent, well-informed ancient reader at least a plausible candidate for truth.

## 4.1 The Principle of Opposites

The argument relies crucially on a principle whose truth Socrates claims is clear (436b9), though he is careful enough to note that, for the purposes of the discussion with Glaucon and the others, it has and retains the status of a hypothesis (437a3–8). This is the so-called Principle of Opposites (PO; 436b9–10):

> PO: The same thing cannot do or undergo opposites in the same respect, in relation to the same thing, and at the same time.

The principle stated, Socrates proceeds to defend it against two apparent counterexamples, thereby clarifying significantly what it is meant to come to. The first apparent counterexample is a person who stands still but moves her arms and head. Socrates rejects this as a counterexample to PO, analyzing it not as a case of

---

4. "No tutor," wrote Gilbert Ryle in 1947, "would accept from a pupil the reasons given by Plato for...the doctrine that the Soul is tripartite." That statement is from his review of Popper's *The Open Society and Its Enemies*. Ryle's dim view of the argument is revived by Myles Burnyeat, in "The truth of tripartition," *Proceedings of the Aristotelian Society* 106 (2006), 1–4.

the same thing being simultaneously at rest and in motion but, rather, as a case of one part of the person being at rest while another is in motion (436d1–2). Just as in the parallel case of the archer, whose one arm pushes the bow in one direction while the other arm pulls it the other way (439b8–c1), Socrates accepts that the predicates in question are opposites and that they apply at the same time. In both cases, he holds that the opposite predicates belong to distinct bearers. Strictly speaking, it is the person's arms and head (or whatever) that are in motion, while other parts of her body remain at rest. This need not mean that it is false that the person is in motion and at rest at the same time, only that by saying this, one does not succeed in accurately pinpointing what it is that is, respectively, in motion or at rest. As we might say, by saying this, one fails to pick out the proper subjects of the predicates in question.

The second apparent counterexample to PO that Socrates considers is a spinning top, which, according to an imaginary interlocutor, is as a whole in motion and at rest at the same time (436d4–6). The point of this more sophisticated example (note 436d4) seems precisely to be that it cannot be resolved by identifying distinct subjects for the opposites motion and rest.[5] Socrates rejects this, too, as a counterexample to PO. He points out that a top has a certain complexity and can undergo motion in more ways than one. Given that it has an axis, it can incline or wobble in a certain way. Given that it is suitably curved, it can rotate without coming to occupy a different place. On Socrates' analysis of the spinning top example, the top is "at rest with respect to its axis" (436e1–2), which is to say that it does not incline or wobble. At the same time, he notes, it is "in circular motion with respect to its curved surface" (436e2–3).

This analysis distinguishes between two different ways in which a top may be in motion or at rest: it may undergo motion that affects the axis of its rotation, or it may undergo motion that affects its curved surface, sending the surface around in circles (cf. Aristotle, *Physics* 6.9, $240^{a}28$–$^{b}7$). This is not to say that what it is about the top that is in circular motion is specifically and exclusively its curved surface. It is plainly not the case that the top's surface is going around in circles, whereas the other parts of the thing remain at rest. Rather, Socrates quite reasonably identifies rotation, as opposed to inclination, in terms of its being a form of motion that affects the top's curved surface—namely, by sending it around in circles. This allows him to accept the imaginary interlocutor's nice point that, at the same time, a spinning top is as a whole at rest and in motion. As far as inclination or motion with respect to the top's axis is concerned, it is at rest and is at rest as a whole. As far as rotation or motion with respect to the top's curved surface is concerned, it is in motion and is in motion as a whole.

By disarming these two apparent counterexamples to PO, Socrates has made available two importantly different methods for dealing with cases in which a given subject does opposites at the same time. One method treats the subject as a

---

    5. This is pointed out by C. Bobonich, *Plato's Utopia Recast: His Later Ethics and Politics* (Oxford, 2002), 226–35.

composite and ascribes the one opposite to one part of it and the other to another. The other method distinguishes between different respects in which something or other can do the opposites in question, so that one can say that the subject as a whole does the one opposite in one respect and the other in another. We may add that the first method treats the opposites in question, such as unqualified motion and unqualified rest, as full-on opposites, taking it that nothing can simultaneously serve as their proper subject. The second method, by contrast, amplifies the predicates in question by attaching appropriate qualifications and thereby shows the situation not to involve a clash of full-on opposites. Nothing prevents a suitable object from simultaneously serving as the proper subject of both members of such a pair of qualified opposites.

The argument for tripartition presupposes that desire and aversion are op-posites in the sense of the word that is in play in PO. Desire and aversion are not logically incompatible, and so it will not do to interpret PO as a purely formal truth to the effect that logically incompatible predicates cannot apply to the same subject at the same time, in relation to the same thing, and in the same respect. Socrates is quite explicit about the fact that he does take desire and aversion, as well as assenting and rejecting, to be opposites in the relevant sense (437b1–c5). It is somewhat unclear on what basis he takes that view. It may well be that he takes them to be opposites in the relevant sense simply because they are extremes that delimit a range of states or attitudes, much as Aristotle takes black and white, for instance, to be opposites because he thinks that they delimit the range of colors. In that case, Socrates' acceptance of PO commits him to the view that, for any such range, nothing can at the same time serve as the proper subject of both extremes in the same respect and in relation to the same thing.

Moreover, Socrates evidently takes desiring something and being averse to it to be full-on opposites, treating a case of desire for something and simultaneous aversion to the same thing like the case of the archer's arms pulling the bow in one direction and at the same time pushing it the other way (439b3–c8). One thing this makes clear is that he thinks of the parts of the soul that the argument brings to light as the bearers of psychological states like desires and aversions.[6] That this is the way he conceives of the parts of the soul is corroborated when later on in the *Republic* he also ascribes to them emotions, pleasures, and beliefs.[7]

Why does he treat desiring something and being averse to it as full-on op-posites? There is some indication that he takes desires and aversions to involve motions or impulses of the soul towards, or away from, the object of desire or aversion. He repeatedly describes parts of the soul as pulling or dragging the rest of the soul toward the object of desire (439b4, d1, 604a10, b1–2, etc.), sometimes with another part pulling the other way (e.g., 439b3). When Aristotle uses the same kind of language (e.g., *Nicomachean Ethics* 1.13, 1102$^b$16–18), we know not to take it

---

6. *Contra* T. Irwin, *Plato's Ethics* (Oxford, 1995), 204–5.

7. Emotions are ascribed as follows: excitement at 439d7; anger at 441c2; indifference at 581b8; plea-sures at 580d6–7; beliefs at 442c9–d2, 571d1–4, 603a1–2.

literally because he takes care to make clear in book 1 of the *De Anima* that he takes the soul not to effect motion by itself engaging in some kind of motion (1.3, 406$^b$24–5, 1.4, 408$^b$30–1). But in the same context, he criticizes Plato, among others, for having held precisely the view that the soul imparts motion to the animal by itself engaging in motion (*De Anima* 1.3, 406$^b$26–8). Thus it is probable that Plato conceived of desires and aversions in straightforwardly directional terms, as a matter of the soul impelling you toward something or away from it. This seems a rather natural thought, and it would make it reasonable for Socrates to analyze his cases of psychological conflict like the case of the archer's arms simultaneously pulling the bow one way and pushing it the other way, rather than like the case of the spinning top, which is as a whole in motion in one respect and at rest in another.

Now, one might think that if desire and aversion are opposites in the sense relevant to PO, and if desiring something and being averse to it are full-on opposites, then the psychological conflicts to which Socrates appeals in the course of the argument for tripartition prove PO to be false. For if desiring to φ and being averse to φ-ing are full-on opposites, then the fact that people can at the same time desire to φ and be averse to φ-ing just shows, one might think, that there are things that can at the same time do opposites in the same respect and in relation to the same thing. After all, a person or soul plainly is one thing.[8] However, having attended carefully to the way Socrates resolves his first apparent counterexample to PO, we can see that this objection depends on a questionable understanding of what PO is meant to come to. Considering the case of a person standing still and, at the same time, moving her arms and head, Socrates takes care to pinpoint what precisely it is that, respectively, is in motion or at rest. Strictly speaking, it is only some parts of her body that are in motion, while other parts remain at rest. Thus the case is no genuine counterexample to PO. Note that Socrates' analysis does not require denying that a person is one thing. It only requires treating the person as a composite, so that one can identify distinct parts that will serve as the subjects of the relevant predicates.

Likewise, Socrates can accept that a given soul is one thing, without having to accept that his examples of psychological conflict, as he analyzes them, show PO to be false. He will only have to say that if people do sometimes desire this or that and are at the same time averse to it, this shows that the soul is a composite, with distinct parts of it available to serve as the bearers of conflicting desires and aversions. This he is ready to say. What PO, strictly speaking, rules out, then, is not that opposites can simultaneously apply to the same thing in the same respect and in relation to the same thing. Rather, what it rules out, strictly speaking, is that one and the same thing can simultaneously serve as the proper subject of two opposite predicates, which apply to it in the same respect and in relation to the same thing. There is no reason to think that any of the examples of psychological conflict considered in the argument for tripartition, as Socrates analyzes them, shows PO to

---

8. Thus Burnyeat, "Truth of tripartition," 4.

be false, once it is understood along those lines. It is to Socrates' examples of psychological conflict that we now turn.

## 4.2 The examples of conflict

The first example concerns someone who simply is thirsty, so that Socrates can apply the Principle of Relatives to obtain the result that what the person wants is simply to drink. It happens frequently, Glaucon agrees, that someone who is thirsty in this way is averse to drinking (439c5). Suppose that the person understands that, given his medical condition, he should abstain from drinking anything at all. Given that the person is averse to precisely the thing he wants, Socrates has a case of something simultaneously doing opposites in relation to precisely the same thing. If desiring to $\varphi$ and being averse to $\varphi$-ing are full-on opposites, then Socrates can at this stage infer, and infer validly, that the soul must be a composite of at least two parts. Moreover, he holds that the two parts that have come to light are reason and appetite, on the grounds that the aversion to drinking, in the case considered and in others like it, stems from reasoning or calculation, while the desire to drink arises from "affections and diseases," by which he means physiological imbalances such as dehydration (439c10–d2).

Later remarks, in book 4 and beyond, yield a rather detailed picture of reason and appetite, as well as of spirit, to which we turn presently. According to that picture, reason, at any rate if it is tolerably well developed, is "always wholly straining to know where the truth lies" (581b6–8), and so Socrates also calls it the learning-loving and philosophical part of the soul (581b10–11). It is also the natural ruler of the soul: a properly developed reason is knowledgeable about what is advantageous for each part and for the soul as a whole (441c4–7). It issues directives about how to act and how not to, and it gives rise to corresponding desires and aversions, which are desires and aversions of reason itself. The desires of appetite are related both to physiological imbalances (439d1–2) and to indulgences and pleasures (439d6–8). The objects of appetitive desire prominently include the pleasures of food, drink, and sex (436a10–b2, 442a7–b1), but if and when the person in question comes to take pleasure in a broader range of activities, appetite's interests expand as well. Thus people may form appetites to have a bit of fun by participating in philosophical discussion or by sounding off in political debates (561c6–d4). What unifies appetitive attitudes is that they are impulses toward perceived or expected pleasures or away from perceived or expected pains.

In arguing for the existence of the spirited part of the soul, Socrates relies on two more examples of psychological conflict to show the distinctness of spirit first from appetite and then from reason. Although he does not specify or analyze those examples as explicitly as one might wish, it seems clear that they are meant to follow the pattern set by his first example of psychological conflict: in all three cases, a person experiences a conflict between wanting to do something or other and at the same time being averse to doing it. Leontius, probably a notorious necrophile, wants to take a close look at some corpses lying by the side of the road and is, at the same time, averse to doing so (439e5–440a4). Odysseus can hardly restrain his impulse to punish the maids there and then, but he does manage to control himself, knowing that it would be unwise now to reveal himself as the legitimate king of Ithaca (441b3–c2).

It would have been easy enough for Plato's contemporaries to see that Leontius' aversion to gazing at the corpses is a spirited attitude, one that springs from his sense of what is and what is not praiseworthy and respectable. Before running up to the corpses, Socrates says, Leontius feels disgust, turns himself away, and covers his face. For a while he does battle with himself, then appetite defeats him (440a1–2). As he runs toward the corpses, he angrily addresses his eyes, saying, "Look for yourselves, you evil wretches, take your fill of the beautiful sight!" (440a3–4). Socrates takes the story to indicate that anger sometimes does battle with the appetites—and hence that anger and appetite are distinct from one another, since it takes two parties to do battle (440a6–7). This, in turn, he takes to show the distinctness of spirit from appetite. To understand what he has in mind, we need to recall that he has already noted the psychological link between anger and the character trait of spiritedness, by associating being impelled to act from anger (436a10) with the spiritedness that he takes to be particularly notable in the ideal city's military class (435d9–436a3).

How Plato and his contemporaries conceive of spiritedness is a complicated matter.[9] For present purposes, a sketch may suffice. It is a character trait or psychological tendency that includes as a central aspect eagerness to distinguish oneself and to gain and maintain the esteem and respect of others in one's community. It crucially involves an awareness of one's social position and of one's merits. It also involves solicitude that one's status be duly noted and respected by others and that such merits as one might have be recognized and honored. Hence the spirited person's sensitivity to slights, insults, and the like, and the connection between spiritedness and anger. One thing that being notably spirited must involve is a vivid sense of what does and does not count as praiseworthy and respectable by the lights of one's community. Socrates and Glaucon are agreed at the outset of the argument for tripartition of the soul that each of us has this characteristic, at least to some extent (435d9–436a3). The idea is presumably that every ordinarily constituted and developed human being is spirited, at least to some extent. This entails, among other things, that we all have a more or less vivid sense of what does and does not count as praiseworthy and respectable by the lights of our community, and also that we are all motivated to behave as that sense demands, at least to some degree, and to avoid acting in ways that would violate it.

Against this background and given Socrates' purpose at this stage in the argument, the Leontius anecdote is exquisitely chosen. Leontius' angry exclamation, addressed to his own eyes, dramatizes the frustration of his passionate aversion to

9. A good place to start is A. Hobbs, *Plato and the Hero: Courage, Manliness and the Impersonal Good* (Cambridge, 2000), 1–31.

the very course of action that at the same time attracts him irresistibly. Like the anger that wells up in him as he fails to maintain control over himself, the aversion that in the end is overcome by appetite is naturally and plausibly thought of as being intimately connected with Leontius' spiritedness. It is an aversion that springs from his awareness that gratifying oneself by gazing at the corpses would be an ugly and disreputable thing to do. That is why he feels disgust as he struggles with himself (439e8), and that is why he refers to the sight of the corpses, with grim irony, as a beautiful one.

## 4.3  Comments on the argument

It is worth noting that reason is not even mentioned in Socrates' analysis of the Leontius episode. Leontius is brought in to show that spirit is not, contrary to what Glaucon is initially inclined to think (439e1–4), an aspect of the appetitive part, but is a part of the soul distinct from appetite. For all that Socrates says, the rational part of Leontius' soul might have been entirely inactive, both at the time of conflict between appetite and spirit and when Leontius ran toward the corpses, impelled by appetite. Perhaps the idea is that Leontius' reason was incapacitated by intense emotion. Perhaps it did take the view that it is better to abstain and lent support to spirit's aversion.

In any case, there is no indication at all in the text that Socrates takes reason somehow to assist appetite in forming the desire that Leontius proves unable to control. Socrates' analysis treats appetite as being capable both of forming determinate, situation-specific desires and of getting a person to perform a certain action. The appetitive desire that overcomes Leontius is not a mere craving for pleasure or sexual gratification. It is a desire to take a close look at the corpses lying by the side of the road (439d7–8). All it takes for Leontius to start running toward the corpses is for this appetitive desire to overcome the aversion that resists it. Socrates goes on:

> Don't we often see in other cases, too, that when appetite compels someone contrary to reasoning, he reproaches himself and gets angry with that in him that's doing the compelling, so that of the two factions that are fighting a civil war, so to speak, spirit allies itself with reason? (440a9–b4)

It is part of the picture that appetite may find itself at war with the allied forces of reason and spirit, and that it may compel a person to act contrary to reason, much as Leontius' appetite compels him to run toward the corpses for sexual gratification. Again, this presupposes that appetite can by itself form determinate impulses to act in certain ways. This, in turn, requires that appetite is equipped with cognitive resources that enable it to apprehend suitably determinate and specific objects of desire.

That the psychological theory of the *Republic* treats even appetite as being equipped with considerable cognitive resources, such as are required for the apprehension of quite specific objects of desire, becomes perfectly clear at the beginning of book 9, when Socrates describes some of the lawless desires that arise in people while they are asleep:

> Then the brutish and savage part, full of food and drink, casts off sleep and seeks to find a way to gratify itself. You know that there is nothing it won't dare to do at such a time, free of all control by shame or reason. It doesn't shrink from trying to have sex with the person's mother, as it supposes, or with anyone else at all, whether man, god, or beast. (571c3–d3)

The Socrates of the *Republic*, then, takes even the appetitive part of the soul to be able to form impulses to do specific things, as well as to get a person to act in certain ways without having to be assisted in some way or other by the other parts of the soul. It is important, and has been duly stressed, that the psychological theory of Plato's *Republic* takes reason not to be inert but to have its own attachments and desires.[10] It is equally important that the theory takes appetite, and no doubt spirit as well, not to be blind but to have their own forms of sensitivity and cognition.

This is not to say, however, that appetite and spirit are equipped with the same cognitive resources as reason. For instance, there is good reason to think that Plato's theory takes neither appetite nor spirit to be capable of means-end reasoning.[11] To begin with, Socrates refers to the appetitive part as *alogiston*—that is, as being such as not to engage in *logismos* (439d7; cf. 441c1–2). In Plato's *Timaeus*, a later dialogue that restates the theory of the tripartite soul, the main speaker Timaeus says that appetite has no share in *logismos* at all (*Timaeus* 77b3–6). Since Plato treats straightforward cases of means-end reasoning as cases of *logismos*,[12] not engaging in *logismos* excludes engaging in means-end reasoning.

Moreover, if the nonrational parts of the soul can reason about how best to satisfy their desires, and can form desires and aversions on the basis of such reasoning, there seems to be no satisfactory way for Plato to rule out the simultaneous occurrence within appetite or spirit of both a desire and an aversion in relation to the same thing. For instance, having a burger right now may seem a very pleasant thing to do, but it may also seem an obstacle to one's full enjoyment of the exquisite dinner party one expects to attend in an hour's time. Suppose that appetite, on that basis, forms a reasoned aversion to having the burger now. If the person in question nonetheless continues to have a pleasure-directed desire to have the burger right away, that desire must belong to appetite.

Notice that we now have a situation that is relevantly like the example to which Socrates appeals in order to show the distinctness of reason and appetite (439b3–d2): a physiologically based desire for something or other and a simultaneous

---

10. Cooper, *Reason and Emotion*, 121–26; M. Frede, Introduction to M. Frede and G. Striker (eds.), *Rationality in Greek Thought* (Oxford, 1996), 5–7.

11. *Contra* (among others) J. Annas, *An Introduction to Plato's* Republic (Oxford, 1981), 129–30; Bobonich, *Plato's Utopia Recast*, 244.

12. For instance, *Republic* 553d2–4, 604d4–5; cf. *Timaeus* 30a6–b6, 33a6–b1.

reasoned aversion to the same thing. Socrates' argument presupposes that conflicts of this kind show that what undergoes the conflict, the soul or whatever it may be, must have at least two distinct parts, which constitute the conflicting parties. Furthermore, he takes the conflicting parties in question to be appetite and reason. This crucial step in his argument would be undermined if he thought that appetite by itself can form desires and aversions based on its own reasoning about how best to satisfy its desires. In that case, he would have no basis for holding that his first example of psychological conflict brings to light appetite on the one hand and reason on the other. It might equally well be taken to show the complexity of appetite. On the other hand, Socrates can reasonably hold that the example brings to light appetite and reason, if he takes reason, but not appetite, to be responsible for reasoned desires for, and aversions to, this or that as a means, or obstacle, to the achievement of some given goal.

The strongest prima facie support for the view that the *Republic* takes even appetite to be capable of means-end reasoning is that Socrates holds appetite to be a lover of money (or property) and profit, explaining that it is most of all through money that appetite's desires for food, drink, sex, and the like are satisfied (580e2–581a1). In saying this, he may have in mind that appetite loves money specifically as a means to the satisfaction of its primary desires. But the idea may also be that appetite tends to form and maintain an intense, pleasure-directed attachment to money itself, because it, more than anything else, provides access to the pleasures of eating, drinking, and the like; as a result, suitable psychological mechanisms bring it about that thoughts of money come to be intimately associated with thoughts of such pleasures.

Now, if appetite cared about money specifically as a means to the satisfactions of its other desires, that would make it hard to resist the conclusion that it is capable of at least basic means-end reasoning. But Socrates never says that appetite cares about money specifically as a means. In fact, he makes clear that his paradigmatic man of appetite, the moneymaker, loves money not as a mere means but in the pleasure-directed way that is characteristic of appetite. Comparing the philosopher, the honor-lover, and the money-lover in terms of how truly pleasant their lives are, he notes that the moneymaker will say that "the pleasure of being honoured and that of learning are worthless compared to that of making profit, if he gets no money out of them" (581c11–d3).

The moneymaker is endowed with reason and capable of means-end reasoning, of course. He knows that money is an effective means to the satisfaction of all sorts of pleasure-directed desires, and his interest in money no doubt rests in important part on his awareness of this fact. However, what Socrates says makes clear that the moneymaker's concern for money rests not only on his awareness that it is an effective means, the way one might care for some pills only because one knows that they are effective against headache. Socrates says that the moneymaker takes pleasure in making profit, the way an honor-lover takes pleasure in being honored and a lover of wisdom takes pleasure in learning. The thought is that the moneymaker is passionate about money and its acquisition in part because it is something that is, for him, in itself a potent source of pleasure. Moreover, Socrates holds that while the love of wealth is particularly prominent in the moneymaker, it is a psychological tendency that is to some degree or other present in everyone (435d9–436a3). This chimes in well with the fact that he takes money and profit to be among the canonical objects of appetitive desire and pleasure (581a3–7). In every ordinarily constituted and developed human being, Plato seems to think, appetite is at least somewhat attached to money as something that is, for it, in itself a source of pleasure. One thing this presupposes is that there are psychological mechanisms by which reason-endowed creatures, if they live in a suitable cultural environment and participate in suitable practices, will typically form attachments to money and its acquisition as things that in themselves give them pleasure.

The *Republic* does not offer anything like a systematic account of the psychological mechanisms that are at work when people form such attachments. Plato may well think that such attachments tend to be prefigured in early childhood, as people internalize the beliefs and values of the culture that surrounds them—for instance, by way of hearing the stories and myths in which those beliefs and values are given concrete expression. In his remarks about poetry in books 2 and 3 of the *Republic*, Socrates emphasizes that in the corrupt culture of his contemporary Athens, even young children are already busy absorbing false and damaging beliefs, including ones that are apt to turn them into people in whom the love of wealth is unduly prominent (390d7–391a2; cf. 377a11–b8). In this way, even young children may already find themselves with, say, the unreflective belief that wealth is a delightful and wondrous thing. Later on in their lives, as they begin to reason about how to achieve their various goals (note 441a7–b2), their own recognition that money is an effective means to the satisfaction of this or that appetite may not just provide their attachment to money with a new basis. It may also serve to reinforce their appetitive, pleasure-directed attachment to money, as it establishes fresh connections in their minds, and perhaps strengthens old ones, between money and various pleasant things that money can buy: delicious meals, fine wines, and so forth.

In any case, once one accepts that reason-endowed creatures, given a suitable cultural environment, will tend to form a pleasure-directed attachment to money, it is easy to see how the appetitive part of the soul can come to be attached to money and its acquisition, as Socrates evidently holds that it can do and, in fact, very much tends to do. Note that the formation and maintenance of such appetitive attachments does not require that appetite itself be capable of means-end reasoning or of recognizing that money is an effective means to the satisfaction of certain other desires it may have. It may well be the case that from appetite's own point of view, eating, drinking, having sex, making a profit, and the occasional bit of philosophizing or speechifying are all on a par: at the appetitive level, all of these activities seem attractive, if and when they do, simply because, at the time, they seem pleasant things to do.

## 5. DESIRE AND THE GOOD

The psychological theory of the *Republic* is a dramatic departure from the intellectualism of earlier dialogues. From the point of view of the later theory, it may seem as if the Socrates of the *Protagoras* and the *Gorgias* is blind to the fact that humans are not only driven to pursue whatever they take to be the good but also find themselves with desires and aversions that flow directly from their natural aspiration to distinguish themselves and from their equally natural anxiousness to maintain and enhance their social status, as well as from their natural and immediate attraction to what they perceive or expect to be pleasant and their equally natural and immediate aversion to what they perceive or expect to be painful.

But it is not only that the Socrates of the *Republic* sharply disagrees with the views expressed by the Socrates of the *Protagoras* and the *Gorgias* in holding that adult, ordinarily developed humans frequently find themselves with desires, even intense, pressing ones, for various sorts of things that they know, or anyhow believe at the precise time, it would be better for them to keep away from. This in itself would be a significant theoretical development and surely one to be welcomed as representing a cluster of important insights about the human condition. However, the Socrates of the *Republic* goes further beyond the earlier dialogues than this, by taking it that appetitive and spirited desires can by themselves get even adult, ordinarily developed humans to act in certain ways, either because the desire in question is not resisted by the person's rational part or because it overcomes any resistance that reason might put up. On this view, then, it is not just that not every human desire aims at the good or even at what seems to the person to be the good. It is also that not every human action aims at the good in either of these ways. It is a fact of human psychology, the Socrates of the *Republic* is committed to thinking, that adult, ordinarily developed humans are quite capable of doing things that they think are thoroughly bad, even at the precise time of action, all the while believing that a better course of action is available to them.

One thing this makes clear is that a much-quoted passage in book 6 of the *Republic* needs to be handled carefully. Many readers have thought that the passage restates at least a somewhat qualified version of Socratic intellectualism.[13] In that passage, Socrates says about the good that

> every soul pursues it and does everything for its sake. It divines that the good is something but is perplexed and cannot adequately grasp what it is or acquire the sort of stable beliefs it has about other things, and so it misses the benefit, if any, that even those other things may give. (*Republic* 6, 505e1–5)

It is worth noting that Plato's Greek in the first sentence quoted can quite naturally be interpreted as meaning that every soul exerts itself immensely for the sake of the

13. For example, G. Carone, "*Akrasia* in the *Republic:* Does Plato change his mind?," *Oxford Studies in Ancient Philosophy* 20 (2001), 132–35; M. Anagnostopoulos, "The divided soul and the desire for good in Plato's *Republic*," in G. Santas (ed.), *The Blackwell Guide to Plato's* Republic (Oxford, 2006), 181–83.

good,[14] rather than that every soul does whatever it does for the sake of the good.[15] On the first interpretation, Socrates is making the substantial claim that one thing that everyone is immensely concerned to obtain or promote is the good. This leaves it open that there might be things other than the good that people pursue and also that they sometimes do things without, in doing the thing in question, acting for the sake of the good. It thus leaves open the possibility that people sometimes do this or that without supposing that, in doing what they are doing, they are making progress in obtaining or promoting the good.

On the alternative interpretation, the claim is that everyone acts for the sake of the good in everything he or she does. In other words, people always do whatever they do because they suppose that doing the thing in question will conduce to obtaining or promoting the good, however they may conceive of it. But no one who has read book 4 with the care it deserves will be inclined to prefer this alternative interpretation to the other. For it is plainly part of the psychological theory that is presented and argued for in book 4 that people are capable of doing something or other not because they think that acting in this way conduces to obtaining or promoting the good, however they may conceive of it, but, for instance, because they are overcome either by a powerful pleasure-directed impulse or by an angry desire to retaliate or inflict punishment. In acting in such ways, people may do things that they themselves realize are seriously detrimental to their pursuit of the good, as they conceive of it.

Given the context of the *Republic*, then, Socrates' remark in book 6 about every soul's pursuit of the good is best understood as the claim that the good is something that every soul pursues and for the sake of which it exerts itself immensely. In saying this, the Socrates of the *Republic* is not reverting to the Socrates of the earlier dialogues. He is only highlighting the fact that even though the psychological theory of the *Republic* does depart dramatically from the intellectualism of earlier dialogues, it nonetheless preserves and accommodates what certainly is one of its central and most important commitments: that all of us, in virtue of being endowed with reason, are naturally oriented toward the good, no matter how misguided or confused our views about it may be.

# BIBLIOGRAPHY

Anagnostopoulos, M. "The divided soul and the desire for good in Plato's *Republic*," in G. Santas (ed.), *The Blackwell Guide to Plato's* Republic (Oxford, 2006), 166–89.
Annas, J. *An Introduction to Plato's* Republic (Oxford, 1981).
Bobonich, C. *Plato's Utopia Recast: His Later Ethics and Politics* (Oxford, 2002).

14.  On *panta prattein* at 505e1–2, see T. Irwin, *Plato's Moral Theory* (Oxford, 1977), 336 n.45.

15.  The notion of acting for the sake of the good is not explicated in the context of the remark in *Republic* 6. In the *Gorgias*, it is introduced as apparently equivalent to the notion of doing something supposing it to be better—better, that is, than not doing it (*Gorgias* 468b1–8).

Burnyeat, M. "The truth of tripartition," *Proceedings of the Aristotelian Society* 106 (2006), 1–22.

Carone, G. "*Akrasia* in the *Republic:* Does Plato change his mind?," *Oxford Studies in Ancient Philosophy* 20 (2001), 107–48.

Cooper, J. (ed.) *Plato: Complete Works* (Indianapolis, 1997).

———. *Reason and Emotion* (Princeton, 1999).

———. "Plato's theory of human motivation," in his *Reason and Emotion*, 118–37.

———. "Socrates and Plato in Plato's *Gorgias*," in his *Reason and Emotion*, 29–75.

Frede, M. "Introduction," in M. Frede and G. Striker (eds.), *Rationality in Greek Thought* (Oxford, 1996), 1–28.

Hobbs, A. *Plato and the Hero: Courage, Manliness and the Impersonal Good* (Cambridge, 2000).

Irwin, T. *Plato's Ethics* (Oxford, 1995).

———. *Plato's Moral Theory* (Oxford, 1977).

Moss, J. "Shame, pleasure, and the divided soul," *Oxford Studies in Ancient Philosophy* 29 (2005), 137–70.

CHAPTER 11

......................................................................................................

# PLATO'S ETHICS

......................................................................................................

## JULIA ANNAS

ETHICS, in the sense of a concern to act rightly and to live a good life, is pervasive in Plato's work, and so we find Plato's ethical thinking throughout the dialogues. Even the *Sophist*, whose major theme is the problem of being and not-being, examines this in the context of discovering what is distinctive about sophistry, which can corrupt our attempt to live well. For Plato philosophical inquiry, however far it may get from the immediately practical, is never detached from the framework of living a good, worthwhile life.

Ethical concerns are found in dialogues of the most varied types, from those in which Socrates shows other people that they fail to understand the claims they make about courage, friendship, or virtue to those in which he, or another person, gives long, sometimes uninterrupted speeches on a variety of topics. And we find ethics treated sometimes on its own, sometimes in political contexts, and sometimes in a framework of metaphysical theorizing.

Given this, it is clearly always important, when examining Plato's ethical arguments, to pay attention to their role in the dialogue in which they occur. Nonetheless, it is legitimate to extract ethics, as a subject, from the dialogues and to outline a Platonic theory of it. Differing as they do between dialogues, his discussions of ethical concerns do fall into patterns which can be brought together and seen to have a distinctive structure. In antiquity, Plato is (apart from fragmentary ideas in Democritus) the first philosopher to form a tradition of specifically ethical theory. We find recurring themes, which Plato can reasonably be seen as the first to unify into a recognizably ethical theory. This, of course, does not exclude noticing differences between dialogues, and some of these are best explained as suggesting changes of mind on Plato's part.

With some issues, it makes a large difference whether an interpreter takes there to be an overall development in Plato's thought or, rather, a continuing overall concern allowing for particular changes. In this chapter, I do not take a stand on this very contentious issue. The so-called Socratic dialogues in which Socrates displays what is wrong with the thoughts of others on virtue are often taken to be an early stage of Plato's thought, one in which he had not yet developed positive ethical views of his own.[1] They can just as well, however, be read as complementary, rather than prior to, the passages where Socrates puts forward positions in his own right, and this is how I read them, especially since they contain passages important for understanding the positive exposition. I will continue to refer to as "late" the dialogues generally so labeled, but nothing depends on chronological claims about these or other dialogues.

Plato's ethical thought begins, rather surprisingly, from something everyone accepts. We all seek to be happy; we seek everything for the sake of this, while we do not seek this for the sake of anything further.

> "Suppose someone . . . asked," says Diotima to Socrates in the *Symposium*. "Now, Socrates, the lover of good things has a desire; what does he desire?" "That they become his," I said. "And what will he get, when good things become his?" "That's easier to answer," I said. "He'll be happy." "It's by the possession of good things," she said, "that happy people are happy, and there's no need to ask the further question, "Why does someone want to be happy?" The answer has the final end." (*Symposium* 204e–205a).[2]

In the *Euthydemus,* in a passage famous in the ancient world as a "protreptic" to philosophy, Socrates and a young boy agree that it makes no sense even to ask whether everyone wants to do well and be happy; nobody would deny it. It is equally obvious that everyone thinks that they will be happy by having (and making use of) good things. The discussion proceeds from there, showing a deep difference between Socrates and conventional opinion on what things are good but leaving unchallenged the point that we all seek happiness (*Euthydemus* 278e–282d).[3]

Elsewhere, Plato is completely unimpressed even by unanimous common belief. Here, however, he does not, as elsewhere, find fault with it or challenge it philosophically. Rather, he holds that everyone is, indeed, on to something important; our problem is, rather, that our grasp of happiness is extremely dim. For most, if not all, people go radically wrong in their views about what things are good and thus about how we shall actually succeed in becoming happy. Much of Plato's

---

1. Some scholars take these dialogues to present positive "Socratic" views which differ from "Platonic" views in dialogues such as the *Republic,* taken to be later.

2. All translations are my own. I am very grateful to the large number of excellent contemporary translations of Plato that have become available in the last two decades.

3. At *Philebus* 20b–23a, 60a–61a, Socrates puts forward as obvious the ideas that a good life must meet the conditions of being complete (we seek it for its own sake and not for the sake of anything further) and self-sufficient (it lacks nothing we have reason to seek). As with the other two passages, Plato takes it that nobody would deny this, so that no argument is needed. See Daniel Devereux's essay on Socratic ethics, chapter 6 in this volume, for a more detailed treatment of the *Euthydemus'* eudaimonistic framework. For the importance of this framework, see G. Vlastos, *Socrates, Ironist and Moral Philosopher* (Cambridge, 1991); T. Irwin, *Plato's Ethics* [*Ethics*] (Oxford, 1995); and J. Annas, *Platonic Ethics, Old and New* [*PEON*] (Ithaca, N.Y., 1999). For a dissenting view, see N. White, *Individual and Conflict in Greek Ethics* (Oxford, 2002).

effort in discussions of value is devoted to improving our views about goodness and thus about what things are good.

Why does Plato take most people to be drastically wrong about goodness but not about happiness? Might we not expect him to take the sorry state of most people's views about goodness to show that they are no authority on happiness, either, or its place in the way we think about our lives? Given Plato's radically anti-commonsensical approach to metaphysics and epistemology, why is the framework of his own ethical thinking found in the few passages where we can be confident that he is telling us what most people actually think?

The answer here lies in the notion of happiness, which is how we have hitherto rendered *eudaimonia*. Since "being happy" in these passages is treated as interchangeable with "doing (or acting) well," it obviously does not fit closely onto the predominant modern notion of happiness. What the ancients took us uncontroversially to be seeking in everything we do is something achieved over life as a whole, not a feeling or episode, as happiness is often now construed. Importantly, for the ancients, *eudaimonia* is itself a highly indeterminate notion. That everyone aims at *eudaimonia* leaves open that there are many divergent and, indeed, mutually incompatible ways of so doing. In noting the fact that everyone agrees that *eudaimonia* is our universal aim, Plato does not recognize any great achievement on our part. We cannot go wrong because what we agree on is so indeterminate that there is extreme disagreement as to how to achieve it.

Plato's ethical thought is, then, structured by a broad eudaimonist assumption. His main concern is to challenge the views most people have about goodness, for it is here that they go disastrously wrong in trying to live happy lives. Most people think that virtue is a minor good, or even an impediment to living a happy life. Plato thinks this utterly wrong; it is *only* by being virtuous that we can hope to be happy. This is a radical claim, one that demands that we reject a lot of things intuitively considered needful for happiness, and can on its own seem to reconceive happiness on theoretical grounds. But Plato is in fact never prepared to pull happiness away from the intuitive idea that the happy life is a pleasant one. His preoccupation with virtue is matched by a preoccupation with pleasure and its relation to virtue. The main lines of Plato's ethics are thus best followed by doing the following: looking at his theoretical answer to the question about virtue and happiness, then examining the way he discusses virtue, and then exploring his positions on pleasure. I shall conclude by looking at the relation of Plato's ethics to his political and his metaphysical thought.

In the *Euthydemus* passage already mentioned, Socrates gets the young boy Cleinias to list things most people would take to be good and thus components of a happy life: health, beauty, power, status, and the like; he includes the virtues but gives them no particular prominence. Socrates argues him into accepting that there is a crucial difference between virtue and all these conventional goods. The value of conventional goods in a life is conditional on their being used wisely, as a craftsperson makes wise use of her material in producing the results of her skill. Thus there is a radical distinction among things that we call good: no conventional good will do what we expect of a good—namely, benefit us and so make us happy—

unless it is put to proper use by the kind of wisdom that will make us good. A similar distinction is drawn in two passages of the *Laws* (631b–d, 661a–e) between human goods—health, beauty, strength, and wealth—and the divine ones, the virtues, on which they depend. For both a city and an individual, the goodness of, and so the benefit from, conventional goods depends on the possession of the virtues, which depend, in turn, on the wise use of reason.

Clearly, Plato is making the point that most people, who think that they will achieve happiness by becoming rich, or famous, or powerful, are fundamentally mistaken and need to revise their priorities radically. As Socrates tells his fellow Athenians in the *Apology*, they are wrong to care for wealth, for wealth does not bring about virtue, whereas "from virtue wealth and all other things become good for people, both privately and publically" (*Apology* 30a–b). But what exactly is the relation between living virtuously and being made happy by having health and wealth?

Once raised, this question dominated ethical philosophy; ethical theories were differentiated by their answers to it. Plato does not distinguish between two distinct positions clearly separated by later debate. Plainly, he always thinks that being virtuous is necessary for *eudaimonia*. Happiness cannot be a matter of how wealthy, good-looking, or powerful you are; it must lie in what we do with these things in our lives. If we take them as our ultimate goals, we have no hope of being happy; without the divine goods, every person and city loses the human ones, too (*Laws* 631b–c). Plato's position, however, allows of two interpretations, both with textual support.

One is that, while conventional goods do not make us happy independently of virtue, they can make a virtuous life better. Thus in the *Euthydemus,* we find that the correct account of conventional goods is that "if ignorance guides them, they are greater evils than their opposites . . . ; but if practical intelligence and wisdom are the guides, they are greater goods" (281d). And in the *Laws,* the Athenian says that "although what are called evils are in fact evil for the just, they are good for the unjust; and what are called goods, while actually good for the good, are evils for the evil" (661d). This may seem commonsensically appealing: if a virtuous person with chronic disease is cured, it seems obvious than her life has become better just by acquiring health. The consequence is very uncommonsensical, however: that if you are vicious, you are actually better off being poor and ill than rich and healthy—indeed, it is best for you also to be stupid and deaf (*Euthydemus* 281b–d). The claim that the value of conventional goods in a life depends on the use to which they are put commits Plato to thinking not only of health, for example, as making a good life better but also as making a bad life worse, by providing more opportunities for the wicked person to live wickedly.

Sometimes, however, Plato claims that virtue is the *only* good thing. "[Of the other things,] none of them is either good or evil, but of these two, wisdom is good and ignorance evil" (*Euthydemus* 281e). Hence virtue, being the only thing which is good, and thus of benefit to us, will be sufficient for happiness. The only correct account, says the Athenian, is the one that insists that "the good man, being temperate and just, is happy and blessed, whether he is big and strong or small and weak, rich or poor; and thus that even if he is richer than Midas . . . but is unjust, he is miserable and lives wretchedly" (*Laws* 660e–661a). On this view, nothing besides virtue should properly be called good at all (and the same for evil and vice).

These two positions have different implications for the role in the happy life of health, wealth, and power, later called external goods or goods of fortune, implications which Plato does not distinguish. Plato notably does not face a problem which would have forced him to make a distinction: How, if nothing but virtue is good, can the virtuous person have a reasonable basis for selecting among other things? If health does not make a virtuous life better, why should the virtuous person bother trying to be healthy? In practice, much of what Plato says about virtue and happiness suggests that health and wealth, while they cannot in themselves make us happy, do make good lives better, suggesting the weaker interpretation. Yet the language of some of the more uncompromising passages about virtue shows that later Stoics had a point in claiming affinity with Platonic ethics:[4] often, Plato suggests that there is such a gulf between the kind of value that virtue has and the kind found in conventional goods that we would be wrong to think that we should just care *more* about virtue than we do; we need a complete change of perspective on value. To do justice to Plato's ethical thought, we need to find both positions in the dialogues and to recognize that they are not distinguished and often juxtaposed.[5]

Uncompromising insistence that we need to change utterly to be happy chimes with many passages where Socrates asserts radical ethical positions most people reject (though he claims that if they submitted to Socratic questioning, he could show them that they do, deep down, believe them—*Gorgias* 471e–472c). A good person cannot be harmed (*Apology* 41c–e); other people can unjustly accuse and execute him, as happened to Socrates, but if he is virtuous, this does not harm him. If you cannot live virtuously, there is nothing to be gained by staying alive; life in itself has no value for you (*Crito* 47d–48a). Doing wrong is worse for you than suffering wrong (*Crito* 49 a–d; *Gorgias* 472d–476e); it is so much worse that if you do wrong, the best thing for you is to seek out punishment for it (*Gorgias* 476a–479e). It is irrelevant to a person's happiness whether he is rich and powerful, only whether he is wise and good (*Gorgias* 470c–471a).

There is a reason why these passages became famous in antiquity: they give us a stark choice between conventional views of happiness and an utterly different perspective. The starkness of the choice shocks us into asking whether we are, as Socrates thinks we are, committed to this extreme divergence from convention.

4. Antipater, one of the heads of the Stoa, wrote a three-book work claiming that Plato converged with the Stoics on many points, particularly in taking virtue to be the only good, and sufficient for happiness. Annas, *PEON,* argues that this is a reasonable interpretation of Plato's ethical thought overall. See Irwin, *Ethics,* for interpretations, particularly of the *Republic,* defending the weaker view.

5. Hence there is debate whether the evidence supports scholars who take the stronger view to characterize dialogues taken to be early and the weaker view to characterize later work.

The stronger claim, that virtue is sufficient for happiness, is marked in the *Apology, Crito,* and *Gorgias.* In the *Republic* we find it too, but not distinguished from the weaker claim. The *Republic* is structured as an answer to the question, how one ought to live (*Republic* 344e). Glaucon and Adeimantus make a challenge to Socrates, which he answers, referring back to it at the end of book 9 (366d–367e, 588b–592b). He is challenged to show that virtue[6] is worth having "in itself" and for what it does for us "in itself," as opposed to external rewards which could equally well be obtained from a successful cynical pretense. The challenge is put in two forms, juxtaposed but not equivalent.

Glaucon describes two extreme cases: the virtuous person who suffers every misfortune, including that of being traduced as wicked, and the wicked person who successfully puts up a front of being virtuous (360e–362c). In the case of the virtuous person, virtue has been stripped of everything that it could possibly owe to appearance and pretense; and so when we ask whether it is in our interests to live justly, we can appeal only to what virtue can do for us by its own nature. Socrates is challenged to show that even in the worst circumstances the virtuous person is happier than the wicked person (361d). This is compatible with the virtuous person not being *happy* in terrible circumstances, only happier than he would be were he not virtuous. The argument proceeds by way of Plato's sketching the structure of an ideal society, whose structure exhibits the same form as the virtuous person's soul; those brought up in such a society, Plato claims, would be completely virtuous and, so, happy. In such a society virtuous people would, it appears, be happy because they are virtuous in circumstances where virtuous people have circumstances organized for them to flourish. It looks, therefore, as though Plato is claiming that, while virtue is necessary for a happy life, it is not sufficient, since the virtuous are happy only in a society where they have favorable external circumstances. Still, even in the worst circumstances of the actual world, the virtuous person will always be happier than the wicked, however favorable the circumstances of the wicked.

Other passages in the *Republic,* however, appear to defend the claim that virtue is sufficient for a happy life. In the very passage where the challenge is posed, Socrates states it in terms of virtue simply benefiting you and being in your interests (367c). And when Socrates refers back to this challenge at the end of the main argument, this is the claim defended. It is in your interests to be virtuous, it has been argued, because this is best way for your soul to be organized, without reference to your being in ideal or in actual circumstances (588b–591b); indeed, the virtuous person will be concerned with conventional goods and evils only insofar as they conduce or the reverse to their being in this internal state (591b–d). The happiness of the virtuous in the ideal state is thus not a part of Socrates' answer to

---

6. The *Republic* is about *dikaiosunê,* often translated "justice," since part of the argument concerns the ideal society, but the main argument concerns the individual, where "justice" may be misleading and "virtue" is a safer rendering.

the challenge to show that being virtuous is in your interests even in the worst conditions of the actual world.[7]

At the theoretical level of ethical thinking, then, we find that Plato does not have a single determinate answer to the question whether virtue will make us happy; for he does not distinguish between the claim that being virtuous is sufficient for living a happy life and the claim that it also needs favorable circumstances, although even in the worst circumstances, it will render you happier than the most prospering wicked person. The sufficiency claim can reasonably be seen as lying behind the most uncompromising claims by Socrates in some dialogues, but it is blurred with the weaker claim in Plato's best-known work, as well as in the passages where he comes closest to the kind of theoretical discussion of virtue and happiness that we find from Aristotle onward.

Even the weaker claim conflicts dramatically with the conventional assumption that health and wealth contribute to happiness in their own right. We find Socrates continually calling into question ordinary assumptions about virtue. This is a two-pronged attack. Positively, Socrates develops a conception of virtue in which it is taken as having the structure of a practical skill, accepting the prominence this gives to the cognitive and intellectual elements in virtue. And negatively he shows a variety of people with such strong views about virtue that they do not comprehend what they are talking about, since they cannot "give an account" (*logon didonai*) of virtue or a given virtue. What they fail to provide is the kind of ability to explain and justify what they are doing which is typically found among those with mastery of a practical skill. The positive and negative approaches work together.

In the *Euthydemus*, virtue was readily identified with mastery of a productive skill, and, although it sometimes surprises modern readers, the idea that being virtuous is like having mastery of a practical skill is quite intuitive. Becoming good is learning to act well, as a skilled person does things well; in both cases, what is exercised is practical knowledge, which has the feature that it is normally learned from someone who can convey expertise to the learner, while also requiring of the learner that she come to master the relevant field of activity for herself. Where practical expertise can be conveyed, we have more than a natural talent or happy "knack"; we have a cognitively structured way of thinking. The impetus for Plato's "intellectualist" account of virtue thus comes from virtue's sharing with practical skill familiar features of practical reasoning.

Plato engages with the skill analogy for virtue in a variety of ways. Virtue is practical, thus a matter of getting down to the task of living; Socrates' anxiety about his fellow citizens' drift and lack of concern for living well is an urgent one. What they need to do, he insists, is to start paying attention to themselves; they need to exercise *epimeleia*, proper attention and diligence (*Apology* 29d–30b). One entire

---

7. In the bulk of the *Republic*, there are many passages suggesting the stronger, sufficiency thesis: for example, 387d–e, 472b–e, 427d, 444e–445a, 580c, 613a–b. Irwin, *Ethics*, and Annas, *PEON*, give different interpretations of these passages.

dialogue, the *Alcibiades,* is devoted to this point. The young Alcibiades is confident of happiness, backed as he is by looks, wealth, and influence. Socrates convinces him that all these apparent advantages are utterly worthless until he begins to pay attention to himself. Alcibiades comes to see that he needs to get working on his own lazy and self-satisfied state before he can understand virtues like justice and their importance for happiness. The historical Alcibiades did not do this; he went spectacularly to the bad. The reader is encouraged to do a better job of paying attention to his own deficiencies.[8]

Living virtuously is, in the light of the skill analogy, thought of as actively living in a way which is the product of exercising your own intelligence, taking charge and working at living with a clear overall goal in view, rather than drifting along with uncritical views of what matters in life. The skill analogy emphasizes the cognitive side of virtue: the ability to learn how to perform a task, to figure out how to respond to diverse situations, and to explain what you are doing—all analogous to what mastery of a practical skill requires.

The kind of understanding required to be virtuous emerges from the *Laches,* where Socrates turns a discussion of the educative value of fighting in armour into an examination of two generals' understanding of courage. (One of them, Nicias, remarks that a conversation with Socrates inevitably turns into an examination of your own life (187e–188b).) Laches begins by characterizing courage as standing firm, and then, more widely, as endurance, but fails to grasp the kind of understanding we require in endurance that we admire. Nicias then suggests that courage *is* a kind of understanding. This is found intuitively bizarre, but the objection which sinks it is that if courage is a kind of understanding, it cannot be limited to its intuitive area, that of what is and is not to be feared. A right understanding of what is to be feared requires understanding what is to be feared or not in general, at any time; and to know in general what is worth fearing amounts to knowing what in general is valuable; and this kind of understanding would amount to virtue, not just one aspect of it, as courage is usually taken to be.

Whatever puzzles the reader is supposed to take away from this dialogue, we can see here the force of the thought that what underlies a virtue is practical understanding—the ability to discern and to respond to what is truly valuable—and that this will be something all the virtues will share. An account of virtue which starts by taking it to be cognitively rich will tend toward some form of the unity of the virtues.

It is then no surprise that in other dialogues various interlocutors are shown by Socrates that they fail to understand what they think they know about virtue. In the dialogues named after them, Euthyphro fails to understand piety, Charmides and Critias fail to understand temperance, Meno fails to understand virtue, and Hippias fails to understand the fine or *kalon,* what virtuous people aim at.

8. The notion of "care" here is dominant in the interpretation of Plato, particularly his use of the figure of Socrates, in the work of Hadot (for example, P. Hadot, *What Is Ancient Philosophy?* (Cambridge, Mass., 2002).

In all these cases, the interlocutors fail because they cannot "give an account" of what they think they know; they cannot explain what it is nor justify their own judgments about it. Their failure is persistently likened to failure to possess mastery of a practical expertise. In the case of virtue it involves a failure to appreciate that having a virtue involves more than just learning from society how to behave, even reliably, in certain contexts. This kind of piecemeal socialization may leave the person with no clue as to its point and hence no way of linking in his understanding the different circumstances in which the virtue is exercised. Coming to understand what virtue, or a specific virtue, is, thus requires, if it is to pass the test of "giving an account," an ability to give a unifying and explanatory account of actions and reasons over your life in general, not merely in one area conventionally associated with, say, courage or virtue. In the virtuous person's reasonings, virtue is dominant over her life as a whole, in a way that unifies her priorities over a variety of different circumstances. The virtuous life has the kind of unity characteristic of the product of expertise (*Gorgias* 500e–501b), suggesting the metaphor used by Stoics and later Platonists of virtue as the skill of molding the material provided by your circumstances into a life unified by its overall achievement of *eudaimonia* by way of virtuous activity.[9]

In the *Protagoras,* we find that this kind of distinctive way of thinking about your life might be amenable to some degree of formalization. The sophist Protagoras has expounded his own view: that people are socialized into virtue the way they pick up their native language. Socrates pushes him into discussing the idea that it might, rather, be something more like a precise expertise, "the skill of measurement." He also introduces the idea that what we are trying to measure is pleasure and pain (a controversial move we shall return to). Socrates develops the idea that what will "save our lives," make us able to live securely whatever life faces us with, is a skill which will measure the pleasures we want and the pains we want to avoid, objectively, in a way that avoids our bias toward what is here and now, as well as our bias toward favoring what presents itself or "appears" to us as appealing or unappealing at a given moment:

> The power of appearance confuses us and often makes us take and then regret the same things back and forth in our actions and choices of both great and small things, while the art of measurement would have taken authority from this appearance and, by showing us the truth, would have given us peace of mind resting on truth, and would have saved our lives. (356d–e)

The *Protagoras* is the only dialogue in which Plato even entertains the idea that pleasure might be an adequate final goal for our lives, and he is careful to have Socrates introduce it merely as a thesis to be discussed. But the wider thought has continuing appeal for him: that our lives should be lived in a way unified by pursuit

---

9. The development of the idea of skill (*technê*) in Plato is well set out in P. Woodruff, "Plato's Early Theory of Knowledge," in S. Everson (ed.), *Epistemology: Companions to Ancient Thought,* vol. 1 (Cambridge, 1990), 60–84.

of an overall final goal that has objective value, a pursuit to which we have to be summoned away from our tendency to be misled by the power of "appearances," the way things attract or repel us. Living well requires us to reject being at the beck and call of our likes and dislikes and the ways things affect us, and to organize our life overall in a way that has objective value. For Plato, it is always our reasoning powers which enable us to do this, and to counteract our tendency to follow our desires, which are fixated on their own fulfillment in a way unresponsive to wider concerns. To varying degrees in different dialogues, he is open to the idea that this achievement of our reasoning powers might ultimately be, or rest upon, thinking that is rigorous and precise beyond the achievement of everyday arguing of the Socratic kind—indeed, as rigorous and precise as that of mathematicians.

In the *Gorgias*, living a good life requires imposing on our life the kind of structure that an expert imposes on her materials to come up with a unified product; there are hints, however, that it requires a deeper kind of understanding of a formal, even mathematical kind (507c–508a). In the central books of the *Republic*, Plato explores the idea that a proper grasp of ethics requires profound mathematical and metaphysical study, which takes years to acquire. But, despite the different level of background demanded, the basic thought remains constant: we come to live virtuously by coming to have overall understanding, expressed in practice, of what is worth pursuing as our aim in life; achieving this is difficult and requires detaching ourselves from caring about the kinds of desire that most people invest most of their time and energy in gratifying. It is no surprise, then, that Socrates shows his interlocutors that where virtue is concerned, they have little or no idea what they are talking about; the kind of understanding that virtue really requires demands attention and effort that most people are not prepared to put in, and puts you at odds with most people's views of what life is all about and what is worth doing and having (*Gorgias* 485a–e).

Grasping what is truly valuable in life will, then, pull us away from uncritical identification with the satisfaction of our desires for particular things and our pursuit of what we find appealing. How radical is the required detachment? Plato does not have a single answer to this. Throughout a good part of his work, he is tempted in two different directions on this, and this leads him to conceive of the dominance of reason in the life of virtue in two discrepant ways, both powerfully presented.

The first account is most memorably put forth in the *Republic*, where the virtuous person is the person whose soul is rightly ordered. In this and some other dialogues,[10] Plato distinguishes three parts of the soul—reason, spirit, and desire—rather than simply contrasting reason with desire, but this does not alter the general point made here. Each part has its proper function; that of reason is to rule, since only it can discern what is good for the whole soul, whereas the other parts

---

10. *Timaeus* and *Phaedrus*. There is considerable scholarly discussion of the differences, if any, made to other central ethical claims by the tripartition of the soul. C. Bobonich discusses the issue in depth in *Plato's Utopia Recast* (Oxford, 2002). See also Hendrik Lorenz's essay, chapter 10 in this volume.

can register only what is attractive to them (441d–443e). Reason's rule does not imply that the other two parts should be repressed but, rather, that they should play the parts assigned to them by reason, given its superior understanding of what is good for the whole which the parts make up. Thus reason aims not to extirpate desires but to bring it about that they are fulfilled only in ways which encourage, rather than conflict with, the overall pursuit of goals set by reason (588b–591b).

Famously, there are two ways in which the obedience of the other two parts to reason is construed, each reflected in metaphorical descriptions of the person. One is that of education.[11] The parts of the soul can agree, in a harmonious way, and thus are taken to be capable of the kind of communication that is capable of agreement and disagreement, as opposed to blank conflict of mutually uncommunicative forces. Plato develops the idea that desire and spirit, in particular, which in actual societies are recalcitrant in accepting the conclusions of reason, can, in principle, and in ideal conditions, be formed and, if necessary, reformed, by education of varying kinds, ranging from the attractive to the coercive. This depends on the thought that reason and the nonrational parts of the soul share enough by way of cognitive structure that communication is possible (442c–d, 443c–444a, 586c–587a). It also depends on the thought that nonrational aspects of ourselves are plastic and can be successfully molded by social forces. This assumption underlies the highly transformative program of education in the early books of the *Republic* and becomes explicit in the similar program of the *Laws,* where even sexual desires are taken to be so plastic that a regulated society could eliminate same-sex sexual attraction (838a–841e).

The other way of construing the dominance of reason over other parts of the soul is in terms of force. Reason is a stronger kind of item than the nonrational parts of the soul; they cannot grasp what reason can, but the kind of force that reason can produce is more effective than what they can bring to bear. This idea is often expressed by representing reason as a little person within the whole person whose good it alone discerns, the other parts being represented as nonhuman animals, which reason is capable of controlling. This produces Plato's most famous metaphors: the soul as inner person controlling beasts and as a chariot whose rider controls two powerful horses (*Republic* 588b–589b; *Phaedrus* 246a–e, 253d–256e). Clearly, reason and the nonrational parts do not on this construal share enough cognitive structure for communication and agreement to be possible.

These are not only different but mutually incompatible ways of thinking about reason's dominance in the soul. That Plato does not clearly make up his mind between them shows that he continues to be drawn both by the thought that good psychological functioning is a matter of putting into practice, in differing ways, shared overall principles of organization, and by the thought that, even in ideal psychological functioning, there are elements which are potentially resistant to overall organization and direction and thus have to be coerced. In the *Phaedrus*

---

11. On Plato's complex views about education, see Rachana Kamtekar's essay, chapter 14 in this volume.

passage, the bad horse pleads and argues with the other horse and the charioteer but is deaf (253e, 254c–e)! As has often been pointed out, Plato's ambivalence here reflects his ambivalence as to whether the producer class in the *Republic* fit their assigned roles unconstrainedly or whether force is always needed to keep them from usurping the rule of the Guardians.[12]

There is a second picture of virtue as reason's dominance in the soul: reason's exercise reveals to us the utter insignificance of human life. If we take this seriously, we become detached from all worldly things. In the *Phaedo*, Plato vigorously stresses that to achieve grasp of the Forms, the philosopher must "practice dying" (64a); he must detach himself from the everyday way in which we identify with our beliefs and, especially, our desires. Relatedly, true virtue does not deal with the matters of everyday life but consists in an escape or "purification" from them (69a–d).

On this austere construal, virtue consists not in dealing with the material circumstances of life but in rising above them, aspiring to living a life in which they have no part. A life free from the encumbrances and drawbacks of the human condition is the Greek idea of the life of the gods, and Plato does not hesitate to say that a life of virtue, construed as fleeing or being purified from the everyday world, is a life which is godlike or aspires to become like god. The most famous statement of this is in the "digression" in the *Theaetetus,* where Socrates says that human life must unavoidably contain evil, "so we should try to flee from here to there as quickly as we can; and flight is becoming like God to the extent that we can. And becoming like God is becoming just and pious, with wisdom" (176a–b; cf. *Republic* 612e–613b).

In these passages, flight to escape our world rests on the sharp metaphysical and epistemological divide between the world of our experience and the true world of the Forms revealed to the person willing to use his mind in a rigorous way and pursue lengthy courses of mathematical and dialectical thinking.[13] We cannot, however, miss the point that grasping what is transcendent to our world renders us aware of the insignificance of human concerns. In the *Laws*, this awareness of insignificance comes with awareness of God rather than Forms (644d, 803c–804c).

In the later dialogues, the idea of the individual's becoming like god is found in another context: the idea that reason in the person is a small-scale version of what reason is in the cosmos as a whole (*Philebus* 28c–30e). Reason's function continues to be that of unifying and ordering, and thus living our own lives in a rational way comes to be seen as participating in the large-scale workings of reason in the cosmos, which is seen in different ways in the later dialogues (as a causal element in the world in the *Philebus,* as the rational plan of a divine Craftsman in the *Timaeus,* as the rationality of a cosmic soul in the *Laws*), but always as divine. The work of the divine reason is to organize things for good, since the divine is good and,

---

12. The relation between the partition of the soul in the *Republic* and the structure of the ideal state is much disputed. G. R. F. Ferrari, *City and Soul in Plato's Republic* (Sankt Augustin, 2003), is a recent contribution to this debate.

13. It is controversial how determinate is the idea of the objects of such thinking in the *Theaetetus* passage, and hence how appropriate it is to call them Forms.

lacking envy, seeks to spread goodness in the way it orders things. Becoming like God thus comes to be construed as aspiring to identify with the goodness-producing works of the divine reason, which makes it less surprising that this is a characterization of virtue. Virtue continues to be seen as imposing rational order on potentially refractory materials, but this is linked to, rather than contrasted with, transcendent divinity.[14]

These two construals of "becoming like God" are not unified in Plato's thought. We can see how they might be put together. The flight idea stresses our need to detach from everyday thoughtless engagement with our everyday world and to recognize a new kind of value, by comparison with which our everyday values are dross. This is then followed by the realization that we respect this new kind of value by identifying with its workings in the cosmos and cooperating, as far as we can, in its functioning; in our own lives, this consists in living in a way in which this value is dominant in our lives, and reflection shows us that this is what the life of virtue is. Stoic ethics brings these two ideas together, stressing both the distinctive nature of virtue's goodness and the way in which we honor its value in the way we live our lives, and setting this in a cosmic rather than specifically political framework. We can thus agree with the Stoics that their ethical ideas converge with Plato's, even though they reject his transcendental understanding of the divine and of reason in the world.

Plato's various claims about virtue all have in common that virtue is either the only or the dominant element in a life which can achieve what we all dimly grope for—happiness. We might expect, given these strong claims, that he would defend a much reconfigured view of what happiness is, one in which the role of pleasure is reduced or even eliminated. But we find that, for Plato, pleasure presents a continued invigorating challenge to his ethical thinking, producing a variety of spirited responses. In the ancient world, this was taken to show that Plato was the source of a whole range of later theories of pleasure; modern scholarship has tended to use the differences between the accounts to support a variety of accounts of Plato's alleged overall development.[15] Plato's engagements with pleasure show us different responses in his continuing concern with the central issue of how we are, through living a virtuous life, to achieve *eudaimonia,* which is happiness, and thus in some way satisfying and enjoyable.

In some passages, pleasure appears as what we seek by fulfilling our desires, where these are taken to be paradigmatically short-term urges for fulfillment. In the *Gorgias, Philebus,* and the treatment of pleasure in *Republic* 9, this goes with the idea that pleasure is the replenishment of a lack (*Gorgias* 492e–495a; *Philebus* 42c–47d; *Republic* 585b–586b). Standard examples are hunger, thirst, and sexual need: these are natural to the kind of beings that humans are, and will in the normal course of things standardly recur. If we accept this picture of pleasure, it is clear

14. For a recent development of this aspect of the idea, see J. Armstrong, "After the Ascent: Plato on Becoming Like God," *Oxford Studies in Ancient Philosophy* 26 (Summer 2004), 171–83, criticizing Annas, *PEON,* and D. Sedley, "The Idea of Godlikeness," in G. Fine (ed.), *Plato,* vol 2 (Oxford, 1999).

15. We find the ancient claim in Aulus Gellius *Attic Nights* 9. 5.

why it would be a mistake to seek pleasure as our overall end. For pursuing pleasure will simply be a matter of filling the lacks coming from our recurring needs to eat, drink, and so on. This is not an organizing principle for a life, but simply a way someone might drift through life, reacting to the pressures of felt need but never giving her life overall direction from within. Only reason can provide the organizing power to get the person to focus on an end which will give the life a shape. Thus it is rational organization, not the fulfillment of desires, which should shape our lives.

Plato makes the significant claim that having reason give overall direction does not lead to a loss of pleasure, as the pleasure-seeker might fear. The overall dominance of reason will stop or inhibit the fulfillment of many desires which without it would just have gone ahead, so the person will lack many pleasures which she would otherwise have had. But this should not be construed as a lessening of pleasure, since it is crucial for the happiness of a life what *kind* of pleasures are had.

> So when the entire soul follows the philosophical part, and there is no civil war in it, it comes about that each part does its own work and is just, and in particular each has enjoyment of its own pleasures, the best and truest pleasures it can have. . . . But whenever one of the other parts gets control, it comes about that it cannot even discover its own pleasure, and it compels the others to pursue a pleasure that is alien to them, and not true. (*Republic* 586e–587a)

Behind this picture lies Plato's conviction that our capacity to have pleasure is plastic and can be formed and, if necessary, re-formed, by education and training of various kinds, ranging from teaching and practice to punishment. This conviction underpins, as we have seen, the educational programs of the *Republic* and *Laws;* the latter work especially focuses on the differences between kinds of pleasure and our capacity to be educated to enjoy activities and entertainments quite different from those we start with. Legislation and social opinion have brought it about that people not only stifle incestuous desires but do not feel frustrated by this and, indeed, are appalled by the thought of finding incest enjoyable; Plato claims that the same could be true of homosexual sexual desires (*Laws* 838a–841c). Similarly, he thinks that a rightly ordered and focused educational program could produce citizens who not only perform the approved songs and dances that they are taught but unforcedly enjoy them and feel no need for innovation, the young enjoying the same songs and dances as the old (652a–660c). Much of Plato's confident authoritarianism in political matters rests on his conviction that our capacities for enjoyment are plastic, as well as on his conviction that firm understanding is possible on the issue of what humans ought to enjoy if they are to lead happy lives.

Hence alongside passages which stress the dominance of virtue we find passages, sometimes surprising to the modern reader, such as: "We choose less pain with more pleasure, do not choose less pleasure with more pain and when they are equal find it hard to be clear about what it is we want." Pleasure and pain influence our wishes, and so our decisions, because of their "number, size, intensities, equalities and the opposites." "Since things are thus ordered," we desire a life in which pleasure predominates over pain, whether the feelings are frequent and intense or few and weak: "We should regard our lives as all being naturally bound up in these; and therefore if we say that we wish for anything beyond these, we are speaking as a result of some ignorance and lack of experience of lives as they are" (*Laws* 733b–d). Plato sees a problem here, which is soluble once we realize that most people have little clue about which activities are really pleasant. It is the task of education to change people's priorities so that they find living virtuously to be their overriding aim in life. In giving up attachment to their pursuit of pleasures they may think that they are losing out, but they find themselves mistaken; the virtuous life turns out to be the most pleasant they could lead.

In the light of this thought, we can see why some of Plato's discussions of pleasure treat it as a competitor with our aspiration to be virtuous, while others claim that the greatest pleasure comes from being virtuous. Plato is not confused here; he is developing the view that pleasure is not a feature of your life independent of your activities and the value these have. People whose characters differ will take pleasure in different things; and Plato holds that some of these, the virtuous, are right and the others wrong. Hence his continuing detailed concern with the education of enjoyment and the censorship and filtering of culture this requires. Aiming at happiness in the right way, by living virtuously, will bring it about that you find a different way of life, and different activities, enjoyable, and reveal to you that your previous view of what activities were pleasant was profoundly mistaken.

Plato also thinks, interestingly, that conventional understandings of pleasure actually lead to underachieving it. Most people take pleasure to be nothing more than release from pain (an idea obviously linked to the thought that it is a replenishment of a lack). But, then, most pleasures will be "mixed" with pain: experiencing the pleasure of drinking when thirsty will involve being aware of the disappearance of the thirst, for example. Plato vehemently denies that this exhausts the nature of pleasure. It is not true of pleasure, he holds, that it is simply release from pain; the claim that it is comes from limited experience and reflection. In dense and fascinating passages of the *Republic* and *Philebus,* he argues that pleasures which depend for their pleasantness on release from pain are "false" and "impure." Pure pleasures are those which do not rely for their pleasantness on any release from pain and thus will not come from filling lacks or needs:

> There are many others, but a particularly good example to notice are the pleasures of smell. They suddenly become very intense without your having had any preceding pain, and when they cease they leave no pain behind.
> (*Republic* 584b)

The *Philebus* adds the pleasures of experiencing pure colors, shapes, and sounds, not to be confused with the pleasures of enjoying these as representations of something. Plato also adds the pleasures of learning, which do not rely on release from any pain (*Philebus* 51e–52a). Pure pleasures enhance and improve the state of freedom from pain, without being more of whatever produces that (*Republic* 584c–585a).

Epicurus later defended the position that the extreme of pleasure just is freedom from pain (bodily and mental), a state he identified with "tranquillity." Plato already takes this to be inadequate as an account of all that pleasure contributes to the happy life. One of the most fascinating aspects of Plato's ethical thought is his combination of a rigorous insistence on the dominance of virtue in a happy life, and the dominance of reason in virtuous living, with equally tenacious insistence not only that the happy life is pleasant but also that pleasure forms a positive contribution to it.

Clearly, the account of pleasure in the *Protagoras* is not part of Plato's general project of locating the place of pleasure in the happiness achieved by a virtuous life. In that dialogue, the assumption is that pleasure can be a final goal in a way that pays no regard to the values of the people seeking it, something quantifiable without regard to the activities in which pleasure is taken. I have suggested that in the *Protagoras* Socrates puts the idea forward just in the service of a larger argument. If, however, Plato does want Socrates to be committed to this view of pleasure, and does so because he is himself committed to it, the *Protagoras* illustrates a change of mind from his predominant view of pleasure.[16]

Happiness, virtue, and pleasure are in most of the dialogues in which they figure discussed in the context of an individual life, but in Plato's two longest and most magisterial works, *Republic* and *Laws,* the happiness of the individual's life, and the role in it of virtue and pleasure, are set in an ideal society, one that in the *Republic* is lightly sketched and in the *Laws* thoroughly, indeed ponderously, worked out.

In one way, Plato's thoughts about the individual's happiness are unaffected by this. As we have seen, there are continuities in the argument about happiness and virtue in the *Republic* from the *Apology, Crito,* and *Gorgias.* Plato clearly, when writing the *Republic,* thought that the argument that an individual lives happily only by living virtuously is given additional support by his analogy of individual and state, which shows that virtue has the same form in both. For, given this, virtue in soul and state cannot be adequately understood merely by studying only one of them; it requires a more abstract level at which the virtue which is studied will be applicable to both. Hence the ethical argument remains but is supported by discussion of the ideal state and of the Forms which both state and soul exemplify.

The context of the ideal state does, however, serve to enable Plato to develop his views on education of character. In both *Republic* and *Laws,* he sets out a program where individuals are, from infancy onward, to be socialized and educated in ways that encourage attraction to virtue and repulsion from vice. In both dialogues, Plato goes into some detail as to how the culture of his time will have to

---

16. For a recent treatment of pleasure in Plato's work overall, see D. Russell, *Plato on Pleasure and the Good Life* (Oxford, 2005).

be modified to do this, in ways that lead to large-scale censorship and rethinking of the contemporary arts. Thus Plato needs to show us individuals as citizens of a society in order to show us the kind of education and formation that would make us virtuous, and so livers of pleasant and happy lives.

Do we, however, need the *ideal* state to make this point? Could Plato not have noted the importance of education for character and left the reader to think of the appropriate development? He seems to be thinking that we will not fully understand either the power or the importance of education in the formation of character unless we are given a *good* example, and for this we need the ideal state. This also serves to weed out the irrelevancies that any example of non-ideal education would bring along.

Some features of Plato's political thought have dominated consideration of his ethics—in particular, the elitism defiantly present in both his longest works. In the *Republic,* Plato insists that the individual's life must be ruled by reason, his or her own if it is adequate, but that otherwise

> in order that someone like that should be ruled by what is similar to what rules the best person, we say that he should be the slave of that best person who contains within himself a divine ruler. It is not for the harm of the slave that we think he should be ruled . . . but because it is better for everyone to be ruled by divine intelligence, preferably his own that he has within himself, but otherwise imposed from outside, so that as far as possible we may all be alike and friends, steered by the same thing. (*Republic* 590c–d)

Since Plato thinks that only a very few people will have adequate reason, properly trained, this means that for most people the living of their lives will be structured largely by the deliberations of others. Only a few, then, will be living lives which are virtuous in a way that depends on their own thinking. If we take it that the living of an ethically good life excludes such radical dependence on another's thinking, then Plato is excluding all but a few from living a genuinely ethical life. The *Republic,* however, is a sketch of an ideal state based on the principle of rule by those with ideal understanding, and Plato is clear that in the actual world nobody can come up to this standard. This aspect of the ideal society is thus not part of the main argument that any individual in the actual world will be happy by being virtuous even in the worst possible conditions. The elitism of the ideal state is not part of a practical political proposal about the actual world (a point that has been frequently misunderstood).

This does not get rid of all legitimate worries about Plato's elitism, however. The *Laws* depicts a society which is ideal but in which there are no longer the *Republic*'s huge divisions of understanding among the citizens. All of them will be educated in the same way, will live in fairly egalitarian circumstances in which extremes of wealth and poverty will be avoided, and will live under institutions which encourage them to see themselves as members of a community of equals taking turns at ruling and being ruled. But this community whose efforts are so strenuously devoted to making themselves virtuous itself depends for its conditions of existence on the labor of others who are sharply kept outside that community, the resident aliens and slaves who do the work that enables the citizens to enjoy the leisure to educate themselves. Plato never envisages a community in which all are equal members of the entire functioning community, and so it can reasonably be argued that his conception of the individual's virtue is always based on the assumption of this being supported by someone else's labor and efforts. There is thus a serious and ineliminable elitism even in Plato's more egalitarian ideal state. His conception of virtue always requires leisure and education, which has to be supported by the work of others.

This is important, for it is an ironical result for a philosopher who insists so strongly[17] on the irrelevance for happiness of material goods, bodily well-being, and social goods like status. It was left to the Stoics to see that insisting on the sufficiency of virtue for happiness leaves us with a conception of virtue that does not actually require for its exercise circumstances of leisure or the specific context of the Greek city state, and thus does not require the exploitation of others who are thereby excluded from the pursuit of virtue and happiness.

It is also in the *Republic* that we find Plato's ethical position in the context of perhaps his most striking and elaborate presentation of Forms. As with the political background, there is a sense in which this does not make a profound difference to the ethical ideas that have already been developed in other contexts. Plato always takes virtue to require an overall grasp of what is good to take as a guide for one's life as a whole, and takes this to be an objective matter which requires intellectual effort. As between various dialogues, his view differs as to how much such effort is needed and what form it takes. This varies in stringency from mastery of a practical skill to mastery of mathematical and dialectical thinking that requires years of effort. The increased intellectual demand comes from putting ethics in the larger context of metaphysics, where a different range of intellectual skills will be required.

The metaphysical background is itself not something which itself remains static as a background to Plato's ethical thinking. In the later dialogues, as already touched on, the individual's life is related to the workings in the universe of divine reasoning. In our small way, each of us tries to do in our own life what cosmic reason does in the universe as a whole: organize things for the better to the extent that we can. In some ways, this metaphysical picture makes the larger whole of which we are parts less remote than Forms; ethics is seen in the dynamic larger whole of the cosmos rather than being located on the far side of a lot of mathematics and abstract reasoning.[18]

In other ways, however, the picture makes us, as individuals, smaller, since, though the important educative and sustaining role of society continues, the individual's basic ethical relation is with the cosmos and with others in the cosmos.

17. Though not always consistently, since Plato does not clearly distinguish between the weaker and stronger positions about the relation of virtue to happiness (see above, pp. 270–73).

18. Mathematics is still needed in order to discern the regular and mathematically comprehensible structure of the universe, as the *Laws* insists, but the dialogue also suggests a certain division of intellectual labor between the experts and the rest of the citizens.

This is another way in which Plato, at least in the later dialogues, can be seen as a precursor of the ethics of the Stoics. It is a notable difference, however, that Plato never envisages the kind of cosmopolitanism which we find in Stoic ethics, in which we are related ethically to all rational humans and the context of the city-state recedes in importance. Plato's stress on our relation to the cosmos coexists with a continued and, indeed, in the *Laws,* strengthened insistence on the crucial importance of the culture of the city-state in developing and sustaining the individual's ethical development.[19]

# BIBLIOGRAPHY

Annas, J. *An Introduction to Plato's Republic* (Oxford, 1981).
———. *Platonic Ethics, Old and New* (Ithaca, 1999).
———. "Wickedness as Psychological Breakdown," *Southern Journal of Philosophy* 43 (Supplement, Spindel Conference 2004) (2005), 1–19.
Armstrong. J. "After the Ascent: Plato on Becoming Like God," *Oxford Studies in Ancient Philosophy* 26 (Summer 2004), 171–83.
Bobonich, C. *Plato's Utopia Recast* (Oxford, 2002).
Ferrari, G. R. F. *City and Soul in Plato's Republic* (Sankt Augustin, 2003).
Gill, C. "Plato and the Education of Character," *Archiv fuer Geschichte der Philosophie* 67 (1985), 1–26.
———. *Greek Thought, Greece and Rome.* New Surveys in the Classics 25 (Oxford, 1995).
Hadot, P. *What Is Ancient Philosophy?* (Cambridge, Mass., 2002).
Irwin, T. *Plato's Ethics* (Oxford, 1995).
Kahn, C. *Plato and the Socratic Dialogue* (Cambridge, 1996).
Kraut, R. (ed.) *Plato's Republic, Critical Essays* (Lanham, Md., 1997).
Russell, D. *Plato on Pleasure and the Good Life* (Oxford, 2005).
Santas, G. (ed.) *The Blackwell Guide to Plato's Republic* (Oxford, 2006).
Sedley, D. "The Idea of Godlikeness," in G. Fine (ed.), *Plato,* vol. 2, Oxford Readings in Philosophy (Oxford, 1999), 309–28.
Taylor, C. C. W. "Platonic Ethics," in S. Everson (ed.), *Ethics: Companions to Ancient Thought* vol. 4 (Cambridge, 1998), 49–76.
Vlastos, G. *Socrates, Ironist and Moral Philosopher* (Cambridge, 1991).
White, N. *Individual and Conflict in Greek Ethics* (Oxford, 2002).
Woodruff, P. "Plato's Early Theory of Knowledge," in S. Everson (ed.), *Epistemology: Companions to Ancient Thought,* vol. 1 (Cambridge, 1990), 60–84.

19. I am grateful to Gail Fine for helpful comments.

CHAPTER 12

# PLATO ON LOVE

## RICHARD KRAUT

## 1. *ERÔS* AND *PHILIA*

Two families of Greek words, each with its distinctive semantic content, can properly be translated as "love." On the one hand, there is the verb *philein* and its cognates (*philia* is the noun, *philos* the adjective)—a word we use all the time when we talk about philanthropy, philosophy, philharmonic, and the like. On the other hand, "to love" is also the proper translation of the verb *eran* (*erôs* is the name of this psychological force, *erastês* designates a lover, and *erômenos* is the one who is loved). Those Greek terms are of course no less familiar to us than the "phil..." family: from them we have "erotic," "erogenous zones," and so on. Although our terms "erotic" and "sexual" are by no means interchangeable (a depiction of sexual organs, for example, need not be erotic), no discussion of the place of eros in human life could possibly ignore sexual desire and sexual activity. Similarly, Greek texts that concern *erôs*—the subject of Plato's *Symposium*, and one of the central topics of *Phaedrus*—must address themselves to sexuality, though they can encompass far more than that. *Erôs*, unlike *philia*, picks out a type of desire that drives people, under certain conditions, to physical contact—to touch, to kiss, to embrace, to "make love"—and also to think obsessively of the person who is loved and to be filled with longing when he or she is absent.

But *philia* is not necessarily low in affect. Although it can be applied to nearly any group of cooperative associates, it is the word that would most naturally be used to name the strong feeling and close relationship that exists among family members and also among close friends, whether or not they are sexually attracted to each other. To call two people *philoi* is to suggest neither that there is nor that there is not an erotic component to their relationship.

So there is no semantic oddity in the thesis, which Plato endorses (sec. 4 below), that there is *philia* in the best kind of erotic relationship. He does not single out sexless relationships for special commendation—although we will see how such a misreading of his thought might arise. To call a friendly relationship that is devoid of sexual attraction or interaction "Platonic," as we often do, is therefore to misrepresent him. On the contrary, he is especially interested in sexually charged relationships and is aware of their potential to do great good—though also great harm. One of his principal motives, in writing about *erôs*, is to teach us how to make that distinction.

For the best and fullest discussion of *philia* in antiquity, we should turn not to Plato but to Books VIII and IX of Aristotle's *Nicomachean Ethics*. But there is a remarkable gap in those books: Aristotle sees no need to say much about *erôs*, for he assumes that his theory of *philia* can be applied to those bound together by sexual love no less than to those who are "just friends." He remarks at one point that when *philia* is strong, it can be felt toward only a few people, and then he adds that *erôs* is an extreme form of *philia*, because it is felt toward one person (IX.10 1171a10–12). The sexuality of *erôs* (as opposed to its intensity and narrow focus) has little interest for him, as a philosophical writer.

We would have to say the same about Plato, had he written only *Lysis*, but not *Symposium* and *Phaedrus*, for there is hardly a word about *erôs* in this short work (widely assumed to have been composed before the other two). Instead, it searches but does not find a proper account of *philia*. The problems it raises about that notion have nothing to do with *erôs* but apply to all *philoi* whatsoever—whether or not their relationship is erotic. But Plato, unlike Aristotle, is fascinated by *erôs*. He considers it a subject from which philosophers have a great deal to learn and upon which philosophy can cast much light. His greatest contributions to the study of intimate human relationships, which are contained in *Symposium* and *Phaedrus*, have to do with *erôs* and with *philia* only insofar as erotic relationships should involve *philia* as well. He does not have, as Aristotle does, a robust and systematic theory about *philia* in its own right. Instead, he offers us, in his *Lysis*, a series of puzzles about *philia*; and then, in *Symposium* and *Phaedrus*, a series of contrasting speeches about *erôs*. The heart of his theory of intimacy, affection, and sexuality lies in those speeches.[1]

Every Platonic dialogue presents its own riches and difficulties of interpretation. Readers of his *Symposium* cannot be criticized for paying special attention to the speech delivered by Socrates (that is the approach I adopt here), for it is reasonable to suppose that this is the most important segment of the dialogue—the one that contains the correct theory of love, which Plato himself accepts and recommends to his readers. That supposition can be supported by the fact that the

---

1. For further study of the speeches of these two dialogues, I recommend G. R. F. Ferrari, *Listening to the Cicadas: A Study in Plato's Phaedrus* (Cambridge, 1987); C. Griswold, *Self-Knowledge in Plato's Phaedrus* (New Haven, Conn., 1986); and R. Hunter, *Plato's Symposium* (Oxford, 2004). Valuable discussions of both works are presented by T. Irwin, *Plato's Ethics* (New York, 1995), 298–317; and M. Nussbaum *The Fragility of Goodness: Luck and Ethics in Greek Tragedy and Philosophy* (Cambridge, 1986), 165–233. A comprehensive treatment of *Lysis* is offered by T. Penner and C. Rowe, *Plato's Lysis* (Cambridge, 2005).

speech within that speech—particularly the ascent to the form of beauty described by Diotima—fits hand in glove with the metaphysical scheme propounded in such other dialogues as *Phaedo*, *Phaedrus*, and *Republic*. The middle books of *Republic* are an especially close match to the ascent Diotima prescribes in *Symposium*, for there too we are told about the process by which a philosopher-in-training will be led to a great discovery: the form of the good. But however important the speech of Socrates is for an understanding of *Symposium*, Plato must want his readers to pay careful attention to the other speeches as well—to see how they bear on each other, complementing each other in some respects but conflicting in others. Similarly, although the party-crashing of Alcibiades adds immeasurably to the dramatic impact and comedy of the dialogue, we must ask ourselves what that denouement has to do with the content of the other speeches. Can it be that Plato gives the final word to Alcibiades because his encomium contains some corrective to what has gone before? The problem of understanding *Symposium* as a philosophical work is in part a problem of seeing how all of its material hangs together.

*Phaedrus* creates rather different obstacles. It seems to be a work about two subjects—love and rhetoric—and yet it contains a theory of composition that insists that every discourse must contain an organic unity, each part contributing to a larger organizational plan (264c). Plato is apparently prodding his readers to ask themselves what the principle of organization of this dialogue is. In this essay, I must bypass that question and so give short shrift to *Phaedrus* (though see secs. 9 and 10) in order to concentrate on Diotima's speech.

## 2. *Erôs* and Desire

The centrality of Diotima's ascent (210a–212b) in the scheme of *Symposium* is undeniable, but some of the ideas it contains cannot be understood on their own, since they build on earlier material. For our purposes, the best place to begin an examination of this dialogue (if that is the right word for it) is the passage in which Socrates, by cross-examining Agathon (199e–201c), shows that there is a close connection between *erôs*, desire, need, and futurity. More precisely, when someone loves (*erai*), there is something or someone he wants and, therefore, something or someone he needs and lacks. Plato realizes that this thesis requires defense, and so he has Socrates show Agathon that apparent counterexamples to it can be redescribed in ways that make them conform to it. We say: "I want to be healthy, and I have what I want." But can we really mean what this seems to mean? If I already am healthy at the present time, what would be the point of wanting to be healthy at the present time? A desire is a motivator; its role is to move us to do something. Properly understood, then, when someone who already is healthy says, "I want to be healthy," he should be taken to mean that he wants to continue to be healthy. He wants to have his health in the future, but that is something that he does not yet have. He lacks and needs future health.

*Erôs* is characterized here as a desire. That does not mean that whenever someone wants something, he loves it. The relationship goes in the other direction: whenever someone loves, he wants. This thesis says nothing about what kind of desire one has, when one loves. It may be a desire that Plato would locate in the appetitive part of the soul, but it need not be. The word Plato most often uses for desire in this passage, as so often, is *epithumia*. But an *epithumia* can be any sort of desire—it is not necessarily an "appetitive" desire for food, drink, or sex.[2]

Plato might be accused of making a mistake here: people can want things that have nothing to do with themselves, and so desiring is not the same thing as needing and lacking. Suppose I want someone else's needs to be fulfilled. That does not show that *I* have a need or a lack. If I act on my desire, that is not because I need or lack something but because someone else does.

Perhaps this criticism of Plato can be sustained. But even if it can, it does not reveal a defect in his conception of *erôs*. Whether or not there are desires that reflect no need or deficiency in the subject, what matters to Plato, in *Symposium* and *Phaedrus*, is the distinctive psychological phenomenon that goes by the name of *erôs*. He can insist that *this* type of desire always arises out of the subject's needs, even if he were to concede that other desires might not.

# 3. Birth in Beauty

Let us pick up the thread of the conversation several pages later, where Diotima, in her cross-examination of Socrates, insists on a connection between *erôs* and good. Up to that point, it is assumed that the object at which *erôs* is directed is beautiful—or, at any rate, is taken by the lover to be beautiful. Agathon claimed in his speech that love is never of ugliness but always of beauty (197b), and that assumption is allowed to stand in Socrates' conversation with him (201a–b). But then Diotima asks Socrates a series of questions about the relationship between *erôs* and good, and this interchange eventually leads to the thesis that "*erôs* is wanting to possess the good forever" (206a11–12).[3] Is Plato here inviting us to infer that because

---

2. See, for example, *Republic* 431d1, 554e1, 580d7, 587b1–4. Plato's division of the soul into three parts (reason, spirit, appetite) is most fully presented and defended in *Republic* 435e–441c, but, to understand what spirit and appetite are, it is important to read his critique of defective political regimes and their corresponding character types in 545a–580a. His conception of the rational part of the soul and the values with which it is associated are contained in his depiction of philosophical training in Books VI and VII. A helpful introduction to this subject is provided by H. Lorenz, "The Analysis of the Soul in Plato's *Republic*," in G. Santas (ed.), *The Blackwell Guide to Plato's Republic* (Malden, Maine, 2006), 146–65.

3. There is no word corresponding to "wanting" in the Greek text, and so a translation that mirrors only what is on the page would be "*erôs* is of the good to be one's own forever." But the insertion of "wanting" is justified by the context. See 204d5, where one of Plato's several terms for "want" (*erai*) is used to express a similar idea, and the conversation then moves back and forth between this and several other such terms (*bouletai* at 205a3, *epithumia* at 205d2). I am grateful to Tushar Irani for discussion of these passages.

290 THE OXFORD HANDBOOK OF PLATO

goodness is the object of love, beauty is not—that beauty has no bearing on *erôs*? That would be too great an about-face.

It is more plausible to take him to mean that the relation between love and beauty is not quite as simple as Agathon and Socrates had been assuming (206e2–3). The object of one's desire, when one loves, is always something that is good—but it is never claimed, during the remainder of the dialogue, that it must be something beautiful or taken to be such. Diotima insists (204e–205d) that each person's desire for the goods that he equates with happiness (the ultimate object of desire: 205a1–3) should be classified as *erôs*, and that since everyone wants happiness, everyone should be classified as a lover, despite the fact that this term (*erastês*) and its cognates are normally reserved for only one kind of love—the kind that consists in "making love" (as we would put it). Diotima is complaining that ordinary ways of using *erôs* and related terms are arbitrary and should therefore be reformed. Someone who loves money, or wisdom, or sports is no less a lover (*erastês*) than someone who seeks sexual intercourse, even though that term is normally reserved for lovers in the conventional sense (205d). The Greeks use *philein* rather than *eran* to talk about the love of philosophy (*philosophia*) or sport (*philogumnastia*), but Diotima sees no reason to avoid the semantic field of *erôs* to describe our passion for these activities.

Presumably, then, she would also say that it is arbitrary to deny that a parent is an *erastês* of his children or to insist that his feeling for them is *philia* but not *erôs*. That would not commit her to saying that parents should have sex with their children but only that *erôs* and kindred terms should be applied more broadly than common usage allows. Note that since Diotima drops Agathon's idea that the object of *erôs* must be taken to be beautiful (206e2–3), she would not be forced to concede that in having *erôs* for their children, parents find them beautiful, alluring, or attractive.

The thesis that "*erôs* is wanting to possess the good forever" is obviously an extension of the point Socrates makes in his discussion with Agathon. What someone who loves health desires is not that he be healthy now but that he be healthy in the future. If health is part of his conception of happiness, surely he will want to be healthy not just for some short period of time but for a very long one—in fact, indefinitely into the future. Being mortal, he cannot have his health for as long as he would like, and so his love of health leads to the pursuit of some approximation to his possessing health eternally. This is the thought process that lies behind Diotima's thesis that every lover seeks "birth in beauty"[4] (206b7–8)—the striking formula by means of which she allows beauty to be readmitted to the theory of love. She draws on the assumption that as sexual beings we cannot help being responsive to beauty (206c–d) and that the outcome of this responsiveness,

---

4. The Greek term translated "birth," *tokos*, applies both to a process and its product: that is, both to giving birth and to the child. Diotima immediately explains herself by ascribing to all human beings a desire to go through the process (*tiktein*, 206c4), but she also uses her theory to explain our love of children, both those made of flesh and blood and those composed of ideas (see, e.g., 208b and 209c–d).

in sexual intercourse and pregnancy, is the production of a new generation that extends the lives and often the projects of its forebears.

She then (208e–209e) broadens the basic ideas of her theory by elaborating on the notion that someone can be pregnant in soul and not merely in body. Someone who loves wisdom and justice, for example, cannot possess these qualities forever, but even so he can get closer to this goal by inculcating them, through reasoning and education (209b–c), in the next generation, which will, in turn, reproduce its virtues in others. In this way, one can come as close as mortality allows to the eternal possession of what one takes to be good. But, Diotima insists, one cannot do this in the absence of a sense of beauty (209b). Just as the desire for sexual intercourse is aroused by the sight of physical beauty, so the desire to give birth to discourse in the education of a younger person is aroused by some perceived beauty in that person's soul.

She even applies her theory to animal reproduction: *erôs* exists among these winged and many-footed creatures as well (207a–d). She is not merely making the obvious point that they copulate. Rather, her idea is that for them sexual activity serves a purpose that they know nothing about: the production of a new generation and, therefore, membership in a chain that extends without end into the future. She might even be assuming that they too are responsive to beauty—if her statement that "it is impossible to beget in ugliness, but only in beauty" (206c4–5) is meant to be exceptionless. Animals do not have a conception of happiness or good, but if the thesis that "*erôs* is wanting to possess the good forever" (206a11–12) is meant to apply to them as well, then the good that they want forever must be life itself.

What of human beings who are not pregnant in soul but only in body? Is Diotima saying that the function—whether acknowledged or not—of their sexual intercourse, like that of all animals, is the eternal possession of life itself? Perhaps, but she must also make room in her theory for the fact that nearly all parents want to transmit their values to their children. If what they love (and what they therefore wish they could have forever) is not merely life but also money or health or sports, then they will do what they can to reproduce the love of these goals in their children. To have a simulacrum of life forever merely requires being part of an unending generative chain, but human beings can, in a way, also have health or wealth forever by giving to their children a passion for these goals and the resources needed for sustaining them. There is no reason, in fact, why Diotima should deny that ordinary parents (pregnant in body but not soul) might also love justice and virtue in general and try to possess these goods eternally by engendering this love in their children.

She also mentions a way of eternally possessing the good that bypasses sexual reproduction but falls short of the pregnancy of soul that issues in reasoned education. The great heroes of the past, she claims, sought honor and glory for their acts of courage and wanted to possess these goods forever (208c–e). They do not give birth to flesh-and-blood children or to reasoned discourse but, rather, to beautiful deeds, and if these are celebrated by poets whose words live on, then the fame they seek will live forever, as will the reputation of the poets who memorialize those deeds (209d). We seem to have here a threefold division that corresponds to the tripartition of the soul (into appetite, spirit, and reason) in Plato's *Republic*: appetitive people seek such low-level goods as eternal life, or eternal wealth, or eternal physical well-being; those who love honor in battle or a reputation for excellence—goods that Plato associates with the spirited part of the soul—can possess these goods eternally by being the subjects or creators of song; but the best sorts of people employ philosophical methods of reasoning to pass along a full understanding of what is good.

# 4. SELF AND OTHERS

*Erôs*, so conceived, is necessarily self-involved. Even when it is directed at another person, it nonetheless expresses a desire for the lover's own good. The self-involvement of *erôs* is implicit in the thesis that to love is to want to possess the good forever; for that must be taken to mean that to love is to want *oneself* to possess the good forever. But it must be emphasized that, according to Diotima, the self that is involved in all love is not genuinely single because it is ever-changing: the stuff of the body is constantly being replenished; new desires, beliefs, and habits replace old ones; and even knowledge depends on fresh memories (207d–208a). When the present self plans for the satisfaction of its desires, it is already reaching out to something that is merely similar to rather than identical to what it is now.

That, Diotima, claims, is why all living things care for their offspring (208b). An animal, she notes (207b), will die for her young out of *erôs*, and in doing so it obeys the law of nature that whatever ages seeks to replace itself with younger versions of itself (208b). Love of life (one's own life, that is) lies behind efforts to preserve not only one's own body and soul but also the lives of one's offspring. Similarly, if one loves justice—that is, if one wants it to be the case that one possesses this good forever—then one will not only see to it that one's future soul possesses this good but also look for ways in which other people who bear some similarity to oneself and will take one's place also possess this good. If one propagates what one loves by having and raising a family (that is, if one is pregnant in body but not soul), one will try to inculcate a love of justice in one's children. But Diotima claims that there is a superior way of wanting to possess the virtues eternally. Some are pregnant in soul rather than body; in other words, they have within them notions about justice that they want to expose to the light of public discourse, in the hope that they can create just conditions for others who will outlive them. There is something self-involved even in that moral drive, because its beneficiaries are thought of as extensions of the self and not utterly alien to it.

Diotima's conception of *erôs* is a far cry from the self-forgetting kind of love that cares only for others and is devoid of all thought of oneself—the kind that does not care whether it is I who helps others but only that they be helped by someone. That selflessness, whether praiseworthy or not, is rare among human beings and therefore accounts for very little of the good that they have achieved. By contrast, *erôs* as Diotima conceives it—a complex combination of self-involving and other-regarding motives—has great motive power and has achieved more impressive results. Although Diotima does not propose that we regard all humans as members of a single family, her theory of *erôs* does rest on the idea that some sense of likeness to others (and not only to blood relations) elicits a willingness to forego comforts, resources, and even life itself.

The idea that all human beings, when they reach a certain age, are pregnant in one way or another, either in body or soul, contains the suggestion that we all are overfull with self-love—in other words, that our love for something within us eventually leads to our dedication to something outside us, as pregnancy leads to the birth of a new individual who receives its mother's loving care. Here too, as in her reflections on the continuity of body and soul, Diotima finds a form of self-involvement in the love of other people. Her tacit assumption is that a mother loves her child because that child was once inside her. When she likens a poet's songs or a statesman's laws to their children (209d–e), she is drawing on the idea that those products were once inside their minds and is suggesting that they are loved at least partly for that reason.

But the main idea that she is driving at when she uses the metaphor of the pregnant soul is that the best form of love among two human beings is one in which there is reasoned discussion about *sophrosunê* (moderation) and justice—and presumably all of the other topics that Socrates loved to discuss (209a). In such a relationship, the *erastês* gives birth to ideas that have been within him for a long time by finding someone capable of philosophical discussion—someone who, in this sense, has a beautiful soul. Their relationship will be all the more intense if the *erômenos* is also physically attractive, although it is not necessary that he be so (209b). What they produce in their philosophical discussions, if it is nurtured well, will itself become a thing of beauty, for if a poem can be beautiful so too can other forms of discourse when the ideas in them fit together harmoniously. Diotima claims that the relationship between these two—the philosophical *erastês* and his *erômenos*—is a firmer love (here her word is *philia*) than parents have, because they have far more in common with each other than those whose only bond is their joint production of children (209c). It is important not to lose sight of the fact that these two philosophers love *each other*—far more so than many other couples do—and not only their discursive offspring, however beautiful their jointly produced philosophical theory may be. In this respect, at least, Diotima's theory of love has become familiar and widely accepted: couples who talk to each other about serious matters and arrive at a meeting of minds enjoy a better form of love than do those whose relationship rests on nothing but the physical attraction that initially brought them together and their responsibilities as parents.

Diotima briefly indicates, at one point, that the well-nurtured offspring of this philosophical couple has more to be said in its favor than its beauty and the way in which it binds them together. When she starts to explain the notion of the soul's pregnancy, she says that the offspring that it is most fitting for a soul to produce is wisdom and that by far the greatest and most beautiful form of wisdom is the one that organizes the affairs of cities and households—namely, justice and moderation (209a). This suggests that the beautiful product that arises from the discussions of a philosophical couple is not merely of interest and value to *them*—rather, it can also benefit the entire political community. The way in which two people love each other matters to everyone else, not only when the offspring of such love is a child who will enter the political community and affect it for better or worse but also when the offspring is a theory about how the community should arrange its affairs. Presumably, one of Diotima's reasons for claiming that this product of a pregnant soul is most beautiful by far is precisely the potential it has for improving the life of the whole city. Of course, the philosophical couple is unlikely to have had this motive for establishing their relationship. But Diotima's reason for thinking so highly of their bond has to do, in part, with the great good it can do for others, not only for them.

The communal benefits of the love felt by a male couple is a theme that enters Plato's *Symposium* almost from the start. It plays an important role in Phaedrus's encomium to *Erôs* (178d–179a); although it drops out of sight for a while, it returns in Diotima's speech, and she continues to dwell on it when she includes such civic founders as Lycourgos and Solon among her examples of individuals who love the products of their own minds (209d–e). We are briefly reminded once again of the connection between *erôs* and politics when Diotima describes the ascent to the form of beauty: the beauty of *laws* is one of the steps of her ladder, and that connection cannot be far from the reader's mind when Alcibiades crashes the party. It cannot be an accident that Plato chooses to bring the *Symposium* to a close by bringing on stage a *political* figure and that the theme of that last speech is the failure of his erotic pursuit of Socrates. Plato is perhaps suggesting that Alcibiades' failure to understand what *erôs* is and how to be an *erastês* is connected in some way to his larger failure in the political arena. I return to Alcibiades below (sec. 9).

## 5. Aristophanes and Diotima

The conception of *erôs* contained in the speech of Aristophanes (189d–193d) is, in some respects, the converse of the one that Diotima proposes. She conceives of the *erastês* as overfull—as containing within himself so much that he must, with the help of another, get it outside of himself. The additional life within him is reasoned discourse that can benefit another person of the right sort—the *erômenos* whose soul is beautiful—but, as we just noticed, it can be of value to the entire community as well. Throughout the duration of the relationship of these two friends, each continues to have a mind of his own; that, surely, is what enables their discussions to be worthwhile and capable of leading to a beautiful product. By contrast, Aristophanes takes love to be nothing but an effort to overcome the burdens of distinctness and separation. It is a sense of isolation that drives distinct individuals to want to meld into one and to do nothing for each other but embrace. For them, fusion, not sexual satisfaction, is the goal of physical contact; the satiation of their sexual desires happens to serve a useful purpose, in that it temporarily induces them to separate and attend to their quotidian tasks (191c). Their desire to eliminate all physical distance between themselves is an expression of a deeper longing to be melded into one body with one soul. This is the opposite of the Socratic inquiry that Diotima assumes will take place when the *erastês* educates his *erômenos*; it is the *un*examined life par excellence—the life of someone who wants nothing more than to lose his mind and to become one with the person he loves. Remarkably, the simple point that offspring of some sort—flesh-and-blood children, or psychological transformation—is the product of love is a matter of no significance for Aristophanes. He entirely ignores the political implications of his conception of *erôs*.

The Aristophanic lover is seeking one person in particular: the one to whom he was once joined. But, of course, neither Aristophanes nor anyone else believes that each of us was once literally joined to another half. When his allegory is interpreted, it must be taken to mean that although we long to be joined to some one person, there is no way to articulate why we long for fusion with precisely this person and no other. We just have a strong sense that *this* is the right person for us, and our longing to become one with him or her is a brute force that can have no justification.

But the unique appropriateness of the object of love is not an idea for which Diotima has any use. What a lover teeming with ideas is looking for is someone who can help nurture those ideas and turn them into something substantial, and beauty of soul consists in those qualities of mind that make someone a good conversational partner in this endeavor. A lover should have no trouble articulating the features of the person to whom he is drawn and whom he finds attractive. (Admittedly, he has nothing to say about why he finds certain *bodies* beautiful: he simply does.) Nothing Diotima says suggests that for each of us there is one uniquely appropriate partner in love. In fact, the multiplicity of suitable objects of affection is already implicit in Socrates' idea that to want something is to want all of the many future replacements for one's present self to have it. The "wide sea" of objects of love then becomes one of the themes of Diotima's description of the ascent to the form of beauty (210d4). If there is anything in her speech that provides an analogue to the one object of love that an Aristophanic lover seeks, it is the form of beauty. The *Phaedrus* has a great deal to say about the way in which *erôs* reunifies us with the forms that we observed when, in a previous life, we were able to see them far more clearly than we can now. So, some truth can be salvaged from Aristophanes' speech, but it must be transformed almost beyond recognition before Diotima can accept it.

# 6. THE ASCENT TO BEAUTY

We are now ready to examine the final stage of Diotima's presentation, in which she describes a series of steps by which a lover-in-training is educated and brought to the recognition of an "amazing beauty" and thereby to the achievement of the "goal" of his erotic education (210e4–5). At that highest point of the ascent, the lover arrives at an understanding of what beauty is (211c8–d1). That should be taken to mean that he can articulate and defend a theory that explains what makes all beautiful things beautiful. But Plato's way of talking about this unchanging object and its location at the pinnacle of a series of objects, each of which is beautiful, implies that the unchanging entity about which the fully educated lover achieves an understanding is itself a supremely beautiful object. It is pure, un-mixed, divine, uniform, and devoid of the great silliness that mars the beauty of human things; their beauty is a mere image of its true beauty (211e–212a). All of this suggests that the form of beauty, untainted by any imperfection, has a beauty that surpasses the sullied or short-lived appeal of all else. That is why the life of the lover who reaches this stage is greatly enhanced, so much so that it becomes godlike (212a). Not only can the lover explain why imperfectly beautiful things are beau-tiful; he has gazed on the greatest beauty of all.

The first step of this staircase (*epanabasmos*: 211e3) is to love one body and, in doing so, to beget beautiful ideas (*logoi*). The next step is to generalize—to rec-ognize that there are many other beautiful bodies as well and that there is something identical in the beauty of them all (210a–b). The outcome of this second stage will be that the lover-in-training's extreme fascination with the single body that occupied his attention during the first stage will diminish, and he will realize that this was a small thing (210b). Diotima does not say, in her all too brief description of the first stage, what the learner's words will be about or what their purpose is. Are they simply the lover's verbal depiction of the beauty of the person whose form he finds so alluring? Another question we wish Diotima had answered is how the transition from loving just one body to loving many is to be brought about by the teacher who is guiding this process (mentioned at 211c1). How does that guide induce the lover-in-training to broaden the field of things he loves? And what transpires between the lover and the one he loves (and later with the many)? We are perhaps given some help by an idea Socrates expresses in the *Republic*: an erotically inclined man will be attracted to many different physical types and not only to a few (474d–e). Pre-sumably, then, Plato thinks it will not be difficult, at least for someone who has a receptivity to physical beauty, to see what is alluring in bodies of different types and to put his appreciation of each type into words. The more difficult task that must be accomplished, to arrive at the second stage, is to describe what all of these kindred kinds of physical beauty have in common. That, of course, is a project akin to the one pursued in several of Plato's shorter ethical dialogues. Even if it is easy for someone to appreciate the allure of many different beautiful bodies, it is a task for philosophy to put into words the common element in them all.

Diotima never claims that the lover who has moved from the first to the second stage is no longer a lover of bodies. On the contrary, she says that he becomes "a lover of all beautiful bodies" (210a4–5). Presumably, that means that he recognizes and enjoys the perception of the beauty of any body that is beautiful. It is not the thing that all beautiful bodies have in common—the property they share—that is loved, but those concrete bodies themselves. Physical beauty is not to be treated as something that is entirely without value.[5] Rather, what occurs when the lover moves beyond the first stage of the ascent is a diminution in his extreme concentration on one body. He has become a lover of many things and is no longer transfixed by any one of them. He now sees how defective his initial response to beauty was because it excluded so much. These points are important to recognize because doing so keeps us from mistakenly supposing that in the ascent to the form of beauty the lover, as he moves from each stage to the next, stops loving and finding beautiful what he appreciated at some earlier stage. What the lover constantly learns as he ascends is that his outlook at each earlier stage was defective because it included too little. So, when he reaches the final stage and recognizes the greatest beauty of all, he does not stop thinking that other things—including bodies—are beautiful as well and responding affectively to their attractiveness. Their beauty may be small by comparison with that of the form of beauty, but they nonetheless participate in its beauty and because of that participation they too have some degree of beauty, however small.

Having arrived at stage two, the lover-in-training now moves up to a new ontological level by turning his attention to the beauty that a soul can have—a beauty that he should recognize to be superior to that of the body (210b). Here again Diotima tells us less than we would like to know. How precisely is this recognition achieved? Perhaps she is assuming that since the lover-in-training has been admitted to the mysteries of love because of his suitability he has the philosophical talent and character that will make it possible for an experienced guide to show him, through philosophical discussion, that having a well-ordered soul is far more important than having a good-looking body. It is better to have the virtues of the soul than those of the body—but best to have both kinds. Someone who can be persuaded of that can also be brought to place the beauty of a virtuous person in a higher order than the beauty of an alluring body.

Diotima does not explicitly say that the student of *erôs* will go through soul-loving stages that recapitulate the numerical difference between body-loving stages, but that is clearly what she has in mind. Having passed through stages one and two, the next step is to fix one's attention on one soul, to care for that one individual, and to give birth to the kind of discourse that can educate young minds (210c). Diotima then describes a number of other items—practices, laws, types of

---

5. Though some translations unfortunately imply as much. Thus the generally excellent translation by A. Nehamas and P. Woodruff, *Plato, Symposium* (Indianapolis, 1989), has Diotima say at 210c5–6 that the ascending lover thinks that "the beauty of bodies is of no importance." So too R. Waterfield's translation, *Plato, Symposium* (Oxford, 1994): "he comes to regard physical beauty as unimportant." The Greek, *smikron ti*—"something small"—does not imply that the lover's estimation of physical beauty sinks to zero. He never becomes completely indifferent to physical beauty.

knowledge—whose beauty the lover-in-training will come to appreciate. Just as he was able to say what made all beautiful bodies alike in their beauty, so too with these noncorporeal objects of appreciation. During these stages, the student of love is engaged in the study of politics; that is what is implied by Diotima's reference to practices and laws. He is not becoming a lover of many actual souls, for very few of the people he encounters will have beautiful souls, but he is inquiring into the ways in which the lives of all citizens might be improved, and in this respect he is recapitulating the transition he has already made—a transition from one to many.

In effect, the lover-in-training is becoming a student of political philosophy. Diotima calls him a philosopher when she refers to the "many beautiful words and thoughts" that he will beget in his unstinting love of wisdom (*philosophia*: 210d5– 6). Significantly, she never speaks of the lover-in-training who has reached the stage of political theorizing as someone who undergoes a loss of enthusiasm for the one beautiful soul with whom he discusses practices, customs, and branches of knowledge. She never hints that there is any defect in remaining, at every subsequent stage of the ascent, an *erastês* of one and only one soul—namely, the *erômenos* whom the lover fills with beautiful discourses about political matters. She criticizes Socrates (presumably she does not know him very well) and others for their obsessive desire to look at and be with young boys, and she associates this with a fascination with gold and clothing (211d), but in doing so she is merely elaborating on her earlier critique of overvaluing the beauty of bodies. A beautiful *soul*, she implies, cannot be loved to excess—so long as one goes about loving that person in the right way.

Since Diotima claims that the form of beauty is the most beautiful object there can be, it might be inferred that the lover-in-training, having beheld that magnificent sight, has nothing further to do as a lover beyond continuing to savor his understanding of that supreme object. But that cannot be what she means, because it is a consequence of her theory of love that the earlier discourses constructed by the lover-in-training and his efforts to educate his *erômenos* were defective and therefore need to be improved. After all, this *erastês* did not know at those less than ultimate stages of the ascent what beauty is; his search for it was as yet incomplete. With his new understanding of beauty, he can now construct more beautiful discourses, and these will do a better job of explaining what makes laws well designed, which practices should be adopted, and which branches of knowledge should be studied.

That is what Diotima implies when she says, at the end of her speech, that someone who has seen the form of beauty will "beget not images of virtue . . . but true things" (212a3–4). There are more children, composed of words, to be nurtured. Surely the *erastês*, having seen and understood the form of beauty, will want to engage in conversations with his *erômenos* that will bring him to the same vision of beauty itself that he, the *erastês*, has had. The notional children they nurture together, as they reexamine laws and other social institutions in the light shed by the form of beauty, will be even finer than their earlier offspring, and because they now have all the more to share with each other their friendship will be even more firmly established than it was before (209c). It is implicit in Diotima's allusion to the "true things" begotten through the vision of beauty itself that the ascent to that form is at the same time an intensification of the love that exists between two individuals. And yet it remains a love that can benefit others as well, because what these two have collaboratively achieved is an understanding of laws and institutions that will, under favorable circumstances, lead to the improvement of civic life.

The ideal relationship, then, is one in which two people care for and are friends to each other; one in which they are receptive to much of the beauty of the world, ranging from the beauty of human bodies to the beauty of beauty itself; and one in which they work out, with well-crafted words, ways in which the world can be made more just. This is not a relationship that must be devoid of sexual allure; on the contrary, Diotima makes it clear that responsiveness to physical attraction is always a welcome (though not a necessary) component of such relationships (209b). The *Phaedrus* tells us a great deal about the struggles a lover must endure to prevent sexual allure from playing too large a role in a good erotic relationship. The *Symposium*'s ladder of love affirms that human beings cannot learn how to handle their sexuality except by going through a period in which they are overly responsive to the erotic enticements of a beautiful body. It is left to the *Phaedrus*, however, to depict the psychological conflict that must take place in all of us as we learn through our mistakes to control our response to sexually attractive people.

# 7. EQUAL RELATIONSHIPS: DIOTIMA TRANSFORMED

Diotima's conception of ideal *erôs* is, no doubt, far too narrow. The model she proposes is the relationship of a homosexual male couple in which one (the *erastês*) is the more active and older partner, and the other (the *erômenos*) is reactive, younger, and in some way beautiful. Only one of them—the *erastês*—is pregnant with ideas; the physical appearance of only one of them—the *erômenos*—is a matter of significance (the *erastês* can be ugly, as Socrates is ugly). It is assumed that one of them (the *erastês*) is far older than the other and that he plays the role of educator, whereas the other plays the role of a student. What of women? What of heterosexual couples? What of equal relationships among people of roughly the same experience and education? The speech of Aristophanes, to its credit, is more inclusive and egalitarian: it applies to every sexual proclivity, and the lovers who seek reunification, each being the other's halved counterpart, are equals—equal in their need to lose their parthood and their ability to repair that loss.

Diotima's assumption that *erastês* and *erômenos* are male is probably a mere convenience of exposition. By choosing a woman to be the expositor of this theory of love (a woman who may have been his own invention[6]), Plato in effect acknowledges that women can be experts in this area. And since he sees they can be experts, he must have realized that two women, no less than two men, can enter into ideal relationships. But the male-female sexual relationships with which Plato was familiar were, for the most part, marriages. A man typically sought a marriage partner not to have conversations in which he could unburden his mind and pour out his ideas but to have children. It is only to be expected, then, that Plato's template for ideal erotic relationships should be the *erastês-erômenos* institution with which all of the dialogue's symposiasts were at home and with which all of Plato's contemporary readers were familiar.

Nonetheless, it may seem that Diotima's theory requires there to be a significant difference in age, and therefore in experience and education, between the two partners. That is because she assumes that *erôs* leads us to have an effect on the world that will still be in place after we die—it inevitably leads, in other words, to an attempt to influence the younger generation in some way, either by bringing children into existence or by educating a young mind. A lover wants to possess justice (for example) as far into the future as possible. He cannot possess it forever, but he can create discourses that lead a young person to become just; and as each new generation adds another link to the chain, the lover does, by way of approximation, possess justice eternally. So it might seem that it is essential to Diotima's way of thinking about ideal *erôs* that it be a relationship between people who are a generation apart, and that will inevitably be a relationship between people who are unequal in education and experience. Those may indeed be very good relationships, perhaps even very good erotic relationships. But surely they are not the only good kind.

In fact, however, all the ingredients that Diotima claims are present in ideal erotic relationships can exist in a heterosexual couple of the same age. Consider this contemporary scenario: a man and a woman of roughly equal age (and therefore equal education and experience) fall in love, their relationship is sustained by their conversations about the most serious matters, and they have children because they are eager to nurture and educate people who will make their world more just. They are, to use Diotima's metaphor, pregnant in both body and soul; that is, they have ideas about how the world should be improved, and they want to put those ideas into effect by bringing up their children in a certain way. This relationship differs from the ideal erotic relationship Diotima explicitly describes in only one important respect: for her, there is a division of labor between heterosexual and homosexual love; the former ensures that there will always be a

---

6. As D. Nails, *The People of Plato* (Indianapolis, 2002), 138, notes: "All extant later references to Diotima are derived from Plato." But Nails is noncommittal about whether Diotima is a Platonic invention. If she is not modeled on a real person, she would be a rarity in Plato, because nearly every named character in his dialogues is a representation of someone he knew. (Callicles of the *Gorgias* is, like Diotima, a difficult case; here too scholars disagree about whether he is a Platonic invention.) For reflections on Plato's choice of a female expert on erotics, see D. Halperin, "Why Is Diotima a Woman?" *One Hundred Years of Homosexuality* (New York, 1990), 113–51.

fresh generation, and the latter ensures that some of the members of each new generation will be well educated. But there is no reason propagation and education cannot be tasks performed by the same couple. That, in fact, is a model of a good erotic relationship that has become prevalent in our society. By rearranging the several ingredients of Diotima's theory, but without altering what is most fundamental in it, we emerge with an ideal of eros that is now widely taken for granted.

If we go a step further, and think of God as occupying a similar role to the one played by the form of beauty (which is, after all, a divine thing), the resemblance between her ideal and one that has become familiar to us is even greater. The ideal erotic couple, in that case, would be two equal human beings searching together for a way of extending their love of justice into the future, educating their children to be just and treasuring that additional bond between them, arriving at a fuller appreciation of the beauty of divine existence, and using their enhanced understanding of God to improve their efforts to comprehend and improve the world.

# 8. THE LOVE OF INDIVIDUALS

There is another way in which the Aristophanic ideal may seem, at first sight, more appealing than Diotima's. Each half of an Aristophanic couple loves and is loved *as an individual*. For each of them, no one else but his (or her) other half will do. A loves B not because B plays some role in his life that another person might play equally well or better. It was from B and B alone that A was severed, and so A's relationship with no other person can fill A's need for completion. It is a need that can be completed only by reunification with a particular individual, not by a person of a certain type.

That may seem appealing, but, at the same time, the Aristophanic ideal is burdened by its commitment to the thesis that for each of us there is one and only one other person who can give us what we seek when we look for someone to love and by whom we will be loved. It is far more plausible to suppose (as many people do) that each of us needs a good match and that, although some matches are better than others, no one person is a uniquely best match. It is hard to believe that for each person there is only one other person in the world who is right as a lover.

For Aristophanes, the mythical history of our relationships explains why we each seek one and only one person who will meet our erotic needs. A was once united with B; it was that past state of affairs that accounts for what each is doing, as he or she searches for love. By contrast, Diotima's model can acknowledge the importance of facts about what has actually transpired between a couple. Once a good relationship has been established, a couple nurtures notional children together, and that shared experience is what ties them together so firmly in their friendship (209c). Although Diotima does not point this out, it is obviously true of each lover that there is only one person with whom he has had *these* fine discussions and produced *these* fine children. At this point in their relationship, then, A will care for B and B for A in a different way from that in which each cares about anyone else. If B dies, A will feel the loss of this particular sexual and conversational partner; he will not treat this death in the same way that he reacts to the death of just any human being. If A meets someone even more beautiful in soul and body than B, he will not think about ending his relationship with B, because he is not in the business of loving the most beautiful person he can find. It is B whom he loves, and although he can say what it is about B that he finds so appealing, he is not trying to become the lover of every person who has those qualities or with the person who most fully exemplifies them.

We can find confirmation in his *Phaedrus* that Plato thinks of the best erotic relationships as ones that continue throughout a person's life and even beyond. The couple that is most fully in control of their sexual appetites remains intact even after each has died. Even the second-best sort of relationship, in which the partners are ruled by the spirited part of the soul rather than reason, is one of lifelong fidelity (256a–d). It would be appropriate, then, to say that such lovers as these love each other "as individuals." What each loves is that other individual human being and no other; they do not treat each other as dispensable instruments by which they achieve their goals. And yet there is no illusion, in these relationships, that before each met the other, there was one and only one person who would have been right. Diotima's model of love is able to avoid falling into the trap that undermines Aristophanes' theory: its commitment to a single right lover, one's other half. At the same time, because it recognizes the importance of the history of a relationship, the kind of love it admires can be described as the love of individuals "as individuals."[7]

# 9. BAD *ERÔS*

Diotima says nothing that even suggests that *erôs* can be a destructive force in human relationships—a desire that leads both lovers and those they love to great harm—and yet we know that Plato was fully aware of this possibility. The tyrannical soul Socrates describes in Book IX of *Republic* is ruled by the *erôs* that resides in the lowest part of the soul, and he is a model of everything we should not be. In *Phaedrus*, Socrates says that lovers recapitulate in their earthly existence the character of the god with whom they traveled when they were disembodied. Someone who served Ares (the god of war), for example, will become murderous when he thinks he is being wronged by his *erômenos* and will be ready

7. In this section, my thoughts have been shaped by reflection on G. Vlastos, "The Individual as an Object of Love in Plato," *Platonic Studies* (Princeton, N.J., 1973), 3–42, a great essay with which I profoundly disagree.

to kill himself or his boyfriend (256c). *Phaedrus* offers a sketch of a theory of love that recognizes the duality of *erôs*. It holds that a proper dialectical treatment of this subject must use a system of divisions that contrasts sinister (a word whose Latin counterpart means "left-handed") forms of love with those that are "right-handed" and divine (266a). Here Socrates characterizes his first speech (about why one should succumb to a nonlover) as an exercise in the service of left-handed love, and his second speech (depicting the charioteer and his two horses) as the praise of correct love. Returning to the *Symposium*, we note that several of its speakers make a distinction between a good and a bad form of *erôs* (180d–181d, 186a–c), although others (Phaedrus, Aristophanes, Agathon) do not. So Plato was reflecting on this distinction when he composed this dialogue. But, curiously, Diotima does not mention it. What are we to make of that?

The distinction she draws between those who are pregnant in soul and those who are pregnant in body does not seem to be a division between good and bad forms of love. It is better to be pregnant in soul, she holds; but that does not show that being pregnant in body—conceiving and giving birth to children—is bad. The *erôs* in animals drives them to procreate, and no one could plausibly believe that they go astray in doing so. It would be equally absurd to hold that no human being should engage in sexual intercourse or have children, and there is no evidence that Plato disagrees.

Another possibility that should be considered is this: since "*erôs* is wanting to possess the good forever" (206a11–12), perhaps good forms of human love are those that are based on an understanding—or, at any rate, a true belief—about what is good; and bad forms are those that are false. This proposal is acceptable, I believe, but it does not go far enough. What needs to be added is that *Symposium* contains a paradigm of bad *erôs*: that paradigm, I suggest, is Alcibiades. He is Plato's way of portraying, in this dialogue, how badly one can go astray when one's sexual desires are allied with deeply mistaken assumptions about how one should one lead one's life. Not all mistakes about what is good are equally harmful. For example, someone who thinks that well-being consists in physical health and tries to possess this good far into the future by having healthy children and teaching them to love health is not someone whom Plato wishes to assign to the lowest depths of human misery; nor would anyone say that it is *erôs* that has led such a person astray. There are far worse lives, and Socrates claims in *Republic* that *erôs* can lead us to those depths. This is what has happened to the tyrannical man. He allows the sexual waywardness that is a potential source of misery within all human beings (*Rep.* 571b–572b) to become the leading element in his psychology. His appetite for sex is what shapes his conception of what is worth pursuing, and the results are disastrous. Alcibiades, as portrayed in the *Symposium*, is not at this pitch of depravity, but he is the vehicle that Plato uses, in this dialogue, for showing the reader how badly *erôs* can disfigure us. Diotima's theory of love is not in error, but it is radically incomplete; it must be supplemented by a portrayal of what *erôs* looks like when it goes badly astray.

Plato sometimes uses *erôs* to name the desire that impels us toward sexual activity. When he divides the soul into three parts in the *Republic*, for example, he describes the lowest (appetitive) part as the one by which one loves (*erai*), is hungry, and is thirsty (439d6). Here *erôs* is simply the brute desire to have sex, an instinctive conative force that inheres in our nature no less than thirst and hunger. One would be missing a fundamental component of Plato's psychological outlook if one failed to notice the persistence with which he emphasizes that this desire is an extremely dangerous feature of the appetitive part of the soul—far more so than our desire to eat and drink. That is the lesson he clearly means to convey in his portrait of the tyrannical man. But we should not overlook the warnings that his *Symposium* and *Phaedrus* also issue regarding the destructive potential of *erôs*. What he is suggesting, in these two dialogues, is that human relations inevitably become poisoned when they are dominated by the desire for sexual satisfaction. His *Symposium* is by no means a bouquet laid at the feet of Love: the duality of *erôs* is never far from Plato's mind, as the entrance of Alcibiades makes clear.

Before we consider this episode in greater detail, and before we examine as well Plato's warning, in *Phaedrus*, about the duality of *erôs*, we should linger a bit longer on the tyrannical man portrayed in *Republic*. Can we apply to him the two formulae Diotima proposes: that love is a desire for the eternal possession of good, and that its goal is to give birth in beauty? What is the good that the tyrant wants forever, and in what way does he seek birth in beauty? How these questions are to be answered is by no means certain, but perhaps Diotima's theory and Socrates' portrait of the tyrant can be fit together in this way: As noted above (sec. 2), Diotima applies her theory to animals no less than to human beings. Something in them makes them have sex, although they, of course, have no idea what goal that instinct serves. Something in them wants to replicate life forever by producing copies of itself, and the copulation of animals is its modus operandi. We can reasonably take Plato to be suggesting, in his portrait of the tyrannical man, that his sexual drive, like that of any brute, aims at the replication of his life. The tyrannical man almost certainly does not think of himself as having sex because he wants to live forever, but the impulse to which he gives free rein is a generative force that has eternal life as its goal. He seeks to give birth in beauty: that formula applies to him because his sexual appetite, like everyone else's, is attentive to visual cues and responds to alluring bodies. That does not mean that he wants to have children and raise a family; rather, he sets aside whatever sexual inhibitions most people have and promiscuously chases after young girls and boys, taking every possible opportunity to bed attractive young things (574b–c). It might be asked: Why is it that the sexual instinct of animals leads not only to copulation but also to self-sacrifice, whereas the tyrannical man presumably would not lift a finger for any babies he happens to produce? Plato can reply that human beings are influenced by all sorts of notions about what is worth pursuing, whereas the child-oriented instincts of animals do not have to compete with ideas in their heads, since they have none. Whatever feelings a tyrannical man might have for his offspring can be overpowered by his belief that to be a real man is to move on to the next erotic episode.

Alcibiades does not have every feature that Socrates ascribes to the tyrannical man in *Republic*, but there are some similarities. He is presented as a party-crasher, a drunk, a man in love with flute girls, men, and boys; and all of Plato's contemporary readers would have present to their minds, when they read the *Symposium*, the notoriety Alcibiades achieved as a man in love with power, an untrustworthy traitor to Athens, and a suspected mutilator of religious statues. "Does a drunken man have, in a way, a tyrannical mind?" Socrates asks in *Republic* (573b9–c1), and Adeimantus answers affirmatively. A few lines later (d2–5), Socrates notes the tyrannical mind's love of feasts, revelries, girlfriends, and things of that sort. When Alcibiades first notices Socrates, he immediately becomes jealous and angry, because he sees Socrates reclining next to Agathon (213c). Socrates reacts to Alcibiades' outburst by expressing his fear of the violence that may be done to him (213d). He asks Agathon to protect him, because Alcibiades is full of verbal abuse and can scarcely keep his hands off him: "If he tries to use force, keep him away, because I am very much afraid of his madness and his *philerastia*" (213d5–6). *Philerastia* combines both Greek words for love: it is love of love. Alcibiades, in other words, makes sexual love his favorite pastime. The madness Socrates refers to here is by no means the divine sort of madness praised in the *Phaedrus*—the beauty-inspired ecstasy that is under the control of philosophical reason and is expressed by indifference to wealth and other ordinary human concerns (249d, 251e). Alcibiades' madness is that of the violent tyrant who tries to rule over not only human beings but gods as well (*Republic* 573c)—an apt description for a powerful politician who dares to mutilate religious statues.

The encomium of Socrates given by Alcibiades allows Plato's readers to see that someone can be both an *erastês* and an *erômenos*. No one has more beauty of soul than Socrates, and that is why Alcibiades loves him; and yet he is no merely passive object of sexual interest but an active lover—that is why Alcibiades expects Socrates to make sexual advances toward him. What he discovers is that as an active lover Socrates is highly selective and controlled, allowing himself not the slightest physical expression of affection when such expression would be inappropriate. Plato's dialogues by no means present Socrates as a man who is indifferent to the physical allure of beautiful young men (see, for example, *Charmides* 153e–154d). His refusal even to touch or embrace Alcibiades (217a–219e), despite Alcibiades' best efforts to seduce him, does not arise out of insensitivity to physical allure or a commitment to the avoidance of every physical expression of sexual desire. His second speech in *Phaedrus* acknowledges with approval a lover's longing for physical contact and never says a word in criticism of the lover's kisses and embraces (255e). The bad horse's desire for homosexual copulation must be restrained (253d–254e), but physical expression that falls short of that is accepted as normal and harmless.

So, we must regard Socrates' coldness toward Alcibiades as a refusal to become entangled in the sexual contract that Alcibiades implicitly proposes. Alcibiades assumes that Socrates, lover of attractive young men that he is, wants to penetrate him and that, in exchange for such intercourse, Socrates will pour his wisdom into him. Those assumptions are a colossal misunderstanding of what Socratic wisdom is and how those who love and are loved by Socrates can benefit from it. (The whimsical suggestion that wisdom might flow through physical contiguity, made earlier by Agathon at 175c–d, is a close cousin of Alcibiades' idea that Socratic wisdom might come easily to him, in exchange for sex. A more distant cousin is the hero worship of those who tell the tale of that marvelous night in 416 B.C.— Apollodorus and Aristodemus: they hang on every word Socrates uttered, as though that will bring them understanding.)

The speech of Alcibiades is Plato's device for holding up to our eyes an especially pernicious form of bad *erôs*. When sexual attraction and activity is treated as a mere means to a further end, a chip that can be traded in exchange for something else one wants, the soul becomes corrupted. *Symposium* implies that the public offenses of which Alcibiades was guilty are akin to his private waywardness. A man who would trade sexual penetration for wisdom thinks of human relationships in purely instrumental terms, and little can be expected of a political leader who uses others as stepping-stones to success. At the same time, we cannot help finding something good in Alcibiades. After all, it is wisdom that he seeks from sex with Socrates, and he has enough sense to recognize how remarkable a human being Socrates is and to pay him fitting tribute. He is not the complete tyrant. But Plato's goal, in writing this portion of *Symposium*, is not to show Alcibiades in a good light but to pursue the apologetic agenda of his *Apology* and *Crito*. In effect, he tells the reader: yes, it is true that Socrates loved Alcibiades, but this was a love that came close to making Alcibiades a better person; and it was a love that refused to treat sex as an item to be traded in exchange for a successful career.

# 10. Seduction in the *Phaedrus*, Homosexual Intercourse in the *Laws*

Although we have to do some thinking to see that the gap created by Diotima's omission of a discussion of bad *erôs* is filled by Alcibiades, the *Phaedrus* directly confronts us with bad *erôs*. It creates the category of "left-handed love" and makes this one of its major themes. Plato's way of handling the dangers of sexuality in this dialogue is in line with the approach he takes in his *Symposium*. "Left-handed" *erôs* is at play in the speech of Lysias and the first speech of Socrates, for each of these discourses is a device by which a man tries to persuade a boy to prefer being sexually penetrated by him to having intercourse with someone who, because of his passionate longing, is a genuine *erastês*. These speeches propose a cold-hearted exchange: here are the many benefits you will receive from me, because I am a calculating person who would not profit from harming you; in exchange for what I can give to you, all that I ask is that you give me your sexual favors. The trade being proposed is, in this way, rather like the transaction that Alcibiades thinks Socrates is willing to enter with him.

Although *Phaedrus* treats the theme of a sexual contract at far greater length than does *Symposium*, it does not say, in so many words, what is objectionable about such an exchange of benefits. But it can safely be assumed that Plato expects his readers to find the speech of Lysias a mere piece of cleverness (227c) rather than a truly convincing demonstration that boys should have sex with men who do not love them. Phaedrus is not presented as someone whose sexual attitudes have changed as a result of his admiration for Lysias; rather, Phaedrus admires the speech of Lysias because of its audacious advocacy of a paradoxical thesis that most people would consider shameful. The nonlover who claims that he will confer great benefits merely in exchange for sexual satisfaction is simply not to be believed. He offers no reason to suppose that he has any genuine concern for the well-being of the boy he is trying to seduce. Nothing about the boy attracts him but his physical beauty, which excites the nonlover's desire to have an orgasm with the boy's aid (although he would never express himself so indelicately). Would any father want his son to have sex with someone like that? The nonlover of Phaedrus's speech is transparently a sex-starved and clever manipulator.

This feature of the dialogue goes a long way toward explaining why Socrates assumes, in his second speech, that the charioteer must restrain the bad horse's eagerness to jump all over the *erômenos*. How are an *erômenos* and his father to be assured that an *erastês* really does take the boy's well-being to heart and is not merely making fine speeches in order to relieve his sexual urges? If the lover claims that he has something to teach the boy, that he is offering a boy a philosophical exploration of the most serious matters, that the boy's beauty reminds him of the beauty of the forms he once saw in a previous life, he will not be taken seriously if at the same time he is trying to devise ways to get the boy into bed. It will be difficult to tell him apart from someone who is merely saying these things for the purpose of sexual satisfaction.

Elsewhere, Plato offers other reasons for refraining from homosexual copulation. The speakers of *Laws* agree that in the well-governed city for which they are drafting legislation, such intercourse, though allowed elsewhere, will be banned. Why so? The dialogue's principal speaker, an unnamed visitor from Athens, says that the pleasures of male-male and female-female intercourse are "contrary to nature" (636c6), and this is supported, at a later point, with the claim (one that we now know to be false) that homosexual intercourse is not found among animals (836c). It is difficult to believe, however, that this point by itself carried a great deal of weight with Plato, for nowhere else does he claim that human beings should take animal behavior as a model for their own way of life. It is more likely that what carries most weight for Plato is the assumption that organs should not be used to defeat the purpose for which they are suited by their nature. The production of sperm, we are told in *Laws* (838e–839b) has a generative purpose, and male homosexual intercourse wastes the reproductive potential and weakens the affective ties among husbands and wives. Plato elsewhere rejects the idea that the only sexual intercourse that should be permitted is procreative, for he has Socrates say in the

*Republic* that couples who are past their fertile years may have sexual relations more or less as they please (461b–c).

It is certainly possible that these ideas are at work in *Phaedrus*, for in Socrates' second speech the *erastês* whose disembodied vision of the forms is long past or obscured is likely to "pursue pleasure that is contrary to nature" (251a1), and the context indicates that this is the pleasure of homosexual copulation. But Plato cannot believe that those words by themselves convey a convincing argument for restraint from homosexual intercourse. Rather, the dramatic structure of *Phaedrus* indicates that such restraint is to be practiced because of the way it secures the friendship between *erastês* and *erômenos*. The first two speeches of the dialogue (that of Phaedrus and that of Socrates) are intended to show us how suspicious anyone will be if he claims to be a friend and an educator but, at the same time, pursues sex as a quid pro quo. The argumentative strategy of the dialogue is to show the value of homosexual restraint by presenting it as a safeguard against misunderstanding the motives that lie behind a sexual but not merely sexual relationship. Just as a professional teacher might accept a rule that forbids sexual relations with students, Socrates insists that the highest erotic ideal is one in which the complete physical expression of *erôs* is foresworn. But it should not be forgotten how lenient he is when he discusses those devoted homosexual couples who are occasionally mastered by their desire for genital intercourse (*Phaedrus* 256b–e).

## 11. FINAL THOUGHTS

Cephalus, the first interlocutor Socrates examines in Plato's *Republic*, says that he agrees with Sophocles about one of the great benefits of old age: released from the tyranny of sexual desire, one can at last find peace and freedom (329b–c). Plato, I believe, has some sympathy for this attitude. At any rate, he has Socrates endorse the idea that there is something inherently transgressive in human sexuality. In the dreams of even the best of us, lawless sexual urges—to have intercourse with one's mother, or with gods or beasts or any human being—make themselves manifest (571a–572b). But Plato's recognition of the dark side of human sexuality, which emerges most fully in his portrait of the tyrannical soul, does not blind him to its great value. Without it, there would no future generations, and our deep longing to perpetuate ourselves by making a long-lasting difference in the world—by having children, or transmitting our conception of the good, or both—would be fruitless. Furthermore, receptivity to the sexual allure of the human body is one of the modes by which we take pleasure in the beauty of the physical world. That beauty is not as great as the beauty of souls (which, in turn, pales in comparison with the beauty of the form of beauty), but that does not mean that it would be best for us to be indifferent to it. If old man Cephalus is no longer an *erastês* of all beautiful bodies, that has to be counted as one of the ways in which old age is a period of decline. For the beauty of the human form is one of the ways in which the sensible world offers us reminders of beauty itself.

Plato is perfectly aware that genital intercourse can be intensely pleasant (*Philebus* 45d–e), but he does not take the pleasantness of an experience, in isolation from its cause or object, to be a point in its favor. It is *good* pleasure— pleasure that it is good for someone to feel—that we should seek (*Gorgias* 495d– 499d), and so the intensity of pleasure that can be achieved in genital intercourse is not by itself a reason for engaging in this practice. Plato's denial that every pleasure is good simply because it is a pleasure may be defensible, but even if it is, we should recognize a blind spot in his thinking about sexuality. He recognizes that such gestures as embracing and kissing are appropriate expressions of one person's sexual interest in and love of another (*Phaedrus* 255e–256a); these are things we naturally do, when we are responsive as lovers to another person's physical attraction, and it would be insane to suppose that these expressions of *erôs* are always to be suppressed. Sexual intercourse is a more intense way in which *erôs* is naturally expressed, and Plato knows how strongly we desire it. But he cannot bring himself to believe that because of the greater pleasure it gives sexual intercourse in a homosexual couple can be a fuller expression of affection than kissing and embracing, and that when it carries with it this meaning it is welcome and healthy. What lies behind his disapproval, I have suggested, is his fear that nonprocreative intercourse compromises the trust and affection that people should have for each other: it leads each partner in an erotic relationship to suspect that everything he receives from the other is a mere means to the relief of imperious sexual urges.

We must not take Plato to suppose that we should treat other human beings, beautiful in body or soul or both, as mere stepping-stones on the way to the vision of beauty itself. The best sort of lover is someone who is bursting with ideas about how to improve human life. Because he cannot fully understand or develop those ideas on his own, he needs a conversational partner who will help him nurture those inchoate theories. That he needs a partner in order to fulfill his need to give birth to a better world does not show that it is *only* his needs that matter to him. In the best kinds of *erôs*, self-regard and dedication to others mutually reinforce each other; in the worst kinds, a lover destroys himself as he goes about destroying others.

Above all, Plato insists that the erotic tendencies of human beings—their sexual appetites, their yearning for immortality through propagation, their receptivity to beauty—need to be educated, because they will never lead to anything of great value if they are put in the service of mistaken conceptions of what is truly good and truly beautiful. The desire to change the world so as to invest the future with something of ourselves will merely replicate and rearrange its defective furniture if it is allied to common misunderstandings of what is genuinely good for human beings. Love needs to be turned into something more than an inarticulate yearning for a sexual life partner or a procreative force. It needs to become something better than the intense alliance of two people who care not at all for the larger world—or even for their own families (*Phaedrus* 252a)—but only for their own togetherness and satisfaction. For that to happen on a grand scale, Plato believes, we will need a new kind of political community.[8]

# BIBLIOGRAPHY

Ferrari, G. R. F. *Listening to the Cicadas: A Study in Plato's Phaedrus* (Cambridge, 1987).
Griswold, C. *Self-Knowledge in Plato's Phaedrus* (New Haven, Conn., 1986).
Halperin, D. "Why Is Diotima a Woman?" *One Hundred Years of Homosexuality* (New York, 1990), 113–51.
Hunter, R. *Plato's Symposium* (Oxford, 2004).
Irwin, T. *Plato's Ethics* (New York, 1995).
Lorenz, H. "The Analysis of the Soul in Plato's *Republic*," in G. Santas (ed.), *The Blackwell Guide to Plato's Republic* (Malden, Maine, 2006), 146–65.
Nails, D. *The People of Plato* (Indianapolis, 2002).
Nehamas, A., and P. Woodruff (trans.) *Plato, Symposium* (Indianapolis, 1989).
Nussbaum, M. *The Fragility of Goodness: Luck and Ethics in Greek Tragedy and Philosophy* (Cambridge, 1986).
Penner, T., and C. Rowe. *Plato's Lysis* (Cambridge, 2005).
Vlastos, G. "The Individual as an Object of Love in Plato," *Platonic Studies* (Princeton, N.J., 1973), 3–42.
Waterfield, R. (trans.) *Plato, Symposium* (Oxford, 1994).

8. For their comments on an earlier draft of this essay, I am grateful to Elizabeth Asmis, Gail Fine, Tushar Iranai, and Gabriel Richardson Lear.

# CHAPTER 13

# PLATO'S POLITICS

## CHRISTOPHER BOBONICH

THE dialogues of Plato that are of the most obvious importance for his political philosophy include the *Apology*, the *Crito*, the *Gorgias*, the *Laws*, the *Republic*, and the *Statesman*. Further, there are many questions of political philosophy that Plato discusses in his dialogues (and for others, even if they are not explicitly discussed, we can form reasonable judgments about Plato's views on them). These topics include, among others, (1) the ultimate ends of the city's laws and political institutions, (2) who should rule, and the forms of constitution and their ranking, (3) the nature and extent of citizens' obligation to obey the laws, (4) the proper extent of citizenship, (5) the political and social status of women, (6) the purposes of punishment, (7) aspects of the citizens' material well-being, including the benefits and costs of private property, and (8) slavery.

In a short essay such as this, I cannot explore all of even the most important works in detail and cannot sketch Plato's views on all of the relevant topics without resorting to brief, potted summaries. Whatever other good purposes such overviews can serve, they are deeply antithetical to the basic spirit underlying all of Plato's dialogues: that is, in order to understand anything, the reader must consider all the arguments carefully, working out possible objections and lines of reply. In other words, she must herself engage in doing philosophy.

Although I hope to provide an overall impression of Plato's political philosophy, my aim is not to give a précis of the dialogues that could be read in their stead but, rather, to concentrate on a few of what seem to me to be the most fundamental and persisting issues. In doing so, I focus on three moments in Plato's thought: the "Socratic" dialogues, including the *Apology*, and the *Crito*; the great middle-period work, the *Republic*, along with the *Phaedo*; and two works from Plato's last period, the *Laws* and the *Statesman*.[1]

# I. THE "SOCRATIC" PLATO

Let me begin with two sets of quotations that introduce one of the central topics of the political theory of the Socratic dialogues. In the *Apology*, Socrates compares himself to a gadfly that is set upon the great horse of Athens:

> It is to fulfill some such function [i.e., the gadfly's] that I believe that the god has placed me in the city. I never cease to rouse each and every one of you, to persuade and reproach you all day long and everywhere I find myself in your company.[2] (30e6–31a2)

What is the content of this persuasion?

> I went to each of you privately and conferred upon him what I say is the greatest benefit, by trying to persuade him not to care for any of his belongings before caring that he himself should be as good and as wise as possible, not to care for the city's possessions more than for the city itself, and to care for other things in the same way. (*Apol.* 36c4–d1; cf. 29de and 36de)

What is especially worth noting here is that Socrates claims to benefit Athens by benefiting its citizens, and this benefit consists in getting them to examine themselves and their lives with regard to virtue. Since Plato, throughout his career, believed that virtue was by far the most important contributor to happiness, and that the ultimate end of all of a person's rational actions is that person's own greatest happiness, such encouragement to virtue seems a reasonable way to proceed for anyone seeking really to benefit his fellow citizens.[3]

But we also find the following passages in the same work:

---

1. I take the *Apology* and the *Crito* to antedate the *Phaedo*, and the *Republic* and the *Statesman* and the *Laws* (probably in that order) to follow the *Phaedo*. The *Gorgias'* place is more controversial, but I would place it between the *Apology* and the *Crito* on the one hand, and the *Phaedo* and the *Republic* on the other. More important for this chapter is not the relative date of the *Gorgias* but the fact that it, like the *Apology* and the *Crito*, does not appeal to philosophers as knowers of Platonic Forms, while the *Phaedo* and the *Republic* do. For further discussion of chronology, see Irwin, chapter 3 in this volume.

2. For quotations from Plato, my translations draw on those in Cooper (1997), except for the *Laws* where I draw on Bury (1926) and Pangle (1980). For discussions of Plato's political philosophy from all periods, see Balot (2006), Barker (1960), Irwin (1995), Samaras (2002), and Schofield (2006); for discussions, especially of the Socratic dialogues, with references, see Brickhouse and Smith (1999, 185–229) and Kraut (1984).

3. Socrates gives priority to the well-being of his fellow-citizens (*Apol.* 30a). The literature on Plato's attitude toward rational eudaimonism and the connection between virtue and happiness is extensive (Bobonich [2002] and Irwin [1995]). Here, and throughout, I try to cite work, often more recent, that itself gives further references. In my view, Plato, in all periods, thinks that virtue is the fundamental component of happiness while accepting that there are other parts or components; for discussion of different interpretations, see Bobonich (2002) and Irwin (1995).

It may seem strange that while I go around and give this advice privately and interfere in private affairs, I do not venture to go to the assembly and there advise the city. . . . Be sure, men of Athens, that if I had long ago attempted to take part in politics, I should have died long ago and benefited neither you nor myself. Do not be angry with me for speaking the truth; no man will survive who genuinely opposes you or any other crowd and prevents the occurrence of many unjust and illegal happenings in the city. A man who really fights for justice must lead a private, not a public, life if he is to survive for even a short time. (*Apol.* 31c4–32a3; cf. 32e–33a)

I have deliberately not led a quiet life but have neglected what occupies most people: wealth, household affairs, the position of general or public orator or the other offices, the political clubs and factions that exist in the city. I thought myself too decent to survive if I occupied myself with those things. I did not follow that path that would have made me no use either to you or to myself. (*Apol.* 36b5–c3; the close of this passage immediately precedes 36c4–d1 quoted above)

In the previous passages quoted, Socrates claims that he (i) is a divine gift to the city and (ii) benefits the city. In these latter passages, Socrates (a) suggests that the current state of politics is very bad and apparently must remain so and (b) contrasts his own activity with practicing or engaging in politics.

But there is a natural line of thought that suggests there at least ought to be a connection between politics and benefiting the city. We might hold, to a first approximation, that the proper task of a lawgiver or a statesman is to benefit the city as much as possible and the best way of doing this is by making the citizens virtuous and happy.[4] In the *Gorgias*, we find Socrates suggesting exactly such a line of thought:

I believe that I am one of a few Athenians—so as not to say I am the only one, but the only one among our contemporaries—to undertake the true political art and practice the true politics. This is because the speeches I make on each occasion do not aim at gratification, but at what is best. (*Gorg.* 521d6–e1; cf. 502e–503b)

That is, Socrates attempts "to care for the city and its citizens with the aim of making them as good as possible" (*Gorg.* 513e5–7) and thinks that unless the city is tended in this way, no other action can benefit the citizens (513e8–a3).[5]

Here, unlike in the *Apology*, Socrates claims to undertake the practice of the true art of politics. Understanding Socrates' activities in this way, we can now consider the relation of such a project to Plato's famous claim in the *Republic* that philosophers must rule in a just city. (I leave aside the obvious difference that while philosophers do rule in the *Republic*'s just city, Socrates certainly does not rule in Athens.)

4. Cf. *Hipp. Maj.* 284bd and *Lysis* 209ce. On the relation of this idea to historical understandings of the Greek city, see Manville (1990, 35–54).

5. This is related to a fundamental ethical claim of Plato, the Dependency Thesis: that is, nothing benefits a person who lacks wisdom or knowledge of the good (*Euthd.* 278e–282a and *Meno* 87c–89a).

In the *Gorgias*, Socrates emphasizes his devotion to philosophy but does not claim to know, for example, what justice is, nor does he advocate a political and educational program designed to produce rulers who possess such knowledge. The philosopher rulers of the *Republic* do know the Forms, and this is an important part of why they should rule. In both the *Apology* and the *Gorgias*, Socrates claims that he tries to make the citizens virtuous, but he does not claim to have achieved much success in doing so. If he were able to make others virtuous, this would have striking implications. It is usually thought that, in the Socratic dialogues, Plato holds that the virtuous person must know the definitions of the virtues. Further, only if one knows, for example, the definition of justice will one be able to know of an act whether it is just or not and know what is true of justice—for example, that it is a virtue. Knowledge of the definition is thus necessary for such further knowledge. But Socrates also thinks that people having knowledge of such definitions will succeed: they will have knowledge in ordinary cases where they previously may only have had confident belief and be able to settle hard cases. It will also allow them to know such highly controversial truths such as that it is better to suffer than to do injustice.[6]

There is no attempt in the Socratic dialogues to describe the best possible city or a fully just city. In the *Republic*, this becomes perhaps the fundamental task of political philosophy, and Plato revisits the issue in his later works, the *Statesman* and the *Laws*. In this way, the political philosophy of the Socratic dialogues is radically incomplete. But we can try to work out, drawing on claims and principles found in the Socratic dialogues, what the best possible city would look like. In doing so, we shall both more deeply understand the political implications of Plato's ethical views in these dialogues and come to see that their unresolved issues help set an agenda that carries through the rest of Plato's political philosophy.[7]

Before turning to this topic, however, we must consider Socrates' famous denial of knowledge. Throughout the Socratic dialogues, Socrates claims not to know the definitions of the virtues or principles, such as that it is better to suffer wrong than to do it, and, in my view, this is not to be dismissed as merely "ironic."[8] He has nothing analogous to the knowledge that craftsmen have of their craft or to the sort of knowledge possessed by mathematicians of mathematics. So how should he proceed while lacking knowledge? Socrates provides a general answer in the *Crito* when he responds to his friend's advice to escape from jail before his own death sentence is carried out:

6. These claims are controversial; for a defense of them and discussion of other interpretations, see Benson (2000, 99–163).

7. In recent years, there has been a valuable literature on the more specific question of Socrates' attitude toward the Athenian democracy and its historical rivals. For one of the latest contributions, see Ober (1998, 156–213).

8. In my view, Socrates thinks that there is a better epistemic state than the one he is in and does not claim confidence that no human can attain it. For some starting points on the extensive literature on knowledge in the Socratic dialogues, see Benson (2000) and Brickhouse and Smith (1999, 99–121), as well as Matthews and Taylor, chapters 5 and 7, respectively, in this volume. On the necessity of knowing the definition of, for example, courage for knowing what actions or people are courageous and for knowing what is true of courage, see n. 6.

We must therefore examine whether we should act in this way or not, as not only now but at all times I am the kind of man who listens to nothing within me but the argument that on reflection seems best to me. I cannot, now that this fate has come upon me, discard the arguments I used; they seem to me much the same. I revere and honor the same principles as before, and if we have no better arguments to bring up at this moment, be sure that I shall not agree with you. (*Crito* 46b3–c3)

What Socrates has found, in several dialogues, is that some of his beliefs concerning how to be and how to act have never been refuted in elenctic examination, while beliefs inconsistent with his, when elenctically examined, are inconsistent with other beliefs held by the one examined (and the interlocutor tends to respond by giving up the claim that is inconsistent with Socrates' beliefs). So Socrates intends to continue acting on these beliefs and principles at least until something better comes along. Although we receive no worked-out argument that this is the only (or the most) rational way of proceeding, it is, I think, a reasonable reaction to Socrates' circumstances.[9] Socrates, it seems, can reasonably act in this way without supposing that he possesses knowledge.

In what follows, I take Socrates' epistemic limitations as a constraint on my discussion: that is, I ask what is the best sort of city that is humanly possible, given that no one in it possesses ethical knowledge and no one is (significantly) epistemically better off than Socrates. To put it vividly, what would the best possible city founded by Socrates look like?[10] To begin, we face the issue of what changes—however desirable they may be—are actually implementable. There are some reasons for Socrates to be deeply pessimistic.[11] First, the above quotation from *Apology* 31c–32a suggests that Socrates thinks that it is impossible for him, or others like him who would act to advance justice, to come to rule in Athens and that even any attempts to change laws and institutions for the better (or to prevent them from becoming worse) will lead to the destruction of those trying to do so before they can achieve anything.

Second, in the *Crito*, Socrates claims that

One should never do wrong in return, nor injure any man, whatever injury one has suffered at his hands. . . . I know that only a few people hold this view or will hold it, and there is no common deliberation [*boulê*] between those

---

9. At times, Socrates seems more unwilling to act without better settling the questions under discussion, as in *Laches* 200c–201b; cf. 179a–180a. But this only shows that, in some circumstances, there is no action preferable to further inquiry, not that this is always so. In the *Laches*, the initial options are not exhaustive, and neither seems especially attractive.

10. I put it this way, rather than asking what the best city ruled by Socrates would look like, since we should not assume, without argument, that Socratic principles entail that he should rule in the best city, much less that he should do so without the participation of others. I discuss this issue further below in connection with coercion. Since the ethical expert referred to at, for example, *Crito* 47a–48a has knowledge of the virtues, I shall not consider a city founded by such a person.

11. Cf. Kraut (1984, 194–309).

who hold this view and those who do not, but they inevitably despise each other's resolutions and designs. (49c10–d5)

The word for deliberation that Socrates uses, *boulê*, in addition to meaning "advice" or "deliberation," is politically highly loaded: it is the name of the Council or Senate in Athens.[12] It is sometimes thought that all Socrates means here is that most people will not agree with this principle about not doing wrong until they undergo the elenchus; but given the actual effects of the elenchus on many of Socrates' interlocutors (they leave or grow angry or, even if during the conversation they call their beliefs into question, this seems to have little lasting impact), it is not clear why he would think this. If such changes do not, or cannot, occur, however, those disagreeing over this principle will be unable to engage in the sort of deliberation needed for good collective decision-making. They might not only disagree over a wide range of political issues (e.g., those connected with punishment or warfare or, more generally, with ideals of how to be and how to act), but they may not even be able to sustain productive rational discussion.

This is a good instance of how an unresolved issue in the Socratic dialogues leads to considerable political indeterminacy. From a political point of view, to go further, we need answers to questions such as the following:

1. If enough experience of the elenchus would persuade all (or most) citizens, is it permissible to coerce those who are unwilling to undergo that amount of elenchus?
2. Is there some education (different from that of current Greek cities) that would make citizens more likely to benefit from the elenchus?
3. If not, and there are people who cannot improve in these ways, should they be citizens, and what, if any, political functions could they have, and what restrictions should they live under in the best city?
4. Is there some sort of education not employing the elenchus that benefits such people sufficiently so as to allow them to be citizens and exercise political functions?

If the likelihood of educational success in Athens and other extant cities is sufficiently low and the costs of trying sufficiently high, Socrates might reasonably recommend withdrawal from public activity. But that only answers the relatively specific question of what Socrates and others like him should do in circumstances such as those in which Socrates actually finds himself. It does not answer what the best humanly possible city would be on Socrates' principles or what would be possible, if great changes were made to the laws and political institutions of an existing city or a new colony were founded (a common enough possibility in ancient Greece).

So what would such a city look like? We find no answer to this in the Socratic dialogues and, as I have suggested and we shall see again, this is not accidental,

---

12. For other political language, see *Crito* 49d2–3; there is a common *boulê* for Socrates and Crito at 47c11. For *boulê* as a political term, see Hansen (1991, 246) and Aristotle, *Politics* 1322b12–17.

since we would need to come to some conclusions about issues that are left un-addressed in these dialogues. The first, minimalist option is that Socrates (and others like him) carry out elenctic discussions but have no greater hopes than persuading probably only a few by means of such conversations.

This is not the only option compatible with Plato's commitments in the So-cratic dialogues, however. There are a number of ethical beliefs that Socrates has that have passed elenctic examination:

1. It is better for a person to suffer injustice than to do injustice.
2. If one commits an injustice, it is better to be punished than to escape punishment.
3. Virtue is fine and good for its possessor.
4. No one does wrong willingly.
5. Virtue is necessary for happiness and is the most fundamental part of happiness.

In these dialogues, Plato also accepts some claims as obvious with little disagree-ment and thus little elenctic defense, such as the Principle of Rational Eudaimonism—that is, that the ultimate aim of all of a person's rational actions is his or her own greatest happiness.[13]

It is quite reasonable to ask, even if Plato does not in the Socratic dialogues, what a city might look like if these principles were embodied in its laws. Doing so leads us to four especially important questions:

1. If these principles are embodied in laws and political institutions, they will require sanctions and will sometimes require the people subject to them to give up decision-making authority over various parts of their lives. What legitimates such coercion and removal of decision-making authority? (The Crito has arguments for an obligation to obey the law in general. Here I want to consider what specific grounds there may be for coercing people in accordance with Socratic principles.)[14]
2. In putting Socratic principles into effect, the aim is to make the citizens virtuous and happy. Will all citizens benefit equally, or will the benefit be highly uneven?
3. As we have seen, Plato is pessimistic about the possibility of sustained public action on behalf of justice. How stable could a city based on such laws be?
4. The previous questions focus on what such a city would look like, but we must also consider questions of motivation; in particular, does political activity compete with the development of one's own virtue so that Socrates could not rationally pursue activity in support of such laws?

13. Controversies surround Plato's views on eudaimonism; for some discussion, see Bobonich (forthcoming) and Irwin (1995).
14. On the Crito's arguments, see Harte (1999) and Kraut (1984).

## Coercion

To simplify, here I focus on the costs and benefits to the person to whom the law or institution applies and do not attempt to characterize coercion precisely. If coercion could have the result that the coerced person comes to have knowledge, it is not clear that the Plato of the Socratic dialogues would object. In the *Euthydemus*, Socrates says, "Let him destroy me, or if he likes, boil me or do whatever he wants, but he must make me good" (285c4–6).

For the more common and politically more important cases in which the person does not come to possess knowledge, consider this passage from the *Lysis*:

> Of those matters which we really understand something, everybody . . . will turn them over to us, and there we shall act just as we choose, and nobody will want to get in our way. (*Lysis* 210a9–b4)

In the *Charmides*, Socrates considers some of the implications of a proposed definition of moderation as knowing what it is that one knows and does not know. If this definition were correct,

> it would be of the greatest benefit to us to be moderate, because those of us who had moderation would live lives free from error and so would all those who were under our rule. Neither would we ourselves be attempting to do things we did not understand—rather, we would find those who did understand and turn the matter over to them—nor would we trust those over whom we ruled to do anything except what they would do correctly, and this would be that of which they possessed understanding. (*Charm.* 171d5–e5)[15]

What is striking in these passages from the *Lysis* and the *Charmides* is that Socrates does not seem to take into account the costs of giving up one's decision-making power to someone else. Neither actual coercion nor simply giving up such power would be objected to by Plato as a violation of rights or autonomy if these are understood independently of a person's good. But even in the *Republic*, and especially in the *Laws*, Plato does take it to be vastly better, all other things being equal, to be ruled by oneself than by others.[16] Perhaps something like this is suggested by the passage at *Crito* 46bc quoted above, but Socrates there does not distinguish the value of acting on one's own reasoned judgments from the idea that such a way of proceeding gives one the best chance at correctness.

Yet Plato in the Socratic dialogues also faces a problem: if virtue is knowledge and one benefits through approximating it by having fewer false and, especially, more true beliefs, then doing the right thing for the wrong reason stands in particular need of justification as a benefit. Such justification would seem easier, if the knowledge that virtue consists of is simply instrumentally valuable. (But this is a very controversial claim to attribute to Plato in the Socratic dialogues, and

---

15. Socrates may not accept this definition, but that does not affect the point.
16. For example, *Republic* 590cd and *Laws* 857ce; see Bobonich (2002, 203–5).

I myself would not do so.[17]) One might also appeal to the idea that we have nonrational motivations that are not open to the full range of rational considerations; for example, we might be subject to shame, but that emotion might be sensitive only to thoughts of what others might say of us and not to the ultimate grounds of thinking an action good or bad. It might be possible to argue that a person whose nonrational motivations have been attached to the right objects is better off than one not so trained. But many scholars, rightly I think, hold that Plato does not recognize such motivations in the Socratic dialogues.[18]

Nevertheless, Socrates in the *Gorgias* seems to be confident that ordinary legal punishments, for crimes such as theft, typically improve those subject to them (e.g., 478d–480d). For those scholars who think that Socrates does not have sufficient confidence in his other distinctive beliefs to enforce them by law, perhaps the main change from Athens that he could endorse would be a much more vigilant police force and a more efficient method of public prosecution. If we find this implausible, we should be less inclined to think that Socrates' epistemic limitations require him to reject changing the laws in accordance with some of his other principles.

## Benefit

Determining who in the city can benefit and in what ways they can benefit will require answering a number of challenging philosophical questions. As we have seen, we need to know how many citizens can be brought to have knowledge and how closely the rest can approximate to it. Given the actual results of the elenchus, we might find it hard to be optimistic that Euthyphro, Hippias, or Callicles would be improved by more elenchus. But why are there so many failures? It might be that the defect is simply epistemic; the knowledge that is necessary for virtue may be as hard to attain as knowledge that a proof of Poincaré's Conjecture is correct, so even with the best efforts, few can attain it. Or is the defect owed in part to the effect that nonrational motivations can have in originating and sustaining false beliefs? (As noted, there is a serious question as to whether the Socratic dialogues accept the existence of such motivations.) At least an important part of the problem is that the elenchus as practiced by Socrates, by necessity, takes people as they are, but is there any sort of education that might enable people to make greater progress? To settle these questions, Plato needs to explore, and ultimately to answer, various questions in psychology, epistemology, and the theory of education and learning.

Finally, and perhaps most important, Socrates does not offer definitions or accounts of virtue and happiness in the Socratic dialogues. Even if we grant, for example, that virtue is knowledge of what is good and bad for human beings and that happiness is one's optimal condition, these accounts remain purely formal

17. See Devereux, chapter 6 in this volume.
18. See Bobonich (forthcoming) and Devereux, chapter 6 in this volume.

until we get an account of the good.[19] Without more substantive accounts, it is especially difficult to determine who can benefit, and how much they can benefit, from the various ways in which Socratic principles might be embodied in laws and institutions.

## Stability

Here again, determining the stability of such laws and political institutions requires answering some of our previous questions. How far is there a coincidence of interests among the citizens, and how far can the citizens come to realize that there is such a coincidence? In addition to the question of whether citizens can come to accept the existence of such a harmony of interests, we would need to consider whether their acceptance could rest on what Socrates would count as good reasons. We shall also need to draw on answers about what benefits the citizens in order to determine what are the effective and just means of reducing conflict in the city.

## Own perfection

Some scholars think that in the Socratic dialogues there is an especially strong tension for someone like Socrates between his own perfection and undertaking political action.[20] There are two specific worries here:

1. Since Socrates does not have knowledge, would he not be better off attending to his soul rather than engaging in political action?
2. Since Socrates lacks knowledge, should he be confident enough to enforce his principles on others?

To take up question 2 first, although there are some passages that suggest that one should not undertake politics until one possesses the relevant knowledge, given Socrates' confidence in the Athenian system of punishment, there is no reason to think that it would always be wrong to enforce laws embodying the principles that have survived the elenchus.[21] With respect to question 1, some have argued that the improvement of Socrates' own soul takes nearly absolute priority over benefiting others. Here again, to see whether this is so, we need answers to questions that Plato does not fully address in the Socratic dialogues:

---

19. Bobonich (forthcoming) argues that on the account of virtue that the Socratic dialogues seem to be moving toward — that is, knowledge of good and bad — it is difficult to sustain the claims we find there of the priority of virtue, the necessity and sufficiency of virtue for happiness, and the Dependency Thesis. Plato's middle-period conception of human beings as most fundamentally rational creatures, his understanding of rationality as involving love and knowledge of the truth, and his conception of knowledge as requiring a grasp of Forms are one response to this gap. In the next section, I consider some of the political implications of these middle-period views.

20. For example, Kraut (1984, 207–15).

21. For example, the disputed *Alcibiades* I 118a ff., and Xenophon, *Memorabilia* 4.2.2 and 4.6.

1. Without a theory of happiness, we cannot answer how far others' happiness must compete with mine or whether it could be consistent with, or even a part of, mine.

2. We need to know how far others can benefit from the political activity I might undertake. If the mere enforcement of Athenian laws against, for example, theft, constitutes a significant benefit to the Athenians, how much more would they benefit from laws based on Socratic principles? Other things being equal, it seems that the greater the benefit to others, the stronger will be Socrates' reasons for helping.

3. How much improvement is possible for Socrates? Does he think it possible that human beings can attain knowledge of the definitions of the virtues? If not, how much does he benefit from engaging in further elenchus? How long has it been since his ethical beliefs have changed? Would just more elenchus with the sorts of interlocutors he has already had discussions with really be of significant benefit to him? Would he not eventually just come to see them make the same mistakes again—or others at least as easy to refute?

4. Finally, how valuable to Socrates is it simply to think about the beliefs and arguments that he already possesses? In later dialogues, Plato makes it clear that he thinks that there is enormous value in contemplating the truth. Does Socrates have good reason to believe that the same is true for thinking about his own system of (ethical) beliefs?

# II. THE MIDDLE DIALOGUES

In the most famous of the middle-period dialogues, the *Republic*, Plato invokes philosophers' knowledge of Platonic Forms as part of the reason philosophers should rule. But the *Phaedo*, which is not usually thought to have much political importance, invokes the Forms in distinguishing the two basic groups of people and in giving more content to the notions of virtue and happiness. We can better see the *Phaedo*'s significance if we consider it as a successor of the Socratic dialogues and a predecessor of the *Republic*. In particular, the *Phaedo* helps to give first answers to the sorts of questions noted above that were left unanswered in the Socratic dialogues.

## The *Phaedo*

In the *Phaedo*, Plato thinks that knowledge of Forms is possible (and may come in gradations); for example, knowing the Form of Justice will involve knowing the "real" definition of justice. The Forms allow Plato to distinguish two basic kinds of people: philosophers who seek, and may at least partially attain, knowledge of Forms and who believe that having such knowledge is a prominent part of their ultimate end; and nonphilosophers, none of whom accept the existence of Forms and who have as their ultimate ends the goods of the body, such as wealth and honor (e.g., *Phd.* 68bc and 82d–83e). True virtue requires one to value wisdom— that is, knowledge of the Forms for its own sake—and to use wisdom to guide one's choices. Thus only philosophers possess real virtue, while nonphilosophers have only a "shadow-painting of virtue that is really slavish and contains nothing healthy or true" (*Phd.* 69b7–8). Since happiness for Plato crucially depends on real virtue, only philosophers can be happy. The lives of nonphilosophers are necessarily wretched, and in the afterlife "they lie in mud" (*Phd.* 69c3–6), which is, regardless of the exact details of Plato's views about the afterlife, another way of characterizing the value of the lives they have on Earth. Nothing except being a philosopher can significantly ameliorate this terrible condition, and Plato does not seem to think that the elenchus, or any other education, can succeed in turning most people into philosophers.

Given these views, we can make some progress on the relevant questions left by the Socratic dialogues.

## Coercion and Benefit

There seems to be very little that a city can do to improve significantly the lives of the vast majority of its citizens; no nonphilosopher can have a life that is really worth living for a human being. When they undergo reincarnation, the very best of the nonphilosophers return as bees or ants or members of some other tame and cooperative race (*Phd.* 82ad). If coercion can make some of their characters less bad than they might otherwise be, it can still be justified by minimizing the harm to the person coerced, but the laws and other institutions can bring about no significant benefit for them.

## Stability

Philosophers and nonphilosophers will differ radically in what they take virtue and happiness to be. Such a city cannot be a common association aimed at furthering a shared conception of happiness among the citizens. It could not realize what is commonly thought of as the goal of the city in classical political philosophy: it could not be a shared association in which all the citizens aim at the genuine common good—that is, developing and fostering virtue in each other. Indeed, it is difficult to see how such a city could be stable for long, unless the laws and institutions were simply set by nonphilosophers.

## Own Perfection

On the *Phaedo*'s account of knowledge and its conception of the centrality of reason in undeformed human nature, there would be great value to the individual philosopher not only in improving and perfecting his knowledge but also in continued contemplation of his existing knowledge. Even if he advances no further, the great value of such contemplation would seem to compete strongly with any kind of political action. Also, since so little improvement is possible for nonphilosophers, the tension between seeking one's own good and seeking the good of the city will be all the greater.

Plato's views about nonphilosophers in the *Phaedo* have often been dismissed as a case of Plato simply being caught up in a burst of transcendental enthusiasm. But they are, rather, the consequences of the *Phaedo*'s epistemological and psychological views, and they form the background against which to read the *Republic*. What the *Phaedo* would seem to advise for Socrates and those like him is as complete a withdrawal from politics as possible. This is hardly what the *Republic* recommends for philosophers.

## The *Republic*

The *Republic* is so well known that a detailed description of it is not necessary here, but I shall sketch the points most important for us.[22] The city of the *Republic* is divided into three classes of citizens (there are probably noncitizen slaves as well): (i) the philosopher rulers, (ii) the auxiliaries, and (iii) the producers. All political and legal authority rests with the philosophers. The auxiliaries protect the city from enemies within and without, and the producers engage in the economic activities needed for the city's material life. In the two upper classes (and only there), all private property is abolished, along with the private family. Procreation takes place via eugenically approved temporary matches made by the philosopher rulers; the children are raised communally, and the parents are supposed to be unaware of who their biological children are.

Similarly, education differs for the three classes: for the philosophers, it includes a long education in mathematics, culminating in knowledge of the Forms. The auxiliaries have received an education in music and poetry that "educated the guardians through habits. Its harmonies gave them a certain harmoniousness, not knowledge; its rhythms gave them a certain rhythmical quality; and its stories whether fictional or nearer the truth, cultivated other habits akin to these" (*Rep.* 522a4–9). But there is nothing in such an education to lead people to have any grasp of the Forms or the nonsensible properties that make things fine or good. Such a grasp of nonsensible properties is initiated by the study of mathematics and culminates in the dialectical study of the Forms. Only philosophers receive such an education, and thus the auxiliaries do not have any grasp of nonsensible value properties. The producers do not seem to receive even the musical education that the auxiliaries do.

In Book 4, Plato finally gives an account of the four virtues—courage, justice, moderation, and wisdom—and he does so in terms of parts of the soul. The soul, like the city, has three parts: the Reasoning part, the Spirited part, and the Appetitive part. These parts are the ultimate, nonderivative bearers of things such as beliefs, desires, emotions, and psychic activities. The conventional names for the

---

22. In addition to the references in n. 2, on the *Republic*, see Annas (1981).

parts may be misleading: not all beliefs are located in the Reasoning part, and all three parts have desires. It is in terms of the actions and affections of these that Plato proceeds to define the virtues.

Courage, for example, consists in the power of the Spirited part to preserve, through pleasure and pain, the correct orders of the Reasoning part; justice requires that all three parts of the soul do their own job well and thus requires the presence of the other three virtues (*Rep.* 429c–435c). Since there is no wisdom (*sophia*) without knowledge or scientific understanding (*epistêmê*), only philosophers can possess the virtues. (Whether or not Plato restricted knowledge to Forms in the *Republic*, it is widely accepted that he there thinks that at least knowledge of some Forms is required to know anything at all.) Plato does not offer a complete and exhaustive account of happiness. Nevertheless, the *Republic*'s understanding of human nature places at its center the ability to know the truth and the love of the truth, and both genuine virtue and genuine happiness require the realization of these most fundamental aspects of human nature. Thus genuine virtue requires the possession of knowledge and philosophic contemplation is a major component of human happiness.

### Coercion and Benefit

In the *Republic*, Plato holds that the city's ultimate aim is the greatest happiness of all the citizens (421bc), and these include members of all three classes. So we should expect that the members of all three classes are better off in the ideal city than in others. It is clear that the philosopher rulers benefit by possessing the virtues and engaging in contemplation (I return below to the question whether they benefit by ruling). What of the other two classes? They benefit, rather, by approximating in some way the condition of the philosophers (and Plato gives an ordinal ranking of lives that increase in badness with distance from the philosophic life; *Rep.* 580ac).

The citizens of the two lower classes are not ruled by their own reason, but their characters and especially their Spirited and Appetitive parts are trained by the philosopher rulers so that such people are better off, or at least less badly off, than nonphilosophers in ordinary cities. The auxiliaries' education leads them to love some subset of fine things, although they do not love them for what actually makes them fine. The producers are educated and regulated so that they reliably pursue the orderly satisfaction of their decent appetitive desires. Whatever coercion is involved in this education and regulation as adults—along with the complete denial to both groups of political decision-making authority, as well as decision-making authority over a vast range of other activities—will have to be justified by this sort of improvement of their characters.

But how good or bad are their lives really? They fail to satisfy the Book 4 definitions of the virtues; they do not grasp the Forms at all; and their ends are set, directly or indirectly, by the lower parts of the soul and do not include that which is genuinely good in itself. The deeper explanation of these limitations rests on Plato's epistemology and metaphysics: since nonphilosophers do not grasp the

Forms at all, they do not grasp at all the properties that really make anything fine or good. Consequently, they do not value what is genuinely good and have the further deep misfortune of valuing what lacks genuine value.

These claims about Plato's epistemology, metaphysics, and psychology are controversial.[23] But even leaving aside such controversial claims that explain, I think, why Plato is so pessimistic about the virtue and happiness of the two lower classes, one famous passage from the *Republic* makes it clear that he is very pessimistic:

> When he [one who has left the Cave] reminds himself of his first dwelling place and what passed for wisdom there, and of his fellow prisoners, do you not think that he would count himself happy because of the change and pity the others? . . . Would he not feel with Homer that he would greatly prefer to "work the Earth as a serf to another, one without possessions" and go through any sufferings, rather than share their opinions and live their life? (*Rep.* 516c4–d7)

This is an echo of the famous passage in Homer's *Odyssey*, in which the summoned shade of Achilles tells Odysseus of how deeply undesirable life in Hades is (*Od.* 11.488–91). In the *Republic*, the philosopher and the philosopher alone leaves the Cave. The Cave analogy is not simply an epistemological analogy but is intended to give us a picture of human life, and the picture for nonphilosophers remains bleak.[24]

## Stability

The basic problem from the *Phaedo* remains: the citizens have very different and incompatible views about the good life, and the large majority of them lack genuine virtue. But in the *Republic*, Plato makes a remarkable effort to show that despite this, a just city can exist and remain in existence for some time. There are two especially important ways that Plato tries to ensure the city's stability. First, he thinks that the abolition of private property and families will lead people to extend outward to others the caring attitudes they typically have for family members. Unsure of who one's biological brother is, an auxiliary will treat all those in the appropriate age group as brothers. Whether this could be successful is controversial, but it would only apply to the first two classes, since producers have private property and families and have not received a musical education. Second, Plato thinks that each class benefits from the political association and that this will tend to keep the city together. A significant worry here is whether the two lower classes, given their different conceptions of the good, can recognize this coincidence of interests.

23. For a defense of these claims and, more generally, of this interpretation of the *Republic*, see Bobonich (2002).

24. For a more optimistic assessment of the auxiliaries' lives, see Kamtekar (1998).

In both of these lines of defense, Plato is helped by the fact that in the *Republic*—unlike the Socratic dialogues—he accepts the existence of nonrational motivations. Love of one's own family and affection for benefactors are both emotions that one can feel independently of reason's distinct activity of determining what is best using its own resources. These emotions, in those trained and habituated from birth onward, Plato might plausibly think, can lead many in the just city to have concern for their fellow citizens, even if they have the wrong reasons for doing so. Plato in the *Republic* tries to show that a good city is possible, even while holding epistemological and metaphysical views that are, broadly speaking, similar to those of the *Phaedo*. The worry remains, however, that the lower classes' faulty conceptions of the good and inability to truly understand why they are benefited will ultimately prove destabilizing.

## Perfection

Perfection is one of the most controversial issues in the *Republic*.[25] At *Republic* 519c–521c, Socrates announces that in order for the just city to come into being, philosophers, once they have grasped the Form of the Good, must be "compelled" to return to the Cave and rule. There has been much debate over whether Plato here requires philosophers to make a sacrifice of their happiness in order to serve their fellow citizens, or whether he thinks that ruling in these circumstances is, in fact, what most conduces to their own good. Fortunately, we need not resolve this issue, but we should note that the problem is especially acute because the philosopher has to return to the Cave. There are only a few people that he will be able to bring up to the light (i.e., to grasp the Forms and have knowledge of them), but for the rest, all he can do is make their existence in the Cave less bad. It remains very difficult to see how a life spent entirely in the Cave could be in itself a significant good for a human being, however, and thus one's own perfection, for philosophers, seems still to compete strongly with any political activity open to them.

# III. THE LATE DIALOGUES

Throughout most of the twentieth century, the ethical and especially the political aspects of Plato's views in the late dialogues have received little attention. Moreover, what has been written has tended to focus on fairly narrow and, in my view, less than fundamental issues. But in the past twenty years, interest and scholarship have grown, although much needs to be done and a scholarly consensus has yet to form on many issues.

---

25. For a recent discussion, see Brown (2000).

# The *Statesman*

The *Statesman*'s declared goal is to provide an account of the ideal statesman (*politikos*), and it proceeds by trying to find an account of the art or science that he possesses.[26] Nevertheless, especially toward its end, the dialogue takes up basic issues such as the nature of a good political community, the nature of the relations among citizens, and the revisability of laws and other rules, as well as important topics in Plato's psychology and views about education.

There are, the *Statesman* tells us, two basic kinds of people, the "courageous" and the "moderate": the former are quick and spirited, while the latter are slower and more intent on leading a private life. Both of these character types, before receiving a very specific sort of education, are defective and prone to ethical and political errors: the courageous tend to violence, and the moderate are unwilling to assert themselves even when they should (*Stsmn.* 307d–308b). The fact that those having such characters go wrong in these ways shows that they are not genuine and full virtues. Indeed, the seriousness of these mistakes shows that the original forms of courage and moderation do not even closely approximate genuine virtues. Plato's views about how such characters can and must be improved are bound up with significant changes in his conception of citizenship from the *Republic*.

One of the most fundamental differences between the *Republic* and the *Statesman* is that, in the latter, citizenship has much greater ethical significance and the qualifications for it are much higher. The just city of the *Republic*, as we saw, counted as citizens the members of the two lower classes, and none of them had just characters. The *Statesman*, however, gives a criterion for citizenship in terms of character: only just people can be citizens in a good or just city (*Stsmn.* 309e–310a). Those who cannot become genuinely virtuous are entirely excluded from citizenship (*Stsmn.* 308e–309a). Thus those having the original character types of "courage" and "moderation" cannot be citizens; only those whose characters have been moderated and improved so that they come to possess genuine virtue will be citizens.

The most important way of effecting such improvement is by education, specifically one that results in their having "really true and secure opinion about what is fine, just, and good" (*Stsmn.* 309c5–7). This education, unlike that in the *Republic*, is common to all the citizens of the good city. Because of this sameness of education and similarity of finished characters, the just city is not stratified by class as it was in the *Republic*. Indeed, with the exception of the single ruler who possesses scientific knowledge, there are no classes of citizens differentiated by their conceptions of happiness or the kind of virtue they can attain.[27]

26. In addition to the references in n. 2, on the *Statesman* specifically, see Annas and Waterfield (1995), Cooper (1999), and Rowe (1995a) and (1995b).
27. We are not told how large the city in the *Statesman* will be, but it is large enough to provide for its own defense. The citizen body will thus be much larger than the class of philosopher rulers in the *Republic*; the city described in the *Laws* will have 5,040 citizen households (737eff.).

In this city, all citizens are permitted to have private families and property; possessions are not held in common; at least all able male citizens perform military service; and both the courageous and the moderate serve in political offices on roughly equal terms (*Stsmn.* 311a). All citizens are expected to possess a high level of virtue. Given the important place of virtue in happiness, the same conclusion holds, mutatis mutandis, for happiness.

In sum, with regard to citizenship, the *Statesman* takes a crucial step. It redraws the boundaries of the city so that the just political association has become a community of the virtuous. Political science takes as its task drawing the citizens of a just or good city together "by concord and friendship into a common life" (*Stsmn.* 311b9–c1). It is only in this way that political science can bring about a "happy city" (*Stsmn.* 311c5–6). In such a city, the citizens share the same ultimate goal of fostering virtue in all the citizens. This is only possible because all citizens receive the same education that aims at giving them "really true and secure opinion about what is fine, just, and good." We cannot determine precisely what such opinions are or how they are inculcated, but they appear to rest much more on reasoned explanations than the musical education of the auxiliaries in the *Republic*.[28]

These changes from the *Republic* are what I think is most important for us in understanding Plato's political philosophy. But I shall briefly discuss another issue that has received considerable attention. Some scholars think that, in the *Statesman* (297c–302b), Plato holds that all cities that are not ruled by someone with scientific understanding should never change any of their laws. But this is an implausible view to attribute to Plato. After all, some of the established laws of extant constitutions can surely be highly defective: the laws may be self-contradictory or outmoded, or they may require the commission of flagrant and serious acts of injustice. Why would Plato forbid changing any of them? Even if there is now no scientific ruler available to correct them on the basis of knowledge, this does not place contemporary citizens at an epistemic disadvantage to the original establishers, since they, too, lacked knowledge. Indeed, if Plato thinks that there are ethical differences among people who still fall short of knowledge, contemporaries may well be ethically superior to those who originally established the laws. I can think of no plausible line of thought that would show that the costs of change must *always* outweigh any possible gain.

We see in the *Statesman* some significant changes in Plato's political theory with regard to the education of the citizens, the political activity allowed to them, and the goal of city. If this is right, we need some explanation of them. Are they simply changes in Plato's political philosophy that stand alone, or do they rest on developments or revisions in Plato's ethics, psychology, and epistemology? I return to this point in the *Laws* section. But we saw that Plato's middle-period political views depend on deeper aspects of his psychology and epistemology. It would be surprising if his late-period political views did not also rest on other aspects of his philosophy.

---

28. For support, see Bobonich (2002, 412–16) and Cooper (1999). McCabe (1997) and Nightingale (1996) suggest that a related lesson can be drawn from the *Statesman*'s cosmological myths.

# The *Laws*

In addition to the stylometric evidence, we have Aristotle's testimony that the *Laws* is later than the *Republic*. The *Laws*' text shows some signs of being unfinished; there is some ancient evidence that Plato died while composing it and, given that it is the longest of the dialogues, it is reasonable to think that its composition overlapped with some of his other late works.[29] Let us begin with the most quoted passage from the *Laws* in which Plato characterizes the city he will go on to describe:

> Anyone who uses reason and experience will recognize that a second-best city is to be constructed.... That city and that constitution are first, and the laws are best, where the old proverb holds as much as possible throughout the whole city: it is said that the things of friends really are in common.... If the constitution we have been dealing with now came into being, it would be, in a way, the nearest to immortality and second in point of unity.... First, let them divide up the land and the households, and not farm in common, since such a thing would be too demanding for the birth, nurture, and education that we have now specified. (*Laws* 739a3–740a2)

Scholars have sometimes assumed that this passage settles the question of the relation between the political theory of the *Republic* and that of the *Laws*. Plato here endorses the city sketched in the *Republic* as the best possible city, but now he thinks that the demands it places on its inhabitants are too high: the city in the *Laws* is the second-best, although it is the best that is likely to be compatible with human nature.

But such an interpretation clearly misreads the passage. What is most important is that, in fact, Plato here does not endorse the *Republic*'s method for making the city one by introducing a certain kind of community of property and families. In the *Republic*, these institutions are restricted to the first two classes but are rejected for the third class, the producers. The *Laws* passage presents as the "first-best" city not that of the *Republic* but one in which there is, throughout the entire city, a community of property and of women and children. So the claim that the city sketched in the *Laws* is second-best does not suggest that the *Republic* still represents Plato's ideal political arrangement. What the *Laws* represents as the ideal—which is to be approximated as closely as possible—is a city in which all citizens are subject to the same high ethical demands. The *Laws* thus early on rejects the notion that the *Republic*'s city is the ideal. Something new is going on here, although it is easy to overlook or dismiss it as a sign of the carelessness of Plato's old age, especially if one comes to the text of the *Laws* with the implicit assumption that the more canonical *Republic* (which almost all students and scholars have read first and far more often) represents the essence of Plato's political thought.

---

29. Aristotle, *Politics* 2.6. For the report that the *Laws* was unfinished at Plato's death, see Diogenes Laertius 3.37. In addition to the references in n. 2, on the *Laws* specifically, see Laks (2001, 2005) and Saunders (1991).

The *Laws* also announces, with great fanfare, an innovation in the relation between the laws and the citizens: "None of the lawgivers has ever reflected on the fact that it is possible to use two means of giving laws, persuasion and force.... They have used only the latter; failing to mix compulsion with persuasion in their lawgiving, they have employed unmitigated force alone" (*Laws* 722b5–c2). In several earlier dialogues, Plato appealed to the analogy between the statesman and the doctor to justify harsh treatment and coercion of citizens for their own ultimate benefit.[30] The doctor should employ cuttings and burnings and so on to benefit the patient even if, as is typically the case, the patient does not see that the treatment is beneficial and so is unwilling to undergo it. This same analogy of the statesman as doctor is used to make a very different point in the *Laws* (the Athenian Visitor in general speaks for Plato in the *Laws*):

> ATHENIAN   What pertains to the laying down of laws has never been worked out correctly in any way.... What do we mean by this? We did not make a bad image, when we compared all those living under legislation that now exists to slaves being doctored by slaves. For one must understand this well: if one of those doctors who practices medicine on the basis of experience without the aid of theory should ever encounter a free doctor conversing with a free man who was sick—using arguments that come close to philosophizing, grasping the disease from its source, and going back up to the whole nature of bodies—he would swiftly burst out laughing and would say nothing other than what is always said about such things by most of the so-called doctors. For he would declare, "Idiot! You are not doctoring the sick man, you are practically educating him, as if what he needed were to become a doctor, rather than healthy!"

> KLEINIAS   Would he not be speaking correctly when he said such things?

> ATHENIAN   Maybe—if at any rate, he went on to reflect that this man who goes through the laws in the way we are doing now, is educating the citizens, but not legislating. (*Laws* 857c2–e5)[31]

In the *Laws*, Plato proposes attaching persuasive preludes to the individual laws and the law code as a whole. One of their main purposes is to give to all the citizens a rational understanding of the laws and of the more general political and ethical principles underlying them.[32] The rest of the citizens' education has the same aim, and it includes the study of calculation and arithmetic, measurement of

---

30. For example, *Gorgias* 515b–522b, *Republic* 389bc, and *Statesman* 296a–297b, but as Cooper (1999, 188–89) notes, it is not clear that the *Statesman* is in genuine tension with the *Laws*.

31. Karl Popper (1971, 139 and 270), for example, is so convinced that the *Laws* must hold the same view as the *Republic* that he claims that the remark beginning with "Idiot!" states Plato's own view. But Plato clearly rejects it and attributes it to an ignorant slave doctor who treats slaves (*Laws* 720be and 857ce).

32. For a defense of this view, see Bobonich (2002, 97–119) and Samaras (2002, 305–30); for different interpretations, see Laks (1990) and (2005) and Nightingale (1993).

lengths, surfaces and solids, and astronomy (*Laws* 817e–818a), as well as the study of plane and solid geometry, acoustics, and kinetics. Such an education fosters in all citizens the awareness that there are nonsensible properties—in the first place, mathematical ones.

The sophisticated cosmological and theological arguments found in Book 10 (which are intended as a prelude to the laws on impiety) draw on this education and are meant to be studied, repeatedly, by all the citizens (*Laws* 890e–891a). They are designed to bring the entire body of citizens to recognize that souls exist and are nonmaterial and nonsensible first causes of change in the universe, and that the universe itself has been structured by god in a beautiful and orderly way in accordance with mathematical principles and properties. The citizens should thus come to recognize that these nonsensible principles are themselves principles of order and value. This mathematical education goes far beyond anything that the *Republic*'s auxiliaries received, and in the *Republic* it was a mathematical education, as we saw above, that marked the transition to grasping nonsensible value properties. (In the *Laws*, those whose education and work are similar to that of the producer class in the *Republic*, are visiting workers with no political rights.)[33]

The differences from Plato's middle-period positions are clear. The *Laws'* view that nonphilosophical citizens can be educated to have, to some significant extent, a reasoned grasp of basic ethical and political truths extends the line of thought found in the *Statesman*, and it is a crucial difference from the *Phaedo* and the *Republic*. This difference has important implications for Plato's political philosophy; I shall note two of them. First, we saw that in the *Statesman* Plato suggested a new conception of a good city as an association in which all citizens aim at leading virtuous lives and at fostering virtue in the other citizens. In the *Laws*, Plato is much clearer and more emphatic in building on this conception of a good city and, as we have seen, restructures the citizens' education accordingly. Second, since the citizens are more capable of exercising good ethical and political judgment and engaging in rational discussion, they will be able to hold office and exercise political authority. The *Laws'* just city is not ruled by a single philosopher or a group of philosophers. There is an Assembly open to all the citizens and a Council elected from the citizen body. There are also a wide variety of other political and judicial offices open to the citizens. Such political participation is not only something that is now possible for the citizens, but it is also good in itself for them as a central expression of their virtue.[34]

There is also a second important set of differences from Plato's middle-period views. In the *Phaedo* and the *Republic*, Plato's characterization of nonphilosophers

33. Bobonich (2002, 378).

34. The *Laws'* account of political institutions is complex. Its views on changing the laws, the Nocturnal Council, property classes, and women complicate the above picture but do not, I think, change its essentials. Regardless of how disputes about the role of women and the use of property classes are to be settled, political office is not restricted to philosophers. With respect to the Nocturnal Council, I do not think that it exercises sole or dominant political authority, and it is not composed exclusively or predominantly of fully trained philosophers. For a defense of these views with references to other interpretations, see Bobonich (2002, 374–408); on the goodness of political activity, see Bobonich (2002, 450–73).

rests on his epistemology and psychology. The developments and changes I have suggested that we see in the *Statesman* and the *Laws* thus should also rest on developments in Plato's epistemology and psychology. Although examining these issues would take us far afield here, I think that this is correct. In particular, in the later dialogues, we see two important shifts in Plato's views. First, he comes to think that a grasp of nonsensible properties is much more deeply embedded in human thought and is not restricted to mathematical or philosophical knowledge. Thus there is no longer such a sharp discontinuity between the ethical cognitive capacities of philosophers and nonphilosophers. Second, Plato develops a more unified conception of the soul that emphasizes the role of reason in shaping all of the soul's capacities.[35]

Accepting, at least in broad outline, the account of the *Laws* that I have sketched—especially the account of the citizens' education and of what they can attain—let us return for a final time to our questions.

## Benefit and Coercion

If this interpretation is correct, we can see why Plato would think that he had made considerable progress on the issues of coercion and benefit. It is the case, of course, that there will be criminals in the city of the *Laws* who must be coerced and citizens too stupid or too absorbed in their nonrational desires and emotions to benefit from the preludes and the system of education more generally. But Plato accepts that many citizens will benefit from the preludes and the education and acquire some grasp, even if not a full understanding, of the ethical principles underlying the laws (of the sort that the auxiliaries in the *Republic* never attained).

Although the laws still have sanctions, Plato explicitly and sharply contrasts coercion with the sort of persuasion embodied in the preludes and the citizens' education. Citizens will benefit precisely because they are rationally persuaded and educated, and not coerced. Moreover, the possible benefit to citizens is much greater than before. Their grasp of ethical and value principles will enable them to lead lives that are genuinely and significantly good for them.

## Stability

In the *Laws*, Plato is perhaps more acutely aware of human frailty than he is in any other dialogue. He is especially sensitive to the influence that pleasure and pain have on the character and the choices of all human beings (662d–664c, 732d–734e) and is highly doubtful that it is possible for anyone, even one possessing full philosophical knowledge, to withstand the temptations of autocratic rule (689b, 691cd, 713cd, 875ad, 902ab). Nevertheless, this city should be considerably more stable than previous ones, since the citizens' education fosters a common

---

35. Plato's later epistemological and psychological views are controversial. For interpretations that differ in some respects from that in the text, see Lorenz, chapter 10 in this volume and Scott (1995).

conception of the good. In particular, it inculcates the understanding of a city as a shared association in which all aim at fostering and maintaining virtue in all their fellow citizens.

## Perfection

For similar reasons, the conflict between one's own perfection and political activity will be minimized even for the highest officials. Most of the citizens of the *Laws'* city will engage in political activities and sometimes exercise legal and judicial authority. Since such activities are a primary way in which their virtue is expressed, they will benefit the citizens. And insofar as political activity can help bring about genuinely virtuous states in others, the value to the agent of so acting seems to increase. This lack of competition between political activity and one's own perfection is emphasized by the theology of Book 10. There human ethical and political activity is seen as a form of cooperation with god in bringing good order to the universe as a whole, and god acts to guarantee that it is always the case that what is best for the individual is best not merely for the whole city but for the whole cosmos (e.g., *Laws* 906ab and 903bd).

# IV. CONCLUSION

I argue in this chapter that we can gain a deeper understanding of Plato's political philosophy by seeing it as, at least in part, a response to certain unresolved issues and problems that arise in the Socratic dialogues. In particular, I argue that Plato tries to address these issues in the political views of the Socratic dialogues by using the resources developed in the epistemological, metaphysical, and psychological theories found in dialogues such as the *Phaedo* and the *Republic*. I also argue that some of Plato's views on these fundamental issues—especially those concerning coercing and benefiting citizens, the nature and stability of the political association, and the tension between one's own perfection and political activity—change and develop in later dialogues, such as the *Statesman* and the *Laws*. I also suggest that these later views themselves depend on developments in other parts of Plato's philosophy, especially his epistemology and psychology.

As I note, a number of aspects of the account that I offer are controversial and may be modified by future research. This is an exciting time in the study of Plato's political philosophy. Greater attention is now being paid to the *Statesman* and the *Laws*, and these later dialogues are, at last, being read in the context of the psychology, epistemology, ethical theory, and metaphysics (including the metaphysics of value) of the other late dialogues. This increased discussion of the late dialogues should also lead to more work on the issues and problems that recur throughout Plato's political philosophy from the *Apology* and the *Crito* to the *Statesman* and the *Laws*. As scholarly debate on these topics increases and new lines of research are identified, our understanding of Plato's political philosophy should grow.[36]

# REFERENCES

Annas, J. 1981. *An Introduction to Plato's Republic*. Oxford: Clarendon Press.

Annas, J., and Waterfield, R. eds. 1995. *Plato, Statesman*. Cambridge: Cambridge University Press.

Balot, R. 2006. *Greek Political Thought*. Oxford: Blackwell.

Barker, E. 1960. *Greek Political Theory: Plato and His Predecessors*. London: Methuen.

Benson, H. 2000. *Socratic Wisdom*. Oxford: Oxford University Press.

Bobonich, C. 2002. *Plato's Utopia Recast: His Later Ethics and Politics*. Oxford: Oxford University Press.

———. Forthcoming. "Socrates and Eudaimonia," in *The Cambridge Companion to Socrates*, ed. D. Morrison. Cambridge: Cambridge University Press.

Brickhouse, T. C., and Smith, N. D. 1999. *The Philosophy of Socrates*. Boulder, Colo.: Westview.

Brown, E. 2000. "Justice and Compulsion for Plato's Philosopher-Rulers." *Ancient Philosophy* 20, pp. 1–18.

Bury, R. 1926. *Laws*. 2 vols. New York: Putnam's.

Cooper, J. (ed.) 1997. *Plato: Complete Works*. Indianapolis: Hackett.

—— 1999. "Plato's *Statesman* and Politics" in J. Cooper *Reason and Emotion*, 165–91. Princeton, N.J.: Princeton University Press.

Hansen, M. 1991. *The Athenian Democracy in the Age of Demosthenes*. Oxford: Blackwell.

Harte, V. 1999. "Conflicting Values in Plato's *Crito*." *Archiv für Geschichte der Philosophie* 81, pp. 117–47.

Irwin, T. 1995. *Plato's Ethics*. Oxford: Oxford University Press.

Kamtekar, R. 1998. "Imperfect Virtue." *Ancient Philosophy* 18, pp. 315–39.

Kraut, R. 1984. *Socrates and the State*. Princeton, N.J.: Princeton University Press.

Laks, A. 1990. "Legislation and Demiurgy: On the Relationship between Plato's *Republic* and *Laws*." *Classical Antiquity* 9, pp. 209–29.

———. 2001. "In What Sense Is the City of the *Laws* a Second Best One?" in *Plato's Laws and Its Historical Significance*, ed. F. Lisi, 107–14. Sankt Augustin: Academia Verlag.

———. 2005. *Médiation et coercition: Pour une lecture des Lois de Platon*. Villeneuve d'Ascq: Presses Universitaires du Septentrion.

Manville, P. 1990. *The Origins of Citizenship in Democratic Athens*. Princeton, N.J.: Princeton University Press.

McCabe, M. 1997. "Chaos and Control: Reading Plato's *Politicus*." *Phronesis* 42, pp. 94–117.

Nightingale, A. 1993. "Writing/Reading a Sacred Text: A Literary Interpretation of Plato's *Laws*." *Classical Philology* 88, pp. 279–300.

———. 1996. "Plato on the Origins of Evil: The *Statesman* Myth Reconsidered." *Ancient Philosophy* 16, pp. 65–91.

36. I thank Alex Coley, Aditi Iyer, and Christine Kim for their comments, and I am especially indebted to Gail Fine for her many helpful suggestions.

Ober, J. 1998. *Political Dissent in Democratic Athens*. Princeton, N.J.: Princeton University Press.

Pangle, T. 1980. *The Laws of Plato*. New York: Basic Books.

Popper, K. 1971. *The Open Society and Its Enemies*. Vol. 1. Princeton, N.J.: Princeton University Press.

Rowe, C. 1995a. *Plato: Statesman*. Warminster, England: Aries and Phillips.

———. (ed.) 1995b. *Reading the Statesman: The Proceedings of the Third International Symposium Platonicum*. Sankt Augustin: Academia Verlag.

Samaras, T. 2002. *Plato on Democracy*. New York: P. Lang.

Saunders, T. 1991. *Plato's Penal Code*. Oxford: Oxford University Press.

Schofield, M. 2006. *Plato's Political Philosophy*. Oxford: Oxford University Press.

Scott, D. 1995. *Recollection and Experience*. Cambridge: Cambridge University Press.

CHAPTER 14

..................................................................................................................

# PLATO ON EDUCATION AND ART

..................................................................................................................

## RACHANA KAMTEKAR

CONCERN with education animates Plato's works: in the *Apology*, Socrates describes his life's mission of practicing philosophy as aimed at getting the Athenians to care for virtue (29d–e, 31b); in the *Gorgias*, he claims that happiness depends entirely on education and justice (470e); in the *Protagoras* and *Meno*, he puzzles about whether virtue is teachable or how else it might be acquired; in the *Phaedrus*, he explains that teaching and persuading require knowledge of the soul and its powers, which requires knowledge of what objects the soul may act on and be acted on by, which, in turn, requires knowledge of the whole of nature (277b–c, 270d); in the *Laws*, the Athenian Stranger says that education is the most important activity (803d) and that the office of director of state education is the most important office of the state (765d–e). Each of Plato's two longest works, the *Laws* and *Republic*, tirelessly details a utopian educational program. And Plato's outlook on the arts (poetry, theater, music, painting) is dominated by considerations of whether they help or hinder correct education.[1]

To bring Plato's vast and multifaceted concern with education into focus, it will be helpful to begin by looking through the lens of his differences with those he styles Socrates' educational rivals: sophists like Protagoras, teachers of rhetoric like Gorgias, and, ultimately, poets like Homer. Plato sees the differences between these educators and Socrates not only as a difference over what subject matter is worth learning but

---

1. On the issue of the educational as opposed to aesthetic value of art, see C. Janaway, *Images of Excellence: Plato's Critique of the Arts* [*Images*] (Oxford, 1995).

also as a difference over the nature of would-be learners' powers to learn. By under-standing these differences, we will gain insight into the motivation for Plato's positive educational proposals in the *Republic* and *Laws*.[2] For Plato's educational proposals go hand in hand with his psychology:[3] his distinctive account of human capacities to learn specifies the good human condition at which his educational proposals aim.

# 1. Socrates and the Rival Educators

The fifth and fourth centuries were a period of great intellectual and cultural productivity in Athens, but, at the same time, elite Athenians came to see a need for an education beyond the traditional immersion in culture and military training. We find ample evidence of this in the writings of Isocrates in the fourth century, but also in the phenomenon, well documented by Plato, of itinerant teachers in a variety of subjects, most importantly in persuasive speaking, flocking to Athens during Socrates' lifetime. A number of factors can explain this new interest in education beyond the traditional. Athenian political life had changed radically through the fifth century, with reforms in democratic institutions making possible greater popular participation (for example, jury duty and assembly attendance were now compensated for by a day's wage), at the same time as Athens' imperial pursuits greatly complicated its political affairs. Would-be political leaders now had to communicate effectively with a wider cast of people than previously and on a wider range of affairs. Now successful political leadership called for expertise in public speaking; expertise in military strategy, once a prerequisite for leadership, became dispensable (cf. Aristotle, *Politics* 1305a11–15).

## 1.1 The teachers

The teachers who came to Athens to meet this new demand promised tomorrow's politicians the means to personal and political success. According to Plato, Prota-goras claimed to teach "sound deliberation, both in domestic matters—how best to

2. There are important contexts for Plato's thoughts about education other than the one I consider here. For example, S. Menn, in "On Plato's Politeia," in J. Cleary and G. Gurtler (eds.), *Proceedings of the Boston Area Colloquium in Ancient Philosophy* 21 (Leiden, 2005), argues that the education described in the *Republic* is a correction (a "Socratization") of Laconizing ideal constitutions, of which the best-preserved example is Xenophon's *Constitution of the Spartans*, in that the *Republic*'s educational system counterbal-ances gymnastic education (which would otherwise make the spirited element harsh and the guardians not sufficiently gentle to fellow citizens) with a musical education that begins with love of wisdom and ends with the establishment of wisdom to guide the spirited part.

3. For a fuller view of how I see the connections between Plato's psychological accounts and edu-cational projects, see R. Kamtekar, "Speaking with the Same Voice as Reason: Personification in Plato's Psychology," *Oxford Studies in Ancient Philosophy* 31 (2006), 167–202.

manage one's household, and in public affairs—how to realize one's maximum potential for success in political debate and action" (*Protagoras* 318e–319a), and Gorgias claimed to teach "oratory" (*Gorgias* 449a)—that is, "the ability to persuade by speeches judges in a law court, councillors in a council meeting, and assemblymen in an assembly or in any other political gathering that might take place" (452e).[4] An expertise in public speaking could involve a great many subordinate subjects: in the *Phaedrus*, Socrates attributes to figures such as Protagoras and Gorgias the identification of many different elements of a successful speech, such as correct diction, indirect praise and censure, preambles and recapitulations, claims to plausibility, and so on (267d–269c). We can also plausibly take as subordinate to an expertise in persuasive speaking Protagoras' expertise in literary criticism, grammar, and diction (Plato, *Protagoras* 339a; Aristotle, *Rhetoric* 1407b6–9, *Sophistical Refutations* 165b20–21, *Poetics* 1456b8–18), the production of arguments for contradictory conclusions (Diogenes Laertius IX.52, 55; cf. Plato *Sophist* 232d), and epistemology—Protagoras is still famous for the doctrine, "man is the measure of all things" (*Theaetetus* 151e).[5]

Plato's take on the market in higher education in the Athens of Socrates' day[6] is clear from the beginning of the *Protagoras*: the merchandise is potentially dangerous, and the eager buyers are but poor judges of the value of what they are getting. Protagoras' prospective student Hippocrates tells Socrates of his desire to study with Protagoras to receive "a gentleman's education" (rather than to become a professional sophist himself), in response to which Socrates warns, when you go to a teacher, you hand your soul over to him. But while when you buy food in the marketplace you can take it away and test it before eating it, "you cannot carry teachings away in a separate container. You put down your money and take the teaching away in your soul by having learned it, and off you go, either helped or injured" (314b). It is dangerous to study with a sophist, not just because you might be throwing away your money but because you might end up with a damaged soul.

But how could studying with a sophist damage your soul? One might think that it is because the sophists corrupt their students by teaching them such things as that what goes by the name "justice" is a convention established by the weak to control the strong (*Gorgias* 483b–484a) or by the strong to control the weak (*Republic* I. 338c–339a).[7] Yet when Plato discusses these supposedly corrupting views, he does not put them in the mouths of the teachers who are the targets of his

---

4. All quotations from Plato's text are from the translations in J. Cooper and D. S. Hutchinson (eds.), *The Complete Works of Plato* (Indianapolis, 1997).

5. Hippias seems to have been a true polymath: expert in astronomy and geometry, diction, ancient history, and mnemonics (*Hippias Major* 285c–d; cf. *Protagoras* 318e–319a), as well as in the crafts of engraving, cobbling, and weaving (*Hippias Minor* 368b–c). But these figures would have made much of their money as private tutors to young men with political ambitions, so for teaching public speaking, and it is in this capacity that Plato's engagement with them is most extensive and intensive.

6. On Plato's rivalry with his own contemporary Isocrates, see Schofield, chapter 2 in this volume.

7. See T. H. Irwin, "Plato's Objections to the Sophists" ["Sophists"], in A. Powell (ed.), *The Greek World* (London, 1995), 568–90. My discussion above builds on Irwin's thesis that Plato does not fault the sophists for undermining the authority of Athenian moral values but, rather, for being uncritical of these values; I argue that Plato thinks the sophists dangerous because they make it intellectually respectable

criticisms, such as Gorgias and Protagoras.[8] Instead, he puts the charge that the sophists corrupt the young in the mouth of Anytus (*Meno* 91c–92e) and shows that, like Anytus' charge that Socrates in particular corrupts the young (*Apology* 24c–25c), it is based on ignorance and unconcern for the truth. In the *Republic*, Socrates generalizes the point and says that those who charge the sophists with corrupting the young are themselves the real corrupters (indeed, they are "the greatest sophists"), when they sit together in assemblies, courts, theaters, and other public gatherings, collectively praising some and blaming others (492a–c). As a result,

> Not one of those paid private teachers, whom the people call sophists and consider to be their rivals in craft, teaches anything other than the convictions that the majority express when they are gathered together . . . what the sophists call wisdom [is] learning the moods and appetites of a huge, strong beast . . . how to approach and handle it, when it is most difficult to deal with or most gentle and what makes it so, what sounds it utters in either condition, and what sounds soothe or anger it. . . . [The sophist] calls this knack wisdom, gathers his information together as if it were a craft, and starts to teach it. In truth, he knows nothing about which of these convictions is fine or shameful, good or bad, just or unjust, but he applies all these names in accordance with how the beast reacts—calling what it enjoys good and what angers it bad. He has no other account to give of these terms. (493a–c)

Let us grant, then, that the sophists are not the source of corruption but are merely reflectors of popular opinion and that the real source of corruption is the opinion of the crowd. Our question can be sharpened: If all the sophists teach is popular opinion, how does studying with them make one worse off than not studying with anyone at all?

The *Republic* passage quoted above faults the sophists on two counts: first, they do not know whether the popular convictions they reflect are fine or shameful, good or bad, just or unjust (cf. *Gorgias* 454e, 461b); second, they call the ability they teach—to tell which are the convictions of the majority and presumably to use these convictions to persuade the audience of some particular course of action— "wisdom." The sophists do not differ from the average Athenian in holding ignorant opinions about the fine, good, and just, but it is the sophists who make ignorant opinion intellectually respectable instead of acknowledging that it is a shortcoming. So, for example, Protagoras argues that what appears to be true to each subject is true for that subject (*Theaetetus* 152a, 160c). And Gorgias brags that rhetoric enables one to persuade an audience on any subject whatsoever even more effectively than the expert on that subject could—and without having to bother to

---

to seek nothing surer than opinion, and that he responds to this counsel of despair by developing a psychology to show how knowledge is possible.

8. Hippias draws the nature-convention distinction at *Protagoras* 337d, but to make peace between Protagoras and Socrates, saying that the assembled wise men, since they are alike in being wise, are kinsmen by nature even though not by convention.

learn the subject oneself (*Gorgias* 456b–c, 459e).[9] So the sophists combine skill in persuasive speaking with the elevation of mere opinion. In the *Phaedo*, Socrates suggests that when unskilled people experience arguments that are sometimes true and sometimes false, especially in the study of contradiction (of which Protagoras' work *On Conflicting Arguments* and Gorgias' *On Non-Being* would be star examples[10]), they acquire the beliefs that they are wise and that reason is not to be trusted. They come to believe that "there is no soundness or reliability in any object or in any argument" and as a result become closed off to true, reliable, and understandable arguments (90b–d). This is the harm of studying with sophists.

If a sophist only reflects popular opinion, then perhaps the cross-examination by which Socrates exposes Protagoras' ignorance about the virtue he claims to teach is also an examination of traditional Athenian education in values. Protagoras himself insists that his sophist's profession is continuous with what the familiar and celebrated poets, prophets, artists of various kinds, and even athletes of Greece practice (316d–317a). To the extent that Protagoras is the mouthpiece of Athenian values, contradictions within Protagoras' assertions about the relationship of the virtues to one another and to virtue as a whole (brought out by Socrates at 329b–333e and 349e–360e) also reveal the inadequacy of Athenian ideas about the virtue that Athens claims to teach. This hypothesis would explain at least three puzzling moments in the *Protagoras*. First, when Socrates expresses his doubts as to whether the virtue Protagoras claims to teach can in fact be taught, he gives as reasons what the *Athenians* must believe about virtue's teachability, which he infers from Athenian practices[11]—but the Athenians' beliefs give Socrates reason to doubt that virtue is teachable only because he here (incredibly) counts the Athenians as wise (319b). So Protagoras is constrained to show that the belief in the teachability of virtue is implicit in Athenian practice because of the way Socrates first framed the issue.[12] But why would Socrates do this? Second, when Protagoras

---

9. Plato does not call Gorgias a sophist, and indeed in the *Gorgias* Socrates distinguishes sophistic and rhetoric, insisting that although alike and often confused, they are different activities, sophistic making itself out to be the craft of legislation and rhetoric the craft of justice (465c). Yet in virtue of their likenesses—making themselves out to be parts of political expertise while in fact aiming at pleasure rather than the good, and guessing rather than knowing (464c–d)—both sophistic and rhetoric are captured by the description of the so-called sophists in the *Republic* passage quoted above.

10. Irwin, "Sophists," 586, suggests that Gorgias' *On Non-Being* could have been written to demonstrate that arguments as rigorous as the Eleatics' could prove conclusions opposite to theirs, the lesson of this being that persuasiveness, the product of rhetoric, should be the ultimate standard of success in speech.

11. So, for example, the Athenians cannot believe that virtue is teachable since they allow any Athenian to advise the assembly about city management even though he cannot point to a teacher who taught him this, whereas in technical matters the assembly listens only to established experts (319d–e). Further supposed evidence of the unteachability of virtue is that good men such as Pericles (whom he calls a gratifier of appetites at *Gorgias* 517b–c) provide their sons the best possible education and so clearly must value it—and yet fail, themselves and through other teachers, to make these sons good (320b; cf. *Meno* 93a–94e).

12. So Protagoras too argues from beliefs implicit in Athenian practice: virtue must be teachable because we are angry at the vicious and punish them to deter them (323d–324a); the practice of punishment for vice requires us to think that virtue is teachable (324a–c); given the high value of virtue, it must be that everyone tries to teach it to everyone, which would explain why the sons of the virtuous aren't especially virtuous (324d–327c).

says that he would be ashamed to say that the person acting unjustly is temperate, even though many people say it, Socrates proceeds to examine the view of the many on the grounds that he is primarily interested in testing the argument and regards the testing of Protagoras and himself as a possible by-product (333c). But just a couple of pages earlier, Socrates has said he is not interested in examining arguments premised on an unendorsed assumption, for "it's you and me I want to put on the line" (331c). So why the reversal? Third, when Socrates introduces, into the examination of whether knowledge can be overpowered by anything else, the opinion of most people that one can know what is best and yet fail to do it because one is overcome by pleasure (352b–353a), Protagoras asks, "Socrates, why is it necessary for us to investigate the opinion of ordinary people?" (353a). Why indeed? All three moments fall into place when we recognize that Protagoras is Socrates' target: not qua individual to be improved by cross-examination but qua sophist and reflector of popular opinion.

Protagoras (who tellingly has more to say about traditional Athenian education than about his own educational program) mentions three elements in traditional education: children are educated by living examples (their parents or nurses teach them, "this is just, that is unjust," "this is fine, that is shameful," etc.), by the traditional aristocratic curriculum of poetry, music, and gymnastics and by the laws, which constitute patterns for behavior (*Protagoras* 325c–326d). This account gives substance to the idea, mooted by Protagoras and popular within the democracy, that every Athenian teaches virtue (328a), and suggests that education is ongoing and pervasive, not restricted to the period and methods of formal schooling.[13] It will be a short step to the outlook of the *Republic* and *Laws* that every feature of the environment—stories, works of art, fellow citizens—is a vector in the education of citizens. Plato's account of "musical"[14] education in these two works suggests that Plato agrees with Protagoras that the actual praise and blame of parents and teachers, and the projected praise and blame of culture heroes and the law, teach people what to value and how to behave; he differs from Protagoras because he questions whether it is *virtue* that the Athenians teach.

Plato's positive proposals for an educational curriculum in the *Republic* discuss the content of poetry at length, so we may defer discussion of poetry's content to section 2. For the moment, however, it is worth noting that Plato criticizes the poets on grounds quite similar to those on which he bases his criticism of the sophists and orators. First, all three are indifferent to the truth, and poetry (like rhetoric and sophistry) aims at giving pleasure to a crowd without any regard to what in fact is good (*Gorgias* 501d–502e; cf. 465b–c). This judgment of poetry is in some tension with Socrates saying in the *Apology* (22b–c), *Ion* (533e–535a), and

---

13. Cf. *Apology* 24e–25a; *Meno* 92d–93a. Pericles' funeral oration describes the city of Athens as a whole as a means for the education of Greece (Thucydides 2.41). M. F. Burnyeat discusses Plato's idea that educational influences include one's "total culture" in "Culture and Society in Plato's *Republic*," in G. B. Peterson (ed.), *The Tanner Lectures on Human Values* 20 (Salt Lake City, 1997).

14. So-called after the Muses, a musical education would include learning to sing, to play an instrument, to recite and interpret poetry.

*Phaedrus* (245a) that works of poetry are produced by divine inspiration. The tension could be eased if Plato meant to criticize poets but not poetry or if he meant to exclude great works from criticism. Second, Socrates criticizes poets on the grounds that they cannot critically assess poetry, for although the critical assessment of poetry is part of the rhapsode's art and of a traditional aristocratic education (*Ion, Protagoras* 339a), it takes knowledge or at least dialectic to do it. For example, Socrates is able to resolve an apparent contradiction within Simonides' poem using the distinction between becoming and being (*Protagoras* 340b–d). In the *Ion*, Socrates argues that for Ion to be in a position to judge Homer's poetry as good, Ion must show the poetry to give us the truth about what it represents, and this, if Ion were to attempt it, would require Ion to know the truth about what it represents (531e–532a).[15] Indeed, in the *Republic*, Socrates relegates all the critic's concerns with rhythm, mode, diction, and so on (Protagoras' "correct speech" [*orthoepeia*]) to second place by saying that these must follow what is said, and what is said must conform to the character who supposedly says it (400d)—and presumably knowledge of good and bad character (which the poets do not have) should determine what characters appear in a poem.

For his own part, Socrates denies that he is any kind of teacher (*Apology* 33a–b). He does not charge fees as do the sophists,[16] but there is also a deeper reason: lacking knowledge of virtue,[17] he *cannot* teach others, not even if his own beliefs (e.g., 28b–d, 29b) are true—which they might be as a result of luck or divinity or of extensive elenctic self-examination.[18] Of course, he has, or tries to have, an effect on his interlocutors in discussion, at the very least showing them that their beliefs are inconsistent and as a consequence that they have intellectual work to do. This is not teaching, however, for teaching he glosses as "producing conviction with knowledge," which he contrasts not only with rhetoric ("producing conviction without knowledge") but also with inquiry, his own practice of refutation aimed at clarifying the subject at hand and rooting out false beliefs (*Gorgias* 454c–455a, 458a).

---

15. T. Penner takes Socrates' claim to be that Ion cannot know what Homer is saying (i.e., what Homer means) about medicine if he does not know the relevant truths of medicine. See Penner, "Socrates on the Impossibility of Belief-Relative Sciences," in J. Cleary (ed.), *Proceedings of the Boston Area Colloquium in Ancient Philosophy* 3 (Lanham, Md., 1987), 263–325. This is not right: Socrates is making a claim about what Ion needs to know in order to judge whether Homer speaks *well*, not about what he needs to know in order to know what Homer is saying. It's true that Socrates begins to question Ion by asking about his ability "to explain better and more beautifully" Homer's than Hesiod's verses on the same things (531a–b), but the content of this explanation is not "What does it mean?" It's, rather, "How is it *well said?*" Socrates' point is that just as one would have to have medical knowledge to judge whether the passages on healing wounds are well composed, one would have to have ethical knowledge to judge whether the passages on the relations between men, and gods and men, are well composed. And that is what both Homer and Ion lack.

16. *Apology* 19d, 33b

17. *Apology* 20c. Elsewhere, knowledge seems to require having an "account" (cf. *Meno* 97e–98a; *Gorgias* 465a), which would seem to enable its possessor to teach others.

18. That Socrates takes some claims to be true on the grounds that they have not been refuted in his elenctic experience is suggested by G. Vlastos, "The Socratic Elenchus" ["Elenchus"], in G. Fine (ed.), *Plato 1: Metaphysics and Epistemology* (Oxford, 1999), 36–63, 58.

Now as long as elenchus produces only puzzlement, it can be contrasted with both teaching and rhetoric, since it produces no conviction (save that one is ignorant), but once elenchus identifies certain beliefs as false, it seems to be producing a conviction: namely, that such-and-such beliefs are false. This characterization of elenchus' results raises a famous problem about how showing that someone's beliefs are inconsistent with one another can help to eliminate their false beliefs (Which of the inconsistent beliefs are they to reject?) and how consistency among beliefs attests to their truth (Why couldn't a set of false beliefs be internally consistent?).[19]

In the *Gorgias*, Socrates also attributes to interlocutors beliefs that they do not say they have, even beliefs they expressly deny having (466d–e, 474b–c, 495e, 516d). One possible explanation for this is that Socrates attributes these beliefs to interlocutors on the grounds that they are entailed by beliefs the interlocutors hold explicitly. In this case, we might expect that he would attribute false as well as true beliefs to his interlocutors, because surely some false beliefs are entailed by the beliefs his interlocutors hold explicitly. In fact, however, it is true beliefs in particular that Socrates attributes to them—which may call for the more extravagant hypothesis that he attributes true beliefs to interlocutors on the grounds of a doctrine that these truths are innate, perhaps to be recollected. This brings us to our next topic, the students.

## 1.2 The students

Gorgias' *Encomium of Helen* purports to demonstrate the power of persuasion by exculpating the universally blamed Helen of Troy; internal to the speech too are claims about the force or magic by which speech sways its audience (8–15): words

> become bearers of pleasure and banishers of pain; for, merging with opinion in the soul, the power of incantation beguiles it and persuades it and alters it by witchcraft. Of witchcraft and magic twin arts have been discovered, which are errors of the soul and deceptions of opinion. (10)

According to Gorgias, our poor epistemic condition makes us dependent on opinion, and opinion is vulnerable to persuasion, which "when added to speech can impress the soul as it wishes"; we can see this in the way in which meteorologists, skilled speechwriters, and philosophers influence their audiences' opinions (13). Indeed, he says, although "the mode of persuasion is in no way like that of necessity," "its power is the same" (12), for "the effect of speech upon the structure of soul is as the structure of drugs over the nature of bodies" (14).[20]

That Plato thinks that there may be something to Gorgias' account of the soul as epistemically deprived and so as impressionable by persuasion is suggested by

19. For discussion, see Vlastos, "Elenchus."

20. Gorgias' *Encomium of Helen*, in J. Dillon and T. L. Gergel (eds. and trans.), *The Greek Sophists* [*Greek Sophists*] (London, 2003).

Socrates' report of a wise man saying that "the part of the soul in which our appetites reside is actually the sort of thing to be open to persuasion and to shift back and forth" (*Gorgias* 493a). In the *Republic*, Plato seems to accept that Gorgias' characterization of the soul as a whole does accurately characterize the nonrational parts of the soul.[21] So Socrates describes musical and gymnastic education's effects on the soul using images from metallurgy (410d–411b) and dyeing wool (429c–430b), saying that prerational souls are "most malleable and take on any pattern one wishes to impress" on them (*Republic* 377a–b; cf. *Laws* 664a).[22] I consider the nonrational parts of the soul at greater length in section 2; for the moment, however, I note that the characterization of the nonrational elements in the soul as easily persuaded (malleable, able to be dyed any color) is highly cognitive, attributing to them the capacity for something like belief or appearance.

Plato's real difference with Gorgias lies in his conception of reason. Whereas Gorgias boasts that persuasion "can impress the soul as it wishes" by means of a force akin to that of witchcraft (13), Plato describes education as a process in which the natural capacities of the soul—and especially of reason—are awakened and developed. Thus, in the passage immediately following the famous cave allegory of the *Republic*, Socrates says,

> ...the power to learn is present in everyone's soul and ...the instrument with which each learns is like an eye that cannot be turned around from darkness to light without turning the whole body.... education is the craft concerned with...turning around [the whole soul until it is able to study...the good].... It isn't the craft of putting sight into the soul. Education takes for granted that sight is there but that it isn't turned the right way or looking where it ought to look, and it tries to redirect it appropriately. (518c–d)

Reason's powers are not content-neutral, as Gorgias imagines. Rather, just as sight is a power to grasp visible contents, reason is a power to grasp intelligible ones—which is why it needs only to be directed appropriately in order to learn. By contrast with the "so-called virtues of the soul," which "really aren't there beforehand but are added later by habit and practice," "the virtue of reason seems to belong above all to something more divine, which never loses its power but is always useful and beneficial or useless and harmful, depending on the way it is turned" (*Republic* 518d–519a).

Just how this power to learn works varies across dialogues. In the *Republic*, reason has a desire—to know the truth—that is fulfilled by knowledge (581b). Elsewhere, Socrates suggests that the immortal soul, having acquired knowledge in

21. In the *Republic*, Socrates' language for describing what the rulers must be able to resist in order to retain their educated beliefs seems to echo Gorgias': "neither compulsion nor magic spells" (*mête goêteuomenoi mête biazomenoi*) should lead them to give these up (412e); " 'the compelled'... [are] those whom pain or suffering causes to change their mind,...[and] 'victims of magic'...are those who change their mind because they are under the spell of pleasure or fear" (413b–c).

22. That music and physical training target the spirited and wisdom-loving parts of the soul (411e) is consistent with this training being prerational (402a).

its disincarnate state, can recollect this knowledge when incarnated—for example, when we are asked the right sorts of questions, or when we judge that sensible particulars are deficient in the possession of some property, or when an experience of beauty reminds us of the Form of Beauty (*Meno* 81b–86b; cf. *Phaedo* 72e–76d, *Phaedrus* 246d–250e).[23]

While the *Republic*'s idea of the mind as a power requiring appropriate direction differs in detail from Plato's doctrine(s) of recollection (according to which when we learn we are reminding ourselves of truths latent in our minds), the two have in common the rejection of Gorgias' implicit conception of the soul and consequently the rejection of his conception of education. Whatever its exact nature, reason's power to grasp the truth is such that it needs not a teacher to pour doctrines into it, but instead some stimulus to inquiry, whether a questioner like Socrates or conflicting experiences that summon the understanding (*Republic* 523c–524d).

Plato's difference with Protagoras is subtler. According to Protagoras, Zeus gave all humans justice and a sense of shame (*Protagoras* 322c–d); however, those who live in cities are much more virtuous than those who do not (327c–d), because cities educate their citizens by the processes discussed above (sec. 1.1). Now Protagoras does conceive of human beings as having a capacity for virtue rather than as being purely blank and impressionable. However, he characterizes this capacity as purely receptive: we learn what is fine and base, good and bad, from living and literary examples and from the example of the laws. How do we determine whether a new case is similar to or different from the cases we have learned? Do we generalize? Do we somehow pick up underlying principles? While Protagoras is silent about these vital questions, Plato attempts to answer them by describing the powers, objects, and activity of reason.

## 2. UTOPIAN EDUCATION

As much as Plato's *Republic* is a defense of justice against Glaucon's challenge to show how justice, and not only its consequences, is in our interest, it is equally a work on education, and to see this, we only need follow Socrates' interlocutor Adeimantus through the dialogue. Adeimantus remarks about Glaucon's challenge, "The most important thing to say hasn't been said yet" (362d), and goes on

---

23. The doctrine of recollection raises many questions beyond the scope of this chapter: What is the range of things about which we have innate opinions (the *Meno* speaks of "all truths" and does not mention forms)? Do innate opinions play any role in ordinary cognition, and if so, what? What enables us to tell which of our opinions are innate and therefore guaranteed to be true? Just what is the relationship between recollection as a result of repeated questioning and the account of the reason why that turns true opinions into knowledge (97e–98a)? Do we only have innate true opinions or also innate knowledge (cf. 85d)? For discussion of recollection, see Taylor, chapter 7 in this volume. Outside this volume, see also D. Scott, *Recollection and Experience: Plato's Theory of Learning and Its Successors* (Cambridge, 1995); Scott, *Plato's Meno* (Cambridge, 2006); and G. Fine, "Inquiry in the Meno," *Plato on Knowledge and Forms* (Oxford, 2003), 44–65.

to explain: the things conventionally said in *praise* of justice in fact undermine its claim to intrinsic value because they praise the good consequences of appearing to be just, such as high reputation and all that derives from this, and favor from the gods (362e–363e); further, poets and ordinary people alike say that justice is hard and injustice sweet, and they willingly honor unjust people and declare them happy; finally, they say that the gods can be bribed so as not to punish unjust deeds (363e–364c). Adeimantus raises a general concern about the effects of cultural environment on values, and—by contrast with Glaucon's immoralist challenge, which may be written off as purely theoretical[24]—the effects of culture and education on values are real effects. The commonsense "sayings" of an actual culture—the culture of Socrates and his interlocutors—are, Adeimantus suggests, a breeding ground for a casual attitude toward the concerns of justice which shades easily into immoralism. While Socrates' description of the ideal constitution is likely a response to Thrasymachus' observation that all existing constitutions serve the interests of their rulers (338d–e), his long treatment of the education that produces just citizens (376c–415d) and just individuals (including the perfectly just philosopher-rulers; 514a–540c) is a response to Adeimantus' concern; indeed, it is at Adeimantus' urging that Socrates describes the education of the guardians at all (376c–d).

Before we turn to the details of Plato's educational proposals, it may be helpful to have a synoptic view of the whole educational program of the *Republic*, and to that end, see table 14.1

Musical and physical education, which are designed for the whole guardian class (future philosopher-rulers and their helpers, the military and police force), aim to produce habituated political virtue in the soul (430a–c, 522a).[25] I will say nothing further about physical education, but it is interesting to note that its object is also to train the soul rather than (as one might expect) only the body (410b). The higher education in mathematics and dialectic is designed for future philosopher-rulers. Mathematical education turns the soul around to the realm of the things

24. B. Williams writes, "Glaucon claims...that someone armed with Gyges' ring act unjustly, as (effectively) an exploitative and self-seeking bandit. An immediate objection to this is that, with regard to many people, it is not very plausible...[for] it is likely that, if an ethical system is to work at all, that the motivations of justice will be sufficiently internalized not to evaporate instantaneously if the agent discovers invisibility. Moreover, it is not clear in any case how much such a thought-experiment tells one about justice in real life" (Williams, "Plato against the Immoralist," in O. Höffe [ed.], *Platon, Politeia* [Berlin, 1997], 59). One might reply that such a thought experiment tells us that in those real-life circumstances in which we can commit injustice without likely punishment, it is rational to commit injustice, and that this is evidence that justice is not preferable to injustice in every way. For an argument along these lines, see T. H. Irwin, "*Republic* 2: Questions about Justice," in G. Fine (ed.), *Plato 2: Ethics, Politics, Religion, and the Soul* (Oxford, 1999), 170–75. Still, it may be that acceptance of Glaucon's argument could not actually undermine the motive to justice because of the way in which this motive is internalized. Adeimantus, by contrast with Glaucon, focuses on actually held beliefs that do undermine the motive to justice.

25. In R. Kamtekar, "Imperfect Virtue" (*Ancient Philosophy* 18 [1998], 315–39), I argue that such education-inculcated political virtue, while not based on knowledge as is philosophical virtue, is nevertheless genuine: its possessors value virtue for its own sake rather than for the sake of its consequences, for as a result of their education, they have an internalized standard of conduct that they try to live up to even in the absence of rewards and punishments.

Table 14.1 Educational Curriculum in the *Republic*

| Stage | Education |
| --- | --- |
| First, when the soul is most malleable (377b) | Poetry and music: false stories containing something of the truth (377a and ff.); heard, perhaps enacted (395c) |
| After poetry and music (403c), for 2–3 years (537b) | Physical training (403c) |
| In childhood, in play (536d–e) but not during physical training (537b) | Mathematics: arithmetic, plane and solid geometry, astronomy, harmonics (525a–31d) |
| From the age of 20 on | Synthesis of earlier studies into a unified vision of their kinship with one another and with the nature of what is (537c) |
| 30–35, after the mathematical "prelude" | Dialectic (532a–39e) |
| 35–50 | Practical experience (539e–40a) |
| 50 | The Good itself (540a) |

that are (521d–525b). Dialectic results in knowledge of the Forms, including the Forms of the virtues, culminating in a grasp of the Good itself.

As we have seen, in the *Protagoras*, Socrates distinguishes between education as mere cultural reproduction and education as cultivating genuine virtue by requiring knowledge for the latter. In the *Republic*, at the end of his account of musical education, Socrates once again cautions that

> neither we nor the guardians we are raising will be educated in music and poetry until we know the different forms of moderation, courage, frankness, high-mindedness, and all their kindred, and their opposites too, ... and see them in the things in which they are, both themselves and their images. (402c)

Consequently, when Socrates acknowledges that what he has to say about the soul and the virtues is only adequate to the standards of their present discussion (504a–b; cf. 435d), we might reasonably conclude that his account of education, too, is subject to revision on the basis of knowledge of the Forms of the virtues. Since Socrates does not give (and may well not have) accounts of these forms, it is worth approaching his educational proposals with the following question: Where do his educational goals and standards come from?

## 2.1 Musical education

Education begins, Socrates says in the *Republic*, with stories told to young, impressionable children. The education is designed for guardian-children, and it is unclear whether the producing class will receive any part of this education, but it would seem difficult (and pointless) to exclude them. To know their place in society, they would need to hear the Noble Lie (414b–415d), and some of them might turn out to be guardian material (415a–c). In any case, if the goal of the city is, as Socrates says repeatedly, to make the city as a whole as happy as possible, and if education is the route to happiness, it would make no sense to deprive them of any education they are capable of benefiting from. He argues that women in the ideal city ought to be educated in the same way as men also on the grounds that this makes them as good as possible.[26]

Socrates says the stories told to the young are "false on the whole, though they have some truth in them" (377a). This requirement that stories have "some truth" is vague. Socrates says that children should not hear stories that would cause them to take into their souls beliefs that are "opposite to the ones they should hold when they are grown up" (377b) and proceeds to censor the verses of Homer, Hesiod, and others on the basis of the vicious behavior these verses attribute to the gods and hence license for humans. In any case, Socrates lacks knowledge about the virtues. As a result, it may seem that musical education is only concerned with mind- and behavior- control and not at all with truth.

Yet the truth is the foremost concern in musical education. The first grounds for rejecting stories is if they "give . . . a bad image of what the gods and heroes are like, the way a painter does whose picture is not at all like the things he's trying to paint" (377d–e). So a bad image is not merely one that leads to undesirable consequences like antisocial behavior; it is inaccurate. But if the stories as a whole are false, as Socrates says at the outset, what is the objectionable inaccuracy that justifies throwing out verses?

Socrates says that we are all ignorant of ancient events involving the gods (382c–d), yet these stories are all about such events, so the stories must be (blamelessly) false in this sense: they are inventions, fictions. In what sense, or about what, then, may they not be false? Socrates says, somewhat vaguely, that all gods and humans hate "true falsehoods"—that is, falsehoods "about the most important things" and "the things that are" (382a–b). This suggests that what the stories must be accurate about is how we should live, so about happiness and what does and doesn't conduce to it. Stories that convey moral untruths are objectionably inaccurate and must be thrown out.

For example, Socrates' criteria for judging stories about the gods are (1) what is pious (which presumably requires accuracy about the gods), (2) what is advantageous to us (which may, since the god is good, be a proxy for truth), and (3) what is consistent (380b–c). Socrates seems to assume that these criteria, which could in principle conflict, converge.[27] His "patterns for . . . stories about the gods" (379a) follow from the hypothesis of god's goodness: first, since nothing good is harmful, and nothing that is not harmful can do harm, and nothing that does no harm can do or be the cause of anything bad, it follows that a god is not the cause of bad things; on the other hand, since good things are beneficial or the cause of doing

26. I argue for this in R. Kamtekar, "Social Justice and Happiness in the *Republic*: Plato's Two Principles," *History of Political Thought* 22 (2001), 189–220.

27. Again, one could explain this after Vlastos ("Elenchus," 58), as assumed on the basis of his elenctic experience.

well, a god is the cause of good things (379b–c). Again, since the best things are most resistant to change, the gods would not want to change, for that would be to make themselves worse (380e–381c). Finally, being perfectly good, the gods have no need of falsehoods, no need to change or deceive anyone; instead, they hate falsehoods (382d–383a).[28]

In this discussion, Plato focuses not on the truth of statements but rather on the truth or falsehood of the beliefs that people form on the basis of statements, for it is beliefs that influence actions and form characters, virtuous or vicious. Thus Socrates dismisses the observation that the stories he is banning come out true if read allegorically: "the young can't distinguish what is allegorical from what isn't, and the opinions they absorb at that age are hard to erase and apt to become unalterable" (378d). To know how to read a poem allegorically, one would need to have an independent grasp of the truths that one hopes to find in the poem; these poems, however, are people's first teachers.

Hearing stories and taking them to be true is the most obvious of mechanisms by which opinions are impressed in the soul. The human being to be educated is a desirer after happiness, and he looks to the gods and heroes for both excusing precedents (391e) and positive ideas about how to seek happiness. Listening to traditional stories about Zeus, a listener might reason, Zeus is good and lives the most blessed life, so it cannot be contrary to happiness to be led by one's lusts or to harm one's father and so it cannot harm me to do these things—I am just doing as Zeus does. Or he might reason, satisfying one's lusts and acting on one's anger are part of what living a happy life involves—look at Zeus! Although the focus of the discussion is on eliminating passages that might lead people astray, Socrates sometimes retains a verse to prescribe behavior. For example, to model the virtue of self-control, he includes the passage about Odysseus' "exhibiting endurance in the face of everything" when he controls his angry impulse to slaughter his maids as they carouse with Penelope's suitors (390d).

Imitation *may* be a separate mechanism by which people acquire opinions. As a prelude to his prohibition on guardians taking on the roles of vicious or weak characters (leaving it open whether they will play any parts at all[29]), and ultimately on all craftsmen representing vicious characters (401b), Socrates says that

28. Socrates delays specifying the stories that may be told about human beings until after he has shown "what sort of thing justice is and how by nature it profits the one who has it, whether he is believed to be just or not," lest his interlocutor find that he has "agreed to the very point that is in question in our whole discussion" (392b–c). However, stories about the gods and heroes help to set the guardians' standards as to how they may behave, and Socrates seems to rule out certain passages because they represent the gods and heroes behaving unjustly. For example, they may not hear stories about gods warring, fighting, plotting against one another, or hating their families or friends (378b–c; for other stories that seem to be censored because they attribute injustice to the gods and heroes, see 377e–378a, 390d–e, 391d). Even if these passages are censored for attributing other vices to the gods (enmity, impiety, immoderation, cowardice), if human justice is closely connected to these other virtues, Socrates is in the very danger he warns of at 392b–c, of prematurely assuming what justice is.

29. Socrates says, "*If* they do imitate, they must imitate…what is appropriate for them" (395c; emphasis mine)

"imitations practiced from youth on become part of nature and settle into habits of gesture, voice, and thought" (395c). He is talking here about the effects of playing the part of a character in a play or poem, in theatrical performance, or perhaps simply in reading aloud. He has just distinguished two kinds of narration (*diêgesis*): narration in the voice of the poet and imitation (*mimêsis*), which is narration in the voice of a character (392d–394b). Socrates defines imitation (of a person) as "making oneself like someone else in voice or appearance" (394b–c).[30] The evidence is not conclusive whether Plato thinks that we have a basic propensity to imitate (seen perhaps in the way babies mimic facial expressions) which is not (at least initially) hooked up to our happiness-seeking behavior, or whether he just thinks that we imitate those we regard as happy. Socrates says that one can't help but imitate the things we associate with and admire (500c), but this makes admiration a precondition of imitation, and Plato may well think that we admire those whom we think are happy.

The mechanisms by which poetry can affect the soul are also illuminated by Socrates' account of the divided soul in *Republic* X. He contrasts an inferior part of the soul, which persists in believing appearances despite the witness of measurement, with the part of the soul that "puts its trust in measurement and calculation" (602e–603a), obeys the law, and commands us to deal with our misfortunes by fixing them as best we can rather than grieving over them (604b–c).[31] If we are decent, we are ordinarily able to keep in check the desires of the inferior part of our soul for "the satisfaction of weeping and wailing," desires it has "by nature."[32] Yet

---

30. There is a problem about how to square this account of imitation as impersonation with the account of imitation in *Republic* X, according to which any artistic representation would seem to count as imitation, for on the *Republic* X account, what painters as well as poets do is to make imitations of what craftsmen make (597d)—or, more precisely, make imitations of the appearances of these products of the crafts (598b). Janaway, *Images*, 126, observes that despite their divergent senses of mimesis (impersonation vs. appearance-making), these two discussions are about the same thing: poetry "insofar as it is mimetic" (595a5) is poetry that involves dramatization and so involves the actor in impersonation.

31. This discussion distinguishes only two parts of the soul, whereas in *Republic* IV, Socrates distinguishes three; some scholars hold that the two parts distinguished in *Republic* X are two further parts into which rational part of the soul is divided; others hold that the inferior part is the spirited part, and still others that it is the appetitive part. But Plato's periphrastic characterizations of the lower part(s) of the soul in *Republic* X seem designed to block any precise mapping to the parts of *Republic* IV: in *Republic* X, he characterizes the lower part in two ways. The first way is by what it does in the very situation under consideration, as the lamenting element (606b1), the pitying element (606b7–8), the element forcibly restrained by the reasoning (606a3), the thing in the soul which judges contrary to measurement and reasoning (603a7), the element which grieves and impedes deliberation (604c3–5), the thing that is insatiable for recalling and lamenting our sufferings (604d8–9), and so on. The second way is by contrast with the best part of the soul, as "base" or "inferior" (603a, 603b: *phaulon, elatton*; 604d: irrational, idle, a friend of cowardice; cf. 605c). Often, he refers to it/them simply by "*toiouton*," of this sort. This elusiveness suggests that what is important to Plato in this discussion is not the details of the soul-divisions of Books IV.436b–441c and IX.580cd–581b (how many parts, the internal logic of each part, the part's characteristic object of desire) but, rather, the opposition between the reasoning part and the other(s), and the inferiority of the other(s) to the reasoning part.

32. It is unclear why the inferior part desires to grieve. Perhaps we enjoy strong feelings (and in the theater can enjoy them without suffering the real misfortunes that ordinarily cause them). T. Gould suggests there is a particular pleasure in the spectacle of the innocent victim and explores this in *The Ancient Quarrel between Poetry and Philosophy* (Princeton, N.J., 1990).

when we watch a tragic performance—for example, one in which a supposedly great man grieves excessively for the loss of his son—we think that we may relax rational control over the inferior part, on the grounds that there is no shame involved in praising and pitying the grieving character (after all, it is not ourselves but another person we are praising and pitying), and because doing so gives us pleasure.[33] The effect of this, however, is to make it difficult to control our desire to grieve when we ourselves suffer (606a–b).

We might wonder why pitying a character in a play should affect our real-life attitudes, but Plato suggests that the attitude we have to the character in the play is also a real-life attitude. The reason we allow ourselves to pity him—that is, to share in his lamentation—is not that we say to ourselves, "no harm done; it's only a play," but, rather, "it's not me and mine I'm lamenting, so there's no shame attached." So we already believe "the loss of a son is a terrible thing," and, inconsistently, "it's shameful to lament the loss of my own son"—and because the theater presents us with the loss of a son not our own, we deem our shame response irrelevant and indulge our desire to grieve.

Socrates attributes the desire to grieve to the inferior part of the soul, the beliefs of which follow appearances and are unresponsive to reasoning, calculation, and measurement.[34] The indifference of the nonrational part(s) of the soul to truth suggests that the musical education's concern with the truth of beliefs about value is really a forward-looking concern for when the soul's rational powers develop; the truth of beliefs about value does not engage any power or propensity of the nonrational part(s). Further, the nonrational part(s) may not respond to considerations such as that grieving on behalf of a tragic character brought pleasure but no shame, whereas grieving on one's own behalf brings shame and interferes with future-directed deliberation.[35]

Plato's remarks on painting and poetry in the first thirteen pages of *Republic* X, which I have been mining for what they tell us about belief formation, have attracted much scholarly and popular attention. Does Plato finally banish the artists from his ideal city?[36] How can Plato reconcile the banishment of dramatization from ideal education with his own practice of dramatization in the

33. It may indicate our lack of education that shame and pleasure are our only considerations (cf. 606a).

34. D. Scott has argued that that the *Gorgias* and *Republic* I depict Socrates' failures in education and attribute these failures to intransigent beliefs supported somehow by the interlocutors' good-independent appetitive desires. Scott argues that the *Republic* suggests two sources of intransigent (false) beliefs: they may have been imprinted on the very young soul (377ab), thereby becoming indelible (378de), or they may be caused or sustained by (bad) appetitive desires (412b, 429c–430a, 560c–d, 494d, 605b) (Scott, "Platonic Pessimism and Moral Education," *Oxford Studies in Ancient Philosophy* 7 [1999], 15–36).

35. Or, more precisely, it may be that the evaluative powers of the appetitive part do not extend to considerations of honor or what is all-things-considered best, but are restricted to what brings pleasure by satisfying a preference.

36. This is suggested by I. Murdoch's title, *The Fire and the Sun: Why Plato Banished the Artists* (Oxford, 1977). Murdoch's book is concerned rather with Plato's hostility to artists.

dialogues? Does Plato reserve his criticisms for imitators of appearances, leaving the door open to artists who imitate Forms?[37]

Although he begins his criticisms of "imitative" (595a) poetry by arguing that painters produce imitations of appearances which are "third from the . . . truth" (597e),[38] Plato does not ban painting—even though, for example, a painter who knows nothing about carpentry can paint a representation of a carpenter that children and fools mistake for a real carpenter when it is distant enough (598b–c).[39] It is true that paintings are like poems in being imitations, and that imitations are inferior to the things they imitate. But Socrates uses this point not to banish all imitations but to argue, against those who think that the poets "know all crafts, all human affairs concerned with virtue and vice, and all about the gods" (598d–e), that producers of imitations cannot be teachers. For if they could produce virtuous deeds, they would not devote themselves to producing imitations of them in poetry (599a–b); and as it happens, they have no good laws, successful wars, inventions in the crafts or sciences, ways of life, or virtuous individuals to their credit (599d–600c).[40]

It is a much-debated question how the banning of imitative poetry in *Republic* X (595a) compares with the restrictions on poetry in *Republic* III (to which *Republic* X refers). Clearly the ban on representations of vicious behavior (*Republic* X) is more extensive than the ban on guardians' playing the parts of vicious characters (*Republic* III 395c), but the representation of vice—in *all* the arts, not just in poetry—was already banned in *Republic* III (401b). Finally, the only poetry admitted into the city is "hymns to the gods and eulogies to good people" (607a). This, it seems, is the poetry Plato thinks could be informed by the knowledge of Forms that Socrates says must underwrite and be the goal of a proper education. This is the same type of poetry that the *Phaedrus* describes as divinely inspired by a madness that comes as a gift from the gods, one of its powers being to awaken the soul to a "Bacchic frenzy of songs and poetry that glorifies the achievements of the past and teaches them to future generations" (244a–245a).

Many have challenged Plato: even if the poets have no knowledge of the truth, and can only reflect back to their audience the uninformed opinions that circulate in society (602a–b), surely poets can also raise critical questions about these

---

37. On Platonism in art, see the introduction in S. Halliwell, *Republic Book 10* (Warminster, 1988).

38. J. Annas points out that the analogy between poetry and painting in *Republic* X supports a criticism of poetry as unimportant, which is distinct from and in some tension with the criticism of poetry as dangerous (Annas, "Plato on the Triviality of Literature," in J. Moravcsik and P. Temko [eds.], *Plato on Beauty, Wisdom and the Arts* [Totowa, N.J., 1982], 1–28). But perhaps Plato's two criticisms can be reconciled as follows: (1) poetry is of little value even if it represents the truth as accurately as possible because it can only represent the truth dimly, and as a result poetry can contribute far less to making people virtuous than can legislation or teaching, and (2) poetry is of great disvalue, even danger, when it does not represent the truth accurately.

39. E. C. Keuls, *Plato and Greek Painting*, (Leiden, 1978); A. Nehamas, "Plato on Imitation and Poetry in *Republic* X," in J. Moravcsik and P. Temko (eds.), *Plato on Beauty, Wisdom and the Arts* (Totowa, N.J., 1982), 47–78.

40. Socrates makes a similar point without the machinery of imitation in the *Phaedrus*, when he says that the dialectician, who can improve souls through conversation, won't regard his writings as his serious work (276c–277a).

opinions? The problem with this is that poetry provides no resources to answer these questions other than opinion all over again. What help can poetry give to a reader of Sophocles' *Antigone* who wonders, "What is justice, after all? My former answers, obedience to the law or the king, and upholding the traditional customs, conflict!" Plato can offer at least a way ahead, dialectic.

## 2.2 Mathematical and dialectical education

While the goal of musical education is that citizens acquire true beliefs about how to live well, about such things as what actions are courageous and what institutions just, this is clearly inadequate if our souls have the capacity to know what courage or justice is. Indeed, it is inadequate even if our souls only have the power to *ask* what courage or justice is. The *Republic* discussion of dialectic describes the corrosive effect of such questions on even a person committed to the convictions with which he has been brought up. The dialogues in which Socrates pursues "What is . . . ?" questions about courage, justice, and so on amply illustrate the shortcomings of true beliefs. Since a person who has only true beliefs is limited in his comprehension of courage or justice to identifying instances of courage or justice,[41] such as endurance in battle or returning what is owed, when he offers these as accounts of courage or justice, he will find that they turn out to be courageous or just in some cases but cowardly or unjust in others. As a result of being repeatedly refuted, Socrates says in the *Republic*, he will start to believe that "the fine is no more fine than shameful, and the same with the just, the good, and the things he honored most"; he will lose his former commitments; and even philosophy will lose its standing in his eyes (*Republic* 538c–539a, 539c).

Avoiding asking "What is . . . ?" questions is not an option. If it is a natural power of the soul to ask such questions, then an education that thwarts or even ignores it will not be a good education. Further, Socrates says that there are certain experiences in which our conflicting judgments "summon the understanding"—make us ask, in other words, about the qualities we ascribe to things, what they are. If the same object appears great or small depending on what it is seen next to, the soul is puzzled: How can the same thing be great and small, these being opposite qualities? The soul then summons the understanding to inquire: Are the great and the small distinct? What is the great? What is the small? (523b–524d).[42]

41. By "instances," I do not mean particulars. A. Nehamas shows that the problem with the candidate definitions given by Socrates' interlocutors is not that they supply particulars where Socrates asks for universals but that the universals they supply are incorrect (Nehamas, "Confusing Universals and Particulars in Plato's Early Dialogues," *Virtues of Authenticity: Essays on Plato and Socrates* [Princeton, N.J., 1999], 159–75).

42. That this is an activity of the rational part of the soul is indicated by Socrates' remark that the irrational part "cannot distinguish the greater and the smaller but believes that the same things are great at one time and small at another"—for example, that the once-great hero is now small, reduced by misfortune (605b–c). I diverge from the Grube-Reeve translation in this passage to substitute "great" for their "large," because the moral context seems to require it. I also translate "greater" and "smaller" (for *meizô* and *ellatô*) at 605c1, as does C. D. C. Reeve in his translation, *Plato, Republic* (Indianapolis, 2004).

Number is such a summoner: from the point of view of sense experience, each thing is both one and many, but, since one and many are opposite qualities, this puzzles the soul. This is why the study of arithmetic and calculation reliably summon the understanding, turning our attention away from counting particulars given to us in experience and toward number itself, which can be grasped only in thought. So the study of mathematics, apart from influencing the orderly ranks that warriors must observe, turns potential philosophers from becoming to being (525b–c). Likewise, plane and solid geometry, astronomy that seeks out the true motions approximated by the observable heavenly bodies (529c–530c), and harmonics pursued by way of "problems" (531b–c) all "purify" and "rekindle" the soul's most valuable instrument (527d–e), making it easier to see the Form of the Good (526e). Finally, the different mathematical studies must be integrated and consolidated to "bring out their association and relationship with one another" (531c–d). These mathematical studies are preparatory for dialectic, but they are also intrinsically good for the soul.[43]

Properly practiced, dialectic uses reason alone to find the being of each thing and continues until the understanding grasps the Good itself (532a–b); it enables the student to give an irrefutable account of the being of each thing, including of the Good (534b); it produces an understanding of how all the subjects formerly studied fit together into a unified whole (537c); finally, unlike the mathematical disciplines, it achieves unhypothetical knowledge (533c–d). Socrates describes the Good grasped at the culmination of dialectic as the cause of both our power to know and of the truth of what is knowable. (508d–e) Many scholars see the grasp of the Good as a kind of direct acquaintance with a self-certifying or self-evident first principle from which all the Forms may be derived. But it can also be seen as a synoptic understanding of a coherent teleological structure of which the Forms are parts.[44] In either case, prior to grasping the Good which is the condition of unhypothetical knowledge, students have their dialectical studies interrupted by a fifteen-year practical experience requirement, the point of which seems to be to ensure that future rulers are at least the equals of their fellow-citizens in experience and that they remain steadfast in their values (539e–540a). Unlike the other studies,

43. See Scott, chapter 15, and Taylor, chapter 7, both in this volume. See also M. F. Burnyeat, "Plato on Why Mathematics Is Good for the Soul," in T. Smiley (ed.), *Mathematics and Necessity: Essays in the History of Philosophy* (Oxford, 2000), 1–81, which argues that mathematics in the *Republic* does not have the purely "instrumental" value of sharpening the mind (as Isocrates and others seem to have thought) but is constitutive of ethical understanding since it provides a (low-level) articulation of objective value. Concord, for example, can be understood both mathematically (in harmonics) and ethically. A more minimal view would be that while Plato insists that mathematics ought not to be valued only as a tool for solving practical (e.g., agricultural or navigational) problems, the intrinsic value he accords to mathematics seems to *be* that it rekindles and purifies the soul and orients it toward being. This is not valuing mathematics in a content-indifferent way as a tool for sharpening the mind so that it can be exercised on other (intrinsically valuable) subjects but, rather, thinking of intrinsic value as that which puts the soul in a better condition—which is what mathematics does.

44. This is the view of Taylor, chapter 7 in this volume, and of G. Fine, "Knowledge and Belief in *Republic* V–VII," *Plato on Knowledge and Forms* (Oxford, 2003), 109–16.

the practical experience requirement does not seem to contribute to knowledge of the Form of the Good, but rather only to competence in political rule.

At the level of the individual soul, knowledge of the Good is a perfection of reason and, Socrates says, in addition to providing reason its characteristic pleasure of knowing the truth, it allows the nonrational parts of the soul "the truest pleasures possible for them" (586d–e). But Socrates says that even the truest pleasures of the nonrational parts are inferior in truth (they fill us up with "what is never the same, and mortal") and purity (they follow or are followed by pain) (585b–d). Their presence in a virtuous life seems to be more a matter of making the best of bodily and psychological necessity than of realizing any perfectible powers of the nonrational parts.

# 3. PLATO'S LAST THOUGHTS

Aristotle reports in the *Politics* that the *Republic* and *Laws* set out the same program of education (II.6.1265a6–8). This is a surprising claim, in view of the prominence in the *Laws* of striking educational institutions absent from the *Republic*, such as the use of the *Laws* itself as a teaching text (811c–e), drinking parties to test and reinforce the education of old men in self-control and modesty (645d–649d, 665c–666d, 671b–e), and persuasive preambles to the laws (719e–723c)[45]. But Aristotle may not regard the last as part of an educational program, and he may regard the former two as minor innovations. Certainly the Athenian's initial description of education echoes Socrates' description of musical education in the *Republic*: education channels a young child's pleasures and pains toward the right things before he can understand the reason why, so that when he later comes to understand, his reason and his emotions agree, virtue being a harmony between reason and emotion (*Laws* 653b; cf. *Republic* 401c–402a).

We may approach the question of how similar or different the *Laws'* educational proposals are to the *Republic's* by considering again how these educational proposals reflect, and are guided by, a conception of the soul that is to be educated. We may inquire whether or not any institutional differences we find reflect a difference in Plato's conception of the soul's powers to learn, and also whether or not institutionally identical educational proposals are described in terms that indicate a new conception of how they work on the soul to produce virtue. We cannot do all this here, but we can make a preliminary exploration.

Table 14.2, on the educational curriculum prescribed in the *Laws*, will allow us to consider at a glance a rather long-winded discussion.

---

45. On the way in which these preambles persuade rationally, as befits a free citizen, see C. Bobonich, "Persuasion, Compulsion, and Freedom in Plato's *Laws*," in G. Fine (ed.), *Plato 2: Ethics, Politics, Religion and the Soul* (Oxford, 1999), 373–403.

Table 14.2 Educational Curriculum in the *Laws*

| Stage | Education |
| --- | --- |
| Prenatal–3 years | Movement (788d–793e) |
| 3–6 | Play, wrestling, dancing (814e–816e), music |
| ? until they are old enough for the Chorus of Apollo? | Choral singing and dancing (in the chorus of the Muses) |
| ? from the time they are "tiny tots" at play | Arithmetic, to be followed by geometry and astronomy (819b–822c) |
| ? ongoing | Fighting, including with weapons (813d–e) |
| 10–13 | Reading and writing (809e–810b), the text of the *Laws* (811c–e) |
| 13–16 | Lyre-playing (809e–810a), to be in unison with singing (812d–e) |
| 18/20–30 | Choral singing and dancing (in the chorus of Apollo) (664c) |
| 30–60? | Choral singing and dancing (in the chorus of Dionysius) (653d, 665a, 666b, 670b, 812b–c) |
| ? | "Advanced education" for guardians (965b–968c): a grasp of the one over many, and a rational account; theology, the priority of soul and the power of reason |

An immediately striking difference in this account of citizens' education is the importance of certain kinds of movement, certainly in the first six years but presumably continuing throughout life in the form of choral dancing. The Athenian says that the souls (and bodies) of the young are always in motion (653d, 664e, 787d), are internally agitated (791a), and are wild due to the presence of unchanneled reason (808d–e), and it is all this unruly internal movement that calls for external movement (e.g., being carried about, dancing) to calm down the young soul (790c–d) and make it orderly. But we might note that the source of disorder is not purely "internal": according to the *Timaeus*, sense perceptions too cause unruly movements; the real cause of the soul's disorderly motion is embodiment (43a–c). In any case, the importance given to movement in the *Laws* accompanies Plato's new interest in the soul as the source of motion and so as a self-mover (*Laws* 895a–896a; cf. *Phaedrus* 245c–e).

Musical education in the *Laws* is aimed like musical education in the *Republic* at cultivating citizens' virtue; nevertheless, the *Laws*' discussion of musical education says little about the belief content required for this virtue. The Athenian does make the general point that poets and everybody else in the city must affirm that the best life is the most pleasant (662b–664b) and that the criterion of correctness in music—since music involves making likenesses and imitation—is accuracy in representing its model, beauty (667c–668b), which requires knowledge of what has been represented and how correctly and well the copy represents it (669b). The Athenian also repeats that authors may not compose as they like but must bear in mind the effects of their compositions on virtue and vice (656c), that poets are bound to express the society's notions of virtue (801d), that tragic poets may enter the city only if their doctrine agrees with the city's (817d–e), and that the elder chorus admits only virtuous representations in music to guide the citizens' souls to virtue (812c). But there are few details about correct belief content comparable to those in *Republic* II–III. Detailed accounts in the *Laws* are about things like the kinds of dances representing the movements of graceful people that may be performed (814e–816e).

So far, we have seen a difference in emphasis: although the two works insist on the importance of both doctrinal truth and enjoyment of true value, where the *Republic* discussion emphasized correct belief content, the *Laws'* discussion emphasizes pleasure: a well-educated person sings and dances well, singing and dancing good songs and dances, and, above all, takes pleasure in just these songs and dances (hating the other kinds)—the last of these being more important than correctness in voice, body, or thinking (654b–d).

These two new emphases in the *Laws*—on the soul's movements and on pleasure—seem to be related. Although the Athenian describes the young soul as malleable and impressionable (*Laws* 664a, 666c, 671b–c) as Socrates did in the *Republic*, he also observes that even very young humans have a sense of order and disorder in movement (653e–654a, 664e–665a); his point seems to be that even though they are disorderly, young souls are already responsive to and appreciative of order.[46] After all, their motion, erratic and disorderly as it is, is just the soul's natural, rational, circular motion disrupted. By contrast in the *Republic*, young guardians have to be habituated to take pleasure in fine things, and the point of such habituation is to prepare the soul for the development of rational appreciation of these things (401c–402a). In the *Laws*, the pleasure a young child takes in the orderly movements of choral dancing seems to be evidence that his prerational soul itself has been put in a good state for it. If these thoughts are on the right track, then musical education in the *Laws* is not a matter of impressing prerational souls with belief contents that turn out to be appropriate to them only when their rational powers have developed. Instead, the direction of pleasures and pains is a development of protorational powers to perceive goodness.[47]

---

46. This is argued in C. Bobonich, *Plato's Utopia Recast* (Oxford, 2002). However, Bobonich relates this judgment to (what he argues is) Plato's late rejection of the *Republic* view of the soul as composed of three independently motivating parts. According to Bobonich, Plato's late writings instead depict reason as contributing conceptual content to even nonrational psychic movements like sensory pleasures. Thus, for example, the *Timaeus* and *Philebus* treat sensory pleasures as involving appreciation of fineness or good order and as perfections of our power of perception rather than as restricted to fulfilling the bodily ends of the appetitive part of the soul (350–73). H. Lorenz, *The Brute Within* (Oxford, 2006), differs from Bobonich in allowing the nonrational parts of Plato's late dialogues independent motivating power; according to Lorenz, the nonrational parts here are capable of representational content but not belief (95–110). The contrast between the *Republic* and *Laws* sketched above is compatible with, but does not require, the rejection of independently motivating parts in a divided soul.

47. Thanks to Gail Fine and Rachel Singpurwalla for their comments on an earlier draft of this chapter.

# BIBLIOGRAPHY

Annas, J. "Plato on the Triviality of Literature," in J. Moravcsik and P. Temko (eds.), *Plato on Beauty, Wisdom and the Arts* (Totowa, N.J., 1982), 1–28.

Bobonich, C. "Persuasion, Compulsion, and Freedom in Plato's *Laws*," in G. Fine (ed.), *Plato 2: Ethics, Politics, Religion and the Soul* (Oxford, 1999), 373–403.

Bobonich, C. *Plato's Utopia Recast* (Oxford, 2002).

Burnyeat, M. F. "Culture and Society in Plato's *Republic*," in G. B. Peterson (ed.), *The Tanner Lectures on Human Values* 20 (Salt Lake City, 1997), 217–324.

Burnyeat, M. F. "Plato on Why Mathematics Is Good for the Soul," in T. Smiley (ed.), *Mathematics and Necessity: Essays in the History of Philosophy* (Oxford, 2000), 1–81.

Cooper, J., and D. S. Hutchinson (eds.) *The Complete Works of Plato* (Indianapolis, 1997).

Dillon, J., and T. L. Gergel (eds. and trans.) *The Greek Sophists* (London, 2003).

Fine, G. "Inquiry in the Meno," *Plato on Knowledge and Forms* (Oxford, 2003), 44–65.

Fine, G. "Knowledge and Belief in *Republic* V–VII," *Plato on Knowledge and Forms* (Oxford, 2003), 85–116.

Gill, C. "Plato and the Education of Character," *Archiv für Geschichte der Philosophie* 67 (1985), 1–26

Gould, T. *The Ancient Quarrel between Poetry and Philosophy* (Princeton, N.J., 1990).

Halliwell, S. *Republic Book 10* (Warminster, 1988).

Irwin, T. H. "Plato's Objections to the Sophists," in A. Powell (ed.), *The Greek World* (London, 1995), 568–90.

Irwin, T. H. "*Republic* 2: Questions about Justice," in G. Fine (ed.), *Plato 2: Ethics, Politics, Religion, and the Soul* (Oxford, 1999), 164–85.

Janaway, C. *Images of Excellence: Plato's Critique of the Arts* (Oxford, 1995).

Kamtekar, R. "Imperfect Virtue," *Ancient Philosophy* 18 (1998), 315–39.

Kamtekar, R. "Social Justice and Happiness in the *Republic*: Plato's Two Principles," *History of Political Thought* 22 (2001), 189–220.

Kamtekar, R. "Speaking with the Same Voice as Reason: Personification in Plato's Psychology," *Oxford Studies in Ancient Philosophy* 31 (2006), 167–202.

Keuls, E. C. *Plato and Greek Painting.* (Leiden, 1978).

Lorenz, H. *The Brute Within: Appetitive Desire in Plato and Aristotle* (Oxford, 2006).

Menn, S. "On Plato's *Politeia*," in J. Cleary and G. Gurtler (eds.), *Proceedings of the Boston Area Colloquium in Ancient Philosophy* 21 (Leiden, 2006), 1–55.

Murdoch, I. *The Fire and the Sun: Why Plato Banished the Artists* (Oxford, 1977).

Nehamas, A. "Confusing Universals and Particulars in Plato's Early Dialogues," *Virtues of Authenticity: Essays on Plato and Socrates* (Princeton, N.J., 1999), 159–75.

Nehamas, A. "Plato on Imitation and Poetry in *Republic* X," in J. Moravcsik and P. Temko (eds.), *Plato on Beauty, Wisdom and the Arts* (Totowa, N.J., 1982), 47–78.

Penner, T. "Socrates on the Impossibility of Belief-Relative Sciences," in J. Cleary (ed.), *Proceedings of the Boston Area Colloquium in Ancient Philosophy* 3, (Lanham, Md., 1987), 263–325.

Reeve, C. D. C. (trans.) *Plato Republic* (Indianapolis, 2004).

Scott, D. "Platonic Pessimism and Moral Education," *Oxford Studies in Ancient Philosophy* 7 (1999), 15–36.

Scott, D. *Plato's Meno* (Cambridge, 2006).

Scott, D. *Recollection and Experience: Plato's Theory of Learning and Its Successors* (Cambridge, 1995).

Vlastos, G. "The Socratic Elenchus," in G. Fine (ed.), *Plato 1: Metaphysics and Epistemology* (Oxford, 1999), 36–63.

Williams, B. "Plato against the Immoralist," in O. Höffe (ed.), *Platon, Politeia* (Berlin, 1997), 55–67.

# CHAPTER 15

# THE *REPUBLIC*

## DOMINIC SCOTT

## I. A BIRD'S-EYE VIEW

Arguably the greatest of Plato's works, and nowadays the best known, the *Republic*
is certainly among his most complex. From its title, the first-time reader will expect
a dialogue about political theory, yet the work starts from the perspective of the
individual, coming to focus on the question of how, if at all, justice contributes to
an agent's happiness. Only after this question has been fully set out does the work
evolve into an investigation of politics—of the ideal state and of the institutions
that sustain it, especially those having to do with education. But the interest in
individual justice and happiness is never left behind. Rather, the work weaves in
and out of the two perspectives, individual and political, right through to its
conclusion. All this may leave one wondering about the unity of the work. My
purpose in this introduction is to show that, despite the enormous range of topics
discussed, the *Republic* fits together as a coherent whole.[1]

The need to defend justice arises in book I, when Thrasymachus claims that
justice is merely a matter of giving benefit to another at one's own expense (343c).
Deep down, what we all really admire is not justice but the very opposite: the ideal
of the tyrant, someone who holds everyone else in his power so as to satisfy any
desire he pleases and with no fear for the consequences (344a). Thrasymachus is as
forceful and memorable as any of Plato's characters, but Socrates eventually wears

---

1. There is no shortage of books devoted to the *Republic*, many of which serve both as introductions
and as scholarly monographs. For example, R. Nettleship, *Lectures on the Republic of Plato*, 2nd ed. (London,
1901); R. Cross and A. Woozley, *Plato's Republic* [*Republic*] (London, 1964); N. White, *A Companion to
Plato's Republic* (Oxford, 1979); J. Annas, *An Introduction to Plato's Republic* [*Introduction*] (Oxford, 1981).
Also, chs. 11–18 of T. Irwin, *Plato's Ethics* (Oxford, 1995), focus on the *Republic*.

him down, and it is left to the brothers Glaucon and Adeimantus at the beginning of book II to renew the challenge. Even though Thrasymachus has been subdued, they still feel his underlying position remains intact. With less heat and more light than before, they ask Socrates to show that justice is better for the agent than injustice, even if one has the power to commit injustice with impunity.

Socrates accepts the challenge but wants to proceed more methodically than before. First, they must define the nature of justice and begin by looking at the state before turning to the soul. Justice, he claims, will be easier to see in the larger entity (368d–369a). This creates the first great shift of focus in the work, from ethics to politics, and sets off an inquiry that lasts right into the middle of book IV. Imagining themselves as the founders of a perfectly just state, they ask what such a state would be like.

The answer turns out to be a city composed of three classes—producers, auxiliaries, and guardians: the first to provide for the material needs of the state, the second for its defence, and the third to rule. Each has a specific function of its own, and none is to interfere with the others. Above all, the just city will be unified, ordered, and harmonious. The rulers and auxiliaries, the two classes Socrates discusses at most length, will be dedicated to protecting the good of the state as a whole, and every aspect of their education, as well as the conditions under which they live, will be minutely engineered to ensure they fulfil their roles as best they can. In a particularly famous passage, Socrates devotes considerable attention to the arts, proposing radical censorship of the kinds of poetry and music to which the would-be guardians and auxiliaries may be exposed (376c–398b).

The ideal state now established, Socrates returns to the individual (IV 434d). Since justice in the city is a matter of the harmonious arrangement of its three parts, the same ought to apply to the individual—if, that is, it also has three parts. This he shows to be the case with an argument that divides the soul into reason, spirit, and appetite, each of which is an analogue of one of the three classes in the state. Reason is able to direct the soul and determine its good overall.[2] Spirit is the source of such feelings as anger, pride, and shame. Appetites are typically desires for physical pleasures, and they need to be kept carefully in check by an alliance of reason and spirit. Justice in the soul obtains when each part performs its own function and does not interfere with that of the others—in particular, when neither spirit nor appetite usurps the ruling function of reason. As such, justice is a form of psychic harmony or health. By contrast, injustice is a condition of inner turmoil, a civil war between the parts, where one vies against another for overall control. If this is correct, Socrates concludes, we can answer Glaucon's challenge: justice, as psychic health, is inherently good for the soul (445a–b); injustice, as the polar opposite, is quickly rejected as any sort of good, losing all the appeal it had earlier on in the work.

---

2. "Reason" is perhaps a somewhat misleading translation of *to logistikon*, since it may suggest pure reason, with no desires, which is clearly not Plato's view; his view is that each part of the soul has its distinctive kind of desire (580d–583b). Others may prefer "the rational part" as a translation.

the reason part

This is meant to provide the defence of justice demanded at the beginning of book II. But neither Socrates nor his interlocutors want to end the conversation there: Socrates, because he wants to establish his conclusion more firmly and clarify the nature (and hence unattractiveness) of injustice; his interlocutors, because they have a question they want him to answer about the ideal state (V 449c). Back at book IV 423e–424a, Socrates had casually stated that the rulers of his state would have "wives and children in common."[3] With this brief remark, he had at a stroke abolished the traditional family unit. Now in book V, when challenged to explain what he meant, he admits that this is only one of three of proposals that will evoke consternation. Not only does he propose to do away with the family, he would also sweep aside all barriers to the participation of women in ruling and defending the state. Men and women differ only in respect of their role in reproduction; there are no differences between them that are relevant to ruling and hence no reason why a woman, just by virtue of being a woman, should not be a fully fledged member of the guardian or auxiliary classes (451c–457c).

But he has a third, even more controversial proposal up his sleeve—philosopher-rulers:

> Until philosophers rule as kings or those who are now called kings and leading men genuinely and adequately philosophise, that is, until political power and philosophy entirely coincide . . . cities will have no rest from evils . . . nor will the human race.[4]

Socrates anticipates such hostility to this proposal that he spends the rest of book V and much of book VI defending it. He then turns to consider what sort of education would be required to produce these philosopher-rulers, which takes him all the way to end of book VII.

The first step in Socrates' argument for philosopher-rulers sounds innocuous enough: the rulers of the ideally just state will need knowledge—of justice, for a start. But it turns out that, on its own, no amount of practical experience will yield such knowledge. Rather, one needs to grasp the Form of Justice in itself, an entity distinct from particular cases of justice, the essence of justice, apprehended only by intellect. Without knowledge of the Form of Justice, one will never be able to understand what makes any particular action or state of affairs just. In fact, the philosopher-rulers will need knowledge of all the Forms—not only Justice but also many others, including Beauty, Temperance, and, above all, the Good. Much of book VII focuses on the extraordinary difficulty of apprehending the Forms and, in what is one of the most memorable passages in Plato, Socrates compares the process of learning to the slow, painful ascent from the darkness of a cave into the sunlight (VII 514a–517b).

The feeling of bewilderment described in the allegory might well be shared by some of Plato's readers as the book goes on. It turns out that the education of the trainee rulers will last thirty years (and this is on top of the education in the arts

---

3. He had already attacked the institution of private property for the guardians at 416d–417b.
4. At 473c–d. All translations are from G. Grube, *Plato: Republic*, rev. C. Reeve (Indianapolis, 1992).

that was described in books II–III).[5] Starting at the age of twenty, they will have to spend an astonishing ten years devoted to mathematical studies before they can even begin "dialectic," the process of inquiring directly into the Forms. And even after five years of dialectic, it is not for another fifteen years, involving military and administrative tasks, that they finally apprehend the Form of the Good and assume control of the state.

By the beginning of book VIII, Socrates seems to have satisfied his interlocutors' curiosity about the rulers of the ideal state and returns to the project he was about to take up at the end of book IV, which was to enumerate and describe the main forms of vice: timocracy, oligarchy, democracy, and tyranny, each of which can appear in either the state or the soul. In either case, timocracy aims at honour, oligarchy at wealth, democracy at freedom, and tyranny at the unbridled pursuit of the worst form of appetite. Throughout, Socrates presents this taxonomy in a narrative of decline. The political version shows an ideal state degenerating into a timocracy, where the military hold power (545c–548d); in time, this becomes unstable and lapses into an oligarchy, a state sharply divided into rich and poor (550d–553a). Civil war eventually breaks out, resulting in the victory of the poor, who impose a radical democracy where freedom and toleration rule supreme (555b–558c). But, in time, a demagogue emerges who persuades the citizens to let him take power; this he subsequently abuses, reducing them to the status of slaves. The result is tyranny, the most extreme form of injustice (562a–569c).

To distinguish the four kinds of vice in the individual, Socrates recalls the theory of the divided soul and develops it further. A timocratic soul is one in which spirit dominates over reason and appetite (548d–550c). The other three types of vice are explicated in terms of the domination of appetite: the oligarch gives priority only to those appetites whose fulfilment is necessary for bodily health (553a–555a); the democratic individual indulges all sorts of desires, be they for necessities or for luxuries, and he insists that all pleasures and desires are equal in worth (558c–562a). Finally, the tyrant enslaves himself to the worst kind of desires, "lawless" appetites (571a–580c).

When Socrates invites his interlocutors to rank the five characters in terms of happiness (580a), they place the just person at the top and the other four in the order in which they appeared. The tyrant, despite Thrasymachus' eulogy at the beginning of the work, turns out to be the most miserable. After giving two more arguments to justify the same ranking, based on the pleasure that each life brings (580d–588a), Socrates ends book IX with a graphic image that warns against allowing either the appetitive or spirited part to take control of the soul (588b–592b).

This seems to conclude the overarching project of the *Republic*, the defence of justice. But in book X, Socrates returns to some unfinished business: the status of poetry in the ideal state. Using the psychology from book IV, he imposes further restrictions on the kind of poetry he is prepared to allow into the ideal state. He bans all imitative poetry, including Homer, as well as tragedy and comedy, arguing that such poets have no expertise in political affairs and, further, that they corrupt the

5. For further discussion of the arts in books II–III, see Kamtekar, chapter 14 in this volume.

souls of their audiences, helping the nonrational parts to grow and assume control over the rational. Finally at 608c, he returns to the subject of justice and discusses some of its further benefits—in particular, the rewards it brings us in the afterlife.

As I said above, the *Republic* starts as a work of ethics, investigating the link between justice and happiness in the individual. Initially, politics only appears on the stage as a heuristic device to help define justice in the soul. But as the dialogue goes on, it acquires an interest in its own right and, once centre stage, helps broaden the scope of the work still further, to embrace such topics as the arts in books II–III and X and epistemology, metaphysics, and mathematics in books V–VII. But although political theory goes on to have a higher profile than we might initially have expected, it in no way diverts the work from the ethical course on which it started. Quite the reverse: Plato uses his politics to deepen his ethics. In books II–V, the ideal state provided merely an analogue for understanding justice and happiness in the individual; by the end of book VII, it also provides the context in which the good of the individual is fully attained, for it is only in the ideal state, with its ability to provide exactly the right kind of philosophical education, that human nature can be perfected.

Although this chapter has to be highly selective, I try to focus on a cluster of issues that are genuinely salient to an understanding of the work. The first section concerns the central question of the work, about the value of justice, and examines a fundamental objection to Plato's argument. The second section turns from ethics to politics and focuses on what for modern readers is the least palatable aspect of the work: its authoritarianism. In the third section, I focus on the nature of philosophy as discussed in the central books.

# II. THE DEFENCE OF JUSTICE

At the beginning of book II, Glaucon challenges Socrates to show that in and of itself justice benefits the agent and that the life of justice is superior to that of injustice. Most people, he claims, see it as a good of some sort, but only as a burden. Ideally, we would commit injustice whenever it furthered our own interests. But since, as individuals, we usually lack the power to stop others from committing injustice against us, we accept the restrictions of justice as an agreement to secure mutual protection. Glaucon develops the point with the story of Gyges, who discovered a ring that would make him invisible and used it to commit injustice with impunity and to acquire the greatest goods. Glaucon's point is that, if any of us had a similar opportunity, we would cast all thoughts of justice aside. To put the challenge in its starkest terms, he imagines two people: one is actually just but has a reputation for injustice; the other is unjust but through cunning has acquired the greatest reputation for justice. The first is imprisoned and tortured for his apparent injustice, while the second enjoys all the external benefits of justice without actually having it. Glaucon ends by challenging Socrates to explain why anyone would prefer to be the first than the second. His brother Adeimantus then reinforces the challenge with a long speech of his own.

What Socrates is being asked to provide here is a definition of justice and injustice, as well as an account that explains "what power each itself has when it's in the soul" (358b) or, as Adeimantus puts the point several times, "what effect each has because of itself on the person who has it—the one for good and the other for bad—whether it remains hidden from gods and humans beings or not" (367e). As this last clause suggests, what they do not want is an assessment of justice in terms of the benefits that most people associate with it. The point of the Gyges story and the choice of lives is that such benefits are "detachable" from justice per se. The good repute that usually follows from being just depends on contingent circumstances that may sometimes not obtain. The challenge is to argue for the *inherent* superiority of justice over injustice.

Notice how strong this challenge becomes by the time Glaucon sets out the choice of lives: the just person whom he envisages may have no other good apart from justice—in fact, not only does he lack any physical goods, he is beset by the worst kinds of physical evil; and yet his life is still meant to be preferable to that of unjust person who enjoys the maximum of other goods. This is tantamount to claiming that, once you lack justice and possess injustice instead, no amount of other goods can compensate.[6]

Socrates' response is to define justice as psychic harmony and injustice as the opposite: internal disorder and conflict. Once he has redescribed the two states in this way, he expects us to reverse the preference between the just and unjust lives that seemed so tempting in Glaucon's original challenge. In book IX he reinforces this strategy by focusing on the very extreme of injustice, the tyrant. At the end of book I, Thrasymachus had held him up as the ideal because of his unlimited freedom to satisfy any desires he wanted, but by the end of book IX Socrates has probed deep into his soul to reveal him for what he is: frustrated, tormented, isolated, and enslaved. Such is the power that injustice has "in and of itself" on the soul (cf. 358b).

This at least is the strategy, but it faces a well-known objection.[7] What Socrates was meant to defend has been referred to as "conventional justice": that is, a disposition to behave in certain intuitively specified ways, such as to keep one's compacts and promises, to honour one's parents, and not to steal. Also, the actions or abstentions in terms of which justice and injustice are conventionally understood

---

6. Glaucon's challenge has provoked considerable scholarly controversy. A notorious problem is that he appears to contradict himself, by starting with the need to praise justice in itself and not for its consequences, and then asking Socrates to explain what "power it has in the soul" (358b; cf. 366e), which sounds very much like a reference to its psychological consequences. For two opposing solutions to the problem, see N. White, "The Classification of Goods in Plato's *Republic*," *Journal of the History of Philosophy* 22 (1984), 393–421, and T. Irwin, "*Republic* 2: Questions about Justice," in G. Fine, ed., *Plato 2: Ethics, Politics, Religion and the Soul* (Oxford, 1999), 164–85.

7. For a classic statement, see D. Sachs, "A Fallacy in Plato's *Republic*," *Philosophical Review* 72 (1963), 141–58; reprinted in G. Vlastos, ed., *Plato*, vol. 2: *Ethics, Politics d Philosophy of Art and Religion* (New York, 1973), 35–51.

seem for the most part to concern dealings with other people. But "platonic justice," as defined in book IV, is primarily focused neither on actions nor on our relations with other people; it is essentially an internal state, defined in terms of the relations between the parts of the soul. Just actions are those that develop and preserve internal harmony (443e). One might immediately object that Socrates has replaced the type of justice that Glaucon wanted him to defend with a conception of his own. Therefore his argument is invalid. But Socrates is well aware that the two conceptions differ and is not attempting to defend conventional justice as it stands. Nevertheless, there remains a subtler objection: he has not shown that there will be significant overlap between the kinds of action someone might perform according to the two conceptions. In other words, why couldn't someone with a harmonious soul still commit acts of conventional injustice—for instance, by breaking their promises or failing to honour their parents? What is it about inner harmony that prevents such actions?[8]

## The psychological defence

For the most part, commentators have found two types of strategy to defend Plato's argument.[9] The first is based on the psychological theory of the *Republic* and is at its most explicit in book IX.[10] One of the premises for this defence is the assumption that the motivation for conventionally unjust behaviour lies in the desires associated with appetite and spirit. Ever-increasing appetites demand more and more material resources for their fulfilment; sooner or later, the appetitive individual will exhaust his own supplies and encroach on others' property. Mutatis mutandis, a similar point can be made about spirit, once let out of control: power and honour are limited goods; to maximise one's share of them, one will have reason to ill-treat one's competitors. The second premise in the argument is that increasing the strength of nonrational desires causes at least as much grief to the agent of injustice as to the victim. This grief comes in various forms. For instance, appetites are insatiable. The stronger they grow, the more urgent their demands. This leaves the appetitive individual ever-increasingly in need—in other words, impoverished (579e). Furthermore, anyone in the grip of appetite will have to treat others as mere means to his satisfaction, which makes him (at the extreme) untrustworthy and friendless (580a), and no human being would wish to be in such a state.

All of this helps to show how the class of actions associated with each type of justice, conventional and platonic, might coincide. Although often called psychic "harmony," platonic justice involves more than an inner feeling of calm; it is best

---

8. There is also the problem that someone might commit acts of conventional justice but suffer from inner conflict. The oligarchic man seems a case in point (554d–e).

9. For an excellent overview of this topic, see R. Kraut, "The Defense of Justice in Plato's *Republic*," in Kraut, ed., *The Cambridge Companion to Plato* (Cambridge, 1992), 311–37.

10. G. Vlastos, "Justice and Happiness in the *Republic*," *Platonic Studies*, 2nd ed. (Princeton, N.J., 1981), 133–34.

thought of as psychic *hierarchy*, where reason regulates the desires of the other two parts in accordance with its understanding of the soul's overall good. If the second premise of the argument is correct, it is in the overall interest of the soul to keep nonrational desires within strict limits and to prevent them starting on the cycle of ever-accelerating growth. So in regulating desire for the overall good of the soul, reason will limit precisely those desires that would motivate us to act out of line with conventional justice.

There is another strand in the psychological defence of justice, which relates to a specific form of nonrational desire: unnecessary appetites. These are introduced in book VIII (558d–559c) as appetites that are not needed for physical health (indeed, they tend to harm it) and are also such that they can be eradicated by the right training. But Socrates also thinks that they are "harmful to reason" (559b), by which I take him to mean that they compel it to form beliefs that conform to appetitive goals. This is illustrated in the subsequent portrait of the democratic man, whose appetites grow so strong that he abandons the ethical beliefs of his upbringing, an ethics of thrift, and replaces it with one of indulgence (560e–561b). Now, one reason the platonically just person values the strength and autonomy of the rational part is that it helps keep the soul on course and ensure its overall good. Since certain types of desire threaten this autonomy, they must be restrained, if not entirely eliminated. If, at the same time, these desires also tend to motivate conventionally unjust behaviour, we have found another way to bring about a convergence between platonic and conventional justice.

## The metaphysical defence

The psychological defence of justice makes no use of the metaphysics of the central books. It requires no assumptions at all about the existence of the Forms but, instead, relies on empirical assumptions about state and soul.[11] But there is a second way of supporting Plato's defence of justice that does appeal to the metaphysics and epistemology of the central books. We know from book IV that the platonically just person must have an understanding of the good. In the central books, this turns out to involve understanding the Forms, especially the Good itself, the first principle of all things. This can be used to add a whole new dimension to the theory of book IV, where we had no inkling that the wisdom of the just person would involve ascending such metaphysical heights.

There are two distinct ways in which the added dimension of the central books helps support the defence of justice. First, at book VI 485d, Socrates likens the soul of the philosopher to a stream whose water surges in one direction, thereby drying up other channels. Philosophers are (quite literally) enamoured of the Forms, and

---

11. There is one argument at the end of book IX that does seem to allude to the metaphysics of the central books, when it claims that the pleasures of philosophy are "more real" than those of appetite or spirit (583b–588a). But otherwise, the Forms are completely absent from all but V 476a to VII 541b of the work.

their energy will be so focused on understanding that their desires for physical pleasures or for honour will be greatly weakened, if not eliminated entirely. The lines on which this argument can now be developed are parallel to the psychological argument. As before, the sources of conventionally unjust behaviour lie in nonrational desire; the platonically just person, whom we now know to be gripped by philosophical *eros*, will be too transfixed on the Forms to be interested in the objects of nonrational desire and hence to commit acts of conventional injustice. For these reasons, such a character will be a "friend and relative of justice" (487a).

The second version of the metaphysical defence itself has two aspects. At book VI 500c, the philosopher looks to the order that exists among the Forms and uses it as a model to create order first within his own soul and then, if circumstances require, within the souls of his fellow citizens. One might use this text to support the defence of justice and claim that the order thus imposed on the philosopher's own soul would not allow for the existence of rampant appetitive and spirited desires that would lead to conventionally unjust acts.[12] The other aspect of this version of the metaphysical defence takes its cue from the same text but focuses on a philosopher's desire to imitate the order and balance among the forms directly in his relationships with other people. Failures to fulfil one's compacts and promises or to honour one's parents are all failures to reciprocate, and these disturb the balance in human relations. A philosopher who looked toward the order of the Forms would be repelled by such disorder.[13]

The problem with this version of the metaphysical defence (in either of its aspects) is that the content of the Good is very underdetermined in the *Republic*. (Socrates himself appears to disavows knowledge of it at 506b–e.) So we just do not know enough about what kind of order the philosopher would "read off" the Forms in general, or the Good in particular, to impose on his own desires or on his relations with others. There is no guarantee that the order in question will typically prescribe acts of conventional justice. This is not to say this version of the argument is doomed to fail, just that it is highly provisional and, until we have a more determinate specification of the Good, we might, instead, prefer to rely on the first version of the metaphysical defence: philosophers will be rendered indifferent to the goals of nonrational desire by the intensity of their intellectual *eros*.

But here, too, we should exercise caution. There is a well-known issue in the scholarly literature about why the philosophers, once they have attained knowledge of the Forms, should interrupt their contemplation to rule in the ideal state. Socrates says it is just that they do so, while admitting they will have to be "compelled" to rule "out of necessity" (cf. 501d, 520e, 540b): for them, ruling is something they would rather not be doing. Some commentators have leapt on this passage as a possible counterexample to the basic thesis of the *Republic* that justice

---

12. The order the philosopher imposes on his own soul involves "thinking rational thoughts and satisfying rationally controlled desires of his own" (J. Cooper, "The Psychology of Justice in Plato," *American Philosophical Quarterly* 14 [1977], 156).

13. This is the approach favoured by R. Kraut, "Return to the Cave: *Republic* 519–521" ["Cave"], in G. Fine, ed., *Plato 2: Ethics, Politics, Religion and the Soul* (Oxford, 1999), 247.

benefits the agent.[14] Even without delving into this debate, we can see that the issue raises complications for the first version of the metaphysical defence: the more one leans on the philosophers' indifference to worldly aspirations, including the pursuit of honour and power, the more one emphasises their reluctance to rule, thus seeming to exacerbate the tension between their self-interest and the demands of justice.

There is one important point about the metaphysical defence that needs to be emphasised. In contrast to the psychological defence, which is the strategy that Socrates actually follows in the dialogue to meet Glaucon's challenge, the metaphysical defence is not one that he proffers directly; it is an attempt at "rational reconstruction" on the part of recent commentators. In the books from which it has been constructed, V–VII, Socrates is not explicitly attempting to support his reply to Glaucon as he does in VIII–IX. Rather, he has been interrupted and induced to switch his focus to a series of questions about the rulers in the ideal state, such as what sort of expertise they need and how they are to acquire it. What commentators have done is to take claims made within this section and redeploy them toward a different aim: strengthening the defence of justice given in book IV, something that Socrates himself only explicitly does in books VIII–IX.

This is not to deny that Socrates recommends pursuing such a line of argument. At 504b (cf. 435d), he implies out that the defence of justice that they have mounted so far (i.e., the psychological defence) is a short cut. The "longer route" would require investigating the matter by reference to the Form of the Good— something that will take the trainee guardians in the ideal state many years to achieve. In effect, this would be a much more thorough enterprise than the very provisional line of argument I have called the metaphysical defence.[15] I return to this point at the end of this chapter.

## III. POLITICS

Whether or not Plato can successfully bridge the gap between justice as psychic harmony and conventional justice, the very conception of individual justice that he created in the *Republic* is one of his most enduring legacies. At the heart of this conception is the proposal that reason should rule over the nonrational desires— regulating, limiting, and sometimes eliminating them altogether. But when one turns to the political analogue, one runs straight into one of the less attractive aspects of the work: its authoritarianism, the idea that it is equally appropriate for the guardian class to regulate, restrain, and "remove" awkward citizens where necessary.

14. There is an extensive literature on this subject, but see, especially, R. Kraut, "Cave," and E. Brown, "Minding the Gap in Plato's *Republic*," *Philosophical Studies* 117 (2004), 275–302.

15. On this, see D. Scott, "Metaphysics and the Defence of Justice in the *Republic*," *Proceedings of the Boston Area Colloquium in Ancient Philosophy* 16 (2000), 1–20.

Thanks especially to Karl Popper,[16] the authoritarian nature of the work—in particular, its critique of democracy—has been notorious for decades. But amid all the controversy, the complexity of Plato's critique has sometimes been missed. And complex it certainly is, featuring at several places throughout the work, sometimes explicitly, but often implicitly. Also, the target shifts. Sometimes the argument is against democracy in principle, at others actual democracy, as manifested especially at Athens. The purpose of this section is to chart a route through the *Republic* to separate out the different strands of Plato's argument.

## The organic theory

Before examining democracy directly, we should pause to consider a distinct but related theme. This is the accusation that the *Republic* assumes what Popper called the "organic theory". One component of this theory is metaphysical: that the state is an entity in its own right, a whole distinct from the sum of its parts. Popper claimed to find this implicit in the state-soul analogy:[17] if the state is sufficiently like the soul such that it can bear the same properties of, say, courage, justice, temperance, and wisdom, it must surely have the same metaphysical status as an individual soul and be an entity in its own right. The other component of the organic theory is political: the interests of the state have priority over those of its citizens, which means that individuals' interests may be sacrificed for the good of the higher entity, as the occasion demands.

In fact, there is no explicit or conclusive evidence for the metaphysical claim in the *Republic*. The state-soul analogy cannot be used to make the case on its own, because it is not clear how far one should press the similarities between the two sides of the analogy. Instead of assuming that state and soul have the same metaphysical status, Socrates may just have wanted to point to structural similarities between them.[18]

If the metaphysical thesis fails, one might think the political component of the organic theory collapses with it. Commentators who reject the organic theory as an interpretation of the *Republic* admit there are some passages that talk of individual happiness being sacrificed for the greater good, but they claim these need not be taken in the way Popper supposed. Take, for example, the beginning of book IV. Adeimantus has just complained that the rulers of the ideal state will not have much happiness, given the austere conditions in which they live. Socrates replies that his concern is not to focus on the happiness of some parts of the city at the expense of others but to look to the happiness of the whole. He then compares the

---

16. K. Popper, *The Open Society and Its Enemies*, vol. 1: *The Spell of Plato*, 5th ed. [*Open Society*] (London, 1966). For an excellent recent overview of this topic, see C. Taylor, "Plato's Totalitarianism," *Polis* 5 (1986), 4–29; reprinted in G. Fine, ed., *Plato 2: Ethics, Politics, Religion and the Soul* (Oxford, 1999), 280–96. Another useful article is by J. Ackrill, "What Is Wrong with Plato's *Republic*?" *Essays on Plato and Aristotle*, 2nd ed. (Oxford, 2001), 230–52.

17. Popper, *Open Society*, 79; see also Cross and Woozley, *Republic*, 76–77 and 132.

18. For the point, see Annas, *Introduction*, 180.

city to a statue (420b–421c), saying it would be ridiculous to paint the eyes with the finest colour at the expense of the rest of it. Rather than using this as evidence for the organic theory, some commentators have interpreted this as the proposal to maximise the aggregate happiness of the citizens, which is quite a different matter. Like utilitarianism, and unlike the organic theory, this aggregative approach does not see the mass of citizens as forming a distinct entity. The good to be achieved is no more than the sum of the individual happiness of each citizen.[19]

However, in between the full-blown organic theory and aggregative approach, there is a third option, which I think is the correct interpretation of the *Republic*. Whether or not Plato conceived of the state as an entity in its own right, he does seem to subordinate the interests of individual citizens to a good that is distinct from the aggregate happiness. There can be no doubt that the founders of the state must aim at unity in the state. Although the point is made repeatedly throughout the work (e.g., 422e–423d), it is particularly clear at 462a:

> Then isn't the first step towards agreement to ask ourselves what we say is the greatest good in designing the city—the good at which the legislator aims in making the laws—and what is the greatest evil? . . . Is there any greater evil we can mention for a city than that which tears it apart and makes it many instead of one? *Or any greater good than that which binds it together and makes it one?* (Emphasis added)

He does not say here that unity is a good as a means to increase aggregate happiness; it is the state's greatest good—period.

Another passage that makes the same point comes in book VII, just after Glaucon has complained that compelling the philosophers to rule constitutes an injustice against them. In his reply, Socrates says:

> S. You are forgetting again that it isn't the law's concern to make any one class in the city outstandingly happy but to contrive to spread happiness throughout the city by bringing the citizens into harmony with each other through persuasion or compulsion and by making them share with each other the benefits that each class can confer on the community. The law produces such people in a city, not in order to allow them to turn in whatever direction they want, but to *make use of them to bind the city together*.
>
> G. That's true, I had forgotten. (519e–520a; emphasis added)

---

19. J. Neu, "Plato's Analogy of State and Individual: The *Republic* and the Organic Theory of the State," *Philosophy* 46 (1971), 246, compares Plato to Bentham; see also G. Vlastos, "The Theory of Social Justice in the *Polis* in Plato's *Republic*," in D. Graham, ed., *Studies in Greek Philosophy*, vol. 2 (Princeton, N.J., 1995), 69–103, esp. 80–84, and Annas, *Introduction*, 179. Ironically, utilitarianism itself might be accused of having to assume the organic theory in order to justify maximising aggregate happiness without regard to boundaries between persons. See D. Gauthier, *Practical Reasoning* (Oxford, 1962), 126, discussed in D. Parfit, *Reasons and Persons* (Oxford, 1986), 331–32. If so, utilitarianism would not be the safe refuge that Popper's critics have assumed.

The references to "forgetting" here almost certainly refer back to 462a and to the statue analogy at 420b, specifically the sentence, "We aren't aiming to make any one group outstandingly happy, but to make the whole city so, as far as possible." This means that we should take 519e–520a as an authoritative interpretation of 420b: that is, that the earlier passage was advocating something stronger than the aggregative approach all along. Rather, what Socrates values most of all is a feature of the ideal state—its unity—that is independent of the aggregate well-being of its members, and, in principle, this value could come into competition with the happiness of individual citizens. In other words, structural properties of the state have priority over not only any one individual's happiness but also the aggregate of all individuals' happiness.[20] Though distinct from the organic theory as Popper conceived it, this is still a deeply controversial stance to take.[21]

## The critique of democracy

### The basic argument

In setting up the ideal state in book II, Socrates lays down the principle of specialisation (PoS): each citizen must stick to one type of work alone. Initially, this is just used to insist that different craftsmen spend all their time and energy on a single function. But as the discussion proceeds, the principle is used to generate the three different classes in the state. This happens with the auxiliary class at 374d–376c: while it was standard practice for Greek states to conscript ordinary citizens to fight in times of war, PoS requires the ideal state to have a permanent, professional military class, distinct from the producers. Similarly, when it comes to deciding who should manage (as opposed to defend) the state, PoS requires us to hive off a class of professional rulers (412b–414b).

The use of PoS to create a separate guardian class implicitly rules out democracy. Since the principle lies at the heart of the antidemocratic argument of the *Republic*, it merits a closer look. Socrates adduces two reasons in its support. The first (370a) has to do with the distribution of natural talents: "We aren't all born alike, but each of us differs somewhat in nature from the others, one being suited to one task, another to another." The second (370b) concerns efficiency: "Does one person do a better job if he practises many crafts or—since he's one person—if he practises one?" (Interestingly, that argument only raises a doubt about direct democracy and seems to leave representative democracy intact.) In what follows, I shall not discuss the second of these arguments.

The first argument could only be used to mount an attack on democracy if there really are deep natural differences relevant to political decision-making. But as Plato well knew, there were some who denied this straight out. Well before writing the *Republic*, he himself had articulated the democratic view through the

---

20. On this point, see Kraut, "Cave," 244–45.

21. My interpretation is close to that of L. Brown, "How Totalitarian Is Plato's *Republic?*," in E. Ostenfeld, ed., *Essays on Plato's Republic* (Aarhus, 1998), 13–27.

voice of Protagoras. In the dialogue named after him, he claims that political virtue is shared by almost all humans alike; it is the basic skill that enables us to live together in society (322d–323c). Protagoras agrees that other functions in society require specialisation because of an uneven distribution of talents. But political decision-making is a special case: in terms of the *Republic*, it involves a competence to which the first argument for PoS does not apply.

Although Plato had articulated the democratic position on natural talents so clearly in the *Protagoras*, Socrates in *Republic* II–IV seems merely to assume that it is wrong and that the qualities needed for a political leader are to be found only in a very few. In III 414b–415d, he divides the citizens into gold (guardians), silver (auxiliaries), and bronze (producers) and claims these natures are fixed at birth. But this is more announcement than argument, and a democrat might counter by attributing apparent differences in natural aptitude to nurture rather than nature. If everyone was given the right kind of education, all might turn out to have enough "gold" in their souls to participate in political decision-making.[22]

But Socrates does lend more support to his argument in the central books, which have a great deal to say about the moral and intellectual qualities required of the ideal rulers. Book V (475e–480a) argues that the knowledge needed for ruling is the knowledge of Forms, which is well out of the reach of most people (cf. VI 494a: "The majority cannot be philosophic"). As these books continue, Socrates emphasises again and again the enormous difficulty involved in apprehending the Forms: on top of the poetic or musical education proposed in books II–III, the trainee guardians need thirty years of intellectual and practical training before they are ready to rule. And the natural talents required are not just intellectual: Socrates also argues that one needs specific natural tendencies toward such qualities as temperance, justice, magnanimity, and courage (VI 487a).

Again, the likes of Protagoras will object that everyone has sufficient cognitive and moral resources to participate in the political process and that Socrates vastly overestimates and misrepresents the qualities required for such participation. But to do this, they now have to grapple with the arguments of the central books. Whatever the outcome of that debate, my point here is just to chart the course of Plato's main argument against democracy and to show that, although it begins as early as the second book, it is not until we encounter the metaphysics and epistemology of the central books that we really find its basis.[23]

## A critique of democratic Athens

In the course of defending the proposal for philosopher rulers, Socrates raises objections against contemporary democracy (VI 488c–495c). His critique is at its most explicit in the ship of state analogy (488c) and its aftermath. We are to

22. The earlier dialogue, the *Meno*, does seem to suggest that knowledge (and hence virtue) is equally accessible to all, however difficult it may be to acquire (85c–d).

23. On my view, this makes for a clear contrast between the political and ethical arguments of the *Republic*. In the latter case, the actual defence of justice conducted in the work makes hardly any use of the metaphysics of the central books, whereas those books are designed precisely to develop the political theory of the work, including the critique of democracy.

imagine a shipowner who is "bigger and stronger than everyone else on board" but hard of hearing, a bit short sighted, and with a defective knowledge of seafaring (488a–b). The sailors all vie with one another in persuading him to let them captain the ship, each with the intention of plundering the goods on board for himself. For them, what makes a good navigator is his capacity to persuade the shipowner to put him in control. In fact, the true captain would be someone who understood sufficient astronomy and meteorology to steer the ship on its course. But such a figure would be dismissed as a useless stargazer by the rest of the crew.

In this analogy, the shipowner is the *demos*, the sailors the democratic politicians, and the stargazer the philosopher. Socrates' main purpose is to explain why philosophers were held in such low esteem and why the proposal for philosopher-rulers would meet with such derision. But this passage also functions as a critique of democracy as practised at Athens. This becomes explicit once Socrates unpacks the analogy, focusing on the relation between the sailors and the shipowner. Such is the desire of democratic politicians to curry favour with the *demos* that they do not even exert the kind of control of which they would like to boast. Instead, the power relation is very much the other way around: they spend all their time and energy trying to discover the values of the *demos* and, through a process of assimilation, gradually adopt those values for themselves (490a–495c; cf. esp. 492c). There is a double insult against Athenian democracy here. The *demos* itself is ill equipped to run its own affairs, and the politicians merely ingratiate themselves to it; if they ever did have any finer qualities, they lost them in the process of winning power.

This critique differs from the main argument by focusing not on the problems that democracy has in principle with leadership but on an actual democracy and its "leaders." Lest there be any doubt that Athenian democracy is in Plato's sights throughout this discussion (488c–495c), we need do no more than mention the obvious allusions to such figures as Alcibiades (494c–495b), the sophists (493a), and, not least, Socrates himself (496c).

## Democracy in book VIII

Finally, we come to the most explicit critique of democracy in the *Republic*: book VIII (557a–558c). The democracy portrayed here is a very extreme form, but this should not cause us any surprise, because Socrates' procedure in analysing all the degenerate constitutions in books VIII–IX is to isolate the main forms of political vice. In different combinations with each other, they could form an infinite number of constitutions, but Socrates wishes to focus on the primary colours of political theory, as it were.

Pure democracy is based on the ideal of freedom, just as timocracy was based on honour and oligarchy on wealth. The freedom in question is the freedom to do as one chooses: even convicted criminals are allowed to roam the streets unchecked (558a). There is no condemnation of any way of life or value; it is a society of complete toleration. In this spirit, the democratic state elects its leaders by lot, refusing to admit merit or character as requirements for office. As a result, the state changes complexion according to who holds power on any particular day: it is a political chameleon, a supermarket of constitutions, barely a distinctive constitution in its own right.

For Socrates, the nub of the problem with democracy lies in its instability—at least to the extent that it seeks to realise its core values: freedom and toleration. For as well as being basic to democracy, these are also the source of its undoing. Extreme toleration allows criminal elements to grow strong, create their own bodyguards, and then use them to replace democracy with tyranny. All constitutions are unstable to some degree: even the ideal state would not last forever but would ultimately degenerate into a timocracy. But democracy is especially unstable and, to make matters worse, lies only one step away from tyranny, the very worst kind of constitution.

This is not primarily a critique of any existing democracy, certainly not Athens, which was no model of toleration (witness Socrates' fate at its hands). Nor should we have been expecting him to have any actual target in mind. His methodology in books VIII–IX commits him to finding a constitution that is the political equivalent of a chemical element—perhaps a highly volatile substance that might rarely be found in practice, if at all. This critique also differs from what I have called the "main" argument against democracy. Both can be called arguments against democracy in principle, but one focuses on the democrat's attitude to leadership and its qualifications, the other on the democrat's most basic values and of the dangers of following them through in practice. In this way, the two arguments against democracy in principle are independent of one another.

# IV. Philosophy in the Central Books

We have just seen how the basic argument against democracy finds support in a number of claims developed in the central books: that the knowledge required for political decision-making is philosophical, that such knowledge is extraordinarily difficult to acquire, and hence that those actually qualified to rule in the ideal state would be very few and far between. In this section, I explore these claims further, by looking more closely at how books V–VII distinguish the philosopher from the nonphilosopher, and how they characterise the nature and difficulty of acquiring philosophical knowledge.

The discussion of philosopher-rulers in these books can be broadly divided into two sections. The first defends the claim that only philosophers should rule (V 475e–VI 502a); the second describes their education (VI 504a–VII 540c). Socrates starts the first section by arguing that only philosophers have the requisite knowledge for ruling, and then turns to their moral qualities, claiming that these coincide with the qualities required for political office. At 487b, Adeimantus objects to Socrates' proposal on the grounds that most people would think philosophers the last people suited to running the state. Surprisingly, Socrates feigns agreement, but his real point is that this only applies to those popularly conceived of as philosophers. Genuine philosophers would be utterly different from the useless cranks who have usurped the title, and, if people understood a philosopher's true nature, they would not be so outraged by Socrates' proposal.

The second main section of books V–VII, on the guardians' education, begins with three famous images: the sun, the line, and the cave. The first is an attempt to sketch the nature and power of the supreme object of study, the Form of the Good; the second presents a classification of the four cognitive stages through which their education should apparently pass; and the cave allegory illustrates their ascent from the sensible world to the intelligible and their subsequent return to the world of practical affairs. The rest of book VII goes through the educational curriculum in order, including ten years of mathematics and five of dialectic.

Because the cave allegory (514a–517a) is central to our interests, I need to rehearse some of the essentials. Socrates asks his interlocutors to imagine a group of people sitting at the bottom of a cave, chained to their seats (a fact of which they are quite unaware), with their backs to the entrance. Behind them is a fire, and in front of the fire people are moving artifacts and puppets above a wall. This creates shadows in front of the prisoners, which they think constitute reality. Next, we have to imagine what would happen if one of them were released from his chains and turned around. He would be initially dazzled by the fire, finding it difficult to make out the puppets, and would much rather return to look at the shadows. The same pain would occur if he was dragged out of the cave into the sunlight, and he would only be able to look at the shadows or reflections of the objects. Eventually, however, his eyes would become accustomed, and he would be able to see everything clearly. In the allegory, the outside of the cave represents the intelligible world and the inside the perceptible world, the fire within it being equivalent to the sun. The prisoners bound to their seats are "like us" (515a): they stand for the normal cognitive condition of most humans.

## The definition of philosophy

At V 474b–c, immediately after announcing the third wave of paradox, Socrates promises to define what a philosopher is, a project that appears to have been completed by the beginning of VI (484a). The definition depends on the distinction between Forms, unitary in nature and apprehended only by thought, and their perceptible manifestations in, for example, colours, shapes, and sounds. Using the Form of Beauty as his example, Socrates contrasts the philosopher, who apprehends the Form itself, with the "lovers of sights and sounds," a group of people who pride themselves on having acquired as much experience of beauty as possible (e.g., by frequenting cultural and dramatic festivals). Their problem, according to Socrates, is that they do not apprehend the Form of Beauty itself. What they call "beauty" they conceive of as a range of different sensible properties, differing from one context to another: they would say, for example, that what makes an object beautiful in some cases is bright colour and, in others, dark colour.[24]

But they deny that there is a single, distinct entity that underlies and explains these perceptible phenomena, an entity apprehended only by thought. Because they confuse Beauty itself with its instances or likenesses, Socrates compares them to people in a dream: they "think that a likeness is not a likeness but rather the thing itself that it is like" (476c). Accordingly, he says that such people do not have knowledge of beauty, merely opinion about it. It is only the philosophers who have knowledge, because they grasp the nature of the unitary Form in itself and distinguish it from its instances. The cave allegory confirms this distinction, insofar as the prisoners think that the shadows, which are ultimately mere likenesses of the objects outside the cave, constitute reality. As the objects outside the cave are the equivalent of the Forms, we find the same point that the prisoners, who are "like us," are in a dreamlike state, thinking that a likeness is the very thing of which it is the likeness.[25]

What this shows is that in books V–VII Socrates defines philosophy by reference to its objects. Philosophy is not simply a matter of abstracting away from concrete particulars to apprehend general patterns and structures[26] but involves a commitment to a peculiar metaphysical stance—that there exist unchanging, nonsensible objects of which sensible properties are mere likenesses.

In articulating the distinction between philosopher and nonphilosopher, Socrates leaves no room for doubt on one point: the nonphilosopher has no awareness of a nonsensible reality. This much is beyond dispute. Nevertheless, it leaves room for the following question: Might the nonphilosophers have a latent grasp of the Forms (cf. 518b–c), which they use unconsciously to structure their thought about the sensible particulars around them? Although they do not possess explicit knowledge, they still manage to classify just things as just and beautiful things as beautiful, and they have a vocabulary that they use in making such classifications. (Recall that their classification of just and unjust actions is not so far off the mark: in fact, the Platonic conception of justice converges to a striking degree with the ordinary one.) The question arises of how they manage to do this, and the suggestion just made would provide an answer.[27]

This interpretation, however, is controversial. Nowhere in the *Republic* does Socrates even allude to nonphilosophers using their latent resources to form opinions or classify objects of perception, which we would expect given the importance

24. For this reading of the passage, see G. Fine, *On Ideas* (Oxford, 1993), 58–59.

25. The allegory also complicates the distinction set out in book V, because there are different levels of similarity in the cave: the shadows are images of the puppets, which are themselves images of the objects outside. Unfortunately, there is not space in this essay to unpack the complex imagery of the cave in any detail.

26. Contrast the view of E. Havelock, *Preface to Plato* (Oxford, 1963), who thinks that for Plato a philosopher "is at bottom a man with the capacity for the abstract" (282). For a wide-ranging and innovative treatment of Plato's attempt to define philosophy, see A. W. Nightingale, *Genres in Dialogue* (Cambridge, 1995).

27. For this view, see M. Ferejohn, "Knowledge, Recollection, and the Forms in *Republic* VII," in G. Santas, ed., *The Blackwell Companion to Plato's Republic* (Oxford, 2006), 214–33; see also V. Harte, "Language in the Cave," in D. Scott, ed., *Maieusis: Studies in Honour of M. F. Burnyeat* (Oxford, 2007), 195–215.

of the idea. So an alternative view is that nonphilosophers may indeed have a latent grasp of the Forms, but this remains entirely inactive. They acquire their concepts and opinions from experience—even about beauty, goodness, and the virtues. If one is sceptical that Plato would ever have subscribed to such a view, one should turn to *Phaedo* 68d–69b, where Socrates criticises nonphilosophers for having (what is in effect) a naturalistic conception of the virtues. Most people, he complains, conceive of temperance as abstaining from one pleasure for the sake of a greater one in the future; or of courage as facing one danger to avoid facing a greater one. In each case, the virtue is "cashed out" by reference to experience—that is, in terms of the feelings of pleasure and pain. He states that a parallel account of justice could be given, without saying what it is (69b), though Glaucon's social contract theory could provide such an account, insofar as it analyses justice as a balance between expected benefits and burdens. All this suggests that for Plato it is quite possible to form evaluative concepts without any recourse to the Forms, latent or explicit; and as far as nonevaluative properties are concerned, we should note that *Republic* VII 523a–524c clearly states that sight sees such properties as largeness and smallness; what it cannot do is understand the nature of each.[28]

Although there is not space to pursue this controversy any further here, it is worth mentioning because it invites us to press the question of exactly how sharply Plato draws the distinction between philosopher and nonphilosopher: What degree of continuity exists between the two perspectives? How the controversy is resolved might also rebound on our assessment of the argument against democracy: If nonphilosophers have a latent grasp of Forms that they actually use in their everyday thinking, shouldn't Socrates be prepared to take their contributions to political debate more seriously than he does?

## The difficulty of the transition

Even on the more optimistic of these interpretations, there remains a substantive gap between philosophical and nonphilosophical perspectives. We now turn to the difficulty of bridging this gap, a point reinforced throughout the central books. In discussing the lovers of sights and sounds, Socrates claims not only that they fail to apprehend the Form of Beauty but also that they could not be led to do so even if someone actually tried to help them (476b–c, 479e). The point is immediately generalised: "There are very few people who would be able to reach the Beautiful itself and see it by itself" (476b). So it is no surprise that later on, at VI 493e, he claims that "the many" cannot accept the reality of the beautiful itself, and cannot become philosophers.

The cave illustrates the difficulty of making the transition by its use of the light metaphor. Both when the prisoner first turns around to the fire and when he steps outside the cave he is dazzled. Initially, he just wants to return to his seat and stay there. The allegory shows how apprehending the different levels of reality is not just

28. On this, see D. Scott, *Recollection and Experience* (Cambridge, 1995), 83.

a matter of looking but of accustoming oneself, a process that is both arduous and time consuming. Specifically, the allegory brings out the problem of moving from the sensible world to the intelligible, the movement from inside to outside the cave. Socrates talks of the prisoners being chained to their seats. At first, one might be tempted to view this in a political light, perhaps seeing them as the prisoners of the puppeteers. Thoughts of 1984-style scenarios readily come to mind. But the kind of imprisonment in question is epistemological, not political. At *Phaedo* 81b–83e, Socrates also talks of the soul as a prisoner, explicitly of the bodily senses and feelings. What he means is that when a person perceives something or feels physical pleasure, he also thinks that what he is experiencing is "most real" (cf. 83c). The vividness of the perception or the intensity of the pleasure imposes a perspective that makes it almost impossible to understand how there could exist a nonsensible reality, of which the sensible is merely a copy. The prison of the cave allegory is Plato's way of representing a similar point in the *Republic*.

Another passage that emphasises the difficulty of making the transition to the Forms is the section discussing the role of mathematics in the education of the would-be guardians. They must spend two years each in the study of arithmetic, plane geometry, solid geometry, astronomy, and harmonics: ten years in all. Why? At several points Socrates states that arithmetic and geometry are useful in warfare (521d, 522e, 525c, 526d, 527c) and also remarks that people who study arithmetic tend to be mentally sharper as a result (526b). But neither of these reasons can begin to explain the length and intensity of the rulers' mathematical studies. To find a better explanation, we might point to a brief but significant remark made at 531c: that harmonics is useful for studying the Beautiful and the Good. The point may be that harmonics seeks to understand the principles underlying the order and beauty of audible phenomena. The same applies to astronomy: Plato bids us to leave behind the visible beauty of the heavens and move back to its mathematically explicable order (530b). The more general point is that the perceptible world exhibits goodness and beauty, which we can begin to understand if we investigate the underlying mathematics. But, ultimately, mathematics itself requires explanation, and this will only be provided by knowledge of the Good, the Beautiful, and the other Forms.[29] Nevertheless, mathematics is worth studying because it cultivates an intellectual appreciation of beauty and order, thus preparing us for understanding the nature of the Forms.

Still, one might ask why we should have to go through such a long mathematical training. Once we have become aware of the mathematically intelligible order underlying sensible phenomena, why not advance as quickly as possible to dialectic and investigate the Form of the Good without further delay? Again, the answer lies (partly) in the peculiar difficulty of moving from the sensible world to the intelligible, the movement from inside to outside the cave. Although, as we have just seen, this point had already been made in the *Phaedo*, what is new in the

29. On the role of mathematics in the philosophers' education, see M. Burnyeat, "Platonism and Mathematics: A Prelude to Discussion," in A. Graeser, ed., *Mathematics and Metaphysics in Aristotle* (Bern, 1987), 213–40, and Burnyeat, "Plato on Why Mathematics Is Good for the Soul," in T. Smiley, ed., *Mathematics and Necessity: Essays in the History of Philosophy, Proceedings of the British Academy* 103 (2000), 1–81.

*Republic* is the role of mathematics as the bridge to help us make the extraordinarily difficult transition from perceptible to intelligible. When we start mathematical study, we start to think about the perceptible world in more abstract terms. But this really is just a start and is quite different from believing that there exists a distinct intelligible realm to which the sensible is merely an approximation. It is only after a long period of mathematical study that such a mindset starts to form.

## Pretenders to philosophy

In the *Republic*, therefore, philosophy involves a complete reorientation toward a distinctive subject matter, a process that goes directly against the cognitive grain. This, in turn, helps explain a theme that runs throughout the central books: that true philosophers are so few and far between. There are, of course, many who style themselves as philosophers, but for Socrates they are in one way or another only pretenders to the title. The lovers of sights and sounds claim expertise in beauty and are said to be "like philosophers" (475e). Yet, for all their experience, they fail to grasp Beauty in itself. In book VI (495a–496a), Socrates complains that those who genuinely have a talent for philosophy tend to be deflected from it, and those who attempt to take it up instead are for the most part sophists. But philosophy, being distinguished by the nature of its objects, requires much more than logical agility and an appetite for abstraction. Socrates makes a similar point at VII 537d–539d, complaining that, as things are, people engage in (what they take to be) dialectic too early in life. He is referring to young men who debate about the just and the beautiful, asking and answering definitional questions. The problem is that they enjoy the battle of argument more than the pursuit of truth. Again, despite their ability to operate at a relatively abstract level, such people are not true philosophers, and their debates have only the appearance of true dialectic.

But if most of what passes for philosophy is just a poor imitation, and true philosophers are so thin on the ground, what are we to say about Socrates' interlocutors—or, indeed, ourselves as readers of the *Republic*? As we follow the arguments of the work, what sort of activity are we engaged in? Is it, in fact, philosophy in the true sense of the word?

I argue above that the defence of justice actually mounted in books II–IV and VIII–IX makes almost no reference to the Forms. For the most part, it appeals to empirical assumptions directly about human psychology and politics. In the central books, there is talk about Forms, about the knowledge based on them, and about the way in which such knowledge can be attained. But this is not dialectic in the true sense—that is, direct inquiry into the nature of the Forms. We are just peeping outside the cave but then finding the light too strong; or perhaps we have not even been that far, but someone else, who has stepped outside, is telling us what it is like. The central books are best described as metaphilosophy and the remaining books as preparation for philosophy. By its own lights, the *Republic* is not really a work *of* philosophy.

# BIBLIOGRAPHY

Ackrill, J. "What Is Wrong with Plato's *Republic?*" *Essays on Plato and Aristotle*, 2nd ed. (Oxford, 2001), 230–52.

Annas, J. *An Introduction to Plato's Republic* (Oxford, 1981).

Brown, E. "Minding the Gap in Plato's *Republic*," *Philosophical Studies* 117 (2004), 275–302.

Brown, L. "How Totalitarian Is Plato's *Republic?*" in E. Ostenfeld, ed., *Essays on Plato's Republic* (Aarhus, 1998), 13–27.

Burnyeat, M. "Platonism and Mathematics: A Prelude to Discussion," in A. Graeser, ed., *Mathematics and Metaphysics in Aristotle* (Bern, 1987), 213–40.

———. "Plato on Why Mathematics Is Good for the Soul," in T. Smiley, ed., *Mathematics and Necessity: Essays in the History of Philosophy, Proceedings of the British Academy* 103 (2000), 1–81.

Cooper, J. "The Psychology of Justice in Plato," *American Philosophical Quarterly* 14 (1977), 151–57.

Cross, R., and Woozley, A. *Plato's Republic* (London, 1964).

Ferejohn, M. "Knowledge, Recollection, and the Forms in *Republic* VII," in G. Santas, ed., *The Blackwell Companion to Plato's Republic* (Oxford, 2006), 214–33.

Fine, G. *On Ideas* (Oxford, 1993).

Gauthier, D. *Practical Reasoning* (Oxford, 1962).

Grube, G., trans. *Plato: Republic*, rev. C.Reeve (Indianapolis, 1992).

Harte, V. "Language in the Cave," in D. Scott, ed., *Maieusis: Studies in Honour of M. F. Burnyeat* (Oxford, 2007), 195–215.

Havelock, E. *Preface to Plato* (Oxford, 1963).

Irwin, T. *Plato's Ethics* (Oxford, 1995).

———. "*Republic* 2: Questions about Justice," in G. Fine, ed., *Plato 2: Ethics, Politics, Religion and the Soul* (Oxford, 1999), 164–85.

Kraut, R. "The Defense of Justice in Plato's *Republic*," in R. Kraut, ed., *The Cambridge Companion to Plato* (Cambridge, 1992), 311–37.

———. "Return to the Cave: *Republic* 519–521," in G. Fine, ed., *Plato 2: Ethics, Politics, Religion and the Soul* (Oxford, 1999), 235–54.

Nettleship, R. *Lectures on the Republic of Plato*, 2nd ed. (London, 1901).

Neu, J. "Plato's Analogy of State and Individual: The *Republic* and the Organic Theory of the State," *Philosophy* 46 (1971), 238–54.

Nightingale, A. W. *Genres in Dialogue* (Cambridge, 1995).

Parfit, D. *Reasons and Persons* (Oxford, 1986).

Popper, K. *The Open Society and Its Enemies*, vol. 1: *The Spell of Plato*, 5th ed. (London, 1966).

Sachs, D. "A Fallacy in Plato's *Republic*," *Philosophical Review* 72 (1963), 141–58; reprinted in G. Vlastos, ed., *Plato*, vol. 2: *Ethics, Politics and Philosophy of Art and Religion* (New York, 1973), 35–51.

Scott, D. "Metaphysics and the Defence of Justice in the *Republic*," *Proceedings of the Boston Area Colloquium in Ancient Philosophy* 16 (2000), 1–20.

———. *Recollection and Experience* (Cambridge, 1995).

Taylor, C. "Plato's Totalitarianism," *Polis* 5 (1986), 4–29; reprinted in G. Fine, ed., *Plato 2: Ethics, Politics, Religion and the Soul* (Oxford, 1999), 280–96.

Vlastos, G. "Justice and Happiness in the *Republic*," *Platonic Studies*, 2nd ed. (Princeton, 1981), 111–39.

————. "The Theory of Social Justice in the *Polis* in Plato's *Republic*," in D. Graham, ed., *Studies in Greek Philosophy*, vol. 2 (Princeton, N.J., 1995), 69–103.

White, N. "The Classification of Goods in Plato's *Republic*," *Journal of the History of Philosophy* 22 (1984), 393–421.

————. *A Companion to Plato's Republic* (Oxford, 1979).

# CHAPTER 16

# THE *PARMENIDES*

## SANDRA PETERSON

PLATO's *Parmenides*[1] contrasts with Plato's other works in several ways. For example, Socrates is depicted as "very young" (127c5), perhaps fifteen or perhaps nineteen. Parmenides questions Socrates, who contradicts himself; in other dialogues of question and answer, Socrates typically questions others, who contradict themselves. Parmenides refutes Socrates on the topic of forms, items such as justice itself and good itself, while the older Socrates of other dialogues presents forms as central to philosophy; the dialogue thus raises the question whether its criticism of forms signals Plato's revision of views expressed in previous writings. The *Parmenides* is the only dialogue in which forms are the main topic. The dialogue's second part, 137c–166c, is the longest passage of unrelenting argument in Plato's writings. Its arguments are his most puzzling.

## SECTION 1

Socrates enters the dialogue asking Zeno what he means (127e1). The renowned Zeno had argued that it is impossible that there be many things (127e7). Socrates says Zeno wished to contend something unusual ("to fight against all the things commonly said"; 127e9–10): this gives us some ground to think Zeno's conclusion is the incredible, barely intelligible, thesis it appears to be.

Socrates seems brash, even rude, both to Zeno and to his more famous mentor, Parmenides. At 127e8–128b1, Socrates questions Zeno mockingly:

---

1. Quotations from the *Parmenides* are from the translation of M. L. Gill and P. Ryan in *Plato, "Parmenides"* [*Parmenides*] (Indianapolis, 1996), with an occasional change. Gill and Ryan used mainly the text of J. Burnet, in *Platonis Opera*, vol 2 (Oxford, 1901).

> Then is this what your *arguments* are aiming at: nothing else but to contend, against *all the things* commonly said, that there are not many things? And do you think that *each of the arguments* is a proof for you, so that you also offer *as many proofs as* you have written *arguments*, that there are not many things? . . . *Hugely many* and very great *proofs*.

With repeated plurals and quantifying vocabulary, Socrates indicates bluntly that Zeno commits himself to many beings despite arguing otherwise.

Socrates mentions that Zeno says almost the same as Parmenides (128a6–7), who had maintained, "All is one" (128b5). Socrates complains that Zeno attempts to impress his audience by saying something that looks different from what Parmenides said but actually isn't that different.

Zeno agrees that he said almost the same as Parmenides, but he protests that Socrates mistakes Zeno's motive: Zeno wrote, when young, out of love of victory, to defend Parmenides' thesis against detractors who said it implied "many ridiculous things and contraries to that very thing" (128d1–2). Zeno wanted to show that the detractors' proposition implied "yet more ridiculous things" (128d5).

At 127e1, Socrates summarizes a representative argument of Zeno's:

1. Suppose that beings are many. (Assumption for reduction to absurdity)
2. It they are many, they are both like and unlike.
3. So things are both like and unlike. (From premises 1 and 2)
4. It is impossible that unlike things be like or like things unlike.
5. Therefore, beings are not many.

Our natural reaction to this is that the parts of Zeno's argument are of unequal merit. The strategy of reduction to absurdity or indirect proof—temporarily assuming some statement for exploration and presupposing that the actual cannot imply what is impossible—is familiar and unobjectionable. And premise 2 is highly plausible. (Perhaps Zeno argued that many beings would, as beings, be alike, but as plural and hence different from another would be unlike in some respects.)

Premise 4, by contrast, seems highly implausible: of course, the same things can be like and unlike—for example, Antiphon and his grandfather Antiphon are alike in their names but unlike in their ages. The ordinary Greek hearer would agree, since Parmenides later defines being like as bearing the same attribute (148a3). To be unlike is then to differ in some attribute. So it is easily possible for the same thing to be both like (something) and unlike (something else).

# SECTION 2

......................................................................................................................

Compare our reaction to Zeno's argument with Socrates' reaction:

> Don't you acknowledge [*nomizeis*] that there is itself by itself [*auto kath hauto*], a form [*eidos ti*] of likeness, and again something contrary to such a thing, what

unlike is [*ho estin anomoian*], while the things we call many—me and you and the other things—together get [*metalambanein*] these two things that are? Don't you and I and the other things we call many together have those two things that are? And don't things that together get likeness become like in that way and to the extent that they together get it, and the things [that together get] unlikeness [in the respect and to the extent to which they together get it become] unlike, and [things that jointly get] both, both? Even if all things together get both contrary beings, and are, by together having both, like and unlike, themselves to themselves, what is wonderful [about that]? (128e6–129b1)

I make several separate points before examining Socrates' response.

At 129a1, Socrates asks Zeno about "a form [*eidos ti*] of likeness."[2] A usual meaning of our word "form" is "specific variety," as when we say, "That form of rudeness is typically adolescent." But Socrates emphatically does not here mean by "form of likeness" "variety of likeness." Rather, he means "likeness that is *not* any specific variety of likeness," or "likeness considered solely as likeness."[3] Socrates' phrase "itself by itself" builds on our ordinary focusing use, as when I say, "I want to discuss shampoo itself, not pet shampoo or medicinal shampoo."[4]

Socrates uses the phrase "likeness itself by itself" (128e6–129a1) as parallel to the phrase "what unlike is" (129a1). We may infer that the phrase "what unlike is" is equivalent to "unlikeness itself by itself" and that the phrase "likeness itself by itself" would be interchangeable with the phrase "what like is." The phrase "what like is" is ordinary, as when I say: "If those twins aren't like each other, I don't know what like is." We could also say, especially because like things come in pairs, "If those twins aren't like each other, I don't know what likes are." Accordingly, at 129b1, Socrates uses the plural phrase "the likes themselves" interchangeably with the previous "likeness itself by itself." "Likeness itself by itself," "likeness itself" (Parmenides' phrasing at 130b3), "the form of likeness," "what like is," "the likes themselves," "what likes are," "the like," and "the like itself" are interchangeable.[5] (At 135c9–d1, Parmenides speaks of "something beautiful and just and good, and each one of the forms." So "something good" is there equivalent to "the form, good itself.")

Characters in Plato's dialogues talk of forms, these items often labeled with "itself," prominently.[6] Scholars speak of "Plato's theory of forms."[7] Some scholars

---

2. To be consistent with other translators, I translate *eidos* by "form." But I note "aspect" as an alternative, because it is closer in etymology to *eidos*: both *eidos* and aspect are literally what is visible about something—present to our sight or, more widely, to our thought. In its widest meaning *eidos*, like "aspect," amounts to something like "attribute." "I want to talk about the aspect of likeness" means "I want to concentrate on likeness, apart from other attributes."

3. An advantage of thinking of aspects here is that "aspect of" in English never means "variety of."

4. See topic-focusing uses of "itself" at *Republic* 437–38 on thirst; *Phaedrus* 258d ("writing speeches itself"); *Euthydemus* 281d; and *Gorgias* 496d1 (hunger itself).

5. The phrases are more interchangeable in Greek than in English, since in Greek the neuter plural subject takes a singular verb.

6. For example, *Phaedo* 75d, 76d7–9, 96a–101e, 100b; *Republic* 475b–484a, 523a–525b, 596a–597e; and *Symposium* 209e–212a, where Diotima speaks of beauty itself, although she doesn't use the word "form" for it.

7. See T. H. Irwin, "The Theory of Forms," in G. Fine (ed.), *Plato 1: Metaphysics and Epistemology* (Oxford 1999), **143**–170. See also G. Fine, "Vlastos on Socratic and Platonic Forms," *Apeiron* 26 (1995), 67–83.

say the *Parmenides* represents the young Socrates as advocating the theory of forms.[8] Because of the differences in what different dialogues say about forms, I avoid phrasing that suggests that there is one determinate, recurrent collection of principles about forms.[9] Although later I take note of possibly different theories of forms, for now I simply observe exactly what Socrates says to Zeno about forms.

Socrates asks Zeno, "Do you not acknowledge [*nomizeis*] . . . ?" *Nomizein* means "recognize the customary usage" or "genuinely accept." Socrates is asking about what Zeno customarily acknowledges, not introducing something innovative or technical. What Socrates says about forms at this point belongs as much to Zeno, as depicted, as to Socrates.

Socrates is aware that "like" and "unlike" are incomplete opposite predicates that require further qualification clearly to apply to something or to exclude one another: he speaks of things becoming like and unlike *in a respect* and *to an extent*.

The verb "together (or jointly) get" (*metalambanein*; 129a3), like the verb "together have" (*metechein*; 129a8), has the prefix *meta*, which adds the sense "together" or "jointly" to the root verbs "have" (*echein*) and "get" (*lambanein*). Customary but less revealing translations are "share," "participate," and "partake." The more literal translations bring out the verbs' ordinariness. To say that someone gets or has courage is perfectly ordinary. So it is also ordinary to say, if each of two people gets and has courage, that the two of them together get and jointly have it. Socrates is not using the phrases "together get likeness" and "together have likeness" as metaphors for something new and difficult to express or as technical terms for which Socrates owes Zeno an explanation.[10] Socrates expects that Zeno customarily says that things become (*gignesthai*; 129a4) like to the extent to which—that is, if and only if—they jointly get likeness and that they are like if and only if they together have likeness. Socrates' verb phrases are banal equivalents to "together become like" and "together are like."

These preliminaries prepare us to see that Socrates refutes Zeno with three distinct moves.

---

8. For example, M. Miller, *Plato's "Parmenides"* (Princeton, N.J., 1986), 37; R. E. Allen, *Plato's "Parmenides"* (New Haven, Ct., 1997), 67, originally published Minneapolis, 1983; S. Rickless, "How Parmenides Saved the Theory of Forms" ["Saved"], *Philosophical Review* 107 (1998), 502; Gill, "Introduction" to Gill and Ryan, *Parmenides*, 12; C. Meinwald, *Plato's "Parmenides"* (Oxford, 1991), 5; K. Sayre, *Parmenides' Lesson: Translation and Explication of Plato's "Parmenides"* (Notre Dame, Ind., 1996), 61–62; Proclus, *Commentary* Bk I 729–30.

9. See the caution of J. Annas, *Introduction to Plato's "Republic"* (Oxford, 1981), ch 9, "The 'Theory' of Forms," 217–241.

10. C. H. Kahn, *Plato and the Socratic Dialogue: The Philosophical Use of a Literary Form* [*Plato*] (Cambridge, 1996), 334–35, cites pre-Plato occurrences of *metechein*, such as "sharing in military prowess." He calls them "metaphorical." To me they seem ordinary and not metaphorical. *Gorgias* 468a says that sitting, making sea voyages, and sticks sometimes partake of what is good and sometimes of what is bad: that clearly means that they are sometimes good and sometimes bad. *Sophist* 223c1–2 says that sophistry is "not a sharer [*metochon*] in an ordinary art, but in a variegated one." This means that sophistry isn't ordinary, but is variegated.

When the subject of one of these *meta*- verbs is singular, the translation "share" is preferable to "together-has," since the latter leads us to expect a plural subject—that is, explicit mention of a partner in having. (Thanks to Constance Meinwald here.)

First, from 127e to 128b, having clarified that Zeno's argument is a reduction to absurdity of the statement that beings are many, Socrates leads Zeno to display Zeno's own belief that many things are like and unlike, as, for example, when Zeno implies that he and Parmenides are like in that they say the same things (128b5) and unlike in that Zeno says "not many" and Parmenides says "one" (128b3–5). By implying that there are several beings like in some respects and unlike in others, even while he contends there cannot be several beings both like and unlike, Zeno is conspicuously inconsistent.

Second, Socrates explicitly states the deeper and devastating objection (128e5–129a3) that Zeno, in conducting his reduction to absurdity, presumes that there *are* two opposites—likeness and unlikeness—each of which is a being ( *toutoin de duoin ontoin*; 129a2). Zeno presumes that likeness itself is one item and unlikeness is a second and opposite item.[11] Zeno's premises imply the denial of his conclusion. And that is disastrous. Naturally, in order to argue via reduction to absurdity, you assume, or temporarily treat as a premise, the denial of what you want to prove. But if the denial of what you want to prove is a consequence of your actual premises, your argument is entirely unconvincing.

Third, Socrates' final question to Zeno denies Zeno's premise that it is impossible for anything to be both like and unlike:

> Don't things that together get likeness become like in that way and to the extent that they together get it, and the things that together get unlikeness [in the respect and to the extent to which they together get it become] unlike, and [things that jointly get] both, both? (129a1–b1)

Socrates emphasizes that the predicates "like" and "unlike" are incomplete ("in that way and to the extent") and that ordinary talk recognizes many things that are both like and unlike or have likeness and unlikeness in various respects.

Socrates' third objection, though identical with our own natural reaction, seems somewhat anticlimactic after his devastating second objection. But it is worth dwelling on. If not properly understood, it will seem worthless. Many commentators understand it to involve the introduction of a new theory of forms, where forms are special technical or theoretical entities. So understood, it would be entirely superfluous to Socrates' simple and devastating refutation of Zeno that ends at 129b1.[12]

Besides adding nothing to Socrates' objections to Zeno, a technical theory would subtract something. If we think Socrates brandishes a new technical theory with unfamiliar entities, without defending it, we miss the genuine power of his simple refutation and cannot explain why Parmenides and Zeno admire the spirit of Socrates' response at 130a6–7. Spirit that produces a superfluous undefended

---

11. Cf. *Parmenides* 149e8–150a1.

12. Gill, "Introduction" to Gill and Ryan, *Parmenides*, 12–14, drawing on the *Phaedo*, explains how the assertion that there are forms could dispel Zeno's apparent absurdity and not be superfluous. But Socrates does not give her explanation here.

proposal against Zeno's argument would not be admirable. Zeno and Parmenides, as depicted, would see that.

I mention as an aside here something I discuss later. When Parmenides begins questioning Socrates, there do appear some new proposals that may very well be part of someone's technical theory. But up to 129b1 there is no reason to ascribe to Socrates premises apart from the ordinary commitments he has called attention to. (For example, there is no reason to introduce capital letters, not in the Greek.)

If we avoid saying that Socrates invokes an unhelpful and gratuitous new technical theory, we can say that up to 129b1 his three-part refutation of Zeno is decisive. Socrates simply points out undeniable presuppositions of customary speech. He deserves Zeno's and Parmenides' admiration.

# SECTION 3

Socrates next offers a challenge and then responds to Parmenides' questions. Both Socrates' challenge and his responses indicate that he has not thought enough about the forms he deployed so successfully in refuting Zeno.

This is Socrates' challenge:

> If someone showed the likes themselves coming to be unlike or the unlikes like—that, I think, would be a marvel; but if he shows things that together have [*metechonta*] both as having undergone [*peponthota*] both, it seems to me, Zeno, nothing out of the way, nor if someone shows all things are one by together having unity and these same things many by again together having multiplicity. But if—what one is—he will show this itself many and again the many one, I would at that point wonder at it. And so for all the others: if he should show the kinds and forms themselves in themselves bearing these conditions that are contraries, it would be worthy of wondering at.(129b1–c3)

Seven points are worth mentioning.

1. Socrates' examples of statements that would surprise him, in fact, do not seem surprising. At 129b, Socrates says he would be astonished if someone showed that the likes themselves come to be unlike or the unlikes like: that is, if someone showed that likeness itself is unlike and unlikeness itself is like. Since, at 129a, he recognized that things are like or unlike in certain respects, it would be odd if Socrates were not well aware that Zeno's (conjectural) argument—that the many beings are like in that each is a being, while they must be somehow unlike to be distinct from one another—obviously applies to likeness itself and unlikeness itself. Since this obvious argument does not deter Socrates from his challenge, it seems probable that the simple feat of showing that likeness itself is unlike in some way would not meet his challenge. Socrates' challenge suggests a new conviction not implied by his refutation of Zeno. For now, I formulate Socrates' new conviction

vaguely: in some as yet unclear way, different from the way of being unlike that he has already implicitly accepted, what like is cannot be unlike; more generally, in some yet unclear way, an opposite cannot be its own opposite.

2. Socrates' second example of what would surprise him is being shown that "what one is, this itself" is many or that the many is one. He then gives a general formulation of his challenge: "And in the same way for all the others:... if [someone]... should show the kinds and forms themselves in themselves undergoing these conditions that are contraries, it would be worthy of wondering at" (129c1–3). His general formulation contains a new phrase, "in themselves" (*en hautois*; 129c2). If we take this phrase merely to emphasize that the word "itself" occurs in locutions for forms, the simplest interpretation of his challenge is to prove that the many itself is one in some way or other. But since there was reason to reject this simplest interpretation of Socrates' challenge for likeness, we may reasonably suppose that the phrase "in themselves" is more here than reminder that the word "itself" occurs in phrases for forms. A similar phrase occurs at 129e1:

> But if someone first distinguishes as separate (*chôris*) the forms themselves by themselves of those things I was just now speaking of, such as likeness and unlikeness and multitude and unity and rest and motion and all such things, and then shows these things *in themselves* (*en heautois*; 129e1) able to be combined and to be thoroughly distinguished, I would admire it wonderfully.

To acknowledge Socrates' new phrase, I reformulate the conviction behind Socrates' challenge: an opposite itself, *in itself,* cannot be its own opposite.

3. What might his phrase "in itself" add to his challenge? We have already noticed one ordinary role of "itself" as a topic-narrowing device. The older Socrates of other dialogues gives the word "itself" a second role to initiate definitional conversations through such questions as "What is the fine itself?" (*Hippias Major* 288a8–9). Although Socrates in the *Parmenides* does not ask a characteristic definition-seeking question such as "What is the unlike itself?" he shows interest in definitions in that he uses the phrase "what unlike is" (129a1). The phrase "what unlike is" has a close connection to definition. An analyzing answer to the question "What is the unlike itself?" reveals what unlike is. What unlike is is unlikeness itself, defined. What a square is is the square itself, analyzed as an equal-sided rectangle. Since Parmenides noticed (135c8–d2) that Socrates was trying to mark off or define too soon in a previous conversation, perhaps Parmenides heard Socrates ask such questions as "What is the just itself?"

This definition-seeking "itself" does somewhat more than narrow a topic. Merely to narrow a topic for discussion is not yet to start a definitional conversation. If I invite conversation about mud itself, and your first comment is to say that mud is annoying on rugs, I would be inept to grumble, "That's not what I wanted. You are telling me something extra about mud—where mud is or what it is like. I just wanted to talk about it, itself, that is, what it is." For in some conversations "Mud is annoying on rugs" might acceptably respond to "Tell me about mud itself." Even the question "What is mud itself?" doesn't confine us to definition as response. If I want a definition as answer, I must say more. For example, it would be helpful to say, as the older Socrates would, that I want to know that *by which anything that is mud* is mud.[13] "By which" translates a dative pronoun. Plato uses this instrumental dative often. In the *Hippias Major* (287c–d), Hippias agrees that people are just by justice and that justice is something. Hippias is agreeing that there is some content to the notion of justice. We cite that content to explain how just things are just. Defining is stating that content. In contrast, consider slithiness. It is not something. There is no answer to the question "What is slithiness?"—nothing to cite by which anything could be slithy. So nothing is slithy.

Socrates does not use this instrumental dative here but says that like things are like by together *having* likeness (129a8). However, Parmenides uses the instrumental dative: large things are large by largeness (132a–b). Aristotle, an interlocutor later in the dialogue, assents to relevant statements with "by": "If being is different, and the one is different, then not by the one is the one different from being, nor by being is being other than the one, but by the different . . . they are different from one another" (143b3–6). I take it that Parmenides understands such statements with instrumental datives as ordinary, obvious truths, just as Hippias understands them.

The definition-seeking role of "itself" permits at least two possible meanings of Socrates' challenge to show him that an opposite itself, *in itself*, is its own opposite. One possibility is that Socrates' challenge means "Show me that an opposite itself can be defined as its own opposite." So understood, his challenge is insuperable. After all, to be opposites is to have definitions excluding one another. A second possibility is that he is requesting a demonstration solely from the definition of likeness itself that it is unlike. We will not be able to meet this request by the easy argument that likeness is both like and unlike because its *being* implies likeness to beings and its *difference* from other beings implies unlikeness to them in some respect. If Socrates thinks it challenging to demonstrate that likeness itself, as defined, entails or necessitates unlikeness, and vice versa, he would seem to pre-suppose what I will number as the first in a list of convictions that go beyond what he said in his refutation of Zeno.

> I. It is not the case that an opposite itself is in itself—that is, as necessitated by its definition—its opposite.

Why would he think this? Perhaps he is convinced that information about something's definition does not necessitate about it *anything* that is not explicitly mentioned in its definition. This putative conviction seems wrong. Though being is not mentioned in the definition of unlikeness, nevertheless, if unlikeness has a definition that says what unlike *is*, then unlikeness is something and hence a being. (Again contrast slithiness. It has no definitional content; hence it is not anything; hence it is not a being.) But the putative conviction seems close to something that is right: the

13. At *Euthyphro* 6d10 Socrates wants Euthyphro to tell him "that form itself by which all the pious things are pious." See also 6d11–e.

definition of unlikeness does not mention that it is a being or is like other beings. The definition of unlikeness does not mention anything apart from what unlike is.

4. At 129d6–e3, Socrates would be surprised if someone first distinguishes separately forms themselves by themselves and then shows them capable of being combined and also distinguished. He does not mean that (a) he would be surprised if they could be combined and that (b) he would be surprised if they could be distinguished. He would definitely not be surprised that they could be distinguished. He has just said that he and Zeno distinguish likeness from unlikeness. What would surprise Socrates is if, *given that these forms have been distinguished separately*, these separate forms, themselves by themselves, could be combined.

5. At 129d7 is Socrates' first use of the word "separately" (*chôris*). Here the word indicates that the various forms are separate from one another.[14] Socrates is apparently reinforcing his thought (129d6) that the forms are distinguished from (i.e., not identical with) one another by saying that they are distinguished separately. Many commentators immediately but for no clear textual or logical reason take 129d7 to say that forms are separate from their participants.

6. At 129d8–e1, Socrates lists as forms separate from one another likeness, unlikeness, multitude, the one, rest, motion, "and all such." It would surprise Socrates if these separate things could be combined. Previously, we saw that to say that likeness and unlikeness are opposites guarantees that there are at least two (or as we can now say, two separate) things. Now we learn that, for example, likeness and motion, though not opposite to one another, are separate from one another.

Socrates does not explain how exactly all these forms are distinguished separately from one another. In the case of likeness and unlikeness, there is strong reason to say that they are separate in that they exclude one another: you and I disagree if you say that certain things are alike in a certain respect and I say that those same things are unlike in that respect. But you and I do not disagree if I say that certain things are like and you say that they are one. We simply give different information. Socrates suggests here that something besides opposition is a basis for certain forms being distinct from one another. That speaking of them gives different information would provide such a basis. Parmenides later brings that basis to the surface:

> There would be the being of the one, which is not the same as the one. For [if it were] ... to say one is would be like saying one one(s). But this is not now the hypothesis, if one one(s), ... but if one is. ... Is it then that "is" means something other than "one"? (142b7–c5)

The passage gives the following argument in a different order:

1. To say "one is" is different from saying "one ones."
2. So "is" means something other than "one."
3. Therefore being is not the same as the one.

14. 139e9–140a1 shows that *chôris* can be used to say that one form is separate from another. S. Peterson discusses the passage in "New Rounds of the Exercise of Plato's *Parmenides*" ["Rounds"], *Modern Schoolman* 80 (2003), 255–58.

7. Socrates' challenge is offered in three different stages. First, he would be surprised if the like itself were unlike or the one many; that is, he'd be *surprised if one of a pair of opposite forms were in itself its own opposite* (129b). Second, he would be surprised if someone could show that forms themselves in themselves bear opposite attributes. So far, he has mentioned only the opposites likeness and unlikeness, one and many. If he included all pairs of opposites, his general claim would be that he would be surprised *if any form in itself had any pair of opposites*. Third, at 129d6–e3, Socrates would be surprised *if separate forms in themselves could be combined*: for example, if someone showed that motion itself is in itself like. The putative conviction speculated at (3) would explain his surprise.

The seven points above suggest that in issuing his challenge Socrates has left unclear in what way opposites cannot be their own opposites and why separate forms cannot be both distinguished and combined.

# SECTION 4

Parmenides now repeats Socrates' word "separate" and extends Socrates' application of it. Parmenides asks, "Have you yourself distinguished as separate in the way you speak of certain forms themselves, and also as separate the things that together have them?" (130b). Here Socrates introduces something not previously asserted. At 129d7–8, where "separate" first occurs, he only said forms were separate from one another. Now he says as well that they are separate from the things that jointly have them.

Of the two reasons we have so far seen to say that forms are distinguished or separate from one another (first, incompatibility; second, different informational content of associated predicate), neither is a reason that likeness might be separate or distinct from things that jointly have likeness. Like twins and likeness itself clearly are not separate by excluding one another. Nor do speaking of likeness itself and speaking of what has likeness convey different content in the way speaking of likeness conveys different content from speaking of motion. That likeness and unlikeness and plurality are separate is a condition of normal discourse about many like and unlike things, as Socrates' refutation of Zeno showed. In contrast, that I who have likeness am separate from likeness by being distinct from it is a happy accident for me. (I might not have existed at all.) My being separate from it is not a condition of discourse.

It might be proposed that "separate" means "independently existing" and that here Parmenides means that likeness is separate from, say, like twins because it can exist when they do not. That would be a coherent position. But a form's separation in that way from what jointly has it would be very different from the way paired opposites are separate from another. Separate opposites must exist in tandem: there is such a thing as likeness if and only if there is such a thing as unlikeness.

Though the word "separate" might unambiguously cover two different ways of being distinct, Parmenides has not prepared us for this extended application. His question requires a new ground for "separate," obviously not the same as, and not obviously related to, Socrates' earlier likely grounds. Socrates should ask for clarification because Parmenides is pressing the word "separate" into service beyond the role in which Socrates introduced it.

We have now a second addition to the minimal description of forms that Socrates used in his refutation of Zeno up to 129b. Our second new principle is the general claim of which an instance would be:

II. Likeness itself is (in some way not yet clarified) separate from what has likeness.

Parmenides extracts a third new claim from Socrates, asking: "Do you think that likeness itself is something separate from the likeness we have [*echomen*; 130b4]? And one and many and all the things you heard Zeno read about a while ago?" (130b3–5). Parmenides has now introduced, in addition to the likeness we jointly have (*metechonta*; 130b3), a likeness that we have but apparently not jointly. *Echomen* at 130b4 lacks the prefix *meta*, "together" or "jointly." That Parmenides drops the prefix suggests that he distinguishes between each having (*echomen*) and both having. An instance of Parmenides' new general claim would be:

III. Likeness itself, which we jointly have, is separate from the likeness we (each) have.

Claim III suggests that your likeness, which only you have, my likeness, which I alone have, and likeness itself, which we both have, are distinct items. The *Parmenides* does not further develop this suggestion.[15]

Parmenides next asks whether there are forms for several examples. Socrates is at first uncertain whether there is a form itself of human being, fire, or water. Though Socrates might have argued that there is a form of man because what a man is is different from what a cat is, he wouldn't have been able to argue that there is one form of man because it and its opposite must be two, since man has no opposite. Commentators have speculated that Socrates hesitates because he believes that there are forms only for predicates that have opposites.[16] I will not enter this among Socrates' commitments because the text does not compel it.

Socrates is surer that there are no forms of hair or mud, but he worries that he might be wrong. Parmenides elicits their dismissal by saying they might "seem

15. Some interpreters accept the consequence and call the likeness in you and the likeness in me "immanent characters," a type of being apart from forms. The opposite position is that the likeness that you have and the likeness that I have are, after all, the same item as likeness itself, only differently described, just as my cat, your cat, and the cat in the basket are the same cat if we co-own the cat in the basket. For the issues, and for argument that forms in things are "not a distinct ontological category from forms, but (parts of) forms themselves, when they are in things," see G. Fine, "Immanence," *Oxford Studies in Ancient Philosophy* 4 (1986), 71–97; reprinted in Fine, *Plato on Knowledge and Forms: Selected Essays* (Oxford, 2003), 301–25. The quoted phrase is from p. 305 of the latter.

16. Gill, "Introduction" to Gill and Ryan, *Parmenides*, 22.

laughable" (130c5) and are "most lacking in honor" (130c6) and "most inferior" (130c7). But Parmenides says that Socrates will not dismiss these when he is older and pays less attention to people's opinions (130e). Parmenides implies that there is a form of mud, and he flatly diagnoses that Socrates mistakenly believes:

> IV. There are forms themselves by themselves for what F is only where what is F is considered worthy of honor.

Parmenides thus explicitly finds in Socrates a mistake that lacks any connection to the insight, displayed in Socrates' refutation of Zeno, that making distinctions in speech commits us to belief in distinct aspects. Attention to the ordinary roles of "itself by itself" might ward off that mistake.

# SECTION 5

Now the discussion proceeds differently: Parmenides not only asks questions to clarify Socrates' beliefs about forms but also, for the first time, draws fresh consequences from Socrates' answers—consequences so unacceptable that Socrates finally expresses incapacity to speak about forms (135c). Parmenides asks, "Does each thing that shares (*metalambanon*) [it] share the whole form or a part? Or might there be some other sort of sharing apart from these?" (131a4–6). Socrates thinks there is no other kind of sharing. Parmenides says that if the form as a whole, one and the same form, is shared, "it will be at the same time as a whole in things that are many and separate, and thus it would be separate from itself" (131b1–2).

In reply, Socrates compares the form to the same day—in many places at the same time, yet not separate from itself. Parmenides ridicules this proposal. He infers: "So the forms themselves are divisible, and things that jointly get them would both get a part, and it [the form] would no longer be in each thing as a whole, but a part would belong to each thing" (131c5). Socrates vigorously dissents when Parmenides asks: ' "Do you want to say then, Socrates, that our one form is truly broken up into parts and yet will be one thing?' 'In no way,' he said" (131b9).

Parmenides' questions seem to assume that there must be an answer whenever someone asks whether things that jointly get something get the whole or a part. But in numerous instances we say that things share something without feeling bound to answer the question whether they get or have all or part of it. Antiphon and his grandfather share the name "Antiphon." Antiphon and Adeimantus both have the same mother. Even if we were to say that what gets a name gets the whole of it, we would not then worry that the name two people jointly have is separate from itself. So even if Parmenides' question is appropriate, it is not clear that every answer is worrisome. Parmenides fastens on one kind of having-together, and not obviously the relevant kind. Parmenides asks the sort of question that would be appropriate to ask about together having a pie for lunch.

Parmenides' inference from several items all having the whole form to the whole form's being *in* each of the several things is equally uncompelling. That things share a (whole) name does not imply that it is in any of the things that have it.

Parmenides argues that if the form is in each of several things, then it is "separate from itself." Whereas previously "distinguished separately" as applied to forms conveyed something like "have different defining contents," here "separate from" seems to mean "in a spatially separate location." It is not obvious that Parmenides is entitled to mean by "in" the "in" of spatial location.

Although it's not yet clear what leads Socrates into confusion, one possibility is that he at least needs to attend more to various actual uses of "in" and "have."

# SECTION 6

Parmenides now extracts, and argues from, several new admissions that again go beyond the minimum Socrates used to refute Zeno. Parmenides considers the form, the large itself. His argument has been called the "third man" because Aristotle so labels an argument about the form, man, with the same logical pattern.[17] Aristotle takes the argument to be a severe objection to what Plato says about forms.[18]

Parmenides says,

> I suppose you think that each form is one on the following ground: whenever some number of things seems to you to be large, perhaps there seems to be some one aspect [*idea*], the same as you look at them all, and from that you conclude that the large is one. (132a1)

What Parmenides supposes is not quite accurate. Previously, Socrates clearly did not take as ground for there being one form or aspect, the F, that there are several Fs; on the contrary, he expressed doubt (130c) that there was a form of human

---

17. Aristotle, *Metaphysics* 990b17–1079a13; *Soph. El.* 178b36, and *Metaphysics* 1039a2. The ancient commentator Alexander of Aphrodisias presents the argument in *In Metaph.* 84, 23–85, reproduced in G. Fine, *On Ideas: Aristotle's Criticism of Plato's Theory of Forms* [*Ideas*] (Oxford, 1993), 19.

G. E. L. Owen, "The Platonism of Aristotle," in G. E. L. Owen, *Logic, Science, and Dialectic: Collected Papers in Greek Philosophy*, ed. M. Nussbaum (Ithaca, N.Y., 1968), 200–220, thinks this argument provoked Aristotle to create his own theory of predication and categories, which is the ground for his own theory of (Aristotelian) forms. For dissent to Owen, see G. Fine, "Owen, Aristotle, and the Third Man," *Phronesis* 27 (1982), 13–33.

18. The twentieth century saw a tsunami of literature on the third man argument, initiated by G. Vlastos, "The Third Man Argument in the *Parmenides*," *Philosophical Review* 63 (1954), 319–49; reprinted in R. E. Allen (ed.), *Studies in Plato's Metaphysics* (London, 1965), 231–63. P. T. Geach responds to Vlastos in "The Third Man Again," in R. E. Allen, *Studies in Plato's Metaphysics* (London, 1965), 265–77. See also C. Strang, "Plato and the Third Man," *Proceedings of the Aristotelian Society* 37(suppl.) (1963), 147–64; S. M. Cohen, "The Logic of the Third Man," *Philosophical Review* 80 (1971), 448–75; and G. Vlastos, "Plato's 'Third Man' Argument (*Parm.* 132a1–b2): Text and Logic," *Philosophical Quarterly* (1969), 298–301, reprinted in G. Vlastos, *Platonic Studies*, 2nd ed. [*Studies*] (Princeton, N. J., 1981), **342–360**.

being. However, since Socrates agrees to Parmenides' supposition, we may add as a new statement about forms a schema, the one-over-many premise, that yields such statements as the following as instances:

> V. Whenever it seems that several things are large, there is one form, the large (that is of them all).

Socrates also agrees when Parmenides proposes:

> VI. Given the large itself and the other large things, there is one form by which all of these appear large. (132a7–8)

"Appear" does not here contrast with "really are" but amounts to "plainly are." If so, Socrates' agreement to claim VI gives us

> VII. The large itself is large.

In the secondary literature, the general claim of which this is an example is called the "self-predication assumption."[19] The general formulation implies, for example, that the dog itself is a dog. Such a result has seemed odd to readers since the dog itself is certainly not an ordinary dog. However, such a self-predication does not imply that the dog itself is an ordinary dog.

One argument that Socrates should accept such self-predications is as follows.[20] The dog itself is what a dog is, the content of the analyzing answer to the definition-seeking question, "What is the dog itself?" Suppose the answer to the definitional question is that the dog is a barking quadruped animal. Definition gives us analysis of a predicate. Analysis is interchangeable with what it analyzes in most contexts, including the present one. Since what a dog is is a barking quadruped animal, it follows that the dog itself is a dog.

Although self-predications have an apparently odd syntax—a form-term as subject and a predicate applicable to ordinary things—many sentences that we accept have that same syntactical pattern. If we rejected self-predications because of their odd syntax, we would have to give up many ordinary statements, such as the biblical statement "Charity suffereth long" or encyclopedia statements such as "The tiger is a carnivore."[21] Accepting self-predications is no more than facing up to consequences of our definitions.[22]

After claim VII, Parmenides infers:

19. See S. Peterson, "A Reasonable Self-Predication Premise for the Third Man Argument" ["Self-Predication"], *Philosophical Review* 82 (1973), 451–70; J. Malcolm, *Plato on the Self-Predication of Forms* (Oxford, 1991); and Fine, *Ideas*, 61–64.

20. Meinwald, *Parmenides*, 15–17, crediting Michael Frede, gives a different argument that self-predications are acceptable. See also Meinwald, "Good-Bye to the Third Man," in R. Kraut, *The Cambridge Companion to Plato* (Cambridge, 1992), 344.

21. Peterson, "Self-Predication," esp. 457–62, argues that there are several accounts of the semantics of our self-predications that would explain how they are true, and that Plato in effect chose one.

22. Parmenides later shows he accepts some self-predications: the different is different at 139c4–5; at 150 c7, largeness and smallness themselves "have … their power of exceeding and being exceeded … in relation to each other."

Then another aspect of largeness will appear having come to be alongside [i.e., different from] largeness itself and the things that together have it, and again another over all these, by which all of them will be large. (132a10–b2)

When Parmenides speaks of the large itself and the things that together have it, he suggests this assumption:

VIII.  Largeness does not together-have (partake of) itself

(Parmenides later at 158b1–2 says similarly that things that partake of the one are different from it.) I won't discuss claim VIII here except to distinguish it from a quite different principle that Socrates implicitly commits himself to in accepting the inference to "another aspect of largeness" and to "again another." I call this the "non-self-explanation" principle:

IX.  The large itself is not large by (or in virtue of) itself.

It is odd that Socrates lets this go by. As we understand the instrumental "by," claim IX is an obvious falsehood. (That the triangle itself is a triangle by itself, or because of what-a-triangle-is, is an equally obvious truth.)

Parmenides draws a conclusion that troubles Socrates: "No longer will each of your forms be one, but they will be infinite in multitude" (132b2). I take this conclusion to mean that there is an infinite regress of forms of, for example, largeness.[23] Parmenides and Socrates do not explain in detail why the regress should trouble Socrates, but, presumably, the reason is that it appears incompatible with Socrates' conviction that each form is one (131b5–6, 131b11, 132a1).

Claims V, VI, VII, and IX validly yield an unending regress for largeness; analogous premises yield a regress for every form.

To make it plausible that Socrates would accept the argument, I've supplied the implicit, though false, premise IX. This makes the argument valid. It seems more likely that Socrates accepts a valid but unsound argument than that he accepts an invalid argument.

# SECTION 7

In a new phase of the discussion, Socrates volunteers some claims instead of simply accepting Parmenides' proposals. To avoid the conclusion of the third man argument and to preserve his conviction that each form is one, Socrates suggests a new way for each form to be one: perhaps each form is a thought and occurs only in minds (132b5).[24] Socrates appears to think the one-over-many premise got him

---

23. Rickless, "Saved," and Rickless, *Plato's Forms in Transition* [*Forms*] (Cambridge, 2006), thought-provokingly finds a different meaning.

24. M. Burnyeat discusses this passage in "What Descartes Saw and Berkeley Missed," *Philosophical Review* 91 (1982), 20–23. See also Fine, *Ideas*, 131–34.

into trouble, so he now replaces it. This replacement is immediately refuted and dropped, so I don't enter it into our list of Socrates' current commitments. But his offering it emphasizes that Socrates believes that

X. Each form is one.

(This, unlike my other numbered principles about forms, was actually part of Socrates' refutation of Zeno.) That each form is one implies immediately that the form multitude (or what many is) is one. That implication is perfectly reasonable: it means that many cats and many problems and many numbers are one thing: they are all many. What many is is a single aspect of things—that is, a single form.

Socrates' explicitly accepting claim X confirms our rejection of the simplest interpretation of his challenge at 129b to show him that the many is one, as does Parmenides' giving no hint at 132a that he thinks Socrates' saying that each form is one might conflict with Socrates' predicted surprise if someone should prove that the many itself, in itself, is one.

At 132d1, Socrates volunteers something else new in an attempt to avoid difficulties. He proposes that "the forms are patterns set in nature": "Other things are like them and are likenesses and . . . this partaking of the forms is nothing other than being like them." This is reasonable. The dog itself, what a dog is, is a barking quadruped animal. In that respect, every dog is like it.

Parmenides now generates an infinite regress of likenesses from the premises Socrates grants him.[25] In the course of his argument, Parmenides elicits from Socrates a new admission:

XI. Every form is like the things that share it and that are like it. (132d7–8)

Socrates' agreement commits him to the immediate consequence that unlikeness itself is like the things that share unlikeness. So Socrates has for the second time assented to one of the statements that he said would surprise him (129b1)—that unlikeness itself is like. And, again, Parmenides refrains from hinting that Socrates might be inconsistent. Parmenides apparently thinks Socrates' challenge worth pursuing. Parmenides' reticence alerts us to attend to the phrase "in themselves" and further confirms our rejection of the simplest interpretation of Socrates' challenge.

In summing up these difficulties and in introducing his final, and what he will call his "greatest" problematic consequence about forms, Parmenides comments:

> Do you see, Socrates, how great the impasse is if one marks off forms that are themselves by themselves. . . . You almost do not yet touch on it—how great the impasse is if you will posit one form for each of the things that are whenever you make a distinction. (133a8–b2)

---

25. Some readers think the argument here is very similar to the third man argument and produces an infinite regress for any form. M. Schofield convincingly explains that the argument is specifically for likeness in "Likeness and Likenesses in the *Parmenides*," in C. Gill and M. M. McCabe (eds.), *Form and Argument: Studies in Late Plato* (Oxford, 1996), 49–77. See also Allen, *Parmenides*, 181–83. For a different account of the argument, and a defense of its similarity to the third man, see Fine, *Ideas*, 211–15.

In warning Socrates about positing "one form for each of the things that are, whenever you make a distinction," Parmenides recalls Socrates' reason for recognizing forms in the refutation of Zeno: to acknowledge distinctions we make in speaking.

# SECTION 8

Socrates now no longer volunteers anything but simply accepts new proposals from Parmenides. It becomes Socrates' responsibility to maintain consistently what he accepts.

Parmenides outlines his last difficulty, the "greatest":

> Suppose someone should say that they are not fit to be known, if the forms are such as we say they ought to be. To someone saying these things one will be incapable of showing that he [the objector] is saying something false, if the objector did not happen to be experienced in many things and not unsuited by nature, but [rather] was willing to follow while the one giving the demonstration carried out his business from a long way off. (133b4–9)

Even as he prepares to confront Socrates with his most damaging conclusion, Parmenides encourages Socrates by alluding to an adequate, though lengthy, response.

Parmenides then extracts his first premise for the greatest difficulty:

> "You and anyone else who posits that there is for each thing some being itself by itself would agree, to begin with, that none of these beings is in us."
>
> "Yes, for how could it still be itself by itself?" replied Socrates. (133c)

Socrates has agreed to a new extraneous claim:

XII. Nothing that is a being itself by itself is in us.

Fortunately, Parmenides now clarifies this somewhat mysterious claim: he states a general principle applicable to forms associated with relational predicates. Examples of relational predicates are "master of," "slave of," "knowledge of," and "equal to":

> Then as many of the forms as are what they are in relation to one another, these have their being in relation to themselves but not in relation to the things alongside us, whether likenesses or in whatever way one posits those things, together-having which we are named as being each. The things that are among us that have the same names as those are again themselves in relation to themselves but not in relation to the forms, and again as many as are thus named [are named] of themselves but not of those. (133c8–d5)

Just as "what it is" signals the answer to the definitional question, "What is it?" so the phrase "are what they are" amounts to "are defined as." Similarly, "have their being" means "have their defined content." Then a more compact formulation of the general principle, where the F and the G are relations coordinate with one another, is this:

XIII. The F itself is defined in relation only to the G itself.

For example, since master and slave are coordinate relata, the master itself—that is, the master pure and simple—is defined as of the slave itself: the slave, pure and simple. (The master itself is not defined as of the Ethiopian slave or the male slave.) The principle tells us that only items themselves, forms, get mentioned as relata in the definitions of relational forms. The principle follows from a more general principle that definitions of something itself will never mention anything extra beyond the topic focused on. For example, the account of what a dog is does not mention paw size.

Claim XIII is plausible. Socrates accepts as an instance of it:

For example, if one of us is somebody's master or somebody's slave, he is surely not a slave of master itself—of what a master is, nor is the master a master of slave itself—of what a slave is. Rather, being a human being, he is both of these of a human being. (133d7)

But Parmenides' example, though perfectly acceptable, is not an instance of claim XIII. Claim XIII provides no reason to think, as we presumably do, that our neighborhood master is not a master of what a slave is. Claim XIII leaves that open: it implies, rather, that our neighborhood master will not be mentioned in the definition of the slave itself.

Just as Socrates agrees on the insufficient basis of claim XIII that our mastery cannot be of the slave itself, so he agrees that our knowledge cannot be of any form and that only knowledge itself can be of a form, and "we neither have the forms themselves nor are they such as to be among us . . . So none of the forms is known by us, because we don't partake of knowledge itself" (134b). But claim XIII does not warrant these results. Rather, it warrants such results as that neither the forms' being among us nor their being known by us is mentioned in the definition of knowledge itself. Socrates' assents reveal misunderstanding of claim XIII and of the definition-eliciting role of "itself by itself."

The full passage presenting the greatest difficulty deserves detailed scrutiny that is not possible here.[26] But I call attention to one telling moment: "Surely you would say that if in fact there is knowledge—a kind itself—it is much more precise than is knowledge that belongs to us. And so for beauty and all the others" (134c). This is plainly wrong. Given the topic-focusing and definition-eliciting use of "knowledge itself by itself," knowledge itself by itself is knowledge considered

---

26. See B.-U. Yi and E. Bae, "The Problem of Knowing the Forms in Plato's *Parmenides*," *History of Philosophy Quarterly* 15 (1998), 271–83.

without any further qualifications whatsoever. It is what knowledge is, pre-supposed when we speak of geometrical knowledge or of less and more precise knowledge. But it is not the case that knowledge itself is either geometrical or less or more precise. Knowledge itself, knowledge pure and simple (so to speak), as opposed to further specified knowledge, could not be knowledge more precise than the knowledge we have, any more than the dog itself could be shaggier than any dog we have.

Parmenides continues: "Well whatever else shares knowledge itself, wouldn't you say that god more than anyone else has the most precise knowledge?" (134c). Granted, any gods there are presumably have the most precise possible knowledge. But Socrates then in 134d1–d8 accepts an unwarranted conclusion.

> If this most precise mastery and this most precise knowledge belong to the divine, the gods' mastery could never master us, nor could their knowledge know us or anything that belongs to us. . . . They are neither our masters, nor, being gods, do they know human affairs. (134e7)

Socrates assumes incorrectly that knowledge itself is to be identified with "this most precise knowledge" that the gods have. Moreover, even if the gods do have knowledge itself, Socrates is wrong to think that claim XIII implies the "too as-tonishing" result (134e7) that they don't have knowledge of us. Rather, it follows that the definition of knowledge itself does not mention that it is of us.

Though Parmenides winds down his examination of Socrates by alluding to many other difficulties (134e8–135a3) that follow "if there are these aspects [*ideai*] of what is, and someone marks off [*horieitai*] each form as something itself," Parmenides still encourages investigating forms.

> [It is the part] of a naturally capable man to learn that there is a certain kind [*genos*] of each [one] and a being (*ousia*) itself by itself. . . . If someone will not allow that there are forms of the things that are, and will not mark off (*hor-ieitai*: define) a form of each one, he will not have anywhere he may turn thought, not allowing there always to be an aspect (*idean*), the same one, of each of the things that are, and thus he will totally destroy the possibility of conversation. But you seem to me to have perceived that sort of thing even more. (135a7–135b1)

Parmenides' reference to what Socrates "has perceived even more (than most people)" is to the insight displayed in Socrates' remarkable refutation of Zeno: if we can make distinctions in speech, then there are distinguishable aspects, something "itself by itself" in each case.

Parmenides offers more diagnosis and he advises Socrates to exercise: "So-crates, you are trying to mark off (*horizesthai*) something beautiful and just and good and each one of the forms too soon, before having been exercised" (135c8–d2). We will be interested to see both how the exercise Parmenides now displays might help Socrates and whether it leads to anything like our own tentative re-actions to Socrates' troubles. Our reactions were that

1. Attention to the ordinary roles of "itself by itself" would protect Socrates from his adolescent fault of thinking that forms are especially honor-bearing entities.

2. He should have rejected the question whether things have the whole form or part.

3. He should have questioned Parmenides' extended application of "separate."

4. He should have resisted the non-self-explanation principle.

5. He should have better understood principle XIII.

6. It also seemed there was an ambiguity or confusion in the challenge Socrates issued.

7. But—on the bright side—since Parmenides did not point out the apparent inconsistencies between Socrates' challenge and Socrates' admissions under examination, Parmenides seemed to see something in the challenge.

# Section 9

Parmenides says that Socrates needs exercise "in the manner of Zeno" (135d). But Parmenides adds a restriction that Socrates' challenge imposed.

> You didn't allow him [Zeno] to remain among visible things and observe their wandering, but [you asked him to observe wandering] concerning those things that one might above all grasp by means of speech . . . and might think to be forms. (135d–e)

The "wandering" Socrates wanted to see consisted in forms bearing opposites (135e) as perceptible objects unsurprisingly do. So Parmenides urges Socrates to exercise by arguing that forms truly bear opposites.

It would be pointless to discuss forms characterized by the whole collection of admissions that Socrates now realizes are not sustainable all together. But the exercise might usefully concern forms as Socrates first introduced them into the conversation, minimally characterized and untouched by Parmenides' questioning. Those were items (a) that are labeled with the focusing device, "itself"; and (b) that are what a definition spells out. (We may, however, learn during the exercise that Parmenides allows himself to say more about forms than the minimum Socrates' refutation of Zeno deployed.)

What Parmenides recommends so far seems a lot like the very thing that Socrates' challenge asked for, but Parmenides adds, "you must not only hypothesize if each thing is, and examine the consequences of that hypothesis; you must also hypothesize, if that same thing is not" (135e). Parmenides advises Socrates to exercise on "*whatever* you might ever hypothesize as being or as not being or as undergoing any other attribute" (136b7–c1): that is, Parmenides advises many rounds of exercise. Parmenides stipulates further:

> You must examine the consequences for the thing you hypothesise in relation to itself (*pros hauto*) and in relation to each one of the others (*pros hen hekaston tôn allôn*) . . . and in turn you must examine the others, both in relation to themselves (*pros hauta*) and in relation to whatever other thing you select on each occasion, whether what you hypothesize you hypothesize as being or as not being. (136b8–c5)

So Parmenides makes three twofold stipulations. First, generate consequences (i) from a hypothesis that a certain form is and (ii) from the negation of that hypothesis. Second, generate consequences (i) for the hypothesized form and (ii) for forms other than it ("the others"). Third, in considering the hypothesized form or considering the others, generate consequences (i) in relation to the form itself (*pros heauto*) and in relation to the others themselves (*pros heauta*) and consequences (ii) in relation to the others than the form (*pros ta alla*) and in relation to the hypothesized form other than they (*pros to allo*). Since we have three sequential twofold tasks, we have $2 \times 2 \times 2$, or eight, total tasks.

Parmenides' illustrative exercise consists of 195 arguments. His hypothesized item is the one itself. Parmenides generates consequences first from the hypothesis that the one is (I'll call it "H") and then from the hypothesis that the one is not (I'll call it "not-H"), as he predicted at 135e8–136a2. Parmenides' exercise has eight clearly announced sections, beginning at (i) 137c, (ii) 142b, (iii) 157b, (iv) 159b, (v) 160b, (vi) 163b, (vii) 164b, and (viii) 165e. The first four sections are derivations from H. The final four are derivations from not-H. Under each of H and not-H there are two sections clearly about the one and two sections clearly about the others. Each section obviously meets one part of each of Parmenides' first two stipulations. It would be elegant if each one of his eight sections met exactly one part of the third two-part stipulation: to generate consequences with reference to itself or themselves (*pros heauto/a*) or with reference to the others or the other (*pros ta alla/to allo*).[27] Adopting this elegant reading will prove illuminating.

Parmenides' directions do not predict a further salient feature of his actual performance: under each hypothesis, one of the two sections about the one generates entirely negative consequences (e.g., that the one is not many, not the same as another thing or itself, and not different from itself or another thing), while one section has mostly positive results (e.g., that the one is many, is the same as itself, and is different from itself). So the results of the negative section about the one appear to contradict results of the positive section about the one. Similarly, one of the two sections about the others has entirely negative results, whereas one has

---

27. However, because Parmenides does not label any section or any result with his phrases, *pros heauto/a* or *pros ta alla/to allo*, some commentators think that the arrangement of 195 results is not the elegant arrangement that would isolate *pros heauto/a* results into unmixed sections and isolate *pros ta alla/to allo* results likewise. Some scholars take as a clue that results within sections are mixed the fact that phrases similar to *pros heauto* and *pros ta alla* occur, though rarely, within the same section.

mostly positive results. Moreover, even within the positive section, some results seem to conflict with other results.

Parmenides sums up his first four sections:

> Thus if one is, the one is all things and is not even one, both in relation to itself and in relation to the others, and the others likewise.[28] (160b2–3)

Parmenides sums up all eight sections thus:

> Whether one is or is not, it and the others both in relation to themselves and in relation to each other both are and are not, and both appear and do not appear, all things in all ways. (166c)

By repeating his phrases "in relation to itself" and "in relation to the others" in these summaries he emphasizes their importance to the exercise. But his summary reinforces the odd appearance that both hypotheses led to contradictory results.

# SECTION 10

Parmenides does not explain the phrases *pros heauto* and *pros ta alla* either in his directions for or in his summaries of the exercise. I accept the controversial proposal of Constance Meinwald[29] that in those occurrences *pros heauto* in effect means "as included in its definition," and *pros ta alla* amounts to "in the manner of its relation to attributes other than its own definitional content." For example, the square is a rectangle *pros heauto* in that the square's definition mentions being a rectangle. The square is different from the circle *pros ta alla* in that the square's definition does not mention that it is (necessarily) different from the circle. (Meinwald does not propose that Plato now reserves these phrases for technical, specialized use. Rather, they continue to be available for their ordinary use.)[30] I also accept Meinwald's controversial claim that the eight sections have the more elegant plan: each of the eight is governed by just one of these key phrases.

Meinwald's proposal that each section is governed by a single qualifier that attaches to every one of its results has the advantage that it most simply removes the appearance that Parmenides has deduced contradictions from H and its negation and has left us with nothing to believe. For instance, on Meinwald's account, the first section's entirely negative results are all *pros heauto* results that tell in some

---

28. I accept the conjecture of F. Heindorf (ed.), *Platonis Dialogi Selecti*, vol. 3 (Berlin, 1806), discussed in Meinwald, *Parmenides*, 142–44.

29. In Meinwald, *Parmenides*, esp. chapter 3, 46–75.

30. The first appendix to S. Peterson, "The Language Game in Plato's *Parmenides*" *Ancient Philosophy* 20 (2000), 19–51, discusses the objections of Miller, Sayre, and Gill against Meinwald's understanding of the phrases in Parmenides' directions and summaries and indicates that they infrequently occur within a section with their ordinary meaning.

detail what the one is *not* defined as. A sample result is that the one is not many—that is, not *pros heauto* many, or not defined as many. That result does not conflict with the second section's result that the one is many—that is, many *pros ta alla*.

The first section's results are all obviously true as statements that distinguish what the one is from other separate forms.[31] And because the first section separates the one from much else, it goes some distance toward meeting Socrates' challenge, which was,

> If someone first distinguishes as separate the forms themselves by
> themselves ... and then shows that in themselves they can be combined
> and thoroughly distinguished ... I would admire it wonderfully. (129d–e)

Each first section of future exercises, by distinguishing its hypothesized form from many others, will record the insight of the young Socrates that forms are separate from each other.[32]

The second section of exercise under Meinwald's interpretation reaches only *pros ta alla* results. It goes more distance toward meeting Socrates' challenge: it reveals that the one, now thoroughly distinguished from many other forms, can be combined (in some nondefinitional way) with anything from which it was distinguished in the first section. Parmenides' second section establishes such results as that the one is its own opposite, many, and that it is of necessity in motion, and older and younger than itself, and neither older nor younger than itself. Parmenides is ingenious enough to find a variety of appropriate arguments. His midpoint and endpoint summaries make the large claim that he has shown that everything holds of the one ("all things" [160b]; "all things in all ways" [166c]). Presumably he means, in some way or other, or with suitable qualifications.[33]

So far, even without having considered the third through eighth sections of the exercise, we can see that on Meinwald's interpretation the exercise responds to Socrates' challenge. Its first section shows that the one is separate (*pros heauto*) from many forms. Its second section shows the one to be combined (*pros ta alla*)

---

31. S. Peterson argues for the ultimate obviousness of the few that are not immediately obviously true in "Plato's *'Parmenides'*: A Principle of Interpretation and Seven Arguments," *Journal of the History of Philosophy* 34 (1996), 167–92.

32. For some thoughts on what the first and second sections of other rounds of exercise would look like, see Peterson, "Rounds."

33. A sample argument from the second section is instructive.

> "What about when I say being and one. Haven't both been mentioned? ... Can things that are correctly called both be both but not two?"— "They cannot."—"If there are two things, is there any way for each member of the pair not to be one?"—"Not at all."—"Therefore since in fact each pair taken together turns out to be two, each would be one." (143c–d)

Here the one is one on the same ground—in the same way—as being is one. It is not merely because it is defined as one that the one is one. That something other than the one itself must be one implies that there is a way of necessarily being one that is distinct from the way in which the one itself is one as so defined or *pros heauto*. The present proof shows that the one itself is also one in the way that other things are one, *pros ta alla*.

with those many forms.[34] The second section also responds to Socrates' specific request to be surprised by an argument that the one itself is many (142d9–e7). The exercise highlights something good about Socrates' challenge and something unclear. Socrates was correct to think that different forms (such as what one is and what many is) are separate in that they have different definitional contents. He was confused to think that thoroughly separated forms could not enter into combinations necessitated solely by their definable content.

# SECTION 11

Several worthwhile rival interpretations of the *Parmenides* attempt to connect the exercise to the arguments that precede it. All disagree with Meinwald's distinctive interpretation of the phrases *pros heauto* and *pros ta alla*.[35] Some think the *Parmenides* signals Plato's development from his "Middle Period Theory of Forms" to a sparer theory of forms in dialogues such as the *Sophist* and *Philebus*. On this developmental view, the *Parmenides* reduces to absurdity a theory of forms that Plato held in previous writings. There is dispute about what that theory was and which provisions are now obsolete. Meinwald more subtly maintains that the *Parmenides* represents Plato's clarification of views that earlier were underspecified.[36]

I propose instead that the *Parmenides* depicts an occasion on which the adolescent Socrates, who has put forward impressive minimal insights about forms, then makes a confused challenge. In youthful eagerness to show off by answering Parmenides readily, Socrates is prodded into taking short-term ownership of various additional statements.[37] He cannot coherently maintain them. He forth-

---

34. The text at 143b3–7 shows that the second section, while establishing *pros ta alla* consequences that combine forms, uses premises that separate forms:

> If being is something, and the one is something different, it is not by its being one that the one is different from being, nor by its being being that being is other than the one. On the contrary, they are different from each other by difference. . . . And so difference is not the same as oneness or being.

Here the separate forms difference, oneness, and being are all different by difference. Because being and one are separate forms from difference, neither being nor one is that by which they are different.

35. The interpretation of Rickless sketched in "Saved" and developed in detail in *Forms* contrasts sharply with Meinwald. Other worthwhile treatments incompatible with Meinwald's are, for example, Gill, "Introduction" to Gill and Ryan *Parmenides*; Allen, *Parmenides*; and Sayre, *Lesson*. (All of these, unlike my account, take the young Socrates in his first words to Zeno as a proponent of some full-fledged technical theory of forms.) Gill's bibliography is a good starting point for more literature.

36. Meinwald, *Parmenides*, 170–72, and Meinwald, "Good-bye," 389–91. A now discredited view that Plato took none of the *Parmenides'* objections seriously is P. Shorey's in *The Unity of Plato's Thought* (New York, 1980; reprint of Chicago, 1903), esp. 86.

37. That they do not surprise him suggests as much that they were already in the air as that he himself had previously embraced them. Glaucon in unsurprised by form-talk at *Republic* 476a. The Pythagorean

rightly admits that he doesn't know what to say (135c). Now disabused of the unsustainable collection he briefly adopted, he can, however, continue to believe the minimum about forms he deployed in refuting Zeno. Parmenides cast no doubt on that.

Our impression of the currently silenced adolescent Socrates (inevitably partly formed by Plato's vivid picture of the mature Socrates) is that in the future he will not speak confusedly about forms or aspects. Parmenides' questioning gives Socrates a mild case of a disease I will call "aspect-itis." Socrates quickly recovers, now immunized and free from such symptoms as the belief (item IV in my list) that forms, themselves by themselves, are especially worthy of honor, and from readiness to misunderstand principle XIII.[38]

Those who think the older Socrates of other dialogues enunciates claims about forms that the young Socrates of the *Parmenides* gives up may explain Socrates' different views by the hypothesis that Socrates enunciates what Plato believed at different times in his writing career.[39] The hypothesis I prefer for explaining why differing views about forms appear in different dialogues is that the older Socrates of the "middle" dialogues does not endorse every statement about forms that he places into the conversation. I cannot here give all my grounds for my hypothesis. The details differ for each dialogue.

A first step is the reminder that it is clear that Socrates in the aporetic dialogues does not have ownership of the answers he gets to his questions.[40] A next step is the observation that in each middle dialogue Socrates is explicitly giving a persuasive speech, often for a conclusion assigned to him by his interlocutors. Conclusions assigned to Socrates may or may not be conclusions he thinks are capable of proof from true premises. Persuasion is very different from doctrinal instruction. Any well-crafted attempt at persuasion builds on beliefs of the persuadee, independent of what the persuader thinks. So Socrates' persuasive speeches must reflect what appeals to his interlocutors.[41] He does not own declarations that persuade his

---

Timaeus of the *Timaeus* speaks familiarly of forms. At *Phaedo* 100b Socrates makes explicit that what he says about forms is not novel but familiar to his interlocutors (also 74a–b ["we say"] and 78d). At 76d the phrasing "we always babble about" and at 100b "the much babbled about items" (*poluthruleta*: perhaps "notorious items" or "the buzz-words" [100b]) indicates that forms were a current topic and that not everything said about them has been sufficiently examined for Socrates to believe it. G. M. A. Grube, *Plato's Thought* (Boston, 1958; reprint of London, 1935), 291–94, argues that "much babbled about" refers only to conversation within the *Phaedo*. But it is at least equally likely to signal that the topic of forms was trendy and not always carefully considered. I, of course, do not count Socrates as a careless babbler, though he might very well say something provocative for his eager companions to ponder.

38. Some evidence for the immunizing effect of the Eleatic Parmenides' examination and exercise is that the Eleatic Stranger of the *Sophist*, a likely graduate of Parmenidean examination and exercise, marks off distinct forms in a careful way that shows no signs of aspectitis.

39. G. Vlastos, *Socrates: Ironist and Moral Philosopher* [*Socrates*] (Ithaca, N.Y., 1991), 117 n.50, formulates his "grand methodological hypothesis" on which his account of Socrates as depicted in Plato rests. The hypothesis is that the character Socrates says what Plato at the time of writing considers true.

40. On Socrates' relation to the answers he gets when in questioning mode, see M. Frede, "Plato's Arguments and the Dialogue Form," *Oxford Studies in Ancient Philosophy* 9(suppl.) (1992), 201–19.

41. Some examples: in the *Republic* Glaucon asks Socrates now to produce a counterspeech (358c–d, in comparison with 348a) that justice is advantageous to the just agent. The rest of the dialogue is his speech.

hearers when he is in persuasive mode any more than he owned the proposals granted to him in questioning mode. Further, our evidence that Socrates believes his declarations cannot solely be that he makes them. Our evidence must also include his purpose in making them, their consistency with other parts of the same conversation, and the probability that they would survive his critical scrutiny (which we must sometimes attempt to approximate by our own critical scrutiny).

To answer the likely question, "Why would Socrates be interested in persuading his interlocutors, sometimes of conclusions for which he sees no compelling reason?" my hypothesis has this further clause: Socrates' persuasive projects are part of his lifelong project, displayed throughout the dialogues, of examining the beliefs people live by for their benefit and his own.[42] Since revealing to a persuadee where his (possibly false) inclinations lead reveals him to himself, it is a first step toward critical self-examination. If someone should ask why Socrates would not rather persuade every interlocutor only with arguments that convince Socrates himself, I'd reply that such persuasion would not constitute examining an interlocutor. Concerning the greatest matters, persuasion via ready-made arguments would be attempted teaching of the most objectionable kind.

Because I think that many of the views about forms presented in various dialogues appeal to Socrates' various interlocutors and not to Socrates, as depicted, I do not have to explain how Plato can hold conflicting views. The *Parmenides'* serious objections to one theory of forms give me no motive to reconcile the objections with alleged doctrine of Plato's.[43] Though Plato, as a thoughtful person, surely changed his mind occasionally, his writings, whatever chronology we accept for them, are not compelling evidence—though they are of course possible evidence—for such change.

I still have the question what Plato himself believed about forms, and that interests me. To answer that question, we must look to what Socrates, the figure at the center, believes. Yet it is exceedingly hard to tell exactly what he believes, either from what he says in persuasive mode or from what he asks in questioning mode. Because of my strong impression that the character Socrates and the author Plato believed about forms what best survives examination, whatever that might be, my only way to decide which of the views in the dialogues Plato believed is to make my best efforts to see which best survive my—admittedly imperfect—examination.

I am convinced by the youthful Socrates' refutation of Zeno that there must be those distinguishable aspects—forms themselves—that make discourse possible. My own reflection convinces me that self-predication, properly understood, is

---

Socrates' interlocutors in the *Phaedo* want to be persuaded that Socrates should not be unwilling to die. They want proof that the soul is immortal, so Socrates goes into persuasive mode.

42. As G. Vlastos emphasizes in *Socratic Studies* (Cambridge, 1994), 10, Socrates (though Vlastos means only the Socrates of the early dialogues) habitually examines people's lives. My hypothesis that the Socrates of any dialogue is engaged in an examination appropriate to each dialogue's interlocutors—whether via questioning or via persuasive speech—also accounts for Socrates' making different proposals in different dialogues.

43. For a different view, see R. Kraut, "Plato," *Stanford Encyclopedia of Philosophy* (summer 2004 Edition), at http://plato.stanford.edu/archives/sum2004/entries/plato/.

reasonable and non-self-explanation is not. So I have those starting points toward saying what Plato thought about forms. I am also pretty sure, however, that anything accurately describable as a "grandiose metaphysical theory" or a "boldly speculative metaphysical system" is not what Plato believed.[44] Those are descriptions appropriate to a quaint antique curio or to an extravagant mythology, not to what has survived Plato's examination.

Those who ascribe an objectionable theory of forms to the older Socrates of other dialogues and to a Middle Period developing Plato leave unanswered this question: Why did Plato choose the adolescent Socrates to be disabused of a "Middle Period Theory of Forms" in the *Parmenides*? Creating an adolescent Socrates disabused of a theory of forms after creating an older Socrates attached to that theory yields a fragmented or discontinuous character. On this developmental picture, to make Socrates whole, we need an intervening dialogue that shows a relapse into the disease of aspectitis after the lesson of the *Parmenides*. But instead, at the age of seventy, the character Socrates expresses great and apparently long-standing admiration for his conversation with Parmenides (*Theaetetus* 183e; *Sophist* 217c).

On my hypothesis, the talk about forms discredited in the *Parmenides* occurs in other dialogues because some interlocutors suffer from an affliction from which Socrates early on was fortunately immunized. The immunized older Socrates can recognize the condition in others. When called on to persuade, he can use persuasive speech to elicit symptoms of aspectitis from interlocutors for the eventual benefit of us all.

# BIBLIOGRAPHY

Allen, R. E. *Plato's "Parmenides"* (New Haven, Ct., 1997).

Annas, J. *Introduction to Plato's "Republic"* (Oxford, 1981).

Burnet, J. *Platonis Opera*, vol. 2 (Oxford, 1901).

Burnyeat, M. "What Descartes Saw and Berkeley Missed," *Philosophical Review* 91 (1982), 3–40.

Cohen, S. M. "The Logic of the Third Man," *Philosophical Review* 80 (1971), 448–75.

Fine, G. "Immanence," *Oxford Studies in Ancient Philosophy* 4 (1986), 71–97; reprinted in Fine, *Plato on Knowledge and Forms: Selected Essays* (Oxford, 2003), 301–25.

———. *On Ideas: Aristotle's Criticism of Plato's Theory of Forms* (Oxford, 1993).

———. "Owen, Aristotle, and the Third Man," *Phronesis* 27 (1982), 13–33.

———. "Vlastos on Socratic and Platonic Forms," *Apeiron* 26 (1995), 67–83.

Frede, M. "Plato's Arguments and the Dialogue Form," *Oxford Studies in Ancient Philosophy* 9(suppl.) (1992), 201–19.

Geach, P. T. "The Third Man Again," in R. E. Allen (ed.), *Studies in Plato's Metaphysics* (London, 1965), 265–77.

---

44. Vlastos, *Socrates*, 53.

Gill, M. L., ed. and trans., and P. Ryan, trans. *Plato, "Parmenides"* (Indianapolis, 1996).

Grube, G. M. A. *Plato's Thought* (Boston, 1958; reprint of London, 1935).

Irwin, T. H. "The Theory of Forms," in G. Fine, (ed.), *Plato 1: Metaphysics and Epistemology* (Oxford, 1999), 143–70.

Kahn, C. H. *Plato and the Socratic Dialogue: The Philosophical Use of a Literary Form* (Cambridge, 1996).

Kraut, R. "Plato," *Stanford Encyclopedia of Philosophy*, at http://plato.stanford.edu/entries/plato/.

Malcolm, J. *Plato on the Self-Predication of Forms* (Oxford, 1991).

Meinwald, C. "Good-bye to the Third Man," in R. Kraut (ed.), *Cambridge Companion to Plato* (Cambridge, 1992), 365–96.

———. *Plato's "Parmenides"* (Oxford, 1991).

Miller, M. *Plato's "Parmenides"* (Princeton, N.J., 1986).

Owen, G. E. L. "The Platonism of Aristotle," in *Logic, Science, and Dialectic: Collected Papers in Greek Philosophy* ed. M. Nussbaum(Ithaca, N.Y., 1968), 200–220.

Peterson, S. "The Language Game in Plato's *Parmenides*," *Ancient Philosophy* 20 (2000), 19–51.

———. "New Rounds of the Exercise of Plato's *Parmenides*," *Modern Schoolman* 80 (2003), 245–78.

———. "Plato's *Parmenides*: A Principle of Interpretation and Seven Arguments," *Journal of the History of Philosophy* 34 (1996), 167–92.

———. "A Reasonable Self-Predication Premise for the Third Man Argument," *Philosophical Review* 82 (1973), 451–70.

Rickless, S. "How Parmenides Saved the Theory of Forms," *Philosophical Review* 107 (1998), 501–54.

———. *Plato's Forms in Transition* (Cambridge, 2006).

Sayre, K. *Parmenides' Lesson: Translation and Explication of Plato's "Parmenides"* (Notre Dame, Ind., 1996).

Schofield, M. "Likeness and Likenesses in the *Parmenides*," in C. Gill and M. M. McCabe (eds.), *Form and Argument in Late Plato* (Oxford, 1996), 49–77.

Shorey, P. *The Unity of Plato's Thought* (New York, 1980; reprint of Chicago, 1903).

Strang, C. "Plato and the Third Man," *Proceedings of the Aristotelian Society* 37(suppl.) (1963), 147–64.

Vlastos, G. *Platonic Studies* (Princeton, 1981).

———. "Plato's 'Third Man' Argument (*Parm.* 132a1–b2): Text and Logic," in G. Vlastos, *Platonic Studies*, 2nd ed. (Princeton, N.J., 1981), 342–360.

———. "The Third Man Argument in the *Parmenides*," in R. E. Allen (ed.), *Studies in Plato's Metaphysics* (London, 1965), 231–63.

———. *Socrates: Ironist and Moral Philosopher* (Ithaca, N.Y., 1991).

———. *Socratic Studies* (Cambridge, 1994).

Yi, B.-U., and E. Bae. "The Problem of Knowing the Forms in Plato's *Parmenides*," *History of Philosophy Quarterly* 15 (1998), 271–83.

# CHAPTER 17

# THE *THEAETETUS*

## MI-KYOUNG LEE

Is it possible to explore and settle questions about the nature and possibility of knowledge without also considering what the possible objects of knowledge are? That is, can epistemology be done independently of metaphysics? Or must epistemology always go hand in hand with consideration of what kinds of things there are and of what can be said about them and how?

This question is raised most vividly for readers of Plato when assessing the central epistemological claim of the *Republic*: that knowledge is impossible unless one grasps the Forms, and that those who do not recognize the existence of the Forms can at best achieve "opinion" (*Rep.* V. 475e–480a). It may then come as a surprise, when one turns to Plato's late dialogue the *Theaetetus*, which is devoted to the question "What is knowledge?," that Plato nowhere explicitly makes or even considers this claim, that knowledge is not possible without the Forms. For one thing, the dialogue is filled with examples of knowledge where the objects known include ordinary, mundane, individual objects like Theaetetus, Theodorus, oxen, wagons, and stones, as well as colors, smells, and sounds. Socrates and his interlocutor discuss examples of knowledge, including knowing that a stone is white, knowing that So-and-so is guilty of such-and-such a crime, knowing that this person standing here is Theaetetus.

Of course, this by itself does not indicate a change in view—if Plato thought that Forms are required for knowledge, but are not the only possible objects of knowledge, then it would be possible to have knowledge of things other than Forms.[1]

---

1. Cf. Gail Fine, "Knowledge and Belief in *Republic* V," *Archiv für Geschichte der Philosophie* 60 (1978), 121–39, and Gail Fine, "Knowledge and Belief in *Republic* 5–7," in Stephen Everson (ed.), *Epistemology* (Cambridge: Cambridge University Press 1990), 85–115. For a recent defense of the "Two Worlds" interpretation of Plato, according to which Plato argues in *Republic* V that the only possible objects of knowledge are the Forms and the only possible objects of opinion sensible particulars, see Francisco J. Gonzalez, "Propositions or Objects? A Critique of Gail Fine on Knowledge and Belief in *Republic* V," *Phronesis* 41 (1996), 245–75.

However, it is striking that the Forms are nowhere explicitly mentioned in the dialogue. One might even suppose that the *Theaetetus* offers evidence that Plato eventually gave up the theory altogether;[2] or, at any rate, one might arrive at the impression that Plato has decided, in the *Theaetetus*, to make a fresh start by considering what knowledge is, while remaining agnostic on the question of what the possible objects of knowledge might be.

This view is, in a way, both right and wrong. In the *Theaetetus* Socrates does not assume the existence of the Forms. Indeed, he tends to use premises about the nature of reality which are incompatible with the Forms. In that sense, the *Theaetetus* is free of the Forms. But this does not mean the Forms have been abandoned. Plato adopts a complex strategy for examining the nature of knowledge in the *Theaetetus*: he sometimes has Socrates examine a conception of knowledge purely on its own terms. In other parts of the discussion, he has Socrates examine a proposed conception of knowledge with the help of substantial metaphysical claims about the nature and kind of objects that are known—claims that conflict with what Plato argues for elsewhere. Plato's strategy appears to be to allow a fairly generous set of assumptions about the nature of the objects of knowledge, assumptions that are introduced for dialectical reasons, and not because he endorses them himself. He explores various conceptions of knowledge without assuming that the only things that can be known are Forms or that knowledge is not possible unless there are Forms. Nevertheless, although Plato does not prove the impossibility of knowledge for one who does not acknowledge the existence of Forms,[3] some of the problems do appear to come from premises belonging to a Forms-free metaphysics.

But before we examine these issues in detail, let me briefly consider the main contours of the dialogue and of Plato's method of argumentation in it. After the introductory section (*Tht.* 145c–151d), in which a preliminary attempt at defining knowledge is rejected,[4] three further definitions of knowledge (K1–K3) are proposed, examined in detail, and then rejected. At the end of the dialogue, Socrates and his interlocutors express puzzlement about what knowledge is, but Socrates declares Theaetetus better prepared now to take up these questions again on a

---

2. McDowell tends to favor this as a working hypothesis; see the passages cited at John McDowell, *Plato: Theaetetus* [*Theaetetus*] (Oxford: Clarendon Press, 1973), 159.

3. Contrast Cornford, who holds that the implicit moral of the *Theaetetus* is that "True knowledge has for its object things of a different order—not sensible things, but intelligible Forms and truths about them" (Francis Macdonald Cornford, *Plato's Theory of Knowledge: The Theaetetus and the Sophist of Plato Translated with a Commentary* [*Theaetetus*] (London: Routledge and Kegan Paul, 1935), 162). For a discussion of some shortcomings of Cornford's thesis and how it might be improved, see Gökhan Adalıer, "The Case of 'Theaetetus'" ["Case"], *Phronesis* 46/1 (2001), 2–3; Timothy Chappell, *Reading Plato's Theaetetus* [*Theaetetus*] (Indianapolis: Hackett, 2005), 20–21.

4. This section includes Socrates' famous comparison of himself to a midwife (*Tht.* 148e–151d); for discussion, see Myles F. Burnyeat, "Socratic Midwifery, Platonic Inspiration," *Bulletin of the Institute of Classical Studies of the University of London* 24 (1977), 7–16; Myles F. Burnyeat, *The Theaetetus of Plato* [*Theaetetus*], trans. M. J. Levett (Indianapolis: Hackett, 1990); David Sedley, *The Midwife of Platonism: Text and Subtext in Plato's Theaetetus* [*Midwife*] (Oxford: Clarendon Press 2004).

future occasion (*Tht.* 210bd). The *Theaetetus* is thus an aporetic dialogue, sharing that form with early "Socratic" dialogues like the *Euthyphro*.

According to the first definition (K1), knowledge is the same as perception (*Tht.* 151e). This leads to a long and extended attempt to spell out what exactly this amounts to and how one might support it. Plato has Socrates introduce a number of metaphysical theses, belonging to the so-called "Secret Doctrine,"[5] in support of the definition. In the end, the supporting metaphysical theory is rejected as incompatible with the proposed definition (*Tht.* 181c–183c); furthermore, the definition is rejected on its own for independent reasons (*Tht.* 184b–186e). According to the second definition (K2), knowledge is true opinion or judgment (*doxa*) (*Tht.* 187b).[6] Plato has Socrates explore this definition by seeing whether it is possible to explain how false belief is possible. Their repeated failure to be able to explain how it is possible to think about something, and at the same time make a mistake about it, strongly implicates the definition of knowledge itself (though, admittedly, Socrates does not make the connection clear). The definition is also rejected in a more straightforward fashion by pointing to contexts in which we would clearly want to say that true judgment is not sufficient for knowledge (*Tht.* 200d–201c).

Finally, the third proposed definition of knowledge (K3) states that knowledge is true judgment with an account (*logos*) (*Tht.* 201cd). Socrates and his interlocutors explore this definition in two stages. First, they explore it in terms of a "Dream theory," which includes various metaphysical assumptions about the kinds of objects that can and cannot be known, along with various reasons why some things can be known and others cannot (*Tht.* 201d–203c). The thesis of asymmetry in the knowability of objects is first rejected by making explicit use of those metaphysical assumptions of the Dream theory (*Tht.* 203e–205e), and then rejected in a more straightforward fashion (*Tht.* 206ac). Second, they examine what an "account" (*logos*) is (*Tht.* 206c–210a). Each notion of account they examine encounters problems, and in the end it is not clear whether and what kind of account is necessary for knowledge—but their failure is partly due to the kinds of assumptions retained from the Dream theory, and indeed from earlier parts of the dialogue, about what kind of objects can be known and what can be said about them.

In what follows, I pursue two themes concerning the relation between epistemology and metaphysics in the *Theaetetus*. The first theme concerns Plato's methodology: sometimes Socrates examines a thesis on its own, and sometimes he examines it by assuming premises on behalf of that thesis. These ancillary theses introduce metaphysical ideas and commitments that are meant to describe sufficient conditions under which the proposed definitions would be true. But they turn out to create problems for the very definitions they were meant to support. In the case of K1 and the Secret Doctrine, Socrates argues that K1 is not true if those metaphysical ideas are true. And in the case of K3 and the Dream theory, Socrates argues that if one makes certain apparently reasonable assumptions about the

---

5. Socrates introduces this as a doctrine Protagoras taught his students "in secret" (*Tht.* 152c).
6. For a discussion of these and other possible translations of *doxa*, see Burnyeat, *Theaetetus*, 69–70.

nature of things, then it is not possible to maintain, as K3 does, that some things can be known and others cannot.

The second theme of the discussion concerns the kinds of objects of knowledge under consideration. For the reader of the *Theaetetus*, the Theory of Forms is the elephant in the room—Socrates never mentions it, but that does not mean it has gone away. Socrates nowhere argues that knowledge requires a grasp of the Forms—much less that knowledge can only be had of the Forms. But the repeated failure to arrive at a definition of knowledge when assuming a metaphysics incompatible with the Forms suggests (though it does not require) that progress could be made if we admitted certain assumptions characteristic of Plato's metaphysics of Forms.

# 1. KNOWLEDGE IS PERCEPTION (K1)

The first definition of knowledge Plato examines in the dialogue is the thesis that

(K1) Knowledge is perception (*aisthêsis*). (*Tht.* 151e)

Now this definition is of great interest because it articulates two ideas about knowledge and perception which get short shrift in other dialogues such as the *Phaedo* and the *Republic*: the idea that our senses are accurate and informative about their proper objects—that is, colors, sounds, smells—and the idea that knowledge depends on and is built up from perception. It becomes clear that Plato is particularly interested in exploring the first idea, for he quickly connects the definition of knowledge as perception with another thesis, Protagoras' measure doctrine, according to which "man is the measure of all things, of what is that it is, of what is not that it is not" (*Tht.* 152a). This is construed as the claim that

(P) Whatever appears to be the case to one is the case for one.

Claim (P) appears to have been introduced for the following reason: Plato understands Protagoras as focusing on what is the "measure" or criterion of truth. Protagoras' thesis—that each of us is the measure of truth—derives its plausibility from the fact that the senses are the criterion of what is and what is not, at least in the case of things like hot, cold, sweet, bitter, and so on.[7] Thus, the senses are a criterion of truth, and what they perceive in the case of sensible qualities is true. But if Protagoras' measure claim is true in the case of sensible qualities, such as hot, cold, and the like, then it follows that perception "is always of what is, and free from falsehood" (*Tht.* 152c), and from this we are to[a] infer that it must be the same as knowledge. This, then, represents one version of the empiricist claim: since

---

7. For further discussion, see Mi-Kyoung Lee, *Epistemology after Protagoras: Responses to Relativism in Plato, Aristotle, and Democritus* [*Epistemology*] (Oxford: Clarendon Press, 2005), 8–29.

perception is infallible with respect to the sensible qualities, it should be regarded as a kind of knowledge. What the senses tell us is always true, and hence their claims to knowledge should not be dismissed. Furthermore, K1 implies that every instance of knowledge is a case of perception and that the senses do tell us about everything; thus, it implies that nothing exists that is not perceived. Thus, (P), when restricted to sensible qualities, implies and is implied by (K1), at least on a certain interpretation.[8]

Plato proceeds to explore the Theaetetan-Protagorean proposal (K1 and P) by working out in detail the kind of metaphysical assumptions that would make the thesis true. He introduces a set of Heraclitean theses, which include the idea that everything is in motion and changing, and the thesis that, if something is F, then it also is or will be its opposite, not-F (*Tht.* 152de). Drawing on this set of ideas, he shows that you can describe a world in which perception is always true and that whatever appears to be the case in perception is the case for one (*Tht.* 153d–160e). In this world, the object of perception and the perceiving organ together generate perceptible properties and perceivings which are unique to each encounter and which are each "of" the other (*Tht.* 156a–157c). That is, when I perceive a stone, I perceive the whiteness that was generated together with my perception. One obvious question is why we should suppose that these two "offspring" should always be generated together and why it's not possible to have one without the other. The answer is that these are assumptions which are simply brought in—ad hoc or otherwise—under the rubric of the Heraclitean doctrine in order to make good on Theaetetus' and Protagoras' claims.

The exact nature of the connection between (K1) and (P), on the one hand, and the Secret Doctrine, on the other, is controversial. There are, in fact, two related issues: first, how exactly to interpret (P); second, how (K1) and (P) are related to the metaphysical theses in the Secret Doctrine. There are a number of possible answers to the first question: Protagoras' measure doctrine can be variously interpreted as (i) the thesis of relativism about truth, according to which truth is relative, and nothing is true absolutely; (ii) the thesis of infallibilism, according to which all beliefs and appearances are true *simpliciter*; and (iii) relativism of fact, according to which whatever appears to be the case to one is the case for one—a position that resembles (i) in emphasizing the importance of the relativizing move but is more like (ii) insofar as it is noncommittal on the question of whether truth itself is to be relativized.[9]

---

8. On some interpretations of (K1), this entailment does not hold true; see R. M. Dancy, "Theaetetus' First Baby: *Tht.* 151e–160e," *Philosophical Topics* 15/2 (1987), 61–108.

9. Point (i) can be found in Myles F. Burnyeat, "Idealism and Greek Philosophy: What Descartes Saw and Berkeley Missed," *Philosophical Review* 91/1 (1982), 3–40. Point (ii) can be found in Gail Fine, "Protagorean Relativisms," in J. Cleary and W. Wians (eds.), *Proceedings of the Boston Area Colloquium in Ancient Philosophy*, vol. 19 (Lanham, Md.: University Press of America, 1996), 211–43, and in Fine, "Conflicting Appearances: *Theaetetus* 153d–154b," in C. Gill and M. M. McCabe (eds.), *Form and Argument in Late Plato* (Oxford: Oxford University Press, 1996), 105–33. I have given arguments for point (iii) in Lee, *Epistemology*, 30–45; see also Sarah Waterlow, "Protagoras and Inconsistency," *Archiv für Geschichte der Philosophie* 59 (1977), 29–33.

As for the second issue, two general lines of interpretation are possible:

1. (K1), (P), and the Secret Doctrine are connected by relations of mutual entailment, so that each one requires and is required by each of the others. On this view, there is no way to maintain Protagoras' measure doctrine without also being committed to a radical doctrine of flux.
2. (K1), (P), and the Secret Doctrine are not connected by relations of mutual entailment but by a narrower set of relations: the Secret Doctrine is sufficient for the truth of (P), which, in turn, is sufficient for the truth of (K1). On this view, Plato does not think, or argue, that the relations among the three positions is one of entailment; rather, Plato is trying to characterize, on the basis of the Secret Doctrine, a world of which (P) and thus (K1) hold true.[10] All this requires him to do is to find metaphysical assumptions on which the truth of (K1) and (P) would follow—and these are found in the Secret Doctrine.

The two issues—concerning the exact interpretation of (P), and its connections with (K1) and the Secret Doctrine—are not unrelated. If one adopts the view that interpretation 1 describes Plato's strategy, then we have a problem since relativism about truth does not appear to commit one to the metaphysical doctrine of flux, and, indeed, seems to be incompatible with it, since the doctrine of flux would appear to be presented in the *Theaetetus* as being true *simpliciter*, whereas relativism about truth denies that there are any such truths. But perhaps (P) is not (i) relativism about truth but, rather, infallibilism, (ii) above. On this view, all appearances and beliefs are true *simpliciter*. But if contradictory beliefs are true together without relativization, then doesn't this imply that contradictory states of affairs are simultaneously true? It is in order to save (P) from this problem that Plato introduces the flux doctrine: contradictory beliefs can simultaneously be true without contradiction because they turn out to be true of different things. On the other hand, if one adopts the view that interpretation 2 describes Plato's strategy, then Plato is not arguing that (K1) or (P) commits one to any metaphysical thesis at all, but only that, on certain metaphysical assumptions, (K1) and (P) turn out to be true—or so it seems.

On interpretation 2, the interpretation I favor, Plato argues that if one accepts the "Heraclitean" metaphysical doctrine, then Theaetetus' and Protagoras' claims follow. So do the dual theses in fact find support in the Heraclitean doctrine that Socrates introduces? His own answer is "yes" and "no." At first glance, the theory of perception Socrates works out on the basis of the Secret Doctrine seems effective in showing how Theaetetus' and Protagoras' claims could be true. It can even handle problem cases like sickness and dreaming; as Socrates notes, if perceptions are always generated together with perceptible properties, and these "offspring" are generated in different ways over time, then there is no reason to suppose that

---

10. Sufficiency here is a one-way entailment, which is weaker than mutual entailment: if the Secret Doctrine is true, then (P) and (K1) are true, but (P) and (K1) do not imply that the Secret Doctrine is true.

someone who is supposedly awake is more authoritative about her perceptions than one who is asleep (*Tht.* 157e–160e).

But in the end, they have to conclude that the dual theses are insupportable on the Heraclitean hypothesis, for the reason that the thesis that "everything is changing" implies not just the truth of Protagoras' and Theaetetus' claims but the opposite as well (*Tht.* 181c–183b). For if everything is changing, then it will certainly be the case that for every perception, there is a perceptible property matching it that will come into being with it. But *ex hypothesi* the perception and perceptible property themselves will be undergoing change (*Tht.* 182de). For example, whiteness and the perceiving of white—that is, the "twin births" in the Heraclitean story of perception which Socrates tells on Protagoras' behalf—themselves are constantly changing, so that whiteness becomes not-white and perceiving becomes not-perceiving. What exactly this means is not clear; at the very least, it suggests that a person's perceiving that the stone is white is no more true than it is false.

The Secret Doctrine is a metaphysical doctrine which leaves no room for the existence of anything like Forms. It says that everything is both F and not-F, that everything is always changing, that everything is what it is relative to something else (*Tht.* 152de). The Forms, by contrast, are never both F and not-F (e.g., *Phaedo* 74bc; *Republic* 478e–479e). The Forms do not undergo change. And the Forms are not what they are relative to something else—for example, relative to a perceiver—but are whatever they are in themselves. Its total lack of stability—such as would be provided by theory of Forms, if one accepted it—is part of the reason that the Secret Doctrine comes to grief. For it says that things like perceptible properties and the perceptions of those properties themselves do not remain stable. Thus, on this view, nothing can be said to be white (as opposed to not-white) or to be perceiving, since whiteness itself and perceiving are always changing.[11]

When Socrates says that the Secret Doctrine tells us that "whiteness" itself is becoming not-white (*Tht.* 182d), it is unclear whether he has in mind the universal color white or a particular instantiation of white. Either way, the lesson remains the same: one cannot make perceptions true in a world which lacks the kind of stability that Forms would provide. For in a world without that stability, things like whiteness and perceiving themselves undergo constant change, such that someone who is perceiving something as white cannot be said to have a true perception—since even if they are right, because there is something white out there, they are at the same time wrong, because what is out there is at the same time not white. This argument cannot stand alone as a proof for the existence of Forms, for nothing has yet been said about why there must be entities which never change at all—it only shows that there must be some necessary truths or that the nature of what it is to be white cannot change. (For example, whiteness is necessarily white, and it is

---

11. On interpretation 1, according to which Protagoras is committed to the theory of flux, it is difficult to explain why Protagoras is committed to such an extreme thesis of flux. Why couldn't he simply say that things are sometimes changing in some respects—not everything in every respect? On interpretation 2, however, flux is introduced as a part of a metaphysical doctrine that is meant to provide sufficient conditions for (P). On this view, Plato is not arguing that Protagoras is committed to the radical thesis of flux.

impossible for perceiving to become something other than perceiving.) So (K1) and (P) can only be true in a world in which some such limits have been placed on the extreme thesis of flux and opposites found in the Secret Doctrine—limits such as can be found in Plato's own view about the place of Forms in a world of flux.

Theaetetus' definition (K1), then, cannot be given any support by the Secret Doctrine. Socrates proceeds to examine Theaetetus' definition on its own, independently of the doctrine of opposition and flux, at *Theaetetus* 184–86.[12] This argument is of interest because it comes the closest of Plato's arguments in the *Theaetetus* to ground familiar from *Republic* Book V: as in the *Republic*, Plato has Socrates argue here that perception is not sufficient for knowledge because it cannot "get at being." But whereas in the *Republic* the reason for this has to do with the nature of the objects of perception—namely, the fact that they are changeable and variable—the reason given here has to do with the nature of perceptual states and activity.

At 184–86 Socrates argues that perception is infallible about the proper objects of sense: sight is authoritative about colors, hearing about sounds, and so on. But unlike Epicurus, Plato does not make much of this fact, if indeed he thinks it's true. Though he thinks that the senses are authoritative about their own objects, he is interested rather in their limitations: they cannot tell us about anything beyond their own special objects. Thus, for example, the sense of sight is capable of determining about colors but not about sound, much less about anything like "being," which is needed to determine truth. And if the senses are not capable of getting at "being" or any of the other common objects of thought, and "being" is necessary for truth, which, in turn, is necessary for knowledge, then it follows that perception is not sufficient for knowledge.

What does it mean to say that perception cannot get at "being," which is necessary for truth and for knowledge? Perception consists of a bare sensory awareness and lacks even the basic ability to apply concepts and form judgments. But grasping being is, in the first instance, saying what things are. What we do with the senses does not even rise to the level of making a judgment of the form "x is F," such as "the stone is white"; the senses do not "say" anything at all. Perception by itself has no propositional content; all that we do with the senses is to apprehend some color, experience some texture, and the like. Knowledge, however, requires at the very minimum the propositional complexity involved in making judgments.[13]

---

12. Socrates also examines (P) independently of the doctrine of opposition and flux in the celebrated refutation of Protagoras at *Theaetetus* 169e–171d. The classic treatment of this argument is Myles F. Burnyeat, "Protagoras and Self-refutation in Plato's *Theaetetus*," *Philosophical Review* 85 (1976), 172–95.

13. This accords with one of the two interpretations offered in John M. Cooper, "Plato on Sense-Perception and Knowledge (*Theaetetus* 184–186)," *Phronesis* 15 (1970), 123–46, and is endorsed by Myles F. Burnyeat, "Plato on the Grammar of Perceiving," *Classical Quarterly* 26 (1976), 44–45. However, Plato does not consistently adhere in this passage to a neat distinction between perception as sensory awareness and the mind's conceptualizing activity; for one thing, it seems that perception includes not just sensory awareness but some use of concepts in order to label things as "sweet" "hot," and so on, which, in turn, suggests that use of concepts does not necessarily require the use of *einai*. For this reason, Cooper prefers the second interpretation, on which perception is taken to be the activity of the mind in apprehending things by means

Socrates then rejects the claims of perception to be knowledge because, on his newer and narrower understanding of perception,[14] perception constitutes bare sensory awareness and never attains the level of making judgments about how things are. This argument does not imply that knowledge is not possible without the Forms. But at the same time, it doesn't tell us that knowledge *is* possible without the Forms—nothing here suggests that Plato has renounced the view that knowledge requires grasping the Forms. What the argument here tells us is that knowledge is not possible without grasping "being," where that includes not merely the ability to make judgments and claims about how things are (which is why perception falls short) but also the ability to make expert judgments about what is true, an ability that requires the grasp of objective standards for each subject matter (*Tht.* 186bc).[15] And this point is consistent with the claim in the *Republic* (though, again, it does not imply) that only the person who grasps the Forms is in a position to know whereas the person who is ignorant of the Forms is not.

What the argument here at *Theaetetus* 184–86 does leave open is that it might be possible to know things about the objects of perception. For the argument here focuses not on the unsuitability of the objects of perception for being objects of knowledge but, rather, on how perception relates to its objects. Since perception fails to count as knowledge because it doesn't even rise to the level of making statements about them, this leaves open the possibility that sensible objects could be objects of knowledge. This could explain why, in the next section where Socrates examines a new definition of knowledge as true judgment, he consistently uses examples of knowledge about sensible objects to illustrate his points.

## 2. KNOWLEDGE AS TRUE JUDGMENT (K2)

The second proposed definition—according to which knowledge is true belief or judgment—flows from the rejection of the first definition of knowledge as perception. Perception is rejected as insufficient for knowledge since it is limited to the

---

of the senses. Perception then does attain the use of sensory concepts and can determine by itself whether something is white or red or sweet or hot (*Tht.* 184de). But it fails to be knowledge because it does not attain objective validity. For whereas it is possible to "read off" from sensory data whether something is hot, cold, wet, or dry, it is not possible to determine in the same way whether something is (really) beneficial or valuable, same, different, and so on. On this interpretation, what the senses do falls short of what is needed to determine what is really the case. For problems with this interpretation, see Sedley, *Midwife*, 106–7 n.29.

14. For the argument that *Theaetetus* 184–86 signals a change in Plato's conception of perception, see Michael Frede, "Observations on Perception in Plato's Later Dialogues," *Essays in Ancient Philosophy* (Minneapolis: University of Minnesota Press, 1987), 3–8.

15. This is why perception falls short, according to the second interpretation argued for by Cooper.

apprehension of proper sensibles (such as hot, cold, red, sweet, etc.) and lacks propositional content and so cannot even get at "being." That is, perception cannot by itself deliver judgments about what is the case. But that then raises the question whether true judgments about what is the case might be sufficient for knowledge (187bc).

The proposal is not innocuous. It says that getting something right—making a correct judgment about something—is enough to count as having knowledge about it. But Plato already pointed out in the *Meno* that there is a significant difference between true belief and knowledge: true belief is presumably just as good as knowledge as long as it "stays put." But true belief is easily dislodged; someone who only has true belief and not knowledge will easily be persuaded of the falsity of her belief and will quickly change her mind. What is needed to make one's belief stay put is an "account of the reason why" (*aitias logismos*) that will make the belief stable (*Meno* 98a).

Another way of putting this is to say that true belief is not a capacity or ability. You can make a true judgment once, by accident or randomly, for the wrong reasons or perhaps because you made a good guess. Judging correctly about something on one occasion is quite compatible with making mistakes about it on other occasions. Saying that true belief is sufficient for knowledge thus violates the idea of knowledge as expertise, the idea that knowledge is a capacity that makes one the source of authoritative and infallible judgments about a thing. Surely someone who knows something can't also make mistakes about it.

To say, then, that knowledge is the same as true judgment is to maintain that true judgment itself is the (sole) source of authority and infallibility with respect to knowledge. Getting things right—no matter how one manages to do so and how reliably one is able to do so—is enough in itself to count as having knowledge. Note that this was implied by the earlier proposal that perception is knowledge; perception was deemed to be knowledge because perception is infallible, and truth is sufficient for knowledge (152c).[16] This definition of knowledge as true judgment gives Plato the opportunity to examine the assumption contained in the definition of knowledge as perception—an idea otherwise taken for granted up to now—that what makes *anything* a suitable candidate for knowledge is its getting things right.

Like the definition of knowledge as perception, the definition of knowledge as true judgment is examined in two phases. First, Plato has Socrates examine it indirectly, by seeing whether it is possible to explain how false judgment is possible, if we suppose that true judgment is sufficient for knowledge. Socrates' repeated failure to explain the possibility of false judgment—five attempts in all at (1) *Tht.* 188ac, (2) 188c–189b, (3) 189b–191a, (4) 191a–196c, and (5) 197a–200d—is an indirect

---

16. The connection of this section with Protagoras is reinforced by the fact that much of this section is devoted to the apparent impossibility of false belief; the *Euthydemus* (285e9–286c9) attributes the denial of falsity to Protagoras. In antiquity, Proclus also thought that this section was a continuation of the discussion of Protagoras in the first part of the dialogue (*In Plat. Prm.* 657.5–10; cf. David Sedley, "Three Platonist Interpretations of the *Theaetetus*," in C. Gill and M. M. McCabe [eds.], *Form and Argument in Late Plato* [Oxford: Oxford University Press, 1996], 82 n.3; Sedley, *Midwife*, 119).

indictment of the definition of knowledge on which the discussion depends.[17] The fundamental problem is that it doesn't seem possible to explain how one can be thinking of something (as opposed to something else) and make a mistake about it (say, by misidentifying it as something else entirely, Y). The source of the problem is the very definition of knowledge as true judgment itself, for on that view, as we noted earlier, knowledge is not an enduring capacity that can be exercised or not on various occasions but, rather, consists simply of true or correct judgment, whenever it happens to occur.

Thus, if knowledge is the same as true judgment, then whenever you make a correct judgment, you have knowledge. But to think about something, you must be thinking about it and not something else, and so you must be judging it truly (about what it is)—but then by definition you know it. And if you know it, it seems impossible to make a mistake about it, since it is not possible to know and not know the same thing. In other words, if even thinking of something requires that one know what one is thinking of, then it seems to follow—at least according to the line of thought Socrates and Theaetetus pursue[18]—that it is not possible to think of something and make a mistake about it at the same time. This is the fundamental obstacle that Socrates and Theaetetus keep confronting and trying to find a way around.

For example, consider the fourth attempt to explain false judgment, the "Wax Block" model of thinking (*Tht.* 191a–196c), according to which there is a wax block or tablet in our souls onto which we imprint our perceptions, thereby gaining the ability to call up those thoughts long after the sensory affection has passed. The wax block itself seems to represent the faculty of memory and of thought. Socrates introduces it to solve the problem that it seems impossible to think of something as X and at the same time to think of it as something else, Y. He solves it by finding a way to have something in mind without thinking of it as X: by perceiving it. Socrates says that we perceive things and then imprint the images of those things into the "wax block" in our minds—that is, in our memory. Thus, having a wax imprint of something in our minds represents the capacity to call up an image of, and think of, that thing. But when one perceives an object, the object is presented to one without one's being aware of what it is.[19] Thus, it is possible to have something in mind and to misidentify it without knowing it. One can have an object presented to one in perception (e.g., Theaetetus), and when one matches this to the wrong imprint in one's wax block (e.g., that of Theodorus), one is

17. See also Gökhan Adalıer, "Materialism in Plato's *Theaetetus*" ["Materialism"](Ph.D. dissertation, Duke University, 1999), and Adalıer, "Case." Gail Fine, "False Belief in the *Theaetetus*" ["False Belief"], *Phronesis* 24 (1979), 70–80, also thinks the definition of knowledge as true judgment is implicated in the failure to explain how false judgment is possible.

18. This follows only if we assume that all judgments are identity statements (see note 20), or if we assume that knowing what one is thinking of is knowing everything about what one is thinking of (cf. the "all-or-nothing" view of knowledge as acquaintance discussed in Fine, "False Belief").

19. This passage continues to assume, in line with *Tht.* 184–86, that perception has no propositional content, though perhaps it differs from it in allowing that what we see are objects like Theaetetus, not just the special sensibles.

effectively making a mismatch without being guilty of knowing Theaeetus and making a mistake about him. For the reason is that the wax block allows one to perceive Theaetetus, but in perceiving Theaetetus, one is not perceiving Theaetetus *as* Theaetetus; in other words, one can perceive an object without having any thought whatsoever about what it is.

So according to the proposal, one has a wax block in one's mind, which allows one to have an imprint of X, which represents the thought or memory of X, and one is also capable of having perceptions of X (though one does not perceive X *as* X), and in making judgments about things, one either successfully or unsuccessfully matches perception with imprint. A mismatch then represents the thought that "this is Y," where "this" in fact refers to some X that is not the same as Y. This appears to be a successful explanation of false judgment. But it is rejected because it is unable to explain how false judgment can occur in cases where perception is not involved (*Tht.* 195b–196c). And it is clear that false judgment occurs even about things which we grasp by means of the mind; for example, one can make a mistake about 12, thinking that it is the same as 5 + 6.

One noteworthy feature of the entire section on false judgment is that Socrates focuses almost exclusively on judgments of identity about particular things, such as judging Theaetetus (i.e., judging who he is) or judging Socrates (i.e., judging who he is).[20] In my view, the focus on identity statements does not vitiate the argument; even if it does not cover all judgments, such as judgments like "Socrates is snub-nosed," Socrates is still quite right to think that it is a problem, given their initial assumptions, to explain how one can know something and make a mistake about it. More significant, in my view, is the fact that they tend to focus on judgments about particular things. Here, as elsewhere in the dialogue, we find an ecumenical tendency toward the question of what kind of objects can be known.

Though the problems of explaining false judgment cannot be laid at the doorstep of this focus on judgments about unique particulars,[21] we will see that it will later give rise to a problem for the final definition of knowledge as true judgment with an account. The problem raised there is that anyone with true

---

20. At *Tht* 188c5–7, Socrates draws the conclusion that it is impossible to judge that one thing is another—that is, that false misidentifications are impossible; he then infers that one cannot make any false judgments (188c7–8). Since there seem to be more forms of judgments than identifications, such as mis-descriptions, it would appear that the inference does not follow (cf. Burnyeat, *Theaetetus*, 70–123, esp. 70–73, for a statement of the problem). Either the argument is meant to be limited to identity judgments (Cornford, *Theaetetus*, 113; Frank Lewis, "Two Paradoxes in the *Theaetetus*," in J. M. E. Moravcsik (ed.), *Patterns in Plato's Thought* (Dordrecht: D. Reidel, 1973), 123–24; Nicholas White, *Plato on Knowledge and Reality* (Indianapolis: Hackett, 1976), 164; McDowell, *Theaetetus*, 195), or more than identity judgments are considered (C. F. J. Williams, "Referential Opacity and False Belief in the *Theaetetus*," *Philosophical Quarterly* 22 (1972), 298–99; Fine, "False Belief," 74; and David Bostock, *Plato's Theaetetus* [*Theaetetus*] [Oxford: Clarendon Press, 1988], 172–73). A Cornford-style approach has recently been argued for by Adalier, "Materialism," who thinks these assumptions are characteristic of a position Plato is arguing against, one which assumes that all judgments are judgments of identity, precisely because it does not admit Forms and therefore the possibility of predication.

21. Unless one supposes that this entire section implicitly presupposes an ontology of particulars; cf. Adalier, "Materialism," and Adalier, "Case."

judgment already appears to be in possession of an account, if having an account is having the distinguishing mark that sets off what one knows from everything else; hence, adding "with an account" adds nothing to true judgment that it didn't already have (*Tht.* 208d–210a). As we've already seen, if having a true judgment about X consists of having X in mind, and no one or nothing else, then it does seem that true judgment already carries with it the ability to distinguish X from everything else. But this problem disappears, as I argue below, if one takes kinds, rather than unique individual objects, as the objects of knowledge.

Besides the indirect examination of the definition of knowledge as true judgment, Plato also has Socrates examine it directly: Socrates dispatches it fairly quickly, in an argument that takes barely two paragraphs (*Tht.* 201ac). As Socrates notes, juries can be correctly convinced that certain events occurred—for example, that the defendant committed a murder at a particular time—even though they did not themselves witness the event. But only someone who has actually seen the event could be said to know that it occurred. That is, in order to have knowledge, one needs proper evidence or justification for one's belief. The members of the jury could be said to have, at best, correct judgment, not knowledge.[22] The striking thing about this argument, for our purposes, is that it clearly implies that knowledge is possible for things like particular facts and events and, furthermore, that perception may have a role to play in acquiring the proper evidence or justification required for knowledge. Here again is evidence that Plato is prepared to entertain a wide range of possible objects of knowledge, though the argument still leaves open the possibility that Plato thinks that knowledge of the Forms is necessary even to know, for example, that some event occurred.

# 3. KNOWLEDGE AS TRUE JUDGMENT WITH AN ACCOUNT (K3)

The refutation of the definition of knowledge as true judgment shows that true judgment by itself is not sufficient for knowledge: one needs something additional, playing the role that first-hand witnessing of an event plays in the case of knowing what happened on a particular occasion. This point leads Socrates and Theaetetus to their final proposal concerning knowledge, (K3), that knowledge is true judgment with an account (*logos*) (*Tht.* 201cd). This definition is the most likely to be endorsed by Plato himself, since there are many passages in other dialogues where something like K3 is endorsed—most famously, the statement in the *Meno* that

---

22. For further discussion, see M. F. Burnyeat, part 1, and Jonathan Barnes, part 2, of "Socrates and the Jury: Paradoxes in Plato's Distinction between Knowledge and True Belief," *Proceedings of the Aristotelian Society* 54(suppl.) (1980), 173–91 and 193–206.

"true beliefs are not worth much until one ties them down by reasoning about the cause" (*aitias logismôi; Meno* 98a).[23]

The central idea in Theaetetus' definition of knowledge is that "things of which there's no account are not knowable ... whereas things which have an account are knowable" (*Tht.* 201d). This introduces an asymmetry between things which do and do not have an account (call this "asymmetry of *logos*," or "AL"), which together with the requirement that everything known must have a *logos* (call this "knowledge requires a *logos*," or "KL"), gives rise to an asymmetry between things which can be known and things which cannot be known (call this "asymmetry of knowledge," or "AK").[24] K3 explicitly says that some things can be objects of knowledge (namely, those things which have an account) and that other things cannot be objects of knowledge (namely, those things of which there is no account). But as it stands, K3 is extremely abstract; it is unclear what exactly a *logos* or account is and why certain things admit of an account, whereas others do not.

Socrates begins his examination of this definition with a move familiar from the perception section of the *Theaetetus*: he introduces another thesis—or, rather, a set of theses which are meant to illustrate and support the proposed definition. That is, he examines the definition by offering a set of ideas that is sufficient for the truth of the definition; he introduces what he refers to as a "dream" to show how Theaetetus' definition could be true (*Tht.* 201d–203d).

In particular, the "dream" is meant to answer the second question above, why some things can't be given a *logos* and hence can't be known, whereas others can. According to the Dream theory, the asymmetry exists because things fall into two different kinds: "primary elements (*stoicheia*), as it were, of which we and everything else are composed" (*Tht.* 201e–202a) and those things which are composed out of them. It is unclear what these primary elements are and how they figure as constituents in everything else. We are simply told that (1) elements can only be named; (2) that one cannot say anything else of an element—such as "is," "is not," "itself," "that," or "each"—since that would be to add something to it which does not belong to it alone; and (3) that an element can be perceived, not known. By contrast, things composed out of elements (a) can be given an account, (b) which consists of names woven together, and (c) can be known (201e–202b).

Like K3, the Dream theory is abstract and open to multiple interpretations. Are the primary elements material stuffs, or are they parts out of which other material objects are constituted? Such an interpretation is encouraged by the fact that Socrates talks of primary elements "out of which we and everything else are composed" (201e), as well as by his later remark that elements "have no account and are unknowable, but they're perceivable" (202b). Or is the Dream theory a

---

23. See also *Phaedo* 76b5–6, 97d–99d2; *Symposium* 202a5–9; *Republic* 534b3–7; *Timaeus* 51e5. For further discussion, see Taylor, chapter 7 in this volume.

24. Cf. M. F. Burnyeat, "The Material and Sources of Plato's Dream" ["Dream"], *Phronesis* 15 (1970), 101–22; Gail Fine, "Knowledge and *Logos* in the *Theaetetus*," *Plato on Knowledge and Forms: Selected Essays* ["Knowledge"] (Oxford: Clarendon Press, 2003), 225–51, originally published in *Philosophical Review* 88 (1979), 366–97.

theory about meaning, where the primary elements and things which are composed out of them are the meanings of our words and meanings of sentences or propositions constructed out of them? One could cite in support of this Socrates' speaking of the elements being "woven together" into a complex, just as the names are woven together into a *logos* or account (202b). So understood, there is a resemblance between the Dream theory and Wittgenstein and Russell's Logical Atomism, a resemblance noted by Wittgenstein himself.[25] There are no doubt other possible spheres of application—and perhaps this is a sign of how potentially powerful the theory is. But, in my view, none of these does justice to Plato's intentions. Plato deliberately leaves it open what the "primary elements" are,[26] for he only wants to focus on certain features of ontology and language and not others. Plato leaves many features of the Dream theory vague in order to make it sufficiently general and hence widely applicable to a variety of possible objects of knowledge.

The Dream theory focuses on the following three features of ontology and language:

1. It tells us that things fall into two kinds: elements and those things which are composed or "woven together" out of them. That is, the distinction between things that can and can't be known appears to correlate with a distinction between things that are ontologically basic and others that are made up out of them.

2. Elements can only be named (not given an account), and they can only be perceived (not known). That is, their ontologically basic status gives rise to the fact that they cannot be given a *logos* (AL) and thus the fact that they cannot be known (AK); they are spoken of and grasped through other means.

3. A *logos* says of a thing what is proper to it. This effectively restricts all *logoi* to identity statements—that is, statements or definitions of what a thing is.[27] The Dream theory continues to assume, as in the false judgment section, that all judgments are judgments of identity about particular objects.

Next, Socrates considers what the Dream theory would say about the following case: take letters to be primary elements and syllables to be complexes made up out

---

25. Cf. Burnyeat, *Theaetetus*, 149–64; Chappell, *Theaetetus*, 208–11, offers a reply to Burnyeat's objections to the "Logical Atomist" interpretation of the Dream theory.

26. This is a theme of Burnyeat's discussion of the third definition of knowledge (Burnyeat, *Theaetetus*, 129, 131–32, 164).

27. The oddity of this stricture—that one should not, in general, say anything of a thing which doesn't belong to it, and that one should only say of a thing what belongs to it alone—has historically put people in mind of Antisthenes, partly because Aristotle seems to suggest that Antisthenes had the strange view that the only way you can talk about a thing is to name it; hence, both subject-terms and predicate-terms in sentences serve the same function—that is, to name—and a sentence itself is nothing other than an extended name. Whether or not Plato has him in mind is not clear, partly because we know so little about Antisthenes. For an even-handed judgment on this matter, see Burnyeat, "Dream," and Burnyeat, *Theaetetus*, 164–73.

of them (*Tht.* 202e). Thus, the first syllable of Socrates' name, "SO," is a complex, and the letters "S" and "O" are the elements out of which the syllable is composed. The account of the complex "SO"—given in answer to the question "What is 'SO'?"—would be that it is "S" and "O." However, "S" and "O" cannot themselves be given an account; as Theaetetus says, "How could one express in an account the elements of an element? In fact, Socrates, 'S' is one of the unvoiced consonants, only a noise, which occurs when the tongue hisses, as it were" (*Tht.* 203b). One will wonder, of course, why what Theaetetus has just said about the letter "S" could not count as an account of an element. But the reason is evidently that it does not refer to the parts of a letter, because a letter has no parts *ex hypothesi*. We can thus infer that in the Dream theory we are to assume that the account of a thing is simply an enumeration of its elements (EE) and, furthermore, that the elements are a thing's parts. The Dream theory is thus reductionist because it takes a thing to be no more than its parts and therefore to be wholly analyzable into its parts.[28] But why should we assume that?

To answer this, let's look at Socrates' two refutations of the Dream theory—or more precisely, his refutations of the thesis of asymmetry in knowledge between elements and complexes. One of these assumes this controversial point, that the relation between an element and a complex is that of part to whole and that the whole is the same as the sum of its parts (call this "WP"); the other does not. In the first argument, WP is assumed in order to argue that the thesis of asymmetry in knowledge between element and complex is untenable: either they are equally knowable, or they are equally unknowable (not-AK) (*Tht.* 203d–205e). The second argument does not assume WP; it simply points out that our experience in coming to know things is the opposite of AK: far from it being the case that the elements are unknowable, we find that in our own experience of learning, the elements are better known than those things that we know by means of their elements (*Tht.* 205e–206b). For example, when we learn to read, we concentrate on learning the letters first and only later on recognizing the syllables constructed out of them. As Socrates says, "the class of elements admits of knowledge that is far clearer, and more important for the perfect grasp of every branch of learning, than the complex" (*Tht.* 206b).

Plato's strategy in offering two different arguments against AK seems to be to start both from premises (such as WP) that he would probably not accept and from premises that he might accept. The advantage of this strategy is that it covers his bases; insofar as WP is widely accepted, even if not by Plato himself,[29] an argument showing that WP is incompatible with AK would strongly suggest that AK should

---

28. Cf. A. E. Taylor, *Plato, the Man and His Work* (London: Methuen, 1926), 344–46; K. Sayre, *Plato's Analytic Method* (Chicago: University of Chicago Press, 1969), 120–30; Adalıer, "Materialism," 207–48, esp. 234–41; Sedley, *Midwife*, 158.

29. Cf. Burnyeat, *Theaetetus*, 191–209, esp. 199–201; Verity Harte, "Plato's Problem of Composition," in John J. Cleary and Gary M. Gurtler (eds.), *Proceedings of the Boston Area Colloquium in Ancient Philosophy 2001*, vol. 17 (Leiden: Brill, 2002), 1–26.

be rejected. The second version clinches the argument, showing that we have good reason to reject AK even if we do not accept WP.

What follows if we reject AK, the thesis of asymmetry of knowledge between elements and complexes? Either elements and complexes are likewise knowable or likewise unknowable. That we are meant to conclude the former is suggested by the second argument Socrates gives against AK, in which he says that our experience of learning our letters suggests that, far from it being the case that we have no knowledge of the elements, knowledge of the elements of a subject matter is fundamental in coming to learn it. Supposing that elements and complexes are both knowable (not-AK), what should we say about KL, AL, and EE, since KL, AL, EE, and not-AK are inconsistent?[30]

A. One option is to reject KL: not everything requires a *logos* to be known.[31] For example, one might suppose that certain Forms—in particular, the Form of the Good—will figure in Plato's answer to the question of what the elements of everything are but that the Form of the Good itself cannot be given an account, since it is the most fundamental of all. This option would be particularly compelling if one thought that Plato was committed to EE as a model of what an account is—that is, if one thought that accounts can only be one-directional, from the more complex to the simpler, from explanandum to explanans. (Note that EE does not commit one to WP, since the elements in terms of which one gives an account of a thing need not be parts of that thing.) Arguably, Aristotle took this option, since he distinguishes first principles or elements which are known by other means than demonstrative knowledge[32]—namely, by nous.

B. Another option is to retain KL and reject AK and AL: both elements and complexes can be known, and since knowledge requires an account, both elements and complexes can be given accounts—albeit accounts of different sorts. The key here is to reject EE, according to which an account is an enumeration of a thing's elements.[33] The reason the Dream theory gave for denying accounts to simples was that simples don't have parts. But Theaetetus' own reply when explaining that the letter "S" does not have an

30. Cf. Fine, "Knowledge," 236.

31. Some argue that knowledge for Plato requires some kind of nondiscursive, intuitive grasp of its objects (e.g., I. M. Crombie, *An Examination of Plato's Doctrines*, 2 vols. (London: Routledge and Kegan Paul, 1962, 1963), 2:1131–34; Richard Robinson, "Forms and Error in Plato's *Theaetetus*" in his *Essays in Greek Philosophy* (Oxford: Clarendon Press, 1969), 52–55). Alternatively, one might think that the point of giving up KL is to acknowledge that not everything can be defined without circularity, and hence at least the most basic Forms must be known by some other way (Stephen Menn, "Collecting the Letters" ["Collecting"], *Phronesis* 43/4 [1998], 201).

32. Aristotle says that knowledge is always "with an account" (*Posterior Analytics* II 19. 100b10; *Nicomachean Ethics* VI 6. 1140b33) but distinguishes demonstrative knowledge with the self-explanatory, undemonstrated knowledge of first principles (*Posterior Analytics* I 3. 72b19–24, II 19. 99b20).

33. "The endorsement of KL, coupled with the rejection of AK, suggests that AL and, correspondingly, EE are also to be rejected: since elements are as knowable as compounds, and since all knowledge requires accounts, there must be accounts of elements" (Fine, "Knowledge," 237).

account—that it has no account because there are no letters in a letter, that it is simply an unvoiced consonant—shows that one could give a different kind of account of "S," one that did not analyze a thing in terms of its parts, but which placed it in a classification scheme relative to other letters and sounds: vowels versus consonants, voiced versus unvoiced, and so on. So elements could receive accounts not in terms of their parts—since they don't have any—but rather in relation to other elements and ultimately in relation to the whole field to which they belong.

Deciding which option Plato intends us to go for would be too large and complex an undertaking for this chapter.[34] For our purposes, it is sufficient to note that whether one thinks we are supposed to carve out a different conception of knowledge besides the kind of knowledge that is true judgment with an account, as in option A, or to defend the viability of K3 as a definition of knowledge by jettisoning some of the problematic features of the Dream theory, as in option B, there is no reason to suppose that Plato is committed to the assumption that a whole is identical to the sum of its parts (WP). According to option A, Plato retains the idea that a *logos* is, fundamentally, an enumeration of a thing's elements—though the elements of what is known are not necessarily a thing's parts (i.e., not WP). Instead of expanding the conception of *logos*, we're supposed to realize that knowledge does not require a *logos*. Whatever the most basic items of ontology are, they are not going to be known by means of a *logos* but, instead, will be perceived or known in some other way. According to option B, Plato rejects WP, and also EE, as imposing an unnecessarily restrictive conception of *logos* on the definition of knowledge as true judgment with an account (which then points forward to *Theaetetus* 206c–208b, especially 208ab, where he makes this point explicitly). If one expands one's conception of *logos*, then one might think that both elements and complexes can have *logoi*, and, correspondingly, both elements and complexes can be known, albeit in different ways.

What we ultimately think of the definition depends on getting clear about what a *logos* is, as is made clear in the final section of Socrates' examination of K3, where he considers three different conceptions of *logos* and raises problems for each one (206c–210a). The first proposed interpretation of *logos*—according to which it is simply "speech"—is quickly dismissed, since presumably adding speech to true judgment doesn't get one anything more than true judgment (*Tht.* 206ce). The second account of *logos* holds that one gives a *logos* of a thing when one goes through its elements (*Tht.* 206e). For example, to give a *logos* of a wagon is to name the parts it has—for example, "wheels, axle, body, rails, yoke" (*Tht.* 207a). Though the Dream theory did not explicitly state what it is to give a *logos*, this account articulates what was assumed in the Dream theory: that the *logos* of a thing is an enumeration of a thing's elements. For this reason, Socrates suggests that "our

34. Recommended readings include Fine, "Knowledge"; Bostock, *Theaetetus*; Burnyeat, *Theaetetus*; and, more recently, Adalıer, "Materialism"; Sedley, *Midwife*; and Chappell, *Theaetetus*.

man"—the one who came up with the Dream theory—would scoff at one if one gave as the account of a wagon "wheels, axle, body, rails, yoke" (207ab). He would say that these were no more the elements of a wagon than syllables are of a name; rather, a proper account of a wagon would refer to the wagon's "hundred timbers"—that is, the many individual elements out of which it is made.

This way of conceiving of a *logos* is clearly inadequate. For example, no mention is made of the importance of structure or arrangement or the relationship between the parts of a thing for understanding what it is. Presumably any account of the syllable "SO" should mention not only the letters that make it up but also their order and arrangement—after all, "SO" is different from "OS." An account of a wagon should name not only its parts but also their order and arrangement; a wheelbarrow and a wagon could conceivably be made up out of the same materials and parts but be distinguished by different arrangements of those materials.

Plato does not say this; his point is deeper. The objection he has Socrates raise to this way of thinking of *logos* shows that a *logos* cannot consist simply in being able to name the elements or parts of a thing (207d–208b). Socrates objects that someone might be able to go through Theaetetus' name, spelling it correctly and giving a correct account of all the letters making it up. But that person might at the same time make a mistake about the first syllable of Theodorus' name, spelling it "TE" instead of "THE." And similarly, he might make a mistake about the syllable "AI" when he finds it in another word, though he spelled it correctly in the name "THEAITETOS." Such a person does not know how to spell Theaetetus' name.

The point, then, is that knowledge of something does not simply consist of enumerating the elements of a thing; one must also be able to recognize those elements as such when they occur elsewhere. The mistake the novice speller makes when he spells Theaetetus' name correctly, but mispells Theodorus', shows that he doesn't have a systematic grasp of the rules of spelling and of phonetics. Indeed, Plato uses the same example of spelling and letters in the *Philebus* to illustrate the methods of collection and division (*Phlb.* 18bd). The novice speller is unable to "collect" the letters correctly: he does not recognize letters and syllables as of the same kind when they are found in different words, as when letters and syllables have been combined in different ways.[35] This objection then points toward a different conception of what it is to have a *logos*: it is to have the capacity to *recognize* the parts of an individual thing (e.g., letters in a particular word) as its elements, where those elements can only be identified in terms of a larger, inter-related system characterizing an entire field or genus, one which can explain, for example, how all the words of a language should be spelled. Such a grasp of an entire field or genus is the province of the expert.[36]

---

35. Cf. Burnyeat, "Dream"; Burnyeat, *Theaetetus*; Fine, "Knowledge"; Menn, "Collecting."

36. The importance of this point in reading this part of the *Theaetetus* is emphasized in Burnyeat, "Dream"; Julia Annas, "Knowledge and Language: The *Theaetetus* and the *Cratylus*," in Malcolm Schofield and Martha Craven Nussbaum (eds.), *Language and Logos: Studies in Ancient Greek Philosophy Presented to G. E. L. Owen* (Cambridge: Cambridge University Press, 1982), 95–114; and Alexander Nehamas, "*Episteme* and *Logos* in Plato's Later Thought," *Archiv für Geschichte der Philosophie* 66 (1984), 11–36.

For option A—according to which we are supposed to give up the requirement of *logos* for knowledge because some things are known by means of a *logos* of their elements, whereas the elements themselves are known, but not by means of a *logos*— this comes as a welcome amendment to the conception of *logos* at work in the definition of knowledge as true judgment with a *logos*. That is, we are to understand that giving the *logos* of a thing in terms of a thing's elements does not simply consist of naming its parts. And it will insist that the elements themselves do not have *logoi* and are known in a different way. Option B—according to which we should retain K3 as the definition of knowledge, and reject AK and AL—can also admit this amendment to the conception of *logos* at work in the definition. For the objection helps to make the point that having a *logos* of a thing should not be thought of as simply being in possession of a list of the parts of a thing but, rather, as having the ability to locate and recognize the relevant elements for a thing, an ability which would require one to relate that thing to other things of the same kind.

Finally, Socrates considers a third conception of *logos* according to which having a *logos* consists of "being able to state some mark by which the thing one is asked for differs from everything else" (208c). For example, the sun is "the brightest of the heavenly bodies that go round the earth" (208d). An account must, then, "get hold of the differentiation of anything, by which it differs from everything else, whereas as long as you grasp something common, your account will be about those things to which the common quality belongs" (208d).

Socrates raises the following difficulty for the definition of knowledge that results with this meaning of "logos" (208e–210a): it would seem that even in order to judge correctly about Theaetetus, one has to have in mind and grasp Theaetetus as he is different from everyone else. After all, if one has in mind those features that Theaetetus shares with anyone else, then one will no more be thinking of Theaetetus than anyone else. Hence, even in correct judgment about a thing, one must already grasp the features that distinguish it from everything else. But then this seems to render "with an account" empty; one will not have added anything to true judgment when one adds an account to it. Thus, adding an account of how something differs from something else to a correct judgment will not add anything informative to what was already contained in the judgment itself.

One might insist that adding an account consists of getting to know rather than judging the differentness. But this will not help, because adding "knowledge of the differentness" to a true judgment would simply make the definition of knowledge circular: knowledge is true judgment about a thing plus knowledge of how it differs from everything else (209e–210a).

What are we supposed to make of this conception of *logos*, as well as of Socrates' reasons for rejecting the resulting definition of knowledge? On the one hand, one might think that there are reasons for regarding it with some suspicion. Socrates' marking something as "what most people would say" (208c) is never a recommendation in favor of the proposal.[37] Furthermore, this "popular" con-

---

37. Burnyeat, *Theaetetus*, 191, draws attention to this remark.

ception of knowledge seems to assume that knowledge is always of unique individual objects, like the sun, Theaetetus, and so on, and that knowing a thing means being able to say how it differs from other unique individuals. For this reason, Socrates slips comfortably back into the language of the wax block when he discusses this proposal. He says that one won't have Theaetetus in one's judgment "until precisely that snubness [of Theaetetus'] has imprinted and deposited in me a memory trace different from those of the other snubnesses I've seen, and similarly with the other things you're composed of. Then if I meet you tomorrow, that snubness will remind me and make me judge correctly about you" (209c). What allows one to judge that this is Theaetetus and not someone else is the fact that Theaetetus' unique individual qualities—for example, the particular snubness of his nose—have been imprinted in Socrates' memory, his wax block, so that on future occasions, he is able to make a correct judgment by matching the person he perceives with an imprint possessing exactly those features that he happens to have.

On the other hand, one might think that the problem lies not in the idea itself but in its application. One might argue, for example, that the idea that to give an account of a thing is to give the *sêmeion* or distinguishing mark of it and thus is very close to what Plato says in other dialogues[38] but that the way this interpretation is applied in the *Theaetetus* is problematic and the cause of the difficulty. For it is assumed that the things for which we are to give *sêmeia* are particular individual objects; thus to know Theaetetus is to be able to recognize him and distinguish him from everyone else. And here, giving the *sêmeion* does seem to be something one who has a true *judgment* about Theaetetus should already be capable of doing, if they are judging correctly about him as opposed to someone else. That is, if one is thinking about Theaetetus, as opposed to someone else, one must be picking him out of the crowd not by means of general features that Theaetetus shares with others but by means of particular features that are unique to him. However, if one gives up the assumption that the objects of knowledge are unique individual objects, there is no reason to think that one would be capable of giving the *sêmeion* if one had a true judgment about a *kind* of thing. For example, one might be able to recognize and make true judgments about zebras without being able to give the *sêmeion* of zebras—to say how zebras are different from other species. After all, that is the special province of the expert in biology. In other words, the *sêmeion* of a particular individual object serves to distinguish that object from other objects—in particular, objects of the same species. Hence, what one looks for to distinguish Socrates from Theaetetus is, for example, the particular bend of his nose, or the color of his skin, or the height and weight of the individual—or some combination of these features. But the *sêmeion* of a kind of thing—of human beings, of justice, or of beauty—serves to distinguish it from other kinds of things. (Think, for example, of Aristotle's conception of definition: to give a definition of a thing, you have to give the genus plus its differentiae.[39]

---

38. Fine, *Knowledge*, 228; Sedley, *Midwife*.

39. *Topics* VI 4. 141b26: "A correct definition must be given through the genus and the differentiae, and these are better known without qualification and prior to the species."

The differentiae are obviously not the *sêmeion* or the distinguishing mark of an individual particular concrete object but, rather, what distinguishes a species from other things belonging to the same genus.) Thus, the third conception of *logos* is only vulnerable to Socrates' objection if one assumes that what we have knowledge of are particular things like Socrates or Theaetetus. If one focuses on knowledge of kinds, there is no reason to think that being able to judge truly about a kind carries with it the ability to give any kind of account of what distinguishes that kind from others; for example, even if I correctly judge my neighbor's tree to be an oak, there is no reason to think I can also give an account of what distinguishes oak trees from all the other kinds of trees that there are. Hence, the definition of knowledge as true judgment with an account of the distinguishing mark remains a promising contender as an account of knowledge.

Although Plato gives no indication here in the *Theaetetus* that this is what he has in mind, it is consistent with his interest in genus-species hierarchies in other late dialogues.[40] And if we apply the third conception of logos in this way to kinds, rather than particulars, then it is also consistent with Plato's claim in the *Republic* that all knowledge requires grasp of the Forms; here the point of the definition would be that understanding something requires that one be able to give an account of it in terms of what it is to be that kind of thing, which, in turn, requires one to relate it to and distinguish it from other kinds that belong to the same genus. Again, nothing here requires a commitment to Plato's theory of Forms specifically. But it does suggest—along with other passages in the dialogue—that a metaphysics consisting entirely of particulars, with no room for kinds of things to which these particulars belong, would have less chance of success in sustaining what would otherwise seem to be a promising definition of knowledge, namely (K3).

# 4. CONCLUSION

Plato examines three definitions of knowledge in the *Theaetetus* using a variety of methods. One feature of his strategy is to examine a particular definition of knowledge using two different methods—one of which explores the definition by offering metaphysical premises in support of that definition, the other of which explores and refutes the definition on its own terms, without any such metaphysical commitments. Thus, for example, Plato tests and examines the thesis that knowledge is perception both on its own (at 184–86) and in conjunction with a number of metaphysical theses, including the thesis that everything is always changing and the thesis that everything is always characterized by opposites (*Tht.* 152c–183c). Similarly, Plato tests and examines one aspect of the definition of knowledge as true judgment with an account both on its own (206ac) and in

---

40. Taylor, chapter 7 in this volume.

conjunction with a number of metaphysical theses, contained in the Dream theory—in particular, the thesis that a thing is nothing more than the sum of its parts (203c–205e).

It is beyond the scope of this chapter to try to determine what Plato intended us to conclude (Taylor discusses some options in chapter 7). Instead, I conclude with a more limited point: Plato introduces various metaphysical theses in order to provide support for a definition of knowledge. But they are not necessarily ones which he himself would endorse. Plato's purpose in assuming metaphysical premises that are incompatible with the Forms is analogous to the role of the hedonist hypothesis in the *Protagoras* (353c–354e). There, Socrates assumes the truth of hedonism—that the good is the same as pleasure—in order to show that there is no such thing as being overcome by pleasure. He puts this forward as a working assumption, on behalf of the ordinary folks whom he and Protagoras are addressing (353a, 354b), which will help Socrates to show that no one is ever overcome by pleasure: in particular, that reason cannot be outweighed by pleasure. In my view, neither the character Socrates nor Plato endorses the hedonist hypothesis.[41] Rather, Socrates' purpose in introducing the hedonist hypothesis seems to be to convince those people who are already committed to hedonism—which would presumably include most readers and, perhaps, most people in Socrates' audience—that it's never the case that anyone is overcome by pleasure. But even if one is not committed to the hedonist hypothesis, one can see that Socrates could in principle offer another argument along the same lines that doesn't depend on that assumption—as indeed the Stoics would much later.

Similarly, in the *Theaetetus*, Plato repeatedly introduces metaphysical doctrines he does not himself endorse on behalf of epistemological theses he wishes to explore. Thus, he introduces the flux doctrine in order to flesh out a picture of a world in which knowledge is the same as perception and in which all appearances are true. As it turns out, the flux doctrine implies both that these are true and that they are not true. Hence, the conclusion is, minimally, that the flux doctrine cannot provide support for Theaetetus' definition of knowledge as perception after all. More robustly, Socrates and his interlocutors conclude that the flux doctrine is incompatible with any kind of knowledge. This hardly constitutes a proof for the existence of the Forms. But it does suggest that there need to be limits on the extent of flux—such as are provided by Plato's theory about Forms.

In the case of the Dream theory, Plato assumes the thesis that a thing is the same as the sum of its parts (WP) on behalf of the definition of knowledge as true judgment with an account. Plato goes on to show that the thesis of asymmetry in knowledge is untenable. But he also argues that the thesis of asymmetry is untenable even if one does not assume WP. And he then goes on to show what is wrong with conceiving of a *logos* as a list of the parts of a thing, which, in turn, suggests that we shouldn't conceive of things as being nothing more than the sum

---

41. This is not uncontroversial; some think that Plato accepted hedonism at the time of the *Protagoras* (see, for example, T. Irwin, *Plato's Ethics* [Oxford: Oxford University Press, 1995], 85–92).

of their parts. Again, this hardly constitutes a proof for the existence of the Forms. But it does suggest the shortcomings in theories that locate knowledge in one's grasp of the parts of a particular thing—rather than in the understanding of what it is to be that kind of thing, an understanding involving a grasp of the systematic relations it has with other kinds of things, such as can be found in the conception of knowledge advocated in other Platonic dialogues.

As we have seen, Plato does not offer anything quite as straightforward as an argument that knowledge is impossible without the Forms. But three aspects of the metaphysical theories he introduces on behalf of the various definitions of knowledge he considers in the *Theaetetus* prove to be problematic. First, the theses of flux and opposition—according to which everything is changing, and everything is F and not-F—are ultimately deemed to be incompatible with the first definition of knowledge and indeed with any conception of knowledge. In particular, these problems result if whiteness is always "flowing" or coming to be not white, and if perceiving is always coming to be not perceiving—that is, if the nature of things is subject to change. Acknowledging that some things, such as the nature of things, cannot change may not yet commit one to the theory of Forms, but it certainly resembles the claim Plato often makes elsewhere that the Forms do not admit of their opposites. Second, Socrates tends in the dialogue to suppose that what is known are sensible particulars rather than kinds to which sensible particulars belong. Expanding the range of possible objects of knowledge to include kinds does not, of course, commit one to the theory of Forms. But it takes one in a direction that is more congenial to the theory of Forms than to an ontology exclusively composed of material particulars. Finally, Socrates adopts the viewpoint in the final section of the dialogue that a thing is nothing other than the sum of its parts and, therefore, that to say what a thing is is to say what it is made out of. His rejection of this kind of reductionism again does not commit him to the theory of Forms. But it does suggest that understanding what a thing is depends not on finding out what a thing is made out of but on finding out how it relates, in a system, to other kinds of things—an idea that Plato goes on to explore in other late dialogues.

# BIBLIOGRAPHY

Adalıer, Gökhan. "The Case of 'Theaetetus,'" *Phronesis* 46/1 (2001), 1–37.
———. "Materialism in Plato's *Theaetetus*" (Ph.D. dissertation, Duke University, 1999).
Annas, Julia. "Knowledge and Language: The *Theaetetus* and the *Cratylus*," in Malcolm Schofield and Martha Craven Nussbaum (eds.), *Language and Logos: Studies in Ancient Greek Philosophy Presented to G. E. L. Owen* (Cambridge: Cambridge University Press, 1982), 95–114.
Barnes, Jonathan. "Socrates and the Jury: Paradoxes in Plato's Distinction between Knowledge and True Belief (Part 2)," *Proceedings of the Aristotelian Society* 54(suppl.) (1980), 193–206.

Bostock, David. *Plato's Theaetetus* (Oxford: Clarendon Press, 1988).

Burnyeat, Myles F. "Idealism and Greek Philosophy: What Descartes Saw and Berkeley Missed," *Philosophical Review* 91/1 (1982), 3–40.

———. "The Material and Sources of Plato's Dream," *Phronesis* 15 (1970), 101–22.

———. "Plato on the Grammar of Perceiving," *Classical Quarterly* 26 (1976), 29–51.

———. "Protagoras and Self-refutation in Plato's *Theaetetus*," *Philosophical Review* 85 (1976), 172–95; reprinted in Stephen Everson (ed.), *Epistemology* (Cambridge: Cambridge University Press, 1990), 39–59.

———. "Socrates and the Jury: Paradoxes in Plato's Distinction between Knowledge and True Belief (Part 1)," *Proceedings of the Aristotelian Society* 54(suppl.) (1980), 173–91.

———. "Socratic Midwifery, Platonic Inspiration," *Bulletin of the Institute of Classical Studies of the University of London* 24 (1977), 7–16.

———. *The Theaetetus of Plato*, trans. M. J. Levett (Indianapolis: Hackett, 1990).

Chappell, Timothy. *Reading Plato's Theaetetus* (Indianapolis: Hackett, 2005); originally published, Sankt Augustin, Germany: Academia Verlag 2004.

Cooper, John M. "Plato on Sense-Perception and Knowledge (*Theaetetus* 184–186)," *Phronesis* 15 (1970), 123–46.

Cornford, Francis Macdonald. *Plato's Theory of Knowledge: The Theaetetus and the Sophist of Plato Translated with a Commentary* (London: Routledge and Kegan Paul, 1935).

Crombie, I. M. *An Examination of Plato's Doctrines*, 2 vols. (London: Routledge and Kegan Paul, 1962, 1963).

Dancy, R. M. "Theaetetus' First Baby: *Tht.* 151e–160e," *Philosophical Topics* 15/2 (1987), 61–108.

Fine, Gail. "Conflicting Appearances: *Theaetetus* 153d–154b," in C. Gill and M. M. McCabe (eds.), *Form and Argument in Late Plato* (Oxford: Oxford University Press, 1996), 105–33.

———. "False Belief in the *Theaetetus*," *Phronesis* 24 (1979), 70–80.

———. "Knowledge and Belief in *Republic V*," *Archiv für Geschichte der Philosophie* 60 (1978), 121–39.

———. "Knowledge and Belief in *Republic 5–7*," in Stephen Everson (ed.), *Epistemology* (Cambridge: Cambridge University Press, 1990), 85–115.

———. "Knowledge and *Logos* in the *Theaetetus*," *Plato on Knowledge and Forms: Selected Essays* (Oxford: Clarendon Press, 2003); originally published in *Philosophical Review* 88 (1979), 366–97.

———. "Protagorean Relativisms," in J. Cleary and W. Wians (eds.), *Proceedings of the Boston Area Colloquium in Ancient Philosophy*, vol. 19 (Lanham, Md.: University Press of America, 1996), 211–43.

Frede, Michael. "Observations on Perception in Plato's Later Dialogues," *Essays in Ancient Philosophy* (Minneapolis: University of Minnesota Press, 1987), 3–8.

Gonzalez, Francisco J. "Propositions or Objects? A Critique of Gail Fine on Knowledge and Belief in *Republic V*," *Phronesis* 41 (1996), 245–75.

Harte, Verity. "Plato's Problem of Composition," in John J. Cleary and Gary M. Gurtler (eds.), *Proceedings of the Boston Area Colloquium in Ancient Philosophy 2001* vol. 17 (Leiden: Brill, 2002), 1–26.

Irwin, Terence. *Plato's Ethics* (Oxford: Oxford University Press, 1995).

Lee, Mi-Kyoung. *Epistemology after Protagoras: Responses to Relativism in Plato, Aristotle, and Democritus* (Oxford: Clarendon Press, 2005).

Lewis, Frank. "Two Paradoxes in the *Theaetetus*," in J. M. E. Moravcsik (ed.), *Patterns in Plato's Thought* (Dordrecht: D. Reidel, 1973), 123–49.

McDowell, John. *Plato: Theaetetus* (Oxford: Clarendon Press, 1973).

Menn, Stephen. "Collecting the Letters," *Phronesis* 43/4 (1998), 291–305.

Nehamas, Alexander. "*Episteme* and *Logos* in Plato's Later Thought," *Archiv für Geschichte der Philosophie* 66 (1984), 11–36.

Robinson, Richard. "Forms and Error in Plato's *Theaetetus*," *Essays in Greek Philosophy* (Oxford: Clarendon Press, 1969), 39–73; originally published in *Philosophical Review* 59 (1950), 3–30.

Sayre, K. *Plato's Analytic Method* (Chicago: University of Chicago Press, 1969).

Sedley, David. *The Midwife of Platonism: Text and Subtext in Plato's Theaetetus* (Oxford: Clarendon Press, 2004).

———. "Three Platonist Interpretations of the *Theaetetus*," in C. Gill and M. M. McCabe (eds.), *Form and Argument in Late Plato* (Oxford: Oxford University Press, 1996), 79–103.

Taylor, A. E. *Plato, the Man and His Work* (London: Methuen, 1926).

Waterlow, Sarah. "Protagoras and Inconsistency," *Archiv für Geschichte der Philosophie* 59 (1977), 29–33.

White, Nicholas. *Plato on Knowledge and Reality* (Indianapolis: Hackett, 1976).

Williams, C. F. J. "Referential Opacity and False Belief in the *Theaetetus*," *Philosophical Quarterly* 22 (1972), 289–302.

CHAPTER 18

# THE *SOPHIST* ON STATEMENTS, PREDICATION, AND FALSEHOOD

## LESLEY BROWN

AMONG several striking features of Plato's late dialogue, the *Sophist*, two stand out. First, it divides clearly into two very different parts. In the Outer Part, the main speaker, a nameless visitor from Elea in Italy (hereafter ES, for Eleatic Stranger) embarks on a discourse ostensibly designed to say what is a sophist. Using the so-called Method of Division, the ES offers no fewer than seven accounts of what the sophist is. Interrupting the seventh attempt, the Middle Part provides a striking contrast. There the ES undertakes a lengthy discussion—sparked by problems arising from defining a sophist as a maker of images and purveyor of false beliefs—which, for most readers, is of far greater philosophical interest and value.[1] Though such an ostensible "digression" is not unprecedented in Plato—one may think of the central books of the *Republic*—the disparity between the two parts is arresting.[2]

---

1. N. Notomi, *The Unity of Plato's Sophist* [*Unity*] (Cambridge, 1999), from whom I take the labels Outer Part and Middle Part, ch. 1 usefully compares other Platonic "digressions" with that of the "Middle Part."

2. It is especially hard to envisage how the work was received by anyone who was introduced to it at a reading, unaware of the surprise in store halfway through the work and of the different degree of difficulty and abstractness of the Middle Part.

A second striking feature is the markedly didactic approach. At the start, Socrates asks the ES (217a) to tell the inquirers what the people of Elea think about the issue in hand—namely, the relation between sophist, statesman, and philosopher: Are they three different kinds, or two, or just one? This approach is not the more usual "Let's discuss this matter together." The ES opts to present his material via question and answer with the intelligent Theaetetus but makes it clear that this is just a presentational device, not a true open-ended investigation.[3] Plato has something he wants to convey.

Both features highlight some of the key enigmas of the dialogue: What is the relation between the Outer and Middle Parts? How seriously are we to take the Outer Part, and is there a genuine, and successful, attempt to say what the sophist is? The fact that the ES offers seven alternative definitions, each purporting to be of *the sophist* (and not, as we might expect, of different types of sophist) gives us pause, as does the quirkiness of the "definitions," not least the final one.[4] On my unorthodox reading, we are not intended to regard any of the definitions as correct, especially since the search has assumed something that Plato cannot have accepted: that sophistry is an expertise, a *technē* (denied at *Gorgias* 464d).[5] Nonetheless, Plato ensures that we learn plenty from the dialogue about the many differences between sophistry and philosophy, but also that we note their common ground, especially their shared interest in puzzles, *aporiai*.[6] This will be a theme of the subsequent discussion.

This essay focuses on two key problems discussed and solved in the Middle Part: the Late-learners' problem (the denial of predication), and the problem of false statement. I look at how each is, in a way, a problem about correct speaking; how each gave rise to serious philosophical difficulty, as well as being a source of eristic troublemaking; and how the ES offers a definitive solution to both. As I said above, the *Sophist* displays an unusually didactic approach: Plato makes it clear that he has important matter to impart, and he does so with a firm hand, especially on the two issues I've selected.

---

3. From 217c–e. At d8, ES regrets he will not have a genuine exchange with Socrates. Cf. M. Frede, "The Literary Form of the Sophist" ["Literary Form"], in *Form and Argument in Late Plato,* ed. C. Gill and M. M. McCabe (Oxford, 1996), 138–39.

4. Resumé of first six at 231c–e; cf. 265a. Seventh "definition" at 268c ff: ES: "An imitator, of the contradiction-making sort of the dissembling part of conceit-imitation, of the semblance-making kind of image-making, who's marked off in the human (not the divine) portion of production a magic-trickery with arguments—if someone says such is the lineage and blood of the one who really is a sophist, then I think they'll be speaking the very truth."

5. L. Brown, "Definition and Division in the *Sophist*," in *Ancient Theories of Definition*, ed. D. Charles (Oxford, forthcoming).

6. For different views, see C. C. W. Taylor, "Socrates the Sophist," in *Remembering Socrates*, ed. L. Judson and V. Karasmanis (Oxford, 2004), 157–68; Notomi, *Unity.*

# 1. Lead-in to the Middle Part and Synopsis

Defining the sophist as a maker of images and falsehoods leads us—so the ES proclaims—into matters full of long-standing problems: "How one should express oneself in saying or judging that there really are falsehoods, without getting caught up in contradiction by such an utterance: that's extremely difficult, Theaetetus."[7] The puzzle is not (contra Notomi, *Unity*, 193) "Do falsehood and appearance really exist?" but "How should we express ourselves when saying they do, since to do so involves postulating that not being is?"[8] The ES then develops an exquisite series of *aporiai* about the expression "what is not/not being."[9] He goes on to lard his remarks with pointers to "uttering things correctly," "correct speaking," and so forth and ironically exclaims: "Don't look to me for correct speaking (*orthologia*) about what is not."[10]

The Middle Part proceeds by developing a wealth of problems, then systematically solving them.

(i)  Problems about not being or what is not (237d–241c)
   *Resolve: to show that what is not is in some respect, and what is is not in a way (241d–242a)*

(ii)  Problems about being (242b–251a)
   *Upshot: we're in as much difficulty about what is as we are about what is not (250e).*

(iii)  A new problem: the Late-learners' prohibition on saying that one thing is many things (251a–c)

(iv)  "Partial mixing" must be the correct one of three possible theories, since we can rule out "no-mixing" (Late-learners) and "total mixing" (251d–253b)
   *Greatest Kinds: a four-point program laid out (254b–d2)*

(v)  Five "Greatest Kinds" selected and proofs offered that they are five (i.e., points 1 and 2 of the four-point program) (254d–255e)

(vi)  Points 3 and 4: the Communion of Kinds—investigation of how change combines with the other four kinds; demonstration that change is and is not being; and that being is, in a way, not being (255e–257a)

---

7. From 236e4. I reject the emendation ad loc in the 1995 Oxford Classical Text, *Platonis Opera I*, ed. E. A. Duke, W. F. Hicken, W. S. M. Nicoll, D. B. Robinson, and J. C. G. Strachan (Oxford, 1995). Cf. Frede, "Literary Form," 143–44.

8. This alludes to the locution "say/judge what is not" "for make a false statement/judgment." See below, sec. 3.5.

9. On these *aporiai*, see especially G. E. L. Owen, "Plato on Not-Being," in *Plato 1*, ed. G. Fine (Oxford, 1999), 431–38. In (i), the term *mē on* can't be applied to anything without contradiction; in (ii), nothing that is—such as number—can be applied to it, so that ascribing either the number one (by the appellation *to mē on*, "what *is* not") or plurality (by the label *ta mē onta*, "things that *are* not") involves self-contradiction; in (iii), even the charge that "not being is inexpressible, unsayable and so forth" itself falls foul of the prohibition on treating it as something that is.

10. From 239a8, 239b4, 239b9; cf. 239d1.

(vii) Negation, negative expressions, not being and the parts of difference (257b–258e)

*Upshot: we have shown that, and what, not being is (258e–259e)*

*Remaining tasks: to show what statement is and that falsity in statement, judgment, and "appearing" is possible (260a–261b)*

(viii) What statement (*logos*) is; the difference between "names" and "verbs" and between naming and saying (261c–262e)

(ix) True and false statements (262e–263d)

(x) False judgment and false "appearing" (263d–264b)

# 2. THE LATE-LEARNERS' PROBLEM AND ITS SOLUTION IN THE DEMONSTRATION OF COMMUNION OF KINDS

## 2.1 The Late-learners' problem: summary and rival diagnoses

In these stretches, Plato unveils a problem at (iii), and solves it, after setting up a considerable apparatus, at (vi). He does so using some complex analyses, and this is where the issue of speaking correctly comes in—or, rather, of understanding correctly what has been said. He will tell us that we must not be disturbed by certain ways of speaking, when we say, of two kinds K and L, that "K is L and K is not L," and we will accept this once we recognize the different ways in which each conjunct is said (256a10–b4). So the ES promises a disambiguation, but what is it? A long-standing debate concerns whether his diagnosis of the problem and his solution turn crucially on pinpointing different meanings or uses of "is" (or rather, Greek *esti*).[11]

There are two major schools of interpretation, those I'll call "optimists" and "pessimists." The optimists, who include Ackrill, Vlastos, and others, argue as follows.[12] The puzzle that Plato attributes to certain unnamed people, who are rudely labeled "Late-learners" (*Soph* 251–52), depends on the refusal by these awkward

---

11. The debate is often conducted in terms of different *meanings* of "is," following Frege. M. Frede, "Plato's Sophist on False Statements" ["False"], in *Cambridge Companion to Plato*, ed. R. Kraut (Cambridge, 1990), 397–424, argues for a weaker claim, that Plato distinguishes *uses* but not *meanings* of "is," since different meanings would correspond to different forms, while Plato recognizes only one form of being. For the purposes of this essay, I do not distinguish between the two claims but treat them as interchangeable. Frede's position was developed first in *Prädikation und Existenzaussage* (Göttingen, 1967).

12. J. L. Ackrill, "Plato and the Copula: *Sophist* 251–59" ["Copula"], in *Plato 1: Metaphysics and Epistemology*, ed. G. Vlastos (Garden City, N.Y., 1971), 210–22; G. Vlastos, "An Ambiguity in the *Sophist*" ["Ambiguity"], *Platonic Studies* (Princeton, N.J., 1981), 288 n.44; J. van Eck, "Plato's Logical Insights: *Sophist* 254d–257a" ["Insights"], *Ancient Philosophy* 20/1 (2000), 71–74.

thinkers to recognize that in sentences of the form "A is B," "is" can have two meanings or uses: that of identity (is the same as) and that of the copula, the "is" of predication. Plato (according to the optimists) diagnoses their difficulty as the failure to recognize the two uses of "is," and later (at vi) displays the two uses, by the device of different paraphrases for "is" or *esti*. Triumph! Plato anticipated the great Gottlob Frege. The pessimists accept this distinction between different uses of "is" and agree that it is *needed* to dissolve the difficulty of the Late-learners. But they sorrowfully declare that the passage where Ackrill and others find Plato making this key discovery can't be read in that way; that, alas, Plato did not solve the problem correctly: did not discover the distinction between the two meanings of "is."[13] The optimists and the pessimists share a common premise: if Plato distinguished these two meanings or uses of "is," then he made an important discovery; and if he didn't, he missed making that same discovery. But this assumption is the one I'm going to challenge.

I accept that Plato does not distinguish these two meanings or uses of "is." But (unlike the pessimists), I'll show that he solved the problem in a *perfectly adequate* way, by distinguishing what I'll call "identity sentences" from predications. Indeed, following other writers, I dissent from the tradition (deriving from Frege's "On Concept and Object") of accepting a special "is" of identity. [14] My reading credits Plato with a successful solution to the "Late-learners' problem," one that does not appeal to the rather dubious distinction between the meanings of "is." Our task is to examine the texts and to give as faithful an interpretation as we can; it will be a bonus if, as a result, we can vindicate Plato's so-called logical insights.

At 251a5–6, the Stranger turns to the problem of how we call the same thing by many names (*pollois onomasi tauton touto . . . prosagoreuomen*) and describes the views of the so-called *opsimatheis*, Late-learners.[15]

Str. Well, when we speak of a man we name him lots of things as well, applying colors and shapes and sizes and vices and virtues to him, and in these and thousands of other ways we say that he is not only a man but also good and many other things. And so with everything else: though we assume that each thing is one, by the same way of speaking [*logos*] we speak of it as many and with many names.

Tht. What you say is true.

Str. This habit of ours seems to have provided a feast for the young and some old folk who've taken to studying late in life. For anyone can

13. Pessimists include D. Bostock, "Plato on 'Is-Not' (*Sophist* 254–9)" ["Is-Not"], *Oxford Studies in Ancient Philosophy* 2 (1984), 89–119; J. Gosling, *Plato* (London, 1973), ch. 13.

14. For arguments against isolating an "is" of identity, see F. Sommers, "Do We Need Identity?" *Journal of Philosophy* (1969),499–504; M. Lockwood, "On Predicating Proper Names" ["Predicating"], *Philosophical Review* (1975), 471–498 (who also argues for the interpretation of *Sophist* 255e–256e, which I favor); C. Kahn, *The Verb "Be" in Ancient Greek* (Dordrecht, 1973),e.g.at 372, 400; and B. Mates, "Identity and Predication in Plato," *Phronesis* 24/3 (1979), 211–29. Cf. the discussion in F. A. Lewis, "Did Plato Discover the Estin of Identity?" ["Did Plato"], *California Studies in Classical Antiquity* 8 (1975), 113–42.

15. For discussion of who the Late-learners represent, see F. M. Cornford, *Plato's Theory of Knowledge* [*Theory*] (repr. London, 1960), 254.

weigh in with the quick objection that it is impossible for what is many to be one and for what is one to be many, and they just love not allowing you to call a man good, but only the good good and the man a man. I dare say, Theaetetus, that you often meet people who are keen on that sort of line. Some of them are getting on in years, and their intellectual bankruptcy makes them marvel at that sort of thing and suppose that in this they have made an exceptionally clever discovery.

So this is their position: (i) they object to calling one thing many and with many names (251b3); (ii) they don't allow you to *legein agathon anthrōpon* (251b8–c1) (either "to call a man good" or "to say the man is good"); and (added later) (iii) they don't allow you to call anything something different, since they don't accept that anything has communion with the attribute of another thing (252b9–10, paraphrase).

Presumably they forbid both using a compound description "good man" and saying "the man is good." And presumably this is because they assume that the only function of a word is to name, so they rule out both "good man" and "the man is good" as "making one many" (by naming two things, man and good). They refuse to accept that it is harmless and indeed useful to speak of something "as many and with many names": that is, to apply a number of attributes, as in one of the above locutions.

So much for what the Late-learners don't allow. What do they allow? Here there is a controversy. On some interpretations Plato tells us that they don't allow any sentences at all, but only names or namings.[16] I disagree. I think we are told that the Late-learners do allow some sentences, provided that in whatever you utter you don't "make one thing many"; provided you only call a thing itself, not something else. A sentence may be permitted in which you say that a thing is itself, if the many names it uses are for the same thing. "You must only say a thing is itself, you mustn't say it is something else" (cf. 252b9–10).

"They only allow you to say to say 'the man is a man' but not 'the man is good.' " Must this be read as charging them with a failure to understand "is," with not allowing an "is" of predication, in a sentence such as "the man is good"? Not necessarily. It may just be that they make a mistake about the whole locution—in particular, about the role of what comes after the "is." The Late-learners assume that its role is to name the very same thing as the subject term names. On the same ground they would reject the appellation "good man," with the thought that, since both words are names, and are not synonymous, then two things, not one, would be named by that expression. They do not accept predication, what Plato will later call *methexis*. And it is to answer them that the following sections are written, in which the sharing or *koinōnia* of kinds is described. On this point Ackrill—in my

---

16. J. M. E. Moravcsik, "Being and Meaning in the *Sophist*," *Acta Philosophica Fennica* 14 (1962), 57–59; Gosling, *Plato*, 219–20.

view—is quite correct; but not when he reads Plato as identifying the mistake made by the Late-learners in terms of a mistake about "is."

Confirmation of my diagnosis comes from a later source, the account of the views of the Megarian Stilpo in Plutarch's *Adversus Colotem*.[17] Stilpo apparently, like the Late-learners, rejected statements like "the man is good" but also statements like "the horse runs." In other words, *even sentences without "is" were rejected*, presumably because the second term did not name the same thing as the first term. Stilpo's difficulty, then, does not concern the role of "is." Rather, it is a refusal to accept that parts of *logoi* are used not to name but to predicate, or to attribute, something to the subject.

To sum up: the Late-learners allow only identity sentences, and their mistake is the mistake of not understanding predication, or "sharing in."[18] Some earlier arguments in the dialogue had gone wrong because they treated predicates like names and so treated predicative sentences as identity sentences.[19] Plato's task is to explain the notion of predication, of sharing in, in order to show that the following is possible: K is L (because it shares in L), and K is not L (because K is different from L). *A thing can be what it also is not*: this is what the following section is designed to show, in answer to the mistaken view of the Late-learners. As I have argued, we don't have to construe the problem as a problem about meanings of "is" but, rather, as a problem about types of sentence: identity sentences versus predications. And so to credit Plato with logical insight, we don't have to read his solution as distinguishing different meanings of *esti*—which is a good thing, because he doesn't do so, as we shall see.

## 2.2 The "Communion of Kinds" as offering the solution to the Late-learners problem

We fast-forward through the Middle Part, omitting sections (iv) and (v) in which—inter alia—the ES introduces the notion that dialectic involves investigating the relations of kinds, and draws an analogy between letters of the alphabet and kinds, such that some kinds operate in the way vowels do, enabling the joining of letters while being themselves one type of letter. We omit also the first two points of the four-point program, the introduction of the five so-called Greatest Kinds—*kinēsis* (change), *stasis* (stability), being, same, and different—and the intriguing proofs of their distinctness from one another. We resume where the ES promises to fulfill the remaining points: (3) to see what power of combination they have with one another (4) in order to get hold of *to on* (being) and *to mē on* (not

17. Quoted in N. Denyer, *Language, Truth and Falsehood* [*Language*] (Cambridge, 1991), 34–35.

18. I discuss below (sec. 2.4) Frede's alternative view that the key distinction is between the uses of "is" in self-predications (which the Late-learners allow) and in other-predications (which they forbid).

19. Those at 243d–244b and 250a8–d3. These arguments are designed to be parallel and to be fallacious: the second ends in a contradiction, and the reader is clearly invited to discern what has gone wrong, then to connect it with the Late-learners' *aporia*.

being) and to show that it is safe to say that *to mē on* really is *mē on* (not being really is not being).

## The "Communion of Kinds" (255e–256e): Plato's "four quartets"

It is vital to the understanding of Plato's aims in this section to see how system-atically the passage is organized, as many earlier commentators have shown. The kinds are taken *kath'hen*, one by one. One is chosen, change, and its interrelations with each of the other four kinds are examined in turn. I call these groups of sentences the "four quartets" because in a typical group there are four distin-guishable propositions linking change with the other kind under discussion.

Group 1: Change and stability

|         | 1a | Change is different from stability | (255e10) |
|---------|----|-----------------------------------|----------|
| So      | 1b | Change is not stability           | (e14)    |
| But     | 1c | Change is                         | (256a1)  |
| because | 1d | Change shares in being            | (a1)     |

Group 2: Change and the same

|         | 2a | Change is different from the same | (256a3)  |
|---------|----|-----------------------------------|----------|
| So      | 2b | Change is not the same            | (a5)     |
| But     | 2c | Change is the same                | (a7)     |
| because | 2d | Change shares in the same         | (a7,b1)  |

Group 3: Change and different

|         | 3a | Change is different from different | (256c5) |
|---------|----|------------------------------------|---------|
| So      | 3b | Change is not different            | (c8)    |
| But     | 3c | Change is different                | (c8)    |

[because Change shares in different (not in text)]

Group 4: Change and being

|         | 4a | Change is different from being | (d5)    |
|---------|----|--------------------------------|---------|
| So      | 4b | Change is not being            | (d8)    |
| But     | 4c | Change is being                | (d8–9)  |
| because | 4d | Change shares in being         | (d9)    |

It is clear that Groups 2, 3, and 4 have the same pattern, viz:

|        | a | K is different from L |
|--------|---|----------------------|
| So     | b | K is not L (*denial of identity between K and L, since it follows from a*) |
| But    | c | K is L (*L is predicated of K, as shown by paraphrase at d*) |
| Because | d | K shares in L |

Because Group 2 is the first to exemplify this pattern, Plato treats it at length, taking pains to explain why the apparent contradiction between 2b and 2c is not a real one. He explains that 2b asserts what 2a asserts, and thus does not contradict 2c, which is equivalent to 2d. The same point is made more briefly for Group 3, and at greater length in Group 4, the target of the exercise. The apparent contradiction between the b and c sentences is made possible because the names of the three kinds concerned—same, different, and being—can function both as abstract nouns (as required in b) and as adjectives (as required in c). I return to this point later.

We have noticed a pattern common to the later three groups.[20] What is Plato up to in this carefully worked passage? What are his aims and achievements?

## Common ground to all interpretations

Plato aims to give a careful account of the connections between the sample kind change and the four other kinds, in turn; and to do so by offering analyses, in terms of "sharing in" (*metechein* and similar expressions), of key sentences expressing these connections, sentences which take the form "K is L" or "K is not L" where K stands for change and L for one of the other kinds, in order. He does this to show why conjunctions of the form "K is not L and K is L" are not, despite appearances, contradictory, and why each conjunct can be true, when properly construed.

In particular, he aims to show that "change is not being and change is being" is not a contradiction, that both conjuncts are true and thus to vindicate the status of not being. This is Group 4, the one it was all building up to.

## Accepted by most but not all (Michael Frede has a different view)

Plato uses the device of analysis in terms of *metechein* (sharing in) to distinguish statements of identity from predications. More precisely, he shows that "K is not L and K is L" can be true provided that "K is not L" denies that the kind K is the kind L—that is, denies the identity of K and L—while "K is L" is a predication or

---

20. Group 1 is different at 1c, since the ES has insisted that change cannot in any way share in stability: 252d2–11, 255ab, esp. a11–b1. The text at 256b6–8 considers the counterfactual "if change were to share in stability in some way," clearly implying that this is impossible, despite our expectation that change, as a form, must be stable.

attribution of L to K (in other words, says that K shares in L). I call this the "minimal interpretation" of the section.

Now the important question: how does Plato hope to achieve this?

## The optimists' view: distinguishing meanings or uses of esti

The crucial lines are 256a10–b4. In these lines Plato makes the ES explain why the two previous claims, 2b and 2c (change is not the same and change is the same) must both be admitted.

> Str. Change, then, is both the same and not the same—we must agree and not dispute it. For when we said [it was] the same and not the same, we were not speaking in a similar way, but when [we say it is] the same, we say that because of its sharing in the same in relation to itself, but when [we say it is] not the same, that, by contrast, is because of its communion with the different, through which it is separated from the same and isn't it but different, so that once again it's rightly said to be not the same.

Note, "we were not speaking in a similar way" (ou . . . homoiōs eirēkamen). The optimists argue that this draws attention to an ambiguity, and we may agree. They argue further that the ambiguity in question must be that of the verb "is," since they hold, in the Frege tradition, that this is the correct account. But a major problem is that in these key lines Plato does not draw attention to the word esti; worse, he actually omits it in the crucial sentence. We must indeed supply it, but still, if he had really been signaling an ambiguity in esti, surely he would not have omitted it at the vital moment.[21]

The optimists have a reply here. Even if Plato omitted it, he must still have located the ambiguity in the esti. They argue as follows. Consider the three pairs of contradictory propositions (2b+c, 3b+c, and 4b+c). The esti is the only constituent common to these pairs that could account for the ambiguity in each quartet.[22] Now I agree that we should look for an account of these lines that can also serve as an explanation of the other groups as well, since Plato evidently constructed the passage carefully and means his account of Group 2 to serve also for the two later groups.[23] But optimists are wrong to claim that the only element common to all three that could explain the ambiguity is the verb esti. The three pairs share the

---

21. Defending the "optimist" line, van Eck, "Insights," 71–74, argues that Plato does "distinguish a non-predicative sense of 'is' at 256b3–4," albeit using gegone rather than esti. We may agree that gegone here means "is, as a result of," and that in gegonen ouk ekeino all' heteron (isn't it but something different) the "isn't it" denies identity between change and tauton. But it doesn't follow that Plato is distinguishing a nonpredicative sense of "is."

22. Vlastos, "Ambiguity," 291 n.46.

23. For this reason, we may reject a different interpretation (Gosling, Plato, 218–19) by which the solution is to add different completions to "the same" in the two conjuncts. Such a reading, though possible for Group 2, will not allow an equivalent solution for Groups 3 and 4, which Plato clearly intends.

same *form*, and the ambiguity may be due to that, not to the occurrence of a given word ("is") used in two ways.

## 2.3  Plato's solution: what ambiguity is he pointing out?

There are two alternative solutions that I prefer to the claim that Plato locates the ambiguity in "is."[24]

### *Solution 1*

*Solution 1* locates the ambiguity in what follows the *esti*. In other words, Plato points to a difference in "the same" between 2b "Change is not the same" and 2c "Change is the same," as suggested by Owen.[25] And it is quite correct that the words "the same" play these different roles in the two sentences! Even those who accept two meanings or uses of *esti* must agree that there are *also* two meanings or uses of *tauton*. To say change is not *tauton* is to say it is not the kind, sameness. And the same goes for 3b (change is not the kind different) and 4b (change is not the kind being). It may be helpful to compare the uses of the word "blue" in the following sentences:

- s1 The sky is blue. ("Blue" used as an adjective, to attribute blueness to the sky)
- s2 The color of the sky is blue. ("Blue" used to designate the color, blue)

The crucial item is the word or phrase that follows *esti*; that is, in Group 2, *tauton* (the same).

Now if Plato were being accurate, he should write *to tauton* "the the same" in 2b, to show that the phrase is being used as an abstract noun to refer to the kind sameness. And he should write *to heteron* in 3b, and *to on* in 4b. It is only because he doesn't do so that he is able to produce apparent contradictions. If he had written, at 4b, "change is not *to on*," that evidently does not contradict *Kinēsis estin on*, which means "change is a being (is a thing that is)." One reason he does not use these forms is that Greek, where possible, avoids the definite article after the verb "to be," so Plato felt free to leave it out—in order to achieve his apparent contradictions.[26] To repeat, the word *tauton* plays two different roles, adjectival in 2c (change is *tauton*) but as an abstract noun in 2b (change is not *tauton*). Should we not give Plato credit for pointing out this difference of role, when he offers the elucidation in the key lines 256a10–b5? After all, he does seem to lay the emphasis on *tauton* in the crucial sentence.

---

24. For a number of suggestions about what Plato's solution is, see Lewis, "Did Plato." His preferred solution (134–36) has Plato invoking a special sense of *not* found in 2b, *change is not tauton*, and also in 3b and 4b.

25. Owen, "Not Being," 258 n.63; Lockwood, "Predicating," 479 n.12.

26. This point about Greek usage (cf. Lewis, "Did Plato") answers Bostock's objection ("Is-Not," 93).

To support this interpretation, I make one philosophical point and one appeal to the text. The philosophical point, hinted at above, is that we must admit that there is a dual use of the words "the same," whether or not we accept, with Frege and others, a dual use of the word "is." Usually a different form of the word will be used where the sentence is an identity sentence; for instance, we will say "change is different" (adjective) but "it is not difference" (abstract noun). But where there is the same form (as in the pair "the sky is blue" and "the color of the sky is blue"), we have to assume a different function (once as an adjective, once naming the color blue).

The textual point in support of this interpretation is drawn from some curious lines that follow Group 2.

> Str. And if this very thing, change, were to participate in any way in stability, it would not be at all odd to call it stable (*stasimon*).
>
> Tht. Very true, if we are to agree that some of the kinds are willing to mix with one another and others are not. (256b6–10)

These lines have puzzled commentators. Why are they here? Is something missing (as, e.g., Cornford believed)?[27] At any rate, the ES is evidently not asserting that change does share in a way in stability. Rather, the sentence is a counterfactual: if change were to share in any way in *stasis*, it would not be odd to call it *stasimon* (or, to say it is *stasimon*, stable). Now, we know that change doesn't share in *stasis*, for it has been emphasized several times (cf. n.20). Why does the Stranger revert to it? If I am right that he has just pointed out the different roles for *tauton* in 2b and 2c, then perhaps he is underlining the adjectival role of *tauton*, where "is *tauton*" means "shares in *tauton*," by displaying the parallel with "shares in *stasis*" which becomes "is *stasimon*." This–drawing attention to the adjectival form, *stasimon*, as parallel to the adjectival function in 2c, 3c, and 4c—would partly explain this otherwise out-of-place remark.

## Objection to my proposal and reply

It has been objected that "the names *tauton*, *heteron* and *on* cannot vary in sense within any of the three sentences, for . . . the meaning is fixed unambiguously by Plato's assumption that each name refers to the identical Form within both of the apparently contradictory conjuncts."[28] Reply: Not so, and here is an argument to show it. Suppose Plato had chosen to pursue the Communion of Kinds with the assertions that 5a being is different from stability, so 5b being is not stability, but 5c being is stable. There's no danger here of an apparent contradiction, but still Plato could analyze 5b and 5c on the lines of 2b and 2c, analyzing 5c as being shares in stability. No one would claim that the sole function of "stable" (Greek *stasimon*) in our imaginary 5c is to refer to the form or kind stability, though that is part of its

27. Cornford, *Theory*, proposed a lacuna after 256b7.
28. Vlastos, "Ambiguity," 291 n.46. Bostock, a "pessimist," uses the same argument ("Is-Not," 97).

function. Its evidently adjectival form would make it obvious that its role was different from that of "stability" in 5b. And presumably Plato could have made this point about "the same" as used as an adjective in 2c, despite Vlastos's claims.

### Solution 2: more modest

Perhaps we are wrong to think that Plato identifies one element as the locus of ambiguity. Just because he offers a paraphrase does not mean we must attach each element of the paraphrase to an element of the original sentence. Perhaps instead he simply notes, quite correctly, and shows by means of paraphrase, that in each pair one sentence functions to deny identity between change and the other kind (Change is not the kind being), while the second sentence predicates that kind of change (Change is a being). This would be a holistic solution, rather than an atomistic one. If we seek the correct account of why the pairs of sentences are not contradictory, in spite of appearances, this may be the safest answer. The ambiguity depends on the whole sentence forms, not on any one element. If that is all Plato wishes to convey on the matter, then it is perfectly adequate, in my view.

## 2.4 Different uses of "is": an alternative interpretation

One further line of interpretation remains to be discussed, that of Michael Frede. I label his line "superoptimist" since he too holds that Plato *is* adverting to a crucial distinction in uses of "is"/*esti*, but, unlike the optimists, he holds that this single distinction is the only one needed to solve all the problems in the *Sophist*. (Optimists such as Ackrill, however, hold that at other points Plato is also distinguishing the existential "is.") The key distinction, for Frede, is the one between the use of "is" to say what a thing *is in itself* or *by itself*, and the use of "is" to say what a thing *is by standing in the appropriate relation to something else.*[29] He illustrates the distinction with reference to two uses of "is white." Socrates is white by standing *in a relation to a color* (i.e., second use of "is"). The color white, however, is white *by being this feature*, not by having it (i.e., first, "in itself" use of "is"). Like the optimists, Frede takes his favored distinction to be the key to both the Late-learners' problem and the Communion of Kinds passage. The Late-learners—on his view—allow only "in itself" predications and disallow the second kind, the kind we use when we say "Socrates is white."

   A full discussion of Frede's rich position is beyond the scope of this essay.[30] In brief, I find his account of the Late-learners' position highly plausible, equally plausible with the account I favor, according which Late-learners allow (in effect) identity statements but disallow predications. Each interpretation is compatible

---

29. Frede, "False," 400.

30. In L. Brown, "Being in the Sophist: A Syntactical Enquiry," in *Plato 1*, ed. G. Fine (Oxford, 1999), 474–76, I discuss Frede's claim that this distinction features in the proof of the nonidentity of different and being at 255c–d. At 470–71, I outline the interpretation for which 2.3 above gives a fuller argument.

with the prohibition on calling anything something different. Frede's view would prefer, as the Late-learners' slogan, "you can say what a thing is by itself, but not what it is in some other way," while the identity view would imagine the slogan "you can say a thing is itself, but not anything else." Each fits what we are told about the Late-learners' theory.

However, we want to find Plato demonstrating in the Communion of Kinds section just the distinction that the Late-learners refused to accept, and here—in this later passage—I find Frede's interpretation less plausible. Why? Consider the opening lines of Group 1 above—1a, change is different from stability; 1b, change is not stability. This pattern is repeated, for the first two sentences of the next three groups: K is different from L, so K is not L. We must surely expect to interpret 2b, *Change is not the same*, 3b, *Change is not different*, and 4b, *Change is not being* along the lines of 1b. But 1b surely is a denial of identity. Frede's interpretation wants 2b, 3b, and 4b to be read as denials of "in itself predication," not as denials of identity.[31] Thus 2b is to be understood as "Change is not, in itself, the same," and so on for the remainder. But the equivalent reading of 1b cannot succeed. If Plato had wanted 1b to be a denial of "in itself predication," then he would have written "Change is not by its own nature at rest" (cf. 250c6–7, where the point is made that being, by its own nature, is neither moving nor at rest). Since I find it impossible to read the negative claims in the four quartets in any other way than as denials of identity, I cannot accept Frede's reading.

To conclude this discussion of Plato's treatment of the Late-learners' problem, I raise and reply to two questions. First: "The so-called problem of the Late-learners is so silly that we can't imagine anyone being seriously bothered by it. Did Plato really need to go to such lengths to refute so absurd a view?" In reply, I endorse Ackrill's claim: the thesis was put forward not only by elderly jokers but also by serious thinkers who felt themselves obliged to maintain it for what seemed to them compelling theoretical reasons.[32] We have already seen (sec. 2.1), that it was also maintained by the Megarian thinker Stilpo. And, as Denyer has shown, variants on it have appealed to philosophers such as Bradley, who worried about saying that a lump of sugar is sweet and white and hard: "A thing is not any of its qualities, if you take that quality by itself; if 'sweet' were the same as 'simply sweet,' the thing would clearly not be sweet. And again, insofar as the sugar is sweet it is not white or hard; for these properties are all distinct." And so on.[33] One or both of the following may prompt the thesis: a metaphysical view about what the world ultimately consists in, or a view of language that sees naming as the only function of bits of language. Bizarre though it may seem to us, we cannot dismiss it as a mere sophism unworthy of serious attention from Plato.

---

31. Frede, "False," 422: his chief reason for denying that in this section sentences of the form "X is not Y" are nonidentity sentences is that 263b11–12, which seems to refer back to 256e6–7, must concern denials of predication, not denials of identity. Hence his wish to read this section as also featuring denials of (in-itself) predication. But in my view, this solution to what is a real problem comes at too high a price.

32. Ackrill, "Copula," 215.

33. F. H. Bradley, *Appearance and Reality*, 2nd ed. (Oxford, 1932), 16, quoted in Denyer, *Language*, 44.

The second question asks why, when the Late-learners' puzzle concerns statements about particulars such as "the man is tall and handsome," the solution in the Communion of Kinds section concerns statements about kinds. The answer, I think, is this. In each case (a predication about a particular and one about a kind) we have, in effect, a claim that one thing is many things, and that it *is* what it also *is not*. Now the claim that particulars, such as Socrates, are many things isn't so troubling for Platonic metaphysics. But the claim, of a Form or kind, that it must be many things, and must be what it also is not, needed more defense. *Republic* V had claimed that Forms always are, and in no way are not. But in the Communion of Kinds section, the ES shows not just the difference between identity statements and predications in general but how even Forms or kinds can be spoken of in both these ways. The upshot (in Group 4) is the demonstration that a kind such as change both is a being and is not being (i.e., it shares in being even though it is not the Form being). Thus, we have the first place in which the Resolve is fulfilled (see synopsis in sec. 2): showing that what is not being [i.e., is not the kind being] nonetheless is in a way [i.e., it is a being, and thus lots of other things besides]. In other words, we have been shown not only what the Late-learners denied—how it is legitimate and true to say that one thing is many things, and is what it also is not—but also how a kind (other than being) can be a being and yet not be being itself. Understanding just what is being said in these apparently contradictory locutions is the key to resolving them.

## 3. THE ACCOUNT OF FALSE STATEMENT

Once again we fast-forward, omitting discussion of the most puzzling section (vii) of the dialogue. I say a little about it later; for now we note that it concludes with the declaration that the inquirers have found what the form of not being is.[34] But that, we are told, is not the end of the inquiry. By means of a carefully placed series of signposts (from 260b onward) the ES stresses that fulfilling the Resolve is not enough for demonstrating the possibility of false statement.[35] He emphasizes that showing that kinds mix was necessary but not sufficient to solve all their problems and, in particular, was insufficient to solve the problem of falsehood. To do that, they must also investigate what statement and judgment (*logos* and *doxa*) are, to see if they can be false (to see if "not being can mix with them" (260b10–c4)). Theaetetus repeats the point (261ab), and it's made a third time by the ES (261c).

---

34. "Having demonstrated what the nature of the different is, and that it's parcelled out over all the things that are, set against each other, we've dared to say that the part of it set against the being of each thing—that very thing really is not being" (258d).

35. "Statement" is the best translation for *logos* in this section. It has a range of meanings that include reason, speech, and definition.

Plato was evidently concerned that the reader should see that a fresh topic has been broached and that they are moving to a new discussion.

By almost universal agreement, the section in which the ES explains what a *logos* is and how there can be false ones is one of the most successful and important of the whole dialogue. Though the account is well known, I here outline it once again, discuss how it should be understood (3.2–3.4), then ask what is most valuable in the account (3.5).[36]

## 3.1 The account of what a statement is

The key to understanding how a *logos* can be false lies in first understanding what a *logos* is. Here Plato proceeds with the utmost care. He scripts a scene in which Theaetetus first misunderstands (261d7) and leaps to a wrong conclusion. This allows the ES, in correcting him (262b2), to emphasize the novelty of his new point, which is this. With words as well as with kinds, "partial mixing" is the order of the day, if statements are to eventuate. But the ES informs Theaetetus that the "partial mixing" of words he is about to expound must not be confused with the "partial mixing" of kinds discussed in the four-point program. Words (*onomata*) come in two varieties: names and verbs (*onomata* and *rhēmata*: thus *onoma* has both a general and a more specific meaning). Not any concatenation of words makes a *logos*; rather, a *logos* must combine a name with a verb, where "verb" is the designation used of actions and "name" is the designation used of the doers of those actions.[37] Neither a string of verbs (such as "walks runs sleeps") nor a string of names (such as "lion deer horse") makes a *logos*. A *logos* is special kind of interweaving; someone who interweaves a verb with a name doesn't only name but succeeds in saying something (262d2–6).[38]

Plato here makes a crucial point. Saying something—what the utterer of a statement does—is different from merely naming. To achieve this "saying something" a *logos* needs two parts with different functions: "one part whose function is to name, refer to, identify a subject, and another part by means of which we say something, state something, predicate something of or about the subject."[39] As Frede's terminology shows, we may think of the distinction in a variety of ways.

---

36. My account owes much to that of Michael Frede, "False," sec. III, though I dissent from his understanding of one major issue: how to understand the reference to what is different in the paraphrase the ES offers of what it is for a statement to be false. See also Crivelli, chapter 9 in this volume.

37. "An expression we apply to actions we call a verb" (262a2). The word order, together with the use of *legein* rather than *kalein*, indicate that this is not intended as a strict definition of *rhēma*. Cf. M. Hoekstra and F. Scheppers, "*Onoma, rhēma* et *logos* dans le *Cratyle* et le *Sophiste* de Platon," *L'Antiquité Classique* (2003), 69, who insist, plausibly, that the major point of the passage is not the new assignation of familiar words for words (*onoma, rhēma*) to distinct roles but the recognition that a special kind of fitting together (*harmottein*) is involved in any *logos*.

38. Interweaving, *plegma*; cf. *sumplekōn* (weaving together) at 262d4.

39. Frede, "False," 413–14.

Perhaps the key idea is the distinction between the part of the statement used to refer to the subject (the *onoma*, name, or subject-expression) and the part used to predicate something of the subject.[40] Also with Frede, we can agree that if Plato intends to distinguish word classes, his point that each *logos* has a noun and a verb picks out only a subclass of statements, whereas he seems to want to characterize simple statements more generally "and really is looking for syntactical categories."[41] With the distinction between naming and saying, and with the recognition that a statement is essentially structured, as a special weaving together of parts with different functions, certain puzzles found in earlier dialogues—notably *Euthydemus*—denying the possibility of false statement or judgment and of contradiction are finally put to rest.[42] What the puzzles had in common was that they treated a *logos* as an unstructured whole; many of them portrayed saying and/or judging like naming, using a "scandalous analogy" (Burnyeat) between judging and touching.

## 3.2 The account of true and false statements

After stressing that a *logos* is special kind of structured whole, only one of whose parts has the function of referring to the thing it is about, the ES can at once get Theaetetus to agree that both "Theaetetus sits" and "Theaetetus flies" are, by the above account, statements.[43] Then he proceeds smartly to explain the truth of the one and the falsity of the other. He does so twice over, in what I shall call the two "Final Formulae for Falsehood," the first (which has been much discussed) at 263b4–11, and the second (relatively neglected) at 263d1–4.

> First Final Formula for Falsehood. (A) The true one says of things that are about you that they are; while (B) the false one says different things from the things that are; that is, (C) it says, of things that are not, that they are. In a

40. I cannot agree with D. Sedley, *Plato's Cratylus* (Cambridge, 2003), that in all this *Cratylus* prefigures *Sophist*. Sedley claims Plato in *Cratylus* uses the terms *onoma* and *rhēma* to focus on "the two linguistic acts . . . of naming and predication" and that Socrates shows "awareness that *onomata* and *rhēmata* are functionally disparate items within the statement." Denyer, *Language*, 148–50, correctly remarks that in *Cratylus* (as elsewhere in Plato outside this stretch of *Sophist*) *rhēma* typically means phrase, group of words, as opposed to *onoma*, a single word. Contra Sedley, *Crat* 399ab and 399b7, and 421d–e are best explained in this way. Cf. *Sophist* 257b6–c2 (before the official demarcation and identification of *onoma* and *rhēma*): in support of Denyer, note that at 257b6 *mē mega* (not large) is called a *rhēma*, but at c6 the ES speaks of the *onomata* which follow the "not" in expressions such as "not large."

41. Frede, "False," 413.

42. Frede, "False," 413–17, and M. Burnyeat, "Plato on How Not to Speak about Not-Being" ["How Not To"] in *Le Style de la pensée*, ed. M. Canto and P. Pellegrin (Paris, 2002), 40–65. Burnyeat holds that in the earlier works Plato hints at the vital distinction between the subject of a *logos* and what's said about it, but concedes that prior to *Sophist* there is no "hint of the grammatical or syntactic distinction drawn there between the part of an assertoric sentence that refers to the subject and the part that ascribes to that subject a predicate such as flying or sitting" (45).

43. "Plato quite pointedly lets the Eleatic Stranger settle the question of reference for the sample statements discussed before he lets him go on to consider their truth or falsehood." Frede, "False," 418.

problematic sequel the ES continues, in a highly elliptical manner: (D) (but it says) things that are, but are different (from what is) about you.[44]

To understand all this, we must first eliminate the plural forms, a stylistic device loved by Plato but highly confusing to the reader. The chief warrant for doing so is this: the sample true *logos* "Theaetetus sits," which plainly says one thing about Theaetetus, is described as saying *ta onta*, things that are.[45] Replacing plurals with singulars, and leaving to one side for now a host of problems with this stretch, I recast (A) and (C) in what follows, but postpone discussion of the controversial (B) and (D) until later.[46]

The true one (A) says, of something that is concerning you (viz., sitting) that it is. The false one (C) says, of something that is not (viz., flying) that it is. (Probably we must understand "concerning you" here, too.) In other words, the false one is false because it says, concerning Theaetetus, that what is not (viz., flying) is concerning him. Now, if we confine our attention pro tem to (A) and (C), we recognize how elegantly they dispose of the idea that a false statement simply "says what is not" where this is supposed to be like (the impossible) touching what is not. Plato has distinguished "saying something about something" from "naming." Each statement names Theaetetus, each is about (*peri*) him—that is, is about something that is, and thereby secures its reference—and each says something about him. Plato can now say, without fear, that the false one says, about Theaetetus, what is not, but says that it is concerning him. Even confining ourselves to (A) and (C), we find a fully satisfactory account of true and false statements, at least if we confine ourselves to simple assertions.[47]

44. For a full discussion, including a proof that *hōs estin* at 263b4 must be translated "that they are," not "as they are," see D. Keyt, "Plato on Falsity" ["Falsity"], in *Exegesis and Argument*, ed. E. Lee, A. Mourelatos, and R. Rorty (Assen, 1973), 287–91. D. Sedley, *The Midwife of Platonism* (Oxford, 2004), 133 n.19, proposes a reassignment of speakers in the problematic lines b9–11.

45. Further support for replacing plurals with singulars comes at 263d1–4, where the statement "Theaetetus flies" is said to be "a synthesis of verbs and names" when it is plainly a synthesis of one verb and one name. This licenses us to rewrite the entire sentence replacing plurals with singulars, as discussed below.

46. Those who favor the so-called Oxford interpretation, discussed below, cannot agree that the use of the plurals is merely a stylistic device, for they invoke the plural in (B) 263b7 to indicate that it is correct to import a universal quantifier into the translation. Thus: "Plato could have said in 263b3–4 that the true statement says of something that is that it is. But he wants to get a reference to the whole class of things that are, relative to a given subject, into the characterization of the true statement, as this will be needed to get an adequate characterization of the false statement. This corresponds to the need for a universal quantifier in a proper characterization, first of the use of '...is not...' along Plato's lines, and then of falsehood, a need several commentators have rightly insisted on" (Frede "False," 420). I dispute this line of argument below.

47. Contra Frede ("False," 418), I agree with J. McDowell, "Falsehood and Not-Being in Plato's *Sophist*" ["Falsehood"], in *Language and Logos*, ed. M. Schofield and M. Nussbaum (Cambridge, 1982), 133 n.35, that, as they stand, the Formulae cover only true and false *affirmative* statements. Nonetheless, it is clear how they can be adapted for *negative* truths and falsehoods.

## 3.3 How to understand "different" in the Formulae for Falsehood? Three readings

Now we turn to (B) and (D).

> (B) The false one says different things from the things that are. (263b7)

We have seen this is used as equivalent to "saying things that are not." And I argued above that we may and should replace plurals by singulars, giving

> (Bˢ) The false one says something different from what is.

How should this be understood? One difficulty is immediately evident; I label it the "Problem." Suppose Theaetetus is sitting, and suppose I state, "Theaetetus is talking." Then I have said about Theaetetus something that is different from something that is about him—viz., sitting. But of course he may be talking as well as sitting, in which case my statement is true. But (B) was supposed to characterize a false statement. So, on the simplest interpretation, it is a non-starter.

Two main readings of (B) have gained support, each of which avoids the Problem. Following Keyt, we call them the "Oxford interpretation" and the "incompatibility interpretation."[48] However, I reject them both and defend a less popular, but increasingly supported, reading, as the correct one.

> *Reading 1, the Oxford interpretation.* The false *logos*, "Theaetetus flies," says, about Theaetetus, something that is different from everything that is about him. On this reading the Problem is solved. "Theaetetus is talking" will indeed be false if talking differs from everything which is about him (i.e., which is true of him).
>
> *Reading 2, the incompatibility interpretation.* The false *logos*, "Theaetetus flies," says, about Theaetetus, something that is *incompatible with* what is about him. This too solves the Problem. If I ascribe an attribute incompatible with what is about Theaetetus, I must indeed be making a false statement about him. While talking is merely different from sitting, flying is—or was before the invention of the airplane—incompatible with sitting.

But while both of these solve the Problem, neither of them can easily be extracted from what Plato wrote. The Oxford interpretation faces the objection that there is no good reason to supply, in (B) and (D), that universal quantifier—the "every"—which is so crucial.[49] An even more serious obstacle is the wording of the Second Formula for Falsehood, at 263d1–4, which is rarely discussed.[50]

---

48. Keyt, "Falsity," 294–95. He discusses four alternative readings in all, but not my preferred one, Reading 3. See also Crivelli, chapter 9 in this volume.

49. Cf. n.46. An appeal to the plural in *ta onta* "things that are" at b7 is illegitimate. In 263b4–5 we read: "The true one ('Theaetetus sits') says the things that are that they are about you." Since *ta onta* evidently refers to just one thing/verb, "sits," it must there be understood as "what is." We cannot, with the Oxford interpretation, suddenly read it to mean "everything that is" two lines later.

50. As noted in J. Szaif, *Platons Begriff der Wahrheit* [*Wahrheit*] (Munich, 1996), 492, with whose overall reading I am in considerable agreement.

There we are told that in the false statement, "concerning you, different things are said to be the same, and not beings are said to be beings." Once again we may substitute singulars: "something different is said to be the same, and something that is not is said to be something that is." Now the Oxford interpretation requires different supplements, as follows: in the false statement "something different [from everything that is] is said to be the same [as something that is]."[51] And this is impossibly awkward. My verdict on the Oxford interpretation is that, though it gives an adequate account of what it is for a statement to be false, it is not what Plato intended. It is hard to find in the wording of the First Final Formula, and impossible to read in the Second Final Formula for Falsehood at 263d1–4.

Reading 2, the incompatibility interpretation, also fails for textual reasons, though it has the great strength that the sample statements do indeed feature incompatibles, "sits" and "flies." Sitting and flying, as we noted, are not merely different but incompatible; they exclude each other. Many objections to the incompatibility interpretation have been made on philosophical grounds, and I discuss one of these below. The overwhelming difficulty, however, is not a philosophical one, but that it requires that Plato intend a change of meaning in *heteron*, which up to now has meant "different." Can it be that now, without warning, he uses it to mean "incompatible"? This must be avoided if possible. And we can avoid it with the third interpretation, which is a variant on the "incompatibility interpretation."

> *Reading 3, the incompatibility range interpretation.* Reading 3 allows us to preserve what is good in each of the above—that is, it allows us to keep *heteron* to mean "different," and it takes account of the fact that Plato's sample statements feature incompatible attributes.[52]

I introduce it with the help of an important but difficult text from earlier in the *Sophist* at 257b1–c3, where the ES explains the meaning of negative expressions. There he distinguishes between what is contrary (*enantion*) and what is "only different" (*heteron monon*), and in so doing, he introduces the idea of a range of incompatible attributes such that what is not F has one of the other attributes from the range in question (though not necessarily the contrary of F).

51. The need for a different supplement is concealed in the formulation of J. van Eck: "Things that are different from what is the case concerning him (viz. flying) are described as the same (as what is the case about him)" ("Falsity without Negative Predication" ["Falsity"], *Phronesis* 40/1 (1995), 40). But, as we saw, supporters of Reading 1, including van Eck, have to understand "what is" (or here: "what is the case") differently in the two supplements.

52. Compare M. Ferejohn, "Plato and Aristotle on Negative Predication and Semantic Fragmentation," *Archiv für Geschichte der Philosophie* 71 (1989), 262 ff. To Ferejohn's list of adherents of this Reading (n.9), we may now add Szaif, *Wahrheit*, 487–99, esp. 491, and M.-L. Gill, "Method and Metaphysics in Plato's *Sophist* and *Statesman*", in *The Stanford Encyclopedia of Philosophy*, ed. E. N. Zalta (Winter 2005), available at http://plato.stanford.edu/archives/win2005/entries/plato-sophstate/.Crivelli (chapter 9 in this volume) labels my Reading 3 "quasi-incompatibility" (but opts for Reading 1 in his essay). Below I discuss twentieth-century versions of the same thesis.

(1) "Whenever we speak of not being, we don't speak of something contrary to being, but only different." "How so?" (2) "For example, when we say 'not big' do you think we signify small by that expression any more than equal?" "No." (3) "So when it is said that a negative signifies a contrary, we shan't agree, but we'll allow only this much—the prefixed word 'not' merely indicates something other[53] than the words following the negative, or rather, other than the things which the words uttered after the negative apply to."

The illustration in (2), where the ES is explaining what "not large" means, makes it clear that while "small" is the contrary of large, "equal" is "only different" (see (1)). Plato's point is this: if we think of A's size in relation to B, A may be not large, without being small (the contrary of large), since A may be equal in size to B; so when I say that A is not large, I am not saying that it is small (in relation to B).[54] Here we are introduced to the idea of a range of incompatible properties or attributes F, G, and H, such that what is not F is either G or H.[55] The range may have any number of members; we may think of colors, shapes, and so on. With this in mind, we can retain the translation "different" for *heteron* but recognize that an attribute different from F *taken from that range* will be incompatible with F. In support of this interpretation, think how laughable it would have been if in (2) the ES had chosen a random attribute different from large, and said (for instance), "When we say not big, do you think we signify small any more than yellow?" Being yellow does not rule out being large, so appealing to it in the explication of what "not large" means would be ridiculous.

Using the help offered by 257b–c, where, as I've shown, the account of "not large" invokes the idea of a range of incompatible properties when it labels "equal in size" merely *different* from "large," we can return to defend the incompatibility range interpretation of the Final Formulae for Falsehood, starting with the First Formula.

(B) The false one says different things from the things that are. (263b7)

I've argued that this is equivalent to

(B$^s$) The false one says something different from what is.

We have noticed that this section also features incompatibles, sitting and flying. So we may read (B$^s$) as follows: The false one says something different [from the relevant range of incompatible properties] from what is about you (because it says you are flying, which is a different one of the range of locomotive properties from the one that applies to you—namely, sitting). And we can now read the Second Formula (263d) in a far more natural way than the Oxford interpretation allowed.

Different things are said to be the same, and not beings are said to be beings.

---

53. Literally: one of the others, *tōn allōn ti.*
54. Precisely what his positive account here is is a controversial issue that we needn't go into here.
55. I discuss below an objection to this account of negation.

Again I replace plurals by singulars, yielding

> Something different [from what is about you] is said to be the same [as what is about you].

Now we have the same supplement both times, avoiding the intolerable awkwardness required by the Oxford interpretation. Once again, the different thing, flying, is chosen from the range of incompatible locomotive attributes, so that if I attribute a different thing from what is, I am bound to say something false.[56]

In addition to these two strong indications that Plato has in mind a range of incompatible properties, one may also cite the account of "other-judging" in Theaetetus 189b and following, where a similar idea may be at work.[57]

## 3.4  Objection to Reading 3, and reply

It may be objected that any account of falsehood which makes an essential reference to incompatibility (as both Readings 2 and 3 do) suffers from such a serious flaw that charity requires us to avoid attributing it to Plato. The flaw is this: such an account gives at best a sufficient, but not a necessary, condition for a false statement. (The same objection applies to the equivalent accounts of negation.) For example, the objector points out, it can be false that virtue is square (and true that virtue is not square) without it being the case that virtue is some shape other than square. In reply, I concede that the flaw is indeed serious. Must it have been so obvious to Plato that he could not have held the theory? No. Indeed, such a theory of negation continued to attract leading philosophers into the twentieth century.

It was maintained by J. Mabbott and G. Ryle, two of three contributors to an Aristotelian Society Symposium on Negation in 1929. Ryle wrote that "when a 'predicate' is denied of a 'subject,' that predicate must always be thought of as one member of a disjunctive set, some other member of which set (not necessarily specified) is asserted to be predicable of the subject."[58] Price, the third contributor, made the above objection, insisting that statements such as "virtue is not square" and "the soul is not a fire shovel" were both meaningful and true, in spite of resisting analysis in terms of a range of incompatible properties. And this objection is correct. But though the account which invokes a range of incompatible properties to explain negation and/or falsehood is indeed flawed, it was an attractive candidate, and, as we have seen, Plato's remarks about the meaning of "not large" at 257b–c require it, while his Formulae for Falsehood are best explained by appeal to it—in particular, the comparatively neglected second formula at 263d.

---

56. Van Eck, "Falsity," 26–27, rejects the incompatibility range interpretation (which he numbers 4$^i$) with the protest that the supposed restriction of "different" predicates to ones from a range of incompatible properties is "unannounced in the text" at 257b and at 263. But sentence (2), 257b6–7 comes close to announcing it, as I explain above.

57. Cf. P. Crivelli, "Allodoxia," *Archiv für Geschichte der Philosophie* 80 (1998), 15–16; Szaif, *Wahrheit*, 495–96.

58. G. Ryle, "Negation," *Proceedings of the Aristotelian Society* IX (suppl.) (1929), 86.

## 3.5 Which feature of the account of falsity is more important?

We have now established (by the defense of Reading 3) how Plato means us to understand the reference to the different, which glosses "not being" (*ta mē onta*) in the two Final Formulae for Falsehood. So we can return to take stock of Plato's achievement in this section. We have seen that the account of false statement contains two main elements: (a) the insistence that a *logos*, true or false, is about something and (b) a paraphrase glossing "not being" by "different." Discussions tend to focus on (b), partly because it is the harder to interpret but also because a focus on the problem of not being set the scene originally for the Middle Part. But I contend that (a) both is and is represented by Plato as the major contribution to the account of falsehood. To do so, I must counter the objection of John McDowell.[59] He argues that the *Sophist*'s revelation of the subject-predicate structure of a *logos* is not the key to the solution of the problem of false statement. Rather, Plato clearly indicates that the salient error lay in a mistake about not being, and that the solution is to demolish the Eleatic mistake about negation.[60]

McDowell points out that in the section which develops puzzles about not being/what is not, there are two early definitions of falsehood. I label them "Def A" and "Def B."

> Def A. False saying/judging is saying/judging what is not. (240d9)
> Def B. False saying is (i) saying what is not is or (ii) saying what is is not. (240e–241a)

Def B is a double-barreled definition, of which the first part covers false positive statements such as "grass is red" and the second false negative statements such as "grass is not green."[61] McDowell refers to Def B as the disjunctive definition and to Def A as the definition that conveys "the crude position" about statements.[62] Now, as we have seen, the account of *logos* and of false and true *logos* at 260–63 is well fitted to dispose of the "crude picture" of statements and false statements. For once we insist that a *logos* says something about something, it is at once unproblematic how, having thereby got a grip on reality by that reference, it can go on to say something false about the thing in question.

Why does McDowell reject the familiar account, which sees 260–63 as putting to rest the crude picture by insisting on the need for a subject of a *logos*, as well as something said about the subject? His answer: this does not address the much

---

59. McDowell "Falsehood," esp. sec. 6, 132–34.

60. Likewise, Sedley, *Midwife*, esp. 113–14, 134, holds that it is the account of not being in terms of difference which is the key advance of *Sophist*, rather than the analysis of a *logos* into *onoma* and *rhēma* which (as discussed in n. 40) he thinks is not a new discovery in *Sophist*.

61. The double-barreled definition can cover positive and negative existential statements and judgments, as well as predicative ones. But it should not be understood as confined to existentials.

62. McDowell, "Falsehood," 130. The label "crude" applies to the approach to statements found in *Euthydemus* 285 86 and 283e7–284c6, mentioned in sec. 3.1 above; crude because it leaves no room for a distinction between naming and saying—and hence none for false statement.

subtler Def B of falsehood (the one he labels the disjunctive characterization). Someone who claims to find the locution "is not" puzzling (as importing some contrary of being) will not back down when we add "about you."[63]

But this overlooks two salient features of the discussion of statement and of false statement. First, it is Def A which is prominent when the ES pointedly moves the discussion on to its final stage (260–64). At 260c3–4, he says, "because judging or saying things that are not—that's what falsehood in thought and statements is, surely," and at 260d1–2, he says that the sophist denied the existence of falsehood since "no one can judge or say what is not."[64] These prominent descriptions of false saying and judging set the stage for the final push. The more complex Def B does not get a further mention. Indeed, we may hazard that Plato considered that Def B is not, at bottom, problematic but a rather insightful definition of falsehood, provided, of course, that we add "about so-and-so. A solution to the "crude picture" is, contra McDowell, just what is needed, and it is what we get.[65]

McDowell also overlooks how strongly the account of falsehood emphasizes the need for a statement being about something. We saw how the ES stresses, à propos of his two sample *logoi*, that they are about Theaetetus. Furthermore, after his first pass at the account of true and false *logos*, 263b, discussed above, the ES reemphasizes, first, that the false one is a *logos*; second, that it is about something; and third, that it must be "yours"—that is, it must be of or about Theaetetus.[66] He then moves on to the Second Final Formula, whose first words are "about you." We can safely reject McDowell's analysis, then, and restore the view that Plato is concerned to combat the so-called crude picture, and that a crucial move in doing so is to insist that a *logos*, whether true or false, must be *about something*.

Now one might think, with McDowell, that the second feature of the account must be the more important, given the importance of not being/is not in the architecture of the Middle Part. But remember that the ES offered to vindicate not

---

63. "So it seems to him that when we try to capture the falsity of 'Theaetetus is in flight' by saying that it represents *in flight*, which *is not* (in relation to Theaetetus: given the mistake, the addition does not help) as being, we must be talking nonsense" (McDowell, "Falsehood," 133). Note the clause in parentheses.

64. McDowell, "Falsehood," 130 n.31, correctly queries Owen's claim that back in 237b7–e7, the puzzle (about *legein to mē on*) is "a version of the familiar paradox." But he overlooks 260c3–4 and d1–3, where the locution *legein to mē on* (or a variant) *is* used to designate false speaking.

65. A further objection to McDowell's reading, on which it is the complex Def B, not the simple Def A, which frames the problem about falsehood, is the following. On his reading, any occurrence of the phrase "is not" was held to be problematic, until the "Eleatic error" of interpreting this as "has the contrary of being" or as "utterly is not" is scotched (132). But in that case, even the equivalent formula for true negative statement implied at 240e1, "judging that what is not is not," would be suspect. But no such aspersions are cast against it.

66. The use of the "possessive" pronoun *sos* 263c7 (and *emos*, 263a6) has puzzled commentators, and some (including McDowell, "Falsehood," 130, and Frede, "False," 416) believe that this shows that Plato is invoking the "old" concept of a *logos* as belonging to someone, by "putting that person into words." Frede writes: "Given that the language of 'about' is perfectly clear, and given that the language in terms of possessive pronouns is neither ordinary nor natural, it is difficult not to see in it an allusion to the way of thinking about statements underlying the *antilogia* argument." But "your *logos*" can mean the *logos* which describes you, just as "your picture" is the one that depicts you: that is, we have an "objective" use of the pronoun, not a true possessive, so we need not find the usage puzzling. Cf. Szaif, *Wahrheit*, 464.

being, to clear away misunderstandings that made talk of it contradictory. It should not therefore be one of his aims to dispense with it entirely, and, indeed, the project of dispensing with "not," in an account either of negation or of falsehood, is bound to be a hopeless one, whose success is at best illusory.[67] Note further that in the neglected Second Formula for Falsehood, the ES is happy to use both "different" and "is not," when he describes a false statement as both "saying what is different is the same" and "saying what is not is." Note also, what I remarked above, that the entire Second Formula begins prominently with "about you." If we consider the whole passage in which statement and false statement are discussed, only a tiny portion of it—just a few lines—offer the paraphrases that dispense with "is not" and rephrase the account in terms of the different. Although I believe we can interpret Plato's intentions here, by appealing to what I have called the "incompatibility range interpretation," I do not think it is, for him, the chief lesson he wants to convey. The chief lesson is the one about the kind of interweaving a statement is, with functionally different parts: this is what allows something both to be unambiguously a *logos*, about someone, and to say something false (something that is not) about the subject.

Both in the section devoted to the Late-learners' problem and its solution, and in the discussion of falsehood, Plato is concerned to disclose the nature of statements, particularly predicative statements, and to stress that some parts of a *logos* have a function other than that of naming. Furthermore, for this very reason, a *logos* itself is neither a name nor a string of names. Plato's new account, in emphasizing that a *logos* is a special "weaving together" of terms with different roles, is of major importance. In their different ways, both sections I have discussed make these key points and thereby enable some old puzzles—ones that can be read both as eristic teasers and as revealing deeper philosophical problems—to be finally put to rest.[68]

# BIBLIOGRAPHY

Ackrill, J. L. "Plato and the Copula: *Sophist* 251–59"; repr. in *Plato 1: Metaphysics and Epistemology*, ed. G. Vlastos (Garden City, N.Y., 1971), 210–22.

Bostock, D. "Plato on 'Is-Not' (*Sophist* 254–9)," *Oxford Studies in Ancient Philosophy* 2 (1984), 89–119.

Brown, L. "Being in the *Sophist*: A Syntactical Enquiry," in *Plato 1*, ed. G. Fine (Oxford, 1999), 455–78.

---

67. Critics of interpretations that invoke incompatibility often object that that notion, in turn, needs to be explicated with the help of negation and/or falsity. But the very same point can be made about interpretations that rely on the simple notion of the different, or nonidentical.

68. I am very grateful to the editor, Gail Fine, for her helpful comments on an earlier draft of this essay. Thanks for their comments are due also to Alex Anslow and Stefan Koller. This essay is dedicated to the memory of Michael Frede, who died while the volume was in press, August 2007, in gratitude for his writings and for many discussions about Plato's *Sophist*.

Brown, L. "Definition and Division in the *Sophist*," in *Ancient Theories of Definition*, ed. D. Charles (Oxford, forthcoming).

Burnyeat, M. "Plato on How Not to Speak about Not-Being," in *Le Style de la pensée*, ed. M. Canto and P. Pellegrin (Paris, 2002), 40–65.

Cornford, F. M. *Plato's Theory of Knowledge* (repr. London, 1960).

Crivelli, P. "Allodoxia," *Archiv für Geschichte der Philosophie* 80 (1998), 1–29.

Denyer, N. *Language, Truth and Falsehood* (Cambridge, 1991).

Duke, E. A., W. F. Hicken, W. S. M. Nicoll, D. B. Robinson, and J. C. G. Strachan, eds. *Platonis Opera I*, (Oxford, 1995).

Ferejohn, M. "Plato and Aristotle on Negative Predication and Semantic Fragmentation," *Archiv für Geschichte der Philosophie* 71 (1989), 257–82.

Frede, M. "The Literary Form of the *Sophist*," in *Form and Argument in Late Plato*, ed. C. Gill and M. M. McCabe (Oxford, 1996), 135–51.

Frede, M. "Plato's *Sophist* on False Statements," in *Cambridge Companion to Plato*, ed. R. Kraut (Cambridge, 1990), 397–424.

Frede, M. *Prädikation und Existenzaussage* (Göttingen, 1967).

Gill, M. L. "Method and Metaphysics in Plato's *Sophist* and *Statesman*," The Stanford Encyclopedia of Philosophy (Winter 2005 Edition), Edward N. Zalta (ed.). Available at http://plato.stanford.edu/archives/win2005/entries/plato-sophstate/.

Gosling, J. *Plato* (London, 1973).

Hoekstra, M., and F. Scheppers. "*Onoma, rhēma* et *logos* dans le *Cratyle* et le *Sophiste* de Platon," *L'Antiquité Classique* (2003), 55–73.

Kahn, C. *The Verb "Be" in Ancient Greek* (Dordrecht, 1973).

Keyt, D. "Plato on Falsity," in *Exegesis and Argument*, ed. E. Lee, A. Mourelatos, and R. Rorty (Assen, 1973), 285–305.

Lewis, F. A. "Did Plato Discover the Estin of Identity?" *California Studies in Classical Antiquity* 8 (1975), 113–42.

Lockwood, M. "On Predicating Proper Names," *Philosophical Review* (1975), 471–498.

Mates, B. "Identity and Predication in Plato," *Phronesis* 24/3 (1979), 211–29.

McDowell, J. "Falsehood and Not-Being in Plato's *Sophist*," in *Language and Logos*, ed. M. Schofield and M. Nussbaum (Cambridge, 1982), 115–34.

Moravcsik, J. M. E. "Being and Meaning in the *Sophist*," *Acta Philosophica Fennica* 14 (1962), 23–78.

Notomi, N. *The Unity of Plato's Sophist* (Cambridge, 1999).

Owen, G. E. L. "Plato on Not-Being," in *Plato 1*, ed. G. Fine (Oxford, 1999), 416–54.

Ryle, G. "Negation," *Proceedings of the Aristotelian Society* (suppl. vol.) IX (1929), 80–96.

Sedley, D. *The Midwife of Platonism* (Oxford, 2004).

Sedley, D. *Plato's Cratylus* (Cambridge, 2003).

Sommers, F. "Do We Need Identity?" *Journal of Philosophy* (1969), 499–504.

Szaif, J. *Platons Begriff der Wahrheit* (Munich, 1996).

Taylor, C. C. W. "Socrates the Sophist," in *Remembering Socrates*, ed. L. Judson and V. Karasmanis (Oxford, 2004), 157–68.

van Eck, J. "Falsity without Negative Predication," *Phronesis* 40/1 (1995), 20–47.

van Eck, J. "Plato's Logical Insights: *Sophist* 254d–257a," *Ancient Philosophy* 20/1 (2000), 53–79.

Vlastos, G. "An Ambiguity in the Sophist," *Platonic Studies* (Princeton, N.J., 1981), 270–322.

# CHAPTER 19

# THE *TIMAEUS* ON THE PRINCIPLES OF COSMOLOGY

## THOMAS K. JOHANSEN

## PRINCIPLED KNOWLEDGE

It is a common view in Greek philosophy that in order to master a body of knowledge one needs to understand its principles (*arkhai*). The principles are the basic propositions that explain the other propositions in the body of knowledge while they themselves are not similarly explained by any of the other propositions. Or, if one thinks of the body of knowledge in terms of the entities that are known, then the principles are those basic entities that are responsible for the being or coming into being of the other entities, while their own being or becoming is not similarly dependent on any of the other entities.[1]

If one also holds that there are different bodies of knowledge, it is natural to think that those bodies of knowledge also have different principles. Indeed, one may think that part of what makes those bodies of knowledge different is that they rest on different principles. Aristotle is an exponent of this view: "Different sciences have different principles, for example arithmetic and plane geometry" (*De Anima* 402a21–22). This is not to say that different sciences may not also share some principles. As Aristotle makes clear in the *Posterior Analytics*, there are some

---

1. Cf. Aristotle, *Metaphysics* V.1: "It is common, then, to all [*arkhai*] to be the first point from which a thing either is or comes to be or is known."

principles that related sciences like arithmetic and geometry share, but they are not the ones that define arithmetic as such or geometry as such.[2]

Plato, too, seems to hold that grasping a body of knowledge requires a grasp of its principles. One example is *Republic* VI (510b2–9), where Socrates explains the image of the line. He has divided the line into two sections, the intelligible and the perceptible, each of which he then subdivides. The intelligible section is now divided into the Forms and the objects of hypotheses such as those made by mathematicians.[3] For Socrates, knowledge of what is hypothesized in mathematics requires a grasp of the principle (*arkhê*) on which those hypotheses depend. However, mathematicians commonly make a mistake, not in using hypotheses—Socrates accepts that there are hypotheses appropriate to each discipline—but in behaving as if they were known as first principles that do not themselves require further explanation. The real first principle, Socrates says, is provided by the form of the good. He refers to this principle as the principle "of everything" (*hê tou pantos arkhê*, 511b7). The form of the good is the principle of everything in the first instance because it is the principle of all intelligible beings. But it is also the principle of everything else insofar as everything else is an image, at one or more removes, of the intelligible beings. At the highest level, the form of the good is studied through dialectic, which allows us to ascend systematically to the most basic principle of all.

Later in the *Republic* (521c–534e) Socrates contrasts those disciplines that pull one toward the study of being, and ultimately the form of the good, with those that remain focused on coming into being. He presents a new view of how the mathematical disciplines are to be practiced. They should be used to lead the mind away from the concern with perceptible matters to the study of being itself. The mathematical sciences, including astronomy, should be studied in preparation for the study of being in dialectic. Perceptible objects should be considered only to the extent that they provide the intellect with the opportunity, through problems or examples, to account for the forms. The mathematical sciences provide the first step in the intellect's upward journey from the world of becoming to that of being, an ascent that is completed in the grasp of the form of the good, the last verse, as it were, in "the song of dialectic" (532a1–2).

The *Timaeus*, like the *Republic*, emphasizes the need for us to grasp the proper principle of our disciplines of study. As Timaeus says in his opening speech, "Now in every subject it is of utmost importance to begin (*arxasthai*) according to the natural principle (*arkhê*)" (29b2–3).[4] But what is the natural principle of cosmology? Timaeus' cosmology concerns, we are told (27a5–6), the coming into being of the cosmos, down to and including the nature of man. So our question becomes: What is the natural principle of the study of the coming into being of the cosmos? As we shall see, the principle is a principle of coming into being, not of being.[5]

---

2. Cf. *Posterior Analytics* I.9–10.

3. It is a matter of dispute whether such hypotheses are restricted to special mathematical objects. For the debate and arguments against this restriction, see G. Fine, "Knowledge and Belief in *Republic* V–VII" ["Knowledge"], in G. Fine (ed.), *Plato on Knowledge and Forms: Selected Essays* (Oxford 2003), 85–116.

4. A proverb quoted also at *Republic* 377a12.

5. Cf. 28b6–7, 29e4.

Timaeus accepts that there may be more fundamental principles of everything, but cosmology, as he understands it, does not provide the appropriate method for approaching such ultimate principles.[6] The subject of cosmology is the world as it has come into being, and its method is one that is appropriate to this subject matter. Unlike dialectic in the *Republic*, cosmology, as Timaeus understands it, is not concerned with the principle of absolutely everything.[7] Cosmology is not concerned with being as such; its ultimate principle is not the ultimate principle of being; and its method is not that of dialectic, in the *Republic*'s sense.[8]

It may still turn out that what is ultimately responsible for the coming into being of the cosmos is the same as what is ultimately responsible for all being according to the *Republic*: that is, the form of the good. In that case, there would be a sense in which the principle of becoming and the principle of being are the same. However, since in the *Timaeus*, as in the *Republic*, being is categorically different from becoming, what it is for something to be a principle of becoming is different from what it is for something to be a principle of being. Being responsible in the manner of a principle for the coming into being of something serves a different function from being responsible for the being of something. So even if the same thing answers to both job descriptions, we would still have to say that this thing qua principle of coming into being differs from it qua principle of being.

The fact that the explanatory subject of the *Timaeus* is the coming into being of the cosmos is reflected in a different conception of the mathematical sciences from that of the *Republic*. Timaeus does not justify the study of astronomy and mathematical cosmology by their contribution to the study of being. This is not because he does not value the study of being, for it is clear that he, like Socrates, places it above the study of coming into being. However, he sees the study of being as distinct from that of the cosmos. As he says, the study of coming into being is meant to provide a break from the study of being (59c–d). For cosmology, as we shall see, does not aim to raise questions about being as such; rather, it aims to understand coming into being. We are facing a different explanatory task in the *Timaeus* from that of the astronomers in the *Republic*.

# PRINCIPLES IN THE *TIMAEUS*

My aim in this essay is to articulate the distinctive principles of cosmology, as Plato conceives of them in the *Timaeus*, and so provide the starting point for an understanding of this work. The principles of cosmology emerge in particular from

---

6. Cf. 48c2–d4.

7. Other than insofar as *to pan* means "the universe," but that is a different sense of *pan* from that in the *Republic*.

8. Cf. C. J. Rowe, "The Status of the 'Myth,'" in C. Natali and S. Maso (eds.), *Plato Physicus* (Amsterdam 2003), 30, who presents cosmology, "in the spirit of the *Republic*," as an indirect account "of the truth itself, how things really are," where by "how things really are" we should think of the being of the forms.

two passages of the *Timaeus*, 27d5–30c1 and 47e3–53c3, which set out, as it were, the terms and conditions for the study of the cosmos. We therefore need to look at these passages in some detail.

In the first passage, Timaeus begins (27d5–28b2) by articulating three premises, as follows:

1. Being is that which is graspable by intelligence with an account (*logos*); becoming is that which is graspable by opinion (*doxa*) with unreasoning (*alogos*) perception.
2. Everything that comes into being has a cause (*aition*).
3. When a craftsman uses an eternal model, his product is necessarily fine (*kalon*); if he uses a generated one, the product is not fine.

Timaeus then (28b2–29b2) applies these premises, serially, to the cosmos. First, he argues that the world belongs to what comes into being rather than what is because it is perceptible:

> T1  One should consider first about the entire heaven (or cosmos, or let's call it by whatever other name one might prefer to call it by) a question one should consider about everything in the beginning (*en arkhêi*), namely, whether it always was, having no beginning (*arkhê*) of coming into being (*genesis*) or whether it has come into being, having started from some principle (*arkhê*). It has come into being: for it is tangible and has a body, and all such things are perceptible and perceptible things, being graspable by opinion with perception, appeared to be coming into being and generated.

Applying premise 1, T1 argues that since the world is perceptible, it must have come into being. As part of the argument, Timaeus links having come into being with having a principle of coming into being. In contrast, what always was has no such principle. But what does Timaeus mean by "principle of coming into being"? As for coming into being, I take it that the dominant sense in T1 is that of coming into existence.[9] For Timaeus assimilates what has come into being with what has been "generated" or "born" (*gegonos* with *gennêtos*) at 28b1 and 28c1–2. We are here primarily talking about *genesis* in the sense of generation or coming into existence.

The term *arkhê*, meanwhile, occurs three times in T1. In its first use, the *arkhê* is clearly the beginning or starting point of inquiry. Such a starting point can be understood temporally, or simply as the first in an order of items that need to be addressed, like the first item on a shopping list. In its second use, however, *arkhê* is

---

9. The coupling in premise 1 (28a3) of "coming into being" with "being destroyed" (*apollumenon*) suggests that Timaeus there also, if not exclusively, is thinking of coming into being in the sense of coming into existence. For the interpretation of *genesis* and *gignomenon* in premise 1, see M. Frede, "Being and Becoming in Plato," and A. Code, "Reply to Michael Frede's 'Being and Becoming in Plato,'" both in *Oxford Studies in Ancient Philosophy* (suppl.) (1988), 37–52 and 53–60.

linked to coming into being. Insofar as we think of coming into being as a process in time, it is natural to think that the *arkhê* also represents a temporal beginning.

However, this temporal reading of the coming into being of the world has been disputed since antiquity. Some have taken the temporal description of the cosmogenesis as a mere didactic device, which serves to set out eternal causal relations as if they were a series of events in time.[10] On this view, the claim that the world "has come into being" (*gegonen*) means no more than that it is now and always in a state of having come into being. The principle of its coming into being is the standing cause of its continuous or continual coming into being.

For several reasons, I do not think this is a viable reading. First, the temporal understanding of the principle seems supported by Timaeus' use of tenses. What has come into being (perfect tense) contrasts with what *always was*, in having started from some principle.[11] Second, Timaeus associates the principle of the world's coming into being with its cause (*aition*) and describes the cause in ways that strongly suggest that it is the cause of a temporal process:[12]

> T2    Again, we say that it is necessary for what came into being to have come into being by some cause (*aition*). It is a big job to find the maker (*poiêtês*) and father (*patêr*) of this universe, and having found it, it is impossible to state it to everyone. (28c2–5)

Premise 2, we are told, applies to the cosmos, as we would expect, given that it has come into being. So the coming into being of the cosmos has a cause. T2 leaves us in suspense as to what exactly the cause is. However, Timaeus does tell us something important about the cause: it is the maker and the father of the universe. Now *poiêtês*, like the English "poet," may to a Greek have connotations with the making of verse.[13] However, as the *Symposium* reminds us,[14] we should think more generally of anybody who is responsible for bringing what was not into being as a

---

10. A reading referred to, though not espoused, by Aristotle, *De Caelo* 279b32–280a2. For a recent defense of this nontemporal reading, see M. Baltes, "Γέγονεν (Platon *Tim.* 28B6): Ist die Welt real entstanden oder nicht?" ["Γέγονεν"], in K. A. Algra, P. W. van der Horst, and D. T. Runia (eds.), *Polyhistor: Studies in the History and Historiography of Ancient Philosophy* (Leiden, 1996), 76–98.

11. The supporters of the nontemporal reading point out that the perfect tense in Greek is used aspectually to say something about the present rather than temporally to refer to a past action—for example, F. M. Cornford, *Plato's Cosmology* [*Cosmology*] (London, 1937), 24–25, and Baltes, "Γέγονεν," 91–94. Baltes writes as if the temporal reading could only be firmly established if Timaeus used a finite form of the aorist rather than the perfect. However, *Laws* 781e–782a shows that Baltes is wrong to suggest that we would expect the aorist rather than the perfect if Timaeus had meant to say that the world came into being in the past. Note also (with D. Sedley, *Creationism and Its Critics in Antiquity* ["Creationism"], Berkeley, 2007), *Critias* 106a4, where Timaeus expressly says that the world has come into being a long time ago, using again the perfect tense (γεγονότι). However, even if Baltes were right about the perfect, his argument would fail since the imperfect tenses which Timaeus also uses are sufficient to locate the creation in the past. Sensing this, Baltes dismisses ἦν at 28b6 as "conversational laxness" for what strictly speaking, he says, is meant as ἐστί. But if ἦν is laxness, the repeated imperfects ἀπηργάζετο and ἔβλεπεν (29a1, 3) look like carelessness.

12. Timaeus' use of *arkhê* thus illustrates Aristotle's observation that a standard sense of *arkhê* is "cause" (*aition*); cf. *Metaphysics* V 1, 1013a16–7.

13. Cf. Aristotle, *Poetics* 1447b13–16, 1451b27–29, with S. Halliwell, *Aristotle's Poetics* (London, 1998), 56–59.

14. *Symposium* 205b.

"poet." The temporal aspect of *poiêsis* is made quite explicit by the *Sophist*: "We say…that every power is productive (*poiêtikê*) which becomes responsible for those things that were not earlier (*proteron*) coming into being later (*husteron*)."[15] The Visitor's examples, an animal growing from a seed or a plant from a root, show that "earlier" and "later" are meant temporally. Meanwhile, the notion of the cause as "the father of the cosmos" is one which Timaeus uses throughout his cosmology and reinforces through the language of generation.[16]

On Timaeus' own account of fatherhood,[17] the process of fathering is clearly a temporal one, involving stages of maturation before the coming into being is complete.[18] The process of sowing seeds for growth mirrors Timaeus' account of the actions of the demiurge in creating human souls: the demiurge creates the immortal souls and sows them in the "instruments of time," before handing them over to the created gods to nurture them (41c–d, 42d).[19] Procreation, human as divine, is clearly a temporal process. Both as "the father" and as "the maker," it seems, then, that the cause initiates the coming into being of the cosmos *in time*.

So far, then, I have suggested that the principle of coming into being should be understood as both a causal and a temporal principle.[20] It is that which initiates the coming into being of the cosmos, where the coming into being is to be understood as occurring in time.

The designation of the cause as "maker" is developed next:

T3 But again we need to consider the following point about it [the cosmos]: in relation to which of the models did the builder complete it, in relation to what is the same or in relation to what has come into being. If this world is beautiful and its craftsman good, it is clear that he was looking toward the eternal model. But if that which it is sacrilegious even to say holds, then he was looking toward a model that has come into being. Surely, it is clear to all that he was looking toward the eternal one, for the world is the best of the things that have come into being, and the craftsman is the best of causes. Having come into being in this way it has been crafted in relation to what is graspable by reason and wisdom and is the same. (28c5–29b1)

---

15. *Sophist* 265b9–10, referring back to *Sophist* 219b4–6.
16. Cf. *gennaô* ("to generate") and cognates, for example, at 28c2; 32c1; 34a7, b9; 37a2; 38b6, c4, e6; 41a5; 55b4, 5; 68e4; and 69c4.
17. Cf. 91d1–5.
18. Cf. 91d5: ἀποτελέσωσιν γένεσιν. Fatherhood does not end with impregnation.
19. Sowing the seeds is here, as at 91d, both an agricultural and a procreative notion.
20. The strongest objection leveled at the temporal reading is that it presupposes that there was time before and during the creation, but for Timaeus time only arises with the creation of the planets (37c–38c). The best replies to the objection are those inspired by G. Vlastos, "Creation in the *Timaeus*: Is It a Fiction?," *Socrates, Plato, and Their Tradition*, ed. D. W. Graham (Princeton, N.J., 1995), 271–75. We should distinguish between time as an ordered and measurable succession of past, present, and future and time as a succession of before and after. The creation of the planet introduces the former notion of time, not the latter, and the latter is sufficient to make sense of the temporal succession of chaotically moving appearances in the pre-cosmos (Sedley, *Creationism*, 104–105).

T3 applies premise 3 to the cosmos. The question is now, given that the world has come into being (T1) and given that it has a cause, namely, its maker (T2), which of the two possible models has the maker employed for the coming into being of the world? The answer, that the craftsman of the world looked to an eternal paradigm, confirms our expectations of craftsmanship from other Platonic works. So in *Republic* X, a genuine craftsman was contrasted with a pseudo-craftsman in looking toward an eternal rather than a generated paradigm (597d–598b). We would also expect the choice of eternal model, given that this is the way to make the model fine (premise 3). For in other dialogues, Socrates emphasizes that craftsmanship seeks to make its product as good as possible. So in the *Gorgias*, it is characteristic of a craft like medicine, as opposed to mere knacks, that it considers what is better or worse for those it affects (501c). In *Republic* I, the craft considers the benefit of that of which it is the craft (342c). We expect, then, that a craftsman will do what is required to craft the best possible product, including choosing the right model.

So the world is modeled on an eternal paradigm because the craftsman chose this model, and he chose this model because he is the best craftsman, and as such sought to make the product as good as possible. Now in terms of identifying the principle or starting point of the creation of the cosmos, this makes the eternal paradigm secondary to the craftsman. Strictly speaking, the forms *as a paradigm* are not a principle of the coming into being of the cosmos, for they are not the first factor in the order of explaining or causing the coming into being of the cosmos; rather, the maker is. Alternatively, if we allow for more or less fundamental principles,[21] the formal paradigm is a principle but only a secondary one. After all, it may seem proper to count the forms as a principle of the cosmos insofar as the cosmos is created by being modeled on them. However, since there is a further cause of why the cosmos is modeled on the forms (i.e., the maker), the forms appear only to be a secondary principle.

Note in this context that the paradigm has been selected by the craftsman within the larger kind of eternal beings. So in premise 3, Timaeus said that "when the craftsman looks towards what is always the same and uses *some such thing* as a paradigm, etc.," that is to say, the craftsman looks to the eternal and selects something from that class or kind as his model.[22] When we are told more precisely what the paradigm is, we are told that it is a living being—more specifically, a living being containing all the other living beings within it (30c–31b). Given the range of forms on offer in other Platonic dialogues, it seems unlikely that the paradigm living being includes all the forms there are. The formal paradigm is then a specific instance of the wider kind of eternal beings, chosen by the maker among the

---

21. A parlance licensed, perhaps, by 53d4–7.

22. D. Zeyl, *Plato Timaeus* (Indianapolis/Cambridge, 2000), gets it right: "So whenever the craftsman looks at what is always changeless, *and using a thing of that kind* as his model, . . . "; D. Lee (old Penguin translation) doesn't: "Whenever, therefore, the maker of anything keeps his eye on the eternally unchanging and *uses it* as his pattern . . . " (my emphases).

various eternal beings for its suitability as a paradigm for making the best possible world.

So far I have argued that Timaeus' opening speech is concerned with the identification of the first principle (*arkhê*) of cosmology. Since the cosmos has come into being, the principle is a principle of coming into being rather than a principle of being. The principle of coming into being is implicitly identified with the cause (*aition*) of coming into being. This cause is variously designated as "the maker" and "the father." Both terms seem to confirm that the principle of coming into being should be understood not just as a causal one but also as a temporal one, as a cause that initiates a process of coming into being in time. As a genuine craftsman, moreover, the principle is an intelligent one seeking to make the best work possible and therefore working according to an eternal model.

# THE STANDARDS OF COSMOLOGICAL ARGUMENT

In the next passage, however, Timaeus speaks of another *arkhê*:

> T4 These things being so, again there is every necessity for this cosmos here to be a likeness of something.[23] Now in every subject it is of utmost importance to begin according to the natural principle (*arkhê*), and so, on the subject of a likeness and its model, we need to make the following distinction. The accounts (*logoi*) are of the same kind as the very things of which they are interpreters. So the accounts of that which is stable and certain and transparent to rationality (*nous*) are stable and unchanging—insofar as it belongs to accounts to be irrefutable and invincible, they should not fall short of this— whilst the accounts of that which is made as a likeness by reference to that thing [what is stable, etc.], [these accounts] being of what is a likeness are themselves likely and stand in an analogy to those accounts [the accounts of what is stable], namely, as being stands to coming into being, so truth stands to conviction. (29b1–c3)

Now the second sentence of T4 may seem to suggest that Timaeus will only now tell us the first principle of the cosmos.[24] However, Timaeus is not saying that he is now going to introduce the principle of the coming into being of the cosmos. Rather, he is making a general claim that on any subject matter we need to start with the natural principle, a claim which he then exemplifies by the particular

---

23. "These things being so, etc." introduces a new paragraph, according to the punctuation of the *Oxford Classical Text*; cf. Cornford, *Cosmology*, 23 n.1.

24. So, Proclus tells us (in *Tim.* 337.20–23), the sentence was read by some in antiquity as referring forward to the "most proper principle" at 29e4.

subject matter of a likeness and its model. While confirming, then, Timaeus' general concern with identifying the proper principle of any discipline, T4 does not offer us a new principle of coming into being but, rather, the principle for the particular subject matter of a likeness and its paradigm.

The principle is that "the accounts (*logoi*) are of the same kind as the very things of which they are interpreters." From this principle, it follows that if an account is of being, and being is "stable and certain and transparent to rationality," the account should have the same or related attributes; whereas if the account is of a likeness, then the account should be likely. We should note the normativity of the principle, made explicit at 29b9–c1. For accounts of being, "insofar as it belongs to accounts to be irrefutable and invincible, *should not* fall short of this."[25] Similarly, likelihood for accounts of a likeness is both the maximum and the minimum to which they should aspire.

T4 is emphatic that cosmology is not to be held to the standards of the study of being, as exemplified by dialectic in the *Republic*. The lower argumentative standards are a direct consequence of the subject matter of cosmology, a world that has come into being, albeit as a likeness of being.[26] In a later passage, Timaeus makes reference to this standard, the likely account, to explain why it is inappropriate through cosmological argument to seek the most basic principles of everything:

> T5 We tend to posit them [earth, water, fire, and air] as the elemental "letters" of the universe and tell people that they are its "principles" on the assumption that they know what fire and the other three are. In fact, however, they shouldn't even be compared to syllables. A person with even a modicum of wisdom would not make such a comparison. So let me now proceed with my treatment in the following way: I cannot state "the principle" or "principles" of all things, or however else I think about them, for the simple reason that it is difficult to show clearly what my view is if I follow my present manner of exposition. (*Tim.* 48b7–c6, trans. after Zeyl)

Timaeus is clear that the "present manner of exposition" means arguments based on likelihood (48d2–3). Such arguments are unsuited to demonstrating the principle of all things. I take the contrast to the *Republic*'s notion of dialectic as concerned with ascending to the principle of everything to be deliberate. The alternative offered by dialectic—to ascend to the principle of everything, whereby our grasp of the four bodies might be imagined to turn into the highest form of knowledge—is not an option in the *Timaeus*, since we are methodologically bound to the likely account by our subject matter, the coming into being of the cosmos. Our assumptions about the coming into being of bodies, therefore, have a lower cognitive status than if they were explained in relation to the principle of everything.

25. Cf. M. F. Burnyeat, "ΕΙΚΩΣ ΜΥΘΟΣ" ["ΕΙΚΩΣ"], *Rhizai* 2/2 (2005), 150–52.

26. For a detailed reading of the passage, see Burnyeat, "ΕΙΚΩΣ". My own interpretation is set out in Johansen, *Plato's Natural Philosophy* [*Natural*] (Cambridge, 2004), 48–64.

As an illustration, consider Timaeus' description of the geometrical principle of the construction of the simple bodies:

> We posit (*hupotithemetha*) this principle (*arkhê*) of fire and the other bodies advancing according to the likely account with necessity.[27] But god and, of men, he who is a friend to god know the principles still higher than these. (53d4–7)

Since Timaeus is concerned with the principles lying behind the geometrical construction of the simple bodies, it is likely that the higher principles would be, at least in the first instance, mathematical. These principles may, in turn (if the image of the line still applies), rely on further principles, including, ultimately, the form of the good. However, Timaeus thinks it is justified to leave these higher principles aside in the current context because they do not enter directly into the account of the construction of the simple bodies. From the point of view of cosmology, this is as it should be: our interest in principles only takes us as far as the principles of what comes into being in this world.[28] That there are higher principles than that, principles like the *Republic*'s principle of everything, is assumed, but these do not relate directly to the generation of the world as a likeness and are not, therefore, appropriately dealt with by the method of the likely account.

But how, then, do we arrive at the right principles for cosmology if not through dialectic in the *Republic*'s sense? Note first the reference in T5 to what a man with a modicum of wisdom (*ho kai brachu phronôn*) would assume to be principles. Compare with this Timaeus' claim earlier that "this indeed is in the most proper sense the principle of coming into being and which someone would be most correct in accepting from wise (*phronimoi*) men" (29e2–30a2).[29] We are no doubt meant to think of Timaeus and his audience as examples of wise men. For we have Socrates' assurances that they are uniquely qualified, by nature, education, and experience, to tackle the subject matter.[30] Men of wisdom such as these are used here as a benchmark for the acceptance of the right cosmological principles.[31]

To capture the significance of this benchmark, consider Aristotle's distinction in the *Topics* (100b1–23) between two kinds of argument. One is called "demonstrative" and the other "dialectical," whereby Aristotle has in mind something rather different from the dialectic of the *Republic*. The primary differ-

---

27. See also *hupotithêmi* at 48e6, 55e4, 61d3.

28. It is a matter of debate whether, according the image of the line, the cognitive states in principle are confined to their corresponding objects or whether, as Gail Fine, "Knowledge," argues, it is possible, for example, to have understanding (*noêsis*) of the objects of mathematical hypotheses or thought (*dianoia*) of the forms. *Timaeus* 53d, indirectly at least, appears to lend support to Fine's position. For Timaeus implies that if the mathematical principles used in the construction of the simple bodies were related to the higher principles, they would have a stronger cognitive status than the likelihood they have on our current account.

29. On the significance of the term "accept" (*apodekhomai*) at 29d2, 30a1, see Burnyeat, "ΕΙΚΩΣ" 154–55.

30. From 20a–b; cf. 27a.

31. See also 27c1–2, 55d1–2, 63a6. Ultimately, it is what the gods think that matters (27c7–d1), but we may take it, particularly given the work's view of human wisdom as an assimilation to the divine, that the gods will agree with what wise men think.

ence between demonstrative and dialectical arguments lies in the cognitive status of their premises. In the case of demonstrative deductions, the premises are principles which are true and primitive, commanding belief in and by themselves; in the case of dialectical deductions, the premises express reputable beliefs: that is, beliefs which are accepted by everyone or by the majority or by the wise (i.e., by all of the wise, or by the majority, or by the most notable and reputable of them).

Aristotle's description of dialectical argument suggests two parallels with Timaeus' view of the status of cosmological argument. For Timaeus, too, the arguments of cosmology are, as we have seen, not demonstrative or based on irrefutable and changeless premises, but likely. Moreover, the premises of cosmology are posited repeatedly on the basis of what people, but in particular the wise, would accept.[32] For both Timaeus and Aristotle, reference to the opinions of the wise is a way of establishing principles in subject matters that do not allow strict demonstration.[33]

## THE MOST PROPER PRINCIPLE OF COMING INTO BEING

T4 concludes what Socrates refers to as the "prelude" (*prooimion*, 29d5). The prelude set out certain basic distinctions that have allowed us to outline the nature of the subject matter and the sort of accounts we should expect to be given of it. Timaeus now takes up the account of the creation of the cosmos proper. But first he offers a more precise description of the principle of coming into being and the cosmos:

> T6 Now let us say for what reason (*di' hêntina aitian*) the constructer constructed coming into being and this universe. He was good, and nobody good ever bears any grudge (*phthonos*) about anything. Being without grudge, he wanted all things to become as similar to himself as possible. This indeed is in the most proper sense the principle of coming into being and the cosmos (*geneseôs kai kosmou . . . arkhên kuriôtatên*) which someone would be most correct in accepting from wise men. (29d7–30a2)

Now T6 reads as a corrective. In T1–T2, Timaeus created the impression that the principle of coming into being was the cause (*aition*) of the cosmos. But now we are told that the "most proper" (*kuriôtaten*) principle of coming into being answers not to the cause (*aition*) of coming into being, the maker, but to some-

---

32. See also 27c1–2, 53c5, 55d1–2, 63a6.

33. I take it that it is no accident that one of Aristotle's examples of a dialectical problem (*Topics* 104b8) is whether or not the world is eternal, the very question put to us in T1.

thing referred to as the *aitia* of coming into being. Since Timaeus raises the question of the *aitia* as a new and distinct question, it is clear that he does not think that the question of the *aitia* has been answered by the identification of the *aition* in T2. The *aition* of the coming into being of the cosmos was the maker and father, but the *aitia*, we are now told, is his desire to make the world as similar to him as possible.[34]

"Most properly" (*kuriôtatên*) here suggests that we were not wrong to think that the *aition* was the principle, but that it is not the most proper or precise way of understanding the principle. We can see why that would be so. Being told that somebody made the universe still leaves a question as to why or in what capacity he made the universe. The *aitia* states what exactly it was about the *aition* that made it produce the universe. It is the *aitia*, then, which most properly is the principle of the coming into being, not the *aition*.

One way of thinking about the relationship between the *aition* and the *aitia* is to see it as involving the difference between what after Aristotle we call the "efficient" and the "final cause."[35] The efficient cause initiates the change,[36] while the final cause is the goal toward which the change is aimed. Aristotle holds that, where both are at work (i.e., both in art and nature), efficient causes are generally secondary to final causes, since by identifying the goal we can understand why the efficient cause is at work.[37] With the end or purpose of a building in mind, we can understand why the builder initiates the series of changes leading to a building.

Similarly, we may think that when Timaeus in T2 refers to the father and maker of the cosmos, he has in mind that which initiates the coming into being of the world—the efficient cause, in Aristotle's terms; but when he refers to the *aitia*, he has in mind that for the sake of which the world was made, the "final cause."[38] Moreover, when Timaeus ascribes priority to the *aitia* over the *aition*, calling the *aitia* the "most proper" principle, he would, again like Aristotle, be ascribing priority to the final cause over the efficient. The reason he ascribes priority to the *aitia* would be just that it explains why the *aition* is at work: his desire to make the world as good as possible (the *aitia*) tells us why god (the *aition*) is moving the world in the first place. So we need to understand the *aitia* before we can understand why the maker is at work.

---

34. Timaeus seems to be observing a distinction between *aition* and *aitia*, which can be traced in other Platonic dialogues; M. Frede, "The Original Notion of Cause," *Essays in Ancient Philosophy* (Oxford, 1987), 129. For a clear statement of the distinction in the *Phaedo*, see J. Lennox, "Plato's Unnatural Teleology," *Aristotle's Philosophy of Biology: Studies in the Origins of Life Sciences* (Cambridge 2001), 283. I. Mueller, "Platonism and the Study of Nature," in J. Gentzler (ed.), *Method in Ancient Philosophy* (Oxford, 1998), 85–86, rightly finds the distinction also in the *Timaeus*. The uses of *aitios* at 61b6, 63e8, 76c6, 80a1, and 87e5 (cf. *sunaitios* at 46d1, 76d6, and *summetaitios* at 46e6) can all reasonably be taken to refer to the thing responsible for the causation.

35. Proclus, in *Tim.* 335.28–357.23, suggests that this is a standard way of reading the text.

36. For example, *Physics* 194b29–32, *Posterior Analytics* 94b7, *Generation of Animals* 778b1, and *De Anima* 417b20.

37. *Parts of Animals* I.1.

38. The father is of course Aristotle's standard example of the efficient cause; *Phys.* 194b30.

Yet this account of the relationship between *aitia* and *aition* needs to be modified. We cannot take the *aitia* simply to be the goal of the maker. For the *aitia* is not simply the good that god aimed at but his *desire* to bring about this good, and on Aristotle's plausible analysis of the causation of action, the desire counts as the efficient cause. So it might be said that the *aitia*, while it mentions the goal, is in effect a restatement of the efficient cause. So, the *aitia* states the respect in which the *aition* works as an efficient cause, by desiring a certain outcome for the world. David Sedley, denying that Plato in the *Timaeus* has the concept of a final cause, thus speaks of god's intelligence as "a goal-directed *efficient* cause."[39]

It is clearly right that in stating the *aitia*, the goal cannot be detached from god's desire. However, that does not mean that we should reduce the goal to an aspect of the efficient cause. This would be to ignore the explanatory priority that the goal has in explaining the way the efficient cause works. After all, it is because it appears good to the maker that the world should be thus and so that he desires it to be in this way. There is a sense, then, in which it is the good as it appears to god that is the cause of his desire for the world to be so. To be sure, the apparent good works here not as another efficient cause of god's desire but as a final cause. That is to say, the goal works as a cause by informing and directing god's desire. But if the goal, in this way, has causal priority over god's desire, it cannot be right simply to see it as an aspect of this desire. Rather than reducing god's goal to an aspect of the efficient cause, it seems better to speak, as does Gail Fine, of god's desire to make the best possible world as an efficient cause with a final cause constituent.[40]

We should note Timaeus' exact formulation of this final cause constituent. He does not say simply that the maker wanted to make the universe as good as possible but that he wanted to make the world as like himself as possible. Of course, Timaeus has just emphasized that the maker is good, so saying that he wants to make the world like himself implies that he would also thereby make it as good as possible. However, it might reasonably be thought that goodness can come in different varieties, so it is not obvious that by wanting to make the world as good as possible the demiurge should also want to do so in the way that makes the universe as like himself as possible. In fact, it does seem that the goodness that god as an eternal, intelligible being (37a1) enjoys is not quite the same as the goodness enjoyed by the cosmos as a perceptible, created being. That the world is made good by instantiating somewhat different properties from eternal being is clear, for example, from the creation of time. God created time as a moving likeness of eternity, where eternity is a simple unity, but time has parts: past, present, future. The goodness of the world does not lie in its being a mere carbon copy of its eternal

39. Sedley, *Creationism*, 114, n.47.

40. G. Fine, "Forms as Causes: Plato and Aristotle," in G. Fine (ed.), *Plato on Knowledge and Forms: Selected Essays* (Oxford, 2003), 375. On this interpretation of the *Timaeus*, Aristotle's refusal in *Metaphysics* A.7 (988b6–8) to recognize final causes in the *Timaeus* seems understandable if uncharitable: understandable, because Aristotle would want to keep efficient and final causes distinct in natural causation (*On Generation and Corruption* I.7 324b13–18); uncharitable, because Aristotle presumably himself accepts that in cases of conscious agency final causes are embedded in efficient causes (*De Anima* III.10; in particular, 433a15–20). I am grateful to Robert Bolton for showing me his illuminating paper "The Origins of Aristotle's Teleology" (unpublished) on this subject.

paradigm; rather, it lies in its having properties analogous to those of its eternal paradigm but also appropriate to coming into being.

Consider now god's first actions:

> T7  For god wanted for everything to be good, and nothing, if possible, to be bad, and so when he took over everything that was visible in a state of unrest, moving discordantly and without order, he brought it into order from disorder, believing that order was in every way better than disorder. Now it wasn't permitted (nor is it now) that one who is supremely good should do anything but what is best. Accordingly, the god reasoned and concluded that in the realm of things naturally visible no unintelligent thing could as a whole be better than anything which does possess intelligence as a whole, and he further concluded that it is impossible for anything to come to possess intelligence apart from soul. Guided by this reasoning, he put intelligence in soul, and soul in body, and so he constructed the universe. He wanted to produce a piece of work that would be as excellent and supreme as its nature would allow. This, then in keeping with our likely account, is how we must say divine providence brought our world into being as a truly living being, endowed with soul and intelligence. (30a2–c1, Zeyl trans.)

Now, it was already implied in T3 that the maker was characterized by intelligence (*noêsis*). For he made the world by looking to an eternal paradigm which, as premise 1 told us, is graspable by intelligence. Elsewhere Timaeus makes it clear that the maker is or has intelligence (*nous*).[41] By investing the world with *nous*, as his first task, god has therefore not just made the world as good as possible; he has also made it as good as possible in the way that maximizes its likeness to himself.[42]

The principle of coming into being explains the degree of similarity that obtains between god and the paradigm: the paradigm has been chosen in order to allow the world as far as possible to be like god. Scholars have often noted these similarities, sometimes with a view to assimilating or identifying the demiurge with the paradigm.[43] However, this assimilation gets Timaeus' point exactly the wrong way around. It is not that the demiurge is similar to the formal paradigm because

---

41. Cf. 39e7–9 and 48a2. If god is *nous*, is that compatible with god's having desires, as claimed in T6? Yes, for as the argument for the tripartition of the soul in *Republic* IV shows, *nous* is capable of generating its own desires; cf., for example, T. Irwin, *Plato's Ethics* (Oxford, 1995), 215, and H. Lorenz, "The Analysis of the Soul in Plato's *Republic*," in G. Santas (ed.), *The Blackwell Guide to Plato's Republic* (Oxford, 2006), 154–57.

42. I tend to agree with the view that god is *nous* without soul, where soul is required only for those things that have or come to have *nous*; cf. R. Hackforth, "Plato's Theism," in R. E. Allen (ed.), *Studies in Plato's Metaphysics* (London, 1965), 444–45; S. Menn, *Plato on God as Nous* (Carbondale, Ill., 1995), 19–24; F. Karfik, *Die Beseelung des Kosmos* (Leipzig, 2004), 199–200. If this is correct, the demiurge's first creative act also confirms my point that the maker seeks to maximize the likeness between himself and the creation but in a way that it is appropriate to something in the category of coming into being.

43. Baltes, "Γέγονεν," 88; E. D. Perl, "The Demiurge and the Forms: A Return to the Ancient Interpretation of Plato's *Timaeus*," *Ancient Philosophy* 18 (1998), 81–92; F. Ferrari, "Causa paradigmatica e cause efficiente: il ruolo delle Idee nel *Timeo*," in C. Natali and S. Maso, *Plato Physicus* (Amsterdam, 2003), 88–91.

he just is the same as the paradigm; instead, the formal paradigm has been chosen by the demiurge because it is in the relevant respects similar to him. The principle of creation is god's desire to make the world as similar to him as possible and the choice of the eternal paradigm is instrumental to that end.

That god should make another thing like himself makes good sense also in view of that fact that he is not only the craftsman but also the father of the universe (T2). Normally, a craftsman does not make another thing such as himself. A carpenter does not make another carpenter but, say, a chair. However, in generation the cause is like the offspring. As the *Symposium* says, generation works by producing another thing such as oneself.[44] Or as Aristotle says, "man generates man." As the father of the cosmos, god makes another thing like himself: a unitary, immortal, intelligent god.[45]

Another reason to keep in mind god's paternity of the world is that it helps explain what he can and cannot be responsible for in the creation of the world. At 41a–d he prepares to hand over the creation of the mortal creatures to the lesser, generated, gods: "Those things which came into being and came to participate in life through my agency would be equal to gods' (41c2–3). One might ask why a divine craftsman should not also make mortal beings. The answer cannot be that since immortal beings are of more worth than mortal ones and god as a good craftsman always makes the best possible product, god can only make immortal beings. For Timaeus clearly thinks that the universe overall is better or more beautiful by the inclusion of mortal beings. So from the point of view of the cosmos in its totality, god would act as the best craftsman by making also the mortal beings. The answer is, rather, that he is prevented by his nature as a father from creating merely mortal beings: as a father, one can only generate something of the same nature as oneself. It is no accident, therefore, that one context in which the language of procreation is rife is where Timaeus refers to the cosmos as a god. As a father, the maker generates another thing like himself; being a god, his offspring, too, are immortal and divine (34b9, 37c7, 68e4).

If, finally, we ask why god, the father, should *want* to make a world as like himself as possible, Timaeus' answer in T6 is that it is because he lacks envy (*phthonos*). But what does lacking envy have to do with wanting something else to be like oneself? Aristotle's definition of "envy" (*phthonos*) in *Rhetoric* II.10 suggests a partial answer. Envy, for Aristotle, is "a kind of pain in respect to *one's equals* for their apparent success in things called good, not so as to have the thing oneself, but [solely] on their account" (1387b23–25).[46] Envy is thus a vice specifically concerned with the goods that others who might be considered one's equals would enjoy. In his goodness, the demiurge, however, is so far removed from envy that he wants to create something which as far as possible is his equal such that it can enjoy, as far as

44. *Symp.* 207d3–4, 208a6–b2. For the idea of similarity between parent and offspring, see also *Republic* 506e3.

45. Cf. 38b6–9, 41a7–b6, 92c8–9.

46. Translation from D. Konstan, *The Emotions of the Ancient Greeks: Studies in Aristotle and Greek Literature* (Toronto, 2006), 112–113; my emphasis.

possible, the same goods as he.[47] Given his complete lack of envy,[48] it makes sense that god's creative desire should take the form of wanting to create another being like himself to enjoy the good that he enjoys.

So far I have argued that Timaeus' introduction is concerned with identifying the proper principle of cosmology. The principle is associated with the maker of the creation, but in its most proper sense Timaeus identifies it with the maker's desire for the world to be as similar to himself—and hence as good—as possible. It is this principle that prescribes the choice of an eternal model, and specifically, the choice of a living being, for the creation of the cosmos.

# NECESSITY: ANOTHER PRINCIPLE
# TAKES THE STAGE

In 47e2–48e1, a passage brimming with references to *arkhai*, Timaeus advises us that we need another principle or starting point (*arkhê*) for our cosmology.[49] What is the second principle and why is it called for? At 47e2–48a5 Timaeus tells us that intelligence for the most part guided necessity toward the best in the creation of the universe and that we have so far considered the universe, with a few exceptions,[50] insofar as intelligence so guided necessity. That intelligence had to persuade necessity to create the world but only managed to do so for the most part shows how necessity is a causal principle independent from intelligence.[51] But what does Timaeus mean by "necessity"?

Timaeus refers to "necessity" also as "the wandering cause" (48a6–7). The two designations may appear incompatible: necessity suggests causal determinacy and regularity, "wandering" indeterminacy and irregularity. However, "wandering" is to be understood in contrast to the goal-directedness of the intelligent cause, and not to determinacy or regularity: the intelligent cause does what it does for the sake of the good, whereas the wandering cause brings about its outcome without regard to its goodness. Calling necessity "the wandering cause" does not mean that it is indeterminate or irregular, only that its outcome is not determined by considerations of what is good. "Wandering" underlines that necessity is not goal-directed.

---

47. For an alternative view of envy in T6, see F. G. Hermann, "φθόνος in the World of the *Timaeus*," in D. Konstan and N. K. Rutter (eds.), *Envy, Spite and Jealousy: The Rivalrous Emotions in Ancient Greece* (Edinburgh, 2003), 53–83.

48. Note the strongly emphatic negatives, *oudeis peri oudenos oudepote . . . phthonos*, 29e1–2.

49. See, in particular, 48a7–b3.

50. I take one of the exceptions to be the account of mirror images at 46a2–c6; cf. the reference to "necessity" at 46b1.

51. On the sense of persuasion, see G. Morrow, "Necessity and Persuasion in Plato's *Timaeus*," in R. E. Allen (ed.), *Studies in Plato's Metaphysics* (London, 1965), 421–37, and Johansen, *Natural*, 99–103.

Already 46d–e suggested that there was a notion of necessity which belonged to bodies. Now we are seeking to understand necessity as a principle independently of the intelligent cause. We are therefore invited to consider what the bodies and their affections were before the intelligent cause ordered them in the creation. That is to say, we are going to look at the "nature and affections" of earth, water, fire, and air (48b3–5) before the intelligent cause acted on them in order to see what properties bodies necessarily give rise to in and of themselves. It is to meet this request that Timaeus introduces a third kind of entity, alongside the two we know from premise 1. The third kind is of a mysterious nature, having no inherent properties, yet serving an indispensable role as the "receptacle" of the coming into being of bodies.[52]

Remember that we are interested in the nature of fire, earth, air, and water before the coming into being of the cosmos. The receptacle is introduced first (49b–50b) because of a certain difficulty in talking about fire, earth, air, and water as being *anything*. The problem is that they always seem to be changing into each other and never appear to be the same. So it is difficult to say which of them is which. Later Timaeus refers to the pre-cosmic bodies as "traces" (*ikhnê*, 53b2) of earth, fire, water, and air.[53] While the term "traces" suggests that they are reminiscent of the cosmic version of the four bodies, it also suggests that they are not the real thing. We can see why: not yet having been invested by god with forms and numerical order, the bodies did not have the integrity to be reliably identified. In these circumstances, Timaeus says (50b1–2), it seems safer when asked what each of them is to refer to the receptacle, just as if when asked what some gold was which is constantly changing shape it would be safest to say that the thing was gold.

It may seem natural to take the comparison with the shapes in gold to imply that the receptacle is the matter out of which the pre-cosmic bodies are composed. However, later Timaeus refers to the receptacle as the "space" (*chôra*) that provides a place for all the things that come to be (52a9–b1). The issue whether the receptacle should be understood as the matter out of which bodies are constructed or the space in which they are located has been intensely discussed. My own view, which I cannot argue for here, is that the two views are not incompatible: we can understand the receptacle as space[54] and at the same time allow that there is a sense in which space is that out of which bodies, understood as geometrical figures, are constructed.[55] It is worth noting, however, that as far as god's creation of the four basic bodies is concerned, Timaeus presents not the receptacle itself but the traces as that out which the bodies are created (*ex hautôn*, 53a7; cf. 53b1–6). Of course, one might say that since the traces are in some sense just qualifications of

---

52. For detailed interpretation, see D. Miller, *The Third Kind in Plato's Timaeus* (Göttingen, 2003).

53. I take no position here in the debate whether the appearances at 49a6–50a4 should be understood as phenomenal particulars or recurrent types. For a summary of the debate with further bibliography, see Zeyl, *Plato Timaeus*, lvi–lxiv.

54. For reasons for prioritizing the spatial description of the receptacle, see Johansen, *Natural*, 118–36.

55. See V. Harte, *Plato on Parts and Wholes* (Oxford, 2002), 247–64, in particular 250–51; see also Zeyl, *Plato Timaeus*, lxi–lxiv.

the receptacle, god also orders the four bodies out of the receptacle, but if so, that is only indirectly. Moreover, saying that the receptacle itself is ordered is problematic since it is supposed to remain without any inherent properties if it is to serve properly as a receptacle (50d–51b).

The description of the four bodies as ever-changing appearances in the receptacle suggests a condition that is specific to the pre-cosmos. Yet it is clear that Timaeus is seeking to set up a description of the pre-cosmos that allows us to draw certain parallels with the behavior of the bodies in the cosmos. So, in describing the transformations of bodies, he refers in the present tense to what we see (49d4) or think that we see (49b8–c1), and at 52e4 he refers to the three kinds as having been *also* before the world came into being. Later (54b–c) he says that the appearance that all the four bodies change into each other was wrong, since earth, given its different geometrical composition, stands apart from the transformations. If this claim is to count as a correction, then it seems that Timaeus cannot have meant earlier to refer merely to the pre-cosmic state of the four bodies.

Timaeus seems then to have adopted a viewpoint on the pre-cosmos that to some extent carries over to the cosmos. The account of the motions of the bodies in the receptacle is a good example. Timaeus tells us (52e–53a) that in the pre-cosmos the four bodies—that is, their traces—shook and were in turn shaken by the receptacle, somewhat like a winnowing basket separating grains. The result was that the bodies joined with their kindred bodies in different parts of the receptacle. It is clear that this process continues in the cosmos (57c). The difference is that the distribution according to likeness and unlikeness now reflects the geometrical natures of the four bodies. Similarly, while the bodies changed into each other also in the pre-cosmos, they continue to do so in the cosmos, albeit now according to rules of geometrical composition.

There is then a viewpoint from which one can describe the pre-cosmic and cosmic bodies in the same way: namely, the viewpoint that abstracts from the mathematical order whereby god shaped the bodies (53b4–5). It is instructive for Timaeus to adopt this viewpoint because he can thereby show the properties that the materials of the creation contribute to the bodies in the cosmos: already in the pre-cosmos, bodies come into being as likenesses of forms, possessed with tendencies to move toward kindred bodies and to change into each other. The materials continue to contribute such properties to the bodies in the cosmos.

Timaeus understands the way that pre-cosmic bodies contribute properties to the cosmic bodies as a matter of necessity. His concern in 47e–68d as a whole, indeed, is to explain the properties of bodies from the bottom up, starting with the most basic constituents of the creation. As I understand it, necessity here attaches to the consequences of bodies' having a certain material composition. Properties that bodies have by necessity are those properties which the bodies take over from their material constituents.

Three examples illustrate the way Timaeus uses necessity to explain the properties of bodies from the bottom up, from the point of view of their material constituents. First, if a body has depth, he says, it is necessary that it has surfaces (53c–d). Second, if the faces of earth are made of isosceles triangles, it is necessary that earth be stable and immobile (55e). Third, if the head is fleshy, then it is necessary, given the character of flesh, that it lacks sensitivity (75a–b). Necessity here attaches to the consequence of having certain properties given the properties of the materials at a lower level of composition. On this understanding, the so-called works of necessity are staggered in such a way that a body at each level $n + 1$ has certain properties necessarily because of the properties of its constituents at level $n$.

Understanding necessity in this way, as relative to a certain level of composition, helps us with two problems. One is that the passage at 53c–68d cannot be meant to account for the "works of necessity" to the exclusion of intelligence. The geometrical composition of the simple bodies is explicitly assigned to god at 53b4–5 and again at 56c3–7. It cannot then be Timaeus' intention to account for the composition of bodies and their compounds by reference to necessity to the exclusion of intelligence. On my suggestion, in contrast, we would expect intelligence to operate alongside necessity at each level of composition. Necessity is a separate explanatory principle at each level because it refers back to those properties the materials have in virtue of the lower level of composition. But this is compatible with the materials having been composed at the lower level by the gods: recall here the case of flesh bringing certain necessary properties to the head because of the way the gods had composed it.

Another problem, rarely addressed by commentators, is that if the receptacle is meant to account for necessity, it is curious that there is not a single mention of necessity during the entire passage discussing the receptacle. Rather, after 48a, the first mention comes again at 53c5–6, with, as we saw, the discussion of the geometrical composition of the simple bodies. The omission is to be expected, however, if necessity attaches to the consequences of the materials' having certain properties at level $n$ for the composition of a body at level $n + 1$. Since the traces in the receptacle represent level 0 from the point of view of composition of bodies, we should not expect necessity to enter our account at this level but only at the next level, that of the composition of the simple bodies, as in fact we found at 53c. Put differently, necessity as the modality of bottom-up causation does not apply to items at the bottom level itself but only to the relationship between items at the bottom level and those at the next level up and subsequent levels.

# CONCLUSION: BRINGING THE TWO PRINCIPLES TOGETHER

At the end of the account of "the works of necessity" (68e–69b), Timaeus considers the relationship between the necessary and the intelligent or "divine" causes. It is clear that explanatory priority rests with the divine cause: the necessary cause was introduced so that we could better grasp the divine. For the necessary cause was used by the divine cause, as an auxiliary cause, in bringing about his fair design. Timaeus is clearly thinking of the necessary cause in extension of the craftsmanship model: the necessary cause provides the means by which the divine craftsman realizes his design. Necessity may present an obstacle to design, as we saw in the case of the human head which could by necessity not both be covered in flesh and be sensitive, even if that would have been preferable. However, Timaeus is suggesting that we may also think of necessity not as an obstacle but as an aid to the intelligent cause. For if there were not materials which necessitated certain outcomes, then the materials could not reliably help the craftsman realize his design. If heating up metal did not necessarily make it pliable, then the furnace would be of less use to the blacksmith. We need to understand necessity, then, both as a constraining and as an enabling cause in relation to the divine cause. Plato's cosmology is based on these two causal principles, which from opposite ends of the creation together allow us to see why this, rather than any other, world came into being.

In the end, then, we are left in cosmology not with one highest principle of being as in the *Republic* but with two principles, both of which are specifically geared to explaining the world as something that has come into being.[56] The specificity of the principles to coming into being is obvious in the case of necessity, since this principle attaches to bodies as such. However, the highest principle, god's benevolence, is also a principle of coming into being, not a principle of being. As we have seen, the highest principle, in the manner of the craftsmanship and fatherhood, is essentially a cause of coming into being of what was not before. To understand the *Timaeus* properly, we need to read the principles of cosmology as fundamental and specific to the study of the visible world. In the *Timaeus*, the notion of cosmology as a mere means to the study of being has been left well behind.[57]

# BIBLIOGRAPHY

Baltes, M. "Γέγονεν (Platon *Tim.* 28B6): Ist die Welt real entstanden oder nicht?" in K. A. Algra, P. W. van der Horst, and D. T. Runia (eds.), *Polyhistor: Studies in the History and Historiography of Ancient Philosophy* (Leiden, 1996), 76–98.
Bolton, R. "The Origins of Aristotle's Teleology" (unpublished).
Burnyeat, M. F. "ΕΙΚΩΣ ΜΥΘΟΣ" *Rhizai* 2/2 (2005), 143–66.

56. The argument of this essay lends indirect support to D. Sedley's thesis in "The Origins of Stoic God" (in D. Frede and A. Laks [eds.], *Traditions of Theology* [Leiden, 2002], 41–83) that the Stoics could have derived their two-principle physics from a reading of the *Timaeus*. For the later ancient answers to the question, how many principles of cosmology in the *Timaeus*?, see D. Runia, "Plato's *Timaeus*, First Principle(s) in Philo and Early Christian Thought," in G. Reydams-Schils (ed.), *Plato's Timaeus as Cultural Icon* (Notre Dame, Ind., 2003), 133–51.

57. I am grateful to Gail Fine for many helpful comments on this essay.

Code, A. "Reply to Michael Frede's 'Being and Becoming in Plato,'" *Oxford Studies in Ancient Philosophy* (suppl.) (1988), 53–60.

Cornford, F. M. *Plato's Cosmology* (London, 1937).

Ferrari, F. "Causa paradigmatica e cause efficiente: il ruolo delle Idee nel *Timeo*," in C. Natali and S. Maso (eds.), *Plato Physicus* (Amsterdam, 2003), 83–96.

Fine, G. "Forms as Causes: Plato and Aristotle," in G. Fine (ed.), *Plato on Knowledge and Forms: Selected Essays* (Oxford, 2003), 350–96.

Fine, G. "Knowledge and Belief in *Republic* V–VII," in G. Fine (ed.), *Plato on Knowledge and Forms: Selected Essays* (Oxford, 2003), 85–116.

Frede, M. "Being and Becoming in Plato," *Oxford Studies in Ancient Philosophy* (suppl.) (1988), 37–52.

Frede, M. "The Original Notion of Cause," *Essays in Ancient Philosophy* (Oxford, 1987), 125–50.

Hackforth, R. "Plato's Theism," in R. E. Allen (ed.), *Studies in Plato's Metaphysics* (London, 1965), 439–47.

Halliwell, S. *Aristotle's Poetics* (London, 1998).

Harte, V. *Plato on Parts and Wholes* (Oxford, 2002).

Hermann, F. G. "φθόνος in the World of the *Timaeus*," in D. Konstan and N. K. Rutter (eds.), *Envy, Spite and Jealousy: The Rivalrous Emotions in Ancient Greece* (Edinburgh, 2003), 53–83.

Irwin, T. *Plato's Ethics* (Oxford, 1995).

Johansen, T. K. *Plato's Natural Philosophy* (Cambridge, 2004).

Karfik, F. *Die Beseelung des Kosmos* (Leipzig, 2004).

Konstan, D. *The Emotions of the Ancient Greeks: Studies in Aristotle and Greek Literature* (Toronto, 2006).

Lennox, J. "Plato's Unnatural Teleology," *Aristotle's Philosophy of Biology: Studies in the Origins of Life Sciences* (Cambridge, 2001), 280–302.

Lorenz, H. "The Analysis of the Soul in Plato's *Republic*," in G. Santas (ed.), *The Blackwell Guide to Plato's Republic* (Oxford, 2006), 146–65.

Menn, S. *Plato on God as Nous* (Carbondale, Ill., 1995).

Miller, D. *The Third Kind in Plato's Timaeus* (Göttingen, 2003).

Morrow, G. "Necessity and Persuasion in Plato's *Timaeus*," in R. E. Allen (ed.), *Studies in Plato's Metaphysics* (London, 1965) 421–37.

Mueller, I. "Platonism and the Study of Nature," in J. Gentzler (ed.), *Method in Ancient Philosophy* (Oxford, 1998), 67–90.

Perl, E. D. "The Demiurge and the Forms: A Return to the Ancient Interpretation of Plato's *Timaeus*," *Ancient Philosophy* 18 (1998), 81–92.

Rowe, C. J. "The Status of the 'Myth,'" in C. Natali and S. Maso (eds.), *Plato Physicus* (Amsterdam, 2003), 21–31.

Runia, D. "Plato's *Timaeus*, First Principle(s), and Creation in Philo and Early Christian Thought," in G. Reydams-Schils (ed.), *Plato's Timaeus as Cultural Icon* (Notre Dame, Ind., 2003), 133–51.

Sedley, D., *Creationism and Its Critics in Antiquity* (Berkeley, 2007).

Sedley, D. "The Origins of Stoic God" in D. Frede and A. Laks (eds.), *Traditions of Theology* (Leiden, 2002), 41–83.

Vlastos, G. "Creation in the Timaeus: Is It a Fiction?," *Socrates, Plato, and Their Tradition*, ed. D. W. Graham (Princeton, N.J., 1995), 265–79.

Zeyl, D. *Plato Timaeus* (Indianapolis/Cambridge, 2000).

CHAPTER 20

..............................................................................................................

# THE *PHILEBUS*

..............................................................................................................

## CONSTANCE C. MEINWALD

THE *Philebus* discusses the good human life and the claims of pleasure on the one hand and a cluster containing intelligence, wisdom, and right opinion on the other in connection with that life. Plato includes extended treatment of metaphysics and methodology: this is his typical supplement to the procedure of his own Socratic dialogues, which considered human questions in isolation from other issues. Some parts of our dialogue are intelligible locally as we read them, and some tricky bits have benefited by treatment in the secondary literature. Yet the text as a whole remains elusive and hard to grasp. We do not understand why the discussion develops as it does and how all this is supposed to work together. This means we do not understand the characteristic Platonic move of addressing human questions with the aid of what he takes to be more fundamental investigations. Moreover, we do not grasp the dialogue as an artistic success. Surely a work studying good mixtures and thematizing the harmony (that is, the fitting together) of unlike elements should itself fit together in some intelligible way. But Plato may well have given the *Philebus* an obscure unity that we are challenged to find.[1] In this essay I provide an overview of the dialogue, with special attention to parts not already patent. Then I use my interpretation of the metaphysics and method passages as a basis from which to develop ideas about how these work with the discussion of pleasure and reason.

---

1. Our dialogue fits the idea of M. F. Burnyeat, *The Theaetetus of Plato* (Indianapolis, 1990), xii–xiii and interspersed throughout, that in advanced work Plato sets us challenges that we must do philosophy to meet.

# CHARACTERS AND SETTING

The *Philebus* is a minimalist dialogue: it contains no action outside the philosophical conversation, and Plato has not specified when or where that conversation occurs. We have become used to such settings as wrestling schools, the homes of the wealthy, the prison, and the lush countryside. Also usual is temporal location: after the first victory of the tragic poet Agathon, at the time of the Great Panathenaea, in the days leading up to the death of Socrates. The *Philebus* not only omits any real-world setting but differs from many of its predecessors[2] in being presented to us without mediating characters. In the latter respect it returns to the compositional form of works like the *Apology* and *Euthyphro*, a form replaced in such elaborate works as the *Symposium*, *Theaetetus*, and *Parmenides*. In the more elaborate form, the conversation constituting the core of the dialogue is fictively reported by a narrator, thereby adding another layer to the embedding of the philosophical conversation in a fictional world that has been built up to resemble the real world as it was within living memory at Athens at the time of composition.

The participants in the "typical" dialogue are often quite fully characterized and usually based on men known to history; readers will have been expected to recognize them. Yet in the *Philebus* the cast is reduced to a minimum. There are apparently (16a4–5, 19c4–5, 19d6–e5)[3] unnamed auditors who are tacit throughout. Philebus himself has retired from official participation by the time the dialogue starts: his role is so minimal that we cannot even tell if he is based on a real person. He functions within the dialogue as the personification of the position he has espoused[4]: holding that pleasure is the human good, he denies that the desirable human life has any need of reason or thought, and he embodies his position by not having enough *nous* (mind, intelligence) to engage in inquiry. Plato thus shows that he is aware, even if Protarchus in his sometimes overstated formulations (e.g., at 21e3–4) is not, that the considerations advanced here do not work on everyone.

Protarchus is taking over the hedonist position as we join the action: note the idiom that he should pay attention to the position he is to defend lest what is said not be "to his mind" (11b1), a subtle touch hinting that Protarchus has a mind; he will prove reasonable and will be convinced by the considerations Socrates brings forward in the course of their discussion. There is some mystery about the identity of Protarchus, but we do have material for speculation. Our character is "son of Callias" (19b5) and has heard Gorgias (58a7–8); thus he may be the offspring of the well-known patron of the sophists (*Apology* 20a2–b9; the main action of the

---

2. I do not wish to engage in controversies of chronology; I hold common views on dating, with the proviso that one's stance should be nondogmatic. Standard opinion assigns the *Philebus* a late position, quite possibly as Plato's last completed work. See C. Kahn, "On Platonic Chronology," in J. Annas and C. Rowe, eds., *New Perspectives on Plato, Modern and Ancient* (Washington, D.C., 2002), 93–127.

3. Citations are to J. Burnet, *Platonis Opera*, vol. 2 (Oxford, 1901).

4. Cf. L. G. Westerink, ed. and trans., *Damascius Lectures on the Philebus* (Amsterdam, 1959), 6–7: Philebus represents the *zôiôdes* (animal type).

*Protagoras* takes place in his house: 311a1–2, 314b8–e2, 315c8–d4.) This famous Callias was at one time the wealthiest man in Greece, though his fortunes declined in his lifetime. Connected by marriage with Plato, he was the father of two sons: we know the name of only one; thus the other may have been Protarchus.

A son of "our" Callias would exhibit many features common among the youth of Plato's fictional world. In particular, the concern of the father for the best education money could buy, along with the failure of the son despite that to amount to much (if we may assume that he actually ⌐failed to earn a place in history ⌐ and isn't just anonymous by accident), would resonate with the dialogue's inquiry into the role of rational accomplishment in the good human life and what that accomplishment involves. Yet this historical person was too young to have conversed philosophically with Socrates.[5] Does this rule out the identification? It could be that Plato does mean him, despite the chronological impossibility; alternatively, it could be that he invents a character about whom he puts in virtually no details. Before we pursue these ideas, I would like to draw attention to the way in which the relationship of Protarchus with Socrates is represented.

Despite the fact that he is assigned the position Philebus originally held, Protarchus seems to me not to be a natural opponent, and not so much to be converted[6] in the course of the dialogue by Socrates, as to have had a relationship with him all along. This interlocutor seems rather dependent on his questioner: he asks Socrates to answer questions in his stead—for example, at 20a1–8 and 28b7–10. He is clingy in a childish way, reminding Socrates "You agreed to be with us"[7] for the purpose of settling the matter at hand; Protarchus insists at 19d6–e4 on his role as the one who gets to say when Socrates may be excused and refuses to let him go at 23b2–4.[8] At the end of the dialogue, the notion (in other works typically expressed by Socrates) that there are points that need further discussion is expressed by Protarchus, as a reason here not (as has been usual) for resuming discussion on another occasion but for not releasing Socrates now (67b11–13). Though our window on the action closes, the idea seems to be that Socrates and Protarchus are continuing their conversation.

These observations can be gathered in the service of a suggestion that would also help answer the question why Plato brings Socrates back as the leading character

---

5. For the historical information in this paragraph, I have relied on D. Nails, *The People of Plato* (Indianapolis, 2002), 68–74, 257. Nails thinks Protarchus is not a son of our Callias: the one we have been discussing was too young, and the possibility that Callias could have had another and undocumented son is remote.

6. A term thematized by D. Frede in, for example, "Disintegration and Restoration: Pleasure and Pain in the *Philebus*" ["Disintegration"], in R. Kraut, ed., *The Cambridge Companion to Plato* (Cambridge, 1992), 427. Frede is also the author of *Platon: Philebos* (Göttingen, 1997) and many other publications on our dialogue; in cases like this of overlapping publications, I will favor the accessible for the convenience of readers.

7. Note *sunousian* at 19c5. Literally "being with," but used commonly for sexual intimacy, this is a favorite way for Plato to refer to philosophical engagement—for example, at *Lysis* 223b3; *Laches* 201c2; *Protagoras* 310a2, 335c3, 347e1; *Gorgias* 461b1; *Symposium* 172b7, 172c1; *Theaetetus* 150d4, 151a3; *Timaeus* 17a5; and *Sophist* 217e1.

8. Compare the role of Callias in marshaling discussion at *Prot.* 317d5–e2, 335c7–d5, 338b3, and 362a1–3.

after writing a series of substantial works in which he did not have this role. The topic—the relative responsibility of pleasure and intelligence for the good human life—and the dialectical style of the work are of course associated with Socrates.[9] Is this the whole answer? It must be admitted that Plato's use of Socrates as a character in general has not been controlled by philosophical overlap with (what we take as) the historical Socrates or the Socrates of Plato's own early dialogues. Perhaps our observations concerning the literary elements may suggest something here. To summarize, we have in the *Philebus* a bare philosophical discussion, unlocated in place and time, with an interlocutor either impossible or fictional and barely characterized, featuring a Socrates who won't go if "we" don't wish it.

Plato—obsessed throughout his compositional career with the death of Socrates—now brings him back one last time. We could thus see the *Philebus* as imagining how Socrates lives on in "Platonic heaven."[10] The death scene in the *Phaedo* had been followed by the resurrection of Socrates narrating the feast of reason when he went down to the Piraeus; this was achieved by setting the *Republic* further in the past than the *Phaedo* had been. That this time was truly lost was underscored early on by the false security enjoyed by Cephalus. (The ruin of the family's fortunes and the death of Polemarchus[11] in the convulsions of war and revolution were known to everyone by the time of composition.) Plato's late period in a way offers a twofold death of Socrates. We know he will be convicted in the trial to which the *Sophist* alludes,[12] and he has been upstaged in Plato's work as well: after having been schooled by the venerable Eleatic in the *Parmenides*, he was a comparatively minor presence in the *Sophist, Statesman*, and *Timaeus*. All this is followed by the last bow of the familiar figure, now outside place and time, engaging in conversation with a partner not available in real life, embracing all of Plato's recent metaphysical suggestions and more, and always ready in this fantasy to continue the association he has promised for as long as his young interlocutor wants.

If this suggestion is too fanciful, we may make use of many of the same observations (though without helping to explain the return to prominence of the character Socrates) by settling for the idea, which seems true to me in any case, that the *Philebus* represents the extreme of the process of leaving out entertaining elements that help draw people in. The later Plato assumes that readers are familiar with ideas developed in previous dialogues; we are no longer like listeners at intro lectures but have, so to speak, taken ethics and been participating in the metaphysics seminar. Thus we have in this latest of completed dialogues the philosophical content stripped down to its essentials.

9. So D. Frede, *Plato Philebus* (Indianapolis, 1993), lxvii–lxxi, and Frede, "Disintegration," 431–33. Frede holds, as I do not, that the *Philebus* also resembles Plato's earlier portrayals of Socrates in representing lively conversation with highly characterized interlocutors.

10. The possibility that after death one has the opportunity to philosophize at leisure was articulated by Socrates at *Apology* 41b5–c4.

11. Made famous by his brother in "Against Eratosthenes" (Lysias XII).

12. By opening with the statement that this is the next day's meeting agreed to at the end of the *Theaetetus*, when Socrates was off to meet the indictment of Meletus.

# THE COURSE OF THE DISCUSSION

As we have noted, as the curtain rises Protarchus is taking over the position originally held by Philebus. The theme question and the rival answers given to it (question and answers are first formally stated at 11b4–c3 and summarized at 60a7–b4; cf. 11d4–6, 13a8, 13b7, 13e4–6, 19c4–d6) are put with some variation, compounded by translators' choices, but the force of Protarchus' position is clearly enough that pleasure alone makes human life good. Socrates, on the other hand, maintains that wisdom, intelligence, right opinion, and such are ... we think he will say the human good, but he pulls back and says more carefully "better than pleasure" (11b9).[13] It will develop that Socrates had reason for his careful formulation, since he will argue that our life requires a mixture of elements to be desirable and fit for a human being.

When one reads through the dialogue for the first time—or, indeed, for the tenth or twentieth—one may well be puzzled by the way in which the discussion now starts to skip around. Socrates, having claimed that pleasures are many and unlike each other (as are forms of knowledge), announces a "One/Many Problem" (14c7–15c3) he considers significant and introduces (16b4–18d2) a method from "some Prometheus" that helps to deal with it. Socrates says this method is based on the fact that things have *peras* (limit or definition) and *apeiron* (the unlimited or indefinite) in them, though he does not explain what this means. The Promethean Method involves dividing subjects into their subkinds and knowing how the subkinds combine with each other; Socrates says he and Protarchus should use the method on their candidates (18e8–19a2; cf. 19b2–3). Protarchus confesses his inability and asks first Philebus, who does not reply (19a3–b4), and then Socrates to do his task for him (19c1–e5, 20a1–8). But Socrates, instead of applying the method, suddenly recollects an argument to show why neither pleasure nor knowledge can be the human good (20b3–22c4).

For pleasure the key intuition (which Protarchus is brought to experience) is that a life of the greatest pleasures in which one did not even know what one was experiencing, and had no awareness of one's past or reckoning about the future (all of which are functions of Socrates' candidate), is not really desirable for a human being.[14] Socrates calls this the life of a mollusk (the higher animals may be thought to have some self-awareness or memory), and evidently the idea is to turn on its head a frequent source of hedonist inspiration: for them, the idea that pleasure is the goal of all other creatures—cattle and cats, dogs and horses—suggests it is our

---

13. Socrates foregrounds different members of his cluster, depending on context, and switches between the infinitives *noein* and *phronein* (11b7) and the nouns *nous* and *phronêsis* (used more pervasively, e.g., at 13e4; cf. 60b4). The idea, though, is uncontroversially that his cluster includes the spectrum of what we might call "correct cognition," or the "mental faculties," or "manifestations of reason."

14. Note the resemblance between the setup here—that the human good must by itself be sufficient to make a life desirable—with what we find in Aristotle (*NE* 1097a8, 1097b14–21).

natural goal as well, while here the thought is that since we have different capacities, our life has a different goal than that of an oyster. Maintaining symmetry, Socrates points out that a life of reason alone would also not be human; in this case, it might rather be divine, but, after all, we are not gods.[15]

For us, then, a mixed life containing both reason and pleasure must be the best, though this does not yet say whether all types of cognition and all pleasures should be included. However, the victory of the mixed life shows already that Protarchus' position, that pleasure is the human good, cannot be right. Similarly, Socrates' candidate cannot enjoy this place, though it may still be, as he put it, better than pleasure. The rest of the dialogue is supposed (22c5–e3) to explore each of the original candidates for the purpose of awarding a prize for second place based on relative responsibility for the good life; the examination, in fact, turns out to prepare us to make the mixture that is that life.

For his exploration of pleasure and reason, Socrates says he needs "new equipment, though perhaps some will be the same" (23b6–9); this introduces a Four-fold Division of things into *peras* (limit or definition), the *apeiron* (the unlimited or indefinite), what is mixed from them, and the cause of the mixture. We will soon turn to understanding this passage and its relation to the Promethean Method. But for now, the thing to note is the way in which our topics follow one another. The introduction of the four fundamental categories leads immediately to the placement of pleasure (27e5–7 with 31a5–6) in the category of the *apeiron*, partly perhaps through misunderstanding on the part of Philebus (evident from Socrates' reaction at 28a1–4), but this is enough to go forward with for now. As we will see, subsequent discussion will be applicable to this point.

Mind, meanwhile, is placed in the category of the cause [of the mixture] in a passage (28a4–31a3) that self-consciously takes off from the views of "all the wise" (28c6–7). The passage trades heavily on the intuition, thought to be self-evident in Greek antiquity (when machines were not as central as they are for us, with our notion of mechanical regularity), that the order observed in the heavens must be due to the operation of a mind.[16] So Socrates and Protarchus adopt the tradition of the sages that mind is the ruler of the cosmos and the mind in us is the ruler of our body. The general setup here, with elemental ingredients in "the all" being the source of the paltry ingredients in us, seems to follow Anaxagoras, and he has been an important precursor for Plato's own views. Also harking back to Anaxagoras is the special role of mind. But Plato famously had made Socrates in the *Phaedo* (97b8–98c2) complain that the natural philosopher, having raised expectations by the extremely promising way in which he introduced this entity, then "did not make use of his mind." Plato may think to do better here: we will see if the balance of the dialogue advances things in this regard.

---

15. Cf. *NE* 1095b14–22 on pleasure as the goal of animals, and 1177a12–18 with 1177b26–1178a8 on contemplation as divine.

16. This section tends to elude reconstruction as a formal argument; it may be better to take it is *expressing* the tradition of the sages.

Why, someone might ask, if the agenda is to find out which of the two candidates is more responsible for the excellence of the mixture, does the placing of mind in the category of the cause not settle the matter? Surely the cause of the mixture is responsible for it, and this is even clearer in Greek where *aition* lies behind both English terms. The answer, I think, is parallel to Socrates' criticism of Anaxagoras in the *Phaedo*. There he said that since the natural philosopher made mind the source of motion in the cosmos, Socrates expected that Anaxagoras would explain the good that mind was seeking to achieve in the unfolding of events, but that this hope was disappointed. So here, that mind is the cause of one's activity is all very well, but a satisfying explanation must go on to tell more about *what one has in mind* in acting. The thing responsible for the desirability of the mixture in this sense may at this point be anything.

In the dialogue's own terms, Socrates says that in addition to placing each of the candidates in its category, they must investigate through which affection it comes about and in what it occurs (31b2–4). Why they must investigate this he does not say here. Taking up Protarchus' candidate, Socrates embarks on a long discussion (31b4–53c3!!), which starts from the idea that a living thing has a harmonious balance of its constituents. When this is disrupted, we have pain, and restoration of harmony is pleasure (31c2–d10). (At 43b1–c6 Plato will add a refinement: only *felt* disruption of a creature's constitution is pain; felt restoration is pleasure.) We are treated to lengthy discussion of varieties of pleasure, generally emphasizing the negative: ways in which they may be called false, their mixture with pain, their unseemliness. This is all capped by two arguments returning to the original idea that pleasure cannot be the good. First is a powerful argument (53c4–55a3) relying on the idea that as a process of coming into being, pleasure is always for the sake of something else, so that it cannot be the good, which must obviously be that for the sake of which other things are.[17]

The next argument (55b1–c1) is highly elliptical and trades on connections between the good, the good man, the good life, and virtue that are standard in the ancient ethical tradition. (The crucial link is that virtue is whatever puts a person in a position to live the good life.) Here Socrates starts with a sort of argument from opposites: if pleasure were really the good, then someone suffering pain would be a bad man—whatever else he were like. And his opposite, the man undergoing pleasure, whatever else were true of him, would have virtue. Protarchus' intuitions reject this.

With the discussion of pleasure over at long last, we get a fairly compact discussion (55c4–59d9) of the arts and sciences, showing how some are purer and more exact than others. Finally comes the production (59d10–64b8) of our mixture, which turns out to consist of every member of Socrates' cluster: all the arts and sciences, from the purest and most hegemonic to the most applied and most empirical, necessary "if we are even to find our way home" (62b8–9), supplemented only by the pure pleasures and those that attend on virtue.

17. Again, the family resemblance to the setup in the *NE* (1094a1–22, 1097a15–1097b6) is striking.

This is followed by reflections (64c1–65a5) on what makes a mixture good. The good is approached under a triple aspect of truth, measure and proportion, and *to kalon*.[18] Finally comes a ranking (65a7–end) of elements responsible for the good life: this is stretched out so as to reduce the pure pleasures to fifth place after which, obeying an injunction from Orpheus (66c9), Socrates and Protarchus cease their song.

The sequence of topics I have just recounted should raise some questions. (Obviously there is a neutral way of recounting the sequence without attempting to explain its unfolding; I have in the past done this myself, and I believe that most people summarizing the *Philebus* do so. One achieves in this way a blandness that decreases the puzzlement naturally present in a reader dealing with the actual dialogue.) It now strikes me as important that we should ask *why* Socrates says he and Protarchus should apply the Promethean Method to their candidates and then veers off when asked to do so on behalf of his interlocutor. We should ask why, if Plato means the Promethean Method and the Four-fold Division passages to work together, he presents them separately. We should ask whether the extended discussions of the kinds of pleasure and later of the cognitive cluster represent the technical genus-species division of the method that was proposed earlier: again, if they do, why does Socrates not do the divisions earlier; and if they do not, then why introduce the method at all? We should ask how the lengthy discussions of pleasure and later of the various rational functions relate to the Four-fold Division: since the placing of pleasure in the category of the *apeiron* and mind in that of the cause is done immediately on the introduction of these categories, do the categories bear at all on the subsequent discussions? We should ask how all this prepares for the final mixing and consequent ranking. To put all these questions in one summary formulation: Why does Plato intercalate the portions of the text dealing with pleasure and reason and those containing the metaphysics and methodological equipment in the involved way he does?

In what follows I do not take up passages in the order in which they occur; we have already traced out this sequence. Rather, since the metaphysical and methodological equipment is meant to aid in the inquiry into pleasure and reason as contributors to the best life, I proceed now by laying out how I understand the passages introducing this equipment. With a detailed reading of these in hand, we then return to issues of how other parts of our dialogue may relate to them.

---

18. It is difficult to render *to kalon* in English. "The beautiful" has too aesthetic a connotation for this passage. "The fine" has good balance between the aesthetic and moral possibilities: *to kalon* is the love object for the *Symposium* ascent (206b1–221a7) and also features in Aristotle's description of the prospective student of ethics, who must love what is noble and hate what is base (*NE* 1179b4–31).

# METAPHYSICS AND METHODOLOGY

I believe the *Philebus* should be understood in the context of Plato's initiative to treat forms by giving genus-species trees:[19] that is, to understand the kinds in question in accordance with the process of "Platonic division."[20] For us today it may be easiest to catch onto the idea by thinking of the program of Linnaeus. We can think of such a scheme as starting with a genus and producing its species by adding differentiae, then adding differentiae to each species, and so on until lowest kinds are reached. An account, or real definition, of each of the lower kinds is then available via genus and differentia(e). Being an animal with a backbone is what it is to be a vertebrate. Plato in the *Parmenides* and *Sophist* marked out assertions with a special force so that this fact could be expressed with the form of words: the vertebrate is an animal with a backbone in relation to itself.[21] The totality of such genus-species structures would map out the underlying structure of reality; the totality of truths "in relation to itself" thus would express comprehensive deep understanding of that reality. While this way of conceiving of forms becomes especially prominent in the late (or technical) dialogues, it was hinted at much earlier: Socrates told Euthyphro that they would have an account of piety if they could say *what part of* justice it is (12d5–e4).[22]

The One/Many Problem of the *Philebus* arises naturally for someone who takes such divisions and the entities involved in them seriously: What preserves the unity of a genus if it is divided into many species?[23] Socrates offers the Promethean Method in this connection, yet to some extent—the extent to which it uses an apparatus of division—it would seem to repeat the basis for the problem. However, there is also material that offers promise of a solution. Our passage emphasizes a systematic and

---

19. The same word, *eidos*, lies behind both many key assertions we put in terms of forms (e.g., *Republic* 476a5) and many central passages (e.g., *Phaedrus* 265e1–2) translated as concerning species.

20. See the groundbreaking M. Frede, *Prädikation und Existenzaussage* (Göttingen, 1967), or C. Meinwald, "Good-bye to the Third Man" ["Third Man"], in R. Kraut, ed., *The Cambridge Companion to Plato* (Cambridge, 1992), 365–96. V. Harte, *Plato on Parts and Wholes* (Oxford, 2002), 6, is agnostic about whether the kinds of the late dialogues are forms. M. Miller, "The God-Given Way," *Proceedings of the Boston Area Colloquium in Ancient Philosophy* 6 (1990), 329–59, denies that the *Philebus* continues Plato's tree program.

21. Plato attaches the same force, on some occasions of use, to elliptical formulations along the lines of "the vertebrate is an animal with a backbone." I hold that the *Parmenides* rejects the reading on which this says that the form exhibits the feature of having a spine (as a sensible cat does). See Meinwald, "Third Man," and M. Frede, "Plato's *Sophist* on False Statements," in R. Kraut ed., *The Cambridge Companion to Plato* (Cambridge, 1992), 397–424.

22. Some scholars, including myself in some other publications, capitalize such expressions. But note that these stylistic choices correspond to nothing in Plato's Greek, in which the capital/lowercase distinction as we use it was not yet operational.

23. For my views on this passage, see C. Meinwald, "One/Many Problems," *Phronesis* 41 (1996), 95–103. R. Dancy, "The One, the Many, and the Forms: *Philebus* 15b1–8," *Ancient Philosophy* 4 (1984), 160–93, has similar motivations. A. Barker, "Plato's *Philebus*: The Numbering of a Unity" ["Numbering"], *Apeiron* 19 (1996), 161–64, makes a suggestion similar to mine. I am glad to find that this essay and Barker's "Text and Sense at *Philebus* 56a" ["Text"], *Classical Quarterly* 37 (1987), 103–9, definitive concerning discussions of music, point beyond music to an interpretation of the dialogue that is consonant with mine.

thorough division of an original genus into all its subkinds, all the subkinds of every one of those, and so on to the lowest kinds that exist. Relatedly, our passage emphasizes that the method is associated with subjects that have a *technê* (an art or body of knowledge), that one must master not just divisions down to *infima species* but also ways of combining the elements so produced, and that seeing how one art is set over all of them (as grammar is set over the letters) is recognizing their bond.

The major addition the Promethean Method passage makes to previous descriptions of division is that now, for the first time, the pair of terms *peras* and *apeiron* is introduced in connection with it: the fact that things have *peras* and *apeiron* in them is said to be in some way foundational, and we are told that after lowest kinds have been reached we release them into the *apeiron* (though our passage underdetermines what exactly this means). The new[24] pair of terms is not really doing much in the Promethean Method passage taken by itself, but they are placeholders for a great deal of foundational information that will be introduced when we come to the Four-fold Division. (Because of this, we will not have a good idea of what the proposed accounts look like until we connect the two passages; I will give illustrations then.)

There is, in fact, disagreement in the secondary literature about whether *peras* and *apeiron* keep the same force in the Four-fold Division passage that they had in the Promethean Method.[25] I am one of those who think that since Socrates repeatedly says they are the same, we should work from that: otherwise we ignore a unifying element Plato has made explicit. As I see it, Plato is challenging us to come up with an interpretation of the two passages that respects the constraint that *peras* and *apeiron* are the same in both, and the interpretation I offer does this.[26] On this interpretation, since *peras* and *apeiron* in the Four-fold Division combine to produce its mixed class, the kinds studied by the Promethean Method (which have *peras* and *apeiron* in them) must all be members of the mixed class of the later passage. The Four-fold Division includes as illustrations of this class music (26a4), health, fineness (*kallos*), strength, and "many fine things in the soul"[27] (26b5–7). The Four-fold Division is a study of wide scope, giving us new insight not just into the subjects of the Promethean Method but also into their constituents.

Even in the earlier passage, the *apeiron* can naturally be understood as exhibiting a blurred condition in which kinds run together with no significant demarcations. Below the level of scientifically distinguished species we must admit a wash of variety not so distinguishable: below the specific vowels is a continuum of sounds into which even Theuth and Henry Higgins must release them; below the

---

24. New, that is, in Platonic descriptions of division. I traced the relationship of the *Philebus* to earlier philosophy in C. Meinwald, "Plato's Pythagoreanism" ["Pythagoreanism"], *Ancient Philosophy* 22 (2002), 87–101.

25. The approach according to which that they do not is associated with G. Striker, *Peras und Apeiron* (Göttingen, 1970), esp. 80–81. For criticism, see J. C. B. Gosling, *Plato Philebus* (Oxford, 1975), ix, 186, 195–96.

26. For details, see C. Meinwald, "Prometheus' Bounds," in J. Gentzler, ed., *Method in Ancient Philosophy* (Oxford, 1998), 165–80, and Meinwald, "Pythagoreanism."

27. Cf. *Republic* 443c9–e2, 591d1–3, and 430e3–4.

specific musical intervals are a blur of indefinitely many other relations in which pairs of notes may stand to each other; below the lowest division into kinds of cats there is still indefinite variation in softness of fur, shape of eye, and so on—even at the level of types.[28] The Four-fold Division's treatment of the *apeiron* is consistent with this but now focuses explicitly on pairs like the hot and the cold, the wet and the dry, the high and the low. Plato may well have thought that what makes each of these pairs an *apeiron* is that its members, left to themselves, run together. To see this we may apply a pattern of thought familiar from other dialogues. The temperature of 40 degrees Fahrenheit is cold in the Ithaca summer yet warm in the Chicago winter, so the hot and the cold run together. The lowest soprano sound would be high for a bass, so the high and the low run together. And so on.

Yet the members of each such pair are capable of being distinguished and made definite for the purposes of some art or science, and then being set into good balances.[29] Medicine must specify what, for its art, the wet and the dry are, and it knows how they are well combined to produce health. Note the correctness of this traditional view in virtually all eyes, from the Hippocratic corpus to the present day. Being dehydrated, for example, is not a matter of the absolute amount of water in one's body but of the proportion of water to dry elements: a football player needs a greater volume of water than a ballet dancer, yet in both cases the ratio between water and ash in the healthy body is the same. Music is a star example in which, having specified what they took the high and the low to be, theoreticians by Plato's time had worked out desirable combinations of them that counted as harmonious intervals and, in turn, desirable combinations of intervals into modes. Harmonious intervals were famously characterized by special ratios.

The factor of *peras*, which in the Promethean Method we could barely deduce would be whatever marked off kinds from each other to make them definite, is revealed in the Four-fold Division to be proportion; Socrates first seems to make all ratios members of this category but then goes back and adds phraseology that gestures at the idea that some ratios are better than others.[30] Music cannot tolerate

---

28. The suggestion that *apeira* in the Promethean Method are at the level of types is due to J. M. Moravscik, "Forms, Nature, and the Good in the *Philebus*," *Phronesis* 24 (1979), 81–104. The overwhelming majority of scholars have assumed, as, for example, Frede still does (*Plato Philebus*, xxv, xxx), that the unlimited multitude of sensible particulars participating in each form is in question.

29. I don't think *emmetron* at 26a8 and 52d1 necessarily picks out members of the mixed class, as J. Cooper seems to suppose in "Plato's Theory of Human Good in the *Philebus*" ["Human Good"], *Reason and Emotion* (Princeton, N.J., 1999), 150, 152 (originally published in *Journal of Philosophy* 74 [1977], 713–30). Consider the following. We have seen that an *apeiron* is a blurred pair of opposites. Before these can be put into a proportion, they need to be separated; once we have something that is just wet, and similarly with dry, we can set them in proportion. What is just wet *admits measure* and can now be set into proportion with what is just dry. Compare the breaking out of measure and proportion at 66a6–b3, whose rationale must be that measure is prior to proportion.

30. Compare the criticism at *Republic* 531c1–4 of those who fail to inquire into which numbers are concordant and why. A. Barker, "Ptolemy's Pythagoreans, Archytas, and Plato's Conception of Mathematics" ["Mathematics"], *Phronesis* 39 (1994), 113–35, identifies someone who isolated a mathematical criterion according to which some ratios are better than others; the *Philebus* seems to presume some such thing.

random pitches, or even pitches reflecting ratios between any chance pairs of integers, but results when the high and the low have the special proportions famously discovered by the Pythagoreans imposed on them. This school took the lead in supposing the ratios that lie behind music to be fundamental throughout the cosmos; the program of the *Philebus* follows this lead. Thus while discussions of division in other dialogues also urge us to look for accounts, the *Philebus* envisages that these accounts take a very particular form.[31] "Promethean" accounts as I understand them will be mathematized in a Pythagorean way: subkinds of a genus will be distinguished from each other by the characteristic proportions each shows between an underlying pair of opposites, with ratios that are better for a mathematical reason being responsible for the desirable qualities of the mixtures they determine.

## SOME THOUGHTS ON DIALECTIC

We have seen that pleasure is placed in the category of the *apeiron*, and this might seem at first to be inconsistent with my understanding of the Promethean Method passage. After all, the method is supposed to be a response to a One/Many Problem that Socrates introduced in connection with the variety of pleasures, and Socrates asks Protarchus to apply the method to pleasure, which the interlocutor rightly understands to mean that he should give its species and subspecies. Yet how can this be, if the method only applies to members of the Four-fold Division's mixed class, while pleasure is *apeiron*? I think that considering this will help us with one of the questions I indicated earlier, the first one to do with the apparent jumping around of topics, especially if we now avoid the trap of making the whole thing into a string of assertions by Socrates, regarded as Plato's spokesman. The piece represents a dialectical exchange, and we should respect the special roles that Socrates and Protarchus have in connection with the examination of the position the youth is supposed to maintain. Thus it is not that *Plato* points out the varieties of pleasures, says they instantiate the One/Many Problem, gives the Promethean Method for dealing with that, proposes using the method on pleasure, and then veers away without doing so.

We can retell the sequence with greater dialectical sensitivity as follows: Protarchus and Socrates each have a candidate, and Protarchus in particular maintains

---

31. On the legacy of the *Philebus* in accounts such as those distinguishing subspecies of birds by talon length, understood in terms of the long and the short, see J. Lennox, "Kinds, Forms of Kinds, and the More and the Less in Aristotle's Biology," in A. Gotthelf and J. Lennox, eds., *Philosophical Issues in Aristotle's Biology* (Cambridge, 1987), 339–59. For the standard scheme for understanding metrical forms as invoked at *Republic* 400a4–c5, see J. Adam, *The Republic of Plato* (Cambridge, 1902; 2nd ed. 1963): the dactyl and spondee belong to the kind where the ratio between rise and fall (the two parts of a foot) is 1:1; other metrical forms are characterized by 2:1 and 3:2.

that pleasure is the good. Socrates supposes that the human good will be treatable by the method, which in general applies to all that is scientifically intelligible. Then he asks Protarchus to give the Promethean treatment of pleasure; Socrates need not suppose himself that this is possible but requires dialectically that if pleasure indeed holds the position Protarchus assigns to it, then it should be treatable in this way. Protarchus' inability to carry out the task thus might indicate not so much personal inadequacy as the fact that the task cannot be carried out. And the awareness of Socrates that a true genus-species treatment of pleasure is not possible would explain why he does not do the job for his companion here but proceeds, instead, to introduce the idea that neither pleasure nor cognition by itself can be the good.

I also think that embracing the idea that pleasure as an *apeiron* cannot be treated by the Promethean Method has another advantage when it comes to the actual discussion of varied pleasures. Here it cannot but be significant that Dorothea Frede, the author of the best treatments of pleasure in the *Philebus*, herself declares that this is not genus-species division of the technical sort, though for her being an *apeiron* does not rule out admitting this treatment (since she holds that the Four-fold Division instantiates the Promethean Method).[32] The position that a technical genus-species treatment of pleasure is possible and that Socrates still gives this lengthy discussion without doing it seems to me awkward. For me, by contrast, the fact that pleasure cannot be treated by the Promethean Method, though that is the way to understand everything that is a subject of *techné*, is a significant step in what Frede has aptly called Plato's "degradation" of pleasure.[33]

On the question why Plato introduces the Four-fold Division and the Promethean Method separately if he means them to work together, I suggest that this presentation highlights what is being added in our dialogue. The Promethean Method passage, as far as describing division goes, is fairly standard: it introduces the Pythagorean terms but does not yet do anything with them. So far, Platonic division looks about as we already thought. Then if we work out an understanding of *peras* and *apeiron* in the Four-fold Division that is tailored to fit both passages, this adds foundational information not present in other dialogues. The whole notion that genera and species—our old friends, the forms!—are made up of *peras* and *apeiron* is new and important; the use of a scheme where the *apeiron* is an underlying blurred pair of opposites while *peras* is the factor of proportion is also new.[34] This proposal allows Plato to suggest a way of integrating the mathematics he emphasized in the *Republic* (522b2–531d4) with his forms, thus revealing their

---

32. Frede, *Plato Philebus*, lvii–lviii, xxxviii; Frede, "Disintegration," 438–39.

33. Frede, "Disintegration," 429.

34. It is attractive to think that the *Philebus* contains the scheme Aristotle had in mind when he reported (*Metaphysics* 987b18–988a17) that Plato made the forms from the One and the indefinite dyad. Cf. K. Sayre, *Plato's Late Ontology* (Princeton, N.J., 1983), 13 and throughout. To see why this emerges on my interpretation, reflect that taking the *apeiron* as picking out blurred pairs of opposites connects the *Philebus* scheme with the notion of the indefinite dyad. I take *peras* as amounting to good or harmonious proportion, and there is evidence that Plato associated goodness, harmony, and unification. See M. F. Burnyeat, "Platonism and Mathematics," in A. Graeser, ed., *Mathematics and Metaphysics in Aristotle* (Bern, 1987), 213–40; Barker, "Mathematics."

study to be not just a matter of mystical revelation but one that holds out promise of an understanding at once articulable and mathematized, scientific and deep.

# PLEASURE

As we have noted, the initial categorization placed pleasure as *apeiron*.[35] I mentioned before that this may not have been for the right reason. But we can now return to consider for ourselves whether and why the idea is correct.[36] In the terms we have been discussing, for pleasure and pain to be *apeiron* means that left to themselves they blur together and are not clearly distinguished. The extensive discussion of varieties of pleasure certainly does emphasize this. The start of the investigation into how pleasure arises is with the idea of the harmony of a creature's natural constitution, the pain when this is disrupted, and the pleasure at restoration—note that this pleasure cannot even be approached without mentioning first the pain that is its precondition. Since we only enjoy eating, for example, while we are still hungry, the pleasure in question is only available when accompanied by the relevant pain. This type of pleasure may still be a necessary part of a good and healthy life; one function of the coming discussion of ways in which pleasure is false is to throw as pejorative a light as possible on pleasures and to make most of the unnecessary ones seem undesirable.

After some general discussion starting at 36c6 of the notion of false pleasure, pleasures considered false in four different ways are discussed.[37] They are, first, pleasure in nonexistent facts (37e5–40d10);[38] second, pleasure overestimated because of perceptual illusions to do with the proximity of pain and the effects of distance (41a7–42c3); third, supposed pleasure, which is really only the cessation of pain (42c5–44a10); and fourth, unseemly and intense pleasure whose precondition is the difficulty of addressing a painful and urgent desire, which introduces a return to the more general idea of *mixtures* of pleasure and pain (44b6–50e2). In all but the first of the four discussions of false pleasures, the inextricability of pain and pleasure is evident. Yet notice that Socrates mentions (47c3–d3) that first kind of case as illustrating one of the subpossibilities of mixtures of pleasure and pain contained in

35. For the context of the contemporary activity that may underlie what we find both here and in the *NE*, see A. Diès, ed. and trans., *Platon Philèbe*, 2nd ed. (Paris, 1978; 1941 orig.), liii–lxx

36. For Frede, an *apeiron* is something with no definite measure or degree in itself (*Plato Philebus*, xxxiii–iv); cf. Cooper ("Human Good," 151–52): the *apeiron* is indeterminate because essentially comparative. For them the claim about pleasure has a different force than I take it to have.

37. See R. Hackforth, *Plato's Philebus* (Cambridge, 1972; published under a different title in 1945), 69–98; Frede, "Disintegration," 442–52.

38. D. Frede, "Rumplestiltskin's Pleasures," *Phronesis* 30 (1985), 151–80, points to the perfect illustration (from the well-known tale) and makes plausible how the nonexistent facts in question may also be present or past. Imagine a woman reveling in what she takes to be her honeymoon with her true love, when in actuality she is with a conman. She *has* pleasure, but with pleasure like this you don't need pain.

the fourth discussion; this is another indication both of the constant running together of pleasure and pain and of the lack of true divisions in this discussion.

Plato has been writing throughout the dialogue so as to decrease the appeal of pleasure, but in this fourth discussion of false pleasure he turns the rhetoric up to maximum. First (46d9–e3) he details the grossly unpleasant case of a putrid inner itch which is extremely hard to get rid of and so sets up an intense pleasure that comes when rubbing and heat finally bring relief. And he follows this (47a3–b7) by the case of sexual activity leading to orgasm, assimilating the sexual case to the disgusting one. He then goes on to show how emotions—both in the theater and in the "tragicomedy of life" (50b2–3)—essentially involve a mixture of pleasure and pain, in a way that suggests that all emotions are pathological (47d5–50d2).

After this lengthy discussion of mixed, false pleasures—which works to help us think about them better and also to reorient our attitude to them—Socrates and Protarchus finally turn to pure, true pleasures (50e5–53c2). These are unmixed (50e6; cf. 51b6, 51e2–3, 52b6–7) with pain, hence must correspond to unfelt lacks (unless they are "bonuses," which do not presuppose specific deficits). The examples we now find are pleasures to do with fine colors, shapes, fragrances, and sounds and with learning.

Let us linger a moment over some apparatus Socrates uses in connection with the fineness of shapes and sounds. These are somewhat laboriously described in terms (at 51c1–d9) that need interpretation: Socrates is not talking of a fineness like that of animals or paintings of them, things that are fine *pros ti* (in relation to something). Fine *kath' hauta* (in accordance with themselves), by contrast, are something straight, curved, and so on or, in the case of sounds, smooth shining sound giving forth a pure phrase. (Here *melos* is often taken as "note,"[39] but this is not a common meaning and, in fact, reflects—and then, in turn, supports circularly—a certain interpretation, which I will reject.)

What is going on with this *pros ti/ kath' hauta* contrast? We should start from the basic fact that the core function of *pros* in this construction, to signal relationality, works with the context to determine what is meant. If we ask what it could mean to say an animal is fine in relation to something, one obvious answer is that it is in relation to some need we have of it: a fine ox does a good job around the farm. Similarly, I welcome the fine sound that answers me from the horn of my comrades when I am hard pressed in the forest. This would contrast with the case—frequent with art, but also occurring in natural cases such as the proverbial stopping to smell the roses—where something is fine without reference to any such consideration. These afford pleasures "not like those from rubbing" (51d1)—that is, not mixed with necessary pains. The contrast as so interpreted would not be that between the ideal and the instance or that between the abstract and the representational, nor would it equate purity with monotony.[40] Rather, it would connect

---

39. When rendering 51d7, see, for example, Frede, *Plato Philebus*, and Diès.

40. I am suggesting we see the examples as applying the criterion, not as further limiting it (for the latter, see Frede, "Disintegration," 452–53, and Frede, *Plato Philebus*, liii). To equate purity and monotony would not only leave us with an unhappily restricted range of pleasures but would surely be a problematic position for a program that enshrines harmony, which, after all, requires more than just one note.

with the surrounding concerns, since it would turn on the issue of whether something's fineness and our pleasure in that are conditioned on a felt need.

So the list of pure pleasures contains those in certain presentations of colors, shapes, sounds, and fragrances and in learning. All of these are free from association with pain and free from unseemliness. Yet none is a strong candidate for our ultimate end: they seem means to or enhancements of a good life rather than what it could be organized to achieve. Even learning in the eyes of Plato and Aristotle is a minor thing compared with knowing. Indeed, if all the pleasures Socrates has been discussing at such length are attempts to achieve the balance of our natural constitution, then we may suspect that the real goal must be not them but what they lead up to: this balance or the consequent functioning of the creature in question. This thought, available through logic-chopping at the beginning of the discussion back in 31c2–32e8, has through the development of so much detail in the cases considered now become intuitively obvious: Plato has managed to describe the particular cases in such a way that the pleasure does not seem very attractive or valuable. Thus we are now ready both intellectually and emotionally for the argument about *genesis* and *ousia* at 53c4–55a3. Becoming in general is for the sake of being; we have over and over seen pleasure as restoration and thus as becoming; therefore it cannot be our goal. The *ousia* at which it aims will be the sort of harmonious constitution studied in the Promethean Method.

## SOCRATES' CLUSTER

Finally we turn to the examination of the arts and sciences, making the transition from the candidate of Philebus to the cluster preferred by Socrates. We already know from the categorization after the Four-fold Division that mind belongs in the category of the cause (it is the cause of the activity of the entity whose mind it is). Notice that cause in the Four-fold Division had been tantamount to Aristotle's efficient cause: we were told at 26e6–7 that "the maker" and "the cause" vary only verbally. Before, we wondered if Plato would be able to develop his account more satisfactorily than he felt Anaxagoras had done. This penultimate section of the *Philebus* will turn out to develop the Anaxagorean tradition to the point of great similarity with what we are familiar with in Aristotle. The *Physics* tells us that while in a sense we may pick out a carpenter as the efficient cause of a house, or a sculptor as that of a statue, more precisely it is the art of each (and ultimately the form in question) that is the real efficient cause (195b21–27, 202a9–12). In the *Philebus*, analysis of what has been identified as the cause is primarily in terms of arts and then of sciences, where the latter clearly operate through their relation to the forms in question.

Is the discussion of Socrates' cluster itself a Promethean division? Considering that mind has been put in the category of the cause rather than the mixed class, the answer, strictly speaking, should be no. But the forms of cognition will clearly be organized, as the varieties of pleasure were not, because of their close relation to their objects, themselves, in turn, clearly distinguishable (even if not by the method). And the objects of the higher cognitive forms, in fact, do admit Promethean treatment, so that the forms of knowledge concerned with them will automatically show an isomorphic structure.

The discussion of Socrates' cluster takes place in two phases: the first (55d5–56c6) concerns crafts or arts of manual skill. These are graded depending on the extent to which their practice incorporates measurement. Carpentry ("Measure twice, cut once!") is emblematic of the more accurate kind of craft. Music, on the other hand, does not—at the moment of performance—admit of measuring the quantities involved, even though they structure it. As Andrew Barker has pointed out,[41] this discussion is perfectly consistent with the treatment of music in the Promethean Method and Four-fold Division even if it takes a little thought to see why: those treatments concerned music theory, this one is about actual performance. If we follow Barker in this, then I believe we might locate the music theory of the Promethean Method actually among the sciences to come in the second phase of the discussion.

In the meantime, we find that measure, weighing, and arithmetic are hegemonic with respect to the manual arts, since as we saw, the more the arts admit measure (etc.), the more accurate they are: without the mathematical component, nothing is left but estimates born of practice. Now it turns out (56d1–57e5) that arithmetic and the other hegemonic parts of the first group afford a further distinction between applied and pure. To see this, we need to keep in mind that for the Greeks there is not a unique series of natural numbers. Rather, a number is a plurality of units, so that any pair of objects is a two, any trio a three. Thus, addition can be done with sensibles, or with ideal nonsensible units. By the lights of the *Philebus*, we have less pure arithmetic when the units are oxen or armies, and we have pure arithmetic when we treat ideal, nonsensible units. This is the most accurate apprehension mentioned to this point.

Now the second phase (57e6–59d9) of the discussion comes when Socrates introduces dialectic as a contender for the most accurate knowledge. Dialectic, from the *Republic* on, has had the task of saying of each thing what it is—that is, giving accounts (532a6–7, 533b1–3, 534b3–4)—and has been developed (see, e.g., *Phaedrus* 265c8–266c1, 277b5–8) in the genus-species way we discussed in connection with the Promethean Method. Thus it is natural to locate the technical understanding we were told resulted from the method here. Now we find that this type of knowledge is most pure—it perfectly and clearly grasps its wholly stable objects—and most deserves the name of *nous* and *phronêsis*. Coming down from this peak, there is a less pure, less accurate type of apprehension (called *doxa*, or opinion), as, for instance, when someone studies not the eternal but subjects like how this cosmos came into being. While this portion of the text contains no mention of the role of any mathematics in the purity and excellence of the knowledge in question, if we do connect it with the Promethean Method under-

---

41. Barker, "Numbering," 158–61, relying on Barker, "Text."

stood in turn in light of the Four-fold Division, then mathematical harmonics will in fact have a hegemonic role to play here that corresponds to that of measuring and arithmetic for the crafts.

# SKETCH OF A FINALE

We come now to the mixture of wisdom and pleasure to find the good life. Note that Socrates is not overambitious: he will do this in a sketch (61a4). Having started the mixing with Protarchus at 61b11, Socrates imagines (63b2–4) the pleasures being asked if they are willing to dwell with the arts and sciences and they (more enlightened than their champion, Philebus!) say that they are; they generously welcome all at once, so confirming the start Protarchus had made. When the cognitive cluster are asked the corresponding question, they are more careful, asking, "What kind of pleasures?" (63c8). It develops that they are happy with pure pleasures and embrace those that go with health and all virtue (probably pleasures like those of eating appropriate food when hungry). They vehemently reject the rest, focusing on the way in which such pleasures are inimical to the development and retention of intellectual achievement. The mixture is rounded out with the addition of truth so that it may truly come into being.

What makes this mixture and indeed all mixtures good is now apprehended under the threefold aspect of truth, fineness, and measure and proportion. (Perhaps we could connect these by thinking: a good mixture must be truly mixed; proportion as we have learned at great length from the Four-fold Division is key to good results and presupposes measure; proportion itself is akin to fineness.) To determine which of the contenders is closer to what makes life good, then, we must evaluate each one three times. That Socrates' candidate is closer to truth is obvious: the cognitive capacities aim at truth. If we had left *to kalon* as beauty, we might have thought Protarchus would win on this count, if he claimed that we take pleasure in beauty. In fact, he admits readily that pleasures are often hidden at night, and he seems to think this is because they can be shameful. Finally, let us consider measure and proportion. My interpretation allows us to see clearly why Socrates' candidate comes out strongly. For on this reading, intelligence and wisdom are the knowledge the Promethean Method amounts to: they grasp forms by giving accounts that state proportions governing underlying opposite constituents. Thus the bodies of knowledge themselves will be structured by the factor of proportion and more particularly by the desirable ratios discovered by the synthesis of mathematics and philosophy that Plato wants harmonics to be.

So the final ranking of elements in terms of relative responsibility for the good life is measure, proportion, intelligence and wisdom, arts/sciences/right opinion,[42]

---

42. Thus the *Philebus* holds back from the Stoic extreme of trying to extirpate opinion.

and pure pleasure in fifth place. A reader who felt comfortable with the internal dialectic of the *Philebus* could go on to ask how this compares with the discussions of the good life in the Socratic dialogues, in the *Republic,* and in other philosophers. But now, if not in accordance with an injunction of Orpheus, then perhaps more in the manner of musical chairs, this essay must come to a stop.[43]

# BIBLIOGRAPHY

Adam, J. *The Republic of Plato* (Cambridge, 1902; 2nd ed. 1963).

Barker, A. "Plato's *Philebus*: The Numbering of a Unity," *Apeiron* 19 (1996), 143–64.

———. "Ptolemy's Pythagoreans, Archytas, and Plato's Conception of Mathematics," *Phronesis* 39 (1994), 113–35.

———. "Text and Sense at *Philebus* 56a," *Classical Quarterly* 37 (1987), 103–9.

Burnet, J. *Platonis Opera,* vol. 2 (Oxford, 1901).

Burnyeat, M. F. "Platonism and Mathematics," in A. Graeser, ed., *Mathematics and Metaphysics in Aristotle* (Bern, 1987), 213–40.

———. *The Theaetetus of Plato* (Indianapolis, 1990).

Cooper, J. "Plato's Theory of Human Good in the *Philebus*," *Reason and Emotion* (Princeton, 1999); originally published in *Journal of Philosophy* 74 (1977), 713–30.

Dancy, R. "The One, the Many, and the Forms: *Philebus* 15b1–8," *Ancient Philosophy* 4 (1984), 160–93.

Diès, A., ed. and trans. *Platon Philèbe,* 2nd ed. (Paris, 1978; originally published 1941).

Frede, D. "Disintegration and Restoration: Pleasure and Pain in the *Philebus*," in R. Kraut, ed., *The Cambridge Companion to Plato* (Cambridge, 1992), 425–63.

———. *Platon: Philebos* (Göttingen, 1997).

———. *Plato Philebus* (Indianapolis, 1993).

———. "Rumplestiltskin's Pleasures," *Phronesis* 30 (1985), 151–80.

Frede, M. "Plato's *Sophist* on False Statements," in R. Kraut, ed., *The Cambridge Companion to Plato* (Cambridge, 1992), 397–424.

———. *Prädikation und Existenzaussage* (Göttingen, 1967).

Gosling, J. C. B. *Plato Philebus* (Oxford, 1975).

Hackforth, R. *Plato's Philebus* (Cambridge, 1972; published under a different title in 1945).

Harte, V. *Plato on Parts and Wholes* (Oxford, 2002).

Kahn, C. "On Platonic Chronology," in J. Annas and C. Rowe, eds., *New Perspectives on Plato, Modern and Ancient* (Washington, D.C., 2002), 93–127.

Kraut, R., ed. *The Cambridge Companion to Plato* (Cambridge, 1992).

Lennox, J. "Kinds, Forms of Kinds, and the More and the Less in Aristotle's Biology," in A. Gotthelf and J. Lennox, eds., *Philosophical Issues in Aristotle's Biology* (Cambridge 1987), 339–59.

Meinwald, C. "Good-bye to the Third Man," in R. Kraut, ed., *The Cambridge Companion to Plato* (Cambridge, 1992), 365–96.

43. I am grateful to Gail Fine for her work as editor. Thanks also to members of an audience at Cornell and Rachana Kamtekar for putting the questions addressed here, and to Patricia Curd, Sandra Peterson, and Marya Schechtman for entertaining my proposed answers.

———. "One/Many Problems," *Phronesis* 41 (1996), 95–103.

———. "Plato's Pythagoreanism," *Ancient Philosophy* 22 (2002), 87–101.

———. "Prometheus' Bounds," in J. Gentzler, ed., *Method in Ancient Philosophy* (Oxford, 1998), 165–80.

Miller, M. "The God-Given Way,"*Proceedings of the Boston Area Colloquium in Ancient Philosophy* 6 (1990), 329–59.

Moravscik, J. M. "Forms, Nature, and the Good in the *Philebus*," *Phronesis* 24 (1979), 81–104.

Nails, D. *The People of Plato* (Indianapolis, 2002).

Sayre, K. *Plato's Late Ontology* (Princeton, N.J., 1983).

Striker, G. *Peras und Apeiron* (Göttingen, 1970).

Westerink, L. G., ed. and trans. *Damascius Lectures on the Philebus* (Amsterdam, 1959).

CHAPTER 21

# PLATO AND ARISTOTLE IN THE ACADEMY

## CHRISTOPHER SHIELDS

Even the more recent among the older thinkers found themselves at a loss, lest it turn out according to them that the same
thing should be at the same time both one and many.

—Aristotle, *Physics* 185b25–27

## I. ARISTOTLE AS A SOURCE OF DATA REGARDING PLATO'S PHILOSOPHY

We need not stray too far into baseless psychobiographical speculation to set aside
two competing but equally monodimensional treatments of Aristotle's relation to
Plato. The first pictures Aristotle beginning his intellectual life as a meek and
dutiful Platonist and coming into his own as a philosopher only after the passing of
his master, some twenty years beyond their earliest association.[1] The second has

---

1. So W. Jaeger characterizes Aristotle: "He had accepted Plato's doctrines with his whole soul, and the
effort to discover his own relation to them occupied all his life, and is the clue to his development. It is
possible to discern a gradual progress, in the various stages of which we can clearly recognize the unfolding
of his own essential nature.... Just as tragedy attains its own ~~attains it own~~ special nature ...'out of
the dithyramb' by leading the latter through various forms, so Aristotle made himself out of the Platonic

him arriving in the Academy as a fully formed Aristotelian, yet as a thinker too immature to grasp the subtlety and force of his teacher's philosophical accomplishments, with the result that he spent his time in the school as an insufferable and captious critic of Plato.[2] Still less is there reason to credit the bewildering contention, common to antiquity and modernity, that Aristotle *never* developed to the point of grasping the rudiments of Platonic philosophy: "In the first place," says Burnet of Aristotle, "it is certain that he never understood the teaching of the head of the Academy."[3] This is not certain; for it is not true and hence not knowable; nor, indeed, is it even remotely credible. Rather, as we should expect in the case of two philosophical geniuses interacting often with one another for two decades,[4] it is entirely likely that each understood much of the other, that each benefited from the criticisms of the other, and that, consequently, each inevitably learned much from the other.[5]

Exactly what they might have learned from each other is hard to say with anything more than the confidence of informed conjecture. What we can do with a reasonable assurance is to observe some obvious points of contact in the surviving writings of Plato and Aristotle. Although he is never mentioned by name in Plato's dialogues,[6] Aristotle offers important data concerning Platonic philosophy, mainly, though not exclusively, through his characterizations and criticisms of Plato. For Aristotle discusses Plato and his views frequently and in illuminating ways in his surviving corpus,[7] and then again, more continuously and fruitfully in his *Peri Ideôn*, or *On Forms*, which survives in a reasonably intact version as a close paraphrase in a

---

philosophy" (*Aristotle: Fundamentals of the History of His Development* [Oxford: Oxford University Press, 1934], 15).

2. An ancient tradition treats Aristotle as "the foal who kicked its mother" (Diogenes Laertius, *Lives of the Philosophers* v 2). The ancient biographical evidence is collected in I. Düring, *Aristotle in the Ancient Biographical Tradition* (Göteborg: Elanders, 1957). A still useful overview of the ancient accounts of Aristotle's life in the Academy may be found in G. Grote, *Aristotle* (London, 1880), 1–26. A much more sophisticated and engaging treatment of Aristotle as moving metaphysically closer to Plato as he matures philosophically is offered by G. E. L. Owen, "The Platonism of Aristotle," *Proceedings of the British Academy* 51 (1966), 125–50. Although he enters many appropriate caveats and cautions, Owen concludes: "It seems now possible to trace [Aristotle's] progress from sharp and rather schematic criticism of Plato to an avowed sympathy with Plato's general metaphysical programme" (150).

3. J. Burnet, *Platonism* (Berkeley: University of California Press, 1928), 56.

4. Their time together during these two decades would not have been uninterrupted. For a succinct assessment of the evidence for Plato's life and activities during the period in which Aristotle was a member of the Academy, see Deborah Nails, *The People of Plato* (Indianapolis: Hackett, 2002), 243–50.

5. This would explain Aristotle's obvious reverence for Plato, whom he characterizes as "a man whom the wicked have no place to praise: he alone, unsurpassed among mortals, has shown clearly by his own life and by the pursuits of his writings that a man becomes happy and good simultaneously" (Frag. 650 R[3], Frag. 673 R[3], Olympiodorus, *Commentarius in Gorgiam* 41.9).

6. The Aristotle mentioned in the *Parmenides* is the son of Timocrates of Thorae (127a2, 136e7, 137c2; cf. *Seventh Letter* 324b–d), who was to become one of the Thirty, not our Aristotle, son of Nicomachus, the philosopher and member of Plato's Academy.

7. Aristotle mentions Plato 54 times in his extant writings. He also mentions Socrates 143 times, where very often—though the matter is permanently complicated—we may reliably treat his references to Socrates as representations of authentic Platonic views. He also mentions by name fourteen of Plato's dialogues, some such as the *Apology* and *Euthydemus* only once or twice, but others much more frequently. Most often mentioned is the *Timaeus*, at eighteen.

commentary on Aristotle's *Metaphysics* by Alexander of Aphrodisias, written in the late second or early third century AD.[8] Aristotle's criticisms are sometimes harsh and sometimes mild, and they are sometimes astute and other times curiously under-developed. Very often, however, they are not what they first seem: indeed, as I argue here, the process of becoming clear about some of Aristotle's criticisms of Plato helps us appreciate not only their real force but also the strength of Plato's resilience in the face of them. In this way, more than any other, it is possible to learn about Platonic philosophy by studying Aristotle's criticisms of Plato.

Some of the most obvious points of contact between Plato and Aristotle are easy to identify, and they cover the full range of the philosophical topics they each engage individually. The most prominent criticisms are these:

1. Aristotle raises doubts about and rejects aspects of Plato's theory of Forms.
2. Aristotle dismisses Plato's soul-body dualism.
3. Aristotle expresses severe reservations about the tenability of Plato's political philosophy.[9]

Less obvious and more consequential, if also inevitably more obscure and less tractable, are some methodological points of contact. We find in this area:

4. Aristotle is dubious of Plato's habitual and entrenched *univocity* assumption, to the effect that core philosophical notions admit of single, non-disjunctive essence-specifying accounts.[10]
5. Aristotle rejects Plato's method of division as a technique for arriving at essence-specifying definitions, whether univocal or not.[11]

In an effort to come to appreciate some otherwise easily overlooked problems in Plato's theory of Forms, problems whose interest and subtlety point to some

---

8. The authorship of the *Peri Ideôn* is sometimes disputed; and even those who accept it as having a genuinely Aristotelian provenance differ among themselves about the degree of closeness of the paraphrase given by Alexander to an autograph by Aristotle. The fullest and most illuminating treatment of this work is G. Fine, *On Ideas* (Oxford: Clarendon Press, 1993). Fine argues persuasively, with some caution, that the *Peri Ideôn* was indeed written by Aristotle, probably near the end of his time in the Academy, and with the theory of Forms as it is advanced in Plato's middle period as his intended target.

9. As a general point, whenever we speak of Aristotle as criticizing Plato, we should always be mindful of the implicit rider "in one phase of his development" for both philosophers: thus, "In one phase of his development, Aristotle is critical of Plato's conception of the soul, in one phase of *his* development." A serviceable overview of some of the main points of disagreement between Plato and Aristotle can be found in W. D. Ross, "The Development of Aristotle's Thought," in I. Düring and G. E. L. Owen (eds.), *Aristotle and Plato in the Mid-Fourth Century* (Göteborg: Elanders, 1960), 1–18.

10. For a treatment of Aristotle's attitude towards univocity in both Plato's and his own thought, see C. Shields, *Order in Multiplicity* (Oxford: Clarendon Press, 1999). For a more elementary treatment of the same topic, see Shields, "Learning about Plato from Aristotle," in H. Benson (ed.), *The Blackwell Guide to Plato* (Oxford: Blackwell, 2006), 403–41.

11. The subject of Aristotle's criticisms of Platonic division are intriguingly complicated by the fact that Aristotle is himself an unrepentant practitioner of the method. The topic thus provides fertile ground for inquiries into Aristotle's philosophical relationship to Plato. For good approaches to this subject, see W. Cavini, "Naming and Argument: Diaretic Logic in Plato's *Statesman*," in C. Rowe (ed.), *Reading the Statesman* (Sankt Augustin: Akademica Verlag, 1995), 123–38, and P. Pellegrin, "Division et syllogisme chez Aristote," *Revue Philosophique de la France et de l'Etranger* 171 (1981), 169–87.

engaging aspects of their philosophical interaction, we will consider just one of Aristotle's criticisms of Plato, one that seems initially intended to land Plato in a straightforward and inescapable contradiction. In the process of determining the actual force of Aristotle's criticism, we shall see first that it proves to be less straightforward than it initially appears and then also that Plato need hardly be bowed before it. By understanding Aristotle's criticisms of his teacher in the context of their mutual association in the Academy, we will thus also come to appreciate that Aristotle has much of consequence to teach us about Plato.

# II. Aristotle's Criticisms of Platonic Forms

Aristotle has no shortage of complaints about Plato's Forms:

1. They are causally inert and so cannot explain change or generation (*Meta.* 991a8, 1033b26–28).
2. Postulating Forms offends theoretical economy (*Phys.* 259a8).
3. Forms, if ever they existed, would be epistemologically otiose (*Meta.* 991a12–14).
4. Introducing Forms as paradigms is empty metaphor (*Meta.* 991a20–23).
5. Forms cannot be essences if they are separated, since essences are intrinsic features of things (*Meta.* 991b1).
6. Forms are irrelevant to human conduct and so must be set aside from inquiries into ethical virtue (*EN* 1096b32–4).

At his most caustic, Aristotle recommends a "good-bye to the Forms," since "they are jibber-jabber and even if they do exist they are wholly irrelevant" (*APo.* 83a32–4). Different considerations motivate these different complaints, some more and some less perspicuous, and some more and some less compelling. In general, all of these complaints at least admit of rejoinders, in the sense that none of them purports to implicate Plato in any immediate contradiction.

From this perspective, another one of Aristotle's complaints evidently takes on a special significance, since, if cogent, it seems to entail that a feature of Forms clearly accepted by Plato, their *separation*, results in a special absurdity, or even a straightforward contradiction, to which there is no possible response beyond immediate capitulation.[12] In *Metaphysics* xiii 9, Aristotle complains that the successors of Socrates went astray when they separated universals from particulars (*Meta.* 1086a31–b14). Socrates had first provided the impetus for seeking the universal features shared

---

12. This is, for example, how J. Annas understands the criticism: "The whole argument is designed not, as before, to describe the theory of Forms, but rather to subject it to lethal criticism, by showing that its very formulation involves a contradiction" (*Aristotle's Metaphysics Books M and N* [Oxford: Clarendon Press, 1976], 188).

by distinct particulars: philosophers seek knowledge of what is captured in an essence-specifying definition, because an essence-specifying definition states what holds universally and necessarily in its domain of investigation. If we wish to know what piety is, for instance, then we isolate what is common to all and only instances of piety, uncover the presence of that shared feature which makes them pious, and then put this feature on display for the benefit the discerning mind engaged in the project of philosophical inquiry. Since what is laid bare in such an inquiry must be perfectly general, this feature must also be something universal. So, for this reason, says Aristotle, Socrates was right to attend to the universal. For, "without the universal, it is not possible to attain knowledge" (*Meta.* 1086b5–6). Socrates also receives high marks from Aristotle for his admirable intellectual restraint, a virtue lacking, again according to Aristotle, in his immediate successors. Though he sought adequate definitions, "Nevertheless, Socrates surely never separated them from particulars; and in not separating them, he thought rightly" (*Meta.* 1086b3–5). That he thought rightly, Aristotle insists, can be appreciated by observing how those who do separate universals from particulars, the Platonists, go awry (*Meta.* 1086b5).

Aristotle thus suggests that intolerable results follow from the *separation* of Forms, results evidently not attendant upon the mere postulation of universals. So, from his perspective, there is nothing wrong with the bare existence of universal features: after all, Aristotle not only commends Socrates in a general way but approves of his epistemic motives for accepting universals, to the point of offering a highly technical and rigorous theory of scientific taxonomy and inference of his own in which universals play a prominent and indispensable role.[13] Indeed, the language of *universals* (*ta katholou*) belongs to Aristotle, but to neither Socrates nor Plato.[14] Moreover, in other contexts, Aristotle is altogether comfortable with the existence of "common things" (*koina*), even when his primary dialectical purpose is precisely a refutation of Plato's theory of Forms. It is thus evidently not the universality of Forms which earns Aristotle's scorn.[15] It is, rather, as he makes clear, separation and its *results* (*erga*) which render Plato's theory intolerable.[16]

What, though, is the absurdity Aristotle locates in separation of Forms? In *Metaphysics* xiii 9, he foregrounds a single unacceptable consequence, though he does not argue for this result in any detail, preferring instead to allude to fuller discussion elsewhere.[17] That result is this: by separating universals, the Platonists end up swallowing the view that "universals and particulars are practically the same natures" (*Meta.* 1086b10–11), a formulation which softens Aristotle's report earlier

---

13. See S. Mansion, *Le Jugement d'Existence chez Aristote* (Louvain: Éditions de l'Institut Supérieur de Philosophie, 1946).

14. Though one does see clear precursors in Plato, for example, 9th *Meno* 77a6.

15. I agree with M. Frede and G. Patzig, *Aristoteles, "Metaphysik Z": Text, Übersetzung und Kommentar* (Munich: Beck, 1988), vol. 1, 50–51, that attempts to distinguish *koina* and universals fail. Though neither universals nor *koina* need to be regarded as separate, both are shared in the sense sufficient for universality.

16. Indeed, in setting out the *aporiai* of *Meta.* iii, Aristotle suggests that worries we have about universals are really only worries about separated universals, as Platonic Forms are understood to be. See 997b3–12, 999a19–22, 999b17–24.

17. For a brief presentation of the most prominent alternatives, see notes 21 and 22 below.

in the chapter that the Platonists "at the same time make the Ideas, as substances, universal, and then again make them, as separate, belong to the class of particulars" (*Meta.* 1086a32–4). The harsher and the softer complaints are related but nonetheless importantly distinct. Aristotle's first complaint appears to be *categorial* in character: Forms, he supposes, belong to two different categories of being—namely, universals and particulars. This he supposes to be plainly unacceptable Unfortunately, Aristotle does not explain what is so bad about this alleged consequence, perhaps because he takes as an obvious absurdity any commitment to the existence of something which is at the same time both universal and particular. Still less clear is why there should be a problem with the final thought of the chapter, that universals and particulars are practically the same natures. Indeed, it is not entirely clear even what Aristotle means by this complaint.

Hence is not entirely clear why Plato should be so unsettled by these results; nor yet is it clear why, if the results are as problematic as Aristotle supposes, Plato is in fact liable to them. So, there are at least four sorts of questions about Aristotle's brief against Plato's theory of Forms in this regard. First, how does Aristotle argue—if he does so argue—that Plato comes to be committed to the conclusion that Forms are both universals and particulars, or that, for Plato, universals and particulars are practically the same natures? Second, what are the precise relations between these two claims? Does, for example, one collapse into the other? Third, however that may be, are there clear expressions of the elements of Aristotle's argument in the Platonic dialogues themselves, or are we rather to understand Aristotle's criticisms as rooted in principles not directly endorsed by Plato (or not endorsed in the dialogues), so that he may or may not be constrained, upon reflection, to yield to Aristotle's conclusions? Finally, there is a straightforwardly philosophical question about the force of Aristotle's complaints, whatever the Platonic provenance of the view he means to assail: what is wrong with allowing that Forms are both universals and particulars, or that universals and particulars are practically the same natures? Again, pursuant to this last question is the prior question of what Aristotle's final complaint might mean.

The straightforwardly philosophical question should remain open for the time being, at least in the sense that there might be any of a number of *different* things wrong with the results Aristotle foists on Plato. Moreover, at this early stage of our inquiry, it should be regarded as open in another direction as well: it may be a perfectly acceptable consequence, one to which Plato can remain appropriately indifferent. That is, with suitable understandings of the notions of universality and particularity, we may not be constrained to think of these categories as mutually exclusive.[18] Perhaps when the relevant distinction is properly understood, Forms *can*

---

18. Thus, P. Strawson observes that relative to a logical subject criterion *individuality* might be categorially unconstrained: "So anything whatever can appear as a logical subject, an individual. If we define 'being an individual' as 'being able to appear as an individual,' then anything whatever is an individual. So we have an endless variety of categories of individual other than particular—categories indicated by such words as 'quality,' 'property,' 'characteristic' " (*Individuals* [London: Methuen, 1959], 227). For Aristotle's language of particularity, see *Phys.* 189b30, 195a32, *PA* 639b6, and *DI* 17a39–40.

be both universal and particular. Similarly, perhaps we need not be troubled that universals and particulars are practically the same natures. One might say, for instance, that *being good* and *being right* are nearly the same sorts of attributes of certain worthy actions, even while insisting that they are nevertheless importantly distinct features.

In the end, after sorting through these matters, it will turn out that Aristotle does have a point on his side: there is something problematic in the way Plato understands Forms vis-à-vis universals and particulars. Still, Aristotle is wrong if he thinks there is an immediate argument to a self-contradictory conclusion to the effect that, necessarily, every Form is at the same time both a universal and a particular—where these are understood to be mutually exhaustive and exclusive categories of being. The important objection present in Aristotle's criticism has a rather different character. His most telling point turns out to be both more interesting and less lethal that his initial categorial concern—if, that is, we may understand his final remarks in *Metaphysics* xiii 9 as his final thought on the matter. On this alternative approach, Aristotle's contention turns out to be non-categorial: he argues that Plato's conception of *participation* as *imitation* leaves some things about both the synchronic and diachronic unity of sense particulars unexplained. On this understanding, the upshot of the criticism hardly spells the end to Plato's theory of Forms. Instead, insofar as they are legitimate, Aristotle's concerns only force Plato, or a Platonist, to augment and develop a theory that is otherwise overstressed by its own explanatory ambitions.

To reach this conclusion, we may proceed in two stages. First, it is necessary to explore the precise concern Aristotle has regarding particulars and universals in connection with Platonic Forms. Toward this end, we may consider two versions of a standard *categorial interpretation* of Aristotle's criticism of Plato, both initially plausible (as interpretations), but neither ultimately at all forceful. So, if he had only so much to say against Plato, Aristotle's criticisms would be wholly uncompelling. The best Aristotle could hope for would be a kind of unsatisfactory stalemate, a result which would surely fall far short of the sort of refutation of Plato's theory of Forms he is usually thought to offer.

Once that is established, we may turn to the second phase of our discussion. Upon closer examination, it turns out that Aristotle also has in view another, deeper problem in raising his objection to Plato. This deeper problem, unlike the one framed by the categorial version of his objection, locates Aristotle's complaint not in some immediate category error on Plato's part but, rather, in the sorts of explanatory work Aristotle justifiably expects Forms to discharge. While this deeper problem does have more traction, it hardly constitutes a crippling objection to Plato's theory of Forms. So, in the end, what remains viable in Aristotle's anti-Platonic concern about the universality and particularity of Forms does not reduce Plato's theory to a category-based incompatibility. Thus, although Aristotle has put his finger on the pulse of a genuine problem regarding the nature of Forms, his criticism fails to provide a neutral third party with any reason to relinquish a commitment to Forms—if at any rate such a commitment is otherwise independently motivated. Accordingly, Aristotle's criticism, though pertinent, points in the end only to the need for further philosophical work from Plato.

## III. Aristotle's Complaints in *Metaphysics* XIII 9

Aristotle's general critical argument begins rather surprisingly, by locating in Plato a certain lack of philosophical imagination:

> They at the same time make the Ideas, as substances, universals, and again, as separate, belong as well to the class of particulars.[19] Separation is the cause of the resultant difficulties regarding Ideas. These things were shown to be problematic earlier, because this cannot be. The reason why those who say that substances are universal conjoin these things into the same is that they made substances not the same as perceptibles. They thought that in the case of sensibles, particulars are in flux and that none of them remains, whereas they thought of universals as beyond (*para*) these and as being something else. Just as we said earlier, this is something Socrates set in motion, because of his definitions, but even so he did not himself separate them from particulars. And he thought rightly in not separating them. This is clear from the results: for while without the universal it is not possible to attain knowledge, separation is the cause of the difficulties which accrue concerning the Ideas. They [Socates' successors] regarded it as necessary, if there are going to be substances beyond (*para*) the sensible and flowing substances, that they be separate; but they did not have others and instead selected the things predicated universally, with the result that universals and particulars were practically the same sorts of natures. (*Meta.* 1086a32–b11)

The argument here is not especially complex, though the ultimate conclusion seems surprising insofar as it weakens the bolder-sounding claim with which Aristotle begins. He says first that the Platonists "make the Ideas, as substances, universals, and again, as separate, belong as well to the class of particulars" (*Meta.* 1086a32–4), only to conclude ultimately, as we have seen, that they were thus saddled with the view that "universals and particulars were practically the same sorts of natures" (*Meta.* 1086b10–11). The point is not just that he says that they were *practically* (the normal meaning of *schedon* in this context) the same sorts of

---

19. There is a textual problem here. I read *hôs ousias* with the ms. at 1086a33, rejecting Jaeger's seclusion, which is also accepted by W. D. Ross, *Aristotle, Metaphysics* (Oxford: Oxford University Press, 1924), vol. 2, 462. Ross thinks it wrong to stress the substantiality of Forms in this context; but it is appropriate for Aristotle to mention a connection between universality and substantiality, since (i) he himself accepts such a connection in the *Categories*, and (ii) he is here recounting what he takes to be Plato's motives in regarding Forms as universal.

natures but that he demurs from asserting directly that the Ideas were *both* universals and particulars. Rather, he offers the somewhat opaque conclusion that things spoken of universally and particularly are, for the Platonists, effectively the same sorts of natures. That final conclusion is, in comparison with the clear and strident claim with which he opens, both guarded and obscure.

So, there is a question about Aristotle's ultimate objective in this passage. At first, his argument seems to trace the particularity of Forms to their being substances. Since substances are separate, and separate things are particulars, it follows that Forms, regarded as universals by the Platonists, are also particulars. In terms of their reasoning process, the Platonists, as characterized by this approach, were simply at a loss: they could not identify anything other than their own Forms to play the role of the objects of knowledge. Since there do indeed need to be such objects, Plato was generally well motivated, though insufficiently resourceful. After recognizing a need for universal objects of knowledge, seeing no alternatives to their own separated Forms—which as separated must already be substances—the Platonists end up regarding Forms as objects of knowledge as well as substances. This, in turn, implicates them in a contradiction: substances are particular, and objects of knowledge are universal.

Taken this way, laid out schematically, then, the argument of *Metaphysics* xiii 9 is this:

1. If knowledge is to be possible, there must be stable objects of knowledge, immune to the flux suffered by sensibles.
2. Knowledge is possible.
3. So, there must be supersensible stable objects of knowledge, immune to the flux suffered by sensibles.
4. As supersensible and stable, such objects might be: (i) *in rem*, or (ii) *ante rem*.
5. If they are *ante rem*, the result will be that Forms are both universals and particulars.
6. The Platonists, not recognizing 4(i) as an option, endorse *ante rem* objects of knowledge.
7. If they both exist *ante rem* and are also objects of knowledge, then Platonic Forms are both universals and particulars.
8. Hence, Platonic Forms are both universals and particulars.

This approach to Aristotle's generative reconstruction of Plato's motivations for accepting separated Forms proceeds by taking seriously the diagnostic suggestion, whether fair or unfair, that the Platonists saw no alternative to *ante rem* realism, evidently because they did not appreciate that universals might exist *in rem* (*Meta.* 1087b9–10).

In reporting Plato's motivations, Aristotle intimates that he himself accepts premises 1 and 2, and what they entail, which is premise 3, that there are supersensible stable objects of knowledge. He parts company with Plato only at premise 4: he implies that he recognizes the alternatives highlighted in premise 4, even while they are missed by the Platonists. According to his own self-presentation, on this interpretation, Aristotle thereby positions himself to avoid the ensuing results, so that, unlike the Platonists, he can offer forms which are universals but not separate and so preserve the thought that universals and particulars are of radically different natures. Presumably, his unstated conviction is that *in rem* universals are dependent entities, separate at most in thought or definition (*logô(i)*), and so not separate *simpliciter* (*haplôs*). Since separation *simplicter* belongs only to particulars, Aristotle avoids the consequences sketched for the Platonist. This at any rate makes sense of Aristotle's pointed insistence that the Platonists have *separation* and its results (*erga*) to thank for their woes.

Several problems emerge when we consider the merits of this argument. In the first instance, it is a bit difficult to take seriously the suggestion that Aristotle accuses the Platonists of failing to recognize the prospect of *in rem* universals. After all, Aristotle himself, in this very passage, locates in Socrates precisely the wanted remedy: unseparated common definitions which serve as the objects of knowledge. Still, perhaps one can say on Aristotle's behalf that while it is true that Socrates never separated his universals, he never expressly refrained from separating them either. That is, it is compatible with Socrates' not having separated universals that his successors never recognized as a relevant alternative the nonseparation of Forms, even if they were familiar with Socrates' point of view. For, as Aristotle himself suggests, Socrates did not busy himself much with metaphysical questions, which could well result in his never considering either the general question of the nature of his universal definitions or the specific question regarding their separation. When he then took his metaphysical turn, Plato opted for separation without having first entertained the relevant alternatives. He saw that Forms could not be identical with sense particulars, accepted their existence as immune to sensible flux and so in that way superior to sensibles, and consequently invested them with ontological primacy and its attendant separation. So, in principle, Aristotle might fairly accuse the Platonists of failing to discern the relevant alternatives, while in the same breath crediting Socrates with having refrained from going down the Platonist path.

Even so, there is a more serious problem, pertaining to premise 5, the premise that if they are *ante rem*, Forms will be both universals and particulars. Here, in fact, there are two distinct puzzles. The first, already mooted, concerns the force of the consequent, while the second concerns the conceptual connection envisaged between being *ante rem* and having a particular-like nature.

As for the first problem, the conclusion of Aristotle's argument does not seem fatal to the Platonist, since for all that has been established so far, something might be both a universal and a particular. Aristotle must be assuming some views about the natures of particulars and universals and about the relation between separation and particularity—views which the Platonist may or may not accept. Perhaps their natures are not mutually exclusive, and perhaps something may be separate without being particular.

This leads into the second, more consequential form of oddness in the passage. Aristotle does not conclude finally that Ideas will be both particulars and universals or even that universals and particulars will *have* (*echein*) the same natures but, rather, that they will *be* (*einai*) the same natures (*tas autas phuseis einai*; *Meta.* 1087b11). This is not the point Aristotle is usually taken to be making in this passage;[20] and it is moreover a point which is harder to explicate than the simpler suggestion that Ideas are both universals and particulars. For the argument is not simply that since separation belongs to substances and particularity to separate things, the Platonists, having made universal Forms substances, must now also accept their particularity. Rather, the argument holds that finding no other stable objects of knowledge than their own Forms, the Platonists end up accepting as real and separate things those very Forms and that consequently, according to Aristotle, they also end up regarding universals and particulars as being effectively the same natures. This Aristotle supposes to be a problem for the Platonists.

# IV. The Source of Aristotle's Complaint: Two Questionable Contentions

What, precisely, is the final problem? Aristotle does not say but instead prefers to refer back to an earlier discussion, which he fails to identify. Unfortunately, Aristotle's backward reference is a bit hard to pin down. The three most relevant passages, all proposed as the appropriate reference by at least one commentator or other,[21] would seem to be *Metaphysics* iii 6, where the fifteenth and final *aporia* of metaphysics is retailed; *Metaphysics* xiii 4, where Aristotle attacks Platonic Forms in ways parallel to *Metaphysics* xiii 9; and, finally, *Metaphysics* vii 13–15, where Aristotle sketches some of the reasons that nothing spoken of universally is a substance and then draws out the consequences of those reasons for the theory of Forms.

20. The *Revised Oxford Translation* skirts this issue, leaving a misleading impression: "So that it followed that universals and individuals were almost the same sort of thing." Annas has much the same: "With the consequence that universals and particulars were almost the same sort of thing" (*Metaphysics*, 115).

21. Ross rightly observes that *diêporêtai* in *Meta.* 1086a34 "suggests a reference to Book B" (*Metaphysics*, 462). Even so, it is difficult to know which argument in that book Aristotle might intend. It certainly also remains open that Aristotle has another aporetic passage in mind, especially one raising difficulties for the Platonists. J. Owens, *The Doctrine of Being in the Aristotelian Metaphysics*, 3rd ed. (Toronto: Pontifical Institute of Medieval Studies, 1978), agrees that the language suggests a reference to *Metaphysics* iii, but adds that it should not be understood as relying on vii 13–15. He thinks, in fact, that "M 9–10 ... presumes no knowledge in the 'hearers' of M 9, and does not positively refer to ZH" (426). He, too, thinks that it is likely a reference to the last aporia of *Metaphysics* iii, but focuses exclusively on the epistemic horn that if principles are not universal they will not be knowable (1003a15–17). That allusion would be peculiar, however, since that aporia holds quite generally and with no special reference to those who postulate Forms. It is true that the next chapter, xiii 10, does allude to the final *aporia* of *Metaphysics* iii, at 1086b14–20. Owens does not make clear, however, why these are to be treated as so closely linked.

Of these, *Metaphysics* xiii 4 is the least plausible, since it contains no argument which is even indirectly relevant to the claim that Platonic Forms are both universals and particulars or to universals and particulars being practically the same natures.[22]

*Metaphysics* iii 6, by contrast, does seem to bear on this issue, at least orthoganally. There, in the fifteenth *aporia*, Aristotle argues dilemmically, first, that no universal is a source or principle (*archê*) (*Meta.* 1003a7–9) and, second, then that every principle (*archê*) must be a universal (*Meta.* 1003a13–17). The argument for the first horn has it that:

1. Universals are common (1003a8–9).
2. Nothing common signifies *some this* (or, more loosely, *any particular thing—tode ti*; 1003a8–9).
3. So, no universal signifies any particular thing (*tode ti*).
4. Substance (*ousia*) signifies a particular thing (*tode ti*; 1003a9).
5. So, no universal is a substance (*ousia*).
6. The principles of things (*archai*) are substances (*ousiai*) (assumption).
7. So, no principle (*archê*) is universal.

This argument trades on some putative conceptual connections between substantiality, particularity, and the nature of principles (*archai*).

The argument for the second horn, by contrast, finds its impetus in some epistemic theses held in common by both Plato and Aristotle: knowledge (in the sense of *epistêmê*) is in all cases of universals (1003a14–15; cf. *Meta.* 998a24–26, 998b4–6, 1013a14–17; *APo.* 87b28–88a17; *Phys.* 194b16–20); we do have knowledge of principles (*archai*)—or at least such knowledge is possible; so, principles (*archai*) are universal. Since both horns cannot be correct, something must give way.

Now, it is a matter of some dispute as to what gives way, in part because it is also a matter of dispute as to where Aristotle addresses the fifteenth *aporia* later in the *Metaphysics*, if anywhere. This need not concern us here. Rather, for our purposes, it is important only to observe that in mounting his anti-Platonic contention in the opening of our passage from *Metaphysics* xiii 9, Aristotle alludes to both horns of this dilemma. Forms, as objects of knowledge, must be universal, as the second horn contends. But why must they be particular? Tracing out the pattern of inference in the first horn, the argument seems to be:

1. Forms are principles (*archai*).
2. No principle (*archê*) is universal.
3. Whatever is not universal is particular.
4. So Forms must be particular.

22. Annas, *Metaphysics*, along with H. Bonitz, *Aristotelis Metaphysica*, 2 vols. (Bonn: Marcus, 1848, 1849), understands Aristotle's complaint as relying on xiii 4. Annas is right that xiii 4 provides a backdrop of sorts to xiii 9; but it does not contain any argument with the conclusion to which Aristotle here alludes: viz., that Forms are both universals and particulars. Ross is in my view right, then, to suggest, as against Bonitz (and so prospectively as against Annas): "There is nothing in M 4, 5 . . . that quite suits the reference" (*Metaphysics*, vol. 2, 462).

Here, then, we have a rather different point than the direct claim, regularly and rightly ascribed to Aristotle, that if Platonic Forms are substance (*ousiai*), they must be particulars.[23]

This is a welcome result for Plato, since it is doubtful that this sort of anti-Platonic argument will eventuate in anything more than an immediate and unilluminating stalemate. If Aristotle insists that all substances (*ousiai*) are particulars and Plato responds that he rejects the motivating assumption of the inference, then no progress will have been made in either direction. Rather, the case will have been aptly characterized by Grote who, writing in the late nineteenth century, observed that such objections "are founded upon Aristotle's point of view, and would have failed to convince Plato."[24] Moreover, on Plato's side is the retort that Aristotle himself, at least in the *Categories*, recognizes *some* substances, secondary substances, as universal, and even allows degrees among substances by noting that the species is more a substance than the genus in virtue of its being closer to the primary substance, better known than the genus, and prior in predication to the genus, since the genus is predicated of the species, while the species is not reciprocally predicated of the genus (*Cat.* 2a14–15, 2b8–14, 2b20–21). Hence, at least at some periods in his career, Aristotle sees some point in according the status of substance to at least these sorts of universals.[25] So, there seems to be no direct or easy inference from being substantial to being particular. At any rate, Plato is hardly constrained to accept such an inference without some significant ancillary argumentation.

Aristotle's appeal to the status of principles (*archai*) may point to the needed argumentation, though the final *aporia* of *Metaphysics* iii fails to provide it. Consequently, though it is relevant to Aristotle's contention that Forms are both universals and particulars, the final *aporia* of *Metaphysics* iii fails to furnish a fully satisfactory back-reference for *Metaphysics* xiii 9.

We may perhaps therefore turn to a second possible source for a fuller elaboration of Aristotle's complaint. *Metaphysics* vii 13–15 trace some of the consequences of Aristotle's own inquiry into substance (*ousia*) for Plato's theory of Forms. Surprisingly, vii 15 contains a direct and unargued ascription of both parts of the controversial thesis that Forms are universals and particulars to the Platonists. First, Aristotle argues that no Form can be defined, since "Form belongs to the class of particulars, as they say (*hôs phasi*), and is separate" (*Meta.* 1040a8–9). Later in the same chapter Aristotle returns to the epistemic basis for treating Forms as universals but adds a twist by arguing that Forms *must* be universals, on the grounds that "every Idea is such as to be participated in (*methektê*)" (*Meta.*

23. The various connections between form, separability, substance, and particularity in Plato and Aristotle are well discussed by G. Fine, "Plato and Aristotle on Form and Substance," *Proceedings of the Cambridge Philological Society* (1983), 23–47.

24. Grote, *Aristotle*, 560.

25. This assumes that the species and genus of *Cat.* 5 are regarded not as abstract particulars, as sets or aggregations of some kind, but as universals. This assumption is warranted by Aristotle's treating the species and genus as *predicables* (*Cat.* 2b32–35), together with his suggestion that whatever is by nature predicated of many things is a universal (*DI* 17a38–40).

1040a26–27; cf. *Meta.* 990b28, 1079a25). This shows, according to Aristotle, that Ideas cannot consist of other Ideas, since in that case that from which Ideas would be constituted (presumably other Ideas) would equally need to be predicated, under pains of their being simple, and so unknowable, in addition to their being not such as to be participated in. If that is correct, then Ideas, as individuals, do not admit of definitions.

Here, then, we read a rather different basis for the tension that Aristotle locates in Plato's views: Forms are accepted by Plato as the sorts of things which can be participated in, and so must be universals, and yet, "as they say," Forms are also particulars.

Yet it is hard to know *where* they say that Forms are particulars. Plato does on occasion refer to a Form as *hekaston* (e.g., *Phaedo* 78d3), where the language parallels in a nontechnical way Aristotle's technical terminology for particulars, *ta kath' hekasta* (*Meta.* 1086a34). Plato also on occasion uses singular referring terms when mentioning Forms (*Crat.* 389d6; *Parm.* 133d8; *Phd.* 75b1, 75d2; *Rep.* 507b7, 597c9; *Theaet.* 146e9; *Phil.* 62a2). Still, there is a perfectly unobjectionable way in which Forms *are* particulars, whether or not they are also universals. Let us call a *deflationary particular* everything which is a determinate subject of predication.[26] On that score, it is entirely possible to say, for example, that Beauty Itself is a form, or that it is an abstract object, or that it is the most loved Form, and so on. In these cases we are talking about that particular Form, that thing which is Beauty Itself. Aristotle's point cannot simply be that Forms are deflationary particulars as well as universals, for there is nothing objectionable about their being both. Rather, his point must be that Forms are *robust particulars*, those he contrasts with universals as early as *De Interpretatione* 7. In that chapter, Aristotle clarifies his conception of the contrast by explaining that "By *universal* I mean what is naturally predicated over (*epi*) more than one thing, and by *particular* what is not" (*DI* 17a38–40; cf. *Meta.* 1039a1). Particulars thus construed, *robust particulars*, cannot be over (*epi*) many things. Aristotle, at least in this passage, presents universals and particulars as mutually exclusive categories of being. Unfortunately, in this context Aristotle characterizes robust particulars only negatively: they are never over (*epi*) many things.

We know that Plato, in many dialogues, treats Forms as "one over many" (*hen epi tôn pollôn*). Why, though, must he also treat them as robust particulars? According to one common thought, Plato's mimeticism commits him to the particularity of Forms. That train of thought is this. Plato subscribes to mimeticism, the view that a particular *x* is eponymously *F* only by imitating the Form *F-ness*. So, for example, we call Helen beautiful because she somehow imitates the Form Beauty Itself. In general, since nothing could be *F*, except by copying something which is itself *F*, the Form *F-ness* must itself be *F*. For instance, since nothing white could be white by copying something which was not white, the original, the Form, must also be white. Thus, we typically find scholars maintaining that Plato's mi-

---

26. So, a deflationary particular is equivalent to what Strawson calls an *individual* in the sense of a logical subject. See n. 18 above.

meticism commits him to Forms which exemplify the properties copied by the particulars named after them.[27]

The general idea of such scholars is that, without resemblance, copying is impossible. Of interest here is the initially plausible assumption that Platonic mimeticism, the view that a particular *x* is *F* by imitating the Form *F-ness*, by itself commits Plato to a Form of self-predication. The assumption is something more than merely initially plausible, however, only if we assume additionally that mimeticism requires a symmetrical sameness of property instantiation. If we say, for example, that Augustine resembles Rabelais in having a big nose, then we do suppose that there is an attribute, *having a big nose*, had by both Augustine and Rabelais. Indeed, it would be odd to say that they resembled one another in this way if we were also prepared to deny that Augustine had a big nose. This may suggest, then, that resemblance requires symmetry (if Augustine resembles Rabelais with respect to *F-ness* then Rabelais resembles Augustine with respect to this same property) *and* that this symmetry is unpacked only by supposing that any such symmetry is underwritten by shared property instantiation. Taken together, these theses do not commit Plato to the self-exemplification of Forms, since it does not yet follow that Forms are themselves the properties they have; but it does commit him to the view that sense-particulars and Forms share the properties in virtue of which eponymous naming relations become possible.

It is clear, however, that scholars who argue this way are, as a conceptual matter, wrong about resemblance; and they are, moreover, wrong about mimeticism and resemblance in Plato's middle and late periods. Plato seems perfectly aware that the reciprocity restriction fails, as does any notion of resemblance given in terms of shared property exemplification. So, for example, *Republic* iii 395c–d, Plato restricts the kinds of imitation permitted to the guardians to those which imitate actions befitting of their station. They can imitate those who are coura- geous, temperate, pious, and free; but they must avoid imitating the degenerate and slavish, "lest from enjoying the imitation, they come to enjoy the reality." His worry is that "imitations practiced from youth become part of the nature and settle into habits of gesture, voice, and thought." The implication here seems to be that it is possible to imitate someone courageous without *being* courageous. Perhaps this is no surprise: Homer, says Plato, imitates Chryses, though neither Homer nor any verse of the *Iliad* is an old man supplicating the Achaeans (*Rep.* 393d). Poetic imitation requires non-narrative projection, to be sure; but this can be accom-

---

27. A typical example is W. Runciman, "Plato's *Parmenides*," in R. E. Allen (ed.), *Studies in Plato's Metaphysics* (London: Routledge and Kegan Paul, 1965), 158: "If whiteness is white (which must follow if white objects are white by resembling it) then whiteness is one of the class of white objects." W. D. Ross, *Plato's Theory of Ideas* (Oxford: Oxford University Press, 1953), 89, offers a similar judgment, when commenting on Cornford's and Taylor's earlier suggestion that copying is not *mere* resemblance. They had argued, in Ross's characterization, "that the relation of copy of original is not one of likeness, since if *A* is like *B*, *B* is like *A*, but if *A* is a copy of *B*, *B* is not a copy of *A*." Ross responds: "But this defense itself fails. Grant that the relation is not merely one of likeness; it still involves likeness, and likeness between two things involves some Form, some character, that they have in common." Ross is right to contend that *copying* is not the same relation as *resembling* (the latter, but not the former, is symmetrical) but wrong to insist that copying involves resemblance, where that is understood as shared property exemplification.

plished without anything's exemplifying the very property the object represented is represented as exemplifying (cf. *Cratylus* 423c–d).

This last point is worth stressing, since the crucial point about mimeticism in this context is not simply that the original and copy will exemplify *some* of the same properties. For every set of two things share some property or other. Rather, the point is that paradigmatism does not require that paradigms be paradigms by *exemplifying* the properties for which they serve as paradigms.[28] Consequently, nothing in Plato's mimeticism requires that he treat Forms as robust particulars. Therefore, if he thinks that Forms are particulars, Plato does not indicate that this is so simply by embracing paradigmatism. Accordingly, nothing about Plato's mimeticism forces him to accept the robust particularity of Forms.

So far, then, if we suppose that Aristotle's objections in *Metaphysics* xiii 9 ultimately rely on these sorts of considerations, we must conclude that he has failed to achieve his end. We have found instead, by tracing out two versions of the anti-Platonic argument of *Metaphysics* xiii 9, only that we arrive at a stalemate twice over. On the first approach, Aristotle contends that, according to Plato, Forms are substances (*ousiai*) and so particulars, but also that they are *over* many things (*epi tôn pollôn*) and so universals. As we have seen, Plato has an obvious response, that not every (substance) *ousia* is a particular, a retort made all the more ready in view of the fact that at least in some stages of his career Aristotle himself endorses the existence of substancē (*ousiai*) which are universal (*Cat.* 2a14–15, 2b8–14, 2b20–21). On a second version of the same basic approach, Platonic paradigmatism is ultimately the culprit, since it is supposed to entail that Forms are universals and also particulars, because though they are themselves properties, Forms must also exemplify the properties which their eponymous sense particulars copy—namely, the properties they are. Otherwise, the objector contends, Forms could not be the paradigms that Plato holds them to be. This inference relies on a false premise: that shared property exemplification is necessary for mimeticism. It also seems to assume that the only subject capable of exemplifying a property is a robust particular, which is equally objectionable. So, here, too, it is perfectly appropriate for Plato simply to shrug off the Aristotelian barrage. Taken together, Aristotle's criticisms, thus developed, are wholly ineffectual.

# V. A NONCATEGORIAL APPROACH: FORMS AS *ARCHAI*

The shortcomings of these two versions of Aristotle's criticism of Plato stem from a common source: they both understand Aristotle to be arguing that, as a categorial matter, any given Platonic Form impossibly has the property of being both a

---

28. This is a point well expressed by W. Prior, "The Concept of *Paradeigma* in Plato's Theory of Forms," *Apeiron* 17 (1983), 33–42.

universal and a particular ("impossibly" because we are assuming robust particularity, along with the thesis that nothing can be both a robust particular and a universal). To be sure, Aristotle invites this sort of understanding when he suggests, for example, that Forms are both suches and thises (*Meta.* 1038a34–1039a2); that the Third Man results from treating something which signifies a quality or a relation as if it were an individual (*Soph. El.* 178b36–179a10); or that the Platonists make Forms universals even while treating them as belonging to the class of particulars (*tôn kath hekaston, Meta.*1086a33–34; cf. *Meta.* 1086b27). Still, in general, it seems hard to convict Plato of holding explicitly or implicitly that the Forms are particulars in anything more than an acceptably deflationary way. It equally seems difficult to understand mimeticism as issuing in any kind of one-over-many hypothesis which may plausibly be construed as entailing both universality and robust particularity for Forms. So, the categorial approach leads to a dead end for Aristotle.

That dead end, however, counsels rethinking the genesis of Aristotle's concern. In fact, if we focus on his preferred final language in *Metaphysics* xiii 9, we may recall that Aristotle does not ultimately draw the strong categorial conclusion regularly ascribed to him. Returning again with greater care to the wording of the final argument of *Metaphysics* xiii 9, we find a clue to a different direction of investigation. For there at least Aristotle does not draw any direct categorial conclusion. Instead, he offers a conclusion, muted in any case, for the thesis that universals and particulars are almost the same sorts of natures. On closer inspection of Aristotle's conclusion, we see directly that this complaint, at least, is not that Forms will be universals and particulars but, rather, on the contrary, that universals and particulars will be practically the same sorts of natures.

In what sense will they *be*—not *have*—the same natures? In *Physics* ii 1, Aristotle identifies nature with "a principle (*archê*) and cause (*aitia*) of something's being moved and being at rest in that in which it belongs primarily, in itself, and not co-incidentally" (*Phys.* 192b20–23). This he does in part because he distinguishes those things with natures from those things which lack natures by arguing that everything which exists by nature has an internal principle of motion and rest (*archê tês kinêseôs kai staseôs*; *Phys.* 192b13–14). Importantly, what it means to have a principle (*archê*) of motion is here treated quite broadly, so that it encompasses not only locomotion but also growth and diminution, along with alteration generally (*ta men kata topon ta de kat' auxêsin kai phthisin, ta de kat' alloiôsin*; *Phys.* 192b14–15). So, if Aristotle expects a nature (*phusis*) to be a principle (*archê*) and a principle to explain and ground a natural entity's motion, growth, and general alteration, it also follows that he looks to nature (*phusis*) to ground and explain these same phenomena.

This suggests a second, more promising sort of attack on Forms emanating from *Metaphysics* xiii 9. On this approach, Aristotle need not rest with the unsustainable category-based refutation of Platonic Forms. Instead, he will offer a subtler, if less immediately damaging objection. If we grant Plato mimeticism as a specification of participation (*methexis*), then we have not compelled him to suppose that Forms, as *paradeigmata*, must be robust particulars. Still, Plato is not yet out of the woods. For Aristotle is right to insist that among the *explananda* of physics are the following: that there are unified entities which come into existence, grow, change, and die; that one organism may be like another in many respects while nevertheless being numerically distinct from it; and, generally, that individual organisms are unified systems of coordinated activity and directionality. In brief, as students of nature and as metaphysicians, we need to discover the principles (*archai*) of synchronic and diachronic unity.

If it turns out that Forms are virtually both universals and particulars as natures *of* sensible substances, then if they are the principles (*archai*) of such substances, they will fail to ground or explain the unity we observe in sensible substances. If Platonic Forms must be universals, insofar as they are objects of knowledge and definition, then they will explain, or help explain, *what makes human beings be human beings*—what it is that Callias and Socrates have in common in virtue of which they are human. They will also explain what wisdom is—what all and only wise beings have in common in virtue of which they qualify as wise. But then, if we understand that Alcibiades and Socrates are not only wise but also both puckish and charming, while only one is musical and the other is not, then we will need something beyond bare mimesis to explain why just *these* mimetic tokens bundle together with *those* to constitute Alcibiades, and then again why it is that he can remain numerically one and the same with the man whose youthful dark hair has given way to stately blazing grey. In Aristotle's terms, we need to know how Forms, as universals, serve as the grounding principles (*archai*) of these facts. We need to know, that is, why Platonic individuals are anything more than what Sellars aptly termed "leaky bundles of abstract particulars," mere congeries of particularized Form-copies bound together in indifferent regions of space.[29]

It will be by pushing discrete and evidently incompatible *functional roles* onto Forms that Plato will end up with particulars and universals of virtually the same natures. If so much is correct, then a better back reference for Aristotle's under-developed suggestions of *Metaphysics* xiii 9 will be not the last *aporia* but, rather, an earlier *aporia* of *Metaphysics* iii 4, the ninth *aporia*, which again deals with a worry about principles (*archai*), though now of a different character: "if they are only one in form (*eidos*), nothing will be one in number" (999b25–26). Aristotle's dominant worry in this *aporia* seems to be that in order to explain the unity of particulars, it is necessary for a principle to be one in number, presumably for either one of two reasons. First, he may be assuming, as he had at *Metaphysics* 993b23–31, and as Plato had in the *Phaedo*, that the *aitia* of something's being F must itself also be F, so that if a Form is a cause (*aitia*) of a sensible substance's being a *unity*, then it must itself be a unity, in the sense of being one in number. Second, Aristotle seems to suggest that no given Platonic Form can do the job of bundling tropish mirror

29. W. Sellars, "Raw Materials, Subjects and Substrata," in E. McMullin (ed.), *The Concept of Matter* (Notre Dame, Ind.: Notre Dame University Press, 1963), 263.

images into genuine unities. Even the Platonic Form of Unity, as a universal, seems to contribute just one more Form-copy to the bundle of otherwise nonunited and disparate Form copies. This is the point of Sellars's colorful language: the bundle is *leaky* in the sense that it is not properly even a bundle, since it has no internal principle of structure or unification. If the Form of Unity adds just one more mimetic token to the (putative) bundle, it is hard to appreciate how it could serve as a mechanism for unifying or bundling the remaining mimetic tokens in the bundle. Later philosophers may wish to speak of *colocation*, or *coinstantiation*, or *coincidence* in this connection, and their so speaking may or may not be defensible. What is at issue in Aristotle's criticism of Plato is not that no such gambit could succeed but, rather, only that Plato owes some such account. He needs to show how Forms ground both the synchronic and diachronic unity of natural organisms. The bare resources of Forms and Form-copies present in his ontology do not point to any obvious way to discharge this obligation.

It is thus noteworthy that this noncategorial formulation of Aristotle's objection does not seek to force Plato into any immediate contradiction by treating Forms as both universals and particulars. Instead, it treats Forms as overtaxed, from a functional or explanatory point of view. Forms, as universals, permit genuine knowledge; but then, again as universals, Forms fail to provide any principle of unity for sensibles. Hence, they cannot be the principles (*archai*) Plato presumes them to be. Looked at this way, the ninth *aporia* becomes immediately relevant to the argument of *Metaphysics* xiii 9. For now Aristotle seems to have at his disposal the following series of inferences:

1. The principles (*archai*) of unified substances explain both their knowability and their unity, taken both synchroncially and diachronically.
2. If they are the principles (*archai*) which ground (or explain) knowability, then Forms are universal natures.
3. If they are the principles (*archai*) which ground (or explain) synchronic and diachronic unity, then Forms are particular natures.
4. Plato relies on Forms for both of these grounding (and explanatory) functions.
5. So Forms are both universal and particular natures.

In sum, if Forms are both the universal and particular natures of sensibles, then universals and particulars will be virtually the same natures. Note, however, that Forms may be both universals and particular natures without *being* both universals and particulars: the nature of a relative will not itself be a relative—and the nature of a particular need not itself be a particular. If *humanity* is Socrates' nature, and Socrates is a sensible particular, it does not follow that his nature is both a universal and a particular. Humanity is, on the contrary, a universal and not a particular.

Thus, this argument has none of the force of the original categorial argument. It does not seek to reduce Plato's theory of Forms to an immediate or inescapable contradiction. That, though, is a virtue: both versions of the categorial interpretation failed to convict Plato of any egregious mistake or, indeed, of any mistake at all. By contrast, this noncategorial version of Aristotle's concern raises a legitimate worry and points to a bona fide problem in Plato's theory. If he overtaxes Forms by requiring them to function as both universal and particular principles (*archai*), then Plato falls short of explaining either knowability or unity, or both. Perhaps this is why, in *Metaphysics* xiii 9, Aristotle contends that the successors of Socrates found no other principles beyond their own Forms. Their doing so was understandable, but, oddly, if Aristotle is right, unacceptably economical.

Summarizing, then, it is natural to understand Aristotle's complaints about Forms as universals and particulars as proceeding in a categorial vein. If we understand him that way, however, we uncover an argument sown with stridency but ultimately fruitless: nothing about Plato's treatment of Forms as substances (*ousiai*) or as paradigms (*paradeigmata*) enjoins him to treat them as both universals and particulars. Plato is caught, then, in no contradiction, and in no paradox of any kind, categorial or otherwise. Hence, if this is the ultimate purport of his polemic, Aristotle will have missed his mark. If, by contrast, we appreciate Aristotle's aporematic interest in principles (*archai*) as sources of both explanation and unification, then we see that he has a point, though not one that prescribes any immediate rejection of the theory of Forms. Rather, we would want to look first to see whether Aristotle, who himself faces the very tension he justifiably highlights in Plato's theory, fares any better in his own efforts to identify a principle (*archê*) which renders substance (*ousia*) both one and knowable.

# VI. Conclusions

Scholars look to Aristotle as a source of data regarding Plato's philosophy. To some, the data Aristotle provides appear hopelessly tainted, because they are rife with polemic, habitually unsympathetic, and even at times frostily caustic. A closer look at the dialectic of the Academy suggests another vantage point from which to assess Aristotle's contribution to our understanding of Plato. From this angle, many of Aristotle's criticisms prove more multifaceted and less decisive than they may first present.

Indeed, although Aristotle's writings contain many important and perfectly appropriate criticisms of Plato's theory of Forms, no one of them needs to be accepted by a Platonist as unanswerable. Even the criticism which has been judged by scholars to be the most directly devastating, because of its implicating Plato in an immediate categorial contradiction, proves much less damaging than it first seems. It likewise proves, on closer examination, to recommend a subtler and more consequential conclusion than what is derivable from the strongly polemical version advanced in the categorial version of Aristotle's argument. Of course, Aristotle may, in fact, have a multiplicity of motives in his worries about the particularity and universality of Forms; and it remains to be determined how his various worries may relate to one another. However they may, it emerges upon investigation that Plato stands unconvicted of Aristotle's categorial concerns about Forms, at least as they are mounted in their most vigorous formulations.

Even so, it equally emerges upon investigation that among Aristotle's concerns is at least one fair worry about what threatens to be a false economy in Plato's theory of Forms: by introducing Forms as both objects of knowledge and as principles (*archai*) of sense particulars, Plato saddles himself with a problem about the genesis of the unity for sensibles—though, instructively, this is no less problem than that which surfaces repeatedly in Aristotle's own metaphysics in reference to his own positive treatment of sensible substances. This suggests, then, not a linear Academic dialectic given in terms of Aristotle objecting and Plato succumbing, or even an eristic contest given in terms of Aristotle protesting and Plato retorting. Rather, Plato and Aristotle alike must grapple with a fundamental problem of unity, the unity of complex particulars, which arises for them in both its synchronic and diachronic guises.[30] Although in their related ways, both address this problem, neither Plato nor Aristotle emerges as the clear victor in some arena of cleanly traceable intra-Academic dialectic; and yet each, it is fair to conclude, will have learned from the criticisms of the other—as we may yet learn from them both. For the problem of how *many things* may also be *one thing* finds no more ready resolution today than it did in the days of Plato's Academy.[31]

# BIBLIOGRAPHY

Ackrill, J. L. "In Defence of Platonic Division," in J. L. Ackrill, *Essays on Plato and Aristotle* (Oxford: Oxford University Press, 1997), 93–109.

Annas, J. *Aristotle's Metaphysics Books M and N* (Oxford: Clarendon Press, 1976).

Bonitz, Hermann. *Aristotelis Metaphysica*, 2 vols. (Bonn: Marcus, 1848, 1849).

Burnet, John. *Platonism* (Berkeley: University of California Press, 1928).

Cavini, Walter. "Naming and Argument: Diaretitc Logic in Plato's *Statesman*," in C. Rowe (ed.), *Reading the Statesman* (Sankt Augustin: Akademica Verlag, 1995), 123–38.

Cherniss, Harold. *Aristotle's Criticism of Plato and the Academy*, vol. 1 (Baltimore, Md.: Johns Hopkins University Press, 1944).

Düring, Ingemar. *Aristotle in the Ancient Biographical Tradition* (Göteborg: Elanders, 1957).

Fine, Gail. *On Ideas* (Oxford: Clarendon Press, 1993).

———. "Plato and Aristotle on Form and Substance," *Proceedings of the Cambridge Philological Society* 209 (1983), 23–47; reprinted in G. Fine, *Plato on Knowledge and Forms* (Oxford: Oxford University Press, 2003), 397–425.

---

30. An appreciation of this more nuanced form of dialectical interaction is fully in evidence in Owen, "Platonism." Much of his landmark article is dedicated to showing, in effect, that we oversimplify the complexity of Academic dialectic only at the cost of missing much of its real philosophical significance.

31. I thank Gail Fine for her clear and instructive comments on an earlier draft of this chapter. Her generosity has improved the finished offering significantly.

Frede, Michael, and Günther Patzig. *Aristoteles, "Metaphysik Z": Text, Übersetzung und Kommentar* (Munich: Beck, 1988). Editor: 'Patzig' should NOT be deleted. He is an author; that's his last name

Grote, George. *Aristotle* (London, 1880).

Jaeger, W. *Aristotle: Fundamentals of the History of His Development* (Oxford: Oxford University Press, 1934); translated from the original German edition of 1923 by R. Robison.

Le Blond, J. *Aristote, Philosophe de la vie: Le livre premier du traité sur les Parties des Animaux* (Paris: Aubier, Éditions Montaigne, 1945).

———. *Logique et methóde chez Aristote* (Paris: J. Vrin, 1939).

Lennox, James. *Aristotle, On the Parts of Animals I–IV* (Oxford: Clarendon Press, 2001).

Mansion, Suzanne. *Le Jugement d'existence chez Aristote* (Louvain: Éditions de l'Institut Supérieur de Philosophie, 1946).

Nails, Deborah. *The People of Plato* (Indianapolis: Hackett, 2002).

Owen, G. E. L. "The Platonism of Aristotle," *Proceedings of the British Academy* 51 (1966), 125–50; reprinted in M. Nussbaum (ed.), *Logic, Science, and Dialectic* (Ithaca, N.Y.: Cornell University Press, 1986), 200–221.

Owens, Joseph. *The Doctrine of Being in the Aristotelian Metaphysics*, 3rd ed. (Toronto: Pontifical Institute of Medieval Studies, 1978).

Pellegrin, Pierre. "Division et syllogisme chez Aristote," *Revue Philosophique de la France et de l'Etranger* 171 (1981), 169–87.

Prior, William. "The Concept of *Paradeigma* in Plato's Theory of Forms," *Apeiron* 17 (1983), 33–42.

Ross, W. D. *Aristotle, Metaphysics*, 2 vols. (Oxford: Oxford University Press, 1924).

———. "The Development of Aristotle's Thought," in I. Düring and G. E. L. Owen (eds.), *Aristotle and Plato in the Mid-Fourth Century* (Göteborg: Elanders, 1960), 1–18.

———. *Plato's Theory of Ideas* (Oxford: Oxford University Press, 1953).

Runciman, W. "Plato's *Parmenides*," in R. E. Allen (ed.), *Studies in Plato's Metaphysics* (London: Routledge and Kegan Paul, 1965), 149–84.

Ryle, Gilbert. "Plato's *Parmenides* II," in R. E. Allen (ed.), *Studies in Plato's Metaphysics* (London: Routledge and Kegan Paul, 1965), 97–147; originally published in *Mind* 48 (1939), 302–25.

———. *Plato's Progress* (Cambridge: Cambridge University Press, 1966).

Sellars, Wilfrid. "Raw Materials, Subjects and Substrata," in E. McMullin (ed.), *The Concept of Matter* (Notre Dame, Ind.: Notre Dame University Press, 1963), 259–72.

Shields, Christopher. "Learning about Plato from Aristotle," in H. Benson (ed.), *The Blackwell Guide to Plato* (Oxford: Blackwell, 2006), 403–41.

———. *Order in Multiplicity* (Oxford: Clarendon Press, 1999).

Stenzel, J. *Plato's Method of Dialectic*, trans. D. J. Allan (Oxford, Oxford University Press, 1940).

Strawson, Peter. *Individuals* (London: Methuen, 1959).

Tarán, L. *Speusippus of Athens* (Leiden: Brill, 1981).

CHAPTER 22

....................................................................................................................

# PLATO AND
# PLATONISM

....................................................................................................................

## CHARLES BRITTAIN

## 1. INTRODUCTION

....................................................................................................................

The attempt to understand and develop Plato's philosophical views has a long history, starting with Aristotle and Plato's institutional successors in the Academy toward the end of the fourth century BC. But the development of a specifically Platonic philosophy in the Academy or elsewhere was checked by the advent of the Hellenistic schools, which advocated a more empirical approach to philosophical inquiry. As a result, the idea that Plato's dialogues already presented a well-defined, comprehensive, and essentially correct philosophical *system* seems not to have arisen until the first century BC.[1] And it was probably not until toward the beginning of the second century AD that a disparate set of philosophers who identified themselves as "Platonists" conceived the project of advocating and defending a specifically Platonic philosophy of this kind by systematically interpreting and explaining Plato's texts.[2] Over the next five hundred years (c. 100–600 AD), Platonist philosophers produced a huge corpus of philosophical work inspired by their interpretations of Plato. The aim of this chapter is to introduce the reader to this immensely varied and philosophically exciting—but, as yet, still largely unexplored—tradition.[3] The rest of this section gives some reasons why a modern

---

1. I say "seems" because Antiochus of Ascalon, the originator of this idea in the first century BC, claimed to be returning to the system set out by the early the Academics (see Cicero *Academica* 1.15–18). Antiochus' historical claim is rejected by most scholars; but see D. Sedley, "The Origins of Stoic God," in D. Frede and A. Laks (eds.), *Traditions of Theology* (Leiden, 2002), 41–83.

2. The precise dating of the Platonist revival is disputed; see section 2 and n. 43 below.

3. A magnificent attempt to give a systematic presentation of Platonism through short excerpts with commentaries is found in H. Dörrie and M. Baltes (trans.), *Der Platonismus in der Antike*, vols. 1–5

student of Plato might be interested in historical Platonism; section 2 investigates the origins and evolution of the Platonist movement; and section 3 sketches its shifting epistemological foundations and their relation to the Platonic dialogues.

The Platonist tradition is remarkably heterogeneous in comparison with other ancient philosophical movements because it had neither a physical institution (a school) to regulate membership, as the Hellenistic Stoics and Epicureans did, nor an explicit set of its founder's doctrines to regulate orthodoxy, as later Peripatetics did. The unity of the tradition—that is, the sense in which the philosophers who identified themselves as "Platonists" recognized their affiliation to a wider movement, and the basis for our identification of "Platonism" as a single tradition— thus depends primarily on its participants' adherence to the project identified above: Platonists advocated and defended a "specifically Platonic philosophy." Given the openness of the Platonic dialogues to all sorts of interpretation, however, this schema is too abstract. In practice, we can spell it out as a threefold commitment to (a) the authoritative status of Plato's work as containing in one way or another the correct philosophical doctrines; (b) a shared set of assumptions about the inadequacy of empirical experience as a basis for understanding the world, and about the existence and primacy of certain immaterial principles, including "forms," souls, and a transcendent god, that do explain it; and (c) an increasingly keen interest in a range of religious practices and concerns.

The results of these commitments, when applied by Platonists to the interpretation of Plato's works, are likely to strike a modern student as rather distant from Plato's text. It turns out that (a) is not just an overly enthusiastic version of the principle of charity, but becomes something close to a belief in Platonic infallibility; (b) leads the Platonists into an ever-expanding dialectic of transcendence, producing increasingly complex hierarchies of metaphysical principles that seem more and more remote from Plato's concerns; and, in tandem with (b), (c) eventually introduces an overtly gnostic theory of "theurgy" that seems at first sight to have much more in common with Christian soteriology than with Plato's *Phaedrus* or *Symposium*.[4] It is thus a serious question whether a modern student of Plato should be interested in Platonism, in a way that it is not in the case of later Stoicism or Aristotelianism.[5]

One response to this question would be to argue that some of the Platonists were nevertheless substantially right in their interpretations of Platonic texts (at least on certain central issues). But, while this view might be correct with respect to

---

(Stuttgart, 1987–98). R. Sorabji, *The Philosophy of the Commentators 200–600 AD*, 3 vols. (London, 2004), performs a similar service but emphasizes later Platonism owing to its primary focus on the tradition of commentary on Aristotle.

4. See section 2 on (a); sections 2 and 3 on (b); and n. 62 on (c).

5. The two examples are different, however, in that students of Chrysippus cannot afford to ignore late Stoics like Epictetus or Hierocles because his works are lost, whereas students of Aristotle merely lose out by not reading Alexander of Aphrodisias' great exegetical work. So the Platonic case parallels the second example, if it parallels either.

some details of Platonic interpretation, it does not take into account a basic fact about Platonist exegesis of Plato: the Platonists construed the interpretation of Plato as their primary function *as philosophers*.[6] Since their principal aim was to discover philosophical truths through the study of Plato rather than historical facts about Platonic arguments or texts, and given that we are unlikely to subscribe ourselves to their rather implausible view about Plato's authoritative status ([a] above), it is probably a mistake to read their works as studies in the history of philosophy.

A better case can be made, however, by considering the implications of some general assumptions the Platonists tended to adopt about how to read Plato as a result of their strange view about the status of the doctrines they found in his work. Three prominent general assumptions are: (1) Plato's dialogues (and other work) portray a consistent set of doctrines; (2) his work presents a systematic philosophy; and (3) on most issues, Plato's views are best understood in the light of Aristotle's development of them.[7] We don't need to share any of these controversial assumptions, I suggest, to see how we might benefit by reading the work of the philosophers who made them. At any rate, I will give three reasons to think that we might.

The first is derived from the fact that most modern readers do not share assumption 1, which is a "unitarian" view of the Platonic dialogues.[8] One implication of adopting a unitarian view is that the reader is compelled to consider and resolve the apparent inconsistencies between various dialogues—for example, about the nature of the soul and corresponding conception of virtue in the *Phaedo* and *Republic*. The Platonists offer a range of solutions to such problems, which are often more plausible, and more philosophically stimulating, than modern alternatives.[9] The case above, for instance, which modern scholarship has found particularly perplexing, was resolved by Plotinus by a theory of "grades of virtue" reflecting the stage of self-awareness of the agent in her progress toward a correct understanding of one's *self* as an immaterial and intellectual substance. On this account, the "civic virtues" of the *Republic* are preparatory for the higher "cathartic virtues" of the *Phaedo*.[10] The point here is not to argue that such Platonist views

---

6. Proclus' exegesis of the composition of the world soul in his *Timaeus* commentary is one case in which a Platonist commentator is generally agreed to have solved a difficult question arising directly from the Platonic text.

7. The third point was controversial in the second century AD; see section 2, nn. 51–53.

8. See Irwin's discussion, chapter 3 in this volume.

9. A second case is the apparent inconsistency between the *Phaedo*, the *Timaeus* or the *Republic*, and the *Phaedrus* about the immortality of the nonrational soul. Proclus, e.g., resolved this controversial case by interpreting the two horses in the disembodied stages of *Phaedrus* myth in terms of the circles of the same and the different which are constitutive of reason in the *Timaeus*, rather than the two nonrational parts of the embodied soul in the *Republic*. His view is set out most clearly in his student Hermeias' *Commentary on the Phaedrus*.

10. Plotinus *Ennead* 1.2. See, e.g., J. Dillon, "An Ethic for the Late Antique Sage," in L. Gerson (ed.), *The Cambridge Companion to Plotinus* (Cambridge, 1996), 315–35; C. Brittain, "Attention Deficit in Plotinus and Augustine," *Proceedings of the Boston Area Colloquium in Ancient Philosophy* 18 (2003), 223–63; and below at n. 57.

are essentially correct but, rather, that engaging with them opens up a wealth of philosophically rich and underexploited connections between the Platonic dialogues.[11]

A second reason is that the Platonist assumption that Plato is a systematic philosopher (point 2 above) implies that we can find substantive theoretical answers to the philosophical questions Plato raises. In the case of epistemology, for example, a Platonist expects to discover not just how the apparently conflicting accounts of knowledge in dialogues are consistent but a Platonic theory explaining the roles of perceptual experience and "recollection"—that is, our means of access to non-experiential knowledge—in our acquisition of it.[12] Some of the diverse results of this expectation are examined in section 3, but we can note now that most Platonists found a developed epistemology and theory of rationality in Plato's *Timaeus*. Here, too, we do not need to accept the various interpretations the Platonists offered to benefit from their recognition of the centrality of this dialogue for Platonic epistemology.[13] Another case in which the Platonist assumption of systematicity led them to investigate issues in the dialogues that are usually ignored in modern philosophical scholarship concerns the topics of freedom, self-determination, and divine providence. In the absence of a substantive body of modern scholarship on Plato's views on these questions, the sophisticated work on them by Plotinus, Porphyry, and Proclus is particularly illuminating.[14] (The driving force in this case was their further presupposition that Plato's work contains substantive views about *all* the central questions in philosophy; since these issues had become more salient in the Hellenistic and early Imperial periods, the Platonists felt obliged to seek Platonic responses to the theories of their Stoic and Peripatetic rivals; see section 2.)

The two reasons given so far might be construed uncharitably as the proposal to exploit the vices of Platonist exegesis in pursuit of novel (in our context) and philosophically stimulating ways of reading Plato. The final reason, however, appeals to a significant philosophical virtue of Platonist interpretations, viz. their sympathetic developments of Platonic themes or ideas—often by appropriating

11. In the case of Platonic ethics, Julia Annas has recently shown how using a Platonist text (Alcinous' *Handbook of Platonism*) as a guide for reading Plato can yield illuminating philosophical results; see J. Annas, *Platonist Ethics Old and New* (Ithaca, N.Y., 1999).

12. The *Meno* and *Theaetetus* appear to present a different view about the proper objects of knowledge from the one found in the *Republic* or *Sophist*. The range of problems Platonists saw in this field is set out in D. Sedley, "Three Platonist Interpretations of the *Theaetetus*" ["Three Interpretations"], in C. Gill and M. McCabe (eds.), *Form and Argument in Later Plato* (Oxford, 1996), 79–103.

13. Modern readers have been slow to see this, perhaps because the *Timaeus'* epistemology is hard to fit within a developmentalist account (cf. G. E. L. Owen, "The Place of the *Timaeus* in Plato's Dialogues," *Classical Quarterly* NS 3 [1953], 79–95). A notable non-Platonist exception is D. Frede, "The Philosophical Economy of Plato's Psychology: Rationality and the Common Concepts in the *Timaeus*," in M. Frede and G. Striker (eds.), *Rationality in Greek Thought* (Oxford, 1996), 29–56.

14. For Plotinus and Porphyry's views on these issues, see W. Deuse, *Untersuchungen zur mittelplatonischen und neuplatonischen Seelenlehre* [*Seelenlehre*] (Mainz, 1983). Proclus' short treatises on them have recently been translated into English in J. Opsomer and C. Steel, *Proclus: On the Existence of Evils* (Ithaca, N.Y., 2003); Simplicius' commentary on Epictetus (T. Brennan and C. Brittain [trans.], *Simplicius: On Epictetus' Handbook* [Ithaca, N.Y., 2002]) gives a useful introduction to late Platonist views on these topics.

and adapting Aristotle's earlier, and critical, reworking of them (point 3 above)—into sophisticated and original theories.[15] The remarkable Platonist theories of the first principles, for example, constituted an evolving effort to systematize and defend (by means of a causal theory) the apparently scattered remarks of Plato on the interrelations between soul, intellect, the demiurge, the Forms, the good, and the one.[16] Their complex psychological theories attempted to work out Plato's suggestion that the soul is essentially a rational and immaterial substance that is independent of and prior to the material world, by explaining how such an entity might interact with a body.[17] And their elaborate hermeneutical theories were developed in order to elaborate Plato's diverse treatments of literary theory into a system sufficiently complex to allow them to extract the last ounce of meaning from his texts.[18] These sample cases are of enormous independent significance for the history of philosophy, theology, and literature.[19] But they are also directly relevant to the modern student of Plato, in that they demonstrate some of the promising lines along which someone sympathetic to Plato's central metaphysical views might develop the insights she finds in the Platonic texts.[20]

## 2. The Origins and Evolution of Historical Platonism

Modern research on the origins of historical Platonism stems from the rejection of a traditional picture of a "Platonic School," which was based on the false assumption that Plato's Academy in Athens was an enduring institution that ensured a more or less continuous transmission of Platonic teachings. The traditional picture distinguished five or six discrete stages in the history of this "School":

15. The Platonists, of course, denied that these were original theories rather than systematic expositions of Plato's sometimes obscure meaning. One reason for this was their assumption that they had further information about Plato's metaphysical principles from his (probably spurious) *Letters*, and from various accounts of his "unwritten doctrines"; see Irwin, chapter 3 in this volume.

16. In Plotinus' version, these Platonic principles are reduced to a theory of three *hypostases* (primary ontological types or entities) of Soul, Intellect, and the One or the Good. The Forms are identified as the thoughts that constitute Intellect (and Being), which is the Demiurge; the Good is identified with the One. For Plotinus' use of Aristotle in coming to these views, see n. 58 below.

17. Some of the vast range of Platonist psychologies is reviewed in, e.g., Deuse, *Seelenlehre*, and H. Blumenthal, *Soul and Intellect: Studies in Plotinus and Later Neoplatonism* (London, 1993).

18. R. Lamberton, *Homer the Theologian* (Berkeley, 1986), is a useful modern introduction to Platonist hermeneutics; the anonymous *Prolegomena to Plato* is a less helpful ancient equivalent from the sixth century AD.

19. As the work of Origen and Augustine suggests, a good deal of Christian theology and hermeneutics in the period from 150 to 600 AD is derived directly from Platonism. For a useful overview of their relation, see C. Stead, *Philosophy in Christian Antiquity* (Cambridge, 1994).

20. A parallel history of the Stoic interpretations and adaptations of Plato would perform a similar function for a reader who was unsympathetic to Plato's dualism.

1. The "old" or "early" Academy, which lasted from 348 until 268 BC.[21]
2. The "new" or "skeptical" Academy, from 268 to around 50 BC.[22]
3. A *"transitional"* post-Academic period, from c. 50 BC to c. 70 AD.[23]
4. A *"middle"* or early Platonist phase, from c. 70 to c. 230 AD. [24]
5. A *"Neoplatonist"* or Plotinian phase of Platonism, from c. 230 to c. 300 AD.[25]
6. A *"late Neoplatonist"* or late Platonist phase, from c. 300 to c. 600 AD, including
    6.1. a relatively unattested phase, from c. 300 to c. 400 AD;
    6.2. the "Athenian School," attested from c. 400 to its closure in 529 AD;
    6.3. the "Alexandrian School," attested from c. 435 to its closure in 611 AD.[26]

(The italicized names are avoided in recent work on Platonism for reasons explained below.)

Although the chronological framework of this traditional picture is generally accepted, modern scholars reject the overall picture for three reasons.[27] First, it conflates the notions of a "school" as a physical institution and as a philosophical

---

21. The most prominent old Academics were Speusippus (d. 338 BC), Xenocrates (d. 314 BC), Crantor (d. 276 BC), and Polemo (d. 269 BC). An overview of the extant fragments of their work—which was highly regarded by the Platonists—is given in J. Dillon, *The Heirs of Plato: A Study of the Old Academy, 347/274 B.C.* (Oxford, 2003).

22. The most significant figures in the skeptical Academy were Arcesilaus (315–240 BC), Carneades (214–128 BC), Philo of Larissa (159–84 BC), and Philo's student Antiochus of Ascalon (c. 130–68 BC). Overviews of their work are given in C. Brittain, "Arcesilaus" (2005), J. Allen, "Carneades" (2004), C. Brittain, "Philo of Larissa" (2006)—all in the *Stanford Encyclopedia of Philosophy* at http://plato.s-tanford.edu/—and J. Barnes, "Antiochus of Ascalon" ["Antiochus"] in M. Griffin and J. Barnes (eds.), *Philosophia Togata* (Oxford, 1989), 51–96.

23. Prominent figures in this period include Eudorus (late first century BC), Thrasyllus (d. 36 AD), and Philo of Alexandria (d. 40–50 AD); see J. Dillon, *The Middle Platonists* [*Middle Platonists*] (London, 1977), for an introductory account. (H. Tarrant, *Thrasyllan Platonism* [Ithaca, N.Y., 1993], gives a controversial, maximalist interpretation of Thrasyllus' work, but see nn. 38–39 below.)

24. Notable representatives include Plutarch of Chaeronea (c. 50–120 AD), Alcinous (c. 150–200 AD), Atticus (fl. 176 AD), Numenius (c. 150–200 AD), and Longinus (216–272 AD). Dillon's *Middle Platonists* remains the standard doxographical review of early Platonism in English; more recent accounts of several important figures are given in W. Haase and H. Temporini (eds.), *Aufstieg und Niedergang der Römischen Welt* [*Aufstieg*], Part 2, vols. 36.1–7 (Berlin, 1987–1994); see n. 52. H. Tarrant, *Plato's First Interpreters* [*First Interpreters*] (Ithaca, N.Y., 2000), offers a wide-ranging account focused on Platonic interpretation.

25. Plotinus (204–270 AD) and Porphyry (234–305 AD) are the key figures in this phase. Two excellent introductions to Plotinus' thought are L. Gerson, *Plotinus* (London, 1994), and D. O'Meara, *Plotinus: An Introduction to the Enneads* (Oxford, 1993). On Porphyry, see A. Smith, *Porphyry's Place in the Neoplatonic Tradition* [*Porphyry's Place*] (The Hague, 1974), and the important new editions of two of his works by J. Barnes, *Porphyry: Introduction* (Oxford, 2003), and L. Brisson (ed.), *Porphyre: Sentences* (Paris, 2005).

26. Iamblichus (c. 245–325 AD) is our principal representative of the "lost phase." The leaders of the Athenian school included Plutarch of Athens (d. 431 AD), Syrianus (d. 437 AD), Proclus (411–485 AD), and Damascius (465–540 AD). Notable teachers at the Alexandrian school included Ammonius (c. 440–520 AD), Philoponus (c. 490–570 AD), Simplicius (c. 500–570 AD) and Olympiodorus (c. 500–570 AD). R. Wallis, *Neoplatonism* (1972; 2nd ed. London, 1995), provides a rather out of date account of late Platonism; but the historical circumstances of these philosophers and their work as commentators on Aristotle is comprehensively reviewed in the essays in R. Sorabji (ed.), *Aristotle Transformed* (Ithaca, N.Y., 1990).

27. See J. Glucker, *Antiochus and the Late Academy* (Göttingen, 1978), a groundbreaking account of the actual history of the Platonic Academy and the discontinuous history of Platonism, which investigates the history of the technical terms "Academic," "Platonist," "sect" (*hairesis*), "school-succession" or "transmission" (*diadoche*), and "successor" (*diadochos*).

movement (a "sect" or *hairesis*). But the Platonic Academy had ceased to exist as physical institution by the middle of the first century BC; thereafter, we know something about several "private" Platonist teaching institutions—for example, Plotinus' school in Rome, Iamblichus' in Chalcis in Syria, and the later Athenian and Alexandrian schools—but there was no central "school."[28] Second, it conflates continued philosophical interest in Plato's thought outside an institutional framework with explicitly Platonic "movements"—the skepticism of the "New Academics" or the Platonism of the self-identified "Platonists"—by assuming that there was a continuous chain of Platonic "successors" ensuring the transmission of teaching (*diadoche*) between stages 2 and 4.[29] And third, it conflates philosophical developments within the Platonist "movement" with chronological periodizations and the emergence of particular teaching institutions in stages 4 to 6.[30]

The rejection of this traditional picture for a more accurate view of the various historical forms of Platonic studies allows us to replace ill-defined questions about the origins of Platonism—such as ones framed in terms of the transmission of Platonic authority or teachings or of an evolution toward a specific set of (usually Plotinian) metaphysical doctrines—with a more determinate one about the philosophical movement of stages 4 to 6. Why was the development of an explicit "Platonism" delayed until the late first century AD (stage 4)? A satisfying answer to this question should explain how a group of philosophers came to see a Platonic philosophy as offering the solution to some central difficulties in late Hellenistic philosophy (see section 3). But we might also expect to find a more strictly historical explanation for the fact that it was only at this stage that a group of philosophers came to identify themselves as "Platonists"; and our initial characterization of the movement (commitments a to c, p. 527) suggests that this is likely to depend on the development of Plato's status as an authoritative philosopher (point a).

28. The primary sources for our knowledge of these schools are Porphyry's *Life of Plotinus*, Eunapius' *Lives of the Sophists*, Marinus' *Life of Proclus*, and Damascius' *Life of Isidore* (or *Philosophical History*); see M. Edwards, *Neoplatonic Saints: The Lives of Plotinus and Proclus by Their Students* (Liverpool, 2000), and P. Athanassiadi, *Damascius: The Philosophical History* (Athens, 1999).

29. Some recent scholarship still assumes that we can trace at least the outlines of a continuous transmission between private teachers and their students from Philo of Larissa or his student Antiochus of Ascalon in stage 2 through to Eudorus in stage 3, and perhaps into stage 4; see, e.g., H. Tarrant, *Scepticism or Platonism: The Philosophy of the Fourth Academy* [*Fourth Academy*] (Cambridge, 1985); Tarrant, *First Interpreters*; Dillon, *Middle Platonists*; and nn. 35–36 below. But the traditional institutional picture is not supported or implied by any ancient evidence.

30. "Middle Platonism" is used both as a chronological term, referring to Platonists prior to Plotinus from period 4 (and sometimes their antecedents in period 3), and as a way of classifying doctrinal divergences from Plotinus; as a result, the work of Longinus and Calcidius is chronologically "Neoplatonist" but doctrinally "Middle Platonist," while the reverse is true of Numenius. (The "middle" and "neo-" classifications reflect the assumptions that the Platonism of period 4 was essentially a revival of an original Platonism found in period 1, and that Plotinus' work (in 5) marked a decisive doctrinal shift from these earlier "Platonisms.") The traditional view that the late Athenian and Alexandrian Platonists defended radically distinct forms of Platonism rests on a misreading of the evidence; see, e.g., I. Hadot, *Le problème de néoplatonisme alexandrin: Hiéroclès et Simplicius* (Paris, 1978). (The two schools were tightly connected, both socially and philosophically; Simplicius, for instance, studied in both places.)

The problem of the delayed development of Platonism is an interesting one because the general conditions for its emergence seem to have been in place from at least 50 BC (stage 3). Notable among these conditions were three significant changes in late Hellenistic philosophy. The first was the demise of the skeptical Academy by the middle of the first century BC, which released the interpretation of the Platonic corpus from institutional constraints, and in particular from the skeptical interpretations of Plato the Academics had advocated since the third century BC.[31] The second was the decentralization of philosophy that ensued after the disruption of Athens during the first Mithridatic war (89–84 BC) and the "pacification" of Greece by the Romans. This led to a more pluralistic philosophical culture and paved the way for the development of a tradition of written commentaries on works of recognized importance.[32] And the third was a widespread revival of interest in a set of metaphysical and (crudely) "otherworldly" themes that had been abandoned or neglected by early Hellenistic philosophers but were prominent in Plato: these included theories of transcendent principles and topics such as divination, demonology, and the afterlife of the soul.[33]

The problem becomes more acute when we look at the changes to Plato's status as a philosophical authority that had already occurred by around the middle of the first century BC. One was that philosophers from various Hellenistic schools were now willing to recognize Plato, as well as Aristotle and Pythagoras, as having the privileged status of *classical* figures, whose views were worth considering even when they conflicted in some ways with the orthodox doctrines of one's own school. A second was that the death throes of the skeptical Academy led to two explicit, though incompatible, appeals to the Platonic tradition to validate the historical authenticity of entire philosophical positions. In the case of Philo of Larissa, this meant an appeal to the *continuity* of the Academic tradition—that is,

31. The philosophical demise of the skeptical Academy was caused by Philo of Larissa's shift from radical to mitigated skepticism in the 90s BC, which triggered a revolt by his student Antiochus of Ascalon, who left the Academy to set up a rival dogmatic "Old Academy." This, in turn, led Philo to an attempt to reposition the Academy as part of a critical—rather than skeptical—tradition; see Barnes, "Antiochus," and Brittain, "Philo of Larissa" (2006). Arcesilaus' skeptical interpretations of Plato are examined in J. Annas, "Plato the Sceptic," *Oxford Studies in Ancient Philosophy Supplementary Volume* (Oxford, 1992), 43–72, and Sedley, "Three Interpretations." C. Brittain, *Philo of Larissa [Philo]* (Oxford, 2001), also covers the range of later skeptical Academic interpretations of Plato, Socrates, and the old Academic philosophers (stage 1 above).

32. For a detailed analysis of these developments, and those mentioned immediately below, see M. Frede, "Epilogue," in K. Algra, J. Barnes, J. Mansfeld, and M. Schofield (eds.), *The Cambridge History of Hellenistic Philosophy* (Cambridge, 1999), 771–97.

33. The renewed interest in metaphysics was partly due to the wider dissemination of Aristotle's work in the first century BC, which rapidly generated a cross-party tradition of commentary and debate on the *Categories*. Philosophical interest in Plato's treatment of the whole set of themes is evident in Stoics such as Posidonius (see, e.g., Galen *PHP* 4–5; Plutarch *Proc. An.* 1023b-d; and Cicero *Div.* 1.60–64), and in the revival of philosophical and popular enthusiasm for Pythagoreanism. (These philosophical changes seem to reflect a wider social change away from the optimistic sense that things could be improved by natural and rational means here and now; this perhaps explains the success of the new science of astrology in this period and the proliferation of soteriological sects. On this wider change, see, e.g., E. Dodds, *The Greeks and the Irrational [Greeks]* [Berkeley, 1951], and P. Brown, *The Making of Late Antiquity* [Cambridge, Mass., 1978].)

to "the unity of the Academy," including Socrates, Plato, the early Academics, and his skeptical predecessors—to support his redefinition of Academic philosophy as a nonskeptical tradition of critical inquiry. This was an unusual step for an Academic (although claims that one's views were consistent with a founding orthodoxy were a standard feature of the other Hellenistic schools).[34] But it didn't constitute a return to Platonic philosophy because Philo used the thesis of the unity of the Academy to defend his own empiricist views rather than a set of doctrines drawn from Plato's work.[35]

In the case of his rival Antiochus, however, it meant an appeal to the authoritative *consensus* of the ongoing Platonic tradition—the old Academic and Peripatetic doctrines which the skeptical Academics had misguidedly rejected—to validate the *truth* of the dogmatic philosophical system that Plato himself had established. And since Antiochus' position amounted to an explicit defense of a set of Platonic doctrines—a specifically Platonic philosophy—it is at first sight hard to understand why it did not immediately initiate a Platonist movement.[36] But closer examination of his view provides two reasons to explain this. The first is the content of the Platonic doctrines he advocated: Antiochus' position was an empiricist one, and accordingly substituted an immanent Stoic god for the transcendent metaphysical principles that were central to Platonism. The second is his justification for this substitution: that is, his appeal to Platonic authority in the form of the ongoing consensus of a broad tradition, which allowed him to abandon views that had proven untenable and replace them with later, Stoic, alternatives.[37] These two Antiochian principles directly contradict the central theses of the Platonist movement.

The specific forms that direct appeals to Plato's authority had taken in the early part of the first century BC thus suggest one way to explain why the significant interest in Platonic texts and themes over the next hundred years was not conceived as "Platonism": the philosophers involved had not developed an alternative Platonist ideology that was capable of uniting their specific interest in Plato with their wider philosophical interests in transcendent metaphysical principles. Some prominent examples of these twin interests in the period 50 BC–70 AD include Cicero's trans-

34. Philo's appeal to the tradition contravened the extensive Academic critique of the use of authority by dogmatic philosophers; see, e.g., Cicero *Ac.* 2.8 and *DND* 1.11; traces of this critique remain in Sextus (e.g., *PH* 2.37–45) and Lucian's *Hermotimus*. For general Hellenistic attitudes, see D. Sedley, "Plato's *Auctoritas* and the Rebirth of the Commentary Tradition" ["Plato's *Auctoritas*"], in J. Barnes and M. Griffin (eds.), *Philosophia Togata II: Plato and Aristotle at Rome* (Oxford, 1997), 110–29.

35. *Pace* Tarrant, *Fourth Academy*; see Brittain, *Philo* (2001), 129–265.

36. This seems clear for the reasons given below, as well as the almost complete silence about Antiochus in the later tradition, which is broken only to criticize him someone who attempted to pollute Plato's legacy with Stoicism (see, e.g., Sextus *PH* 1.235; Numenius fr.29 Des Places; and Augustine *Contra Academicos* 3.41). It is denied, however, in, e.g., Dillon, *Middle Platonists*.

37. Antiochus' empiricism is clear from his wholesale adoption of a Stoic epistemology, attested in Cicero *Ac.* 2. His views on Platonic metaphysics are more controversial, since the report in Cicero *Ac.* 1 gives both "old Academic" views and their "corrections" by the later tradition, such as Aristotle's attack on the theory of Forms, which leaves Antiochus' own position unclear. But the section on "old Academic" physics shows that he did agree with the Stoic "correction" that eliminated the Platonic view that god and the soul were immaterial substances (*Ac.* 1.39).

lation of the *Timaeus*, Thrasyllus' work on the Platonic dialogues, Eudorus' work on "Pythagorean" (i.e., Platonic) metaphysics, and Seneca's discussion of Platonic principles in *Letters* 58 and 65.[38] But it is notable that none of these philosophers were considered by themselves or their contemporaries as primarily followers of Plato: their interest in Platonic metaphysics is instead explained by their connections with established (late) Academic, Pythagorean, or Stoic concerns.[39]

The additional element required for the development of an overtly Platonist ideology was a theory that could justify an *unqualified* return to Plato at this late point in the history of philosophy. That is, a theory was needed to explain why it made sense to defend Plato's views as a whole rather than defending some subset of them in light of the intervening Hellenistic philosophical developments, which is what the various Academics, Stoics, and neo-Pythagoreans of the first centuries BC and AD had done. The theory that the Platonists seem to have adapted to serve this purpose drew on what was by this time a popular notion that a common heritage of "ancient wisdom" was encoded in the literature of the established cultures of the world.[40] The point of the theory was to suggest that Plato's philosophy represented the final encoding of this "ancient wisdom" into the form of philosophical writing (in Greek).[41] The Platonists supported this rather surprising claim by an argument from the history of post-Platonic philosophy, which explained the chronic disagreements of the Hellenistic philosophers—and the philosophical dead ends (empiricism, skepticism, etc.) they were driven to—as the direct result of their dissensions from Platonic doctrine.[42] An unqualified return to Platonic wisdom was thus precisely what was required.

38. Eudorus' interest in Plato is attested by his doxographical work on the creation of the world soul in the *Timaeus* (Plutarch *Proc. An.* 1013b) and his neo-Pythagorean views on the first principles (Simplicius *In Phys.* 188). Thrasyllus' work on Plato's dialogues is attested in Diogenes Laertius *Lives of the Philosophers* 3.56–61.

39. Seneca was a Stoic. Thrasyllus was an astrologer known for his Pythagorean bent, who also edited Democritus' works. Cicero was a skeptical "Academic" who admired Plato; his *Timaeus* translation is dedicated to the "Neopythagorean" Nigidius Figulus. Eudorus probably characterized himself as an "Academic," which usually meant a skeptical Academic at this time; but it is more likely that he saw himself as affiliated to the Academic tradition as a whole—that is, a tradition that included the early, nonskeptical Academics of period 1. It is unclear whether this would make him a late Antiochian Academic—a view supported by the thoroughly Stoic ethical work ascribed to him in Stobaeus *Ec.* 2.7—or a significant antecedent for Plutarch's "Academic" Platonism (see nn. 49–50).

40. The (Stoic) origin and evolution of this theory is examined in G. Boys-Stones, *Post-Hellenistic Philosophy* (Oxford, 2001). Its Platonist proponents offer a range of recognized cultures, which varies over time and depending on their aims. Prominent "sages" include the Egyptian Hermes, Persian Zoroaster and Magi, Indian Brahmins, Jewish Moses, and Greek Homer, Musaeus, Orpheus, and Pythagoras. The Chaldean oracles were added rather late to this list of ancient authorities—after they had been forged in the mid second century AD.

41. The exact nature of Plato's relation to the ancient tradition is disputed. M. Frede, "Numenius," in W. Haase and H. Temporini (eds.), *Aufstieg und Niedergang der Römischen Welt*, Part 2, vol. 36.2 (Berlin, 1987), 1034–75, argues that Plato was regarded as the last of the ancients; Boys-Stones, *Post-Hellenistic Philosophy*, sees Plato as the first to *reconstruct* the ancient wisdom correctly and in philosophical Greek.

42. The theory is reconstructed and defended sympathetically in Boys-Stones, *Post-Hellenistic Philosophy*, 99–150. As he shows, the general theory is present in Plutarch (fr. 157, 190 Sandbach), Numenius (fr. 1a Des Places), Celsus (Origen *Against Celsus* 1.14), Plotinus (e.g., *Enn.* 3.5.2), and Porphyry (e.g., fr. 323–24 Smith). The related argument from the history of post-Platonic philosophy is attested in Plutarch (*Stoic. Rep.* passim), Numenius (fr. 24), and Atticus (fr. 5 Des Places), among others.

Something like this view of the development of Plato's status as a philosophical authority seems to give the best available historical explanation for the evidence that the Platonist movement did not take off until the end of the first century AD, despite the revival of interest in Plato a hundred and fifty years earlier.[43] At any rate, it is in the period from c. 70 to c. 230 AD that a disparate group of philosophers accepting an explicitly Platonist ideology set to work to explain and defend the doctrines they found in the Platonic corpus. One result was a large and diverse mass of work, in the form of introductions to Plato, handbooks on Platonic doctrines, Platonic lexica, commentaries on Platonic dialogues and essays on particular problems in Plato—of which only a few samples survive intact.[44] Such works were as necessary then as now to explain textual, linguistic and historical difficulties in the dialogues; interpret their arguments, "myths," and enigmatic (e.g., numerological) passages; elucidate their general intent; and understand how they fit together to produce a coherent philosophical view.[45] But since their authors were primarily philosophers, their central purpose was not to offer interpretations of Plato's dialogues but to identify in them a systematic set of philosophical doctrines and defend these against opposing views— that is, against both rival forms of Platonism and their shared Stoic, Peripatetic, and skeptical philosophical opponents. As a result, the Platonists of this period produced a second mass of more standard philosophical literature, in the form of controversial works, treatises on specific philosophical problems, and systematic treatments of metaphysics.[46]

43. I should note, however, that a number of scholars, including Harold Tarrant and David Sedley, prefer the view that a recognizable form of Platonism had already developed by the end of the first century BC, under the stimulus of Antiochus or Philo. The key disagreement between this view and the one presented above concerns the dating of the anonymous *Commentary on the Theaetetus*, which attests to internal disagreements within a well-developed and explicitly Platonist movement, and hence might support more "Platonist" interpretations of scantily known figures such as Eudorus or Thrasyllus if it were datable to 25 BC or AD. But the arguments for this early date, rather than 100 or 120 AD, strike me as weak, since the controversies in Anon. are exactly those of the later period; see D. Sedley and G. Bastianini (eds.), *Commentarium in Platonis Theaetetum*, *Corpus dei papiri filosofici greci e latini*, vol. 3 (Florence, 1995), 227–562, and Brittain, *Philo* (2001), 249–54. It would also be strange that later Platonists make no reference at all to this hypothetical early tradition of Platonism, beyond a handful of citations of Eudorus and Thrasyllus which do not demonstrate its existence.

44. Some extant examples of the first two categories are Albinus' *Introduction to Plato*, Alcinous' *Handbook*, and Apuleius' *Plato's Doctrines*. Examples of the third and fourth categories are the anonymous *Commentary on the Theaetetus* and Plutarch's *The Creation of the Soul in the Timaeus*. There is a considerable amount of evidence for the views of a number of early Platonists on controversial issues in the Platonic dialogues for which later (fifth or sixth century AD) commentaries are extant, viz. *First Alcibiades*, *Cratylus*, *Gorgias*, *Parmenides*, *Phaedo*, *Phaedrus*, *Philebus*, *Republic*, and *Timaeus*.

45. The Platonist commentary tradition was preceded by an Aristotelian one, which may have taken off in the late first century BC; see H. Gottschalk, "The Earliest Aristotelian Commentators," in R. Sorabji (ed.), *Aristotle Transformed* (Ithaca, N.Y., 1990), 55–81. The aims and scope of the early Platonic commentaries—as manifested by our single example—are explained in Sedley, "Three Interpretations," and Sedley, "Plato's *Auctoritas*." On the later commentaries, see nn. 63–64 below.

46. See the excellent review by P. Donini, "Testi e commenti, manuali e insegnamento: la forma sistematica e i metodi della filosofia in età postellenistica," in W. Haase and H. Temporini (eds.), *Aufstieg und Niedergang der Römischen Welt*, Part 2, vol. 36.7 (Berlin, 1994), 5027–100. Examples for the first category include several extant works by Plutarch—*Stoic Contradictions*, *Common Conceptions* (against the Stoics), and *Against Colotes*, and a summary of *The Impossibility of Living Pleasantly* (against the Epicureans)—as

Given the diversity of this material, we can notice here just two pervasive strands in it. The first is that these Platonist texts share an overriding concern to justify the basic assumptions of Platonism—that the world can only be understood by reference to a set of immaterial principles inaccessible to empirical experience (commitments a to c, p. 527)—against the criticism of their philosophical opponents. This is worth stressing because the nature of our evidence for the period tends to obscure it. Owing to the vagaries of textual survival, it is easy to forget that the "Hellenistic schools" continued to flourish and produce significant work until at least the middle of the third century AD.[47] (This was publicly attested by the emperor Marcus Aurelius' decision in 176/77 AD to establish paid "chairs" for the four dominant "schools" of the period—that is, for the Stoics and Epicureans, as well as for the Aristotelians and Platonists who had emerged over the last century.) But even when we have corrected for our ignorance of the philosophical context in which the Platonist work was produced, the form of the surviving material—which is often fragmentary, or dedicated to religious or cultural topics that may not strike us as obviously philosophical—can make it difficult to reconstruct the underlying philosophical arguments.

The second strand is the struggle to define a narrower Platonist orthodoxy, which is reflected in the variety of philosophical approaches the Platonists adopted for systematizing and defending the doctrines they found in the Platonic texts. Like modern readers of Plato, the Platonists tended to read the dialogues in the light of their own philosophical preoccupations and training.[48] In practice, this resulted in a series of more or less "Academic," "Pythagorean," "Stoic," and "Aristotelian" versions of Platonism, depending on the degree to which their proponents applied the refinements of these traditions to their interpretations of Plato.[49] At issue were both historical questions—such as the role of Pythagoreanism in the formation of Plato's doctrines and the kinds of skepticism adopted by the "New Academics"—

well as the fragmentary remains of Numenius' work, *The Dissension of the Academics from Plato*, and of Atticus' book, *Against Aristotelian Interpretations of Plato*. The second category is represented by Plutarch's extant *Moral Virtue* and pseudo-Plutarch's *On Fate*; later extant examples include most of Plotinus' *Enneads*. There are no extant examples of the third category until Porphyry's *Sententiae* and Proclus' *Elements of Theology*. (The extant material in these categories is thin for the period prior to Plotinus, because it is only in the case of Plutarch that a substantial part of his philosophical corpus survives intact.)

47. In the case of the Stoics, the texts that survive from this period are primarily those of "moralists" like Epictetus and Marcus Aurelius, whose books were valued by later Platonists and Christians for their introductory ethical character, but innovative philosophical work was still being done; see Frede, "Epilogue," 779–81. Skeptical Academics had indeed largely disappeared by this time, but they were replaced by Pyrrhonists; see C. Brittain, "'Middle' Platonists on Academic Scepticism" ["Scepticism"], in R. Sorabji and R. Sharples (eds.), *Greek and Roman Philosophy, 100 BC–200 AD*, vol. 2 (London 2007), 297–315.

48. A possible exception to this is the "literal" interpretation of the creation of the world in time in the *Timaeus*, advocated by Plutarch and Atticus, but rejected by the rest of the tradition. But it is not clear that this is a "literal reading," and it is likely that Atticus' motivation for adopting it has some connection to his opposition to Aristotle.

49. Plutarch regarded himself as an "Academic" (though the later tradition translated this as "Platonist"); Numenius was often described as a "Pythagorean"; and we hear of a "Stoic and Platonist" called Tryphon in Porphyry's *Life of Plotinus* 17.

and philosophical questions about Platonic ethics, psychology, and metaphysics.[50] In ethics, Platonists agreed that the "end" was "likeness to god," but they disagreed about, for example, whether (Plato thought that) the human good was limited to virtue—as the Stoics argued, and the "Socratic" dialogues may suggest—or not— as Aristotle argued, and the later dialogues seem to allow.[51] In psychology, they agreed that the soul was essentially an immaterial and immortal substance, but they disagreed about, for example, its composition (in the *Timaeus*) and whether its partition in some dialogues was compatible with an Aristotelian analysis in terms of faculties.[52] And in metaphysics, they agreed about the existence of Forms and at least one divine intellect, but they disagreed radically about the number and kind of ultimate principles.[53]

A good reason to take the work of Plotinus and his student Porphyry in the period from c. 230 to 300 AD to mark a new stage in the history of Platonism is that their resolutions to many of these questions became standard features of later Platonism.[54] (A less good though understandable reason is that we possess the entire works of Plotinus and a substantial amount of Porphyry's.) Like their predecessors, Plotinus and Porphyry devoted a lot of attention to refuting the Platonists' opponents (al-

50. The debate about the degree of infidelity to Plato shown by the New Academics was fierce: Numenius regarded them (and Antiochus) as complete renegades (fr. 24–8 Des Places); Plutarch thought that their skepticism was largely compatible with Platonism (*Platonic Questions* 1); the anonymous commentator on the *Theaetetus* claimed that "very few" of them were skeptical (cols. 54–55); in his exuberant early Platonist phase, Augustine suggested that they were all esoteric Platonists (*Against the Academics* 3.37– 42). A sympathetic account of the enduring New Academic trend in early Platonism is given by J. Opsomer, *In Search of the Truth: Academic Tendencies in Middle Platonism* (Brussels, 1998). Pythagoreanism was far less controversial, since Pythagoras' influence on or consonance with Plato was generally accepted; see, e.g., D. O'Meara, *Pythagoras Revived* (Oxford, 1989), on the role of Pythagorean mathematical ideas in the development of Platonism.

51. The Stoic (or anti-Aristotelian) line is pursued vehemently by Atticus in fr. 2 Des Places. Plutarch promotes an aggressively Aristotelian (or anti-Stoic) line in his treatise *Moral Virtue*; a more moderate version is given in Alcinous *Handbook* 27–33.

52. On the composition of the soul, see, for example, Plutarch, *The Creation of the Soul in the Timaeus*, and Alcinous, *Handbook* 14; Atticus predictably rejects Aristotle's contributions entirely (fr. 7). The remains of an interesting earlier debate about the faculties of the soul can be seen in the fragments of Porphyry's *The Faculties of the Soul*. Fr. 252 (Smith), cites Numenius' and Longinus' conflicting views on the (originally Stoic) faculty of assent and its relation to the Aristotelian faculty of representation (*phantasia*); see L. Brisson and M. Patillon, "Longinus Platonicus Philosophus et Philologus," in W. Haase and H. Temporini (eds.), *Aufstieg und Niedergang der Römischen Welt*, Part 2, vol. 36.7 (Berlin, 1994), 5215–299, *ad* fr. 9 (pp. 5286–89), and M. Frede, "Numenius," *ad* fr. 45 (pp.1070–74). But this is just one example from a huge range of disputes.

53. These questions are the central focus of much work on the early Platonists; see, e.g., Dillon, *Middle Platonists*. One of the most interesting debates concerned the relation between the Forms and the divine Intellect—that is, whether the former were constitutive of the latter, or superior or subordinate to it. (The Stoics took the Forms to be just thoughts of god, mistakenly hypostasized by Plato. But if the Forms are the "model" and "perfect living thing" of *Timaeus* 29a and 31c, they should be superior to at least the Demiurgic intellect.) See, e.g., Alcinous *Handbook* 9; Porphyry *Life of Plotinus* 18 and 20; and Syrianus *On Aristotle's Metaphysics*, pp. 104–7 (Kroll).

54. Plotinus claimed that his views merely echoed those of his teacher in Alexandria, the shadowy Ammonius Saccas, and Porphyry adverts explicitly to the use of Numenius' and other philosophers' works in Plotinus' classes; see Porphyry's *Life of Plotinus* 3 and 14.

though by this stage they include Christians and other gnostics, as well as Epicureans, Stoics, and Peripatetics).[55] But they also succeeded in integrating enough Stoic and Aristotelian ideas into Platonism to effect the eventual absorption of those rival traditions within it.[56] Two central cases in Plotinus are, first, his integration of Stoic ethics into a Platonic theory of virtue, by identifying its key theses—that rational virtue is the good and, accordingly, that irrational emotions should be eliminated—as the principles of the second of three grades of virtue.[57] And second, his integration of Aristotelian theology into Platonic metaphysics, by identifying the active intellect of *De anima* 3.5 with the unmoved mover and god of *Metaphysics* 12 and both with the Platonic Demiurge, his own second principle. (This meant taking the divine activity of Aristotle's Intellect to be thinking—and so constituting—the Platonic Forms; see section 3.) In both cases, it is notable that Plotinus regarded his predecessors as providing brilliant, but incomplete, insights: the Stoic principles constitute only the *second*, rational, grade of virtue because (Plato showed that) there is a higher virtue corresponding to our life as intellects; the Aristotelian god is only the *second* principle because there must be a higher cause of the unity of Intellect.[58]

Porphyry is known primarily as the disseminator of Plotinus' doctrines through his edition of the *Enneads* and in his own philosophical works. But the remarkable range of his scholarship led him to two further acts of integration that had profound effects on later Platonism. One was the salvaging of Aristotle's *Categories* from Plotinus' critique in *Enneads* 6.1–3 by interpreting it as a work of "logic" rather than metaphysics and writing an introduction and two separate commentaries on it. This allowed him to advocate a strong version of the thesis of "the harmony of Plato and Aristotle"—that is, the claim that, once properly understood, the two philosophers can be seen to be working toward the same (Platonic) goal—which inspired the subsequent Platonist tradition of sympathetic commentary on Aristotle (whose treatises were thereafter read as a propaedeutic to the study of Plato).[59] The second

55. See section 3. Plotinus' method in the *Enneads* is often to start with a critical review of Epicurean, Stoic, and Peripatetic views on a topic before moving the argument to a higher level that resolves the difficulties those views involve; see, e.g., *Enn.* 5.9 or 1.4. But he also directly attacks, e.g., Stoic materialism in *Enn.* 4.7, and the Aristotelian doctrine of the categories in 6.1–3, as well as the Gnostics in *Enn.* 2.9. Porphyry's *Against the Christians* became a notorious work; for controversial works against philosophical opponents, see, e.g., fr. 240–55 Smith.

56. See Frede, "Epilogue," 793–97, citing Longinus' lament at the state of non-Plotinian philosophy in Porphyry's *Life of Plotinus* 20.

57. See n. 9 above.

58. The Aristotelian background of Plotinus' doctrine of Intellect is reviewed in, e.g., S. Menn, *Descartes and Augustine* (Cambridge, 1998), 73–129, and Gerson, *Plotinus*, part 1. Plotinus identified the higher cause as the One of the *Parmenides*, which he took to be the same as the Good in *Republic* 509b, by construing Plato's phrase "beyond being" as meaning "above the Forms, i.e. above the divine Intellect."

59. Plotinus' and Porphyry's work on the *Categories* is examined in S. Strange, "Plotinus, Porphyry, and the Neoplatonic Interpretation of the 'Categories,' " in W. Haase and H. Temporini (eds.), *Aufstieg und Niedergang der Römischen Welt*, Part 2, vol. 36.2 (Berlin, 1987), 954–74, and S. Ebbesen, "Pophyry's Legacy to Logic: A Reconstruction," in R. Sorabji (ed.), *Aristotle Transformed* (Ithaca, N.Y., 1990), 141–71; see also Barnes, *Porphyry: Introduction*. The history of the harmony thesis has not been fully studied; two recent and sympathetic (but controversial) studies are L. Gerson, *Aristotle and Other Platonists* (Ithaca, N.Y., 2005), and G. Karamanolis, *Plato and Aristotle in Agreement?* (Oxford, 2006).

was his attempt to subjoin a set of religious texts and practices to philosophy, as a way of offering a limited measure of ethical progress to nonphilosophers and counteracting the Christian alternative.[60]

Christianity became an increasingly significant force in the Roman empire in the generations after Porphyry's death in 305 AD, as it was gradually adopted as the religion of the imperial elite. In the end, this led to the dissolution of Platonism as an independent philosophical "movement" in the sixth century AD, as its teaching was forbidden and its institutions closed down. (Its ideas survived, however, in the new forms of Christian and, later, Islamic philosophy.) But the two hundred and fifty years between these events were anything but a period of decline. Three notable innovations—all of them due in the first instance to Iamblichus (c. 245–325 AD)—seem to characterize later Platonism.[61]

The central philosophical change was a major revision of Plotinian meta-physics, involving the postulation of a new series of "unparticipated" principles to ground the "participated" principles of Plotinus' three *hypostases*, Soul, Intellect, and the One. The causal theory driving this innovation led to the proliferation of mediating entities between principles at different ontological levels, which are the subject of the increasingly complex metaphysical and theological arguments in the extant later work of Proclus and Damascius. A second change was the development of a systematic theory of "theurgy"—that is, a theory of ritual or magical practices drawing on Porphyry's first steps in this direction—to bridge the gap the new metaphysics introduced between the increasingly transcendent first principles and our limited capacity for intellection.[62] The effect of this theory on the religious culture of the period was immense, as we can see from the failed attempt of the emperor Julian to establish a theurgical Platonism as the state religion (in 360–63 AD). At first sight, its effect on Iamblichian philosophy looks severe, since it seems to introduce a radical shift toward an unargued and philosophically uninteresting mysticism. But its purpose was not to reject philosophical inquiry but to supple-ment it with something like a theory of divine "special grace." This may strike some modern readers as unhelpful, but at bottom it is no more strange than some of the presuppositions of Christian philosophy (at least in its ancient forms). The

---

60. Porphyry's religious philosophy is partially elucidated in his extant *On Abstinence* and *Life of Pythagoras*. But we have fragments of numerous lost works, and one, *The Return of the Soul*, seems to have contained a program describing various ethnic rituals as a means for moral improvement that could constitute an alternative to the Christian "universal way"; see, e.g., fr. 283–302 Smith (which, however, are largely drawn from Augustine's polemic against Porphyry in *City of God* 10). See Smith, *Porphyry's Place*, Part 2.

61. For an overview of Iamblichus' work, see J. Dillon, "Iamblichus of Chalcis (c. 240–325 A.D.)," in W. Haase and H. Temporini (eds.), *Aufstieg und Niedergang der Römischen Welt*, Part 2, vol. 36.2 (Berlin, 1987), 862–909.

62. The theory is set out in Iamblichus' *De Mysteriis*; see, e.g., Dodds, *Greeks*, 282–311, and the more sympathetic treatment in Smith, *Porphyry's Place*, Part 2. On the later Platonists' rejection of Plotinus' optimism about our intellectual abilities, see C. Steel, *The Changing Self—A Study on the Soul in Later Neoplatonism: Iamblichus, Damascius and Priscianus* (Brussels, 1978), and J. Finnamore and J. Dillon, *Iamblichus De Anima* (Leiden, 2002).

third change introduced by Iamblichus was an intensified interest in commentary on Platonic dialogues, driven by his search for deeper philosophical interpretations than his predecessors had offered.

Iamblichus' innovations were enthusiastically embraced and refined by the remarkable sequence of Platonists who studied and taught at the schools in Athens and Alexandria from c. 400 to 529 and 611 AD (respectively). The massive extant output of these philosophers defies any easy summary.[63] But we can conclude this rapid survey by noting two striking features of their work. The first is that it is no longer profoundly shaped by the need to defend Platonism against "Hellenistic" materialism, empiricism, or skepticism. This does not mean that it had no external opposition; but its (usually unspoken) philosophical opponents were Christians who shared most of its central metaphysical presuppositions. The result is a more hermetic or closed form of philosophy, which, like much of the best philosophical work of our own time, is often inaccessible if one is not already immersed in the tradition. The second is that a great deal of it is in the form of philosophical commentary on Aristotle. The explanation for this is that the later Platonists devised a set curriculum of works of increasing difficulty to provide the rigorous training their advanced philosophical work presupposed. Since they accepted, in varying degrees, Porphyry's thesis of the harmony of Plato and Aristotle, but regarded Aristotle's work as primarily dealing with relatively easy topics, the curriculum included the systematic study of his treatises as a preparation for understanding the more complex metaphysical thought of Plato.[64] It is perhaps unclear whether we should celebrate or regret the effects of this curricular decision on the history of medieval philosophy, but this (along with major strands in Christian and Islamic philosophy) was the legacy of Platonism.

63. For extended summaries of their thought, see n. 3 above. The best starting point for reading the later Platonists is Proclus' *Elements of Theology*, which was translated with commentary by E. Dodds (Oxford, 1933). The Platonist commentaries on Aristotle are being steadily translated into English in the series *The Greek Commentators on Aristotle*, edited by Richard Sorabji. Some of the major commentaries on Plato have been translated into modern English; see, e.g., L. Westerink, *The Greek Commentaries on Plato's Phaedo* (Amsterdam, 1976–77); G. Morrow and J. Dillon, *Proclus' Commentary on Plato's Parmenides* (Princeton, N.J., 1987); and D. Baltzly, *Proclus: Commentary on Plato's Timaeus*, vol. 3 (Cambridge, 2007). There are also excellent French translations of Proclus' *Timaeus* and *Republic* commentaries by A-J. Festugière and, more recently, a steady stream of Budé editions of his works. The older English translations by Thomas Taylor are more reverent than helpful.

64. The late Platonist curriculum started with introductory ethical works, such as Epictetus' *Handbook* or the Pythagorean *Golden Verses*—on which we have extant commentaries by Simplicius and Hierocles, respectively (see n. 14 above, and H. Schibli, *Hierocles of Alexandria* [Oxford, 2002]). The second stage covered Aristotle, especially the "logical works" in the *Organon*, the *Physics*, *Metaphysics*, and *De anima* (for all of which we still have extensive Platonist commentaries). The final stage covered Plato and focused on metaphysics and theology (and especially the *Timaeus* and *Parmenides*). The curriculum and its connection with the commentary tradition is described in detail in L. Westerink, *Anonymous Prolegomena to Platonic Philosophy* (Amsterdam, 1962), and Westerink, "The Alexandrian Commentators and the Introductions to Their Commentaries," in R. Sorabji (ed.), *Aristotle Transformed* (Ithaca, N.Y., 1990), 325–48.

# 3. EPISTEMOLOGICAL FOUNDATIONS

In section 1, I suggested that this broad philosophical tradition was unified by its commitments to the authoritative status of Plato's work and a set of shared assumptions about its fundamental significance; in section 2, I argued that the first commitment is best understood as a reaction to the philosophical failures of the Hellenistic schools. In this section, I sketch some of the ways in which Platonists elaborated the shared assumptions of the second commitment and defended them against their "Hellenistic" rivals.

The basic Platonist assumptions have been crudely characterized as two claims: (I) the world is only intelligible through the structure and order imposed on it by ontologically prior immaterial principles; and (II) knowledge accordingly presupposes (non-empirical) cognitive access to these immaterial principles. The Platonists defended these general claims both positively, by setting out a causal theory to justify (I) and an epistemology to explain (II), and negatively, by arguing for the inadequacy of any materialist alternative to (I) or any empiricist alternative to (II). This section concentrates on the second claim, however, since the defense of the first depends on the possibility of our having access to the principles, and the arguments for (II) tell us something about the nature of at least two of these principles: soul and intellect.[65]

Platonist epistemology depends on a basic set of positive claims about knowledge derived from a (selective) reading of the Platonic dialogues.[66] Three central theses are:

(a) The primary objects of knowledge are immaterial principles (starting with the Forms).
(b) It is in principle possible to apprehend these objects (or at least the Forms) directly through a nonrepresentational faculty of "intellection."
(c) This possibility presupposes that embodied cognitive agents start off with a store of nonempirical information—that is, some form of innate "knowledge."

Since thesis (a) is a fundamental principle of Platonist metaphysics, and (b) amounts to the claim that knowledge is possible, controversy within Platonism centered on (c). The Platonic texts underlying this third thesis—the recollection argument in the *Phaedo*, and its further elaboration, as the Platonists saw it, in the *Phaedrus* and *Timaeus*—raise a number of general problems for any interpretation of Plato. Two

65. On I, see, e.g., L. Gerson, "Neoplatonism," in C. Shields (ed.), *The Blackwell Guide to Ancient Philosophy* (Oxford, 2003), 303–23. Proclus' *Elements of Theology* is a clear exposition of the major later Platonist arguments for (I); some notable earlier arguments are given by Numenius in *On the Good* (fr.1–22 Des Places), Plotinus (see n. 55 above), and Augustine (*De Trinitate* 9–10).
66. Platonist epistemology tended to start from the recollection doctrines of the *Phaedo* and *Pheadrus*, rather than from the apparently belief-centered accounts of knowledge in the *Meno* and *Theaetetus*, because the former lend themselves more readily to Platonist interpretations of the metaphysical and psychological theories of *Republic* 5–7 and 10 and the *Timaeus*.

particularly salient questions concern the relations between perceptual (or "dox-astic") experience and intellectual knowledge in Plato's epistemology, and between the cognitive agent (the soul) and its epistemic objects (the principles). Theories that address these questions could, and Platonist theories did, take many forms, but a brief sketch of two general responses and their reception within the tradition should suffice to indicate some of the ways in which Platonism evolved.

The context for these Platonist theories, however, is not the relatively blank epistemological slate that Plato filled in with his theory of recollection but, rather, the developed empiricist alternatives that the Hellenistic schools had devised in reaction to it. The dominant alternative was the Stoic theory, which derived knowledge entirely from perception, both directly (through the theory of the "cognitive" impression) and indirectly via a process of natural concept formation based on secure perception.[67] The latter process provided a set of contentful "common" or basic conceptions—including concepts of natural kinds, as well as logical notions such as consequence and inconsistency—that the Stoics took to constitute our rationality.[68] On their view, systematic knowledge of the world could be acquired through a process of "articulating" the contentful conceptual knowledge contained in the empirically acquired conceptions we apply in ordinary experience, and using this as the basis for further empirical inquiry. The Stoics thus denied the need for a Platonic theory of recollection—and, since they also con-strued the basic principles of the world, including god and the soul, as material entities, they rejected not just thesis c, but also the existence of both transcendental objects of knowledge a and an immaterial soul that might know them b.

The first challenge for any Platonist theory of recollection (at least prior to late Platonism, i.e., c. 300 AD) was accordingly to clear away the supposed confusions of Stoic empiricism. The basis for this task was, unsurprisingly, the rather disparate set of Platonic arguments designed to show the intrinsic deficiency of doxastic experience—for instance, that the faculty of perception is conceptually im-poverished in certain ways, or that perceptual experience is fallible and restricted to the cognition of material objects or qualities.[69] But this common stock of argu-ments could be mined to support a wide range of positive theories, grounded in very distinct conceptions of perception and the soul. The second challenge for

---

67. See, e.g., M. Frede, "Stoic Epistemology," in K. Algra, J. Barnes, J. Mansfeld, and M. Schofield (eds.), *The Cambridge History of Hellenistic Philosophy* (Cambridge, 1999), 295–322, and Frede, "The Stoic Conception of Reason," in K. Boudouris (ed.), *Hellenistic Philosophy* vol. 2 (Athens, 1994), 50–63. Early Platonists were also concerned to argue against Peripatetic and Epicurean epistemologies (see Plutarch fr. 215f Sandbach), but the surviving texts focus on the Stoics and their Academic rivals.

68. Some Stoic sources suggest that the theory depended on innate dispositions to form the appro-priate set of conceptions, which included moral concepts that may not be derivable from simple perception in early childhood; see D. Scott, *Recollection and Experience* (Cambridge, 1995), 157–210, and the articles in the previous note.

69. The primary Platonic sources for these criticisms of perception are the *Phaedo* and *Theaetetus* (esp. 184–86), and *Timaeus* 28–29 and *Republic* 6–7. An early Platonist catalogue of such arguments is given by Alcinous, *Handbook* ch. 25.3; individual elements are appealed to *passim*; see, e.g., Plutarch *Against Colotes* 1116 a–b and 1118a–b.

Platonist theories of recollection was to deflate the threat of skepticism, which had plagued the Stoics throughout the Hellenistic era and remained a serious obstacle to any positive epistemology.[70] In this case, however, the Platonists shared a strategy, derived from their mutual acceptance of the thesis that divergence from Platonic doctrine inevitably leads to intractable disagreements that can only be solved by an unqualified return to Plato (see section 2): they argued that skepticism picks up on a fundamental problem of Stoic empiricism: viz., its dependence on representations (*phantasia*) that yield only mediated or indirect apprehensions of their objects. The skeptics were correct to argue that such a theory can never provide secure knowledge, but their own skepticism is parasitic on just this theory and falls with it in the face of the Platonist alternative(s).[71] As a result, Platonists were able to supplement their general Platonic criticisms of doxastic experience with a battery of more specific arguments drawn from the skeptical Academic (and, later, Pyrrhonist) critique of Stoic epistemology.[72]

A number of early Platonists seem to have spelled out the Platonic doctrine of recollection as a form of "cognitive dualism" modeled on the sharp distinction between doxastic and epistemic cognitive states in *Timaeus* 28–29.[73] The heart of this view—which is best attested in the sketch of Platonic epistemology in Alcinous' *Handbook*, chapter 4 (from c. 150 AD)—is the thesis that our cognitive faculties flow into two autonomous systems, based on distinct sources and objects. The doxastic system is based on the faculty of perception and geared only for the cognition of material objects and states of affairs. But, Alcinous argues, our or-

---

70. Skepticism was a live option in the second century AD, both in the form of the revived Academicism of Favorinus (attested in Galen, *On the Best Teaching Method*) and in its new guise of Pyrrhonism; see Brittain, "Scepticism."

71. See below. Traces of this strategy in early Platonism are discernible in Numenius and Alcinous; see Brittain, "Scepticism," and Boys-Stones, "Alcinous." It becomes explicit in Plotinus; see *Enn.* 5.5 (and, e.g., Augustine *Trin.* 15.21), and D. O'Meara, "Scepticism and Ineffability in Plotinus" ["Scepticism"], *Phronesis* 45.3 (2000), 240–51.

72. For the Academic criticisms of Stoic epistemology, see the articles cited in nn. 22 and 31 above. Their deployment by Platonists is attested in Plutarch's controversial anti-Stoic works, *Stoic Contradictions* and *Common Conceptions* (passim), and other early Platonist texts such as Plutarch fr. 215 (Sandbach), Anon. *in Theaet.*, e.g., cols. 3.7–15 and 61, and Numenius fr. 24–8 (Des Places), as well as in, e.g., Plotinus *Enn.* 4.6 and 4.7, Porphyry *On the Capacities of the Soul* (fr. 251–54 Smith) and Augustine *Against the Academics* 3.26. These Academic arguments (or Academic developments of Platonic criticisms) are often found in tandem with the Platonic criticisms cited in n. 69.

73. Our sketchy evidence for the period makes it difficult to know how widely shared this sort of theory was. I use Alcinous because recent work on this and related texts has made it possible to get a fairly detailed picture of his theory. On the structure of *Handbook* ch. 4 and its relation to Platonic texts, see D. Sedley, "Alcinous' Epistemology," in K. Algra, P. van der Horst, and D. Runia (eds.), *Polyhistor* (Leiden, 1996), 300–12. On the Stoic and skeptic context that Alcinous aims to undermine, see G. Boys-Stones, "Alcinous, *Didaskalikos* 4: In Defence of Dogmatism" ["Alcinous"], in M. Bonazzi and V. Celluprica (eds.), *L'eredità platonica: Studi sul platonismo da Arcesilao a Proclo* (Naples, 2005), 203–34. Sedley, "Three Interpretations," rightly contrasts Alcinous' views and those of the anonymous *Commentary on the Theaetetus*; but it seems to me that their differences are essentially over how to interpret the dialogues rather than over the epistemological theory they find in it. (The term "cognitive dualism" is owed to Sedley, "Three Interpretations," p. 91, who notes that Scott, *Recollection*, argues for a version of this view as the correct interpretation of Plato's theory in the *Phaedo* and elsewhere.)

dinary cognitive lives—our abilities to make perceptual judgments and to reason about empirical objects—are nonetheless fully explicable in terms of evolved doxastic capacities derived from perception, memory, and a set of empirical concepts they give rise to.[74] The epistemic system, on this view, is thus not required to explain ordinary cognition but, rather, only how philosophical knowledge is possible: that is, how we can acquire the knowledge of immaterial objects (essences and Forms) that is inaccessible to the doxastic system. Alcinous infers that its basis must be some form of innate "knowledge" derived from our preincarnate intellection of the Forms, as Plato suggested. But he elaborates this in terms of our innate possession of a second set of abstract "natural conceptions," which give rise to our capacity for epistemic reasoning. Philosophical inquiry, on this account, is a matter of actualizing or "recollecting" the (abstract and nonrepresentational) content latent in these innate conceptions through a nonempirical process of "articulation," described by Alcinous as applying the methods of Platonic "dialectic"; when successful, it leads to intellection of Forms.[75]

We can see even from this cursory sketch of cognitive dualism that it was conceived as a theory of recollection that could replace the dominant Stoic epistemology of Alcinous' time.[76] The cognitive dualist preserves the Stoic view that our higher (epistemic) capacities are constituted by a set of contentful concepts, but it substitutes a Platonic innatist explanation of their content for the Stoics' empirical theory, which effectively severs the connection between experience and philosophical knowledge in the Stoic theory. It is also clear that this compromise is achieved at some cost. We can note two problems that attracted the attention of later Platonists. The first is that the cognitive dualist's rich conception of "doxastic reason" seems to presuppose some complex rational capacities that are not easily explicable by a Platonist without recourse to concepts derived from "epistemic reason."[77] But once the cognitive dualist allows that our "natural conceptions" play a role in ordinary cognitive life, it is hard to see how he can maintain the firewall between perception and intellection.[78] The road is open for his critics to

74. Alcinous *Handbook* ch. 4.3–5. Alcinous' theory of "doxastic reason" draws on the discussions of perception and memory in the *Theaetetus* and *Philebus*; see Sedley, "Alcinous' Epistemology."

75. The process is called "articulation" in, e.g., Plutarch *Platonic Question* 1 and Anon. *in Theaet.* cols. 46–47. Alcinous' description of "dialectic" and mathematics in chs. 5–7 covers a confusing mixture of methods of argument employed by Plato. The core of it, however, is a version of the doctrine of cognitive "ascent" suggested by the Line simile in *Republic* 6–7.

76. Owing to its form, Alcinous' work does not make the polemical context explicit, but its anti-Stoic intentions are clear from some arguments in the work and the context provided by his contemporaries; see Boys-Stones, "Alcinous." Similar but more palpably anti-Stoic views are found in, e.g., Plutarch fr. 215 (Sandbach); Anon. *in Theaet.*, e.g., cols. 3.7–15 and 61; and Numenius fr. 24–8 (Des Places).

77. The clearest example is the case of moral reasoning, mentioned by Alcinous at the end of chapter 4, which is naturally construed as involving the application of nonempirical moral concepts of value. (*Handbook* 4.8 is confusing, because it seems to conflate the cognitive lives of ordinary and perfect moral agents.)

78. In *Handbook* 25.5, Alcinous describes "irrational souls" as driven by perceptual representation (*phantasia*) and deprived of reasoning, judgment, theorems, and universal apprehensions. In the human case, it is not clear how doxastic *reason* can achieve, e.g., judgment and reasoning, on his view, without actively applying "epistemic" concepts such as "truth" and "being" (see *Theaet.* 184–86).

argue either that such "natural concepts" are derived from perceptual experience by abstraction (the Stoic model) or that all perceptual experience presupposes thick conceptualization (Plotinus' model). Cognitive dualism thus looks like an inefficient theory that unnecessarily undermines the unity of the soul.[79]

A second problem for cognitive dualism is that its explanation for the soul's epistemic potential in terms of innate but latent "natural conceptions" seems too weak to secure knowledge. The cognitive dualist presupposes that once the process of recollection has been triggered, the "articulation" of these natural conceptions is sufficient to culminate in intellection of the Forms. But since the connection between the embodied soul and the Forms is indirect—it depends on the partial grasp of the Forms (the natural concept) being retained unconsciously and re-activated at a temporal distance—it is unclear that it can yield unmediated knowledge. Most early Platonists seem to have assumed that their position was immune to skepticism because the epistemic system was posited precisely to escape the limited and mediated apprehension provided by doxastic representation (*phantasia*).[80] But later Platonists were less confident that the mere avoidance of perceptual or imaginative representation sufficed to avoid a mediated grasp of an object through an "image" or "likeness"—that is, a derivative and incomplete form of knowledge.

The force of these objections to cognitive dualism is particularly evident in Plotinus' radical revision of Platonist epistemology. The *Enneads* are primarily concerned with the interrelations between the divine principles (Soul, Intellect, and the One or Good); but Plotinus devoted a number of his psychological treatises to the elaboration of a novel, and extremely complex, theory of perceptual experience.[81] Plotinus rejected cognitive dualism on the basis of an analysis distinguishing the physiological, sensory, and judgmental aspects of perception. On his realist view, human perception as such is the direct apprehension of an object or quality, i.e., the judgment that it is there. But, while this judgment is occasioned by a (psychological or nonmaterial) sensation triggered by a physiological process, it is realized only through the activation of the "account" of the object or quality— a *logos* or concept—that the agent *already* possesses. For if, as Plotinus argues, the physiological processes involved in perception are in principle incapable of

---

79. Alcinous accepts the standard Platonist view that the soul is essentially an intellectual cognitive agent *constituted* by something like the dualist's "epistemic reason" (*Handbook* 14.1–2, cf. Plato, *Timaeus* 41c–42 and n. 82 below). But the division of "reason" into two discrete systems, when combined with the assumption that the soul's nonintellectual faculties are not essential to it because they depend on the body (*Handbook* 25.5; cf. *Tim.* 69–72), implies that ordinary cognitive life does not involve the soul's essential activity.

80. See n. 71 above. Plutarch, however, may be an exception, since his "Academic Platonism" sometimes drives him to allow that knowledge may not be possible (at least in this life); see his *Platonic Questions* 1, and n. 50 above.

81. See, e.g., *Enn.* 4.3–6. Excellent general accounts of Plotinus' epistemology are provided in Gerson, *Plotinus*, esp. 164–84, and E. Emilsson "Cognition and Its Object," in L. Gerson (ed.), *The Cambridge Companion to Plotinus* (Cambridge, 1996), 217–49. Emilsson's *Plotinus on Sense-Perception* (Cambridge, 1988) is a brilliant reconstruction of the complexities of Plotinus' theory.

transmitting cognitive information, these concepts cannot be generated by abstraction from more primitive sensory inputs. Ordinary perception thus presupposes that the soul, the cognitive agent, has the active use of the set of "natural conceptions" which the cognitive dualist excluded from empirical experience: it is essentially structured by "innate" concepts.

Plotinus' rejection of Stoic empiricism is thus more radical than the cognitive dualist's. His interpretation of the theory of recollection takes it to apply to cognition quite generally: all forms of thinking, including perception, presuppose that the soul actively employs the set of innate "accounts" or concepts that makes them possible. (The theory is based on Plotinus' understanding of *Phaedrus* 249b–c and *Timaeus* 37a–c.) But Plotinus' theory of ordinary cognitive life is also closer to the Stoic model of rationality than the cognitive dualist's: since the (rational) soul is constituted by these immaterial concepts, its existence depends on their continual activation—that is, thinking in one form or another.[82] A consequence of his positive reevaluation of ordinary experience, however, was the downgrading of the philosophical achievement of conscious "recollection"—the startling grasp on "equality itself"—examined in the recollection argument in *Phaedo* 72–78. Recollection in this sense is not the intellection of a Form, as earlier Platonists had thought but, rather, a matter of "comparing new tokens with old ones": that is, becoming conscious of the content and interrelations of abstract concepts the soul already has (or is).[83] Plotinus accepted that "turning inside" in this way was a necessary stage toward intellection; but he argued that an explicit or "articulated" conceptual grasp on an immaterial object was still an "image" or "likeness" of it, albeit one at a higher and more abstract level than a merely perceptual or imaginative representation. If the soul is able to get beyond the derivative knowledge provided by the likenesses of Forms at the rational or conceptual level, it must have direct access to the Forms themselves.

But Plotinus' model for direct access to the Forms is the knowledge of the divine Intellect. As noted in section 2, Plotinus followed Aristotle in taking this Intellect to be constituted by its intellection of itself, and he took the Forms to be the content of its thought, i.e., what it intellects, or itself.[84] The metaphysical significance of his identification of Forms (real being) with the Intellect is, of

---

82. Like Alcinous, Plotinus took the *Timaeus* account of the numerical composition of the (rational and immortal) soul (*Tim.* 35a–37c and 41a–42d) to imply that it is just a set of *logoi*—"ratios" or "accounts"—which were standardly construed as concepts of the Forms. For Platonists, however, the existence or life of immaterial substances like the soul consists in their activity.

83. See *Enn.* 5.3.2 and 4.3.25. Plotinus' explicit treatments of recollection are unsystematic, however: he doesn't distinguish lexically between ordinary "recollection" (memory) and Platonic "recollection," and, since his various discussions of the latter take off from various Platonic texts, he doesn't always remember to reconcile them with his "downgraded" interpretation of the *Phaedo*-type. (*Enn.* 1.2.4 and 3.5.1, for instance, describe the ascent to an actual *vision* of the Forms via beauty in the *Phaedrus* and *Symposium* as "recollection.")

84. For an introduction to Plotinus' extraordinarily complex theory of intellect, see O'Meara, *Plotinus*, 33–53, and Gerson, *Plotinus*, 42–78. A detailed reconstruction in English is forthcoming in E. Emilsson's *Plotinus on the Intellect* (Cambridge, 2007). On the background to Plotinus' theory, see nn. 53 and 58 above.

course, at the heart of Plotinus' Platonism. But our concern here is just with the crucial epistemological implication that Plotinus argues for in *Enn.* 5.3: viz., that the knowledge that constitutes both reality and the Intellect must be an eternal activity of self-knowing.[85] A remarkable feature of taking divine self-knowing as the paradigm of knowledge—and one that Plotinus notes in *Enn.* 5.5.1–3—is that it eradicates any possibility of mediation or representation between the cognitive subject and object (since the two are identical). But once that possibility is removed, there is no further scope for skepticism: the Intellect's existence just is knowledge. (We might doubt the existence of the divine Intellect, of course, but to do so is to undermine the intelligibility of the world, and hence the possibility of thought itself, skeptical or otherwise.)

Thus, if the soul is able to realize nonderivative knowledge, and to do so requires direct access to the Forms, the soul must be able to "conform to" or "become" Intellect. And since Plotinus believes that the soul's capacity for virtue demonstrates that it can have genuine knowledge, he infers that it already has an intellectual capacity over and above the "accounts" that make it a rational substance. But the only possible ground for this capacity is the (active) Intellect itself, which is continually "writing" these accounts on the soul (*Enn.* 5.3.4). Plotinus concludes that the soul is in fact always directly accessing the Forms, although we are not conscious of this: the soul does not entirely "descend" from Intellect, its cause (*Enn.* 4.8.8).[86]

Plotinus' theory of recollection met a mixed reaction in the later Platonist tradition. The thesis that ordinary cognitive experience presupposes the soul's prior possession of at least some nonempirical structuring concepts was widely accepted.[87] The later Platonists' rejection of cognitive dualism was qualified, however, by their development of complex theories of empirical concept formation and a variety of extremely rich and subtle analyses of perception, which remain largely unexplored in modern scholarship.[88] But the radical core of Plotinus' interpretation of recollection—the thesis that it is the means of realizing the direct and necessary connection between the soul and the divine Intellect—was flatly

85. The argument is examined in Emilsson's "Cognition and Its Object" and I. Crystall, "Plotinus on the Structure of Self-Intellection," *Phronesis* 43 (1998), 264–87.

86. See S. Menn, "Plotinus on the Identity of Knowledge with Its Object," *Apeiron* 34.3 (2001), 233–46. As Menn shows, Plotinus thought that this heterodox doctrine was necessary to resolve the "greatest difficulty" in *Parmenides* 133–34; he based his resolution on *Sophist* 238c.

87. See, e.g., Damascius's analyses of the recollection argument in his *Commentaries on the Phaedo* I.253–310 (esp. 1.274) and II.4–20 (esp. II.15). Similar views are expressed by Syrianus in *On Aristotle's Metaphysics*, pp. 104–7 (Kroll), and by Proclus—see n. 9 above.

88. See, however, the works cited in n. 59 on the role of empirical and nonempirical concepts in the acquisition of natural language, e.g., and I. Mueller, "Mathematics and Philosophy in Proclus' *Commentary on Book I of Euclid's Elements*," in J. Pépin and H. Saffery (eds.), *Proclus: Lecteur et interprète des anciens* (Paris, 1987), 305–18, on the role of abstraction in Platonist geometry. Work on the later Platonists' theories of perception has tended to focus on the diverse interpretations of Aristotle's theory in the *De Anima* commentary tradition; but see, e.g., P. Lautner, "Some Clarifications on Proclus' Fourfold Division of Sense-Perception in the *Timaeus* Commentary," in M. Perkams and R. Piccione (eds.), *Proklos: Methode, Seelenlehre, Metaphysik* (Leiden, 2006), 117–35.

rejected by the great majority of later Platonists.[89] Plotinus' theory struck them as naively optimistic about the nature of the fallen (i.e., human) soul and its relation to the hierarchy of transcendent higher principles: the immense gap between the two introduced by Iamblichian metaphysics was in principle unbridgeable by unaided natural reason.[90]

A brief survey of Platonist epistemology can do no more than scratch the surface of the massive body of sophisticated philosophical work by indicating some of the general features of its evolution. But perhaps this is enough to suggest the value of the Platonist tradition for a philosophical reader, both as a stimulus for producing rival interpretations of Plato and as a challenging philosophical movement in its own right.[91]

# BIBLIOGRAPHY

Allen, J. "Carneades," *Stanford Encyclopedia of Philosophy*, http://plato.stanford.edu/entries/carneades (2004).

Annas, J. "Plato the Sceptic," *Oxford Studies in Ancient Philosophy Supplementary Volume*, (Oxford, 1992), 43–72.

Annas, J. *Platonist Ethics Old and New* (Ithaca, N.Y., 1999).

Athanassiadi, P. *Damascius: The Philosophical History* (Athens, 1999).

Baltzly, D. *Proclus: Commentary on Plato's Timaeus*, vol. 3 (Cambridge, 2007).

Barnes, J. "Antiochus of Ascalon," in M. Griffin and J. Barnes (eds.), *Philosophia Togata* (Oxford, 1989), 51–96.

Barnes, J. *Porphyry: Introduction* (Oxford, 2003).

Blumenthal, H. *Soul and Intellect: Studies in Plotinus and Later Neoplatonism* (London, 1993).

Boys-Stones, G. "Alcinous, *Didaskalikos* 4: In Defence of Dogmatism," in M. Bonazzi and V. Celluprica (eds.), *L'eredità platonica: Studi sul platonismo da Arcesilao a Proclo* (Naples, 2005), 203–34.

Boys-Stones, G. *Post-Hellenistic Philosophy* (Oxford, 2001).

Brennan, T., and C. Brittain. *Simplicius: On Epictetus' Handbook* (Ithaca, N.Y., 2002).

89. The standard criticisms deriving from Iamblichus are recorded by Proclus, e.g., in his commentaries on the *Parmenides* (4.946–50 Cousin) and *Timaeus* (3.333–34 Diehl), and in his *Elements of Theology* (§211 Dodds). As these contexts suggest, the criticisms were grounded on the apparent incompatibility of Plotinus' views with Plato's claims about the effects of embodiment on the human soul in *Tim.* 43a–44c and about the possibility of knowledge of the principles in *Parm.* 133–34.

90. See section 2 and n. 62 above. Note, however, that Plotinus himself had pointed the way toward the invocation of superintellectual experiences through his views on the possibility of "experiencing" the ultimate principle, the One or Good.

91. In the case of epistemology, the stimulus is provided by the Platonists' focus on reconciling Plato's disparate arguments into unitary theories. The evolution sketched above could be rephrased as a series of such attempts, centered, respectively, on the recollection argument in the *Phaedo* (for the cognitive dualists), the psychology of the *Phaedrus*, and the theory of rationality in the *Timaeus* (for Plotinus), and all three with the doctrine of principles in the *Parmenides* (for later Platonists, such as Proclus).

Brisson, L. (ed.) *Porphyre: Sentences* (Paris, 2005).

Brisson, L., and M. Patillon. "Longinus Platonicus Philosophus et Philologus," in W. Haase and H. Temporini (eds.), *Aufstieg und Niedergang der Römischen Welt*, Part 2, vol. 36.7 (Berlin, 1994), 5215–299.

Brittain, C. "Arcesilaus," *Stanford Encyclopedia of Philosophy*, http://plato.stanford.edu/entries/arcesilaus (2005).

Brittain, C. "Attention Deficit in Plotinus and Augustine," *Proceedings of the Boston Area Colloquium in Ancient Philosophy* 18 (2003), 223–63.

Brittain, C. " 'Middle' Platonists on Academic Scepticism," in R. Sorabji and R. Sharples (eds.), *Greek and Roman Philosophy, 100 BC—200 AD*, vol. 2 (London, 2007), 297–315.

Brittain, C. *Philo of Larissa* (Oxford, 2001).

Brittain, C. "Philo of Larissa," *Stanford Encyclopedia of Philosophy*, http://plato.stanford.edu/entries/philo-larissa/ (2006).

Brown, P. *The Making of Late Antiquity* (Cambridge, Mass., 1978).

Crystall, I. "Plotinus on the Structure of Self-Intellection," *Phronesis* 43 (1998), 264–87.

Deuse, W. *Untersuchungen zur mittelplatonischen und neuplatonischen Seelenlehre* (Mainz, 1983).

Dillon, J. "An Ethic for the Late Antique Sage," in L. Gerson (ed.), *The Cambridge Companion to Plotinus* (Cambridge, 1996), 315–35.

Dillon, J. *The Heirs of Plato: A Study of the Old Academy, 347/274 B.C.* (Oxford, 2003).

Dillon, J. "Iamblichus of Chalcis (c. 240–325 A.D.)," in W. Haase and H. Temporini (eds.), *Aufstieg und Niedergang der Römischen Welt*, Part 2, vol. 36.2 (Berlin, 1987), 862–909.

Dillon, J. *The Middle Platonists* (London, 1977).

Dodds, E. *The Greeks and the Irrational* (Berkeley, 1951).

Dodds, E *Proclus: The Elements of Theology* (Oxford, 1933).

Donini, P. "Testi e commenti, manuali e insegnamento: la forma sistematica e i metodi della filosofia in età postellenistica," in W. Haase and H. Temporini (eds.), *Aufstieg und Niedergang der Römischen Welt*, Part 2, vol. 36.7 (Berlin, 1994), 5027–100.

Dörrie, H., and M. Baltes (trans.) *Der Platonismus in der Antike*, vols. 1–5 (Stuttgart, 1987–98).

Ebbesen, S. "Pophyry's Legacy to Logic: A Reconstruction," in R. Sorabji (ed.), *Aristotle Transformed* (Ithaca, N.Y., 1990), 141–71.

Edwards, M. *Neoplatonic Saints: The Lives of Plotinus and Proclus by Their Students* (Liverpool, 2000).

Emilsson, E. "Cognition and Its Object," in L. Gerson (ed.), *The Cambridge Companion to Plotinus* (Cambridge, 1996), 217–49.

Emilsson, E. *Plotinus on Sense-Perception* (Cambridge, 1988).

Emilsson, E. *Plotinus on the Intellect* (Cambridge, 2007).

Finnamore, J., and J. Dillon. *Iamblichus De Anima* (Leiden, 2002).

Frede, D. "The Philosophical Economy of Plato's Psychology: Rationality and the Common Concepts in the *Timaeus*," in M. Frede and G. Striker (eds.), *Rationality in Greek Thought* (Oxford, 1996), 29–56.

Frede, M. "Epilogue," in K. Algra, J. Barnes, J. Mansfeld, and M. Schofield (eds.), *The Cambridge History of Hellenistic Philosophy* (Cambridge, 1999), 771–97.

Frede, M. "Numenius," in W. Haase and H. Temporini (eds.), *Aufstieg und Niedergang der Römischen Welt*, Part 2, vol. 36.2 (Berlin, 1987), 1034–75.

Frede, M. "The Stoic Conception of Reason," in K. Boudouris (ed.), *Hellenistic Philosophy*, vol. 2 (Athens, 1994), 50–63.

Frede, M. "Stoic Epistemology," in K. Algra, J. Barnes, J. Mansfeld, and M. Schofield (eds.), *The Cambridge History of Hellenistic Philosophy* (Cambridge, 1999), 295–322.

Gerson, L. *Aristotle and Other Platonists* (Ithaca, N.Y., 2005).

Gerson, L. "Neoplatonism," in C. Shields (ed.), *The Blackwell Guide to Ancient Philosophy* (Oxford, 2003), 303–23.

Gerson, L. *Plotinus* (London, 1994).

Glucker, J. *Antiochus and the Late Academy* (Göttingen, 1978).

Gottschalk, H. "The Earliest Aristotelian Commentators," in R. Sorabji (ed.), *Aristotle Transformed* (Ithaca, N.Y., 1990), 55–81.

Haase, W., and H. Temporini (eds.) *Aufstieg und Niedergang der Römischen Welt*, Part 2, vols. 36.1–7 (Berlin, 1987–1994).

Hadot, I. *Le problème de néoplatonisme alexandrin: Hiéroclès et Simplicius* (Paris, 1978).

Karamanolis, G. *Plato and Aristotle in Agreement?* (Oxford, 2006).

Lamberton, R. *Homer the Theologian* (Berkeley, 1986).

Lautner, P. "Some Clarifications on Proclus' Fourfold Division of Sense-Perception in the *Timaeus* Commentary," in M. Perkams and R. Piccione (eds.), *Proklos: Methode, Seelenlehre, Metaphysik* (Leiden, 2006), 117–35.

Menn, S. *Descartes and Augustine* (Cambridge, 1998).

Menn, S. "Plotinus on the Identity of Knowledge with Its Object," *Apeiron* 34.3 (2001), 233–46.

Morrow, G., and J. Dillon. *Proclus' Commentary on Plato's Parmenides* (Princeton, N.J., 1987).

Mueller, I. "Mathematics and Philosophy in Proclus' *Commentary on Book I of Euclid's Elements*," in J. Pépin and H. Saffery (eds.), *Proclus: Lecteur et interprète des anciens* (Paris, 1987), 305–18.

O'Meara, D. *Plotinus: An Introduction to the Enneads* (Oxford, 1993).

O'Meara, D. *Pythagoras Revived* (Oxford, 1989).

O'Meara, D. "Scepticism and Ineffability in Plotinus," *Phronesis* 45.3 (2000), 240–51.

Opsomer, J. *In Search of the Truth: Academic Tendencies in Middle Platonism* (Brussels, 1998).

Opsomer, J., and C. Steel. *Proclus: On the Existence of Evils* (Ithaca, N.Y., 2003).

Owen, G. E. L. "The Place of the *Timaeus* in Plato's Dialogues," *Classical Quarterly* NS 3 (1953), 79–95.

Schibli, H. *Hierocles of Alexandria* (Oxford, 2002).

Scott, D. *Recollection and Experience* (Cambridge, 1995).

Sedley, D. "Alcinous' Epistemology," in K. Algra, P. van der Horst, and D. Runia (eds.), *Polyhistor. Studies in the History & Historiography of Ancient Philosophy* (Leiden, 1996), 300–12.

Sedley, D. "The Origins of Stoic God," in D. Frede and A. Laks (eds.), *Traditions of Theology* (Leiden, 2002), 41–83.

Sedley, D. "Plato's *Auctoritas* and the Rebirth of the Commentary Tradition," in J. Barnes and M. Griffin (eds.), *Philosophia Togata II: Plato and Aristotle at Rome* (Oxford, 1997), 110–29.

Sedley, D. "Three Platonist Interpretations of the *Theaetetus*," in C. Gill and M. McCabe (eds.), *Form and Argument in Later Plato* (Oxford 1996), 79–103.

Sedley, D., and G. Bastianini (eds.), *Commentarium in Platonis Theaetetum, Corpus dei papiri filosofici greci e latini*, vol. 3 (Florence, 1995), 227–562.

Smith, A. *Porphyry's Place in the Neoplatonic Tradition* (The Hague, 1974).

Sorabji, R. (ed.) *Aristotle Transformed* (Ithaca, N.Y., 1990).

Sorabji, R. *The Philosophy of the Commentators 200–600 AD*, 3 vols. (London, 2004).

Stead, C. *Philosophy in Christian Antiquity* (Cambridge, 1994).

Steel, C. *The Changing Self—A Study on the Soul in Later Neoplatonism: Iamblichus, Damascius and Priscianus* (Brussels, 1978).

Strange, S. "Plotinus, Porphyry, and the Neoplatonic Interpretation of the 'Categories,' " in W. Haase and H. Temporini (eds.), *Aufstieg und Niedergang der Römischen Welt*, Part 2, vol. 36.2 (Berlin, 1987), 954–74.

Tarrant, H. *Plato's First Interpreters* (Ithaca, N.Y., 2000).

Tarrant, H. *Scepticism or Platonism: The Philosophy of the Fourth Academy* (Cambridge, 1985).

Tarrant, H. *Thrasyllan Platonism* (Ithaca, N.Y., 1993).

Wallis, R. *Neoplatonism* (1972; 2nd ed. London, 1995).

Westerink, L. "The Alexandrian Commentators and the Introductions to Their Commentaries," in R. Sorabji (ed.), *Aristotle Transformed* (Ithaca, N.Y., 1990), 325–48.

Westerink, L. *Anonymous Prolegomena to Platonic Philosophy* (Amsterdam, 1962).

Westerink, L. *The Greek Commentaries on Plato's Phaedo* (Amsterdam, 1976–77).

# BIBLIOGRAPHY

This bibliography lists some works that might be useful to readers who wish to pursue the study of Plato further; it is a revised version of the bibliography in G. Fine (ed.), *Plato* (Oxford University Press, 2000), in the Oxford Readings in Philosophy series. That bibliography, in turn, combines the bibliographies in Fine (ed.), *Plato 1: Metaphysics and Epistemology* (1999) and *Plato 2: Ethics, Politics, Religion, and the Soul* (1999). I have focused mainly on fairly recent work and on work in English. The chapters contained in this volume are not listed here, nor have I listed all or only the sources they cite; nor do I cover every topic the various chapters discuss. I refer the reader to the bibliographies at the end of each chapter for many further references. Though many works are relevant in more than one section, I generally cite each work just once.

## ABBREVIATIONS

| | |
|---|---|
| *CCP* | Kraut, *Cambridge Companion to Plato* |
| *EA* | Lee, Mourelatos, and Rorty (eds.), *Exegesis and Argument* |
| *EPS* | Benson, *Essays on the Philosophy of Socrates* |
| *FA* | Gill and McCabe, *Form and Argument in Late Plato* |
| *LL* | Nussbaum and Schofield, *Language and Logos* |
| *LSD* | Owen, *Logic, Science and Dialectic* |
| *MAP* | Gentzler, *Method in Ancient Philosophy* |
| *PKF* | Fine, *Plato on Knowledge and Forms* |
| *PS* | Vlastos, *Platonic Studies* |
| *SS* | Vlastos, *Socratic Studies* |
| *SPM* | Allen, *Studies in Plato's Metaphysics* |
| Fine (ed.), *Plato 1* | Fine, G. (ed.) *Plato 1: Metaphysics and Epistemology* |
| Fine (ed.), *Plato 2* | Fine, G. (ed.) *Plato 2: Ethics, Politics, Religion, and the Soul* |
| Kamtekar (ed.), *Plato's EAC* | Kamtekar, R. (ed.) *Plato's Euthyphro, Apology and Crito* |
| Vlastos (ed.), *Plato 1* | Vlastos, G. (ed.) *Plato 1: Metaphysics and Epistemology* |
| Vlastos (ed.), *Plato 2* | Vlastos, G. (ed.) *Plato 2: Ethics, Politics, and Philosophy of Art and Religion* |
| Vlastos, *Socrates* | Vlastos, G., *Socrates, Ironist and Moral Philosopher* |

# TEXTS AND TRANSLATIONS

The Greek text of Plato is collected in five volumes published by Oxford University Press (Oxford Classical Texts), edited by J. Burnet (1900–1907). These are gradually being replaced with new editions. Two volumes have appeared so far: volume 1, edited by E. A. Duke, W. F. Hicken, W. S. M. Nicoll, D. B. Robinson, and J. C. G. Strachan (1995); and *The Republic*, edited by S. R. Slings (2003). Greek texts, with facing English translations, are available in the Loeb library; the translations are of varying quality. The Budé texts are also worth consulting; they contain a Greek text with facing French translations, and short notes. The Clarendon Plato series provides generally accurate translations into English along with detailed notes. The books in this series include:

Gallop, D. *Phaedo* (1975).
Gosling, J. C. B. *Philebus* (1975).
Irwin, T. H. *Gorgias* (1979).
McDowell, J. *Theaetetus* (1973).
Taylor, C. C. W. *Protagoras* (1976/1991).

Translations (by various authors) of all of Plato's surviving work, as well as of the *spuria* and *dubia*, are in:

Cooper, John M., and Hutchinson, D. S. (eds.) *Plato: Complete Works* (Indianapolis: Hackett, 1997).

Some of these translations appear in separate volumes, with introductions, notes, and bibliographies:

Frede, D. *Plato: Philebus* (1993).
Gill, M. L., and Ryan, P. *Plato: Parmenides* (1996).
Nehamas, A., and Woodruff, P. *Plato: Phaedrus* (1995).
Nehamas, A., and Woodruff, P. *Plato: Symposium* (1989).
Reeve, C. D. C. *Plato: Cratylus* (1998).
White, N. P. *Plato: Sophist* (1993).
Zeyl, D. *Plato: Timaeus* (1999).

Another widely used collection is:

Hamilton, E., and Cairns, H. (eds.) *The Collected Dialogues of Plato including the Letters* (New York: Pantheon, 1961; Princeton, N.J.: Princeton University Press, 1971).

Various journals are devoted to ancient philosophy. These include *Ancient Philosophy, Apeiron, Oxford Studies in Ancient Philosophy*, and *Phronesis*.

The reader new to Plato might begin with:

Benson, H. (ed.) *Essays on the Philosophy of Socrates* (New York: Oxford University Press, 1992). Cited as *EPS*.
Fine, G. (ed.) *Plato 1: Metaphysics and Epistemology* (Oxford Readings in Philosophy series) (Oxford: Oxford University Press, 1999). Cited as Fine (ed.), *Plato 1*.
Fine, G. (ed.) *Plato 2: Ethics, Politics, Religion, and the Soul* (Oxford Readings in Philosophy series) (Oxford: Oxford University Press, 1999). Cited as Fine (ed.), *Plato 2*.

Irwin, T. H. *Plato's Ethics* (New York: Oxford University Press, 1995).

Kraut, R. (ed.) *Cambridge Companion to Plato* (Cambridge: Cambridge University Press, 1992). Cited as *CCP*.

Kraut, R. *Socrates and the State* (Princeton, N.J.: Princeton University Press, 1984).

Taylor, C. C. W. *Socrates* (Oxford: Oxford University Press, 1998).

Vlastos, G. (ed.) *The Philosophy of Socrates* (Garden City, N.Y.: Doubleday Anchor Books, 1971). Cited as Vlastos (ed.), *Philosophy of Socrates*.

Vlastos, G. (ed.) *Plato 1: Metaphysics and Epistemology* (Garden City, N.Y.: Doubleday Anchor Books, 1971). Cited as Vlastos (ed.), *Plato 1*.

Vlastos, G. (ed.) *Plato 2: Ethics, Politics, and Philosophy of Art and Religion* (Garden City, N.Y.: Doubleday Anchor Books, 1971). Cited as Vlastos (ed.), *Plato 2*.

Vlastos, G. *Socrates, Ironist and Moral Philosopher* (Ithaca, N.Y.: Cornell University Press, 1991). Cited as Vlastos, *Socrates*.

White, N. P. *Plato on Knowledge and Reality* (Indianapolis: Hackett, 1976).

Williams, B. A. O. "Plato: The Invention of Philosophy," in his *The Sense of the Past* (Princeton, N.J.: Princeton University Press, 2006), 148–86.


Readers interested in the chronology of Plato's dialogues might look at:

Brandwood, L. *The Chronology of Plato's Dialogues* (Cambridge: Cambridge University Press, 1990).

Brandwood, L., "Stylometry and Chronology," in *CCP*, 90–120.

Cooper, J. "Introduction" to *Plato: Complete Works*, vii–xxvi.

Kahn, C. "On Platonic Chronology," in J. Annas and C. Rowe (eds.), *New Perspectives on Plato, Modern and Ancient* (Cambridge, Mass.: Harvard University Press, 2003), ch. 4.

Young, C. "Plato and Computer Dating," *Oxford Studies in Ancient Philosophy* 12 (1994), 227–50.


A valuable source for information on the people mentioned in Plato's dialogues is:

Nails, D. *The People of Plato: A Prosopography of Plato and Other Socratics* (Indianapolis: Hackett, 2002).


There is dispute about whether the dialogues that are generally taken to be early represent the thought of the historical Socrates. For the view that they do, see:

Vlastos, G. *Socrates: Ironist and Moral Philosopher* (Ithaca, N.Y.: Cornell University Press, 1991).


For a more skeptical assessment, see:

Kahn, C. *Plato and the Socratic Dialogue: The Philosophical Use of a Literary Form* (Cambridge: Cambridge University Press, 1986).

Nehamas, A. "Voices of Silence: On Gregory Vlastos's Socrates," *Arion*, 3rd ser., 2 (1992), 156–86.


See also:

Taylor, C. C. W. *Socrates* (Oxford: Oxford University Press, 1998).

On the question of why Plato wrote dialogues, see:
Frede, M. "Plato's Arguments and the Dialogue Form," in J. Klagge and N. Smith (eds.), *Methods of Interpreting Plato and His Dialogues* (*Oxford Studies in Ancient Philosophy*, suppl. vol.) (Oxford: Clarendon Press, 1992), 201–19.

This topic is also touched on in:
Irwin, T. H. "Plato: The Intellectual Background," in *CCP*, 51–89.
Kraut, R. "Introduction to the Study of Plato," in *CCP*, 1–50.

For discussion of literary and dramatic aspects of the dialogues, and for Plato on art, see:
Annas, J. "Plato on the Triviality of Literature," in J. Moravcsik and P. Temko (eds.), *Plato on Beauty, Wisdom and the Arts* (Totowa, N.J.: Rowman and Littlefield, 1982), 1–28.
Blondell, R. *The Play of Character in Plato's Dialogues* (Cambridge: Cambridge University Press, 2002).
Ferrari, G. "Plato and Poetry," in G. Kennedy (ed.), *Cambridge History of Literary Criticism* (Cambridge: Cambridge University Press, 1989), 92–148.
Gould, T. *The Ancient Quarrel between Poetry and Philosophy* (Princeton, N.J.: Princeton University Press, 1990).
Janaway, C. *Images of Excellence: Plato's Critique of the Arts* (Oxford: Oxford University Press, 1995).
Klagge, J., and Smith, N. (eds.) *Methods of Interpreting Plato and His Dialogues* (*Oxford Studies in Ancient Philosophy*, suppl. vol.) (Oxford: Clarendon Press, 1992).
Murdoch, I. *The Fire and the Sun: Why Plato Banished the Artists* (Oxford: Clarendon Press, 1977).
Moravcsik, J. "On Correcting the Poets," *Oxford Studies in Ancient Philosophy* 4 (1986), 35–47.
Nehamas, A. "Plato on Imitation and Poetry in *Republic* X," in J. Moravcsik and P. Temko (eds.), *Plato on Beauty, Wisdom and the Arts* (Totowa, N.J.: Rowman and Littlefield, 1982), 47–78.
Nightingale, A. *Genres in Dialogue: Plato and the Construct of Philosophy* (Cambridge: Cambridge University Press, 1995).
Rutherford, R. *The Art of Plato: Ten Essays in Platonic Interpretation* (Cambridge, Mass.: Harvard University Press, 1995).
Urmson, J. "Plato and the Poets," in J. Moravcsik and P. Temko (eds.), *Plato on Beauty, Wisdom and the Arts* (Totowa, N.J.: Rowman and Littlefield, 1982), 125–36.
Woodruff, P. "What Could Go Wrong with Inspiration? Why Plato's Poets Fail," in J. Moravcsik and P. Temko (eds.), *Plato on Beauty, Wisdom and the Arts* (Totowa, N.J.: Rowman and Littlefield, 1982), 137–50.

# BACKGROUND AND CONTEXT

Barnes, J. *Early Greek Philosophy* (Harmondsworth: Penguin, 1987).
Barnes, J. *The Presocratic Philosophers*, rev. ed. (London: Routledge and Kegan Paul, 1982).
Bett, R. "The Sophists and Relativism," *Phronesis* 34 (1989), 139–69.

Boardman, J., Griffin, J., and Murray, O. (eds.) *The Oxford History of the Classical World* (Oxford: Oxford University Press, 1991).

Curd, P. K. *The Legacy of Parmenides: Eleatic Monism and Later Presocratic Thought* (Princeton, N.J.: Princeton University Press, 1997).

Dodds, E. R. *The Greeks and the Irrational* (Berkeley: University of California Press, 1951).

Dover, K. *Greek Popular Morality in the Time of Plato and Aristotle* (Oxford: Blackwell, 1974).

Ehrenberg, V. *From Solon to Socrates: Greek History and Civilization during the Sixth and Fifth Centuries B.C.*, 2nd ed. (London: Methuen, 1989).

Field, G. C. *Plato and His Contemporaries: A Study in Fourth-Century Life and Thought* (London: Methuen, 1930).

Gallop, D. *Parmenides* (Toronto: University of Toronto Press, 1991).

Grote, G. *A History of Greece*, 6th ed., 12 vols. (London: Dent, 1872).

Guthrie, W. K. C. *A History of Greek Philosophy 1: The Earlier Presocratics and the Pythagoreans* (Cambridge: Cambridge University Press, 1962).

Guthrie, W. K. C. *A History of Greek Philosophy 2: The Presocratic Tradition from Parmenides to Democritcus* (Cambridge: Cambridge University Press, 1965).

Guthrie, W. K. C. *A History of Greek Philosophy 3: Fifth-Century Enlightenment* (Cambridge: Cambridge University Press, 1969).

Hornblower, S. *The Greek World 479–323 BC*, 3rd ed. (London: Routledge and Kegan Paul, 2002).

Hornblower, S., and Spawforth, A. (eds.) *The Oxford Classical Dictionary*, 3rd. ed. (Oxford: Oxford University Press, 1996).

Hussey, E. *The Presocratics* (London: Duckworth, 1972).

Hussey, E. "The Beginnings of Epistemology: From Homer to Philolaus," in S. Everson (ed.), *Epistemology* (Cambridge: Cambridge University Press, 1990), 11–38.

Irwin, T. H. *Classical Thought* (Oxford: Oxford University Press, 1989).

Irwin, T. H. "Plato: The Intellectual Background," in *CCP*, 51–89.

Kahn, C. *The Art and Thought of Heraclitus* (Cambridge: Cambridge University Press, 1979).

Kahn, C. *Pythagoras and Pythagoreans: A Brief History* (Indianapolis: Hackett, 2001).

Kerferd, G. *The Sophistic Movement* (Cambridge: Cambridge University Press, 1981).

Kirk, G. S., Raven, J. E., and Schofield, M. *The Presocratic Philosophers: A Critical History with a Selection of Texts*, 2nd. ed. (Cambridge: Cambridge University Press, 1983).

Lloyd, G. E. R. *Hippocratic Writings* (Harmondsworth: Penguin, 1978).

Lloyd, G. E. R. *Magic, Reason and Experience: Studies in the Origin and Development of Greek Science* (Cambridge: Cambridge University Press, 1979).

Lloyd, G. E. R. *The Revolutions of Wisdom* (Berkeley: University of California Press, 1997).

Long, A. A. (ed.) *The Cambridge Companion to Early Greek Philosophy* (Cambridge: Cambridge University Press, 1999).

Morgan, M. "Plato and Greek Religion," in *CCP*, 227–47.

Morgan, M. *Platonic Piety: Philosophy and Ritual in Fourth Century Athens* (New Haven, Conn.: Yale University Press, 1990).

Palmer, J. A. *Plato's Reception of Parmenides* (Oxford: Clarendon Press, 1999).

Taylor, C. C. W. *The Atomists Leucippus and Democritus: Fragments* (Toronto: University of Toronto Press, 1999).

The rest of this bibliography lists, first, books that cover a fairly broad range of topics and/ or dialogues, then various other works, listed under the name of the dialogue or topic with which they are primarily concerned. Material already mentioned above is generally not mentioned below.

# GENERAL BOOKS

Allen, R. E. (ed.) *Studies in Plato's Metaphysics* (London: Routledge and Kegan Paul, 1965). Cited as *SPM*.

Benson, H. (ed.) *A Companion to Plato* (Oxford: Blackwell, 2006).

Bobonich, C. *Plato's Utopia Recast: His Later Ethics and Politics* (Oxford: Clarendon Press, 2002).

Crombie, I. M. *An Examination of Plato's Doctrines*, 2 vols. (London: Routledge and Kegan Paul, 1963).

Dancy, R. *Plato's Introduction of Forms* (Cambridge: Cambridge University Press, 2004).

Denyer, N. *Language, Thought and Falsehood in Ancient Greek Philosophy* (London: Routledge and Kegan Paul, 1991).

Fine, G. *Plato on Knowledge and Forms: Selected Essays* (Oxford, Clarendon Press, 2003). Cited as *PKF*.

Gentzler, J. (ed.) *Method in Ancient Philosophy* (Oxford: Clarendon Press, 1998). Cited as *MAP*.

Gill, C., and McCabe, M. M. (eds.) *Form and Argument in Late Plato* (Oxford: Clarendon Press, 1996). Cited as *FA*.

Gosling, J. C. B. *Plato* (London: Routledge and Kegan Paul, 1973).

Gosling, J. C. B., and Taylor, C. C. W. *The Greeks on Pleasure* (Oxford: Clarendon Press, 1982).

Grote, G. *Plato and the Other Companions of Socrates*, new ed., 4 vols. (London: John Murray, 1888).

Grube, G. M. A. *Plato's Thought*, with a new introduction, bibliographic essay, and bibliography by D. Zeyl (Indianapolis: Hackett, 1980).

Guthrie, W. K. C. *A History of Greek Philosophy 4: Plato the Man and His Earlier Dialogues* (Cambridge: Cambridge University Press, 1975).

Guthrie, W. K. C. *A History of Greek Philosophy 5: Later Plato and the Academy* (Cambridge: Cambridge University Press, 1979).

Hardie, W. F. R. *A Study in Plato* (Oxford: Clarendon Press, 1936).

Harte, V. *Plato on Parts and Wholes: The Metaphysics of Structure* (Oxford: Clarendon Press, 2002).

Irwin, T. H. *Plato's Moral Theory: The Early and Middle Dialogues* (Oxford: Clarendon Press, 1977).

Kahn, C. *Plato and the Socratic Dialogue: The Philosophical Use of a Literary Form* (Cambridge: Cambridge University Press, 1996).

Lee, E. N., Mourelatos, A. D. P., and Rorty, R. M. (eds.), *Exegesis and Argument: Studies in Greek Philosophy Presented to Gregory Vlastos* (Assen: Van Gorcum, 1973). Cited as *EA*.

McCabe, M. M. *Plato and His Predecessors* (Cambridge: Cambridge University Press, 2000).

McCabe, M. M. *Plato's Individuals* (Princeton, N.J.: Princeton University Press, 1994).

Nussbaum, M., and Schofield, M. (eds.) *Language and Logos: Studies in Ancient Greek Philosophy Presented to G. E. L. Owen* (Cambridge: Cambridge University Press, 1982). Cited as *LL*.

Owen, G. E. L. *Logic, Science and Dialectic: Collected Papers in Greek Philosophy*, ed. M. Nussbaum (Ithaca, N.Y. : Cornell University Press, 1986). Cited as *LSD*.

Penner, T. *The Ascent from Nominalism: Some Existence Arguments in Plato's Middle Dialogues* (Dordrecht: Reidel, 1987).

Prior, W. *Unity and Development in Plato's Metaphysics* (London: Croom Helm, 1985).

Robinson, R. *Plato's Earlier Dialectic*, 2nd ed. (Oxford: Clarendon Press, 1953).

Ross, W. D. *Plato's Theory of Ideas* (Oxford: Clarendon Press, 1951).

Russell, D. *Plato on Pleasure and the Good Life* (Oxford: Clarendon Press, 2005).

Scott, D. *Recollection and Experience: Plato's Theory of Learning and its Successors* (Cambridge: Cambridge University Press, 1995).

Silverman, A. *The Dialectic of Essence: A Study of Plato's Metaphysics* (Princeton: Princeton University Press, 2003).

Vlastos, G. *Platonic Studies*, 2nd. ed. (Princeton: Princeton University Press, 1981). Cited as *PS*.

Vlastos, G. *Studies in Greek Philosophy*, 2 vols., ed. D. Graham (Princeton, N.J.: Princeton University Press, 1993, 1995).

# THE EARLY DIALOGUES: GENERAL

Allen, R. E. *Plato's Euthyphro and the Earlier Theory of Forms* (London: Routledge and Kegan Paul, 1970).

Beversluis, J. *Cross-Examining Socrates: A Defense of the Interlocutors in Plato's Early Dialogues* (Cambridge: Cambridge University Press, 2000).

Brickhouse, N., and Smith, T. *Plato's Socrates* (Oxford: Oxford University Press, 1994).

Guthrie, W. K. C. *Socrates* (Cambridge: Cambridge University Press, 1971). Originally published as Part 2 of Guthrie, *A History of Greek Philosophy 3* (Cambridge: Cambridge University Press, 1969).

Kamtekar, R. (ed.) *Plato's Euthyphro, Apology and Crito: Critical Essays* (Lanham, Md.: Rowman and Littlefield, 2004). Cited as Kamtekar (ed.), *Plato's EAC*.

Penner, T., and Rowe, C. *Plato's Lysis* (Cambridge: Cambridge University Press, 2005).

Reeve, C. D. C. *Socrates in the Apology: An Essay on Plato's Apology of Socrates* (Indianapolis: Hackett, 1989).

Santas, G. *Socrates: Philosophy in Plato's Early Dialogues* (London: Routledge and Kegan Paul, 1979).

Stokes, M. *Dialectic in Action: An Examination of Plato's Crito* (Swansea: Classical Press of Wales, 2005).

Stokes, M. *Plato: Apology* (Warminster: Aris and Phillips, 1997).

Stokes, M. *Plato's Socratic Conversations: Drama and Dialectic in Three Dialogues* (London: Athlone Press, 1986). (Focuses on the *Laches*, *Protagoras*, and *Symposium*.)

Vlastos, G. *Socratic Studies*, ed. M. F. Burnyeat (Cambridge: Cambridge University Press, 1994). Cited as *SS*.

# THE EARLY DIALOGUES: EPISTEMOLOGY, METAPHYSICS, AND METHOD

Benson, H. "Misunderstanding the 'What Is F-ness?' Question," *Archiv für Geschichte der Philosophie* 72 (1990), 125–42. Also in *EPS*, 123–36.

Benson, H. "The Priority of Definition and the Socratic *Elenchos*," *Oxford Studies in Ancient Philosophy* 8 (1990), 19–65.

Benson, H. "The Problem of the Elenchus Revisited," *Ancient Philosophy* 7 (1987), 67–85.

Benson, H. *Socratic Wisdom* (New York: Oxford University Press, 2000).

Beversluis, J. "Does Socrates Commit the Socratic Fallacy?," *American Philosophical Quarterly* 24 (1987), 211–23. Also in *EPS*, 107–22.

Burnyeat, M. F. "Examples in Epistemology," *Philosophy* 52 (1977), 381–98.

Crombie, I. M. "Socratic Definition," *Paideia* 5 (1976), *Special Plato Issue*, 80–102. Also in J. Day (ed.), *Plato's Meno in Focus* (London: Routledge and Kegan Paul, 1994), 172–207.

Geach, P. T. "Plato's *Euthyphro*: Analysis and Commentary," *Monist* 50 (1966), 369–82. Also in Kamtekar (ed.), *Plato's EAC*, 23–34.

Kraut, R. "Comments on Gregory Vlastos, "The Socratic Elenchus," *Oxford Studies in Ancient Philosophy* 1 (1983), 59–70.

Lesher, J. H. "Socrates' Disavowal of Knowledge," *Journal of the History of Philosophy* 25 (1984), 275–88.

Mackenzie, M. M. "The Virtues of Socratic Ignorance," *Classical Quarterly* 38 (1988), 331–50.

Nehamas, A. "Confusing Universals and Particulars in Plato's Early Dialogues," *Review of Metaphysics* 29 (1975), 287–306.

Prior, J. "Plato and the 'Socratic Fallacy,'" *Phronesis* 43 (1998), 97–113.

Vlastos, G. "Is the Socratic Fallacy Socratic?," *Ancient Philosophy* 10 (1990), 1–16. Revised version in *SS*, 67–86.

Vlastos, G. "Socrates' Disavowal of Knowledge," *Philosophical Quarterly* 35 (1985), 1–31. Also in Fine (ed.), *Plato 1*, 64–92.

Vlastos, G. "The Socratic Elenchus," *Oxford Studies in Ancient Philosophy* 1 (1983), 27–58. Also in Fine (ed.), *Plato 1*, 36–63.

Vlastos, G. "What Did Socrates Understand by His "What Is F?" Question?," in *PS*, 410–17.

Wolfsdorf, D. "Socrates' Avowals of Knowledge," *Phronesis* 49 (2004), 75–142.

Woodruff, P. "Expert Knowledge in the *Apology* and *Laches*: What a General Needs to Know," *Proceedings of the Boston Area Colloquium in Ancient Philosophy* 3 (1987), 79–115.

Woodruff, P. "Plato's Early Theory of Knowledge," in S. Everson (ed.), *Epistemology* (Cambridge: Cambridge University Press, 1989), 60–84. Also in *EPS*, 86–106.

# THE EARLY DIALOGUES: ETHICS, POLITICS, RELIGION AND THE SOUL

Annas, J. "Virtue as a Skill," *International Journal of Philosophical Studies* 3 (1995), 227–43.

Annas, J. "Virtue as the Use of Other Goods," *Apeiron* 26 (1993), 53–66.

Bostock, D. "The Interpretation of Plato's *Crito*," *Phronesis* 35 (1990), 1–20. Also in Kamtekar (ed.), *Plato's EAC*, 210–28.

Brickhouse, T., and Smith, N. "Socrates on Goods, Virtue and Happiness," *Oxford Studies in Ancient Philosophy* 5 (1987), 1–28.

Brickhouse, T., and Smith, N.,*Socrates on Trial* (Princeton, N.J.: Princeton University Press, 1989).

Burnyeat, M. F. "The Impiety of Socrates," *Ancient Philosophy* 17 (1997), 1–12. Also in Kamtekar (ed.), *Plato's EAC*, 150–62.

Burnyeat, M. F. "Virtues in Action," in Vlastos (ed.), *Philosophy of Socrates*, 209–34.

Cohen, S. M. "Socrates and the Definition of Piety," *Journal of the History of Philosophy* 9 (1971), 1–13. Also in Vlastos (ed.), *Philosophy of Socrates*, 158–86, and in Kamtekar (ed.), *Plato's EAC*, 35–48.

Devereux, D. "Courage and Wisdom in Plato's *Laches*," *Journal of the History of Philosophy* 15 (1977), 129–41.

Devereux, D. "Socrates' Kantian Conception of Virtue," *Journal of the History of Philosophy* 33 (1995), 341–408.

Devereux, D. "The Unity of the Virtues in Plato's *Protagoras* and *Laches*," *Philosophical Review* 101 (1992), 765–89.

Harte, V. "Conflicting Values in Plato's *Crito*," *Archiv für Geschichte der Philosophie* 81 (1999), 117–47. Also in Kamtekar (ed.), *Plato's EAC*, 229–46.

Irwin, T. H. "Coercion and Objectivity in Plato's Dialectic," *Revue Internationale de Philosophie* 40 (1986), 47–74.

Irwin, T. H. "Socrates the Epicurean?," *Illinois Classical Studies* 11 (1986), 85–112. Also in *EPS*, 198–219.

Kamtekar, R., "Socrates on the Attribution of Conative Attitudes," *Archiv für Geschichte der Philosophie* 86 (2006), 127–62.

Mackenzie, M. M. *Plato on Punishment* (Berkeley: University of California Press, 1981). (Also discusses this topic in other periods of Plato's thought.)

McPherran, M. *The Religion of Socrates* (University Park: Pennsylvania State University Press, 1996).

Penner, T. "Desire and Power in Socrates," *Apeiron* 24 (1991), 147–201.

Penner, T. "Knowledge vs. True Belief in the Socratic Psychology of Action," *Apeiron* 26 (1996), 199–230.

Penner, T. "Socrates on the Strength of Knowledge: *Protagoras* 351B–375E," *Archiv für Geschichte der Philosophie* 79 (1997), 117–49.

Penner, T. "Socrates on Virtue and Motivation," in E. N. Lee, A. D. P. Mourelatos, and R. M. Rorty (eds.), *Exegesis and Argument: Studies in Greek Philosophy Presented to Gregory Vlastos* (Assen: Van Gorcum, 1973), 133–51. Volume cited as *EA*.

Penner, T. "The Unity of Virtue," *Philosophical Review* 82 (1973), pp. 35–68. Also in *EPS*, 162–84, and in Fine (ed.), *Plato 2*, 78–104.

Rudebusch, G. *Socrates, Pleasure, and Value* (New York: Oxford University Press, 1999).

Santas, G. "Plato's *Protagoras* and Explanations of Weakness," *Philosophical Review* 75 (1966), 3–33. Also in Vlastos (ed.), *Philosophy of Socrates*, 264–98.

Santas, G. "Socrates at Work on Virtue and Knowledge in Plato's *Laches*," *Review of Metaphysics* 22 (1969), 443–60.

Santas, G. "The Socratic Paradoxes," *Philosophical Review* 73 (1964), 147–64.

Segvic, H. "No One Errs Willingly: The Meaning of Socratic Intellectualism," *Oxford Studies in Ancient Philosophy* 19 (2000), 1–45.

Sharvy, R. "*Euthyphro* 9d–11b: Analysis and Definition in Plato and Others," *Nous* 6 (1972), 119–37.

Smith, N., and Woodruff, P. (eds.). *Reason and Religion in Socratic Philosophy* (Oxford: Oxford University Press, 2000).

Taylor, C. C. W. "The End of the *Euthyphro*," *Phronesis* 27 (1982), 109–18.

Taylor, C. C. W. "Socratic Ethics," in B. S. Gower and M. C. Stokes (eds.), *Socratic Questions* (London: Routledge and Kegan Paul, 1992), 137–52.

Vlastos, G. Introduction to *Plato: Protagoras* (Indianapolis: Bobbs Merrill, 1965).

Vlastos, G. "Socrates on *Acrasia*," *Phoenix* 23 (1969), 71–88. Also in G. Vlastos (ed.), *Studies in Greek Philosophy*, vol. 2 (Princeton, N.J.: Princeton University Press, 1995), 43–59.

Vlastos, G. "Socratic Piety," in Vlastos, *Socrates*, 157–78. Also in Fine (ed.), *Plato 2*, 56–77, and in Kamtekar (ed.), *Plato's EAC*, 49–71.

Vlastos, G. "The Unity of the Virtues in the *Protagoras*," *Review of Metaphysics* 25 (1972), 415–58. Revised version with additional notes in *PS*, 2nd ed., 221–69, 418–23.

Woozley, A. D. *Law and Obedience: The Arguments of Plato's Crito* (London: Duckworth, 1979).

Woozley, A. D. "Socrates on Disobeying the Law," in Vlastos (ed.), *Philosophy of Socrates*, 229–318.

Young, G. "Socrates and Obedience," *Phronesis* 19 (1974), 1–29.

Zeyl, D. "Socrates and Hedonism," *Phronesis* 25 (1980), 250–69.

Zeyl, D. "Socratic Virtue and Happiness," *Archiv für Geschichte der Philosophie* 64 (1982), 225–38.

# *MENO*

Bluck, R. S. *Plato's Meno* (Cambridge: Cambridge University Press, 1964).

Charles, D. "Types of Definition in Plato's *Meno*," in L. Judson and V. Karasmanis (eds.), *Remembering Socrates: Philosophical Essays* (Oxford: Oxford University Press, 2006), 110–28.

Day, J. (ed.) *Plato's Meno in Focus* (London: Routledge and Kegan Paul, 1994). Cited as Day (ed.), *Meno in Focus*.

Devereux, D. "Nature and Teaching in Plato's *Meno*," *Phronesis* 23 (1978), 118–126.

Dimas, P. "True Belief in the *Meno*," *Oxford Studies in Ancient Philosophy* 14 (1996), 1–32.

Fine, G. "Inquiry in the *Meno*," in *CCP*, 200–226. Also in *PKF*, 44–65.

Fine, G. "Knowledge and True Belief in the *Meno*," *Oxford Studies in Ancient Philosophy* 27 (2004), 41–81.

Franklin, L. "The Structure of Dialectic in the *Meno*," *Phronesis* 46 (2001), 413–39.

Gentzler, J. "Recollection and 'The Problem of the Socratic Elenchus,' " *Proceedings of the Boston Area Colloquium in Ancient Philosophy* 10 (1996), 257–95.

Moravcsik, J. M. E. "Learning as Recollection," in Vlastos (ed.), *Plato 1*, 53–69.

Nehamas, A. "Meno's Paradox and Socrates as a Teacher," *Oxford Studies in Ancient Philosophy* 3 (1985), 1–30. Also in *EPS*, 298–316, and in Day (ed.), *Meno in Focus*, 221–48.

Nehamas, A. "Socratic Intellectualism," *Proceedings of the Boston Area Colloquium in Ancient Philosophy* 2 (1986), 275–316.

Scott, D. *Plato's Meno* (Cambridge: Cambridge University Press, 2006).

Sharples, R. W. *Plato: Meno* (Warminster: Aris and Phillips, 1985).

Thompson, E. S. *The Meno of Plato* (London: Macmillan, 1901).

Vlastos, G. "*Anamnêsis* in the *Meno*," *Dialogue* 4 (1965), 143–67.

Vlastos, G. "Elenchus and Mathematics," *American Journal of Philology* 109 (1988), 362–96. Also in his *Socrates*, 107–31, and in *EPS*, 137–61.

White, N. P. "Inquiry," *Review of Metaphysics* 28 (1974), 289–310.

Wilkes, K. "Conclusions in the *Meno*," *Archiv für Geschichte der Philosophie* 61 (1970, 143–53. Also in Day (ed.), *Meno in Focus*, 208–20.

# *CRATYLUS*

Ackrill, J. L. "Language and Reality in Plato's *Cratylus*," in his *Essays on Plato and Aristotle* (Oxford: Clarendon Press, 1994), 33–52. Also in Fine (ed.), *Plato 1*, 125–42.

Annas, J. "Knowledge and Language: The *Theaetetus* and the *Cratylus*." See under *Theaetetus*.

Barney, R. *Names and Nature in Plato's Cratylus* (London: Routledge and Kegan Paul, 2001).

Barney, R. "Plato on Conventionalism," *Phronesis* 42 (1997), 143–61.

Baxter, T. *The Cratylus: Plato's Critique of Naming* (Leiden: E. J. Brill, 1992).

Fine, G. "Plato on Naming," *Philosophical Quarterly* 27 (1977), 289–301. Also in *PKF*, 117–31.

Kahn, C. "Language and Ontology in the *Cratylus*," in *EA*, 152–76.

Keller, S. "An Interpretation of Plato's *Cratylus*," *Phronesis* 45 (2000), 284–305.

Ketchum, R. "Names, Forms, and Conventionalism: *Cratylus* 383–95," *Phronesis* 24 (1979), 133–47.

Kretzmann, N. "Plato on the Correctness of Names," *American Philosophical Quarterly* 8 (1971), 126–38.

Mackenzie, M. M. "Putting the *Cratylus* in Its Place," *Classical Quarterly* NS 36 (1986), 124–50.

Schofield, M. "The Dénouement of the *Cratylus*," in *LL*, 61–81.

Sedley, D. *Plato's Cratylus* (Cambridge: Cambridge University Press, 2003).

Silverman, A. "Plato's *Cratylus*: The Naming of Nature and the Nature of Naming," *Oxford Studies in Ancient Philosophy* 10 (1992), 25–72.

Spellman, L. "Naming and Knowing: The *Cratylus* on Images," *History of Philosophy Quarterly* 10 (1993), 197–210.

Williams, B. A. O. "*Cratylus*' Theory of Names and Its Refutation," in *LL*, 83–93.

# *PHAEDO* AND THE THEORY OF FORMS

Ackrill, J. L. "*Anamnêsis* in the *Phaedo*," in his *Essays on Plato and Aristotle*, 13–32. Also in *EA*, 177–95.

Annas, J. "Aristotle on Inefficient Causes," *Philosophical Quarterly* 32 (1982), 311–26.

Bolton, R. "Plato's Distinction between Being and Becoming." See under *Theaetetus*.

Bostock, D. *Plato's Phaedo* (Oxford: Clarendon Press, 1986).

Cherniss, H. F. "The Philosophical Economy of the Theory of Ideas," *American Journal of Philology* 57 (1936), 445–56. Also in *SPM*, 1–12, and in Vlastos (ed.), *Plato 1*, 16–27.

Devereux, D. "Separation and Immanence in Plato's Theory of Forms," *Oxford Studies in Ancient Philosophy* 12 (1994), 63–90. Also in Fine (ed.), *Plato 1*, 192–214.

Dimas, P. "Recollecting Forms in the *Phaedo*," *Phronesis* 48 (2003), 175–214.

Fine, G. "Forms as Causes: Plato and Aristotle," in A. Graeser (ed.), *Mathematics and Metaphysics in Aristotle* (Bern: Haupt, 1986), 69–112. Also in *PKF*, 350–96.

Fine, G. "The One over Many," *Philosophical Review* 89 (1980), 197–240.

Fine, G. *On Ideas: Aristotle's Criticism of Plato's Theory of Forms* (Oxford: Clarendon Press, 1993).

Fine, G. "Separation," *Oxford Studies in Ancient Philosophy* 2 (1984), 31–87. Also in *PKF*, 252–300.

Franklin, L. "Recollection and Philosophical Reflection in Plato's *Phaedo*," *Phronesis* 50 (2005), 289–314.

Frede, D. "The Final Proof of the Immortality of the Soul," *Phronesis* 23 (1978), 27–41.

Gallop, D. "Plato's Cyclical Argument Recycled," *Phronesis* 27 (1982), 207–22.

Gentzler, J. "*Sumphônein* in Plato's *Phaedo*," *Phronesis* 36 (1991), 265–76.

Gosling, J. C. B. "Similarity in *Phaedo* 73b seq., " *Phronesis* 10 (1965), 151–61.

Hartman, E. "Predication and Immortality in Plato's *Phaedo*," *Archiv für Geschichte der Philosophie* 54 (1972), 215–28.

Irwin, T. H. "Plato's Heracleiteanism," *Philosophical Quarterly* 27 (1977), 1–13.

Kelsey, S. "Recollection in the *Phaedo*," *Proceedings of the Boston Area Colloquium in Ancient Philosophy* 16 (2000), 91–121.

Keyt, D. "The Fallacies in *Phaedo* 102a–107b," *Phronesis* 8 (1963), 167–72.

Kirwan, C. "Plato and Relativity," *Phronesis* 19 (1974), 112–29.

Lovibond, S. "Plato's Theory of Mind," in S. Everson (ed.), *Psychology* (Cambridge: Cambridge University Press, 1991), 35–55.

Malcolm, J. *Plato on the Self-Predication of Forms: Early and Middle Dialogues* (Oxford: Clarendon Press, 1991).

Mates, B. "Identity and Predication in Plato," *Phronesis* 24 (1979), 211–29.

Matthews, G., and Blackson, T. "Causes in the *Phaedo*," *Synthèse* 79 (1989), 581–91.

Matthews, G., and Cohen, S. M. "The One and the Many," *Review of Metaphysics* 21 (1968), 630–55.

Mills, K. W. "Plato's *Phaedo* 74," *Phronesis* 2 (1957), 128–74; and 3 (1958), 40–58.

Nehamas, A. "Plato on the Imperfection of the Sensible World," *American Philosophical Quarterly* 12 (1975), 105–17. Also in Fine (ed.), *Plato 1*, 171–91.

Nehamas, A. "Predication and Forms of Opposites in the *Phaedo*," *Review of Metaphysics* 26 (1973), 461–91.

Nehamas, A. "Self-Predication and Plato's Theory of Forms," *American Philosophical Quarterly* 16 (1979), 93–103.

Owen, G. E. L. "A Proof in the *Peri Ideôn*," *Journal of Hellenic Studies* 77 (1957), 103–11. Also in *SPM*, 243–312, and in *LSD*, 165–79.

Rowe, C. J. *Plato: Phaedo* (Cambridge: Cambridge University Press, 1995).

Scott, D. "Platonic *Anamnêsis* Revisited," *Classical Quarterly* NS 37 (1987), 346–66.

Sedley, D. "Equal Sticks and Stones," in D. Scott (ed.), *Maieusis: Studies on Greek Philosophy in Honour of M. F. Burnyeat* (Oxford: Oxford University Press 2007), 68–86.

Sedley, D. "Form-Particular Resemblance in Plato's *Phaedo*," *Proceedings of the Aristotelian Society* 106 (2006), 309–25.

Sedley, D. "Platonic Causes," *Phronesis* 43 (1998), 114–32.

Sedley, D. "Teleology and Myth in Plato's *Phaedo*," *Proceedings of the Boston Area Collo-quium in Ancient Philosophy* 5 (1991), 359–83.

Taylor, C. C. W. "The Arguments in the *Phaedo* Concerning the Thesis That the Soul Is a *Harmonia*," in J. Anton and A. Preus (eds.), *Essays in Ancient Greek Philosophy*, vol. 2 (Albany: State University of New York), 217–31.

Vlastos, G. "Degrees of Reality in Plato," in R. Bambrough (ed.), *New Essays on Plato and Aristotle* (London: Routledge and Kegan Paul, 1965), 1–18. Also in *PS*, 58–75.

Vlastos, G. "A Metaphysical Paradox," *Proceedings and Addresses of the American Philo-sophical Association* 39 (1966), 5–19. Also in *PS*, 43–57.

Vlastos, G. "Reasons and Causes in the *Phaedo*," *Philosophical Review* 78 (1969), 291–325. Also in Vlastos (ed.), *Plato 1*, 132–66, and in *PS*, 76–110.

White, N. P. "Forms and Sensibles: *Phaedo* 74bc," *Philosophical Topics* 15 (1987), 197–214.

White, N. P. "Perceptual and Objective Properties in Plato," *Apeiron* 22 (1989), 45–65.

White, N. P. "Plato's Metaphysical Epistemology," in *CCP*, 277–310.

# *REPUBLIC*: GENERAL

Adam, J. *The Republic of Plato*, 2 vols. (Cambridge: Cambridge University Press, 1902).

Annas, J. *An Introduction to Plato's Republic* (Oxford: Clarendon Press, 1981).

Cross, R. C., and Woozley, A. D. *Plato's Republic: A Philosophical Commentary* (London: Macmillan, 1964).

Halliwell, S. *Plato: Republic 5* (Warminster: Aris and Phillips, 1993).

Halliwell, S. *Plato: Republic 10* (Warminster: Aris and Phillips, 1988).

Joseph, H. W. B. *Knowledge and the Good in Plato's Republic* (Oxford: Clarendon Press, 1948).

Kraut, R. (ed.) *Plato's Republic: Critical Essays* (Lanham, Md.: Rowman and Littlefield, 1997).

Murphy, N. R. *The Interpretation of Plato's Republic* (Oxford: Clarendon Press, 1951).

Ostenfeld, E. (ed.) *Essays on Plato's Republic* (Aarhus: Aarhus University Press, 1998).

Reeve, C. D. C. *Philosopher-Kings: The Argument of Plato's Republic* (Princeton, N.J.: Princeton University Press, 1988).

Santas, G. (ed.) *The Blackwell Guide to Plato's Republic* (Oxford: Blackwell, 2006).

White, N. P. *A Companion to Plato's Republic* (Indianapolis: Hackett, 1979).

# *REPUBLIC*: METAPHYSICS AND EPISTEMOLOGY

These works focus on topics particular to the *Republic*; more general discussions of the Theory of Forms are listed in the section on the *Phaedo* and the Theory of Forms above.

Burnyeat, M. F. "Platonism and Mathematics: A Prelude to Discussion," in A. Graeser (ed.), *Mathematics and Metaphysics in Aristotle* (Bern: Haupt, 1987), 213–40.

Fine, G. "Knowledge and Belief in *Republic* V," *Archiv für Geschichte der Philosophie* 60 (1978), 121–39. Also in *PKF*, 65–84.

Fine, G. "Knowledge and Belief in *Republic* V–VII," in S. Everson (ed.), *Epistemology* (Cambridge: Cambridge University Press, 1990), 85–115. Also in Fine (ed.), *Plato 1*, 215–46, and in *PKF*, 85–116.

Fogelin, R. "Three Platonic Analogies," *Philosophical Review* 80 (1971), 371–82.

Gentzler, J. "How to Know the Good: The Moral Epistemology of Plato's *Republic*," *Philosophical Review* 114 (2005), 469–96.

Gosling, J. C. B. "*Doxa* and *Dunamis* in Republic V," *Phronesis* 13 (1968), 119–30.

Gosling, J. C. B. "*Republic* V: *ta polla kala*," *Phronesis* 5 (1960), 116–28.

Harte, V. "Language in the Cave," in D. Scott (ed.), *Maieusis: Studies in Honour of M. F. Burnyeat* (Oxford: Oxford University Press, 2008), 195–215.

Karasmanis, V. "Plato's *Republic:* The Line and the Cave," *Apeiron* 21 (1988), 147–71.

Santas, G. "The Form of the Good in Plato's *Republic*," *Philosophical Inquiry* (1980), 374–403; abbreviated version in Fine (ed.), *Plato 1*, 247–74.

Strang, C. "Plato's Analogy of the Cave," *Oxford Studies in Ancient Philosophy* 4 (1986), 19–34.

Taylor, C. C. W. "Plato and the Mathematicians," *Philosophical Quarterly* 17 (1967), 193–203.

Wilson, J. S. "The Contents of the Cave," *Canadian Journal of Philosophy* (suppl.) 2 (1976), 111–24.

# *REPUBLIC*: ETHICS, PSYCHOLOGY, AND RELIGION

Annas, J. "Plato and Common Morality," *Classical Quarterly* NS 28 (1978), 437–51.

Annas, J. "Politics and Ethics in Plato's *Republic*," in O. Höffe (ed.), *Politeia* (Berlin: Akademie Verlag, 1997), 141–60. Volume cited as Höffe (ed.).

Bobonich, C. "*Akrasia* and Agency in Plato's *Laws* and *Republic*," *Archiv für Geschichte der Philosophie* 72 (1994), 3–36.

Brown, E. "Justice and Compulsion for Plato's Philosopher-Rulers," *Ancient Philosophy* 20 (2000), 1–17.

Brown, E. "Minding the Gap in Plato's *Republic*," *Philosophical Studies* 117 (2004), 275–302.

Burnyeat, M. F. "Plato on Why Mathematics Is Good for the Soul," *Proceedings of the British Academy* 103 (2000), 1–81.

Cooper, J. "The Psychology of Justice in Plato," *American Philosophical Quarterly* 14 (1977), 151–57.

Dahl, N. "Plato's Defence of Justice," *Philosophy and Phenomenological Research* 51 (1991), 809–34. Also in Fine (ed.), *Plato 2*, 207–34.

Demos, R. "A Fallacy in Plato's *Republic*?," *Philosophical Review* 73 (1964), 395–98. Also in Vlastos (ed.), *Plato 2*, 52–56.

Everson, S. "The Incoherence of Thrasymachus," *Oxford Studies in Ancient Philosophy* 16 (1998), 88–131.

Gill, C. "Plato and the Education of Character," *Archiv für Geschichte der Philosophie* 67 (1985), 1–26.

Heinaman, R. "Plato's Division of Goods in the *Republic*," *Phronesis* 47 (2002), 309–35.

Höffe, O. (ed.) *Politeia* (Berlin: Akademie Verlag, 1997). Cited as Höffe (ed.).

Irwin, T. H. "The Parts of the Soul and the Cardinal Virtues," in Höffe (ed.), 119–39.

Kahn, C. H. "Plato's Theory of Desire," *Review of Metaphysics* 41 (1987), 77–103.

Kenny, A. J. P. "Mental Health in Plato's *Republic*," *Proceedings of the British Academy* 55 (1969), 229–53. Also in Kenny, *The Anatomy of the Soul* (Oxford: Blackwell, 1973), 1–27.

Kerferd, G. B. "The Doctrine of Thrasymachus in Plato's *Republic*," *Durham University Journal* 9 (1947), 19–27.

Kirwan, C. "Glaucon's Challenge," *Phronesis* 10 (1965), 162–73.

Kraut, R. "The Defense of Justice in Plato's *Republic*," in *CCP*, 311–37.

Kraut, R. "Plato's Comparison of Just and Unjust Lives," in Höffe (ed.), 271–90.

Kraut, R. "Reason and Justice in the *Republic*," in *EA*, 331–37.

Kraut, R. "Return to the Cave: *Republic* 519–521," in Fine (ed.), *Plato* 2, 235–54.

Lorenz, H. *The Brute Within* (Oxford: Clarendon Press, 2006).

Lorenz, H. "Desire and Reason in Plato's *Republic*," *Oxford Studies in Ancient Philosophy* 27 (2004), 83–116.

Mahoney, T. "Do Plato's Philosopher-Rulers Sacrifice Self-Interest to Justice?," *Phronesis* 37 (1992), 265–82.

Nicholson, P. P. "Unravelling Thrasymachus' Argument in the *Republic*," *Phronesis* 19 (1974), 210–32.

Penner, T. "Plato and Davidson: Parts of the Soul and Weakness of the Will," *Canadian Journal of Philosophy* (suppl.) 16 (1990), 35–74.

Penner, T. "Thought and Desire in Plato," in Vlastos (ed.), *Plato* 2, 96–118.

Price, A. "Plato and Freud," in C. Gill (ed.), *The Person and the Human Mind: Issues in Ancient and Modern Philosophy* (Oxford: Clarendon Press, 1990), 247–70.

Reeve, C. D. C. "Socrates Meets Thrasymachus," *Archiv für Geschichte der Philosophie* 67 (1985), 246–65.

Robinson, R. "Plato's Separation of Reason and Desire," *Phronesis* 16 (1971), 38–48.

Sachs, D. " A Fallacy in Plato's *Republic*," *Philosophical Review* 72 (1963), 141–58. Also in Vlastos (ed.), *Plato* 2, 35–51.

Santas, G. "Two Theories of the Good in Plato's *Republic*," *Archiv für Geschichte der Philosophie* 57 (1980), 223–45.

Scott, D. "Metaphysics and the Defence of Justice in the *Republic*," *Proceedings of the Boston Area Colloquium in Ancient Philosophy* 16 (2000), 1–20.

Scott, D. "Platonic Pessimism and Moral Education," *Oxford Studies in Ancient Philosophy* 17 (1999), 15–36.

Scott, D. "Plato's Critique of the Democratic Character," *Phronesis* 45 (2000), 19–37.

Stalley, R. "Plato's Arguments for the Division of the Reasoning and Appetitive Elements within the Soul," *Phronesis* 20 (1975), 110–28.

Vlastos, G. "Justice and Happiness in the *Republic*," in Vlastos (ed.), *Plato* 2, 66–95. Also in *PS*, 111–39.

Waterlow [Broadie], S. "The Good of Others in Plato's *Republic*," *Proceedings of the Aristotelian Society* 72 (1972–73), 19–36.

White, N. P. "The Classification of Goods in *Plato's Republic*," *Journal of the History of Philosophy* 22 (1984), 393–421.

White, N. P. "Happiness and External Contingencies in Plato's *Republic*," in W. C. Starr and R. C. Taylor (eds.), *Moral Philosophy* (Milwaukee: Marquette University Press, 1989), 1–21.

White, N. P. "The Ruler's Choice," *Archiv für Geschichte der Philosophie* 68 (1986), 22–46.

Woods, M. J. "Plato's Division of the Soul," *Proceedings of the British Academy* 73 (1987), 23–47.

Young, C. "Polemarchus' and Thrasymachus' Definitions of Justice," *Philosophical Inquiry* 2 (1980), 404–19.

# *REPUBLIC*: POLITICS AND THE IDEALLY JUST STATE

Many of the works listed in the previous two sections are also relevant here.

Ackrill, J. L. "What is Wrong with Plato's *Republic?*," in his *Essays on Plato and Aristotle*, 2nd. ed. (Oxford: Clarendon Press, 2001), 230–52.

Annas, J. "Plato's *Republic* and Feminism," *Philosophy* 51 (1976), 307–21. Also in Fine (ed.), *Plato* 2, 265–79.

Brown, L. "How Totalitarian Is Plato's *Republic?*," in E. Ostenfeld (ed.), *Essays on Plato's Republic* (Aarhus: Aarhus University Press, 1998), 13–27.

Burnyeat, M. F. "Culture and Society in Plato's *Republic*," *Tanner Lectures on Human Values* 20 (Salt Lake City: University of Utah Press, 1999), 215–324.

Burnyeat, M. F. "Utopia and Fantasy: The Practicability of Plato's Ideally Just City," in J. Hopkins and A. Savile (eds.), *Psychoanalysis, Mind and Art: Perspectives on Richard Wollheim* (Oxford: Blackwell, 1992), 175–87. Also in Fine (ed.), *Plato* 2, 279–308.

Ferrari, G. *City and Soul in Plato's Republic* (Sankt Augustin: Akademia Verlag, 2003; Chicago: University of Chicago Press, 2005).

Kraut, R. "Egoism, Love, and Political Office," *Philosophical Review* 82 (1973), 330–44.

Neu, J. "Plato's Analogy of State and Individual: The *Republic* and the Organic Theory of the State," *Philosophy* 46 (1971), 238–54.

Popper, K. R. *The Open Society and Its Enemies*, vol. 1: *The Spell of Plato* (Princeton, N.J.: Princeton University Press, 1971; originally published London: Routledge and Kegan Paul, 1945).

Schofield, M. *Plato: Political Philosophy* (Oxford: Oxford University Press, 2006).

Taylor, C. C. W. "Plato's Totalitarianism," *Polis* 5 (1986), 4–29. Also in Fine (ed.), *Plato* 2, 280–96.

Tuana, N. (ed.). *Feminist Interpretations of Plato* (University Park: Pennsylvania State University Press, 1994).

Vlastos, G. "Does Slavery Exist in Plato's *Republic?*," *Classical Philology* 63 (1968), 291–95. Also in *PS*, 140–63.

Vlastos, G. "The Theory of Social Justice in the *Polis* in Plato's *Republic*," in H. North (ed.), *Interpretations of Plato* (Leiden: Brill, 1977), 1–40.

Vlastos, G. "Was Plato a Feminist?," *Times Literary Supplement* 4, 485, (March 17, 1989), 276, 288–89. Also in Vlastos, *Studies in Greek Philosophy*, vol. 2, 133–43.

Williams, B. A. O. "The Analogy of City and Soul in Plato's *Republic*," in *EA*, 196–206. Also in Fine (ed.), *Plato* 2, 255–64.

# *SYMPOSIUM, PHAEDRUS,*
# AND PLATONIC LOVE

Bett, R. "Immortality and the Nature of the Soul in the *Phaedrus,*" *Phronesis* 31 (1986), 1–26. Also in Fine (ed.), *Plato 2*, 425–50.

Bury, R. G. *The Symposium of Plato*, 2nd ed. (Cambridge: Cambridge University Press, 1932).

Dover, K. J. *Plato: Symposium* (Cambridge: Cambridge University Press, 1980).

Ferrari, G. *Listening to the Cicadas: A Study of Plato's Phaedrus* (Cambridge: Cambridge University Press, 1987).

Ferrari, G. "Platonic Love," in *CCP*, 248–276.

Ferrari, G. "The Struggle in the Soul: Plato, *Phaedrus* 253c7–255a1," *Ancient Philosophy* 5 (1985), 1–10.

Frede, D. "Out of the Cave: What Socrates Learnt from Diotima," in R. Rosen and J. Farrell (eds.), *Nomodeiktes: Greek Studies in Honor of Martin Oswald* (Ann Arbor: University of Michigan Press, 1993), 397–422.

Hackforth, R. "Immortality in Plato's *Symposium,*" *Classical Review* 64 (1950), 42–45.

Hackforth, R. *Plato's Phaedrus* (Cambridge: Cambridge University Press, 1952).

Heath, M. "The Unity of Plato's *Phaedrus,*" *Oxford Studies in Ancient Philosophy* 7 (1987), 150–73.

Heath, M. "The Unity of the *Phaedrus:* A Postscript," *Oxford Studies in Ancient Philosophy* 7 (1989), 189–91.

Hunter, R. *Plato's Symposium* (Oxford: Oxford University Press, 2004).

Kosman, A. "Platonic Love," in W. H. Werkmeister (ed.), *Facets of Plato's Philosophy* (Assen: van Gorcum, 1976), 53–69.

Lesher, J., Nails, D., and Sheffield, F. (eds.) *Plato's Symposium: Issues in Interpretation and Reception* (Cambridge, Mass.: Harvard University Press, 2007).

Mahoney, T. "Is Socratic *Eros* in the *Symposium* Egoistic?," *Apeiron* 29 (1996), 1–18.

Moravcsik, J. M. E. "Reason and *Eros* in the Ascent-Passage of the *Symposium,*" in J. Anton and G. Kustas (eds.), *Essays on Ancient Greek Philosophy* (Albany: State University of New York Press, 1971), 285–302.

Nussbaum, M. "The Speech of Alcibiades: A Reading of the *Symposium,*" in her *Fragility of Goodness* (Cambridge: Cambridge University Press, 1986), 165–200.

Price, A. *Love and Friendship in Plato and Aristotle* (Oxford: Clarendon Press, 1989; 2nd. ed. 1997).

Price, A. "Loving Persons Platonically," *Phronesis* 26 (1981), 25–34.

Rossetti, L. (ed.) *Understanding the Phaedrus: Proceedings of the Second Symposium Platonicum* (Sankt Augustin: Academia Verlag, 1992).

Rowe, C. J. "The Argument and Structure of Plato's *Phaedrus,*" *Proceedings of the Cambridge Philological Society* 32 (1986), 106–25.

Rowe, C. J. *Plato: Phaedrus* (Warminster: Aris and Phillips, 1986).

Rowe, C. J. "*Plato: Symposium* (Warminster: Aris and Phillips, 1998).

Rowe, C. J. "The Unity of Plato's *Phaedrus:* A Reply to Heath," *Oxford Studies in Ancient Philosophy* 7 (1989), 175–88.

Santas, G. *Plato and Freud: Two Theories of Love* (Oxford: Blackwell, 1988).

Scott, D. "Socrates and Alcibiades in Plato's *Symposium,*" *Hermathena* 168 (2000), 25–37.

Sheffield, F. *Plato's Symposium: The Ethics of Desire* (Oxford: Oxford University Press, 2006).

Sheffield, F. "Psychic Pregnancy and Platonic Epistemology," *Oxford Studies in Ancient Philosophy* 20 (2001), 1–35.

Vlastos, G. "The Individual as Object of Love in Plato," in his *PS*, 3–34. Also in Fine (ed.), *Plato 2*, 137–63.

Wardy, R. "The Unity of Opposites in Plato's *Symposium*," *Oxford Studies in Ancient Philosophy* 23 (2002), 1–61.

# *PARMENIDES*

Allen, R. E. *Plato's Parmenides: Translation and Analysis* (Minneapolis: University of Minnesota Press, 1983).

Cohen, S. M. "The Logic of the Third Man," *Philosophical Review* 80 (1971), 448–75. Also in Fine (ed.), *Plato 1*, 275–97.

Cornford, F. M. *Plato and Parmenides* (London: Routledge and Kegan Paul, 1939).

Fine, G. "Owen, Aristotle, and the Third Man," *Phronesis* 27 (1982), 13–33.

Geach, P. "The Third Man Again," *Philosophical Review* 65 (1956), 72–82. Also in *SPM*, 265–77.

McCabe, M. M. "Unity in the *Parmenides*: The Unity of the *Parmenides*," in *FA*, 5–47.

Meinwald, C. "Good-bye to the Third Man," in *CCP*, 365–96.

Meinwald, C. *Plato's Parmenides* (New York: Oxford University Press, 1991).

Mignucci, M. "Plato's Third Man Arguments in the *Parmenides*," *Archiv für Geschichte der Philosophie* 72 (1990), 143–81.

Miller, M. *Plato's Parmenides* (Princeton, N.J.: Princeton University Press, 1986).

Moravcsik, J. M. E. "The "Third Man" Argument and Plato's Theory of Forms," *Phronesis* 8 (1963), 50–62.

Owen, G. E. L. "Notes on Ryle's Plato," in *LSD*, 85–103. Also in Fine (ed.), *Plato 1*, 298–319.

Peterson, S. "A Reasonable Self-Predication Premise for the Third Man Argument," *Philosophical Review* 82 (1973), 451–70.

Peterson, S. "The Greatest Difficulty for Plato's Theory of Forms: The Unknowability Argument of *Parmenides* 133c–134," *Archiv für Geschichte der Philosophie* 63 (1981), 1–16.

Rickless, S. *Plato's Forms in Transition* (Cambridge: Cambridge University Press, 2007).

Ryle, G. "Plato's *Parmenides*," in *SPM*, 85–103.

Sayre, K. *Parmenides' Lesson: Translation and Explication of Plato's "Parmenides"* (Notre Dame, Ind.: University of Notre Dame Press, 1996).

Schofield, M. "Likeness and Likenesses in the *Parmenides*," in *FA*, 49–77.

Sellars, W. "Vlastos and the "Third Man"," *Philosophical Review* 64 (1955), 405–37.

Strang, C. "Plato and the Third Man," *Proceedings of the Aristotelian Society* 37 (suppl.) (1963), 147–64. Also in Vlastos (ed.), *Plato 1*, 184–200.

Vlastos, G. "The Third Man Argument in the *Parmenides*," *Philosophical Review* 63 (1954), 319–49. Also in *SPM*, 231–63.

Vlastos, G. "Plato's "Third Man" Argument (*Parm.* 132a1–b2): Text and Logic," *Philosophical Quarterly* 19 (1969), 289–81. Also in *PS*, 342–65.

# *THEAETETUS*

Ackrill, J. L. "Plato on False Belief: *Theaetetus* 187–200," *Monist* 50 (1966), 383–402. Also in Ackrill, *Essays on Plato and Aristotle*, 53–71.

Annas, J. "Knowledge and Language: The *Theaetetus* and the *Cratylus*," in *LL*, 95–114.

Benson, H. "Why Is There a Discussion of False Belief in the *Theaetetus?*," *Journal of the History of Philosophy* 30 (1992), 171–99.

Bolton, R. "Plato's Distinction between Being and Becoming," *Review of Metaphysics* 29 (1975), 66–95.

Bostock, D. *Plato's Theaetetus* (Oxford: Clarendon Press, 1988).

Burnyeat, M. F. "Conflicting Appearances," *Proceedings of the British Academy* 65 (1979), 69–111.

Burnyeat, M. F. "Examples in Epistemology: Socrates, Theaetetus, and G. E. Moore," *Philosophy* 52 (1977), 381–98.

Burnyeat, M. F. "Idealism and Greek Philosophy: What Descartes Saw and Berkeley Missed," *Philosophical Review* 90 (1982), 3–40.

Burnyeat, M. F. "The Materials and Sources of Plato's Dream," *Phronesis* 15 (1970), 101–22.

Burnyeat, M. F. "Plato on the Grammar of Perceiving," *Classical Quarterly* NS 26 (1976), 29–51.

Burnyeat, M. F. "Protagoras and Self-Refutation in Later Greek Philosophy," *Philosophical Review* 85 (1976), 44–69.

Burnyeat, M. F. "Protagoras and Self-Refutation in Plato's *Theaetetus*," *Philosophical Review* 85 (1976), 172–95. Also in S. Everson (ed.), *Epistemology* (Cambridge: Cambridge University Press, 1989), 39–59.

Burnyeat, M. F. "Socrates and the Jury: Paradoxes in Plato's Distinction Between Knowledge and True Belief," *Aristotelian Society* 54 (suppl.) (1980), 177–91. (Reply by J. Barnes, 193–206.)

Burnyeat, M. F. "Socratic Midwifery, Platonic Inspiration," *Bulletin of the Institute of Classical Studies* 24 (1977), 7–16. Also in *EPS*, 53–65.

Burnyeat, M. F. *The Theaetetus of Plato* (translated by M. J. Levett with revisions by Burnyeat and introductory essay by Burnyeat) (Indianapolis: Hackett, 1990).

Chappell, T. *Reading Plato's Theaetetus* (Sankt Augustin: Academia Verlag, 2004; and Indianapolis: Hackett, 2005).

Cooper, J. "Plato on Sense-Perception and Knowledge (*Theaetetus* 184–6)," *Phronesis* 15 (1970), 123–46. Also in Fine (ed.), *Plato 1*, 355–76.

Cooper, J. *Plato's Theaetetus* (New York: Garland, 1990).

Cornford, F. M. *Plato's Theory of Knowledge: The Theaetetus and Sophist* (London: Routledge and Kegan Paul, 1935).

Crivelli, P. "Allodoxia," *Archiv für Geschichte der Philosophie* 80 (1998), 1–29.

Dancy, R. "Theaetetus' First Baby: *Theaetetus* 151e–160e," *Philosophical Topics* 15 (1987), 61–108.

Day, J. "The Theory of Perception in Plato's *Theaetetus* 152–183," *Oxford Studies in Ancient Philosophy* 15 (1997), 51–80.

Fine, G. "Conflicting Appearances: *Theaetetus* 153d–154b," in *FA*, 105–33. Also in *PKF*, 160–83.

Fine, G. "False Belief in the *Theaetetus*," *Phronesis* 24 (1979), 70–80. Also in *PKF*, 213–24.

Fine, G. "Knowledge and *Logos* in the *Theaetetus*," *Philosophical Review* 88 (1979), 366–97. Also in *PKF*, 225–51.

Fine, G. "Plato on Perception," *Oxford Studies in Ancient Philosophy* (suppl.) (1988), 15–28.

Fine, G. "Protagorean Relativisms," *Proceedings of the Boston Area Colloquium in Ancient Philosophy* 10 ( 1996), 211–43. Also in *PKF*, 132–59.

Frede, D. "The Soul's Silent Dialogue: A Non-Aporetic Reading of the *Theaetetus*," *Proceedings of the Cambridge Philological Society* 215 (1989), 20–49.

Frede, M. "Observations on Perception in Plato's Later Dialogues," in his *Essays in Ancient Philosophy* (Oxford: Clarendon Press, 1987), 3–8. Also in Fine (ed.), *Plato 1*, 377–83.

Holland, A. J. "An Argument in Plato's *Theaetetus*: 184–6," *Philosophical Quarterly* 23 (1973), 97–116.

Kanayama, Y. "Perceiving, Considering, and Attaining Being (*Theaetetus* 184–186)," *Oxford Studies in Ancient Philosophy* 5 (1987), 29–81.

Kerferd, G. B. "Plato's Account of the Relativism of Protagoras," *Durham University Journal* 42 (1949), 20–26.

Ketchum, R. "Plato and Protagorean Relativism," *Oxford Studies in Ancient Philosophy* 10 (1992), 73–105.

Lee, E. N. " 'Hoist on His Own Petard,' " in *EA*, 225–61.

Lesher, J. H. "*Gnôsis*" and *Epistêmê* in Socrates' Dream in the *Theaetetus*," *Journal of Hellenic Studies* 89 (1969), 72–78.

Lewis, F. "Foul Play in Plato's Aviary," in *EA*, 262–84.

Lewis, F. "Two Paradoxes in the *Theaetetus*," in J. M. E. Moravcsik (ed.), *Patterns in Plato's Thought* (Dordrecht: Reidel, 1973), 123–49.

Matthen, M. "Perception, Relativism and Truth: Reflections on Plato's *Theaetetus* 152–60," *Dialogue* 24 (1985), 33–58.

McDowell, J. "Identity Mistakes: Plato and the Logical Atomists," *Proceedings of the Aristotelian Society* 70 (1969–70), 161–80. Also in Fine (ed.), *Plato 1*, 384–97.

Modrak, D. "Perception and Judgment in the *Theaetetus*," *Phronesis* 26 (1981), 35–54.

Morrow, G. "Plato and the Mathematicians: An Interpretation of Socrates' Dream in the *Theaetetus* (201e–206c)," *Philosophical Review* 79 (1970), 309–33.

Nehamas, A. "*Epistêmê* and *Logos* in Plato's Later Thought," *Archiv für Geschichte der Philosophie* 66 (1984), 11–36.

Rudebusch, G. "Plato on Sense and Reference," *Mind* 104 (1985), 526–37.

Ryle, G. "Letters and Syllables in Plato," *Philosophical Review* 69 (1960), 431–51.

Ryle, G. "Logical Atomism in Plato's *Theaetetus*," *Phronesis* 35 (1990), 21–46.

Sedley, D. *The Midwife of Platonism: Text and Subtext in Plato's Theaetetus* (Oxford: Clarendon Press, 2004).

Sedley, D. "Three Platonist Interpretations of the *Theaetetus*," in *FA*, 79–103.

Silverman, A. "Flux and Language in the *Theaetetus*," *Oxford Studies in Ancient Philosophy* 18 (2000), 109–52.

Silverman, A. "Plato on Perception and 'Commons,' " *Classical Quarterly* NS 40 (1990), 148–75. (Also discusses the *Timaeus*.)

Tigner, S. "The "Exquisite" Argument at *Theaetetus* 171a," *Mnemosyne* 24 (1971), 366–69.

Waterfield, R. *Plato: Theaetetus* (Harmondsworth: Penguin, 1987).

Waterlow, S. "Protagoras and Inconsistency," *Archiv für Geschichte der Philosophie* 59 (1977), 19–36.

Williams, B. A. O. "Introduction," *Plato's Theaetetus*, trans. M. J. Levett, rev. M. F. Burnyeat (Indianapolis: Hackett, 1992).

Williams, C. J. F. "Referential Opacity and False Belief in the *Theaetetus*," *Philosophical Quarterly* 22 (1972), 289–302.

# TIMAEUS

Burnyeat, M. F. "*Eikôs Muthos*," *Rhizai* 2 (2005), 143–66.

Calvo, T., and Brisson, L. (eds.) *Interpreting the Timaeus and Critias* (*Proceedings of the 4th International Platonic Symposium*) (Sankt Augustin: Academia Verlag, 1997).

Cherniss, H. F. "A Much Misread Passage in Plato's *Timaeus*," *American Journal of Philology* 75 (1954), 113–30.

Cherniss, H. F. "The Relation of the *Timaeus* to Plato's Later Dialogues," *American Journal of Philology* 78 (1957), 225–66. Also in *SPM*, 339–78.

Cornford, F. M. *Plato's Cosmology: The Timaeus of Plato* (London: Routledge and Kegan Paul, 1937).

Driscoll, J. "The Platonic Ancestry of Primary Substance," *Phronesis* 24 (1979), 253–69.

Frede, D. "The Philosophical Economy of Plato's Psychology: Rationality and Common Concepts in the *Timaeus*," in M. Frede and G. Striker (eds.), *Rationality in Greek Thought* (Oxford: Clarendon Press, 1996), 1–34.

Frede, M. "Being and Becoming in Plato," *Oxford Studies in Ancient Philosophy* (suppl.) (1988), 37–52.

Gill, M. "Matter and Flux in Plato's *Timaeus*," *Phronesis* 32 (1987), 34–53.

Johansen, T. K. "Body, Soul and Tripartition in Plato's *Timaeus*," *Oxford Studies in Ancient Philosophy* 19 (2000), 87–111.

Johansen, T. K. *Plato's Natural Philosophy: A Study of the Timaeus-Critias* (Cambridge: Cambridge University Press, 2004).

Keyt, D. "The Mad Craftsman of the *Timaeus*," *Philosophical Review* 80 (1971), 230–35.

Kung, J. "Mathematics and Virtue in Plato's *Timaeus*," in J. Anton and A. Preus (eds.), *Essays in Ancient Greek Philosophy*, vol. 3 (Albany: State University of New York Press, 1989), 303–39.

Kung, J. "Why the Receptacle Is Not a Mirror," *Archiv für Geschichte der Philosophie* 70 (1988), 167–78.

Lennox, J. "Plato's Unnatural Teleology," in D. O'Meara (ed.), *Platonic Investigations* (Washington, D.C.: Catholic University Press of America, 1985), 195–218.

Mason, A. S. "Immortality in the *Timaeus*," *Phronesis* 39 (1994), 90–97.

Mills, K. W. "Some Aspects of Plato's Theory of Forms: *Timaeus* 49c *ff.*, " *Phronesis* 13 (1968), 145–70.

Mohr, R. *The Platonic Cosmology* (Leiden: Brill, 1985).

Morrow, G. "The Demiurge in Politics: The *Timaeus* and the *Laws*," *Proceedings and Addresses of the American Philosophical Association* 27 (1953–54), 5–23.

Morrow, G. "Necessity and Persuasion in Plato's *Timaeus*," *Philosophical Review* 59 (1950), 147–64. Also in *SPM*, 421–37.

Osborne, C. "Topography in the *Timaeus*," *Proceedings of the Cambridge Philological Society* 34 (1988), 104–14.

Owen, G. E. L. "The Place of the *Timaeus* in Plato's Dialogues," *Classical Quarterly* NS 3 (1953), 79–95. Also in *SPM*, 313–38, and in *LSD*, 65–84.

Owen, G. E. L. "Plato and Parmenides on the Timeless Present," *Monist* 50 (1966), 317–40. Also in *LSD*, 27–44.

Patterson, R. "The Unique Worlds of the *Timaeus*," *Phoenix* 35 (1981), 105–19.

Reed, N. H. "Plato on Flux, Perception and Language," *Proceedings of the Cambridge Philological Society* 18 (1972), 65–77.

Reydam-Schils, G. J. (ed.) *Plato's Timaeus as Cultural Icon* (Notre Dame, Ind.: University of Notre Dame Press, 2003).

Robinson, J. "The Tripartite Soul in the *Timaeus*," *Phronesis* 35 (1990), 103–10.

Sedley, D. *Creationism and Its Critics in Antiquity* (Berkeley: University of California Press, 2007).

Sedley, D. "The Ideal of Godlikeness," in Fine (ed.), *Plato 2*, 309–28.

Silverman, A. "Timaean Particulars," *Classical Quarterly* NS 42 (1992), 87–113.

Strange, S. K. "The Double Explanation in the *Timaeus*," *Ancient Philosophy* 5 (1985), 25–39. Also in Fine (ed.), *Plato 1*, 397–415.

Taylor, A. E. *A Commentary on Plato's Timaeus* (Oxford: Clarendon Press, 1928).

Vlastos, G. "Creation in the *Timaeus*: Is It a Fiction?," in *SPM*, 401–19.

Vlastos, G. "The Disorderly Motion in the *Timaeus*," *Classical Quarterly* 33 (1939), 71–83. Also in *SPM*, 379–99.

Vlastos, G. *Plato's Universe* (Seattle: University of Washington Press, 1975).

Zeyl, D. "Plato and Talk of a World in Flux: *Timaeus* 49a6–50b5," *Harvard Studies in Classical Philology* 79 (1975), 125–48.

# *SOPHIST*

Ackrill, J. L. "Plato and the Copula: *Sophist* 251–59," *Journal of Hellenic Studies* 77 (1957), 1–6. Also in Ackrill, *Essays on Plato and Aristotle*, 80–92, and in Vlastos (ed.), *Plato 1*, 210–22.

Ackrill, J. L. "*Sumplokê Eidôn*," *Bulletin of the Institute of Classical Studies* 2 (1955), 31–35. Also in Ackrill, *Essays on Plato and Aristotle*, 72–79, and in *SPM*, 199–206, and in Vlastos (ed.), *Plato 1*, 201–9.

Bluck, R. S. *Plato's Sophist: A Commentary* (Manchester: Manchester University Press, 1975).

Bostock, D. "Plato on "Is-Not" (*Sophist*, 254–9)," *Oxford Studies in Ancient Philosophy* 2 (1984), 89–119.

Brown, L. "Being in the *Sophist*: A Syntactical Inquiry," *Oxford Studies in Ancient Philosophy* 4 (1986), 49–70. Also in Fine (ed.), *Plato 1*, 455–78.

Brown, L. "Definition and Division in the *Sophist*," in D. Charles (ed.), *Ancient Theories of Definition* (Oxford: Clarendon Press, forthcoming).

Brown, L. "Innovation and Continuity: The Battle of Gods and Giants, *Sophist* 245–259," in *MAP*, 181–207.

Campbell, L. *The Sophistes and Politicus of Plato* (Oxford: Clarendon Press, 1867).

Crivelli, P. "Plato's *Sophist* and Semantic Fragmenation," *Archiv für Geschichte der Philosophie* 75 (1993), 71–74.

Frede, M. "The Literary Form of the *Sophist*," in *FA*, 132–51.

Frede, M. "Plato's *Sophist* on False Statements," in *CCP*, 397–424.

Frede, M. *Prädikation und Existenzaussage* (Göttingen: Vandenhoeck and Ruprecht, 1967).

Heinaman, R. "Being in the *Sophist*," *Archiv für Geschichte der Philosophie* 65 (1983), 1–17.

Heinaman, R. "Communion of Forms," *Proceedings of the Aristotelian Society* 83 (1982–83), 175–90.

Heinaman, R. "Once More: Being in the *Sophist*," *Archiv für Geschichte der Philosophie* 68 (1986), 121–25.

Heinaman, R. "Self-Predication in the *Sophist*," *Phronesis* 26 (1981), 55–66.

Ketchum, R. "Participation and Predication in the *Sophist* 251-60," *Phronesis* 23 (1978), 42–62.

Keyt, D. "Plato on Falsity: *Sophist* 263b," in *EA*, 285–305.

Keyt, D. "Plato's Paradox That the Immutable Is Unknowable," *Philosophical Quarterly* 19 (1969), 1–14.

Kostman, J. "False Logos and Not-Being in Plato's *Sophist*," in J. M. E. Moravcsik (ed.), *Patterns in Plato's Thought* (Dordrecht: Reidel, 1973), 192–212.

Lee, E. N. "Plato on Negation and Not-Being in the *Sophist*," *Philosophical Review* 81 (1972), 267–304.

Lewis, F. "Did Plato Discover the *estin* of Identity?," *California Studies in Classical Antiquity* 8 (1975), 113–43.

Lewis, F. "Plato on 'Not,'" *California Studies in Classical Antiquity* 9 (1976), 89–115.

Malcolm, J. "Plato's Analysis of *to on* and *to mê on* in the *Sophist*," *Phronesis* 12 (1967), 130–46.

Malcolm, J. "Remarks on an Incomplete Rendering of Being in the *Sophist*," *Archiv für Geschichte der Philosophie* 67 (1985), 162–65.

McDowell, J. "Falsehood and Not-Being in Plato's *Sophist*," in *LL*, 115–34.

McPherran, M. "Plato's Reply to the 'Worst Difficulty' Argument of the *Parmenides*: *Sophist* 248a–249d," *Archiv für Geschichte der Philosophie* 68 (1986), 233–52.

Moravcsik, J. M. E. "Being and Meaning in the *Sophist*," *Acta Philosophica Fennica* 14 (1962), 23–78.

Moravcsik, J. M. E. "*Sumplokê eidôn* and the Genesis of *Logos*," *Archiv für Geschichte der Philosophie* 42 (1960), 117–29.

Nehamas, A. "Participation and Predication in Plato's Later Thought," *Review of Metaphysics* 36 (1982), 343–74.

Notomi, N. *The Unity of Plato's Sophist* (Cambridge: Cambridge University Press, 1999).

Owen, G. E. L. "Plato on Not-Being," in Vlastos (ed.), *Plato 1*, 223–267. Also in Fine (ed.), *Plato 1*, 416–54.

Pelletier, F. J. *Parmenides, Plato, and the Semantics of Not-Being* (Chicago: Chicago University Press, 1992).

Prior, W. "Plato's Analysis of Being and Not-Being in the *Sophist*," *Southern Journal of Philosophy* 18 (1980), 199–211.

Reeve, C. D. C. "Motion, Rest, and Dialectic in the *Sophist*," *Archiv für Geschichte der Philosophie* 67 (1985), 47–64.

Roberts, J. "The Problem about Being in the *Sophist*," *History of Philosophy Quarterly* 3 (1986), 229–43.

van Eck, J. "Falsity without Negative Predication," *Phronesis* 40 (1995), 20–47.

van Eck, J. "Plato's Logical Insights: *Sophist* 254d–257a," *Ancient Philosophy* 20 (2000), 53–79.

Vlastos, G. "An Ambiguity in the *Sophist*," in *PS*, 270–322.

Wiggins, D. "Sentence Meaning, Negation, and Plato's Problems of Not-Being," in Vlastos (ed.), *Plato 1*, 268–303.

# STATESMAN

Ackrill, J. L. "In Defense of Platonic Division," in O. P. Wood and G. Pitcher (eds.), *Ryle: A Collection of Critical Essays* (Garden City, N.Y.: Doubleday Anchor Books, 1970), 373–92. Also in Ackrill, *Essays on Plato and Aristotle*, 93–109.

Bobonich, C. "The Virtues of Ordinary People in Plato's *Statesman*," in C. J. Rowe (ed.), *Reading the Statesman* (Sankt Augustin: Academia Verlag, 1995), 313–20.

Cooper, J. "Plato's *Statesman* and Politics," *Proceedings of the Boston Area Colloquium in Ancient Philosophy* 13 (1999), 71–104.

Gill, C. "Plato and Politics: The *Critias* and *Politicus*," *Phronesis* 24 (1979), 148–67.

Gill, C. "Rethinking Constitutionalism in *Statesman* 291–303," in C. J. Rowe (ed.), *Reading the Statesman* (Sankt Augustin: Academia Verlag, 1995), 292–305.

Lane, M. *Method and Politics in Plato's Statesman* (Cambridge: Cambridge University Press, 1997).

Moravcsik, J. M. E. "The Anatomy of Plato's Divisions," in *EA*, 324–48.

Moravcsik, J. M. E. "Plato's Method of Division," in J. M. E. Moravcsik (ed.), *Patterns in Plato's Thought* (Dordrecht: Reidel, 1973), 158–80.

Owen, G. E. L. "Plato on the Undepictable," in *EA* 349–61. Also in *LSD*, 138–47.

Rowe, C. J. (ed. and trans.) *Plato: Statesman* (Warminster: Aris and Phillips, 1995).

Rowe, C. J. "The *Politicus*: Structure and Form," in *FA*, 153–78.

Rowe, C. J. (ed.) *Reading the Statesman: Proceedings of the Third Symposium Platonicum* (Sankt Augustin: Academia Verlag, 1995).

Skemp, J. B. *Plato's Statesman* (London: Routledge and Kegan Paul, 1952; 2nd ed. Bristol: Bristol Classical Press, 1987).

# PHILEBUS

Bury, R. G. *The Philebus of Plato* (Cambridge: Cambridge University Press, 1897; reprinted by Arno Press in 1973).

Cooper, J. "Plato's Theory of Human Good," *Journal of Philosophy* 74 (1977), 714–30. Also in Fine (ed.), *Plato 2*, 329–44.

Cooper, N. "Pleasure and the Good in Plato's *Philebus*," *Philosophical Quarterly* 18 (1968), 12–15.

Dancy, R. "The One, the Many, and the Forms: *Philebus* 15b1–8," *Ancient Philosophy* 4 (1984), 160–93.

Dybikowski, J. "False Pleasure and the *Philebus*," *Phronesis* 15 (1970), 147–65.

Dybikowski, J. "Mixed and False Pleasures in the *Philebus*: A Reply," *Philosophical Quarterly* 20 (1970), 244–47.

Frede, D. "Disintegration and Restoration: Pleasure and Pain in Plato's *Philebus*," in *CCP*, 425–63.

Frede, D. "Rumpelstiltskin's Pleasures: True and False Pleasures in Plato's *Philebus*," *Phronesis* 30 (1985), 151–80.

Gosling, J. C. B. "False Pleasures: *Philebus* 35c–41b," *Phronesis* 4 (1959), 44–54.

Gosling, J. C. B. "Father Kenny on False Pleasures," *Phronesis* 6 (1961), 41–45.

Hackforth, R. *Plato's Examination of Pleasure* (Cambridge: Cambridge University Press, 1945).

Hampton, C. *Pleasure, Knowledge, and Being: An Analysis of Plato's Philebus* (Albany: State University of New York Press, 1990).

Kenny, A. "False Pleasures in the *Philebus:* A Reply to Mr. Gosling," *Phronesis* 5 (1960), 45–52.

Meinwald, C. "One/Many Problems," *Phronesis* 41 (1996), 95–103.

Meinwald, C. "Plato's Pythagoreanism," *Ancient Philosophy* 22 (2002), 87–101.

Meinwald, C. "Prometheus" Bounds," *MAP*, 165–80.

Moravcsik, J. M. E. "Forms, Nature and the Good in the *Philebus*," *Phronesis* 24 (1979), 81–104.

Penner, T. "False Anticipatory Pleasures: *Philebus* 36a3–41a6," *Phronesis* 15 (1970), 166–78.

Sayre, K. "The *Philebus* and the Good," *Proceedings of the Boston Area Colloquium in Ancient Philosophy* 2 (1987), 45–71. (Reply by P. Mitsis, 72–78.)

Striker, G. *Peras und Apeiron* (Göttingen: Vandenhoeck and Ruprecht, 1970).

Taylor, A. E. *Philebus and Epinomis* (London: T. Nelson, 1956).

Thomas, C. "Plato's Prometheanism," *Oxford Studies in Ancient Philosophy* 31 (2006), 23–32.

Waterfield, R. "The Place of the *Philebus* in Plato's Dialogues," *Phronesis* 25 (1980), 270–305.

Waterfield, R. *Plato: Philebus* (Harmondsworth: Penguin, 1982).

# *LAWS*

Bobonich, C. "Persuasion, Compulsion, and Freedom in Plato's *Laws*," *Classical Quarterly* 41 (1991), 365–88. Also in Fine (ed.), *Plato 2*, 373–403.

Bobonich, C. "Plato's Theory of Goods in the *Laws* and *Philebus*," *Proceedings of the Boston Area Colloquium in Ancient Philosophy* 11 (1997), 101–39. (Reply by J. Gentzler, 140–51.)

Bobonich, C. "Reading the *Laws*," in *FA*, 249–82.

Roberts, J. "Plato on the Causes of Wrongdoing in the *Laws*," *Ancient Philosophy* 7 (1987), 23–37.

Saunders, T. "Plato's Later Political Thought," in *CCP*, 464–92.

Saunders, T. *Plato's Penal Code: Tradition, Controversy, and Reform in Greek Penology* (Oxford: Clarendon Press, 1991).

Saunders, T. "The Socratic Paradoxes in Plato's *Laws*," *Hermes* 96 (1968), 421–34.

Saunders, T., and Brisson, L. *Bibliography on Plato's Laws* (Sankt Augustin: Academia Verlag, 2000).

Stalley, R. E. *An Introduction to Plato's Laws* (Indianapolis: Hackett, 1983).

# ARISTOTLE'S CRITICISM OF PLATO

Annas, J. "Aristotle on Substance, Accident and Plato's Forms," *Phronesis* 22 (1977), 146–60.

Annas, J. *Aristotle's Metaphysics M and N* (Oxford: Clarendon Press, 1976).

Annas, J. "Forms and First Principles," *Phronesis* 19 (1974), 257–83.

Cherniss, H. F. *Aristotle's Criticism of Plato and the Academy* (Baltimore: Johns Hopkins University Press, 1944; repr. New York: Russell and Russell, 1962).

Cherniss, H. F. *The Riddle of the Early Academy* (Berkeley: University of California Press, 1945).

Devereux, D. "The Primacy of *Ousia*: Aristotle's Debt to Plato," in D. O'Meara (ed.), *Platonic Investigations* (Washington, D.C.: Catholic University of America Press, 1985), 226–32.

Düring, I., and Owen, G. E. L. (eds.) *Aristotle and Plato in the Mid-Fourth Century* (Göteborg: Elanders Boktryckeri Aktiebolag, 1960).

Fine, G. *On Ideas: Aristotle's Criticism of Plato's Theory of Forms* (Oxford: Clarendon Press, 1993).

Fine, G. "Plato and Aristotle on Form and Substance," *Proceedings of the Cambridge Philological Society* 209 (1983), 23–47. Also in *PKF*, 397–425.

Matthews, G. B., and Cohen S. M. "The One and the Many," *Review of Metaphysics* 21 (1968), 630–55.

Owen, G. E. L. "Dialectic and Eristic in the Treatment of Forms," in *LSD*, 221–38. Reprinted from Owen (ed.), *Aristotle on Dialectic: The Topics* (Oxford: Oxford University Press, 1968), 103–25.

Owen, G. E. L. "Logic and Metaphysics in Some Early Works of Aristotle," in *LSD*, 180–99. Reprinted from Düring and Owen (eds.), *Aristotle and Plato in the Mid-Fourth Century* (Göteborg: Elanders Boktryckeri Aktiebolag, 1960), 163–99.

Owen, G. E. L. "The Platonism of Aristotle," in *LSD*, 200–20. Reprinted from *Proceedings of the British Academy* 51 (1966), 125–50.

Owen, G. E. L. "A Proof in the *Peri Ideôn*," in *LSD*, 165–79. Reprinted from *Journal of Hellenic Studies* 77 (1957), 103–11.

Shields, C. *Order in Multiplicity: Homonymy in the Philosophy of Aristotle* (Oxford: Clarendon Press, 1999).

# LATER PLATONISM

Annas, J. *Platonic Ethics, Old and New* (Ithaca, N.Y.: Cornell University Press, 1999).

Baltzly, D. *Proclus, Commentary on Plato's Timaeus,* vol. 3 (Cambridge: Cambridge University Press, 2007).

Barnes, J. "Antiochus of Ascalon," in M. Griffin and J. Barnes (eds.), *Philosophia Togata* 1 (Oxford: Clarendon Press, 1989), 51–96.

Barnes, J. *Porphyry: Introduction* (Oxford: Clarendon Press, 2003).

Blumenthal, H. *Soul and Intellect: Studies in Plotinus and Later Neoplatonsim* (Aldershot: Variorum, 1993).

Boys-Stones, G. *Post-Hellenistic Philosophy: A Study of Its Development from the Stoics to Origen* (Oxford: Oxford University Press, 2001).

Brennan, T., and Brittain, C. *Simplicius: On Epictetus' Handbook* (Ithaca, N.Y.: Cornell University Press, 2002).

Brittain, C. *Philo of Larissa: The Last of the Academic Sceptics* (Oxford: Oxford University Press, 2001).

Dillon, J. *Alcinous: The Handbook of Platonism* (Oxford: Clarendon Press, 1996).

Dillon, J. *The Heirs of Plato: A Study of the Old Academy, 347–274 B.C.* (Oxford: Clarendon Press, 2003).

Dillon, J. *The Middle Platonists: A Study of Platonism, 80 B.C. to A.D. 220* (London: Duckworth, 1977).

Dodds, E. R. *Proclus. The Elements of Theology*, 2nd ed. (Oxford: Clarendon Press, 1963).

Emilsson, E. *Plotinus on Sense-Perception* (Cambridge: Cambridge University Press, 1988).

Emilsson, E. *Plotinus on the Intellect* (Cambridge: Cambridge University Press, 2007).

Gerson, L. *Aristotle and Other Platonists* (Ithaca, N.Y.: Cornell University Press, 2005).

Gerson, L. (ed.) *The Cambridge Companion to Plotinus* (Cambridge: Cambridge University Press, 1996).

Gerson, L. "Neoplatonism," in C. Shields (ed.), *The Blackwell Guide to Ancient Philosophy* (Oxford: Blackwell, 2003), 303–23.

Gerson, L. *Plotinus* (London: Routledge and Kegan Paul, 1994).

Glucker, J. *Antiochus and the Late Academy* (Göttingen: Vandenhoeck and Ruprecht, 1978).

Karamanolis, G. *Plato and Aristotle in Agreement?* (Oxford: Clarendon Press, 2006).

Morrow, G., and Dillon, J. *Proclus' Commentary on Plato's Parmenides* (Princeton, N.J.: Princeton University Press, 1987).

O'Meara, D. *Plotinus: An Introduction to the Enneads* (Oxford: Clarendon Press, 1993).

Sedley, D. "Alcinous' Epistemology," in K. Algra, P. van der Horts, and D. Runia (eds.), *Polyhistor* (Leiden: E. J. Brill, 1996), 300–12.

Smith, A. *Porphyry's Place in the Neoplatonic Tradition* (The Hague: Nijhoff, 1974).

Sorabji, R. (ed.) *Aristotle Transformed* (Ithaca, N.Y.: Cornell University Press, 1990).

Sorabji, R. *The Philosophy of the Commentators 200–600 AD*, 3 vols. (London: Duckworth, 2004).

Stead, C. *Philosophy in Christian Antiquity* (Cambridge: Cambridge University Press, 1994).

Steel, C. *The Changing Self: A Study on the Soul in Later Neoplatonism* (Brussels: Paleis der Academiën, 1978).

Wallis, R. *Neoplatonism* (London: Duckworth, 1972; 2nd. ed., 1995).

Westerink, L. *Anonymous Prolegomena to Platonic Philosophy* (Amsterdam: North-Holland, 1962).

Westerink, L. *The Greek Commentaries on Plato's Phaedo*, 2 vols. (Amsterdam: North-Holland, 1976–7).

# Index Locorum

**Aristotle**

*Categories*
1a24–25: 15n25
2a14–15: 516, 519
2b8–14: 516, 519
2b20–21: 516, 519
2b32–35: 516n25
13b14–19: 205n38

*De anima*
402a21–22: 463
406b24–25: 257
406b26–28: 257
408b12–15: 252
408b30–31: 257
417b20: 474n36
433a15–20: 475n40

*De caelo*
279b32–280a2: 467n10

*De interpretatione*
16b11–15: 205n38
17a1–2: 240
17a8–9: 240
17a20–24: 240
17a38–b1: 13
17a38–40: 516n25, 517
17a39–40: 509n18
21b9–10: 237n42

*De partibus animalium*
639b6: 509n18

*Eudemian Ethics*
1219a11–18: 161n30

*Generation of Animals*
778b1: 474n36

*Magna Moralia*
1182a15–30: 140
1200b34–37: 149n13

*Metaphysics*
987a29–b7: 140
987a32–b10: 52
987b9–10: 218

987b18–988a17: 496n34
988b6–8: 475n40
990b17–1079a13: 395n17
990b28: 517
991a8: 507
991a12–14: 507
991a20–23: 507
991b1: 507
993b23–31: 521
997b3–12: 508n16
998a24–26: 515
998b4–5: 515
999a19–22: 508n16
999b17–24: 508n16
999b25–26: 521
1003a7–9: 515
1003a8–9: 515
1003a9: 515
1003a13–17: 515
1003a14–15: 515
1003a15–17: 514n21
1013a14–17: 515
1013a16–17: 467n12
1017a27–30: 237n42
1033b26–28: 507
1038a34–39a2: 520
1039a1: 517
1039a2: 395n17
1040a8–9: 516
1040a26–27: 517
1078b12–32: 134
1079a25: 517
1086a31–b14: 507
1086a32–b11: 511
1086a32–34: 509, 511
1086a33: 511n19
1086a33–34: 520
1086a34: 517, 514n21
1086b3–5: 508
1086b5: 508
1086b5–6: 508
1086b10–11: 32, 508, 511
1086b14–20: 514n21
1086b27: 520
1087b9–10: 512
1087b11: 514

*Nicomachean Ethics*
1094a1–22: 490n17
1095b14–22: 489n15
1096b32–34: 507
1097a8: 488n14
1097a15–1097b6: 490n17
1097b14–21: 488n14
1102b16–18: 256
1105a26–b5: 143n6
1113a15–31: 154n18
1140b21–25: 144n7
1140b33: 427n32
1141a9–12: 144n7
1145b23–24: 149n13
1169b28–30: 160n29
1171a10–12: 287
1177a12–18: 489n15
1177b26–1178a8: 489n15
1179b4–31: 492n18

*On Generation and Corruption*
324b13–18: 475n40

*Physics*
185b25–27: 504
185b28–30: 237n42
189b30: 509n18
192b13–14: 520
192b14–15: 520
192b20–23: 520
194b16–20: 515
194b29–32: 474n36
194b30: 474n38
195a32: 509n18
195b21–27: 499
202a9–12: 499
209b11–16: 56n45
240a28–b7: 255
259a8: 507

*Poetics*
1147b11: 37
1147b13–16: 467n13
1151b27–29: 467n13
1456b8–18: 338

*Politics*
1265a6–8: 355
1305a11–15: 337
1322b12–17: 316n12

*Posterior Analytics*
72b19–24: 427n32
83a32–34: 507
87b28–88a17: 515
94b7: 474n36
99b20: 427n32
100b10: 427n32

*Rhetoric*
1387b23–25: 477
1407b6–9: 338

*Sophistici Elenchi* 238
165b20–21: 338
178b27–28: 240
178b36: 395n17
178b36–179a10: 520
183b7–8: 140

*Topics* 770
100b1–23: 472
104b8: 473n32
141b26: 431n39

**Plato**

*First Alcibiades* [?]
118a ff.: 320n21

*Apology*
18a7–20c3: 141
19d: 342n16
19d–20c: 166
20a–c: 166
20a2–b9: 485
20c: 342n17
21–23: 92
21a: 114
21b: 166
21d: 7, 114, 116, 165, 166
21b–e: 128
22b–c: 341
22c–d: 114
22d–e: 114

133d8: 517
134b: 400
134c: 400, 401
134d1–d8: 401
134e7: 401
134e8–135a3: 401
135a7–b1: 401
135b5–c2: 218n4
135c: 394, 407
135c8–d2: 389, 401
135c9–d1: 385
135d: 90, 402
135d–e: 402
135e: 402
135e8–136a2: 403
136b7–c1: 403
136b8–c5: 403
136e–137a: 90
136e7: 505n6
137: 99
137b: 101n58
137c: 403
137c–166c: 383
137c2: 505n6
139c4–5: 396n22
139e9–140a1: 391n14
142b: 403
142b7–c5: 391
142d9–e7: 406
143a3: 384
143b3–6: 390
143b3–7: 406n34
143c–d: 405n33
149e8–150a1: 387n11
150c7: 396n22
152a–e: 89
157b: 403
158b1–2: 397
159b: 403
160b: 403, 405
160b2–3: 404
163b: 403
164b: 403
165e: 403
166c: 404, 405

*Phaedo*
59b: 36, 96
64a: 278
64d4–e5: 197
65d–66a: 53
65d13: 192n3
66a3: 192n3
68b–c: 322
68d–69b: 378
69b: 378
69a–d: 278
69b7–8: 322
69c3–6: 322

72–78: 547
72e: 110
72e–77a: 174
72e–76d: 345
73b–76e: 194n11
74a–b: 407n37
74a–c: 53
74b ff.: 110
74b–c: 417
74b7–c3: 204
74b8: 211n52
74c2: 204n33
74d4–8: 203
75b1: 517
75c10–d5: 197
75d: 385n6
75d2: 517
76b: 12, 334n20
76b5–6: 424n23
76d: 407n37
76d7–9: 385n6
77b–e: 253
77e: 104n67
78–9: 206
78b–80b: 253
78c1–5: 253
78c–e: 54, 53n41
78c–79e: 53
78c10–79a5: 201
78d: 407n37
78d3: 517
78d10–e2: 218
78d10–e4: 210
79a6–7: 202
80d5–e1: 253
81b–83e: 379
82a–d: 322
82d–83e: 322
83c: 379
84d ff. 101
85e3–86d3: 251
88a ff.: 93
88c: 105
90–91: 102
90b–d: 340
92a7–b2: 251
92c: 100
92e5–93a9: 251
93a8–9: 251
94b7–c1: 251
94b8–10: 251
94c3–7: 251
94c9–d6: 251
94c10–d2: 251, 252
94d5–6: 251
94d7–e1: 251
96 ff.: 100
96–106: 193, 195
96a–101e: 385n6

97b8–98c2: 489
97c: 65
97d–99d2: 424n23
100b: 385n6, 407n37
100c: 214
100c2–7: 212
100d5: 207
102–7: 100
102a: 105
102a–b: 100n55
102b–105b: 198
102b1–2: 218
102b3–5: 208
102b3–6: 203, 204
102b5: 203
102b11: 194n10
102d–103c: 198
103b5–c2: 218
103c13: 199
104d1–7: 199n28
105b ff.: 213n62
105c1: 175
105c2–6: 175
107a: 100n55
118a: 37

*Phaedrus*
227c: 307
230d: 96n34
244a–245a: 352
245a: 342
245c–e: 356
246a–e: 277
246a–250c: 254
246d–250e: 345
247b3–5: 254
247b3–6: 254
247c3: 207
248a1–6: 254
249b–c: 547
249b5–249c3: 218n4
249d: 305
251a1: 308
251e: 305
252a: 310
253d–254e: 305
253d–256e: 277
253e: 278
254c–e: 278
255e: 305
255e–256a: 309
256a–d: 302
256b–e: 308
256c: 303
258d: 385n4
262c: 51
264c: 288
265c8–266c1: 500
265d–266c: 187n33

265e1–2: 17n28, 492n19
265e1–3: 220
266a: 303
266b3–5: 218n4
267d–269c: 338
270d: 336
275d–e: 98
276c–277a: 352n40
277b–c: 336
277b5–8: 500
278d–e: 66n13
278e–279b: 51

*Philebus*
11b1: 485
11b4–c3: 488
11b7: 488n13
11b9: 488
11d4–6: 488
12–22: 101
12d5–e4: 492
13a8: 488
13b7: 488
13e4: 488n13
13e4–6: 488
14c7–15c3: 488
16a4–5: 485
16b–18d: 187n33
16b4–18d2: 488
18b–d: 429
18e8–19a2: 488
19: 99
19a3–b4: 488
19b2–3: 488
19b5: 485
19c1–e5: 488
19c4–5: 485
19c4–d6: 488
19c5: 486n7
19d6–e4: 486
19d6–e5: 485
19e–20a: 109
20: 93
20a1–8: 486, 488
20b–23a: 268n3
20b3–22c4: 488
20c–21a: 56
20d–21a: 109
21e3–4: 485
22c5–e3: 489
23a: 103
23b2–4: 486
23b6–9: 489
26a4: 493
26a8: 494n29
26b5–7: 493
26e6–7: 499
27e5–7: 489
28a1–4: 489

# INDEX NOMINUM

..................................................

This index includes only names of modern scholars and philosophers. Other names are listed in the General Index.

Hobbs, A., 259n9
Hoekstra, M., 452n37
Hopkins, J., 31n73
Hornblower, S., 43n18, 59n55, 90n7
Huffman, C., 44n19, 47n26
Hunter, R., 96n38, 287n1
Hutchinson, D.S., 338n4

Irwin, T., 21n42, 21n45, 23n52, 26n59, 32n74, 34n75,
    53n41, 80n73, 83n79, 120, 120n9, 126–27, 126n25,
    130, 134n40, 146n10, 155n21, 159n27, 166n3,
    176n16, 202n30, 203n32, 210n49, 210n51, 221n11,
    222n12, 256n6, 265n14, 268n3, 271n4, 287n1,
    312n1, 312n2, 312n3, 317n13, 338n7, 340n10,
    346n24, 360n1, 365n6, 385n7, 433n41, 476n41,
    528n8
Iyer, A., 334n36

Jachmann, G., 70n38
Jaeger, W., 504n1, 511n19
Janaway, C., 336n1, 350n30
Johansen, T., 471n26, 478n51, 479n54
Johnson, R., 49n32

Kagan, D., 43n18
Kahn, C., 37n1, 46n23, 48n29, 52n39, 53n40, 78n72,
    83n79, 92n15, 96n36, 115, 193n8, 195n17, 196n19,
    386n10, 441n14, 485n2
Kamtekar, R., 4–5, 31, 154n20, 277n11, 325n24,
    337n3, 346n25, 348n26, 363n5, 502n43
Karamanolis, G., 539n59
Karfik, F., 476n42
Kelsey, S., 211n53
Kennedy, G., 49n30
Kerferd, G., 39n8, 48n28
Keuls, E., 352n39
Keyt, D., 236n139, 237n45, 454n44, 455, 455n48
Kidd, I., 68n26
Kim, C., 332n35
Kirk, G., 45n22, 46n23, 46n25
Kirk, G.S., 45n39, 53n40, 54n43
Klosko, G., 433n41
Knorr, W., 46n24, 50n36
Koller, S., 458n68
Konstan, D., 477n46
Krämer, H., 98n43
Kraut, R., 3, 25–26, 28n65, 30n71, 77n71, 92n15,
    142n3, 312n2, 315n11, 317n14, 320n20, 366n9,
    368n13, 369n14, 372n20, 408n43
Kretzmann, N., 225n16
Kripke, S., 131

Laks, A., 329n29, 330n32
Lamberton, R., 530n18
Lane, M., 214n63

Lautner, P., 548n88
Lee, E., 28n65, 28n66
Lee, M., 3, 10–12, 11n17, 414n7, 415n9
Lennox, J., 474n34, 495n31
Lewis, F., 422n20, 441n14, 447n24, 447n26
Linnaeus, C., 492
Lloyd, G., 38n4, 38n5, 38n6
Lockwood, M., 441n14, 447n25
Long, A.A., 192n4
Long, A.G., 88n3, 111n81
Lorenz, H., 4, 5, 27, 21n41, 27n61, 276n10, 289n2,
    332n35, 357n46, 476n41
Ludwigl, W., 65n6
Lynch, J., 45n21, 49n30, 49n31

Mabbott, J., 458
Makin, S., 212n56
Malcolm, J., 396n19
Mansfeld, J., 69n33
Mansion, S., 508n13
Manville, P., 313n4
Mates, B., 441n14
Matthews, G., 5, 6n5, 7, 8, 9, 149n13, 314n8
McCabe, M., 6, 91n12, 102n64, 104n69, 192n1,
    194n12, 214n63, 328n28
McDowell, J., 185n29, 412n2, 422n20, 454n47,
    459–60, 459n59, 459n62, 460n63, 460n64,
    460n65, 460n66
McTighe, K., 153n19
Meinwald, C., 19, 213n57, 213n58, 404–406, 386n8,
    386n10, 396n20, 404n30, 406n35, 406n36,
    492n21, 492n23, 493n24
Menn, S. 192n1, 337n2, 427n31, 429n35, 476n42,
    539n58, 548n86
Metzger, B., 65n6
Mueller, I., 474n34, 548n88
Miller, D., 479n52
Miller, M., 386n8, 404n39, 492n20
Mirhady, D., 49n30
Moravcsik, J., 237n42, 352n38, 422n20, 442n16,
    494n28
Morgan, M., 101n63, 192n1
Morrow, G., 57n49, 58n52, 58n54, 67n18, 75n60,
    478n51, 541n63
Moss, J., 250n3
Motte, A., 195n14
Mourelatos, A., 28n65, 28n66
Murdoch, I., 351n36

Nails, D., 37n1, 84n80, 96n35, 300n6, 486n5,
    505n4
Natorp, P., 192n5
Nehemas, A., 91n12, 92n14, 93n18, 118n8,
    123n15, 203n31, 203n32, 297n5, 352n39, 353n41,
    429n36
Nettleship, R., 360n1
Neu, J., 28n65, 28n66, 371n19

# GENERAL INDEX

Academy, 44, 50, 55–57, 65–66, 70, 530–33
account
  and definitional knowledge
  and knowledge, 185–87, 188–89, 275, 413, 420
  compositional, 186
  of properties, 174
  *See also* definition; *logos*
actions
  and the good, 264, 265n15
  and verbs, 232
  involuntary, 153
  versus objects, 232
  voluntary, 143
Agathon, 288–90 passim
*agathon*, good. *See* good
*aitia*, cause, 10, 172n9, 176, 466, 467, 473–75, 490, 521
*aitias logismos*, 9, 12, 132, 184n26, 420, 424
*akrasia*
  and appearance, 148–49
  and belief, 21–3, 148–50
  and ignorance, 147, 245–46, 249249
  and knowledge, 21–3, 148–50
  and the *Protagoras*, 147–150, 243–46, 249
  common view, 145–47
  kinds of, 21n40
  meaning of, 145n8
  Socratic denial of, 144–50, 244–46
Alcibiades, 303–06 passim
Alcinous, 544
analogy
  of the cave. *See* cave analogy
  ship of state, 373–74
  soul and state, 29–30, 282
  statesman and doctor, 330
  with health, 159
  with perceptual judgments, 148
  See also *technê*
Anaxagoras, 490, 499
Antiochus, 544–45, 526n1, 534n37
Antipater, 271n4
Antisthenes, 36, 50n37, 425n27
Anytus, 339
*apeiron*, the unlimited, 488–96 passim, 494n29, 497n36
aporetic dialogues. *See* dialogues, Socratic
*aporia*, 95, 93, 103, 140
appearance, 148–49, 244

appetite. *See* desire, appetitive; soul, appetitive part
approximation view, 203. *See also* compresence of opposites
Arcesilaus, 68, 531n22
*archê*, principle, 463–465, 466, 467n12, 470, 478, 515–16
Archytas, 44–5, 46–7
Aristophanes, 294–95, 299, 301–02
Aristophanes of Byzantium, 69
Aristotle
  and *philia*, friendship, 287
  and Plato, 16n27, 32–34, 67, 180, 180n19, 355, 504–06, 504n1, 505n2, 505n7
  on argument, 466
  on causation, 474–75
  on definition, 431–32
  on envy, 477–78
  on first principles, 463–64
  on forms, 13–15, 33, 134, 507–24
  on language, 240, 237n42
  on Socrates, 78, 83–84, 134, 140, 507–08, 513, 505n7
  on the soul, 252
Aristoxenus, 56n45, 180n19
art. *See* *technê*
assets, 155–58. *See also* external goods
authoritarianism, 159n27, 369
autonomy, 28–31
auxiliaries, 28, 324–25

beauty, 295–299 passim
behavior. *See* actions
being
  and falsehood paradox, 230
  and knowledge, 177, 192
  and names, 226–27
  See also *einai*, predication
belief, *doxa*
  and *akrasia*, 148–50, 245–46
  and appearance, 148
  and consistency, 128–129
  and falsehood paradox, 230–31, 239–40
  and knowledge 3–12, 9n12, 9n13, 172–73, 178–79, 185–86
  and recollection, 172
  and the elenchus, 125